ARTHUR
MILLER

ALSO BY MARTIN GOTTFRIED

A Theater Divided

Opening Nights

Broadway Musicals

Jed Harris: The Curse of Genius

More Broadway Musicals

Sondheim

In Person: The Great Entertainers

All His Jazz:
The Life and Death of Bob Fosse

Nobody's Fool: The Lives of Danny Kaye

George Burns and the One Hundred Year Dash

Balancing Act:
The Authorized Biography of Angela Lansbury

ARTHUR MILLER

His Life and Work

MARTIN GOTTFRIED

DA CAPO PRESS
A Member of the Perseus Books Group

Printed in the United States of America.

Cataloging-in-Publication data for this book is available from the Library of Congress.

First Da Capo Press edition 2003
ISBN 0-306-81214-2

Text design by Jeff Williams
Set in 10.5-point Berling by the Perseus Books Group

Published by Da Capo Press
A Member of the Perseus Books Group
http://www.dacapopress.com

1 2 3 4 5 6 7 8 9—07 06 05 04 03

For Margo

Contents

Introduction *ix*

Genesis of a Master

1. Escape *3*
2. Epiphany *21*
3. Epic *43*
4. Debut *63*

Prime of Life

5. Hit *87*
6. Inspiration *111*
7. Salesman *133*
8. Movies *157*
9. Betrayal *179*
10. Crucible *203*
11. The Little Red *227*
12. A Bridge *249*

Middle Age and Crisis

13. The Committee 273
14. Movie Star 299
15. Misfits 325

Endurance, Survival

16. The Fall 351
17. Price 375
18. Outcast 401
19. Survivor 423

List of Works 447
Chronology of Premiere Productions 449
Notes 451
Bibliography 463
Acknowledgments 465
Index 467

Introduction

The biography of a writer might seem to be an ironic enterprise, for like many creative people, writers tend to feel that their work—being artfully controlled self-expression—is biography enough and they have no need of another writer to finish the job. Arthur Miller's notion of a biography was a book about his plays. This is perhaps understandable but makes little sense as life history. An artist's work might be his or her most expressive self, even most beautiful self, but it is not the only self and certainly is not the whole self.

Still, this may be the reason why few writers publish autobiographies, although Miller himself did. He might well have been better off letting the plays speak for him. The book, called *Timebends,* does not present him as the warmest or most self-effacing of men. Then again people who are as smart, talented and acclaimed as Arthur Miller are not likely to be endearing but rather immodest, even arrogant and perhaps inevitably self-centered. These qualities have nothing to do with the value of their work and indeed such complexity often makes them more interesting as biographical subjects. More important is the fact of their work, especially if it is of some consequence and value, and Arthur Miller's plays are much more than that.

It is on account of these works' consequence and value that this biography was written, and also because of the shameful disrespect that has been heaped upon this master playwright. Seldom has an artist been so abused in his homeland while being esteemed the world over. "If he comes into a rehearsal room," the British director David Thacker said, "the actors really do believe that they are in the presence of somebody who is as great as Chekhov or Ibsen." Time has already proved the staying power of some of his plays. If he had written only *Death of a Salesman,* it would have been enough to establish him among the giants of drama. Yet in his own country this great artist has gone unappreciated to the point of scorn.

There are, however, more than theatrical reasons for telling this life story. Arthur Miller became a singular and representative figure of his era. There was a historic chemistry in the concurrence of his stage success, his relationship with the most famous of all movie stars and his heroic conflict with the daunting political sensation of the 1950s, the House Committee on Un-American Activities. Thus there are three elements to this book—Miller's plays, considered as both dramatic literature and theater; his role in twentieth-century political history and American popular culture; and embracing these, the eventful story of his personal life.

In his autobiography Miller did not develop a perspective on this fascinating concurrence of art, politics and popular culture. *Timebends*, although original, interesting and valuable in many respects, perhaps stands too close to the subject to paint the whole portrait. Any autobiography is bound to be subjective and this one is no exception, yet it does not even serve Miller's plays well, and it was published at a time when they needed defending. That was 1987, when he was dead, as they say, in the theater, when he had given up hope of having his new plays produced in America and critical hostility was at a peak. "Certainly," Professor Robert Corrigan had written of him, "no modern playwright writes with such moral earnestness and has a greater sense of social responsibility." But America never met a moralist it liked and Miller was derided for being one. *Timebends* was received with startling cruelty, even contempt, as though burning an effigy in print.

Timebends is in many ways an essential work, recounting as it does the playwright's life from his own experience in his own words. It offers colorful anecdotes about his youth and detailed accounts of many of the newsworthy events in his life. It also presents Miller's thinking on a variety of subjects, from the state of the theater to American history and international politics, but as to the unique advantages available to autobiography, many are lacking. The book offers no insights, for instance, into the playwright's creative process, nor does it offer any details of aborted plays or preparatory versions of famous ones. The concentration instead is on productions and reviews, and little is said about the later works. There is also an incompleteness in its chronology—almost nothing about the forty-year marriage that dominated Arthur Miller's middle and later years or the important fifteen years of his first marriage, when he was writing *All My Sons, Death of a Salesman, The Crucible* and *A View from the Bridge*. About those plays *Timebends* offers little in the way of text analysis or thematic discussion. Worthwhile as the book may be, it is abridged and calculated autobiography, selective and sometimes misleading about its author's personal life and unilluminating about his work. These omissions will be addressed.

Arthur Miller decided not to cooperate with the writing of this biography when he realized that it would deal with not only his work but his life. He had previously been of immense help on the subject of *The Crucible*, having provided many hours of interviews for my biography of its original director, Jed Harris. At that time he went into generous detail about the play's background, its research, writing and production. For this book, however, although he was willing to discuss his plays, he would not talk about his life. Such privacy, I would learn, is an essential part of his nature and this constraint was most striking on the subject of Marilyn Monroe. Miller, who had been known to seethe with rage when questioned about her, turned grim and tight-lipped with me merely when asked why an actress had been made up to resemble Monroe in the original production of *After the Fall*. Upon learning that I intended to include his first wife and family in the story of his life, he refused to answer any more questions.

Yet when his indirect cooperation was required, for instance, in gaining access to private collections in research libraries, he graciously provided the necessary permissions. Some information known only to him thus remained unavailable, but there was no Arthur Miller looking editorially over the biographer's shoulder either. In short, this book has advantages and disadvantages of both authorized and unauthorized biography.

As to Miller's role in the general scheme of things, here is a man truly of his century. He has grappled with the world around him in an almost athletic way, as though his life span were game time and current history the arena. He thrived there, having participated in most of the twentieth century's crucial events—the Wall Street crash of 1929, the Great Depression, the socialist movement, the birth of organized labor. In one sense or another his life touched upon the rise of Nazism in Europe, America's emergence as a world power following the Second World War, juvenile delinquency in America, racial and religious prejudice, the development of world communism, the birth of the Atomic Age, the cold war, the anticommunism of the McCarthy era and the Vietnam war years with their social and political reverberations. Miller was even a delegate to the infamous 1968 Democratic convention in Chicago.

During the years of his romance with and marriage to Marilyn Monroe the two were themselves the current event. In that respect his life reflected as well the evolving era of media exploitation and growing American absorption with celebrity culture.

Miller considers himself a "social" playwright, by which he means a playwright concerned with the way people live. His works pursue two of the great themes in contemporary western history: the improvement of society for the benefit of all, and the search for an understanding of the human consciousness. In his finest dramas both themes are present. Frequently and throughout his life he used the word *wonder* in the sense of wondering. "They are waiting for wonders," he wrote of audiences in his celebrated introduction to *The Collected Plays*, and "I have always been in love with wonder—the wonder of how people and things got to be the way they are."

For someone so socially concerned, however, Arthur Miller was a remote person, detached, contained and internalized, a man who would not, could not and did not reveal his innermost feelings. Writing plays would seem a natural outlet for such a personality, since so much of drama depends on the unspoken word, the lines between the lines. "Sssssh!" Miller once told a friend about one of his plays. "I have managed to say things I wouldn't dare say alone." *Saying things alone* means self-exposure, and this is problematic and paradoxical for someone such as Miller, who plainly feels compelled to write about his own thoughts, responsibilities and guilts. At the same time he had to endure his private life becoming a matter of public, even tabloid newspaper interest.

As the story of his life comes into focus, certain resemblances to and parallels with his plays do emerge. Care must be taken, however, regarding any insights that might be gained by finding the sources of his plays in Miller's personal history. Such detective work can be overly zealous, compromising an author's right to be taken at his word, an essential privilege of creation. Given that the work is the main reason for the book, how relevant or useful are such references? When I put this question to the professor and classics scholar Harold Bloom, he replied, "I am much more interested in the influence of the work upon the life than the supposed influence of the life upon the work. The life does matter, everything matters, but you have to bring a sense of balance and proportion into it." In writing this book my effort has been tempered by Professor Bloom's advice so as to bring balance and proportion into the search for the "supposed" influence of the life upon the work, while still searching for the influence of the work—and the career—upon the life.

MARTIN GOTTFRIED
New York City 2003

part one

Genesis of a Master

In the human mind, there is no past:
everything is happening now;
the past keeps rushing up to the present.

1. Escape

EARLY ONE MORNING in May 1940 a tall, skinny, bespectacled, nearly twenty-five-year-old Arthur Miller sat down at his typewriter, much as he did every morning in the cellar of his parents' house. But instead of working on a play he wrote a nine-page, single-spaced letter of despair to Kenneth Thorpe Rowe, who had taught his college playwriting class. The letter was a taking of stock, a looking back over what the young man had accomplished in the two years since his graduation.

He had, he wrote, accomplished nothing and had nothing to show for his efforts. While a few Broadway producers were interested in his plays, there were no takers. The most important of these producers, the Theatre Guild, at least offered what was intended as constructive criticism: Miller's plays were too challenging, not merely in the way they were written, but in what they were saying. The guild's chief play reader, an academic intellectual—indeed, a man to whom Miller had been referred by Professor Rowe, who might be expected to have certain ideals—suggested that the young man broaden his work and make it more positive. He warned Miller not to question an audience's values or discourage its hopes; rather the plays ought to be optimistic and inspiring. The point was to "try to understand the audience. What do they want to see in the theatre? That must temper your work. You must not be too hard with them, Arthur."

Ironically, as Miller pointed out to Rowe, the first play he'd submitted to the Theatre Guild, *The Grass Still Grows*, had hardly been the sort that could be described as too hard on an audience. On the contrary, the play was a family comedy, "Jewish, not bizarre or strikingly novel," and still it was rejected. As far as that play was concerned, it was, Miller said, "dead as a dog."

Next, his summary continued, he'd spent more than a year working on *The Children of the Sun*, an epic play about Montezuma and the Aztec Indians, Cortez and the Spanish conquistadors. Miller considered it not only "a big classical tragedy" but a theatrical one, and he was still "confident that on the stage it would cause a stir." He'd enjoyed writing that play, had even enjoyed rewriting it. "Once it began to draw on my heart," he confessed, "I could not stop until it sucked me dry." Yet producers and even his agent had responded with a spectacularly unanimous lack of enthusiasm and he finally and bitterly had to admit, "I am dry now." Miller thus was writing this letter in hope of "drawing a moral" from his experiences so that he might "grasp your hand and search" for that moral.

At the same time he felt shameful, even unmanly about being unable to support himself. In the preceding two years the only steady income he had earned from his writing had come in the form of artistic charity: six months on the dole with the government-subsidized Federal Theatre and Writers Project that was part of the Works Progress Administration (WPA). Some of the other playwrights in the program could hardly, he thought, be called playwrights, and such wages were unrewarding, unearned by work and paid regardless of quality. Other than that, he continued, "I have been a ward of my brother and father . . . the former is a fine man but I never meant him to support me."

And so he had to face the fact that "I am 25, a grown man as they used to say. Whither away? Have I justified my self-announced and self-appointed existence as a writer?" This was a question gnawing at him, "growing like a weed."

Arthur Miller had come away from college a praised, prized and confidently budding playwright, protected by the conviction that failing to get a drama produced did not mean that it was worthless, nor did having a play produced mean that it was valuable. While such a conviction was fine in theory, his letter resumed, it was of little consolation after he had put so much time, mind and heart into his work. He had begun to question his ability, and not only as a writer of plays. His failure had extended beyond playwriting. Since leaving school, he confided to Rowe, he had also written several radio scripts and a few short stories. Of these a grand total of one radio script had been bought. He couldn't even anticipate selling another, since two subsequent scripts had been rejected. So he drew up the balance sheet: For two years of work, "Net receipts, $200 less ten per cent commission." His only other income for the period had been the $22.77 a week that the government theater paid for his six-month stint.

The disgrace of failure was making him consider "the ways out." One possibility, he mused, was to take the advice of the man at the Theatre Guild and emasculate his plays, soothing the audience with assurances that all is well with their world. He characterized this to be advice from

> the Paraclete, the comforter. . . . He means balm. And while I am with him I hate him for what he means, but when I am alone I know he is helpless. And for moments I say all right, I'll comfort them. I'll keep away from the conflicts,

> the important and wonderful crises in our lives. I'll warp what I see into comforting fancy.

His letter paused, as if to regain its composure. The past two years since 1938, he reasoned, had not been wasted. He had learned much about "the writing game." In *The Children of the Sun* Miller had written an epic in the classical style, a big play that was ambitious, literary and artistic. If he had taken a job instead of depending on his family, he would have had neither the time nor energy to write such a play; but his anger could not be assuaged and the black mood returned as he vowed never again to attempt such a piece. No more history, no more agonizing work to recreate period speech, no more verse to put off potential producers. He would write in the conventional, realistic style, about "contemporary people and subjects"—that is, if he could only find a job that didn't mentally exhaust him; it might even be beneficial. Perhaps, the despairing young man wrote to his professor, an honest job might help him to "overcome or at least better meet the obstacle I see so sharp before me." Perhaps too, he rationalized, a writer might benefit from experience at a real job with real people in the real world instead of working in a social vacuum, alone in a room with only a table, a chair and a typewriter. Indeed that is where and how he would forever feel most comfortable.

The letter could have been shorter, but discursive self-examination would become a way of life for Arthur Miller. So would earnestness, idealism and his enthusiasm for wonderful crises.

Arthur Asher Miller was born in New York City on October 17, 1915, the second child of Isadore and Gittel Miller, thirty and twenty-two years old at the time, respectively. His brother Kermit was already three, and they lived in a splendid apartment in comfort and security high above Central Park.

Isadore Miller was a prosperous man. His Miltex Coat and Suit Company boasted a factory, showroom, front office and more than 800 employees, and its lucrative business of manufacturing women's clothing allowed him to keep his family in fair luxury. They lived on the top floor of a handsome six-story building at a very respectable address, 45 West 110th Street, facing the north end of Central Park just off Fifth Avenue. The apartment was spacious and sprawling, with a formal dining room, a signal of particular prestige in middle-class Jewish circles, and this dining room was a luxury in the purest sense, as it was never used for dining. To have one's children use such a table for homework made the formal dining room not only prestigious but also practical and finally commendable in its contribution to the sacred mission of education. According to Miller family lore, a striking exception to this mission occurred one New Year's Eve, which happened to be Izzy and Gussie (as Gittel preferred to be called) Miller's wedding anniversary.

Gussie actually danced *on top of* that table, a story supporting the notion that she was a vivacious woman despite her weight and occasional moods of darkness.

Impressive too was the apartment's view of Central Park from the windows of the living room that featured two more symbols of middle-class achievement: an oriental rug and baby grand piano. This was a specially built Knabe, with sides not rounded but straight lined and corners squared like a harpsichord's. Only a handful of these pianos had been made and Gussie, the family tastemaker, owned one of them. She sometimes sat at this piano playing and singing popular songs of the day, and such images of dancing and music-making lent the culture-conscious woman a certain glamour in the eyes of five-year-old Arthur, or so he would recall ("diamonds on her fingers . . . she trails a silver fox across the floor"). Indeed he thought his mother was beautiful and admired everything about her, from her lipstick to her velvet shoes—and his admiration was reciprocated. Perhaps the first-born Kermit was the boy scout of the family, but Arthur was his mother's favorite and remained so, even after the birth of a sister, Joan Maxine ("Joanie") in 1922. Her father doted on her. "After waiting so long for a girl," she remembered, "there I was, this pretty angel . . . I was like a doll."

Arthur, though, continued to enjoy his mother's favor, basking in the intimacy of the family gossip she shared with him, such as her low opinion of the women her brothers had married. One sister-in-law was "fat and stupid," while another was a disreputable ex–chorus girl who—as if it served her right—had given birth to a child with Down Syndrome. Nevertheless some relatives he did appreciate, notably, slick Uncle Hymie, who taught him how to whistle with two fingers in his mouth ("one of the greatest gifts anyone ever handed me") and Hymie's wife, Stella, who was too flashy for Gussie's taste but earthy in a way that the youngster found irresistible.

Jewish families tended to be big and all over each other. The extended family of Millers was big enough—Gussie had even more siblings than Izzy, four brothers and three sisters—but that didn't make for an overflow of warmth. Relatives were kept at a distance and even within the immediate family there was a reluctance to be intimate. "It's not like most Jewish families," Joan Miller would later say. "We didn't celebrate birthdays, not even with birthday cards. Nobody would presume to break in on the other person's privacy." This emotional isolation would come to characterize her brother Arthur in profound and sometimes disturbing ways.

In most other cultural respects the Millers were quite usual, certainly in the matter of Jewishness, and although Arthur would later minimize it, Jewishness seemed to pervade his early life. Whatever happened in the world was viewed in terms of how it affected Jews. His friends and classmates were Jewish, as was everyone in the neighborhood or so it seemed. Arthur's parents perhaps were not observant, but Gussie's father, Grandpa Barnett, always wore a yarmulke and both he and Grandpa Miller—both of whom spoke Yiddish most of the time—were at the synagogue for services every

Sabbath. Such observance was not a requisite of Judaism for Isadore, Gussie and the children. Their Jewishness was more a matter of identification, of heritage, and there was a thoroughgoing ethnicity about this household, an atmosphere of Jewish values, style, taste, humor and of course Jewish food. Gussie considered herself just as good at making brisket of beef, gefilte fish and *tsimmes* as she was at interior decorating. Around the Miller family too was a pervasive Jewish manner of speaking, with colorful argot and Yiddishisms. Arthur ("Arty" almost from the start) already had a sensitive ear for these locutions and would soon be able to draw on a fine store of ethnic expressions and colloquialisms.

All, however, was not Jewishness. Each summer the family indulged in a generally middle-class ritual, the exodus from the city to a resort. A good man was supposed to provide such things for his family and if nothing else, Izzy was a good provider. At the end of each school year his wife would lead her troop of children and their grandparents away from the steamy streets of upper Manhattan to a rented bungalow near the oceanic splendors of Rockaway Beach. That escape, along with the apartment, rings, piano and oriental rug, signified the level to which Isadore Miller had taken his family. He even had a uniformed chauffeur take him downtown each morning in an expensive automobile, drive him to work in the Seventh Avenue garment center of Manhattan and wait to drive him home at the end of the day. This did not unduly impress young Arty. Apparently all the men in his building went to work this way, for there was a lineup of chauffeured limousines waiting at the front entrance every morning.

Gussie was well accustomed to this style of living and proud of her husband's success in achieving it. When among his family (a group she held in general contempt and who were rarely seen), she would boast of her Izzy's success. In private Gussie was not quite so respectful, as she regularly demonstrated for the children. Her superiority was expressed in terms of higher cultural refinement and proven by her origins as a first-generation American, whereas Izzy and his family were immigrants from a shtetl in the old country—in this case Austria or Poland or Hungary. At various times he gave one or the other as his birthplace. The borders of Eastern Europe had changed so frequently that many immigrants truly didn't know where they came from. What Isadore Miller did know about his origins—and this he told his children on many occasions—was that he had arrived in America at the age of six still displaying the hand-lettered cardboard sign that had been hung around his neck (and that of many an immigrant child) at the start of the journey. His sign read PLEASE PUT THIS BOY ON THE SS *CLEARWATER*, and at the other end of the Atlantic Ocean, awaiting him on the dock in New York, were the three brothers and three sisters who had been sent ahead to join their father, Shmuel (Samuel). As in so many immigrant families, the provider went first to establish himself, preparing a home for the others, who were sent over in descending order and put to work immediately on arrival.

Was Miller the family name from the outset? If it doesn't quite ring of old Europe, Grandpa Miller didn't remember anyone in the family having any other, and for that matter Gussie's maiden name, Barnett, would seem even more unlikely. The common wisdom is that impatient clerks simplified unpronounceable names upon immigrants' arrival at Ellis Island in New York harbor. Yet record keepers there have insisted that this is apocrypha and suggest that Anglicizing was likelier done during the naturalization process, with the acquisition of citizenship papers. Many years later, faced with a suggestion that he had changed his name to disguise his Jewishness, Miller responded that aside from its being the only name he ever had, *Miller* might have originated in Austria as *Mahler*; it also might have been *Mueller*. For that matter Miller itself was common enough in German-speaking countries. As for Arthur's middle name, Jewish boys traditionally were given additional Hebrew names, and *Asher* was taken from one of the twelve Israelite tribes.

Isadore Miller's first home in America was on the Lower East Side of Manhattan, where so many Jewish immigrants gravitated. He, his six siblings and their parents squeezed into two rooms in a Stanton Street tenement, along with several sewing machines. Samuel Miller was in the clothing business, a family business in the most complete sense—that is, they all worked in it. By the time Isadore was twelve he was operating a sewing machine and not long afterward sold dresses for S. Miller and Sons, as the business came to be called.

Gussie's snobbishness notwithstanding, her background was much the same. Her father, Louis Barnett, had also been "in rags." The crucial distinction between the Barnetts and the Millers, at least in her mind, seemed to be that in addition to being a native-born American, she had not grown up on Manhattan's Lower East Side with the other *greenhorns*. As soon as he could, Louis moved his family uptown from Broome Street to Harlem. Not yet a black ghetto, Harlem was a ghetto nevertheless, if one for German Jews who considered themselves a cut above the vulgarians from Eastern Europe.

Gussie completed enough of her education to become a schoolteacher, but Isadore never finished elementary school; indeed he was barely literate. For these reasons she looked down on him and scorned as well the business that provided her with security and so many comforts. She could even sound anti-Semitic, derogating the materialism of "money-mad cloakies" in the garment business, "Jews who care for nothing but business." This became something of a household litany, and the children regularly overheard their mother belittling Izzy for his grubby ladies' clothing company, his coarse associates, his educational shortcomings and his inability to appreciate *the finer things*. On some occasions she would even complain that her marriage had been involuntary and that she had been "traded" into it "within months," Arthur remembered, "after graduating cum laude from high school."

At six Arty began his education in the same elementary school his mother had attended, P.S. 24 on West One-hundred eleventh Street, a one-block walk from home. Whether in his winter knickers or summer shorts, he was a skinny sight. He squinted constantly, leading to an eyeglasses prescription for which he actually had no need; indeed eyeglasses were unheard of in his family. There were the inevitable snickers from classmates, but ultimately eyeglasses with prominent horn frames were to become his trademark.

A particular boyhood irritant was his Grandpa Barnett, who enjoyed teasing the boy about his looks ("Pull in your ears, we're going through a tunnel"). Yet even this gruff and disliked old man had the patience to sit down with the youngster and teach him how to play popular card games such as seven card rummy and casino. All things considered then, Arty's childhood was a comfortable one and by his own description happily so, even if he had to spend the greater part of his time in school. Unlike his smart older brother, Kermit (always "Kerm"), he was an indifferent student. His gift was for athletics. His big brother, though, was not only a natural scholar but also a better athlete. As Joanie put it, "Kerm was the ideal son," breezing through school collecting top grades while Arty had difficulty paying attention; his teachers would regularly warn (and even smack) him for drifting off, gazing through the window in a reverie.

Around this time his mother took Arthur to see his first play, a melodrama. On some occasions he would remember it as being *Fog* at a theater on Broadway at Eighty-sixth Street, at other times *Tobacco Road,* at the Shubert Theatre on Lenox Avenue at One-hundred fifteenth Street. It was probably the former, since he was eighteen when *Tobacco Road* opened on Broadway, but whichever it was, the play didn't make much of an impression. He was more interested, he remembered, in cowboy movies and adventure serials.

Arty had a best friend in Sidney Franks, who lived in the same building and whose father was a banker. The Franks family was even better fixed than the Millers, but financial distinctions seemed to matter little to the boys. Rainy days they would chase each other up and down the building halls, but if Sid was Arty Miller's best friend, Kerm remained his hero. Arty would watch awestruck as his brother dared to dash across the rooftop, ducking under clotheslines to jump onto the ledge and leap across to an adjacent roof, braving the gap between the buildings and flying over the chasm six stories above the street. Then back downstairs Kerm and his friends would play stickball and the other games that city boys invented, stoopball, punchball, French tennis, marbles and the tag game ring alevio. Arty was soon playing the same city games.

Despite his mother's tutelage, cultural interests were all but nonexistent. He took piano lessons along with Kermit and Joanie. Thanks to that and their mother's regular playing of records, all three would grow up with a lifetime love of classical music; but Arty did not read, even though the public library was a half block away. Kerm could spend entire afternoons there and guided Joanie into the same pleasures. She would always feel that "as a boy, Kermit was really it. He was good. Sweet and energetic and supportive of good things," but he had no such influence on his younger brother. Arthur would say that growing up, he never came closer to a book than a picture of Charles Dickens seen in a children's encyclopedia. His bicycle was more important to him, a ticket to escape.

His mother let him park the bike in the apartment's front hall. After school Arty would bring it downstairs in the elevator, walk it through the lobby then wheel through the streets, cruising his immediate neighborhood and sometimes venturing uptown, across the acknowledged boundary line of One-hundred sixteenth Street into the "colored" section.

He also explored downtown. By the age of twelve Arthur was curious to see where his father went to work and what exactly *the business* was. Manhattan's garment district, which ran up and down the thirties between Broadway and Seventh Avenue, was pandemonium. Trucks lined side streets, loading and unloading woolen clothes in the summer for winter lines and cotton clothes in the winter for summer lines. On the broad avenues sidewalks were crowded with salesmen, showroom models, secretaries and delivery boys who pushed and pulled rolling racks of women's coats and dresses between clanging trolley cars.

His father's Miltex Coat and Suit Company turned out to be an impressive place. Here was a spacious layout of workrooms and showrooms, a handful of clerical people, a squad of salesmen, an army of seamstresses at the many rows of sewing machines and huge cylinders of woolen material stacked on shelves running high overhead in the stockroom. Young Miller watched the delivery boys push racks of finished coats and dresses into the big elevator, to be taken downstairs and rolled out into the bustling streets. All of this activity gave Arthur a new appreciation of his father, and he began to realize that he admired other things too about this man. His height, for instance—over six feet—and his unusual, un-Jewish ("almost Irish") looks, with red hair and a pale complexion that ran through that side of the family, a group oddly described by Miller as looking like "blue eyed bison."

The boy also admired his father's elegant way of dressing and the authoritative manner that commanded respect. Even as an adult, Miller would boast that when his father had walked down the street, "policemen were inclined to salute." He would inherit his father's height and physique, his mother's dark Mediterranean coloring.

As his thirteenth birthday approached, virtually all of Arthur's extracurricular activities ceased, for just like Kerm three years earlier he had a bar mitzvah to study for, and that meant intensified Hebrew lessons after school. In the midst of this preparation a minor crisis occurred at home when six-year-old Joanie was suddenly heard shrieking. As parents and brothers converged on her room, she pointed a trembling finger at her leg.

She'd been bitten, she cried, by a giant fly. When told that these were called "horse" flies, she began to wail.

Izzy cradled the tearful child in his arms and carried her into the living room, setting her down on the sofa. While she wept and as the bite on her leg began to swell, her mother telephoned the doctor. When he arrived, he moved Joanie from the living room couch to the big table in the dining room. Asking for a clean towel, he folded it under her leg and took a bottle of antiseptic from his black bag. Gently sterilizing the wound, he used a scalpel to lance the swollen bite. As the swelling subsided, the doctor looked very seriously at the shaken child and turned to Izzy and Gussie. "If you had waited another five minutes," he said with mock seriousness, "she would have been gone."

The doctor's teasing nearly set little Joanie to crying all over again, but Isadore Miller's essential tenderness came to her rescue. Nodding gravely, he turned and smiled at his daughter, looked at the doctor and said, "Listen, you can't fool a horsefly. You know, those horseflies are very smart. They know what's sweet," and his daughter never forgot it. This was a kind of sensitivity rare among the Millers of One-hundred tenth Street. One often hears of typical ethnic qualities. Arthur himself described Gussie as a "typical Jewish mother" and in many ways she was, doting on the children and dominating her husband. Izzy too fit the stereotype of a Jewish father, strong at his business, browbeaten at home. "He knew the coat business," their son would say, "but he never assumed he had a right to an opinion." Typical Jewish families are also supposed to be emotional, but Izzy's tenderness toward Joanie was not representative of the Miller family. The presence of Arthur's parents at his bar mitzvah would be the last time for several decades that they would attend any landmark ceremony in his life, about which he would express no regrets. As his sister put it, "It's a very strange relationship that our family has, one with the other. It's a nucleus of five people who didn't behave anything like any other family we knew. One didn't have fights in our family and we don't intrude on each other. We don't ask a lot of questions."

Almost exactly one year after Arthur's bar mitzvah his family's life was changed forever. On Black Thursday, October 24, 1929, the Wall Street stock market crashed, bringing down with it not only the economy but America's idea of itself. In an instant the national confidence was shattered, and collapsing with it was a way of life that had been the foundation of this family's world. With one sharp yank all security was pulled out from under them, and it wasn't because Isadore Miller's business had failed. The Miltex Coat and Suit Company would have remained viable, for a time at least, but for one unfortunate fact. As Arthur put it, "like a lot of other people, my father had realized, some time in the Twenties, that while he had a perfectly lucrative business manufacturing women's coats, he could make immeasurably more money on the Stock Exchange." And for a while he had, some of which money he actually got to spend; but like so many Americans, Isadore Miller had entrusted every nickel of his faith in a stock market that seemed to be on a never-ending ascent. All of his savings, all of his capital, everything he had had been invested in common stock. Overnight his holdings were rendered worthless and he was bankrupt.

Izzy held on to the apartment on One-hundred tenth Street as long as he could because his in-laws lived nearby and Grandma Rose Barnett was in failing health. Gussie was not about to abandon her parents, but it was obvious that with an unaffordable rent the family would have to move, and when her mother died, the move was made. This was at the time of Arty's graduation from elementary school, which was at least convenient. He would not have to start high school in Manhattan then transfer to a school in Brooklyn, which was where Gussie found a place for the family, a family that now included her father.

In another sense Brooklyn was where the family found a place for Gussie. Two of her sisters lived side by side in a section called Gravesend, and when they told her of an available house across the street, Izzy agreed to buy it for five thousand dollars. He still had enough credit to be approved for a mortgage that would cost fifty dollars a month.

Gravesend is a section of Brooklyn that sits to the north of Coney Island. One of the borough's six original towns, it was founded in 1643. When the Millers moved there, many of its streets were still unpaved. The outer-lying areas were mostly vacant lots, open fields, wooded patches, cemeteries and even farmland. As for the Miller house at 1350 East Third Street, it was a meek affair. Flimsily built on a pathetic patch of ground, it amounted to no more than six rooms and a pile of clapboard, a sad comedown from the sixth-floor splendor of Central Park North. Adjacent and across the street—aptly enough a dead-end street—were similar signs of domestic surrender. In the two houses immediately facing, witnessing the descent of the Millers, were Gussie's sisters, Arty's aunts Esther and Annie, married to a couple of salesmen who had lost their upstate territories. Isadore Miller of the Miltex Coat and Suit Company was no better off than the men who used to work for him and in the present case still did. He was now employing Uncle Lee (Balsam) and Uncle Manny (Newman), along with various other members of the Miller and Barnett families. He paid them as best he could, when he could.

The Balsams and Newmans were in even worse straits than the Millers. Aunt Annie Newman and Aunt Esther Balsam lived the lives of frontier women. They bought potatoes by the hundred-pound sack to save money and share between them. They grew tomatoes because they had to and canned their own fruits, even kept their own chickens. A child is not concerned with such matters, living in a world as small as he is, and to this point Arty's world had not changed in any devastating way. He even went fishing—an unknown diversion in Manhattan—with his cousins, Abby and Buddy Newman, setting out at dawn and jumping the turnstiles to ride the subway to nearby Sea Gate, or Sheepshead Bay, where they could fish off the rocks. He still had bicycling, only instead of scooting between Manhattan's trolley car tracks he rode past the elm woods and open fields of Brooklyn. He also had games to play because boys will not do without them, inventing new ones to suit their territory. In Brooklyn restrictions were no longer imposed by narrow streets, parked cars and heavy traffic. Instead of stickball and punchball boys could play real baseball and run football games in the empty lots. Arty Miller's height, long skinny legs and sweeping armspan made him a natural at snatching footballs from the air in full stride. His quick reflexes, sure hands, deft footwork and accurate throwing arm as he pegged a ball to first base settled his baseball position as a second baseman. His big brother had clinched the pitcher's spot—the thinking man's position—but being smart and gifted were Kerm's specialties.

Young Miller's adolescence was not yet shaken by the financial earthquake that had upended his family. Perhaps money was the measure of achievement for many men, but in a boy's life in Brooklyn a ticket to acceptance was bought with athletic ability. It was even more valuable than academic achievement, and so life for this boy was not really so different from what it had been on One-hundred tenth Street in Manhattan. Despite the suddenness of his family's rearrangement, Arty Miller had not yet digested the full significance of dislocation. He was only fourteen and his immediate complaint was the permanent presence of his despised Grandpa Barnett, a man with whom he had to share a tiny bedroom. He was a man "no one dared cross," who was stone bald, bearded and "so neat he folded his socks before putting them in the laundry hamper and it took him five minutes to get his two pillows exactly where he wanted them on the bed before he lay down." Especially infuriating to the fourteen year old, as if it summed everything up, was the old man pampering himself with barbershop shaves paid for by a father who "himself had next to nothing."

The Miller boys were enrolled in James Madison High School, a fair distance away on Bedford Avenue between Avenue P and Quentin Road. Most days, Arty and Kerm would keep each other company on the long walk. Their father had a bigger trip each morning, since he still operated the Miltex Coat and Suit Company such as it was. No longer with a car and driver to get him there he had to find his own way, which meant walking a couple of blocks past empty lots and a cemetery to the Avenue M station. There he climbed two flights to the elevated platform, where he caught the Culver Line of the Brooklyn Manhattan Transit, or BMT, subway. Izzy took the clacketing wooden train with its straw seats for the forty-minute ride to Thirty-fourth Street in Manhattan's garment center, where he tried to keep Miltex afloat despite a frightening lack of capital, his own and his customers'.

Although times were difficult, they were not yet disastrous. Perhaps Gussie and Isadore Miller had lost most of the amenities of their old life and all of its security, but education was never considered a luxury and in June 1930 Kermit graduated from Madison High School and was enrolled in New

York University. At about the same time, the new Abraham Lincoln High School was opened on Ocean Parkway near Shore Parkway in Brighton Beach; it was much closer to home than Madison High and Arty was reassigned there. Some mornings he would run much of the way, loping down Ocean Parkway, a wide and beautiful boulevard. He was more fleet than ever, a string bean carrying a mere 120 pounds on a gangling frame that shot past six feet between his fifteenth and sixteenth birthdays. He promptly made the second squad of the school football team playing end, a position for which he was perfectly built, calling as it does for outrunning defenders, reaching beyond their arms to catch the ball then sprinting for the goal line. His cranelike physique was also suited for basketball, which he started playing as well.

Just as in elementary school, Arthur was considerably more successful at sports than in his studies, where he had generally poor grades and several failures in algebra. He was even expelled for a brief time. His extracurricular activities were thoroughly inconsequential—"French Club, Service Squad, Bank Representative." By his own admission his primary interest was "to get out onto the football field with the least possible scholastic interference." He showed no particular ability to write and was so ordinary a student that none of his teachers remembered him even being in their classes, yet he showed intelligence in at least one respect. At sixteen Arthur at last understood that what was happening to his parents' lives was also happening to his own. He watched bitterly as his mother's spirits were permanently dampened. She was forced to pawn her jewelry, sell her furs, forego her vanity and along with it her buoyancy. The glamorous figure from childhood turned slovenly before his eyes. Instead of velvet pumps she wore slippers all day, sometimes not even dressing at all, slogging through what she called "this chicken coop of a house," doling out coal in measured shovelfuls to keep the furnace going at minimal cost. She seemed to summon energy only when being vituperative with her husband. Their relationship was growing ever more acrimonious, and *idiot* was becoming a familiar word around the house. Izzy was an idiot for continuing to pour good money after bad to revive the business; he was an idiot for letting the family fall into its current state of destitution and an idiot for being generally inadequate and clumsy as a husband and a man.

Arthur learned to "stay away from conflict" and not take sides, but in most matters he tended to agree with his mother and would grow up saying that his father had failed the family by being unable to cope with the crisis. He even once claimed, harshly and strangely, but perhaps more revealingly than intended, "One rarely hears of any American writer whose father was to be regarded as in any way adequate or successful. The American writer is supplanting somebody, correcting him, making up for his errors or failures. . . . He is the power that the father lost." Yet at other times he would boast that his father had "built one of the two or three largest coat manufacturing businesses in the country." While this may appear both trivial and a bit of an overstatement, he seems to feel that it captured the best of Isadore Miller. This confusion of contempt, admiration, anger and love for his father would remain with Miller all his life, to surface time and again in his plays.

When not blaming the ruin of his family's fortune and perhaps worst of all the despondency of his mother on Isadore's weakness and stupidity, Miller would blame the American economic system. Such equivocating would become a lifetime habit. In this particular matter there is at least one constant: No matter whether his father or the capitalistic system was responsible for this upheaval and the family's reduced economic circumstances, Miller would cite the Wall Street crash and its aftermath as the formative event in his life. He describes it in an almost incantory way as

> a mystical event . . . odd things happened . . . a drought in the west . . . the sun seemed never to set . . . dust storms . . . it was like nature had decided that we were finished . . . an earthquake [that] changed what America thought about itself. Because the presumption of a permanent prosperity exploded in a matter of weeks. . . . A month ago you were riding around in a limousine, now you were scraping around to pay the rent.

The limousine and the scraping for rent are references to his own family. One must ask whether Arthur Miller's lifelong absorption with the Depression is strictly a matter of social observation. To what extent is his argument with the American economic system and its values a result of and anger about losing the entitlements and security of a monied childhood? Either way, whether he reacted to them subjectively or objectively, the economic events of the Wall Street crash and the Depression were a traumatic time for him. His sister, Joan, said, "Arthur carries scars from that time. It doesn't take a great observer to notice that. It is a memory, in his nerves, and in his muscles, that he just can't get rid of."

In the summer of 1931 Arthur and Kermit were enlisted in the struggle to save Miltex. They made the trip to the garment center each day in the stifling, airless subway. The Depression had settled in for the long haul and its effects were to be seen everywhere, from his mother selling the household's few remaining valuables to the surrender Arty saw in his friends' fathers' faces and domestic quarrels overheard in the pathetic little houses as he walked to the elevated train. Every day seemed to bring more boarded windows and yet another store shuttered on Avenue M, the neighborhood's Main Street. Bars were the only new businesses. Strangers knocked at the Millers' back door asking to wash the windows for a quarter, and if refused, they begged for food or spare change or a night's shelter in the cellar. Grown men, once never seen by daylight because they were at their jobs, now sat idly on front porches playing pinochle. That was a painful image for young Miller: idleness, purposelessness, uselessness and worst of all hopelessness—

the attitude that nothing could be done to make the times better. In later life he would not be able to bear such defeatism.

Miller spent that summer working at the Miltex Coat and Suit Company. The business was in such a state that his father couldn't afford to give the salesmen nickels for the subway, for although there were buyers, nobody was buying. Arty's job was to carry samples for the salesmen while they made their rounds, and one day he was assigned to an especially weary *drummer*, as they were called. This was dreary work in any weather, but miserable in the tar-melting heat of a sweltering July day in New York City. The hot sun only added to the unpleasantness of hugging to his chest a half dozen woolen coats from the winter line while trudging behind the older man from Seventh Avenue to the Third Avenue El, the elevated subway.

The situation became pathetic when the salesman asked to borrow the fare, and downright pitiful as the dispirited fellow—plainly a broken man—tried and failed to make his sales, in the process enduring not merely rejections but insolence and finally humiliation at the various unbuying offices. It was a day young Miller would not forget.

Summer passed and the government assumed the Miller mortgage from the bank, a common occurrence now that many home owners were beginning to miss the occasional installment. Whenever the federal agent came around for a payment, Miller remembered his mother offering the man a chair, a cup of coffee and conversation. Such tactics of distraction didn't fool anyone, but there was still some compassion left in the world. The fellow would sip the coffee, visit with Gussie and "forget" to ask for the payment, at least until the next month. The family ship nevertheless was leaking on all sides, and late that fall Kerm was forced to quit college in the midst of his sophomore year. He went to work full time at Miltex while his father continued the draining effort to bail out the sinking business.

When winter came that year, Arty, thanks to his bicycle, managed to find a before-school job. He was paid four dollars for a twenty-five-hour week delivering bags of bagels, rolls and rye bread for a local bakery. He set out at four-thirty every frozen morning, pulling on a pair of improvised mittens, "long woolen plaid stockings that came up to my elbows." Then he hooked a wire basket to the handlebars of his bicycle, rode to the bakery and loaded in the labeled paper bags. From one customer to the next he tossed the bags at the front doors. If he was to have any pocket money, this was the only way he was going to get it, and so he bicycled through the dark, gripping handlebars as icy as the streets. It was worth it, for after a while he had saved enough money—twelve dollars—to buy lumber for a back porch. Then with his Uncle Lee's help he built that back porch onto the house, in the process discovering that he enjoyed carpentry and had a gift for it.

Arthur's sister was too young to be fully aware of what was happening and didn't notice each day's disappearance of yet another piece of the house as her mother sold a lamp, a carpet, a table. Later Joan would realize that her mother had drawn the line at the piano, which was either symbolic or simply beloved. All through the Depression the girl never missed a lesson, and as Kermit helped with her homework, so he did with her music, along with George Levine, who was his best friend. George was luckier than most because his father was successfully navigating a carpet company through the hard times. At six feet six inches the young man seemed a giant to the ten-year-old girl, but a gentle one. He would ask to hear what piece she was studying and, she remembered, "I would play some Mozart. George would say, 'Very good. Now ask your teacher if you can work on some Beethoven sonatas and some Chopin.'"

So the Depression was an abstraction to the girl. "As long as there was food in my body, I didn't know the difference, and I never missed a meal. My mother was the kind of *balabusta* [homemaker] that, even if there was just a can of tuna fish, all of the relatives could come visiting unexpectedly and there would be a banquet." It never seemed that way to her brother Arthur, and she knew it. To him, she said, "life in Brooklyn was impoverished." That was because he was old enough to know the difference between the way they were living and the way they had lived. His own piano lessons had stopped but he still played, and classical music remained his great love. He was crazy for Debussy's "Prelude to the Afternoon of a Faun," but he also developed a taste for popular songs and the way they were sung by such crooners as Russ Columbo and Bing Crosby. He had a good voice too, a high true tenor. He entertained fantasies of becoming a crooner himself and, with his mother's encouragement, even tried to realize them. Making several trips into Manhattan, Arthur worked his way down the halls of Tin Pan Alley (the Brill Building near Times Square), demonstrating his voice for the assorted music publishers and song pluggers. One of them actually thought he was good enough to sing on the radio and arranged a tryout on a local station. Miller got to sing on the air twice before being replaced.

Better than predawn bagel delivery was a new part-time job, this one at an automobile supplies store. Arthur qualified for a junior driver's license (daytime only) and soon was driving a truck and making deliveries in Brooklyn, the Bronx and Queens. This job lasted nearly a year until he was laid off at the end of summer 1932. That was the pit of the Depression, with long lines of men waiting for free bread and people standing on street corners peddling apples for a penny apiece. If times were hard, however, there was never any consideration of aborting his high school education. In September he was back for his senior year, and that October for Arthur's seventeenth birthday Kermit decided that it was time for the youth to lose his virginity.

Even at a time when "sexuality" was not yet a cliché it was still a drive, though apparently not for this adolescent. Arty's life was dominated by sports, money needs and his mother. To judge from his recollections, his adolescent experiences with girls were nothing more than further reflections of Depression hardships—for instance, his occasional visits to an ice skating rink on Ocean Parkway, "where you had to pay a grim, hard earned quarter to get in and show off for the girls, and hang out till closing time to get your money's worth, half starved though you were by then." This does not exactly ring with the giddiness of youthful sexual exploration. Young people can often find laughter and joy in the darkest time, yet here was perhaps a poor student but a serious fellow, his sensitivities inverted, capable of expressing great vitality and enthusiasm when in action (sports, for instance) but tight lipped in repose. Small wonder that his brother, Kermit, with the wisdom of a twenty year old, decided to give Arty a visit to a prostitute as a birthday present. With a couple of friends as enforcers he ushered the kid into manhood.

The experience proved less than thrilling. "Vacant," Arthur Miller recalled it, and "remote."

One day, however, he did become agitated, and extremely so. As with most events in his young life, Miller identified this one with a moment in Depression history. He even remembered the exact date, March 9, 1933, because it was the day that President Roosevelt announced a bank holiday to prevent a disastrous run on savings withdrawals. Luckily for Arty, the previous day he had emptied his account of all its fourteen dollars. He had negotiated a bicycle trade with another boy and acquired a superior model, a Columbia Racer. Biking home from school on the smart new machine, he stopped to watch a crowd gathering in front of the Bank of the United States. A policeman was explaining why the branch wasn't open for business and Miller would remember the group's "desperation, asking a policeman to describe what had happened to their money. . . . Suddenly, of one morning, they had no assets . . . they had what was in their pockets or what was in a drawer in the house."

When Arthur got home, he parked the new bike in front of the house and went in for a snack. By the time he came out the beautiful Columbia Racer was gone, a cruel reminder of the economic times' effect on human experience large and small. This was for him "a new reality."

Another reality Miller had to face was his looming graduation from high school. Despite the near poverty of his family and mediocrity of his grades, he was determined to go off to college. This was not from a desire like his brother's to get an education; it was a desire to get away from the atmosphere of defeat, to escape the life of the ordinary and bicycle off to adventure. Besides, if he didn't go to college, he faced unemployment or spending his days alongside Kermit at the collapsing Miltex Coat and Suit Company. His sister thought that "he knew, early on, the kind of life he wanted. Not specifically what he would be, but he knew what he *didn't want*. Arthur was determined to get out and live his life not tethered to the home."

Escape was a key element in Miller's emotional core, but not escapism. He would always reach for excitement in life, not the illusory kind but something to make the blood race. Freedom was the meaning of his lifetime love affair with bicycles.

He listed Stanford University as his chosen college in the Abraham Lincoln High School senior yearbook, which was partly wishful thinking but mainly fabrication. Stanford is one of America's elite institutions. He could not afford to go there, he had not even applied and if he had, his grades would have guaranteed rejection. Nor had Miller applied to any other college by the time of his June 1933 graduation, a ceremony his parents did not attend.

Once again Arthur went to work in his father's moribund business, but he continued to research colleges that were respectable, affordable and out of town. The most likely candidate was one of the so-called Land Grant schools at Cornell University, such as the School of Agriculture. Land Grant schools were tuition-free for New York State residents, but the notion of studying agriculture or any other Land Grant area apparently did not thrill him since he never bothered to apply. Instead he went looking for full-time work, armed with a reference from his former employer in the car supplies store. It got him fifteen dollars a week as a stock clerk in a Manhattan automobile parts warehouse. At the same time he applied to the University of Michigan after hearing about it from a neighbor who had just finished his freshman year. The tuition was a manageable sixty-five dollars a semester and so Miller filled out the application forms and mailed them off, along with transcripts of his unimpressive grades and as many reference letters as he could extract (three of the stipulated four) from his reluctant former teachers at Abraham Lincoln High School. Then he started the job at the warehouse.

Chadick-Delameter was a hulking shell of a place with high, wide and open floors holding rows of bins containing generators, clutches, brake shoes, fan belts, spark plugs, hubcaps and assorted gears—virtually every part of an automobile. The building sat at the corner of Tenth Avenue and West Sixty-third Street just off Lincoln Square, an area that thirty years later would be cleared of its inhabitants, demolished, gutted and reinvented as the Lincoln Center for the Performing Arts. At the moment it was far less grand, a run-down stretch of tenements and saloons, a working-class neighborhood for a working class that was largely not working.

Getting there from Brooklyn was an hour-and-ten-minute commute, and arriving at work on time meant getting out of the house by seven-thirty, but with so much time to kill Arthur finally began to read. He started, as best he could recall, with Dostoevsky's *Crime and Punishment*, a book he claims to have mistaken for a detective story.

The warehouse was a depressing place to work, a gapingly barren and airless place with echoing cast-iron floors, freight elevators bigger than Miltex's and windows so grimy that artificial lighting was necessary even in the daytime. Because those windows were sealed the warehouse was steamy in the summer and frigid in the winter, but Miller appreciated his good fortune in having any job at all. As for the men who worked there, they were a crude bunch. Fistfights were an everyday occurrence and here is where Miller first heard anti-Semitic slurs from adults, which he was forced to accept as a fact of life, at least in this place. Meanwhile and unsurprisingly his application to the University of Michigan was rejected by the school's Dean of Admissions, and so he decided to start classes at the City College of New York's night school, which was in the midst of becoming the Harvard of first-generation Americans, especially Jews. Young Miller, still not particularly interested in writing or even literature, registered for courses in history and chemistry. This meant a long trip to the warehouse in the morning, "running around the four story building dragging carburetors and stuff to pack up and send off all over the country," then uptown to the CCNY campus for a class or two and finally a long trip back to Brooklyn. He would fall into bed across from his wretched snoring grandfather only to be awakened by the alarm clock not so many hours later to start yet another day.

The night school education lasted two weeks. It was simply too exhausting, but Miller's positive way of thinking was not just theoretical. Self-determinism began with the self, and reconsidering the University of Michigan situation, he mailed off an audacious letter of proposal to the school's Dean of Admissions. If Black Thursday can be said to have marked the forging of a lifelong attitude for Arthur Miller, then this letter may have marked the day he became a writer. In it he explained with measured urgency that ever since receiving his high school diploma he had been holding a full-time job, saving most of what he earned so that he could go to college. In short, he was no longer the frivolous teenager who had barely managed to squeak by at Abraham Lincoln High School. Now a much more serious fellow, he was once again and more than ever expressing his seriousness of purpose in applying for admission.

The letter worked. The Dean of Admissions responded with an offer of "conditional acceptance" to the university. Before he could enroll in a full schedule of classes for a one-semester probationary period Miller would have to guarantee his ability to pay for tuition, room and board by producing a savings account passbook that showed a $500 balance. Miller responded that he would continue to work until he could do just that, and for the rest of the year he lived on a budget of two dollars a week, saving the remaining thirteen dollars of his pay despite his father's desperate need in merely making mortgage payments. He worked in that automobile parts warehouse and stuck to his budget all through the summer of 1934 until September, when he took the bank passbook and a bus to Ann Arbor, Michigan, and enrolled in the undergraduate school of the University of Michigan.

2. *Epiphany*

THE CAMPUS of the University of Michigan must have looked like the closest thing to heaven. Having spent all of his natural life within the five boroughs of New York City, Arty Miller had taken himself off to the heartland of America. This was not only physical escape but the start of his intelligent life. It was September 1934 and at age nineteen he was in control of his destiny, at least to a point; he would never entirely rid himself of the bitter taste of unfair loss in that chicken coop of a house in Brooklyn. He brought it with him to Michigan, along with a grim serious-mindedness and guilt about his brother, Kermit, "for having left him to prop up the family while I, the inferior student, went off to college."

The University of Michigan was set beside the town of Ann Arbor. What had once been a small town's Main Street—a drugstore, movie house, a few local shops—had grown to include a college marketplace for books, school sweaters and classroom supplies. Beyond this central shopping area were neat frame houses that grew more elaborate as they spread from the school away toward the north, across the Huron River. This river would have been the town's natural dividing line, but the university's vast presence made the school the reference point. Ann Arbor thus was an extension of the university and the university was an extension of the town; in fact the University of Michigan is usually called simply Ann Arbor.

The campus itself was almost urban in feel, certainly as compared to Michigan State University in East Lansing, which resembled a movie college. In Ann Arbor there were no ivy-covered Gothic buildings, no grassy quadrangles, no walks to class across spacious lawns. This place was a series of drab, almost industrial, redbrick administrative and classroom buildings, along with dormitories and imposing libraries divided by a long, slanting walkway everyone referred to as the Diagonal. What lawns did exist looked rather like grass islands within an expanse of pavement, but more important, the place had a great university's intellectual energies, and young Miller would thrive in its atmosphere.

With dormitory space limited and his admission late, he was given a room off campus, in a private home at 122 North State Street, near Catherine Street. His roommate was Charlie Bleich, another Jewish New Yorker. If not intentional, the pairing was at least fortuitous, for the two spoke the same language, Miller's with a pronounced *Noo Yawk* accent he would never lose.

One of their earliest conversations was about the Hopwood Awards—writing prizes that the university dispensed at the end of each school year, famous around campus because they came with cash. Formally these prizes were known as the Avery and Julie Hopwood Awards in Creative Writing. Avery Hopwood had been a Michigan graduate and the author of such successful Broadway farces as *Getting Gertie's Garter* and *Up in Mabel's Room*. He bequeathed one-fifth of his considerable estate to the university "for the encouragement of creative work in writing." The money was given to the Department of Rhetoric and Journalism to serve as a fund for a series of annual awards that amounted to $250 apiece, a not inconsiderable sum in 1934. The prizes "in dramatic writing, fiction, poetry and the essay" were organized into Major and Minor awards for graduate and undergraduate students, respectively. Miller would often recollect that these awards had been his original motivation for attempting a play.

He spent his first week at Ann Arbor registering for classes, yet to decide his major area of study. Evidently English was never considered. He was leaning toward history but was undecided, distracted perhaps by financial concerns. His savings were already being depleted by tuition payments, housing expenses and a meal program. If he were to survive his probationary semester and make it through the freshman year, he would have to find a part-time campus job. A Hopwood Prize, though, would go far toward paying for an entire year's tuition as well as room and board. Miller decided to major in journalism. Essays qualified for the prize. His decision need not be put down as an act of cynicism; it could as well have been an act of necessity.

In school Arthur discovered that if not a scholar, he had certainly become a student. Amazingly to him, considering his lackluster high school career, he was able to pass college courses. Classes were no longer boring distractions that kept him from baseball, basketball and football. Athletics became only occasional (although he would never lose interest in professional sports). Miller found himself actively engaged in studies and a participant in classroom discussions—sometimes even a disputatious one. He was exasperated, for instance, with what he took to be a history instructor's naive opinion that Hitler would respect treaties forbidding invasions. He considered his economics instructor blind to the realities of the Depression, teaching the subject as though the American economy could be analyzed dispassionately while it flattened the social landscape. In short, school was no longer a dreary imposition; classes weren't even enough: he signed on with the school newspaper, the *Michigan Daily*, becoming a junior reporter and learning how to type. At year's end Arthur Miller not only justified the lifting of his probation by passing all of his spring semester courses but also was assured a small loan to help him through the following year.

Yet even a loan and part-time job might not, he knew, be enough to foot the bills and indeed there would be times when the pressure of meeting expenses would lead to thoughts of quitting. The truth, however, was that he was in college to stay. That June he hitchhiked home a young man on his way to maturity. No longer did life exist only in relation to himself. "Hundreds of people were on the road," he would remember. "Everybody was hitchhiking everywhere. . . . Nobody was afraid. . . . It was assumed that [everyone] was simply somebody who didn't have any money, who was a basically honest person." He seemed to enjoy being somebody who was part of everybody.

At the start of his sophomore year in September 1935 he moved a couple of blocks still further from the central campus, to a single in a rooming house at 122 North Thayer Street. Most of his schedule was taken up with required courses, but he was allowed an elective class and signed up for one in creative writing. Beyond the classrooms Miller washed dishes in the school cafeteria to pay for his meals while supplementing his budget with a part-time evening job at the university's cancer research facility, mopping up and feeding the laboratory's thousands of mice. From dishes to mice he apparently relished every minute of whatever he did on that campus, and he still found time to write for the *Michigan Daily*. "It was enough," he remembered. "It was everything."

His assignments at the paper were not restricted to university news. He traveled to nearby Detroit and Flint to report on the efforts of the fledgling United Auto Workers to unionize several General Motors plants. He interviewed the union's charismatic leader, Walter Reuther, whose ultimate success in organizing the automobile industry—a landmark in the history of American organized labor—made the impressionable young reporter "feel safer on the earth." At the time business interests looked on unionism with suspicion bordering on paranoia. Efforts to organize labor were taken as acts of communism and for Miller covering stories about the capital-labor conflict became subjective reporting—"I identified with the workers in no abstract way." His enthusiasm put him in touch with campus action groups supporting the organized labor movement. The university was buzzing with left-wing political activities. Nearby sit-down strikes, designed to force votes on union representation, were the closest thing to a relevant issue that local Michigan had to offer.

Here surely was the origin of Miller's intense left-wing ideology, a chemistry of the Wall Street crash, its cataclysmic effect on his family's fortunes and his chance enrollment in the University of Michigan, which was not only a dynamic center of student radicalism but one located on the cusp of Detroit's automobile industry, where one of the first and greatest battles of American unionism was being fought.

Miller stayed at school during the 1936 spring break, perhaps because of a girl he had met at a party. It was in a basement, she remembered. "The first time I saw Arthur, he came toward me, ducking overhead heating pipes . . . when he asked for a date, I proposed a movie, but he didn't have any money. I treated to the movies, and afterwards to malted milks." Her name was Mary Grace Slattery and she was a pretty, dark-haired, slender coed whose family lived in nearby Lakewood, Ohio. A freshman, one year behind Miller, she was majoring in psychology, planned to become a social worker and shared his increasingly socialistic political convictions as well as his evolving drive to do something about them. They soon realized that they shared opinions about almost everything else, including the obsolescence of religion—an important subject since Mary was not only Arty's first girlfriend but also his first *shiksa*. Apparently free of, or at least freed from, taboos by way of her lapsed Catholicism and his passive Judaism ("Judaism for me and Catholicism for Mary were dead history," Miller said), they were joined by an intense belief in the brotherhood of man and sexual attraction. He'd had scant experience with women, but as usual for even the shyest of young men, once the opportunity was presented it didn't take long to get the idea. A couple of young leftists then and ardent idealists, soon they were making love at night on the lawn in front of the botany building.

If Miller indeed spent spring break at school because of Mary, this didn't stop him from using virtually the entire holiday to clatter away at a typewriter. One Saturday he started a letter in dialogue form that ran so long it had begun to seem like a couple of dramatic speeches. The deadline for that year's Avery Hopwood Awards was imminent. The $500 with which he had come to Michigan had long since been spent. He was now getting by on just the $15 a month he earned tending mice. It was time to seriously "gun," as he put it, for the Hopwood and he gave himself a writing project: a play rather than fiction or an essay, because a play "seemed more tangible," by which he presumably meant that it was acted out and could be seen. Even so, he later wrote, "the theater meant little to me . . . I had seen only a handful of plays and those had seemed so remote and artificial that I could find no connection with myself at all."

Miller had recently played a walk-on part as the Bishop of Lincoln in a school production of *Henry VIII*, Shakespeare's most obscure and probably worst play. The young man must have had some positive reaction to this stage experience because he was already adding characters to his few pages of dialogue and building scenes. Abruptly he jumped up from the desk to dash across the hall and knock on the opposite door in the hallway. It was the room of a graduate student named Jim Doll, whose parents owned the house. Young Miller just had one question: How long was an act supposed to be? Doll, who had designed the costumes for that *Henry VIII*, replied about half an hour, and the newly informed playwright hurried back to the typewriter.

Years later he would say that writing those first scenes made him realize that he could create "the unspoken feelings between the words people spoke, the lines between the lines." Miller was putting his finger on the essential difference between a play and other kinds of writing, simply that a play is made entirely of dialogue. There is no narrative or exposition, no way of explaining what characters mean by the things they say or how others are reacting. Everything must be demonstrable; physical surroundings, moods and atmosphere cannot be described, only established. One could even argue that a play does not exist at all until brought to life on the stage—that drama is strictly a performing art. For that and other literary reasons the classics scholar Harold Bloom does not even consider playwriting to be *writing*. Rather for him literature is an art of the *read* word, denser, more ambitious, complex, allusive and generally more demanding than what the stage can ask of an audience. His singular exception, because he believes it requires reading for full comprehension and appreciation, is Shakespeare. Otherwise, he says flatly, "There are no American dramatists who rank with our great writers of fiction and poetry, Faulkner, Wallace Stevens and so on." Nevertheless it might well be asked, if dramatism doesn't qualify as literature, why do so many professors of literature like Bloom study it?

The theater's "more tangible" element—the presence and vitality of the event—are what seem to have stimulated Arty Miller as he banged away at his typewriter on what now was becoming a series of scenes. He would recall that as the pages rolled out of the machine, there was a transcendent moment when he realized that he was actually writing a play. Never again, he said, would anything match "the total excitement of that discovery and I slept perhaps six hours that week and finished it."

The work was shamelessly autobiographical, "all I knew about my family." He hardly bothered changing the names and sometimes didn't even do that. In his final script, kept at the Special Collections Library of the University of Michigan, the central character, Arny—already close enough to his own name—is once inadvertently called Arty, and the brother, Ben, is once mistakenly typed *Kerm*.

The play is set in "the present"—that is, during the Depression, in the small New York City home of the Barnett (Gussie Miller's maiden name) family. The central characters are Abe, the father, a failing manufacturer of ladies' coats; his embittered wife, Esther; their elder son, Ben, who is helping out in the business; and the younger Arny, a college student in Michigan. Other characters include a young sister, Maxine (Joan Miller's middle name) and numerous extras such as "sixteen workers, five old men in black, a process server, a salesman, a doctor and a Negro elevator man." And, young

Miller points out in his script, those workers in Barnett's shop include "some Communists . . . Arny is one of them."

Had Arty, like Arny, joined the Communist Party at school? If so, there is no evidence of it, although he was never ashamed of his sympathies with the party and the reason for them. "To be Red," he would later say, "was to embrace hope, the hope that lies in action."

At curtain's rise the bickering but close-knit Barnett family is awaiting Arny, who is hitchhiking home from college. The dialogue is Jewish inflected—"I never saw in my life a woman who could enjoy worrying like my Esther"—with the young dramatist demonstrating a sense of idiom, a talent for writing speakable dialogue and playable scenes, and a gift for establishing situations and relationships with a single line—"I suppose it's a marvelous thing that you couldn't even afford to send him bus fare."

The older brother, Ben, having quit college, works with his father but swears that he won't let Arny (who wants to be a writer) "get in that business if I can help it." The play pauses to allow him to explain communism to his mother as well as to the audience. "In other words, there's no profits for a boss—it all goes to the workers. Arny wants to change it to a different system, where we may be able to use [writers, artists]." Abe, the father, insists that although he is a capitalist, "I ain't bad, I ain't no villain," and the talk builds to the end of the act and Arthur Miller's first curtain scene. It is instinctively theatrical, the grandfather praying, "his face turned to the flickering flames, his body suddenly frozen as he cries, 'Odonoi Ellohaynu,' his call to the Lord." With that Miller turned back to the first page, checked his wristwatch and began to read the act aloud. All of his life he would read early versions of his plays to anyone handy, but this first time he did it alone and the first act took just about half an hour.

The second act opens at the father's place of business where a crisis is under way. Abe is selling coats but the orders can't be filled because the shipping clerks are on strike. They are demanding "to organize a union," says Ben. "You can't get any garments through now." Instead of helping out, Arny is at home delivering speeches to his mother. "You strive too much for wealth . . . look down and see what one thing is worth against another . . . we've got to change the world." Miller tries to maintain perspective by giving her the response, "What's the matter with you? The cloak business ain't good enough for you? Arny, you can't . . . be a Communist. You're the son of the owner . . . not the working people."

When Ben arrives, Arny learns that if his father is unable to fill any orders, the bank will foreclose on the loans that have been keeping the business afloat. Abe, a character both coarse and earnest, is torn between trying to understand Arny's new beliefs and needing him at the shop, but Ben now pleads with his brother to come down and help. "We're busted if we don't deliver." Arny's response is that he won't be a scab, a strikebreaker. "I'd be a lie . . . a lie through and through . . . I'd be like an animal." Unionization, he says, "is only the start, the beginning." For a curtain line Ben's retort is "Keep your mouth shut . . . you coward!"

As the third act starts, more orders come in but they are not being delivered. The only reason there are orders at all is because none of the other manufacturers can deliver merchandise either. Abe and Ben decide to make the deliveries themselves, but in the act's second scene the two are back in the showroom, the merchandise destroyed by striking clerks in the street. The bank forecloses on the loans, leaving Ben in charge of the company's future and the playwright with impatience to bring down the final curtain. This act is only eight pages long, and its coda starts almost at once. "For us it begins," Ben says to his father,

> Arny and I . . . For us there begins not work toward a business, but just a . . . sort of battle . . . sort of fight . . . so that you'll know that this will never be in our lives. We'll never have to sit like you sit there now for the reasons you are sitting there . . . Dad, now we not only are working people . . . we *know* we are. Maybe I'm afraid . . . I don't know. But I couldn't start this thing over again. I've got to start something bigger . . . Something that won't allow this to happen . . . Something that'll change this deeply . . . to the bottom . . . It's the only way, dad . . . It's the only way.

That Thursday, six days after Arty Miller had begun his first play, he typed *Final Curtain* on page 120 of the script. On the first page he put the title, *No Villain*, taken from the father's speech early in the play. Beneath the title he typed *By Arthur A. Miller*, distinguishing himself from another Arthur Miller, a playwright whose *Marry the Girl—A Bedroom Farce* had been produced on Broadway a few years earlier in 1932.

In writing about his family Arthur A. Miller was not only following a literary tradition of starting out with a coming-of-age story; he was also laying out a technique that he would use in most of his future work. His plots would, in almost every case, be drawn from experience or research, with characters based on people he had known or studied.

He needed validation, an outsider's reaction to the play, and needed it at once. The obvious choice was Jim Doll, who knew how long an act was supposed to be and was only a few paces away, just across the hall. Doll's reaction, as Miller described it, was ecstatic: "The best student play I've ever read." A freshly exultant young playwright dashed out of the house and "ran uphill to the deserted center of town, across the Law Quadrangle and down North University."

Seeking a more authoritative opinion and with understandable trepidation Miller brought *No Villain* to Erich Walter, who taught his writing class. Walter, he recalled, was "capable of liking half a sentence but not the other half, and here I was, handing him 120 pages of writing." The teacher came into class the next day and announced that he was going to read Miller's entire play aloud. "And," the novice playwright would remember, "when I saw the students laughing, growing tense, absorbed . . . the last doubt disappeared. All that remained was perhaps a few months and I would be produced on Broadway."

In New York, Broadway's foremost producing organization was called the Theatre Guild. The guild was founded in 1919 by the twenty-eight-year-old Laurence Langner after his experiences on Macdougal Street in Greenwich Village with the Provincetown Playhouse. There, such actors as Alfred Lunt, Lynn Fontanne and Edward G. Robinson had been doing the plays of Edna St. Vincent Millay and Eugene O'Neill. Langner moved his operation uptown with the intention of creating an American counterpart to Konstantin Stanislavsky's celebrated Moscow Art Theater (or People's Art Theatre, as it was first called). The following year he was joined by a more realistic partner, a playwright-turned-critic-turned-producer by the name of Teresa Helburn. With Ms. Helburn as its coexecutive director the Theatre Guild rose to prominence, presenting artistic and commercial successes starting with the plays of George Bernard Shaw and continuing with such prestigious hits as Sidney Howard's *They Knew What They Wanted*, William Saroyan's *The Time of Your Life* and Elmer Rice's *The Adding Machine* as well as ten plays by S. N. Behrman and three by Eugene O'Neill—*Ah, Wilderness, Mourning Becomes Electra* and *A Moon for the Misbegotten*. These playwrights, as far as Ms. Helburn was concerned, marked "the high point in the craft of play writing in America."

In short, the Guild was *the theater*, and hoping to seed a new generation of superior playwrights it had inaugurated a Bureau of New Plays in 1934, two years before Miller wrote *No Villain*.

According to Ms. Helburn,

> The Bureau of New Plays [established] a play writing contest for undergraduates or young people who had recently left college. Any play submitted was first to meet with the approval of the drama department of the college. . . . The project was financed in the beginning by the six leading motion picture companies. The chief thing I learned by that first annual contest was that the caliber of the plays submitted seemed to be in direct ratio to the college drama department in which the youngsters had studied. . . [those] who had worked with Kenneth Rowe at the University of Michigan in Ann Arbor were outstanding.

Professor Kenneth Thorpe Rowe was a small, slight, tweedy thirty-seven year old who took a sabbatical leave from Ann Arbor in 1936 to spend the year in New York with the Theatre Guild. If the guild stood to benefit from the academic disciplines of the professor, he stood to be broadened by exposure to the working stage and in particular the commercial Broadway theater. Rowe would be the rare scholar to jump the gap between theoretical principles of drama and the practical demands of professional theater.

Professor Rowe had been invited to New York, in Ms. Helburn's words, to run "a seminar in play writing for the most promising young people discovered through [our] first annual contest." The guild was so pleased with the results that the association with Rowe was rearranged in order that, in the future, he would be able to conduct the seminar at the University of Michigan. Beginning with the second contest, the six winners would receive $1,250 scholarships "to work at Ann Arbor with Mr. Rowe."

While Professor Rowe was in New York with the Theatre Guild, Miller was meeting a March 31 deadline and submitting *No Villain* for consideration in the 1936 Avery and Julie Hopwood Awards in Creative Writing. Rules required that entrants' names be disguised with a pseudonym and he chose Beyoum—perhaps extrapolated from *by you and me*, referring to Mary Slattery, who may have loaned him the typewriter. She might even have typed the final copy, since she often helped him this way. When the play was submitted, it carried the exuberantly noble, youthful and quite incomprehensible dedication "to the indispensable mediators who, between the two producers, stand deserted, waiting to return from whence they came or else to die, not even graced by a battlefield."

The head of the drama division of that year's Hopwood Awards Committee was R. W. Cowden, who chaired the University of Michigan English department. The judges were Edith J. R. Isaacs, editor of *Theatre Arts Monthly*, Alfred Kreymborg, a teacher of playwriting at Olivet College, and Alexander Dean of the Yale University Theater. Their decisions were announced on May 13, 1936, and in the opinion of the most professionally qualified of the three, the editor of *Theatre Arts Monthly*, "The general standard [among graduate student entries for Major awards] seems to me higher than in any contest I have ever judged." But, Ms. Isaacs sourly continued, "regretfully, all of the Minor submissions seem to me quite without indications of talent. I have rated them simply for clarity and general quality of approach." Even among those talentless submissions for the Minor award, she rated *No Villain* second, or even more untalented than the play she put in first place.

Alexander Dean also gave second place to *No Villain* by Beyoum, leaving the playwriting teacher, Kreymborg, in the minority. He awarded Miller's play first place among undergraduate submissions, citing *No Villain* for "An excellent modern theme handled with a tender insight into character."

In any other contest two second places out of three votes would have meant second place, but in the Hopwood competition this tally was as good as a perfect score because rankings were not made public and both authors were announced as winners and given equal $250 prizes. As far as Miller knew he had won this contest and that was a good thing; it encouraged him to write more plays. All of his life he would boast of winning the Hopwood with his first play.

Of course he hadn't. Second place is second place, yet the remarkable thing is not that Miller's talent was recognized at the outset with his first play. Remarkable is that it *wasn't,* because *No Villain* is an amazing accomplishment for someone who had never written a play before, remarkable for a student and superior compared to the level of play generally submitted to agents and producers by unsolicited writers. In future years there would be requests to stage *No Villain,* but Miller refused them all and rightly so. While the product of a significantly gifted young writer, it is a youthful work nevertheless.

Arthur went home that June with passing grades and nearly $250. He withheld $22 of the Hopwood prize money to buy himself a present. Ever since working in the automobile parts store he had been in love with cars, and now he bought one from a graduate student, a 1927 Model T Ford, the first of many collectible cars he would forget to collect. He didn't drive it home, but he did put the Model T into a short story about the salesman who had so saddened him the summer he'd worked for his father.

This story is a more confident work than *No Villain,* almost suitable for publication. Written in the first person, the story describes a sensitive college student carrying coats for a salesman whom Miller calls Schoenzeit. It is set on a steamy day in summertime New York, as the weary man futilely tries to sell a winter line of coats to heartless buyers for the stores. The story attempts to plumb the psyche of the older man, whose profession Miller describes as "dignified slavery." The use of detail is careful and telling: a bow tie and starched collar suggest a brave front that cannot hide the weariness symbolized by the pair of "bulgy toed shoes" in which Schoenzeit trudges along with feet pointed outward. There are signs of youthful writing—such as referring to the man's "countenance" instead of his face—but more important is the emotional force behind the story. Miller creates a student who feels the full weight of this salesman's broken spirit and cringes in the shame of witnessing such defeat in an adult. It is a story in which compassion flows freely and openly.

He called the story "In Memoriam" because of Schoenzeit's death at the end of it, and also because of the actual suicide of the salesman on whom it is based. Upon his return to school in September Miller tried to make a play out of it. He added a family but ultimately was unsatisfied with the way the dramatization was developing and dropped the idea. He saved what he wrote, but apparently the unfinished play was lost some years later in a fire that destroyed many of his materials.

That summer his father finally gave up the ghost of the Miltex Coat and Suit Company. Idle at fifty-one and out of work for the first time since the age of twelve, Isadore Miller began to spend much of each day sleeping, as depressed people so often do. When awake, he joined the community of the jobless, sitting blankly on the front porch of the house in Brooklyn, saddening his son with the look of defeat. When Arty tried to provide company and conversation, his father would turn morbid, talking about the men who used to play cards with him, now dead and buried in the nearby cemetery. Once to change the subject the young man brought up college and his future. He wouldn't say that he wanted to be a writer, certain his father would see no security in it. So he said that he planned to be a journalist, expecting that his father would figure that reporters "work for companies and they had payrolls."

Yet when Miller returned to Ann Arbor in fall 1936 to start his junior year, he changed his major from journalism to English. He also became a night editor at the *Michigan Daily* and joined the radical youth who tended to congregate in and around the newspaper's offices. He never looked down on or condemned the unpoliticized students; he could even appreciate "the fraternity boys sitting on the porches of their mansions [in fact just houses], singing nostalgic Michigan songs as in a movie." Indeed he might have been one of them, but the Wall Street crash had turned Arthur Miller into a have-not, and now he had more in common with these radicals. This would have a profound effect on Miller's thinking, on his work and life, though it could not have seemed much of a departure at the time. On that campus to be a radical was almost conventional. Miller was already angry with what America's economic system had done to his family. Extending these convictions to include an admiration for the Soviet Union probably seemed natural. The Communists claimed to support everything he so eagerly cared about—not just economic injustices and workers' rights and unionism but the fight against fascism in Spain's civil war and the condemnation of racism everywhere. Students, Miller would later recall, "connected the Soviets with socialism and socialism with man's redemption."

Political involvement, with its meetings, demonstrations and, perhaps as the main activity, bull sessions (where "we saw a new world coming every third morning") only added to Arthur's tight schedule of classes, cafeteria dish washing, maintaining the laboratory mice and the night editorship of the *Michigan Daily*. In the bargain Miller decided to enter the second annual student playwright contest sponsored by the Theatre Guild's Bureau of New Plays. Its $1,250 scholarship awards provided motive enough and his notion was to enter the contest with a revised version of *No Villain*—a decision nearly as notable as writing the play in the first place. If all writing indeed is rewriting, young authors seldom have the patience, especially after something is well received. Miller, however, would always be a diligent rewriter, sometimes accumulating thousands of pages before settling on a play's final form or even more disciplined, discarding the whole business. In his revised version of *No Villain*, retitled *They Too Arise*, the story remains essentially the same—a Jewish family's financial straits and a collapsing business in Depression America—but characters are fleshed out. The mother who struggles with the family budget now takes out her frustrations on the father, snapping at him, "Did you ever come and ask me if I got all the bills paid?" Ben, the good Kermitlike brother, defends the old man, replying on his father's behalf that when men do ask their wives about problems, it is "because they know they'll get a nice answer."

Abe, the father, has more backbone, and Miller gives his alter ego more of a voice. Arny like the playwright sees both sides of an issue, telling his father, "I can understand that you're trying to save your business. I can understand that you're trying to make Mother and Maxine rich and happy. I can understand all that. But . . . if the strikers lose, you lose too. . . . Dammit, Dad, you're fighting on the wrong side!"

They Too Arise also has more humor. In one stretch Miller seems to be mimicking a cartoonist named Sid Gross, who had started a craze for Jewish dialect humor in the late 1920s with a newspaper series called *Nize Baby!* Miller's version of this humor runs to "Mahst be something de metter" and "Like clockwoik in a copple days comes by me ah letter." His own Jewish colloquialisms are less cartoonish and truer to character, "What are you talking?" for instance, or "Tell me already" and "God forbid!"

They Too Arise has an additional subplot involving the father's hope of saving his business by marrying off Arny's fair-minded, self-sacrificing brother, Ben, to the daughter of a man who has "a million dollar firm." The core of the play, though, remains as it was, with an added cry of the father's pain, born perhaps in that lost, dramatized version of the short story about a salesman. "It ain't fair," groans Abe, "that I should give my life like this and go out with—with nothing, Ben! Ya hear me Ben? It ain't fair!" *Death of a Salesman*'s Linda Loman is also anticipated in the mother's scolding speech—"Here a man works his life away to give you everything and when it comes to doing a little work for him, just to go downtown a couple of days, you get lazy."

At that late point in the play its author takes yet another step in his artistic evolution with a speech for Arny announcing the assertive social responsibility that Miller himself would champion. The young man tells his mother, "You think that because you close your door in the front of the house then anything that happens outside doesn't have anything to do with you . . . You only want things to 'get better.' Well the time has come when things don't get better unless you make them get better." This moment is important because it is Miller's first full statement of an activist creed he would never abandon. The revised play's title signifies this evolution from passive anger to an imperative of corrective action. If *No Villain* defends innocent victims of the Wall Street debacle, the more militant *They Too Arise* speaks for youths who will right the wrongs that caused it.

Within this rallying cry is a hint of *comes the revolution*. Another example of leftist proselytizing is Arny's rote explanation to his parents of why he is a Communist—"because I want the people to take the power that comes with ownership away from the little class of capitalists who have it now." That the origins of this speech lay in the aggressive, even revolutionary attitudes of Michigan campus radical groups is fair to surmise. If these reflected Communist doctrine, Miller would soon make his idealistic zeal personal. His play sometimes preaches, but beyond its propaganda and beneath the sloganeering and lecturing rests a deep humanity. Also the writing is more assured and theatrical than in the first version. He sent it off to the Theatre Guild in New York in care of its Bureau of New Plays contest, in the meantime attending Professor Rowe's seminar.

The University of Michigan was not, as Miller wrote in his autobiography *Timebends*, "the only school in the U.S. that gave a play writing course," to which he sarcastically added, "Harvard would never have a course in creative writing because they felt that it isn't serious." In fact it was at Harvard that Professor George Pierce Baker originated his legendary 47 Workshop, generally conceded to be America's first college-level seminar in playwriting. (He later took the course to Yale.) Baker taught such students as Philip Barry, S. N. Behrman and Eugene O'Neill. Even so, Rowe's class at the University of Michigan might have been the only one in the United States for Arthur Miller. Rowe, like the Theatre Guild, was convinced of a compatibility between high artistic standards and the realities of commercial theater. The professor would have an immense influence on the budding playwright, not only as mentor but as surrogate father. Years later Miller would tell a Michigan student reporter that Rowe

> administered the kind of criticism that is hardest to take and most necessary of all—based on common sense. Rowe did not lead, he accompanied [offering a] calm, quiet refusal to encourage dreams of sudden glory and at the same time . . . sympathy with those dreams. . . . His example . . . helped to lay up standards and goals of a very private sort for a very public art. The theater was not a carousel one jumped onto but an instrument one had to learn to play.

Rowe began the seminar by making a general comparison of the playwright's role with the director's, describing them as collaborators. He then dealt with a "unified conflict" as the basis of drama, and brought up the simple issues of complications, suspense and "the climactic rhythm of intensity." He drew a sharp distinction between "what is interesting or picturesque, and what is dramatic," and also talked about high drama and low, about classical tragedy and boulevard theater, with its plays of suspense and melodrama. The latter, Rowe said, had to be considered because Broadway was America's only professional theater. The lone dramatic genre beneath his consideration was commercial comedy.

During one session Professor Rowe brought up the crucial subject of how to find dramatic material, suggesting "any familiarly known background. Where," he asked, "does one find a plot? In the lives of the people one knows, first of all. Probably not ready-made, although, as Aristotle says, there is no reason why some real events should not have that revealing orderliness which is the function of art."

Rowe minimized the importance of stories that are completely invented, pointing out that "Aeschylus, Sophocles and Euripides drew upon the storehouse of Greek epic legend . . . Shakespeare and his fellows drew upon whatever collections of narratives, fictional and historical, were available."

But, he added, such histories, legends and lore should not be used as whole cloth. "There must always be added the 'if' of imagination—if, in such a situation, such a thing were to happen, what would follow?" Yet he also pointed out that "a [real] character may be immediately suggestive of plot. There are some people to whom actions seem to gravitate. They do things and things happen to them."

The professor devoted considerable time to discussing dramatic form as an essential, if not *the* essential, in playwriting. It was a lesson Miller would often repeat. "The basic structure of a play," Rowe said, "is the beginning of a conflict, the movement by complications to a crisis or turning point, and the movement to the resolution of the conflict." In light of this he analyzed and even diagrammed, as an example of a "great" play, John Millington Synge's *Riders to the Sea*.

Rowe proceeded to characterization, "integration between character and plot" and the naturalistic approach to dialogue, especially "speakable dialogue." He urged his class to develop "the ear for idiom" and pointed out the necessity of "telling the story by dialogue." Rowe followed this with an intense and prolonged discussion and analysis of Ibsen's *A Doll's House* (in his 1939 book *Write That Play!* his line-by-line examination runs to some 150 pages). And from Henrik Ibsen Professor Rowe brought the seminar back to what he considered the "indispensable first step in the play writing process, the writing of a scenario." This is how Ibsen began to write a play and as far as Rowe was concerned, it is the only way.

> A scenario is simply an outline of the play, and differs from any other outline only in the basis of division, which is acts, scenes, and entrances and exits. Construction is so important in drama, and so complicated in a long play, that the only way to get it right is to strip it bare and look at it. Deformities can be seen then and corrected before they affect the vital functioning of the play. The hard disciplined thinking required in the perfecting of a scenario may check the fine glow of inspiration for a time, but . . . the conception matures during the period of concentration on the scenario.

These lessons from Ibsen—writing scenarios, the problem–complication–crisis formula for dramatic construction—and the precepts of Greek tragedy were perhaps the most enduring lessons that Miller took from his seminars, along with Rowe's final word of advice. "The last thing a dramatist should do," he warned the little group of would-be Broadway playwrights sitting around the long seminar table, "is try to conform to some notion as to what subject or treatment the audience wants."

By chance, when Miller had been home for winter break before starting the seminar, he found a revival of *A Doll's House* playing on Broadway directed by the legendary Jed Harris and starring his mistress, Ruth Gordon. The young man was so impressed that a decade later he would say, "Only once in my life had I been truly engrossed in a production—when Ruth Gordon played in the Jed Harris production of *A Doll's House*."

In this play of Ibsen's, Professor Rowe reiterated, "the antecedent material is no longer introductory but the center of the immediate conflict, the past coming to life in the present and creating drama." This was not a purely academic notion, divorced from the practicalities of the working theater. A half century later the same idea would be expressed in basic stage terms by the Australian director Michael Blakemore.

> The Ibsenite construction has its source in *Oedipus Rex* of Sophocles. He happened to use a terribly effective way of telling stories. First Sophocles is ingeniously giving the audience little bits of the past so that they can see the way it's working on the present. And then suddenly, it *does* work on the present. And Oedipus discovers that he's not only killed his father but slept with his mother. From that moment on, he's doomed. So the past determines the future. And this is a very effective way of telling stories. Because the past *does* work on the present.

Young Miller took advantage of every opportunity to see Ibsen's plays. In Brooklyn during his last college summer he saw *Ghosts* at the nearby Brighton Theatre, part of New York's Subway Circuit. The star was no less than Nazimova, who was considered (by Brooks Atkinson of the *New York Times*) to be—with Laurette Taylor—one of the two greatest actresses of the time. Arthur took fourteen-year-old Joanie to see the production, which greatly impressed her. She would grow up to be a splendid actress, taking the stage name Copeland ("because I didn't want to ride on my brother's coattails"). Ibsen would have an even greater influence on Miller—something for which he would later be attacked. The Norwegian playwright's structures, however, were not the exclusive focus of Rowe's seminar, nor was realism the only mode appreciated. Greek tragedies were studied alongside the German Expressionists Bertolt Brecht, Frank Wedekind and Georg Buechner. Although different in sensibilities and separated by centuries, both schools, Miller was taught, depended on stylized rather than realistic characters. The purpose of such exaggerated figures, for both the ancient Greeks and latter-day Germans, Miller learned, was "to present the hidden forces [rather than] the characteristics of the human beings playing out by those forces on stage."

Even with Professor Rowe Miller was not the docile student, and he could be as contentious as he had been in his freshman economics and history classes. As he grew more involved with leftist causes, he brought his politics into the classroom and refused to separate dramatic purpose from political imperative. Art for him had to be responsive to social realities. O'Neill's plays, he argued, seemed too "cosmic" in a world that cried for practical solutions to immediate problems; based on classical Greek models (as so many of O'Neill's works are), they were compared by Professor Rowe to religious rituals. For Miller this was tantamount to irrelevance: The relations of man to man are primary, not, as in O'Neill, those of man to God. The professor let him have his say.

Rowe surely had something to do with *They Too Arise* winning the Theatre Guild's Bureau of New Plays competition that spring. His connection with the guild was just one of several fortuitous circumstances that seemed to be leading Miller to his future, and the $1,250 scholarship assured him of not only financial security but another seminar with Professor Rowe in his senior year. Luck, however, is not the only element in a successful career; one of the other competition winners was Thomas Lanier—later Tennessee—Williams. Williams at that time wasn't able to take advantage of the scholarship to study with Rowe. Money problems forced him to drop out of the University of Missouri and go to work as a shoe clerk.

Meanwhile at the presentation of the guild scholarships Teresa Helburn particularly noted the "tall, earnest" Miller and would remember him as a "brooding young man burning with all the injustice of the world."

Arthur spent a few scholarship dollars to buy his first typewriter, a used Smith-Corona portable. He could have afforded a new one but was already in the habit of spending carefully. He promptly began a new play. There was a 1937 Hopwood Awards contest to enter and his confidence must have been surging. In March for the first time he saw a play of his own actually staged when *They Too Arise* was given three performances—two evenings and a matinee—in the university's Lydia Mendelssohn Theatre. The Hillel Players, a theatrical club within the campus organization for Jewish students, sponsored the staging, directed by Frederic O. Crandall, then merely a Teaching Fellow. The fledgling playwright was cocky enough to call Crandall's production "very amateurish," but even so, a branch of the WPA's Federal Theatre, which usually specialized in Broadway plays, was sufficiently impressed to restage *They Too Arise* in Detroit, extending the brief run. Thus, Miller recalled, "I became known in that little pond as a playwright," and he probably began to think of himself as one too.

Starting the new play, Miller had no problem coming up with another pseudonym for the Hopwood judges: He got it right off his new secondhand typewriter—*By Corona*—and this play would be more propagandistic than anything he had written thus far. Its setting is a giant automobile parts factory, surely based on one of General Motors' plants, where the protagonist, twenty-three-year-old Max Zibriski, has joined organizers in calling for a sit-down strike to demand a vote on union representation. When a manager offers him a raise and a soft job in exchange for "a little information now and then," Max retorts, "Get yourself another rat. I work for a living," and is not only fired, but hit "a smart whack on the face" and beaten up to conclude the fast-moving scene. It is melodramatic but of the period and not a bad beginning for a second play.

The action shifts to the Zibriski farm in a scene as maudlin as a silent movie. Max's widowed mother, Maria, "a peasant: quiet, shrunken and old," stands at the stove, "slowly stirring soup." A friend keeps her company, a Polish immigrant who, like Miller's father, speaks an illiterate's English. The man has become a farmer, the Depression having cost him a food business that left him with nothing but "the pipe for [to] hook griddle to the gas"—an item never again mentioned in this play but certain to show up in a later one.

Maria's younger son, Harry, is a college junior studying engineering just home from school. While this is beginning to sound like another version of the Miller family, it isn't. Maria and her immigrant friend won't reappear, and Harry is not another stand-in for the author. He is an incipient capitalist, aiming to make a lot of money while doing little of the honest hard labor that Max loves. Harry convinces Max to join him on the easy road to management by going to college and Max, out of a job, agrees. In hard times school is a convenient escape—a notion young Miller expressed on several occasions.

The second act begins at Harry's unidentified university where, needing money for his social life, he is wangling a student loan from the dean. At the same time, through fade-outs and fade-ins, Max's former employer—owner of the strike-threatened automobile factory and a major benefactor of the university—is tyrannizing its president. The industrialist holds out two endowed engineering school buildings as bribes, demanding the dismissal of a certain history teacher who "tries to show . . . these children and the public that men like myself are actually thieves and whatnot," adding that he will no longer hire any graduating engineers who are "union sympathizers, so called liberals, or in simpler terms, Communists." Here is Miller drawing on his *Michigan Daily* experiences covering unionization strikes at General Motors. Did he suspect that the University of Michigan was beholden to the mammoth automobile corporations in Detroit? Many of his fellow campus radicals probably thought so, a notion not so far-fetched.

The craven university president capitulates to the industrialist's demands, promising that "the whole matter will be cleared up to everybody's satisfaction," and moments later he has the dean approve Harry's student loan in exchange for informing on "the people here who are interested in . . . more or less radical activities." These are Max's friends, who protest the expulsion of that "certain history teacher," having written a book that "showed the influence of big business on the universities in this country"—such as, in one of this play's most painfully didactic speeches, "paying an economics professor to preach the virtues of holding companies and the evil of publicly owned electric plants." Yet Max cannot believe that a university would give in to an industrialist's academic censorship. His brother assures him it wouldn't, while jotting down the names of the protesting students.

In the third act Max has changed his mind about the virtues of honest labor. "I don't want to be a sucker. . . . A worker's house is grey. Rain is the only paint they get . . . inside the tears . . . grey houses and grey people." But when his left-wing friends are expelled for supporting the reinstatement of the history teacher (while Miller was at Michigan, three student activists actually were expelled), Max realizes who betrayed them. As Harry comes through the door with a girlfriend, Max grabs his brother "by the collar and lifts him": "Stand up, ya rat! Lift up your head! Y' crept to 'em, didn't ya! Ya went on your hands and knees, didn't ya! . . . like a two bit whore!"

After Harry slinks out in defeat his girlfriend muses, "He was really weak in an ugly way," and now she just wants to leave with Max, who is "the cleanest, rightest thing I ever saw." Here is an endearing example of youthful playwriting: A hero, noble and dynamic but (left unsaid) shy with girls, is provided with a sexually aggressive heroine. Max gallantly replies, "You stay here," then weakening, he tells her, "no don't stay," only to conclude inconclusively, "I don't know what you should do." Such indecisiveness—the obverse of balanced reasoning—occurs several times in this play; indeed the intended equivocations are never explained. This trait is something to watch for in later Miller works.

The play's conclusion is set a year later with a unionization strike in progress and police attempting to maintain order. Max, conveniently in town, at last becomes an activist. A shot is fired and he gets on the public address system, imploring, "Give it all you got!" When the stage clears, he has been hit in the shoulder; "I'll be okay," he tells one of the union men.

> I gotta live now . . . I learned too much to die. They burned a hole in me . . . it's like a stamp on my diploma. . . . Ever hear of anybody graduatin' in a year? With the best diploma education can buy? . . . Y'know? The plant's pretty . . . in the dawn. . . . Listen to a guy who knows. It's gonna be ours.

And the union man agrees, "You graduated, Max. With honors."

Thus the title *Honors at Dawn*.

Not only a student play, it is a youthful one, more ardent than crafty but craftier than anything Miller had yet written and his first venture into plot invention. Much had been learned from writing and revising *No Villain* and this play shows it. Some of the more esoteric lessons from Professor Rowe's playwriting seminar had not yet been applied, particularly the Greek–Ibsen notion of relating events in the present to those in the past. Yet *Honors at Dawn* demonstrates an awareness of developing first-act conflict into second-act crisis, leading to third-act resolution. Moreover, in this first attempt at a fictional plot Miller seems to be taking Rowe's advice in drawing on "the lives of people we know"—in this case the student radicals. As for writing speakable dialogue and developing an ear for idioms, they were among the basic gifts Miller brought to his work. His characters are distinctly drawn with individual styles of speech. The action has propulsion and the acts have definition, conclusion and an overall arc. This play too is more knowledgeable than *No Villain* with regard to stage practicalities such as cast size and number of settings. Entrances and exits remain somewhat awkward and contrived, but the group scenes are well orchestrated, and while the concluding romantic scene is syrupy, cliché-ridden and plainly influenced by period movies, its dramatism is vivid and so, by and large, is the play.

Certainly this is the work of a freshly and intensely politicized young man obviously influenced by the "poster plays" (Harold Clurman's description) of Clifford Odets, who exploded onto Broadway with *Waiting for Lefty* in 1935 and had just followed it up with *Awake and Sing.* To young Miller Odets seemed singularly "pure, revolutionary, and the bearer of the light . . . the only poet . . . not only in the social protest theater but in all of the New York theater." Years later Miller would concede that Odets's plays demonstrated a "Marxist commitment," but he remained loyal to this idol of his youth as being a poet of the theater with "a license for outrage . . . overwhelmingly the clarion playwright." The fact that Odets was also "an American romantic, as much a Broadway guy as a proletarian leader" didn't seem to hurt either.

Honors at Dawn likewise demonstrates a Marxist commitment, at times an elementary example of agitprop (agitation and propaganda) theater, being message-driven and more involved with argument than dramatic values. While not overtly communist (except for "the plant's gonna be ours"), the play is certainly communistic with its malevolent capitalists, saintly workers and idealization of labor. References to fights and battles to change the system may or may not be meant to imply revolution, but there is no mistaking the play's social goal. This sort of polemic leads not only to cardboard villains but also to cardboard heroes, and *Honors at Dawn* suffers at times from two-dimensional characters as well as stretches of idle dialogue that often lead nowhere, with awkward turns of phrase ("thieves and whatnot").

Some of these missteps are the lapses of a dramatist cramped by his own political agenda, but mostly they are the errors of a novice. They are not nearly as important as the overall accomplishment. *Honors at Dawn* is the second in what would be a long series of plays dealing with brother-to-brother relationships, and it marks a sure step forward in Miller's development of playwriting fundamentals. As for rats and squealers, this would not be the last from him on the subject.

Miller not only won the 1937 Hopwood Award for the play—he took first place.

Arty Miller was not prone to making friends easily. His freshman roommate, Charlie Bleich, had felt "all but ignored." Yet one chilly September morning in Miller's senior year a stranger turned up at the door unannounced, a short and slender young man with a mop of dark brown hair and a familiar Brooklyn accent. He came from Coney Island, virtually next door to Gravesend, and without knocking walked into the room and announced, "You Miller? I'm Rosten, Normy Rosten."

A startled Miller asked, "What do you want?"

"I came here on the scholarship. Something about writing plays."

Rosten had been another of the six Theatre Guild winners in Miller's group, and without waiting for a word of welcome or even providing a segue asked, "Where can I get a room?" Ignoring the possibility of an answer, Rosten again changed the subject. "You got any ideas for a play you wanna sell cheap?" Norman sometimes affected an uneducated way of speaking, as if a member of the nobly unpolished masses. An ardent leftist, he liked to remind people that he had once worked as a garage mechanic.

A year older than Miller, Rosten had already graduated from Brooklyn College and was working with the WPA's Federal Theatre and Writers Project when he won the scholarship to study with Professor Rowe. He promptly impressed Miller with his writing credentials, having published "pomes" in *Partisan Review*, *The New Masses* and *Poetry Magazine*. Miller would soon tell the University of Michigan all about that first meeting in an article for the school humor magazine, *The Gargoyle*. Since then, he wrote, Rosten "has become, as they say, the blight of my life." All kidding aside, Miller boasted that his friend was not only publishing "pomes" but also writing radio plays for the university station and stage plays for the campus theater. In fact a "damn big play" of Normy Rosten's was about to be presented titled *The Proud Pilgrimage*. Miller wrote, "there's a bombing right on the stage . . . [to] kill as few people as possible at the same time, not including the author, of course." To that he added, in this affectionate testimonial,

> He can't write without music. He must sit, for instance, with his radio-victrola on full blast and his ear to the speaker, wearing away one Beethoven quartet every month. The pencils on his desk must be as parallel as tracks or he gets panicky. . . . He must fold his sox . . . [along with] his sweater over the chair . . . his shoes must sit in the closet, parallel as the pencils with the shoe laces inside . . . I told him to wait for me outside a man's office and when I returned three minutes later he handed me a "pome" saying, "I wrote it." "When?" I ask. "Just now," he says.

The piece was signed *By Art Miller*. He was growing more dignified; no more Arty.

Rosten not only shared Art Miller's interest in writing plays but his politics as well, perhaps even more ardently: One of the first things he did at Michigan was enroll in the Young Communist League. Ann Arbor was awhisper with warnings about the dangers of joining radical organizations, even of signing campus petitions. Miller had been alerted by a fellow student, "Everything you do is being written down." Rosten scoffed at these fears. Joining the party was daring indeed.

Meanwhile he, Art and Mary became a threesome, then a foursome when she introduced him to her roommate, Hedda Rowinski, a trim, grinning, bespectacled Jewish girl who, like Mary Slattery, was studying psychology with the intention of becoming a social worker. Hedda and Norman would become Arthur Miller's first old friends.

3. *Epic*

WHILE TAKING A second semester of Kenneth Rowe's seminar in the last half of his senior year, Miller went after a third consecutive Hopwood Award. He had trouble coming up with a title for the play and by entry deadline still hadn't thought of one. The script he submitted was simply called *A Three Act Prison Tragedy,* but this time he had no trouble thinking of a pseudonym. Inevitably it was L. C. Smith, the partner of Corona.

Fifty years after starting this, his third and final student play, Arthur Miller would remember it as being the first that wasn't autobiographical, the first to be based on research and the first to deal with social problems that did not affect him personally. This young man was still an ardent admirer of Soviet Russia, still committed to the notion, learned from the Soviets, that art "ought to be of use in a changing society," but he was developing independent views about an artist's right to creative freedom. Indeed Miller wrote his new play in a style distinctly opposed to official Soviet realism. His socialist political ideology evidently was secure, but this too was kept within the limits of personal conscience. Thus while his new play remained involved with the basic issues of the Left, it demonstrated a focus that went beyond the Marxists' signature issue of capitalism and the working class. Miller was moving toward the individual's relationship to society and such matters as responsibility, guilt, action, psychology and fraternity, all of which would recur as themes in his plays.

The idea for *A Three Act Prison Tragedy* came after a visit to a nearby penitentiary. A friend who graduated from the University of Michigan the previous June with only the most rudimentary psychology courses to his credit landed a job as the chief and only psychologist in the 8,000-inmate Jackson (Michigan) State Penitentiary, about 100 miles west of Ann Arbor. Miller was struck by the institution's social significance and dramatic possibility. With the friend's help he spent a number of weekends in Jackson interviewing prisoners, reviewing their records and gathering details of the prison environment.

Coincidentally, a similar subject was being dramatized at that time by Thomas Lanier Williams, a fellow winner of the Theatre Guild's 1937 Bureau of New Plays contest. It is interesting to compare the two approaches. Williams, who would eventually develop a uniquely lyrical and stylized naturalism, came up with a painstakingly realistic semidocumentary about a true and tragic event in a Pennsylvania prison. His play, *Not About Nightingales*—the first to carry the name Tennessee Williams—decries the inhuman conditions in a particularly evil penal institution. Oddly enough, Miller's treatment is the more imaginative, an attempt, as he then put it, at "ex- or impressionistic drama." This take on the subject is at once more personal yet more detached than Williams's. The anomaly reflects Miller himself, who could care intensely about all of mankind but have problems with emotion on the personal level—a typical liberal, some have said.

Miller started the play in October 1937, during the first semester of his senior year. Following Rowe's guidelines, he began with a scenario outlining the plot and characters. Dividing the play into three acts, as was standard at the time, he decided to restrict it to one location. "The entire action," he wrote, "occurs in the office of Dr. Karl Mannheim," who is a psychiatrist "in The Mount Warren State Prison, somewhere in the center of the United States."

The name Karl Mannheim might seem a curious choice for an American character. Miller would always have a weakness for significant names. The play's Karl Mannheim is "responsible for the sanity" of the prison population. In 1937 a real Karl Mannheim was a German anthropologist-philosopher of considerable reputation. He had already published *Ideology and Utopia* and his ideas were commonly taught in undergraduate humanities courses. Mannheim's essential theories had to do with the *sociology of knowledge*, by which he meant science as a social phenomenon, and the title of his book refers to a contrasting of ideology, defined as a justification of an existing social system, with utopia, meaning the total replacement of a system. Mannheim's conclusion is that any society—and the development of knowledge within that society—is a product of its government and economic system. This is intellectual socialism and Mannheim, unsurprisingly, was a prominent European Socialist. His ideas certainly fit in with Miller's and even anticipated the Miller to be, so the choice of Karl Mannheim for the central character appears more than coincidental and rather an echo name.

The setting described in the stage directions is a grim place, its furnishings "institutional and strong," except for the leather couch that was de rigueur for psychiatrists' offices, at least on the stage. Otherwise, *The Jackson Prison Play*, as it was soon retitled, ignores the cells, clanging gates, brutal guards and the rest of the usual business of prison fiction because the play is not really about prison. It is interested in prison as a metaphor for the conditions of the working class under American big business.

The story begins with the entrance of Caroline Matthews, a college friend of Dr. Mannheim, who tells him that her husband, Victor, also a school friend, has just been incarcerated. Victor is not only a meaningful name but one to note in any study of Miller's work. It recurs in several of his plays and is always given to the good brother character: Kermitlike, a moral victor who is benevolent and just but unrealistic and ineffectual.

Mannheim's ignorance of Victor's presence is credible, given that the man was just admitted and that the prison is one of the biggest in the country. Less believable is Karl's chilly reaction when he learns of his old friend's predicament. He asks Caroline to wait in an outer office while he meets with the villainous deputy warden, a walking prison movie cliché, who orders him to punish a young inmate with two months in solitary confinement for "punkin' for a wolf in the power house." Mannheim's response to this example of period homophobia (and slang) is the less than enlightened "How do you know he's perverted?" Nevertheless he complies with the order, leaving the youth to shout, "For God's sake, Doc, not the bottom! I'm no punk I tell ya! I got a wife, for Christ's sake!"

Mannheim berates himself for such craven obedience and asks to see the ex-classmate. Convicted of performing an abortion, Victor is a bitter man, blaming his plight on a former employer, a manufacturer who really prosecuted him because he insisted on certifying workers' injuries as being job-related. Those denied compensation were now being imprisoned for committing crimes of need and Victor vows to avenge this social wrong. His anger is heightened by the belief that his wife is pregnant, which she isn't. In short, Victor is becoming delusional, but Karl promises to "bring him back." That is Mannheim's work, to "bring people back to their senses." Indeed, with a heroic arrogance this would be Miller's lifelong aim.

The Jackson Prison Play pauses to introduce Karl Mannheim's girlfriend, Jean. Like Arthur's own girlfriend, Mary, Jean is an assertive idealist who also helps with the typing. Telling her about the woeful prison conditions, he promises to overcome his passivity and do something about the situation. Mannheim's vow brings down the curtain and the second act begins as, in the words of his trusty-secretary, he is "getting screwed up something terrible." The pictures on his office walls are disappearing, symbolizing a refusal to see what is in plain sight—namely, prison wrongs. Once again his girlfriend urges him to take action. "Is this the way you're strong? . . . Where's the towering mind you were so proud of? You listen to me," she cries, telling him to either act "or else there's one answer. You're afraid." Her strength shames his cautiousness, but the play doesn't act on that as he murmurs, "Believe in me. If I know what to do I can do it . . . I've got to think and make up my mind . . . Give me time, Jean." It is a tender, earnest and touching speech, reasonable perhaps but unassertive. It speaks for Miller's concerns about his own reluctance to act on convictions.

Midway through the second act Jean begins working in the office with Karl, and in a kind of reverie he makes an irrelevant speech that has to be read as—for Miller—a most revealing confession.

> I'm a man without tears . . . as cold as the snow. . . . I'm going . . . back home . . . nobody spoke in our house, even at the table. The lips were tight. I never remember anybody crying, or laughing loud. . . . I was alone when I was young . . . harder . . . stronger, I think. I'll do it again. I'll change as consciously as I did when I was nineteen.

That was Miller's age when he fled his ruined father, his devastated mother and his sacrificial brother, opting out for college and his own life.

Jean reaches up to save the last picture on the wall while tossing a lifeline to coherence. "You're either for them or against them." A moral absolutist, she sees equivocation as evasion, "the shifting, tender ground and it won't hold you very long." This scene is not uninteresting as it explores a Hamletlike character paralyzed by what Miller sees as only reasonableness. He himself would confess, "I am not by nature a man of action. . . . I find myself reflecting at a furious pace when others are clenching their fists. In times of imminent danger, peculiarly enough, I am more coldly objective than ever."

Jean finally spurs Karl to action and he tells the deputy warden, "You're through. Right now I'm big enough to wheel you and this hell house into the biggest public square in America!" Not much later he is indeed triumphant. The deputy warden is replaced and the prison's evil conditions doomed, all symbolized by a new set of pictures on the office wall. Then an archfiend materializes—the manufacturer who had prosecuted Mannheim's classmate. This man, capitalism incarnate, is in the significant company of a senator, for he has the government, like the prison, in his pocket. Victor cries, "You are mutilating hundreds of families with your system!" before being taken off in a straitjacket, and the manufacturer leaves as well, making a lame exit after an unnecessary appearance.

The play heads for the final curtain as a fresh inmate is punished by a new deputy warden. Nothing has changed. Jean again asks Karl to quit, but hearing the sound of a rivet gun, he says, "That gun [meaning capitalist manufacturers] makes maniacs . . . It will have to be true just so long as one man is owned by another like a beast is owned. And," he adds—lest anyone miss the point—"I don't mean only men behind bars. . . . This time we'll show the people of America . . . who their enemies are!" Yes, he declares, he is quitting the prison, but only to take Victor's old job as a workmen's compensation doctor at the manufacturer's plant, to change the system from within.

Yet the final curtain has stopped falling halfway down. Miller needs to explain the significance of the false pregnancy should the audience have missed it, which would be entirely understandable. Victor's wife is in effect the Virgin Mary and "Something," Karl says,

> was actually born in here . . . Victor's son, the one they couldn't kill because things like this . . . belong to mankind. Long ago it was nailed to a cross but it never died . . . it's a conception that lies in the ultimate struggle of men with the masters of men. That is its immaculateness, its divorcement from the single father . . . There must be a new Jesus in tens of thousands walking the earth.

Taking down one of the pictures on the wall, Mannheim leaves the others for the new psychiatrist. "When he can't see the beauty in them anymore, it's time for him to quit or make a great disobedience." Thus the play's ultimate title, *The Great Disobedience*—and disobedience rather than militant uprising would seem to characterize the youthful Arthur Miller's approach to political revolution. As if struggling with the Communist call to violence, Miller is searching for a civil way to change the system and disprove unfair accusations of his inertia and timidity.

While the play marks a good first try at dramatic fiction based on research, it is programmatic and lacks both the idealistic fervor of *Honors at Dawn* and the satisfying wholeness of *No Villain/They Too Arise*. As expressionist drama, *The Great Disobedience* is neither subjective nor exaggerated enough; as for impressionistic, no such theatrical style exists. Miller's inexperience with symbolism (the wall pictures, for instance) also betrays a lack of interior logic: there is no consistent level of reality—or unreality—in *The Great Disobedience*.

The spine of this play (its dramatic backbone) is a connection between psychology and the corporate aggrandizement that is symbolized by the prison, a connection never effectively made. Likewise, the plot device of linking withheld legitimate workmen's compensation payments to the devilish machinations of corporate America is not clear. As to the third act appearance by the villainous manufacturer, the confrontation is fudged. Instead of making for a climax, it wastes a figure of mythic dimension who never should have appeared. Finally and foremost, Karl Mannheim is an inert and bloodless protagonist, constructed as a column of neuroses. Vacillation and compulsive habits simply do not add up to personality, and Mannheim emerges as wishy-washy. Victor is more dynamic, yet what is the implication of his being led off in a straitjacket? Does this suggest that Miller had doubts about the compatibility of sanity (meaning good sense) with absolute morality? There is no clear answer.

Despite these faults, *The Great Disobedience* shows Miller's progress as a thoughtful dramatist. The plot moves smartly from point to point. Professor Rowe's advice for constructing a narrative ("If, in such a situation, such a thing were to happen, what would follow?") was taken to heart. Also in Jean we find Miller's first fully realized female. She is intelligent, righteous, supportive, adult and independent minded, and if she is based on his girlfriend, then Mary Slattery may well have been Miller's captain of conscience. The sudden Jesus Christ speech certainly bears the mark of an outside influence. Such notions as "nailed to a cross," "immaculateness," "divorcement from the single father" and "a new Jesus" are almost in another tongue. Perhaps this is the language of a Mary Slattery reconciling her socialist commitment with a not entirely lapsed Catholicism; or else Art Miller was learning something about Christianity instead of simply fearing it.

Submitted at the March 31 deadline for the 1938 Avery Hopwood Awards, *The Great Disobedience* was turned down by all three judges, whose unsurprising consensus was that it was "muddled" and "turgid." The defeat does not seem to have unduly depressed the young author; he would always be able to cope with rejection, an essential quality for any artist, but particularly a playwright aspiring to the commercial arena. Perhaps he was buoyed by the imminence of graduation, a traditionally bracing time.

In June 1938 the University of Michigan awarded him a Bachelor of Arts degree in Language and Literature, a signal event in Miller's life. Whether by coincidence or destiny, Arthur Miller's artistic career—indeed the life he lived—was made possible at the University of Michigan, where he underwent a personal, moral, political, intellectual and artistic epiphany. His experience was everything that college was supposed to provide, "the testing ground," he would later say, "for all my prejudices, my beliefs and my ignorance, and it helped to lay out the boundaries of my life."

His friends began their postgraduate lives at once. Norman Rosten returned to the WPA's Federal Theatre and Writers Project, which he had left to accept the Theatre Guild's scholarship to Michigan. Familiarly known as the Federal Theatre, the program was directed by Hallie Flanagan (formerly the production assistant to Professor George Pierce Baker at Yale). Subsidizing actors, directors and playwrights, the Federal Theatre also sponsored stagings, most of them performed free of charge, in theaters across the country. Harold Clurman, one of the founders (with Cheryl Crawford and Lee Strasberg) of the Group Theatre and a preeminent stage intellectual of the period, considered the Federal Theatre Project "the most truly experimental effort ever taken in the American theater." It was responsible for the production of classics such as Orson Welles's *Macbeth* for the Negro People's Theatre in New York, as well as such new plays as Sinclair Lewis's *It Can't Happen Here*, T. S. Eliot's *Murder in the Cathedral* and the Marc Blitzstein musical *The Cradle Will Rock*. Perhaps the project's most important achievement, however, lay in helping theater people survive the Depression while doing what they do. In 1938 in New York City alone, where the playwright Elmer Rice headed the program, some 5,000 actors, directors and dramatists were being paid the same $22.77 a week by the Federal Theatre—among them Burt Lancaster, Joseph Cotten, Nicholas Ray, E. G. Marshall, John Houseman and Sidney Lumet.

Also Norman Rosten. He and Hedda Rowinski had come home to New York, were married and found an apartment on Remsen Street in Brooklyn Heights. Mary Slattery was in the neighborhood as well, having dropped out of school to come East with Art. She moved to nearby Pierrepont Street, taking a small apartment that he helped her find to share with a roommate. She used her speedy typing to get a job as a secretary with a publishing house, Harcourt Brace.

Brooklyn Heights was a charming district, beautifully situated, facing the New York harbor with a stunning view of the Manhattan skyline. Along its waterside is the wide Promenade for strolling or bench sitting. Town houses, converted stables, a mews or two and cobblestone streets complete the picturesque scene. The area was becoming an enclave for young left-wing writers and artists, and Art Miller seemed to be the only one of them not living there. He had committed himself fully to playwriting with no means of support. The Federal Theatre, however, offered a way out, and Norman Rosten helped him apply for admission—an arduous and exasperating process, encumbered with bureaucratic requirements and frustrated by delay. In the meantime he could only return to his parents' bitter house on dead-end East Third Street in Gravesend and to the little room that he shared once again with his miserable grandfather. His mother's contempt for his father had grown even deeper as Isadore spent the last of their saved or borrowed monies in a futile effort to start another garment business in those distressed times. The twenty-three-year-old Miller was oppressed as always by any confinement. In a sense he had to find his bicycle; but he could only escape that fractious atmosphere ("I feel a small, size 14 chain around my 15 ½ neck") with occasional overnights at Mary's apartment or in the basement, where he set up a table, chair, lamp, and wrote.

Miller's first project in that dead of August 1938 was yet another version of *They Too Arise*. A family play with Odetsian overtones, it must have seemed his best bet for a commercial production. This was his third take on the autobiographical material. Although he would wonder whether he would "always have to write my plays over after I have 'finished' them once," still, he would tell Professor Rowe, "After pushing that prison play, working with family stuff and comedy was like a holiday."

Now called *The Grass Still Grows* (meaning that there is life after business failure), the play is even better than its previous incarnations. The revision keeps the original's basic plot, while taking full advantage of its author's training and experience at college. The cast of characters is essentially the same, although the young sister is dropped. Arnie is no longer at college but in medical school, as if Miller had to age his alter ego to keep pace with his own life, and perhaps notable is an added reference to the parents' inability to attend the son's college graduation. He gives them a valid excuse—that they can't afford the trip—but it certainly seems as if his feelings were hurt by his own parents not coming to Michigan for his graduation, and that he indeed had feelings to be hurt.

The brother, Ben, now has a tragic pathos in his assorted sacrifices and the father is better loved ("How am I so clever, so wise, that when my son comes to me and tells me he loves a girl, that I should take a life in my two hands and tell him no?"). The mother is angrier: "It's very few people who can be poor and happy. And I want them to be happy. And they're poor. You tell me *love*. I know what love is."

The dialect comedy is gone, although much of the dialogue remains idiosyncratically Jewish ("Before you deliver your message to Congress" or "So where is my fault?"). Employed carefully and neatly, it provides the atmosphere for what Miller considered the play's emotional environment, "the problems of Jewish life and the Jewish character."

The most attractive figure remains the good brother, Ben, rather than the protagonist, Arnie. In this version Ben has become a would-be novelist, sacrificing his aspirations to help support the family and, with foolish benevolence, burning his manuscript—a deed perhaps borrowed from Ibsen's *Hedda Gabler*—while saying without conscious bitterness, "it warmed the house." In one of Miller's more revealing lines, which sounds like Kermit (in the words of his sister, Joan, "the warmest human being you could ever imagine"), the play's older brother confesses, "I look for a loveable trait in everybody . . . I cannot appreciate real evil." Miller himself pointedly and curiously qualified his brother as "a good man to have around, but one with a pathological honesty."

Arnie's opinion is that "Everybody loves Ben because Ben loves everybody. He's soft, that's his trouble," and he advises his big brother to quit the garment business. More to the point of Miller's own development, Arnie can confidently state Arthur's creed of self-determinism, telling his father and brother to stop waiting for some "great event" to "solve everything. . . . People, people, when the hell are you going to learn that it's entirely up to you?"

Then, easing up on the rhetoric, the playwright marries off Ben to his girlfriend and has Abe tell his wife, "let's walk with the time instead of trying to stand on it." The good feelings are almost those of a musical and in this final version the play is gratifying, certainly worthy of a low-key production. Without a doubt its author was a playwright with a beautiful talent. Miller worked at his craftsmanship and now it merged with his intelligence. He was all but ready for the professional stage.

The scenario for *The Grass Still Grows* had taken more than a month to write, but the play itself was finished in only a couple of weeks. By October 1938 Miller was ready to show it to a theatrical literary agent, and he followed Norman Rosten to Leland Hayward and Company, New York's most glamorous agency. The script received a prompt reading, doubtless owing to its author's Theatre Guild playwriting prize. Even so, Miller was startled by the response he got within just a few days from Paul Streger of the Hayward office. A former actor and casting director, the small and slender Streger had just fled the eerie clutches of the notorious Jed Harris, whom Streger grudgingly admired, while privately calling his employer, aspiring producer Leland Hayward, "a road company Jed Harris."

Streger had learned the importance of tempo from Harris, who had revolutionized Broadway in the twenties with such propulsive plays as *Broadway* and *The Front Page*. The agent now told young Miller that in much the same way, *The Grass Still Grows* "moves fast, it is a comedy, there's a hell of a lot of fun in it, and there's body to it." The thrilled young playwright dashed off a letter to his old professor, exulting that Streger not only loved his play ("I thought the man was mad with the raving") but understood it perfectly and had immediately offered a representation contract. Even as he wrote, he said, the script was being submitted to Broadway producers.

The Theatre Guild was not among them, there evidently being no point in sending a revised version of *They Too Arise* to the organization that only a year earlier had given it a college writing award. Given the play's political stance, Jewish milieu and Odetsian manner, the obvious first option was the politically committed, left-wing Group Theatre. After a maddening wait *The Grass Still Grows* was rejected because, Miller wrote to Rowe, "They didn't want to do another Jewish play this year." All the Jewish producers on Broadway were fearful, he insisted, about making waves in a period rife with an anti-Semitism that existed not just in Nazi Germany but also in America. "When trouble brews [they think] it is best for the Jew to hide under the bed."

Streger turned to the "Aryan producers," as Miller put it, but they were just as discouraging. Even his champion at the Theatre Guild, John Gassner, who read it as a favor, was pessimistic about *The Grass Still Grows*. A plump little fellow, Gassner was a theater intellectual, "an intermediary," as Professor Eric Bentley of Columbia University put it, "between the teaching world and the Theatre Guild." Gassner had succeeded Harold Clurman as the guild's chief play reader and had since become a friend of Kenneth Rowe during the professor's year at the guild. Gassner was also a judge in the new playwright competitions, one who put his decisions to work. He had recommended Tennessee Williams to the guild's founder, Laurence Langner, as "a modest young man with a poet's sensitivity, a gift of imagination and a feeling for trenchant dramatic dialogue which [reminds] me of O'Neill." Largely on John Gassner's word, the Theatre Guild was planning to produce Williams's Broadway debut play *Battle of Angels*. Now Gassner hovered above Miller with similar pride of discovery as well as shared political convictions.

The playwright, however, had a more pressing need—namely, income. He was not proud of his dependency on Kermit's generosity. He began writing for radio, which is what Rowe's wife did (she had Miller's "deepest admiration for [sticking] out so many years in radio without losing her sense of values"), and promptly sold a sketch to *The Rudy Vallee Show*. It was called *Joe the Motorman* and Miller chilled at the irony of having "written reams of heartfelt drama and could just as well starve on the street for lack of a job, but on the basis of a specious piece of junk like *Joe the Motorman* . . . an opportunity to live by my pen is opened up."

Junk or no, Arthur Miller was finally being paid for his work—no small matter in a writer's life—and promptly began a serious half-hour radio play called *William Ireland's Confession*. The idea came from a true account of a case involving forgeries of Shakespearean papers in eighteenth-century Ireland. The subject was appropriate for a highbrow radio series such as CBS's *Columbia Workshop*, whose contributors included Archibald MacLeish, a writer Miller admired. The program's producer bought the play and *William Ireland's Confession* was aired on Thursday night, October 19, 1939. Its author was only bemused by the happenstance of a break in radio yet none in theater, and he wrote his professor,

> Success in this business depends in the beginning solely on luck and contacts . . . Nobody seems to be able to judge anything on its merits but if you can get some well known illiterate in the business to think you're a genius, the gates swing wide. Oh the stink of it would pollute the heavens.

One of the Federal Theatre's endless regulations required that an applicant be out of a job and living on welfare. Miller was certainly out of a job, but to qualify for those payments he had to prove himself homeless, or at least living with nonrelatives. To mount such a charade and be prepared for a government inspector's surprise visit, he enlisted the cooperation of Sidney Franks, the boyhood friend of racing-down-corridor days on One-hundred tenth Street. Sid's father, once a prosperous banker, had crawled out from the Wall Street crash to take a job washing dishes at an Automat cafeteria. Sid seemed to have suffered a similar downfall, at least in Miller's view. The Columbia University graduate was now a uniformed policeman living with his father in a seedy midtown Manhattan walk-up, but they were willing to set up a cot where Art Miller supposedly slept. The ruse succeeded. The Department of Welfare accepted his case.

As Miller recounts in his autobiography *Timebends*, the two friends kept in touch for a time before drifting apart once more. Otherwise his recollection of this welfare episode, while vivid, is credible only in broad outline. Five pages of dialogue, ostensibly remembered verbatim from an encounter a half century past, simply defy belief. As for his Federal Theatre application he told Rowe, "My hands shake when I think of it. The red tape is so engulfing." The continuous stream of WPA forms to be filled out must have seemed a Kafkaesque waltz in bureaucratic time.

Theater people were encouraging. Lee Strasberg, a cofounder of the Group Theatre, praised *The Grass Still Grows* to a class in playwriting and even wrote a letter of recommendation on Miller's behalf to the Federal Theatre and Writers Project. Not much later his application was finally accepted ("if nobody has lost the 31st form I filled out") and that helped assuage the disappointment of Streger's signing off on his play. The weekly

$22.77 freed him instantly from his crabbing grandfather, squabbling parents and the household atmosphere of defeat. Miller could now cheerfully confess that while "frightened" at the start of *The Grass Still Grows* ("I did not have a Professor Rowe to consult with") and still without means of support, he had ultimately enjoyed being self-sufficient, and when he finished the play,

> felt so imperious that I laughed out loud in [that] basement! For the first time in my life I felt bigger than the play I was writing . . . I put my arms around the typewriter and . . . that's why I don't weep over Streger's failure to sell the play. And that's how I feel about the prison play . . . *The Great Disobedience*. I laugh at that title. *I* was The Great Disobedience. It dragged me around a whole year with a ring in my nose . . . I know I'm shouting and I'm obscure, but peace, it's wonderful.

If a typewriter (his work) seemed at times the only thing he could put his arms around, peace indeed was what the weekly paycheck made possible: escape from 1350 East Third Street in Brooklyn to a studio apartment, four flights upstairs in a brownstone at 34 East 74th Street in Manhattan. It was just "a large white room, with two windows. . . . But I have a desk," he exulted on November 27, 1938, "and a rug!" The glamorous neighborhood ("yes, right off Fifth Avenue on the WPA") made him feel "like *The New Yorker* magazine," although he did "wish there were just a teeny bit more heat."

Even as Miller started at the Federal Theatre, it was already threatened by a congressional committee with which he was unfamiliar. The committee had been proposed two years earlier by Samuel Dickstein, a Democrat from New York. A Jewish immigrant and the son of a rabbi, Dickstein was apprehensive about Hitler and his Nazi sympathizers in America. He proposed the formation of a standing committee to investigate the Nazi Bund and other anti-Semitic groups. By summer 1938, with such disturbing developments mounting (in February 1939 the largest of all Bund rallies would be held in Madison Square Garden), Dickstein's proposed committee was voted an appropriation of funds. By then, however, and under the chairmanship of Texas Democrat Martin Dies, the new committee had broadened its mandate to investigating "every subversive group in this country." For a time it was simply known as the Dies Committee but soon came to be called the House of Representative's Committee on Un-American Activities—soon contracted to the casual acronym HUAC (which was catchier than the correct HRCUA). Its first public hearings were held in August 1938, only a few months before Miller was accepted into the Federal Theatre program.

Representative Dies was not a strong personality. From the outset he was intimidated by a congressional newcomer, a New Jersey Republican named John Parnell Thomas, who was less interested in fascist subversives than in Communists. By the time the committee held its first session Dies was turning his attention from the extreme right wing to the Left. He still intended to be fair. The committee's sole purpose, he insisted, would be only "to discover the truth."

> The most common practice engaged in by some people is to brand their opponents with names when they are unable to refute their arguments with facts and logic. . . . It is easy to smear someone's name or reputation by unsupported charges, and an unjustified attack, but it is difficult to repair the damage that has been done. . . . This committee will not permit any character assassinations or any smearing of innocent people.

Committeeman Thomas promptly took exception to this. Already reckless enough to accuse President Franklin D. Roosevelt of having "sabotaged the capitalist system," he could hardly have had any compunction about attacking the Federal Theatre and Writers Project. "Practically every play presented under the auspices of the Project," Thomas declared, "is sheer propaganda for Communism or the New Deal." Since Chairman Dies hadn't the stomach for resisting him, Thomas, as committee secretary, was able to make the Federal Theatre the committee's first target.

With hearings begun, the *New York Daily News* reported that according to the Dies House Committee on Un-American Activities, Federal Theatre members were being "coerced into joining and contributing to the Workers Alliance," a budding national theatrical union cited by the committee as a communist organization. On September 13, 1938, the conservative *New York Journal-American* quoted J. Parnell Thomas as calling the WPA "a veritable hotbed of un-American activity . . . because it produces Communistic plays [and] favors giving jobs to radicals." In particular, the *Journal-American* reported, Congressman Thomas cited John Howard Lawson's play *Processional*, condemning this anti–Ku Klux Klan "jazz symphony" for "the tearing up of an American flag and the killing of an American soldier in uniform."

Miller was not fazed by this threat to the Federal Theatre. Perhaps he was too happily rejoicing in his acceptance into the program. Now he shared his joyousness, optimism and innocence with Professor Rowe. Miller's earliest letters to Rowe, written from his parents' Brooklyn basement, were jubilant about his progress and plans. One of these was to "streamline" the prison play, for he had taken its Hopwood Awards rejection as not a defeat but a challenge ("I have secretly felt it beat me"). He intended to replace the play's so-called ex- or impressionist style with "rhythmical speech," by which he meant not "sonnet speech" but dialogue written "metrically without consciously thinking of metrics." To that confusing end (probably meaning nothing more than blank verse), Miller began studying and even writing poetry, which became a new fascination. "My attitude is no longer amateur," he told Rowe, "though my production probably is," and he continued,

> The fine thing about writing in verse is the ease with which revision is made. I somehow enjoy reworking sections because of the compactness and the sectionalized *lineness* of the speech. And the metrics seem to tell one when to stop writing. Perhaps at long last I am getting some dexterity with poetry. At any rate I think it much easier going than prose.

His enthusiasm for poetry spilled over into arty staging. He planned "levels, lights, two choruses" for his new version of *The Great Disobedience,* and next would write a play not only entirely in verse but in the Shakespearean style, "a big classical tragedy."

The twenty-three year old's epic play was going to be about the sixteenth-century confrontation between the Aztec emperor Montezuma and Hernando Cortez, the rogue general of the Spanish conquistadors. Size posed no problem. The Federal Theatre had a huge pool of actors all paid by government subsidy, but this had its drawbacks. The script, even the research schedule, would have to be approved by committee; yet the playwright was at least assured of a production. As for the metric-without-thinking-of-metrics version of *The Great Disobedience,* since the original had been written before Miller joined the program, it did not come under the Federal Theatre's aegis. He told Rowe that Orson Welles's celebrated Mercury Theatre ought to be right for that play, "although they don't know it yet. And if they don't? To hell with them, the Montezuma play will stand Broadway on its ear."

In late November 1938 Miller was ready to tackle the two projects. The Aztec epic had the working title *The Montezuma Play,* and merely referring to it gave him pause. When he contemplated the work ahead—the research, assembling and orchestrating materials, writing and rewriting—he could only characterize the moment of conception as a time to "stare again the mountain in the face." But he was undaunted.

> Tomorrow, Federal Theatre will tell me if it's okay to go ahead with the Montezuma play. I have no reason to doubt that they will okay it since the supervisor was enthused with the story of it which I gave him. [Then] I will read at the library probably every morning, gathering stuff on Montezuma. At the same time, in the afternoons and the evenings, I'll be writing the prison play.

Miller's excitement was palpable but his optimism premature. The Un-American Activities Committee, spurred on by Congressman Thomas, had become unsparing in its attacks on the Federal Theatre. In early 1939 Miller wrote Rowe that he was "dreading the next few weeks," unnerved by rumors that "WPA will be cut drastically and I don't see why I shouldn't be nominated." Congressman Clifton Woodrum, chairman of the House Appropriations Committee, had already vowed to "get the government out of the theater business" and then a number of playwrights were cut from the program,

Miller and Rosten among them. Three months later, in June 1939, Woodrum's committee finished the job, barring the use of Works Progress Administration funds for any theatrical purpose. The nation would be able to sleep securely.

With the loss of his $22.77 a week lifeline, Miller had no choice but to return to his parents' Brooklyn home. From there this disheartened but undefeated young playwright wrote to Professor Rowe that his life was "not easy because I have little money and many debts but somehow I can't get myself to worry over it. I see Norman very often although he does live now at the other end of the city. He will be famous some day, I'm sure." As for himself, he knew he should be grateful for his parents' food and shelter but felt strangled there. Yet even though he had loved college, he was "glad I'm not back there. . . . In Ann Arbor one is a little shy of taking oneself seriously because one suspects that the whole business of collegism is not quite bedrock sincere and that it is a mock serious game played within an outer world of deadly earnestness."

The Federal Theatre finished, Miller decided to concentrate full time on *The Montezuma Play* and give up on *The Great Disobedience*. By the turn of the year the epic was written and, like so many artists, he immediately doubted the quality of what he had done. Miller told Rowe that he'd never put so much work into anything he had previously written, but then again, "By the time I've completed a play in all its revisions, I have little respect for it." Then confidence took over and he decided that, after all, it is "a beautiful play." He gave it a title, *The Children of the Sun*, and invited "three practicing playwrights, an actor, an actress and one Norman Rosten" to be his audience as he read it aloud.

It was the first time anyone would be hearing this dialogue—himself included—and as he nervously turned to the first page of his New World Tragedy, as it was subtitled, he felt "some secret fear." The evening was unusually warm for early autumn, but Miller's audience seemed held. He read on—and on.

The play is set in 1519 and begins in the throne room of Montezuma's mountain palace. The superstitious "king of the Aztec nation, Emperor of the World" is fearful of omens, particularly with regard to the conquistadors of Spain who, led by Cortez, have invaded his Aztec kingdom in Mexico. But like Mannheim in *The Great Disobedience*, Montezuma is an equivocator who won't expel the Spaniards until he is positive that Cortez is an invader and not Quetzalcoatl, the Aztec god who promised a Second Coming.

Cortez is in fact a zealous Roman Catholic conducting a holy crusade—and a greedy one. Spain, he boasts, "is God in Mexico!" Turning to his mistress, a Catholic convert named Marina, he croons, "We'll live in golden palaces, and drink from golden cups, and you shall be a golden queen, rubies in your hair, and from o'er the sea the Kings of the world will come to do obeisance at your feet." Actual poetry comes at the start of the next scene, in a priest's invocation addressed to statues of the Aztec gods Quetzalcoatl, the god of peace, and Huitzilpochtli, the god of war.

> Stir, stir in thy bed of evening clouds,
> Descend, descend, O Huitzilpochtli God of War
> O Battlemaker, possess again the King's faint heart

As this does not prompt the statues to say anything, Montezuma takes the silence as a sign and tells the priest, "Go to Cortez; in my name welcome him to Mexico." Alone, the vacillating emperor asks the gods for divine guidance. "O Tranquil God!" he cries, "The Spaniard bleeds and dies—when did a god die? . . . And yet, what army of men could endure what they endure and live? And yet, they . . . and yet, and yet, and yet!" He implores his god to "speak in thunder . . . It is time for a word! O Eastern Star, oh God of the gentle heart, in what darkness shall I seek for thy word!" And the curtain falls.

As the second act begins, Cortez has entered the city, capitalizing on Montezuma's hesitance. The emperor "sat two days before the gods and no word came," a remark certain to evoke an audience's derisive laughter. The more decisive Cortez is telling his priest, "We are not safe in Mexico until Montezuma is a Christian . . . On the day you are [his] confessor, Mexico is ours." Yet Montezuma does not or will not perceive the danger. He gives Cortez a day to leave the city but wavers even still ("I cannot bring my hand to kill them yet") and orders his generals to hold their arms. They refuse ("Your honor and your state will be defended") and the emperor is fully aware of his own weakness. "Such a proud and pompous fool," he says of himself, so much like Karl Mannheim in the prison play, knowing he should act yet unable to do so. Turning to his daughter he sobs and buries his face in her hair as the curtain falls to end the second act.

In the last act Montezuma is appalled to learn that without his permission, his brother has given the order to attack the Spaniards—once again, passive and active brothers in a Miller play. The emperor believes Cortez's promise to leave Mexico and tells his daughter that the Spanish soldiers who have been arriving in the palace have come to simply "say farewell." As he orders his brother arrested along with the generals, she cries, "Always a reason to pardon the Spaniard—pardon their sacrilege, pardon their murders." Moments later Cortez arrives and makes a prisoner of this holiest of emperors, placing him in shackles; and so the Spaniards rule the Aztec nation. At the royal tomb historic treasures are being looted. The chained Montezuma declares, "This is Mexico you plunder . . . lines of Aztec Kings . . . you are melting down a history." When Cortez threatens to "blow up your city and leave it in ashes," the emperor compromises once again, agreeing to pacify his people. Thus the finale, set at the temple as cannons are heard in the distance while Montezuma delivers a cowardly address urging appeasement and surrender. "We must not live out our lives among ashes! . . . lay down your arms."

Montezuma is cursed for this as "base Aztec," and the thoroughly damning, "the white men have made you a woman!" and with that, he is struck down by his own brother, to lay dying in his daughter's arms. Cortez pleads for a deathbed conversion but Montezuma replies that "your god is bloodier than mine . . . Jesus Christ may be good above all gods, but Christians are debased below all men." Even still, Cortez attempts to baptize him. "Is my blood not enough," asks the emperor, "but I must also render up my soul?" It is not an original expression but a good device that Miller would use again to better effect in *The Crucible*.

Cortez leaves the emperor to a deathbed speech. "Let the history tell how an emperor died in search of the golden years. And by no hand but his own." Thus the play's ultimate title, *The Golden Years*.

With that, Miller lay down the script and looked up at his little audience. He had been reading for three hours. They sat mute. Finally one of the playwrights murmured, "Jesus Christ" and "when he lifted his face, he had tears! If an audience will react the way that group reacted [my play] is a real tragedy," Miller recalled to Professor Rowe. *The Golden Years* is indeed a tragedy in two senses: that of grief for a hero's misfortune, and in the classical sense with Montezuma, victimized by indecision, being the agent of his own undoing. On this subject Miller surely thought and learned much, using tragedy to point up the pitfalls of inertia.

Granted these qualities, the writing has obvious faults. To start, *The Golden Years* is not, as advertised, in verse. The language is merely florid or as Miller later conceded, "purplish." The play is Shakespearean only in the sense of being a period drama involving royalty and armies; and rather than poetry, the dialogue sometimes sounds like a Hollywood epic of the period and on occasion is openly derivative: "Is this the way the world ends? Not with battles, but waiting like old men?" There are anachronisms too, such as Montezuma ordering a lord to "wait outside" and such oddities as an Aztec speaking in the Jewish idiom ("Explain, explain" or "a *man* I can kill"). Epic speech is contrived, using *shall* in place of *will* and the expanding of contractions, *didn't* into *did not he* and *aren't* into *are not we*. Montezuma's people are given Aztec names such as Gujatemotzin, Cuitlahua and Tecuichpo, even though Miller himself conceded that "nobody could be expected to keep all these Indian names straight."

The play is designed to mirror the appeasing of Nazi Germany, with Cortez standing in for Hitler. Its reference point is Germany's occupation of Czechoslovakia and the invasion of Poland while England and America stood idly by. In the course of research Miller had read of lore that despite his unrivaled empire, Montezuma had been paralyzed by his awe of Cortez, notwithstanding the smallness of the conquistador forces. It was, Miller said, as if Montezuma had "mesmerized himself, with the Spaniards' eager help, into believing them emissaries of some half-remembered god, Quetzalcoatl." Young Miller likened this to the hypnotic effect Hitler was having on the United States and England, and drew other parallels, for instance, linking Cortez's promises of nonaggression to Hitler's assurances to Neville Chamberlain. The Aztec empire's "golden cities, roads, gardens, aqueducts and spires" can be easily read as America, "the world's most powerful nation"—a warning that America must avoid complacency and isolationism. Indeed Miller saw in Cortez "the intensely organized energies" of fascism just as he saw in Montezuma America's self-centeredness and delusions of security. The play, however, lacks subtlety; Miller had not yet developed a suggestive touch.

Regarding the play's (and the author's) recurring conflict between action and cautiousness, Montezuma repeatedly delays action, even when he commands it. "We must be wondrous and searching," he says, "not calm." Always word conscious, here Miller uses *calm* to mean smug, while *searching* refers to seeking the truth. As for *wondrous*, the various forms of *wonder* were longtime (and lifetime) favorites of his, used, Miller has said, "in the old sense of that word," meaning curious or musing, as in *wondering*.

In a scholarly analysis the British critic and academic Christopher Bigsby treats *The Golden Years* as Miller's first major play and praises it as "a powerful and accomplished drama." While disagreeing with Miller's characterization of the play as "optimistic" and conceding its language to be "clotted," Bigsby nevertheless respects the writing as "functional, distinguishing a world structured on myth and symbol from one primarily dedicated to fact and engorged with the arrogance of power." His analysis continues,

> Montezuma is a king who lives in fear. His seemingly unchallenged power, his conquests, his role as mediator with the gods, leave him uncertain as to his power, unsure of his destiny . . . He seeks a force greater than himself so that he may prostrate himself before it and thus affirm it and his existence, discovering true power through his obedience to authority . . . Montezuma becomes an appeaser not because he fears he could not defeat Cortez but because he has no wish to do so. On one level, they are close kin . . . because they serve some purpose beyond themselves. Both subordinate the world to an idea.

While he makes an interesting point, Bigsby probably gives the play more credit than is deserved. As chairman of the Arthur Miller Centre for the Advancement of American Studies at the University of East Anglia in Norwich, England, he seems perhaps biased in his suggestion that *The Golden Years* may be as theatrical as Peter Shaffer's *The Royal Hunt of the Sun*, a better known (and better) play on a similar subject. Most likely too Miller never intended the differences in speaking styles of Montezuma and Cortez to express "two different interpretations of experience," as Bigsby suggests. In this respect the analysis seems largely academic, although Bigsby fairly describes the ending of *The Golden Years* as "operatic" (in the best sense). It does pay off to dramatic effect.

Miller would write only one other costume, or period, play, *The Crucible*. By then he would have a much firmer grip on period speech. In that case, however, court records of testimony provided research; he could hardly have researched the speaking style of sixteenth-century Aztecs.

The reception accorded the reading swelled Miller's confidence and he brought the play to his agent. He had "no illusions," he wrote Professor Rowe, "as to the difficulties of selling such a play to a producer . . . but by God if there is a man still left who is not frightened by the magnitude, the play will be produced . . . Despite its ideological breadth [it] is an actor's and director's holiday."

Paul Streger didn't think so. The agent who so "perfectly" understood the family comedy *The Grass Still Grows* didn't understand the Aztec epic at all, saw "next to nothing" in it and could see no reason "why you wrote it in the first place." A wry Miller considered this "pretty thorough damnation." Undeterred, he gave a copy of the script to dramaturg John Gassner at the Theatre Guild and another to Morris Carnovsky at the Group Theatre. The actor responded that he would be "highly honored" to play Montezuma, which Miller used as a springboard to Harold Clurman and the Group Theatre's house playwright Clifford Odets, both of whom were sent scripts. In the meantime Gassner confided that in his report to the guild's Theresa Helburn he called *The Golden Years* "the finest play [I've] read in many years," although he anticipated rejection. "It's the kind of play the Guild would have produced for prestige," he told Miller, "but those days are pretty well passed." Yet he was not discouraging. If the company's first productions of the 1939–1940 season were well received, he felt certain that the Theatre Guild would seriously consider doing *The Golden Years*. He even suggested specific revisions and Miller accepted them in his usual positive way, but the meeting left him gloomy. He wrote Rowe, "I am waiting now for Miss Helburn to say she sees nothing in it . . . I have come to regard the Montezuma play as my major opus and I don't know many people around here who are qualified to pronounce on major opii [*sic*]."

Norman Rosten was in no better shape. His latest play, while more commercial in style than *The Golden Years*, had been dismissed by Streger as unbelievable. The two friends were mutually supportive, although Miller privately conceded, "some of [Rosten's] plot factors could be modified on the side of credibility." They plugged on. For diversion they collaborated on several light pieces, a one-act play called *Listen, My Children* and a sketch for a revue to be presented by the Workers Alliance titled *You're Next!*—a satire of the Dies Committee, which was portrayed, Miller later recalled, as "a mad Star Chamber where witnesses were gagged, bound and tortured." It was never staged because the Workers Alliance had to cancel the show. "They were hard hit," he remembered, "by the collapse of the Federal Theatre." As for *Listen, My Children*, it was, he said, a "farcical sort of play about standing and waiting in a relief office. Nothing ever came of it, I am glad to say." As he told Rowe, "I [couldn't] get my heart in it . . . what with the serious plays I have in mind."

Miller also realized that political satire was not what he did. When he was asked to write a sketch for *Pens and Pencils*, a left-wing revue being put on by student radicals at the City College of New York, he sent a terse response on a postcard: "I don't think comedy is my strong point. Art Miller." Something to remember in later years.

If the death of the Federal Theatre made *The Golden Years* Miller's unencumbered property, perhaps it was too unencumbered. He was never granted the courtesy of a response from Clurman and Odets. Still he would not give up on the play and continued to rewrite it. Finally, in May 1940, more than a year after he'd begun the "tragedy in the Elizabethan mode" with such high hopes, so certain of standing Broadway on its ear, Miller lay down his pen and admitted he was at a "standstill." Beaten down by rejection, writing play after play without seeing any of them produced, performed or realized, he poured out a lament in the form of "a writer's speech to himself"—ten single-spaced pages of futility and defeat addressed to Professor Rowe.

> I can't write again feeling with every word that I'm writing for the dresser drawer . . . I fear that I will never be able to write for the theater . . . How do I face my brother—starting on another writing siege which he knows will last months and no money coming in? . . . How long can I bear, "The question is, Arthur, would anybody risk twenty thousand dollars on it?"
>
> Isn't part of the heat, the inspiration or rather, doesn't part of it come out of the fiery vision that one day living people will laugh and cry at these words I write? How long can one shout and cry and roar laughing into a writing machine before the shouting and crying and laughing become pantomime?

4. Debut

JUST A FEW WEEKS after writing his long ("fat," he called it) letter of frustration and despair, Arthur Miller was invited to accompany a couple of friends who were driving to Mexico. He thought he might accept the invitation too because he had a notion to explore the possibilities of yet another play about the Aztecs. In the course of Miller's research for *The Golden Years* the curator of Mexican archeology at New York's American Museum of Natural History told him that the center of Mexico City, now "the worst slum in the Western World," once had been the royal Aztec burial grounds. These were so sacred, the curator said, that anyone daring to trespass would suffer "all the curses in the heavens." Perhaps, Miller thought, a play could be found in that, a story about "a pure Aztec, so rare in central Mexico, rising out of this slum to meet this century"; but he decided against it. Instead of driving to Mexico with friends, he went to Ohio to get married.

Why the sudden, matter-of-fact decision? Perhaps it was hastened by the looming war. Congress had just passed the Selective Service Act of 1940 that authorized America's first peacetime military draft, and President Roosevelt was about to sign it into law. The act required the registration of all men between ages eighteen and twenty-five. Miller was then twenty-four and would not turn twenty-five for several months, but married men were to be granted deferments, meaning that their inductions would be postponed. If he and Mary were planning to get married, this was certainly a sensible time.

That 1940 summer the couple arrived at Cleveland's Union Station in the middle of a sweltering heat wave. An hour later they were in Mary's hometown of Lakewood, none the cooler on the shores of Lake Erie. There, on the front porch of the Slattery home, Art met the relatives, a group he found distinctly provincial. Not much later he was standing at the counter of a local stationery store, scribbling a postcard to Professor Rowe. First he said that he was sending a script. Next he mentioned that he was where he was "for a week, preparing to get married to my Ohio lass." This was only the second time that he had mentioned Mary in two years of correspondence.

Marrying a Christian—a Roman Catholic—was not easily done by a young man of Arthur Miller's background, even one who considered Judaism to be "dead history." Still more difficult, Mary, the lapsed Catholic, wanted a priest to conduct the ceremony—just, she said, to appease her mother. Art agreed to it, but on the condition that they not be married in a church.

Naturally Miller considered his own hostility reasonable, as opposed to the prejudice he perceived in her family. Mary's mother, Julia Slattery, then in her forties, and her husband, Matthew, an insurance salesman, were "opposed to [their daughter] marrying a Jew," Miller told a British interviewer some years later, failing to mention that Jews tended to feel the same way about their children marrying Christians. "Anti-Semitism," he said, "was quite dense in the United States. Catholics in particular, were very much influenced by the Irish clergy." The ethnic reference is baffling, inspired perhaps by Father Coughlin, the Detroit-based "Radio Priest" who attracted an enormous nationwide audience during the late 1930s with his anti-Semitic and anti-Roosevelt diatribes.

Miller remembered that "Mary reverted to a kind of childish fear and a wish to please her extremely neurotic mother, who feared hell and damnation awaited her daughter for marrying me." Yet this was an encomium compared with Miller's opinion of her father. "Stupidity," he told the British reporter, "was reserved for Mr. Slattery." Fifty years later he would still describe with contempt Matthew Slattery's spitting into a cuspidor, and with lingering distaste, the family living room, with "no bright picture, but only . . . a brown statuette of Christ crucified hanging from the wall." As a parting salute he added, "Something parched touched everything." His disagreements with almost everything Catholic seem to have been scattershot, ranging from generalizations, misinformation and even superstition to scorn regarding "the Church's support of Franco in Spain" and descriptions of his mother-in-law as "foolishly pious . . . prodigiously repressed." Miller nevertheless agreed to make the vows required for intermarriage in the Catholic Church, pledging his respect in such matters as birth control and the religious upbringing of future children. He did not intend to keep the pledges and, he recalled, Mary was in agreement about that.

Miller's suspicions of Christians generally and Catholics in particular and his defensiveness, anger and narrow-mindedness can largely be ascribed to an insulated ethnic background and the psychology of an outsider as well as youthful insecurities. More complicated and interesting is that so many of these feelings were harbored—even nurtured—well beyond his youth and over the course of a lifetime. In his autobiography, written at age seventy, Miller devotes some twelve pages to hostile memories of the Catholic wedding—more space then he gives to the entire marriage. Moreover, as in his account of the visit with Sid Franks, long stretches of ostensibly verbatim dialogue simply are not credible. What comes through, however, is the essential, never-forgotten discomfort of a young Jewish man from New York City dropped into an alien midwestern Christian world. His description is like Woody Allen's *Annie Hall* without the humor, although it is certainly amusing to read of Miller's guilty feelings "about marrying without my family present—for they had made no mention of wanting to come." That is hardly surprising since he didn't tell them he was getting married. "Arthur and Mary were already married," Joan said, "by the time my mother knew that they were going to get married"; and when Gussie delivered the news to Grandfather Barnett, the old man picked up an alarm clock and threw it at her. Gussie herself, Joan said, "was disappointed that Arthur got married by [the] Catholic Church, but there was nothing she could do about it and ultimately, she got to like Mary a lot," as did Joan. "She was upright, a straight arrow [even if] a little bit cool, not emotional." As for Isadore Miller's feelings about his son's intermarriage, it seems that nobody bothered to ask.

Mary Slattery's upright qualities may have had a greater influence on Miller's life than he would ever realize. The moral imperative that drove his work—and the awareness of guilt as an effect of it—possibly, even probably, was developed under the influence of Mary Slattery and her intense moral code, one that surely derived in large part from her religious upbringing that Miller so abhorred.

After a week's delay owing to dispensations required from higher church authorities, the wedding took place on August 5, 1940. Even the reception came in for its share of the bridegroom's abuse, with "scant whiskey bottles and canapes spread as far as they could go on a table." The newlyweds then went directly home to Brooklyn. "We were married without a dime," Mary remembered. "It was all on faith," and she certainly had faith in her husband's future. While she moved on to Harper and Brothers as private secretary to the head of the medical books department, he was going to stay home and write in the little apartment they found at 62 Montague Street in Brooklyn Heights.

He would have to get started later. A few weeks after the couple returned from Ohio, Miller sailed for South America—alone.

If it seems strange that immediately after being married a young man should go off on a two-week sea voyage by himself, that was Arthur Miller at twenty-five. Many years later it even seemed strange to him, but he explains, "This early parting, like our marriage, was a refusal to surrender the infinitude of options that we at least imagined we had." Such a statement speaks for itself. Meant to express a willingness to give each other a measure of independence, it reflects a man who describes his lack of feeling as "a want of empathetic powers."

Miller sailed from Hoboken, New Jersey, on a freighter called the *U.S. Copa Copa* in early September. His purpose was to research a play set on a merchant ship at the dawn of the Second World War, and in 1940 war was obviously imminent. He began this maritime play on September 15, immediately after his return from South America, and writing from a brief outline rather than a full scenario, he finished it on November 29. His protagonist is Mark Donegal, "a fabulous person," Miller wrote Professor Rowe, probably meaning fabulous as in *fable*, "through whom the last two decades have passed. He is now a chief mate on a Chilean freighter which transports Nazi agents into the Gulf ports from South America."

Miller's typing was getting fancy. He used the red half of the typewriter ribbon for the play's title as well as the stage directions and names of the fourteen characters. Dialogue was typed in black and in all, it is the most curious of his trunk, or shelved, plays. It seems to take no part in his development as a playwright. Unlike the "ex- or impressionism" of *The Jackson Prison Play* or the "grand historical tragedy" that was *The Golden Years*, this was a play with no lofty ambitions, essentially a pistol-wielding wartime melodrama. Consciously or not, young Miller may have been trying to write something more commercial.

He considered beginning it with the central character creating "an uproar in the audience, being drunk, and . . . carried out bodily." He decided on a more conventional opening scene: after midnight on "the front of a pier in New Orleans harbor," from which a rusty freighter, the *Bangkok Star*, is to set sail for Chile. As the crew straggles in after an evening of drinking, Donegal, the first mate, speaks of an America "too small" for him. "I gotta go where they need big men!" When a woman named Anna Walden appears, he strikes up a conversation, describing himself as "a swell, crazy guy . . . I'm always drunk . . . on what I see and what I hear and think about." Anna is running away from something undisclosed and hopes to arrange a ride on the freighter. Donegal tells her, "you got good eyes, you know what trouble is." Eyes are important to him, for he sees his past as "a blind man that don't remember me," not the tidiest of metaphors. That past of his includes growing up rich, playing college football, selling airplane equipment in Holland, prospecting for oil in Mexico, running a sugar plantation in Honolulu and playing professional football on the side. He also quit college "to see what it was like to be an iron worker," and was a pilot in the Army Air Force to see "how close you could get to a star."

The well-traveled Donegal invites Anna to come into New Orleans with him and "make it a night, come on, we'll sing, and we'll dance, and we'll tell each other everything now," as the curtain falls on the first act.

The second act is set in the chart room of the *Bangkok Star* where Mark learns that the ship is disguised as a freighter and is actually engaged in piracy. He agrees to take part in the next raid, not for the money but, a shipmate realizes, because "You want to die." That's right, says Mark. "Right and wrong went out of the world." Yet the ship's Captain Shulenberg intends to stand between Mark "and this darkness. You must find something to give yourself to . . . something that . . . if it died, you would want to die with it."

And, he adds for a homosexual surprise, "I am that. You are to me as a white column. . . . I am not a monster! It is not an ugly thing," which enrages Mark. "Why I hated you, and didn't know why . . . why you trailed me around in every port . . . why my women made you puke. And this is what I'm supposed to live for? This is the only clean thing left?"

The captain spies Anna waiting for Mark on the dock and pleads with him. "If we could talk this over. We are reasonable people," but Donegal has no intention of talking over that "lousy, rotten thing." Anna, though, is now certain that he is "the first decent guy I ever met," but Mark is a young man in despair. "I can't stand, like the rest of the millions going round and round the mill like harnessed oxen, never knowing why they're alive, never seeing the thousand, thousand colors in the world!" With that, Anna confesses her secret. She "killed an important man" who molested her, fighting him off "like an animal and we fought on the rocks and he fell on a gray stone and there was blood on me."

Meanwhile Mark learns that insurance money is the ship's real objective. The *Bangkok Star* is in fact controlled by the Nazis, as is the ship they are about to pirate. "They've got torpedoes," he says to the ship's officer, "and you're going to send us under . . . This fish-house is worth thirty times more at the bottom than afloat . . . Berlin needs dollars!" The officer's response is to draw a revolver, crying, "Don't talk or I'll kick your head off!" According to stage directions, *Mark stops, his fists raised, bursting with anger at this symbol of all he hates*, but once again a Miller protagonist cannot act. Donegal's bravado disintegrates into more talk and returning to Anna, he tells her, "I look good to you, heh, strong, handsome, wonderful smile, got an answer to everything . . . yeh . . . in the North there's a girl with a kid of mine!! . . . Anna, you're gonna get off!" Instead they embrace for his second act curtain speech. "Wherever I lay with my blood running out . . . there'll be stars, maybe . . . and we'll stand on the bridge drunk in the belly of the night, and shells come across the water like fiery stars."

The last act has the ship's captain still vainly lusting for Mark as well as smoking marijuana ("That stuff makes you crazy"). Anna is urging her hesitant man to action much as Jean urges Mannheim in *The Great Disobedience*. "The world has got to be changed," she cries, "so we can live, and if you've gotta die, then die changing it!" Yet Donegal, like Mannheim, prefers to orate. "Twenty two years I've been running over the world from one noise to the next, searching, searching for what I didn't know . . . and tonight I know. We're built with half a bridge sticking out of our hearts, looking for the other half that fits so we can cross over into someone else, so we can give ourselves and say . . . all the things."

A clumsy image perhaps, but it does provide the play with a title, *The Half-Bridge*.

In the end it is Captain Shulenberg, the rejected homosexual, who allows Anna and Mark an escape, first allowing Donegal one final heroic declaration.

> Oh you 44 caliber rulers of the world, you slick guys in all languages, throw us to the snails, knock off a billion twenty buck suckers, but a bridge is building, a bridge around the world where every man will walk, the Irish with the Jews, and the black with the white, stronger together than any steel, bone to the bone we'll live to hang you over the edges of the sky! Go on, ya punk, I dare you let me live, or give it to us between the eyes, we're lookin' at you till the dirt's in your mouth!

The play is curious because of negatives—its wartime propaganda, its angry approach to homosexuality, its melodramatics and mawkish romance. It does not, as Miller felt, provide "many characters in a situation, and relationships where they can show what they are." Yet it does mark another phase in his search for a personal signature. Here Miller seems to be influenced by extratheatrical sources, an odd combination of Hollywood B movies and the style-conscious fiction of Ernest Hemingway or William Saroyan. The play reads like the work of a writer who is discovering *writing,* mistaking literary style, a manner of language that has no business in dramatic dialogue, for playwriting style, a manner of dramatizing. Miller would never make this mistake again. Notably in this play, however, two characteristics emerge that would be of lifelong significance to Miller: a drive for a singular and exciting life, and a concern about a protagonist's ability to love.

In November 1940, just as the first version of *The Half-Bridge* was being finished and following his twenty-fifth birthday, Miller was assigned a Selective Service number; so was Norman Rosten, and both got high ones, "which frees us," Miller wrote to the professor, "for at least another year." Rosten, he added, apparently without envy, currently had "things . . . coming a bit his way." Norman had published a collection of poems called *Return Again, Traveler* with a foreword by Stephen Vincent Benet; as a result, he had won a Guggenheim Fellowship. Better still, Rosten was about to make his Broadway debut with a comedy called *First Stop to Heaven*. Miller was hardly making such progress. He sold the occasional radio script, but Mary kept the two of them afloat, working at editorial jobs, even waiting on tables. He appreciated that, appreciated her. "My married life," he wrote Rowe, "if it never changes I shall go to my rest like Euripides, a happy man. . . . I have never felt so solid, so at home in a house, in my life. In these times such a girl is the keel to an otherwise wayward ship. She demands nothing and yet I give her all—paradise." It was a rare expression of warmth, but it did not necessarily represent warmth. It might have been an imitation of emotion, because this happiness and solidity didn't keep him from taking regular breaks by himself, spending a weekend for instance "on a friend's farm. Swell here," he wrote to Rowe, "alone with fine woodshop. Made bookcase, starting coffee table. Run tractor, etc. Understand a little why farmers have the long view."

The journey from writing a play to actual production posed a threat to a young artist's confidence. Near the end of November Rosten's *First Stop to Heaven* opened on Broadway to scathing reviews and closed after five performances. During the same stretch Tennessee Williams's *Battle of Angels* met with an even nastier reception. Before this play ever got to New York it was assaulted by Boston's censors and savaged by the city's moralizing critics. The Theatre Guild put it out of its misery then and there, rather than risking further shame in New York. (Williams would be vindicated when a revised *Battle of Angels* was successfully produced on Broadway in 1957 as *Orpheus Descending*.)

Miller was certain that a better fortune awaited *The Half-Bridge*. He considered it not only "significant—morally" but also "superbly commercial . . . because of its suspense [and] melodrama." It was already in the hands of a producing team, Wharton and Gabel, and Miller excitedly told Rowe that they have "bushels of money . . . the spenders of Jock Whitney's theatrical budget . . . They sent me a $4 Saks Fifth Avenue shirt—for no good reason!" The script had already been submitted to the widely admired Paul Muni in the hope that he would play Donegal, while Morris Carnovsky was being asked to play Captain Shulenberg. The producers were trying to lure Harold Clurman from the Group Theatre to direct it. Luckily for Miller none of that happened, for *The Half-Bridge* is merely a huge play, with a forty-eight-page first act, a forty-five-page second act and a forty-page third act. The play also reflects the author's experiences in radio, with an imbalance of dialogue to action. Its protagonist is florid and absurdly egotistical; its romance is adolescent; yet the piece has drive and heat and several scenes that would probably play well. Even so, had it been produced the young playwright would surely have met with the same mean-spirited reception as had Rosten and Williams.

The Half-Bridge was the last of Arthur Miller's plays to go unproduced. He wiped his hands of the disenchanted, adventure-seeking protagonists with whom he had been identifying. "They are the 'I' that would devour the world and not enter it," he would soon write in his notebook. "They strive for nothing but the scene that has passed. The hero today fights to the death for that which is to come. And now, in my strength, so do I."

In January 1941 Miller applied for—and was refused—a $1,000 Rockefeller Fellowship similar to one that Tennessee Williams had been granted some months earlier. He decided to try his hand at fiction, and even had an idea for a novel. The story comes from Mary's family history, about a young uncle who committed suicide by hanging himself in a barn for no apparent reason. The man had been happily married. He had been successful in business. As his widow put it, "Everybody'd always liked [Peter], he never wanted for a job . . . he was so cheerful."

The *why* of it intrigued Miller; he demanded that life make sense. Why would a man kill himself when he had everything going for him? An editor at Atlantic Monthly Press found the proposed novel's approach to this idea interesting enough to make inquiries about the would-be author to Professor R. W. Cowden, head of the English Department at the University of Michigan. Cowden wrote back, "He is a wide awake Jewish boy and so much interested in writing that every now and then he jeopardized his scholastic standing here at Michigan in order to work on his plays. He does have talent . . . I have been expecting to hear from him somewhere in the field of writing, because his heart is in it."

This recommendation justified a small advance and Miller went to work, calling his novel *The Man Who Had All the Luck*, which he described as "an investigation to discover what exact part a man played in his own fate." Five months later he was stymied. He had been finding lately that he couldn't finish anything. He had never completed *The Half-Bridge* to his satisfaction and now, with his first attempt at prose fiction, he had only half a novel written. That much was sent off to the editor and when it was rejected, he took a break and set out for North Carolina—again, by himself.

In Greensboro Miller began keeping notebooks. He jotted down events that might be dramatized, passing thoughts, possible titles, descriptions of play scenes, brief exchanges of dialogue. These were written in a small, neat script on the ruled pages of a classroom composition book with black-and-white speckled covers. One of his first entries described an official from North Carolina Public Health. "How quickly he dropped his manners, his southern gallantry, and became obscene as a self-suggesting pimp after he had three beers! . . . Vicious, polite, obliging, ambitious in a fatty way. How he tried to push his face into the camera, the mike." And Miller quoted a "beautiful young mother," a farmer's wife, talking to him in a mine yard. "I had a nervous breakdown," she told him. "Three unbroken years in a silk mill." He even wrote a poem about her and her eyes, "so soft by the tall tipple."

He noted a possible play title, *But Cain Went Forth*. He came up with a possible plot, "Two end-of-middle-age people, their two children married, left to themselves. And they discover that they had been existing solely for their children and nothing is left. They are without function." He even put down tentative scenes for a play that, six years later, would become *All My Sons*. The seed had been planted by Mary's mother, who told Miller about a local Ohio girl reporting her own father to the authorities after learning that during the war he had manufactured airplane components and sold them to the Army Air Force, even after learning that they were defective.

Miller was immediately struck by the idea that "a girl had not only wanted to, but had actually moved against an erring father." By the time Julia Slattery finished telling the tale, he recalled, "I had transformed the daughter into a son and the climax of the second act was clear in my mind. I knew my informant's neighborhood, I knew its middle class ordinariness."

He even had working names for the characters: Mom and Pop for the parents, and Chris, Larry, Ann and Pete for children and friends. When the play was finally written, Chris, Larry and Ann would survive, but the parents would be named Kate and Joe Keller. The early use of Mom and Pop suggests that rather than planning to write a realistic play Miller may have had stylization in mind.

His notes include a brief scenario for these characters.

> Act One, Scene two. Ann-Mom. Birthday. Mom sees her need of husband. Mom's feeling this is not their house. Bought it, furniture and all. She feels like she is sitting in one of those complete rooms in department stores. "When you get married, never buy a furnished house. It's like buying a car that comes all assembled . . . A house should be furnished piece by piece. When you sit in a chair it's so nice to remember the trouble you had getting it." Ann: "Do you have any friends here?" Mom "Yes, I get around. Bridge, mostly. But you can't get personal with them. They're very well-mannered people."

In these notes Miller's creative process can be observed. He gave himself another brief scenario to map out the action ahead: "Recap. Pop goes with Pete. Chris feels peculiar. Pete brought it all back. Chris wishes Mom had not invited Pete to stay. Doesn't want it all brought up again. Very distressed."

There are hints of the revealing dialogue that Miller would soon bring to his plays, for instance in this speech for Ann: "If he'd been shot and killed. If there was a battle and he died in it—well all right. It's not so much that I long for him. I do, of course. He was the only fun I ever had. . . . I never enjoy anything alone." Miller's instinct for writing desolate but surviving women was also developing. "They don't even let me wash the dishes," says Mom. "There's nobody here to make the house dirty. I pick up a dust rag—I might as well blow my nose in it." And scattered throughout the notebooks are a young man's heartfelt cries for righting wrongs. "When will the reality of democracy become plain? When the contradictions resolve? Oh the contradictions! Shall we die of them?"

Some months later, on October 8, 1941, a week before his twenty-sixth birthday, he posed the question for himself, "But why, why are you a revolutionary!" to which he replied, "Because the true is revolutionary and the truth I will live by!" The idealistic trumpeting of this serious-minded and earnest fellow was but momentary, as another wave of discouragement washed over him. "Tonight," he wrote to himself,

> after nearly four years of indecision and torment, after passing through the terminable gamut of bourgeois inspiration and bourgeois frustration and fear, I leave that world behind. And with it all I have written and all I have tried to write and failed to finish. The last two works never completed themselves, for at last the mind has exhausted its memories and is left to feed only upon itself.

Miller based most of his work on personal experiences and now considered them spent; inventing plot must have seemed like running into a wall. Suddenly such obstacles became insignificant. The Japanese attacked Pearl Harbor, giving President Roosevelt a pretext for joining the war in Europe as well. This meant fighting on two fronts and a two-ocean sea battle with an immediate need for more ships. Miller promptly (the spring of 1942) got a job at the United States Navy Yard, which was close to home, just under the Brooklyn Bridge at the juncture of Navy Street and Clinton Avenue. Familiarly known as the Brooklyn Navy Yard, it was set at an elbow of the East River opposite Manhattan's Corlears Hook. At the entrance gate where workers' identification badges were checked was an 1864 cigar-shaped submarine, one of the first underwater ships ever built. Beyond it and across acres of shipyard thousands of men were at work building war vessels, from huge battleships such as the USS *Missouri* to "Liberty" ships being speedily assembled for troop and supply transport.

Miller's work slot was shipfitter's helper and he was assigned the night shift, with a lunch break at midnight. His memories of the experience sound much like when he'd worked in the Manhattan automobile parts warehouse, reflecting his appreciation of basic labor. Miller seemed to relish the directness and simplicity of being an assistant shipfitter, enjoying the language of the trade ("Cadmium nuts were used on underwater hull areas, welded with rods of flux, because cadmium did not rust"). He worked not only in the yard but also on ships moored in the river, repairing hulls damaged by weather, wear or occasionally torpedoes. He and his crewmates "straightened steel, and welded cracked struts on depth charge platforms."

He never gave patriotism as his reason for going to work in the Brooklyn Navy Yard, describing it only as "an expression of the . . . wish for community." Perhaps another reason might have been that it was defense work and as such, offered eligibility for military deferment. Otherwise, why wasn't Miller in the service? He would tell the *New York Times* that he couldn't get in the army because his knee was badly injured when he played high school football. In his autobiography Miller states that he was "rejected for military service," but doesn't base it on the knee injury. He never says that he'd been given a 4F classification (that is, physically unfit for duty). To suggest that Miller consciously strove to avoid being drafted would be pure speculation. What can be stated with certainty is that Arthur Miller—whatever the reason—did not go into the service; his brother did. Miller was surely sensitive to this fact.

Kermit was also married, but he enlisted anyway. His wife, Frances, was an intellectually inclined young Jewish woman from Coney Island in Brooklyn, and according to Joan Miller, "Frances felt he should have done more. Her parents were very bright, but they didn't have any money. She honors education, she honors reading. She reads instead of eats. I think perhaps she would have liked Kermit to achieve more in the intellectual field." Kermit, though, felt obliged to quit college and help support his father. Instead of an achievement in the intellectual field he worked as a salesman in the carpet business owned by the father of his friend (and Joan's schoolgirl crush) the tall pianist, George Levine.

Kermit and Frances were only recently settled into married life when he joined the army. He was sent to Officers' Candidate School (because he'd attended college), commissioned a lieutenant and assigned to lead a platoon in the infantry. Arthur, meanwhile, worked nights in the navy yard and used his days to get on with the novel. Finished at last, *The Man Who Had All the Luck* was submitted to another publisher, Doubleday, Doran and Co. The decision came in a letter dated August 14, 1942, addressed to Miller's literary agent at Leland Hayward and Company.

> We have had lots of readings of AM's TMWHATL and the general feeling here was that this is a strange book, almost unique and exceptionally fascinating, but it is so uneven, such a mixture of the good and the bad, that in its present state we don't feel that we can undertake it, without its being almost completely rewritten. There are parts of the book that stand out like a searchlight, yet the connecting links between such flashes of light are dull and awkward and the ending is no ending but a mere petering out. Nor does he make at all clear the theme of the book, that David, from his earliest youth, has lost something and is everlastingly searching for it.
>
> The characterizations are very good and the style almost a combination of Sherwood Anderson and Saroyan, which is, we find, very effective. The inner conflict is often vague and unconvincing. There are the makings of a tremendous book here, but the bigness isn't sufficiently sustained as it stands. We're tremendously interested in Arthur Miller, and I certainly hope that I can keep my eye on him. Would there be any possibility that he would be willing to do a good overhauling of the manuscript and undertake a rewrite job on it? If he would, I'd like to go further into this.

Instead of overhauling the novel Miller elected to dramatize it and devoted the next eight months to doing that while writing radio scripts, still working nights at the Brooklyn Navy Yard. One of the scripts is a propaganda piece called *That They May Win*, urging Americans to not only buy war bonds but report anyone unpatriotic enough to trade on the black market. Here is a rare instance of Arthur Miller encouraging informers. He found a regular outlet in a weekly series called *The Dupont Cavalcade of America*, broadcast on Monday evenings at eight o'clock on NBC's Blue, or prestige, network (as opposed to its Red, or second-class, network). The radio experience served him well. Toward the end of 1943 Miller was presented with a lucrative screenwriting opportunity, $750 a week to write a script based on the celebrated and beloved war correspondent Ernie Pyle. The idea was to somehow contrive a screenplay out of a collection of Pyle's columns that had been published in a book called *Here Is Your War*. A Hollywood producer owned the film rights and already had a screen title, *The*

Story of G.I. Joe. He found Miller through the recommendation of Herman Shumlin, a Broadway producer who was an old friend of Art's agent, Paul Streger. The assignment meant quitting the job at the Brooklyn Navy Yard, but the pay would presumably make up for any lost sense of community, and as for losing a deferment, Mary had become pregnant and fathers were not yet being drafted.

Art wanted to write "a soldier picture which soldiers would sit through until the end without once laughing in derision." The movie's producer arranged permission for him to visit army training bases from Camp Dix (later Fort Dix) in New Jersey to Fort Benning in Georgia. He intended to avoid war movie clichés and military stereotypes. He would bridge "the gulf between combat troops and the 'jokers' in the rear echelons." He would go among the GIs, visit with them in the training camps, and "create a cinematic reality that will satisfy the war-view of all of them." The screenplay, he decided, would follow a group of men, perhaps a half dozen, who are drafted at the same time, take basic training together and then go their separate ways in the infantry before meeting again to "fight together on the same front." Miller intended most of them to be killed in action, but by the time he got to Los Angeles and began dealing with the movie executives, it was decided that just a few of the soldiers would die. The studio finally settled on no more than one dead soldier. "It is very hard to kill a good character in Hollywood," Miller concluded, "because the public seems to prefer pictures where nobody dies."

The Story of G.I. Joe was ultimately made, starring Robert Mitchum and Burgess Meredith, but without an Arthur Miller credit. By that time he had long since been replaced and was back in Brooklyn for the birth of a daughter, Jane Ellen, on September 7, 1944. With military research fresh in his mind, Miller wrote a book about the army he'd observed, about military police and mess halls, "Jeeps" (raw recruits) and homesickness, infantry and paratroopers, rifle ranges and tanks. The writing is breezy and reads like a diary. The book is not political, except for brief references to the racists Gerald L. K. Smith and Father Coughlin. Apart from a mildly impertinent tone, in the manner of Miller's college humor pieces, *Situation Normal . . .* is more or less typical of wartime reportage.

After Jane was born Mary tried "free lance editorial work at home . . . I just couldn't do it. Jane would get sick, everything would go wrong, the publishing house would clamor and I'd stay up until two A.M. trying to get [the job] done." Eventually she did return to work at Harper, this time for Frank E. Taylor, editor in chief of its Reynal and Hitchcock division. He described Mary Miller as more than a secretary, rather "a close office associate," and she promptly recommended her husband's army book. Taylor liked it, he liked its author and he liked its author's politics. The tall, slender, prematurely gray and unusually handsome (a former model, in fact) editor and his pretty wife, Nancy, were serious leftists, and stylish ones. They moved in the artier socialist circles, entertaining politically committed actors, musicians and writers in their Greenwich Village town house. The Taylors soon began spending social time with the Millers and toward the end of 1944 Taylor published *Situation Normal . . .* , which Art dedicated "To Lieutenant Kermit Miller, United States Infantry." It got him his first review.

Writing about the two-dollar, 179-page book on Christmas Eve in the *New York Times,* Russell Maloney said, "As nearly as I can figure it out [Miller's] mission was to find some new cliches to replace the old ones. If that is so, he has succeeded," but all was not negative. "Mr. Miller is at his best," Maloney wrote, "and that is really good, when he is describing actual happenings rather than stalking ideas or impressions . . . and his account of a plane full of paratroops going up for their first jump is almost unbearably detailed and tense."

That passage and several others in *Situation Normal . . .* are written—and were printed—as if they were scenes in a play. Miller made his professional debut as a writer for radio and perhaps now he was a writer of books, but it must have been clear to him that his best talent, greatest interest and most profound ambition lay in writing for the theater. Its fulfillment was hardly in sight. That summer he finished converting *The Man Who Had All the Luck* into a play, and it was not a happy experience. Miller worked on it during Mary's pregnancy (a not irrelevant fact in view of the plot), almost as if his dramatist self had been incubating during the past two frustrating years, when he had been unable to finish anything and didn't write plays at all. He still suffered moods of crushing discouragement.

> I have been bested time and again by writers who I know to be inferior. I have had plays refused insultingly by managements who have gone ahead to buy some monstrosity or other. Had I no faith in my talent I should vent my hatred against these miserable people, But . . . I will go home and write.

Undeterred by these resentments, Miller seemed to be emerging from a chrysalis, transformed into a mature and beautiful artist. This new play was strikingly superior to anything he had yet written. An early version was published in an anthology called *Cross-Section: A Collection of New American Writing,* and then a producer named Herbert H. Harris came forward to present it on Broadway.

The story Mary's mother told him about an unmotivated suicide would hardly seem a basis for dramatic action. Theater is an arena for demonstration and exhibition; how could the unexplainable be explained, let alone shown? Instead of discouraging him the paradox seemed to stimulate Miller. As for the theme, perhaps an existentialist commits suicide simply because life has no point; yet Miller profoundly believed—it was the Karl Mannheim in him (the character, not the social philosopher)—that life must make sense. If not, we would go mad. In real life Mary's uncle probably had been insane when he killed himself—at least that is what Miller thought—but in his play there would have to be a clearer reason. The denouement then could put an exclamation point on the theme; indeed from the outset he had a thorough sense of themes he wanted this play to explore. What he needed was a plot. "However I tried I could not make the drama continuous and of a piece; it persisted, with the beginning of each scene, in starting afresh as though each scene were the beginning of a new play."

Halfway through an early draft Miller decided that the protagonist, David Beeves, had so fraternal a relationship with a friend named Amos that they had to be brothers. As he revised their relationship, he invented. The opening scene's barn is not the place where Mary's Uncle Peter hanged himself. It isn't even used as a barn. It is an extension of a grain and feed store, now used as an automobile repair garage where the twenty-two-year-old David Beeves is employed. Stage directions describe him as "wondrous, funny, naive and always searching," a description that is of little use to an actor. Note, however, Miller's use once again of the word *wondrous*. The location of *The Man Who Had All the Luck* is "a small Midwestern town" and Beeves is telling Shory, his employer, that he is finally going to ask permission to marry Hester Falk, his childhood sweetheart. As he strolls offstage, Beeves is described by fellow workers as a man whose life seems securely destined, in fact predestined, "laid out like a piece of linoleum." He is successful at everything he does, a brilliant salesman and a self-trained, equally brilliant automobile mechanic. Beeves reenters to come upon his father, Pat, and his older brother, Amos, a good-natured, oafish fellow who has been brought up since childhood to be a pitcher in professional baseball.

The two bear some resemblance to earlier brothers in Miller's work. David is an equivocator. ("God!" he cries. "How do you know when to wait and when to take things in your hand and make them happen?") Amos has some of the qualities observed in Miller's various Kermit characters, a big, good-hearted, exceptionally gifted person who can be "in ecstasy at the thought of action" but is not an achiever and can be emotionally manipulated by his father. Incidentally, Kermit was also a pitcher.

David is a decent man, not at all jealous of Amos's favorite son status, possibly because he himself had not been a son in the play's original version. This would explain why the father, Pat Beeves, has a complex relationship with Amos but none with David. Also, David Beeves is the first Miller protagonist who isn't depressed; in fact he is positively cheerful, and unlike earlier Miller heroes who boast about their excellent personal qualities, this one just exhibits them.

David is preoccupied with his darling Hester, but he is fearful of her father, a narrow-minded and priggish farmer who has already threatened him with violence just for sitting in a car with her. After an effective introduction Hester makes a well-timed entrance—feminine, hearty and "breathless with expectation" about David's intention to ask permission to marry her. He is understandably fearful of confronting her ogreish father; but like the Miller heroines before her, she rouses her man to action, telling him, "A person isn't a frog, to wait and wait for something to happen!"

The stage is now set for the frightful farmer's entrance and when he makes it, Miller fills the stage with the character. Falk is an irrational, explosive and intimidating man who orders his daughter home, telling David, "Nobody but me knows what you are," meaning that David is a "lost [irreligious] soul" who has been flagrantly and immorally romancing his daughter. "The man Hester marries," Falk says, will be "a steady man . . . gonna know his God," and he storms out, willing to push his car if he has to, for it won't start. While the exciting scene seems tempered at first by the obvious device—Falk's stalled engine and David's mechanical genius—the maturing Miller won't have any part of such a contrivance.

Beeves tells his friends that with or without her father's permission he is going to elope with Hester, and when his own father disapproves, he cries, "I don't understand why I can't have that girl! I didn't do anything wrong." He demands a reason, insisting that people ought to be able to control their destinies. The father disagrees. "A man is a jelly fish," he says. "A man has very little to say . . . about what happens to him," and thus is the issue joined, one that Arthur Miller would pursue repeatedly. *The Man Who Had All the Luck* becomes a play about predestination as opposed to free will. What had seemed an impossible task—making the irrational suicide dramatic—was now something exciting and original, a play about the thinking process itself, set in the mind of David Beeves. This would be the first of several such plays for Miller.

Just when Beeves demands that circumstance be controllable, the unexpected changes everything. As he is leaving to elope with Hester, they learn that her father has been struck and killed on the road while pushing his car in the dark. It is the start of the play's *fabulous* quality, the first example of David's luck.

Being a good man, he is not grateful for her father's fate, and grimly tells the sobbing Hester, "I could have gotten [his car] started." Nor does he express satisfaction when he learns that she will inherit "a hundred and ten of the best acres in the valley"—another stroke of luck. He simply returns to work, trying to fix an expensive car (a Mammon) whose problems have baffled the most experienced mechanics in town. David too is baffled as, in the second scene, he works on the car deep into the night. Then he experiences yet another turn of fortune. A mechanic wanders into the garage, an Austrian named Gus Emerson. This is quite strange, even magical, considering the postmidnight hour; but Miller wisely tempers the fantastical with a reasonable explanation. Emerson is new in town, he plans to open his own garage and has questions about the local business situation. Beeves tells him, "There's plenty of business for two here," and accepts Emerson's offer of help with the problematic Mammon automobile. While Beeves dozes off, the Austrian proceeds to fix the engine.

In the morning Emerson is gone and Beeves is showered with opportunity and praise. The car's owner, impressed with his mechanical ability, has offered him a vast amount of tractor business. At the same time, David's employer suggests turning the barn into a fully equipped garage in exchange for just 1 percent on the investment. Young Beeves is "wondrous" about all of this too, until Hester notices a jacket that Emerson left behind. When she asks whose jacket it is (the only real contrivance so far), Beeves dashes out to look for Gus, leaving a most effective curtain to fall on the best first act that Arthur Miller had yet written.

The second act is set three years later in David and Hester's home, formerly her father's. It is a joyous atmosphere, almost like a radio comedy and intentionally so, because unreality is at work. The Beeves farm is thriving, the Beeves garage is a booming tractor station and David even considers mink breeding. As one of his friends says, David Beeves is "the only man I ever knew who never makes a mistake." Even Gus Emerson, the first act's heaven-sent mechanic, has become a family friend and now works for David because—more luck—his own garage failed.

Things seem to be good for David's brother, Amos, as well. A baseball scout is expected to watch him pitch that evening, and the future *Death of a Salesman* is foreshadowed in his father's remark, "People laughed when Amos got bad marks in school. Forget the homework, I said. Keep your eye on the ball." Otherwise the only cloud in David and Hester's sky is her failure to conceive a child, which David takes to be the price he is paying for his good fortune. Gus tells him life doesn't work that way, to which David takes exception. "I'll never believe that. If one way or another a man don't receive according to what he deserves inside . . . well, it's a madhouse," and with that, he raises a toast to end the second act's first scene. "In this year . . . everything our hearts desire," which is of course what he has been getting.

That evening, after Amos's marvelous pitching performance, everyone is eagerly awaiting the scout's decision. David anticipates a contract offer because his brother has talent, and talent deserves recognition. It makes him happy, for he "didn't like the idea of me getting everything so steady, and him waiting around . . . Why? Is it all luck?" Hester is certain that "It's good to be lucky," pausing to ask, quite perfectly, "Isn't it?" Here in a nutshell is Miller's core issue: Is one's future controllable or arbitrary?

With fine dramatic timing the impatiently awaited baseball scout arrives, only to reject Amos as perhaps a fine pitcher when the bases are empty but unreliable in tough situations. The fault, he says, lies with Amos's father who, in his obsession with making the boy into a great athlete, trained him year round in the basement of their house. As a result, he had no experience in real-life baseball situations. This metaphor goes directly to an interesting subtheme with regard to practical intelligence: Which is more critical to success, pure talent (Miller sometimes refers to it as genius) or an ability nurtured by ambition and application? Miller thinks the latter. He might well have considered himself less than a natural writer, or not as naturally gifted as his brother, Kermit—but more motivated and self-interested.

Pat Beeves now emerges as the agent of his son's defeat (Miller blamed his father for what he perceived as his brother's unfulfilled life). With that,

Amos flies into a rage. "A man makes mistakes," Pat says in pathetic self-defense, his speech anticipating Willy Loman. "I lie, I talk too much . . . Stop that crying! God Almighty, what do you want me to do! I'm a fool, what can I do!" Also, as Benjamin Nelson of Fairleigh Dickinson University succinctly points out, Amos and David are early versions of subsequent Miller brothers in *All My Sons* and *Death of a Salesman.*

> [O]ne who, anticipatory of Larry Keller and Happy Loman, is destroyed by his father's misguided thinking, while the other, heralding Chris Keller and Biff Loman, manages to survive through a painful exertion of will which enables him to tear away from his father's frenzied devotion.

David promises to contact another baseball scout and urges Amos to meanwhile correct his pitching flaws, telling his brother, "You got a whole life," but Amos insists that "everything the man said was right. I'm dumb . . . I ain't gonna touch a baseball again as long as I live!" Miller gives the act-ending scene to his protagonist, as David proclaims that even he hasn't gotten everything he wanted. "A man is born with one curse at least to be cracked over his head . . . nobody escapes!" His curse is that he is sterile. That, he is sure, must be the reason why he has no children.

Too neatly on cue, Hester announces she is pregnant, but to Miller's credit that is not the curtain line. Instead, as David struggles to express his joy, she provides a better one. "Now, you don't want [the baby]. I don't know what's happened to you, but you don't want it now," and the curtain falls on this new and tantalizing twist as Amos repeats, "Nobody escapes." Thus ends the best *second* act Miller had yet written.

The third act is set six months later, with Hester in labor offstage. Beeves's mink breeding business is now thriving and he seems happy about the expected child. Suddenly there is a stir elsewhere in the house as his wife appears to be miscarrying. David's reaction shows that he isn't surprised; he not only *expected* a miscarriage (she had tripped and fallen early in the pregnancy) but had already acted on it. Confident now that his luck would continue indefinitely, "paid for" with the lost child, he has put all of his money into expanding the mink business. When this cold-bloodedness appalls his friends, he only makes matters worse by suggesting that the baby "doesn't have to be dead . . . It can come wrong . . . A fall can make them that way." This is a peculiar choice, the specter of a handicapped infant, and is superfluous, since the child is born healthy. (It should be noted.)

The finale begins one month later and life is going wrong, signified by a crashing storm. The mink are dying of some mysterious disease; the marriage, once so sweet, is souring and David shows no feeling for his child. Gus fears that his friend is becoming mentally unbalanced—a condition of interest to Miller found in earlier and future plays. Beeves has lost faith in "what a man must believe. That on this earth he is the boss of his life." At this point the playwright appears to be at a loss as to how he might resolve his various themes and end the story. Its last scene is like that of a murder mystery, where the detective explains who did it, why, and how the killer was caught (known in the mystery trade as the Gotcha!). The play's balance and originality go by the wayside as the Austrian mechanic, in a speech addressed to Hester but aimed at the audience, tries to clarify the connection between the child's birth and the meaning of David's good luck. Gus concludes, "The healthy baby stole David from his catastrophe . . . David was left with every penny he owns in an animal that can die and the catastrophe still on its way. He is bleeding with shame because he betrayed his son, and he betrayed you."

Already bewildering, the scene becomes even more confusing as Hester reveals that she herself caused the mink to die by not telling her husband about a warning she had received concerning the animals' food. She fearfully tells David, "You always said something had to happen." He replies, "My boy is a pauper. How is it better?" Miller's hand, so sure an act ago, now grows unsteady as he gropes for easy ways out of the trap in which his play is caught. Hester begins to sound like his earlier heroines instead of the individual he'd created. "I can't live with you . . . I don't want [the baby] to see you this way." David assumes that she is leaving him for Gus—an embarrassingly melodramatic notion. She pleads with him to "start again, start fresh and clean!" He begs her not to go; and then, in still another turn of the plotting wheel, the mink are not dying after all.

The play finally expires of too many twists. An Arthur Miller who is unable or unwilling to decide whether he wants David to commit suicide straddles the issue. Hester asks, "Are you here?" to which he replies, "Yes, I'm here . . . now," which brings the final curtain down with less than finality, leaving the audience all too truly in the dark. Miller himself had become the equivocator, trying to manufacture resolution by passing off indecision as dramatic ambiguity. The problems that were pinpointed in the original novel, "no ending but a mere petering out" and a failure to "make at all clear the theme of the book," are problems that remain within the play.

Miller frankly admitted that *The Man Who Had All the Luck* had got away from him and didn't clearly reflect the theme he had in mind; but which theme? First is "the question . . . how much of our lives we make ourselves and how much is made for us." Then there is "the terror of failure and guilt for success." He described the play in seemingly autobiographical terms as "a brother's question, when one is more favored by parents or life than the other" (a subject he would return to many years later in *The Price*). Elsewhere he calls Beeves a man "destroyed by an illusion of his powerlessness." The process of analysis seems to be self-perpetuating, as if it were an end in itself. Among the major playwrights Miller is second only to George Bernard Shaw in self-exploration and self-explanation. Both seem to be inexhaustible essayists whose lengthy explanations shed scant additional light on plays that are supposed to be self-illuminating (and Miller extended these discussions in countless interviews—two published volumes of them).

Could *The Man Who Had All the Luck* have been fixed? Miller didn't think so, "because the overt story was only tangential to the secret drama [I] was quite unconsciously trying to write." He seems to mean, in his windy way, that the play didn't deliver his intended idea. Even so, it provides plenty to think about, as well as a fascinating mood and an inviting theatricality. Aside from a few loose ends (what is the significance of Gus being an Austrian, or of such symbols of American materialism as cars and mink?), the only real problem with *The Man Who Had All the Luck* is its last scene. Miller had to admit, "I have veered between David committing suicide and the present conclusion and am still not sure which is right."

The original production of *The Man Who Had All the Luck* was directed by Joseph Fields, a writer of light comedies (*My Sister Eileen*) and musical comedy librettos (*Gentlemen Prefer Blondes*). After a tryout engagement in Wilmington, Delaware, it opened in New York on November 23, 1944, at the Forrest Theater. Strangely enough, although Miller had worked so long and hard to reach this point, he never expressed any relief, enthusiasm or pleasure about getting there. It was not strictly a matter of being unable to express emotion. He had expressed plenty of anger, indignation and frustration about the repeated rejections of his plays. Rather, positive emotion seemed difficult for him to demonstrate. Nowhere did Miller recall any excitement about his first Broadway production, nothing from this man who considered almost everything he thought or felt to be worth writing about. Was Mary thrilled? Did his parents come to the opening night? Was he nervous? He left no record of it.

Miller did record, however, his reaction to his play's disastrous reception, five negative reviews from New York's seven newspapers. In the *New York Times* Lewis Nichols could find only "one or two effective moments" amid "the confusion of the script [and] its somewhat jumbled philosophies." The *Herald-Tribune*'s Howard Barnes was nastier ("incredibly turgid in its writing and stuttering in its execution"), while in the *New York Journal-American* the smart but supercilious George Jean Nathan wrote of "confidently expecting the final curtain to come down upon the spectacle of everyone on the stage squirting seltzer siphons at one another."

The producer had little choice but to shut the play down after two previews and four performances. One of them was all that its author could "bear to watch . . . The whole thing," he unhappily concluded, "was a well meant botch." He could scarcely have imagined that decades later *The Man Who Had All the Luck* would become a subject of serious study. Brenda Murphy of the University of Connecticut recognized

> such a close affinity to Ibsen's *Master Builder* that it might be seen as an adaptation if it were not for the fundamental thematic divergence in Miller's play. Miller's appropriation of *The Master Builder* in his writing of *The Man Who Had All the Luck* did not preclude his rejection of the dark romanticism of Ibsen's later plays, which, like the existential angst of the nineteen forties, is

> found wanting in his play. In the face of a universe where good fortune is a matter of random chance, Miller placed his faith in the efficacy of *praxis*—willed action.

Miller seems to have been unconscious of any connection with *The Master Builder*, which does not invalidate the interpretation. But his approach was practical rather than theoretical. In his brilliant introduction to the first edition of *The Collected Plays*, he was in a better position to describe the stylistic flaws in that Broadway debut production.

> In *The Man Who Had All the Luck*, I had tried to grasp wonder, I had tried to make it on the stage, by writing wonder . . . was trying to make this guy both mythic and ordinary at the same time, and succeeded in making him more ordinary than mythical. [But] a character in myth is a persona, he's not an ordinary person . . . It was produced as a realistic folk comedy . . . If it had been produced as a kind of semiwhimsical and yet terribly sad story, it might work.

Thinking in terms of how a play might work is the language of a playwright in the professional Broadway theater and as such, Miller became convinced that his play was fatally flawed. He permitted a "semiprofessional production" in London in 1960, but then decided that he did not "think the play is completed and I have no desire to work on it any further." It would be another forty years before *The Man Who Had All the Luck* was given another chance to work. By then published editions carried the subtitle *A Fable* so as to avoid any mistaking its level of reality. For the British premiere in 1990 the Bristol Old Vic's director, Paul Unwin, worked toward a heightened, or stylized, realism that would be both American and true to the play's period. It was in the style of "Steinbeck," Unwin said, "or Woody Guthrie, or Edward Hopper [because] Miller was trying to find a form to express the scale of the American experience."

The production at the Old Vic was enthusiastically received. Miller had by then become an adopted and revered son in England. It would be another decade until the play's first American revival and then, in a *New York Times* review, Bruce Weber did not let its considerable qualities go unrecognized a second time. "[T]he sound of a new and singular dramatic voice swelling with ambition . . . both flawed and gripping . . . one question it leaves you with is how it could have been so easily dismissed . . . it's downright bizarre that until now the play has been almost entirely forgotten." The twenty-five-year-old Miller could hardly have imagined such a belated validation. In 1944 he was so wounded that he found it "a relief to . . . read about the tremendous pounding of Nazi-held Europe by Allied air power. Something somewhere was real."

His brother, Kermit, was in the thick of that somewhere. Several months earlier, hip deep in the Atlantic Ocean, he had sloshed onto a Normandy beach shore—Omaha Beach, the Americans called it. While Arthur was arriving on Broadway, Kermit was leading his platoon of infantrymen toward the Ardennes Forest on the German-Belgian border. By mid December, after *The Man Who Had All the Luck* had closed, the Battle of the Bulge had begun. That winter would be one of the coldest, snowiest and most bitter in the history of Western Europe. In the thick of it was waged the biggest and most murderous land battle of the Second World War, lasting from December 16, 1944, until January 28, 1945. More than one million soldiers were involved—some 500,000 Americans, 55,000 British and 600,000 Germans. When it was over, there would be 19,000 Americans killed and 81,000 injured, including Kermit. Held down by enemy fire and unable to escape from his foxhole, he was trapped in the blinding snow for a week. By then his feet were frostbitten and potentially gangrenous, a condition that was rife among the troops. Facing the possible amputation of both feet, he was taken from the open trench to a field hospital. While not fully healed, he requested permission to return to his platoon. When it was denied, he got up from his hospital bed, dressed, signed himself out and returned to the front.

Arthur was injured too. He had been trying to succeed as a playwright for more than six years, driven toward that goal by a fierce ambition, only to be repeatedly thrown back. Now, having finally had a play produced, he'd been told that his work was "philosophical and tiresome," a combination of "sincerity of purpose and some inexpert play writing" (Ward Morehouse, the *New York Sun*). In view of such opinions and in the wake of his disastrous debut, he "simply decided I would never write another play," and this time he meant it, he said.

part two

Prime of Life

I have never been able to separate public and private. The way you live your life has consequences for the way everyone else lives his life.

5. *Hit*

TRUE AMBITION KNOWS NO DISCOURAGEMENT. Arthur Miller, once past the immediate fact of a rejection, would always retract any vow he had made to never write another play. There was always a once more. "I can be disheartened [by] failure and sometimes I think it's unfair, but finally I blame myself . . . If you blame the world too much you get depressed and then you're powerless. I come back because I feel I can do it the next time."

He had better do it the next time, he swore, because this time was different. This time, so discouraged after writing so many plays to such repeated rejection, he made one of those youthful bargains with destiny. Miller promised himself that should the *next* play fail, he would "find another line of work." As for the actual pain of rejection, it was expressed as anger about injustice, not self-pity. Negative and positive feelings alike were analyzed; the mind ruled all and disheartened was as depressed as Miller would let himself admit.

Meanwhile the thoroughly emotional Tennessee Williams achieved a resounding success in March 1945 with *The Glass Menagerie*. It was hailed by Broadway's critics and embraced by audiences. Miller appreciated that, for he recognized a "poetic lift" in this "very private play." He does not seem to have been jealous of or competitive with Williams, nor need he have been; their work is as different as are they. If Williams wrote very private plays about the inner self and how people feel, Miller wrote very public plays about the outer self and how people act—about people among people. Interestingly these are precisely the areas where the other had problems.

Miller went back to work, temporarily setting drama aside to write another novel. This was therapeutic activity, providing an escape that comforted the ego while building the bankbook. He finished the manuscript in six weeks, plainly less painstaking about fiction than about playwriting, and only wrote it "because I had been so burned by my first Broadway disaster."

Originally called *Some Shall Not Sleep*, the novel was finally named *Focus*. Its setting is New York City in 1944, and the subject is anti-Semitism. The story at the outset seems possibly inspired by Franz Kafka's "Metamorphosis." A bland, almost faceless man named Newman—lonely, loveless, sex-starved, a conformist, a virtual cipher—works in a huge, unidentified company that is engaged in an unspecified business. His only hint of individuality is a recurring dream about a merry-go-round revolving over an underground factory.

Newman is a personnel manager whose primary responsibility seems to be enforcement of a Christians-only hiring policy. This he is mindlessly capable of doing, for he accepts such prejudicial generalizations about Jews as their being pushy people with beady eyes and big noses, behaving loudly and acting greedily. Then one fine day, as it were, he wakes up to discover that he looks like a Jew and is taken for one. Miller's device for this transformation is a pair of newly prescribed eyeglasses that alter the man's appearance. Symbolically they allow Newman (possibly a meaningful name, possibly not) to see things as they really are—hence the title, *Focus*—and there is a chilling depiction of an anti-Semite's idea of a Jew as he peers into a mirror.

> [T]he eyes fairly popped, glared . . . the [eyeglass] frames seemed to draw his flat, shiny haired skull lower and set off his nose, so that where it had once appeared a trifle sharp it now beaked forth from the nosepiece . . . the smile . . . under such bulbous eyes, it was a grin, and his teeth which had always been irregular now seemed to insult the smile and warped it into a cunning, insincere mockery of a smile, an expression whose attempt at simulating joy was belied . . . by the Semitic prominence of his nose, the bulging set of his eyes, the listening posture of his ears. His face was drawn forward, he fancied, like the face of a fish.

It doesn't take long for Newman to learn what it feels like to be Jewish in an anti-Semitic society. He loses his position, is summarily rejected for jobs that he knows are available and is turned away from half-filled resort hotels, finally finding himself ostracized by his own community and badgered to move away. Although he is known to be Christian, this is disregarded as his Jewish appearance takes precedence with his neighbors. These former friends now join the kinds of Christian Front organizations common during the Second World War. They are the rabble easily aroused by the likes of Father Coughlin, who makes a barely disguised appearance midway through the novel. This is an acceptable fictionalization, although by 1944 Coughlin had long since been reprimanded by the Catholic Church, stripped of his radio pulpit, and was no longer a national force of bigotry.

Newman's situation becomes uncomfortable then dangerous, intolerable and finally violent. Even his wife urges him to join the bigots, although she is herself a Christian who had once been taken for a Jew. This in fact is how

Newman met her, by rejecting her for a job. Ultimately he transcends her cowardice, although the novel is vague about their future together.

The writing begins awkwardly then grows confident as the book moves along, concluding with an earnest plea for humanity and sense.

> The truth was that he was not a Jew. . . . [But] the denial was to repudiate and soil his own cleansing fury . . . He longed deeply for a swift charge of lightning that would with a fiery stroke break away the categories of people and change them so that it would not be important to them what tribe they sprang from. It must not be important anymore, he swore, even though in his life it had been of highest importance.

Primarily a social statement, *Focus* is straightforward in style and makes no pretensions to the kind of stylized writing that was criticized in Miller's first attempt at a novel. Though there is little in the way of plot development or depth of characters (perhaps a direct result of speedy writing), the story holds the attention while capturing and evoking the mood of New York City during the Second World War. The dialogue is more effective than the narrative, but Miller adapts comfortably to the novelistic mode.

While the book does not aspire to the standards of the plays, *Focus* nevertheless maintains a steady pace and rests upon a bed of compelling principle. Within the modesty of its intentions the work is perfectly creditable, although the author would later and understandably dismiss it as of little relevance to his main body of writing.

Mary Miller's boss at Reynal and Hitchcock, Frank Taylor, must have seemed a ready and obvious publisher for the book. He had been satisfied with the publication of *Situation Normal . . .* and to some extent was now socially involved with the Millers. Yet it was not out of friendship that Taylor published *Focus*. He ardently shared its contempt for religious prejudice and was honestly "impressed" with its treatment of the subject. Besides, he considered "acquaintanceship" a more accurate description of his relationship with the author. To Frank Taylor's way of thinking, a friendship with Arthur Miller could only go so far "because Arthur distances himself from intimacy with friends. It can be very frustrating and irritating to be professionally close and at the same time outside [but] Arthur, with or without wives, seldom makes social gestures. You call him, he never calls you."

Reynal and Hitchcock published *Focus* on October 30, 1945, and the 217-page novel was widely reviewed, for the most part, unfavorably. In the *New York Times* Charles Poore called it "too pat . . . does not give his characters sufficient free play. . . . [But] he can write eloquently." A rather fired-up Sterling North wrote in the *New York Post*, "In words that burn like carbolic acid, that flash like tracer bullets, through the midnight of bigotry he has pictured the agonizing fear and revulsion and finally the courage of a little man named Newman." Most notably and with a more composed simile Saul Bellow reviewed *Focus* in *The New Republic*. "The protagonist's heroism," he wrote, "has been clipped to his lapel like a delegate's badge at a liberal convention."

The academic critics tend to set *Focus* aside as a minor effort, unworthy of serious study. An exception is Professor Leonard Moss of the State University of New York at Geneseo, who perceives in it the same theme of active engagement that runs through so many Miller plays. In his excellent study *Arthur Miller* Moss writes of the book as being a novelistic treatment of Miller's convictions regarding activism and man's control over his environment.

> As in several later works (particularly *All My Sons*), in *Focus* the writer first establishes a standard of "normal" behavior, then undermines that standard and initiates a journey from security to disillusionment. . . . Then, in a moment, security and respectability vanish. The "familiar" order becomes transformed into a ghastly, surrealistic parody . . . [Newman] feels sufficiently emboldened [by sex] to protest his demotion in the company . . . sensuality, he finds, was not monopolized by Jews after all. . . . A symbolic dream assists in the exposition . . . a deserted carousel, senselessly rotating above an underground factory. . . . The innocent seeming amusement . . . camouflaged an insidious purpose, the manufacture of irrational hatred and fear. . . . His stand exemplifies the theory of heroic assertion.

In commercial terms *Focus* was successful, selling some 90,000 copies in English and foreign language editions. Evidently the sheer attention of the popular press counterbalanced the mixed-to-negative reviews. Perhaps too the sales were helped by publication that same year of another novel with a similar idea, the best-selling *Gentleman's Agreement* by Laura Z. Hobson. In any case *Focus* earned Miller his first substantial income from writing, including a sale of the film rights. Such financial rewards notwithstanding, he felt

> Somehow a book has always been sort of remote to me. It doesn't offer the same kick that comes from the direct experience of a confrontation with an audience. And when it comes to writing I think my talent has always been fundamentally and essentially for the drama . . . I can do in three pages of dialogue what would take me endless pages of words. . . . There's also a dramatic structure which I find endlessly fascinating. I love to vary and reform it. And I love acting when I write. I'm the whole cast. I play all the parts. And that's not in a book either. And I love real actors too. I love to sit there and change one line and see an explosion happen that wouldn't have happened if the line hadn't been changed.

No question, this writer of plays was a man of the theater who looked beyond play script to performance for full satisfaction. Although grounded in dramatic theory and classical principle, Miller would always gravitate toward the stage with its dynamic and public nature, the commercial stage especially. Thus was he poised between the academy and Broadway, respectful of one, in love with the other.

Toward the end of 1945 Kermit was discharged from the army with a Purple Heart. He'd escaped gangrenous infection and his feet were intact, but he was not. He continued to suffer the effects of what was then called shell shock or battle fatigue. Considering his harrowing combat experience, that would have seemed inevitable, even were he half so sensitive. Following treatment and rehabilitation, Kermit was released from a Veterans Administration hospital, but at the time little was known about battlefield trauma or how to deal with it. Kermit Miller was treated to a series of electric shock therapy sessions before being sent home, where he returned to the old sales job in his friend's family carpet business. When retail sales proved uncomfortable, he went to work directly for the mill, selling carpeting on the wholesale level. "And that's what he did," his sister Joan said, "for the rest of his life.

"He was a wonderful salesman, very successful."

In 1946 electric shock therapy was a relatively primitive technique of psychotherapy. Whether it was permanent battle scars on this peaceful man's psyche or lingering effects of the treatment, Kermit Miller had changed. For the rest of his life he would suffer periods of depression and occasional forgetfulness.

With *Focus* out of the way Arthur Miller turned his attention to a new play, one that, as his notebooks indicate, had been germinating since 1941. It was called *The Sign of the Archer* until the final draft, when the title was changed to *All My Sons*. As he wrote and rewrote, he consciously sought to create a play with built-in audience appeal, one that would have commercial viability. In the language of Broadway, which he was learning rapidly, Miller said that every line was calculated to "land," every scene designed to "work." To that end he was determined "to reverse my past play writing errors," starting with writing this play in a realistic style—one he had not used since *No Villain* back at the University of Michigan. There would be no ex- or impressionism, no period costumes, no verse or fantasy. He wanted audiences "to mistake my play for life itself," and later told the *New York Times*,

> I had written 13 plays, none of which is realistic and none of which got me anywhere. So I decided at the age of 29 that I wasn't going to waste my life in this thing. I already had one child and I couldn't see myself going on writing play after play and getting absolutely nowhere. I sat down and decided to write a play about which nobody could say to me, as they had with all the other plays, "What does this mean?" And I spent two years writing that play

> just to see if I could do it that way. Because I was working in a realistic theater which didn't know anything else.

The dramatic terms *realistic* and *naturalistic* are often used interchangeably but are not synonymous. Their differences are best exemplified by the plays of Ibsen and Chekhov. These great contemporaries of the late nineteenth century set drama on its modern course by turning away from aristocratic environments and florid language to write about characters and conflicts more familiar to middle-class audiences: recognizable characters in recognizable environments facing recognizable crises.

The differences between the realism of Ibsen (*Hedda Gabler, Ghosts* or *An Enemy of the People*, for instance) and the naturalism of Chekhov have been clearly explained by John Howard Lawson, one of the most admired and forgotten playwrights of the 1930s. Clurman called him "the hope of our theater," and he was as essential to the Group Theatre as Odets. The author of such plays as *Success Story* (Noel Coward liked it so much he saw it seven times) and *Processional,* Lawson was the rare playwright with academic credentials. He wrote that while Ibsen and Chekhov each sought to portray "familiar events in a style that corresponds to the experience of the spectators," this is where the similarities end. Ibsen's realism, he explains, is exterior and photographic; it represents objective reality, while Chekhov's naturalism is psychological, capturing such intangibles as insecurity and disappointment, the *nature* of man. Chekhov's dramas are about emotions and the subconscious of humanity; his characters are confused and inconsistent, unwilling and perhaps unable to express what is on their minds. But Ibsen's characters, Lawson writes, "are not driven by irrational impulses." They say everything on their minds, they pursue direct lines of action, and Henrik Ibsen in his realistic plays developed this depiction of such reasonable characters and stories, says Lawson, for a purpose that is also reasonable, the "advocacy of reform . . . protest and concern with social issues." Ibsen's people "try as best they can to exert their will and cope with their environment. If they fail, they fail consciously." This is also the direction Shaw followed, being a disciple and champion of Ibsen. He shared the Norwegian playwright's belief that "human beings can shape their own destiny," a conviction that sits at the very center of Arthur Miller's intellectual being. Indeed George Bernard Shaw could well have been anticipating Miller when he wrote in 1902 that drama "is the presentation in parable of the conflict between man's will and environment."

Shaw and Arthur Miller are certainly the two great issue-oriented playwrights of the twentieth century. Miller's view of Shaw's approach, while competitive, is interesting and perceptive.

> In general, aside from the women, it is the minor characters who are most realistically drawn. The major characters are too completely obsessed with the issues that are being set forth. One of the signs of an abrogation of regular psy-

chology is that people stay on the theme. . . . You read Shaw's plays and see how rarely people get off the subject.

Miller's analysis of the Irish playwright is sharp, lucid and expressed with great clarity. Whoever the character, he writes,

> You always know that it's Shaw speaking no matter what side of the argument is being set forth, and that is part of the charm . . . it isn't psychology he is following, it is the theme. . . . [He] is impatient with the insignificance of most human speech, most human thought, and most human preconceptions. He was funny, and funny in a definitely aristocratic manner that gave him license to preach the virtues of a socialism of wits . . . Shaw the socialist was in love not with the working class, whose characters he could only caricature, but with the middle of the economic aristocracy, those men who, in his estimate, lived without social and economic illusions.

Ibsen had a second, structural influence on *All My Sons*. As Kenneth Rowe had taught, Ibsen applied a principle of Greek tragedy to contemporary playwriting—"the past coming to life in the present and creating drama"—which is precisely what Miller did. As he put it, Ibsen's "insistence upon valid causation" solved the problem of "how to dramatize what has gone before," and how to use it to provoke the play's reaction to that past. "That," Miller claims, "is the 'real' in Ibsen's realism for me." He never would understand complaints about his play being *too much* like Ibsen or *too* realistic, because these were based on different understandings of what Ibsen and realism are about.

For Miller, realism meant facing the facts and being not just pragmatic but sane. Implicit for him is that without sanity, intelligence is of little use.

Miller had in mind only one more thing, what he'd sworn at the outset. This play was going to be a hit.

Five years, a half dozen drafts and some 700 pages after making his first notes about it Miller was satisfied that *All My Sons* was finished. His script sets the action entirely in the back yard of a two-story house in "an American town"—surely Lakewood, Ohio, based on Mary's mother's recollection (and there is in fact a reference to nearby Columbus). The house, "nicely painted . . . tight and comfortable," is the home of Joe and Kate Keller, and the period is "August of our era," just after the Second World War. As the first act begins, the sixtyish Joe Keller is reading a newspaper. Downstage (close to the audience) is a broken sapling, and soon Keller is telling some friends that it was snapped in half "by the night wind."

The tree had been planted in memory of Keller's son, Larry, killed in combat. "Born in August," one of the friends says. "He'd been twenty seven this month and his tree blows down." If he'd been shot down on an astrologically favorable day, the man adds, "it's completely possible he's alive somewhere." Through these casual remarks emerge the basic facts that three years earlier Keller's son Larry was declared missing in action and not everyone wants to believe he is dead—Mrs. Keller especially.

A mood of near mindless conviviality, something like the happy home life of David and Hester Beeves in *The Man Who Had All the Luck*, is created as assorted neighbors make small talk while Joe is established as a prominent town figure. Someone mentions a young woman who has come to visit the Kellers, Ann Deever, who used to live in the house next door. The daughter of Joe's ex-partner, Ann had been Larry's fiancée. Now his brother, Chris, intends to propose to her, which is why he invited her. She is unaware of this, his mother is unaware of it and Joe doesn't want to be reminded. "The girl is Larry's girl," he tells the son. "You marry that girl and you're pronouncing him dead. Now what's going to happen to mother?"

Joe backs off when Chris indicates that he intends to marry Ann even if it means moving away and quitting the family business. "Don't think like that," the father says in panic. "Because what the hell did I work for? That's only for you." With that the matriarch makes her entrance, establishing her power by jumping on her husband ("Do me a favor . . . don't be helpful" "What are you crabbing about?") and expressing her obsession with Larry's continued existence by declaring that Chris "is not going to marry her. . . . [Ann's] faithful as a rock. . . . I won't stand for any nonsense. Because if [Larry is] not coming back, then I'll kill myself!"

With Ann's entrance more of the past is brought into the play's present as Mrs. Keller asks after the girl's parents. "When he gets out," Ann replies, giving the audience a bit of mystery, "they'll probably live together," and Miller further teases with Mrs. Keller's response, "Your father is still . . . a decent man when all is said and done." One of the neighbors begins the clarification, "If an intelligent man like your father is put in prison . . ." while Ann turns aside to ask Joe if everyone is still talking about her father. "Gone and forgotten, kid," he replies. "The only one still talks about it," he chuckles, "is my wife." Ann can only muse, "Gosh, it's wonderful to hear you laughing about it," and she means it. The last thing she remembers from living here, she says, is the neighborhood accusing her father of being a "murderer."

Mrs. Keller says that it's different with Joe, who "was exonerated, your father's still there." With that Joe embarks on an explanation of events that occurred before the play began.

> The day I come home . . . everybody knew I was getting out. . . . Picture it, now; none of them believed I was innocent. The story was, I pulled a fast one getting myself exonerated. . . . I was the beast . . . who sold cracked cylinder heads to the Army Air Force; the guy who made twenty one P-40s crash in Australia. . . . Except . . . there was a court paper to prove I wasn't. . . . Fourteen months later I had one of the best shops in the state again, a respected man again.

"Joe McGuts," Chris beams. Then Joe startles Ann with a suggestion that her father move back after he gets out of prison. This bewilders her. "But he was your partner. He dragged you through the mud." No matter, says the all-forgiving Keller, as opposed to Ann, who harshly refuses to visit or even write her father. "He knowingly shipped out parts that would crash an airplane," she says, "and how do you know Larry's wasn't one of them?" The statement strikes a knife into Mrs. Keller's heart, and she flatly demands, "Put that out of your head . . . He's not dead, so there's no argument."

But Joe can't let go of the subject. "Now look, Ann. . . . Those cylinder heads went into P–40s only . . . You know Larry never flew a P–40." He tries to justify her father's role in that fateful past, but he doesn't try too hard. The plant was "a madhouse," Joe remembers, the air force frantically demanding cylinder heads while a half day's worth of production was emerging with hairline cracks. Her father, all alone in the plant, was desperately covering the cracks. "That's what a little man does," he says. "If I could have gone in that day I'd a told him—junk 'em." This makes Chris adore his father ("Isn't he a great guy?"), and he is so elated that, alone with Ann, he proposes to her. She is not as surprised as one might expect. They have been corresponding for years, and she accepts.

Chris gives his father the news after she goes into the house, but Keller is distracted by a telephone call that Ann has just received from her brother George, who has visited his father in prison. "All these years, George don't go to see his father. Suddenly he goes . . . and she comes here. She don't hold nothin' against me, does she? . . . To his last day in court, the man blamed it all on me." Now it seems that George Deever is headed their way, which should provide the tension to hold the audience through the first intermission.

The second act starts on an edgy note. George's arrival is imminent and there is a sense of trouble ahead. There are rumors that he is in a rage and intends to drag Ann away. Indeed when he shows up, he is in a cold fury, telling his sister that their father "got smaller . . . That's what happens to suckers." With that he informs her, "You're not going to marry [Chris] . . . Because his father destroyed your family."

> I wanted to go to Dad and tell him you were going to be married. It seemed impossible not to tell him. He loved you so much. Ann—we did a terrible thing. We can never be forgiven. Not even to send him a card at Christmas. I didn't see him once since I got home from the war! Ann, you don't know what was done to that man. You don't know what happened.

Now, George provides the final installment on the past events that dramatically come to life in the present. With Keller absent, George tells his father's side of the story: how he reported the crisis to Joe, who did not come down to the plant. By the time there were a hundred defective cylinder heads, "Dad called again . . . Joe told him . . . on the phone, he told him to weld, cover up the cracks in any way he could, and ship them out." Keller himself was suddenly too sick to get out of bed.

> He promised to take responsibility . . . In court you can always deny a phone call and that's exactly what he did . . . and now Joe is a big shot and your father is the patsy. Now what are you going to do? Eat his food, sleep in his bed? Answer me; what are you going to do?

Here was Miller's emotionalism finally going public. By pushing his play to "work," he was finding the words, and the way, to vent his moral passions, and to exploit the theatrical medium so that audiences could feel what he felt. Yet George Deever's speech is only the start of the play's surge, and once the dramatic heartbeat accelerates, it attains a steady and urgent rhythm. Mrs. Keller appears, greeting "Georgie" like a goddess, offering fruits and meat, stroking his hair. Her eerie maternalism and his inability to resist it create an untrustworthy warmth, setting the stage for Joe Keller's strangely innocent entry into the spotlight of guilt.

He welcomes George warmly even as Ann is urging her brother to leave, and talks about the postwar conversion of his plant's production, from airplane parts to pressure cookers and washing machines. Asking George about his father, Keller hears that Mr. Deever is "not well, Joe. . . . It's everything. It's his soul." When Keller blithely says, "as far as I'm concerned, any time he wants, he's got a place with me," George is aghast. "He hates your guts. Don't you know that?" Joe counters with a list of other mistakes George's father had made, to none of which he'd admit. "There are certain men," Keller keeps repeating, "who rather see everybody hung before they'll take the blame."

Ann continues to urge her brother to leave, fearful of his anger even as he is meekly conceding his father's faults, but calm prevails, and he agrees to stay. "I never felt at home anywhere but here," George admits, for everything is so familiar and everyone looks so healthy. "I ain't got time to get sick," Joe cheerfully concedes, and Mrs. Keller adds, "He hasn't been laid up in fifteen years."

With that George freezes, and Joe knows why. "I mean," Mrs. Keller hastily adds, "except for that flu. It slipped my mind." She turns to George. "Don't look at me that way. He wanted to go to the shop but he couldn't lift himself off the bed." Of course it is too late, and with the gaffe Miller brings the long strands of the past to present confluence, and his play to a point of inevitability. From here the story plays out as ritual, Keller's "If I could have gone in that day," and George's "She said you'd never been sick," and "I'd remember pneumonia. Especially if I got it just the day my partner was going to patch up cylinder heads."

Once again the tension is eased off as the astrologically inclined neighbor arrives with good news about the horoscope he mentioned at the start of the play. "Somewhere in this world," he cries to Chris, "your brother is alive!"

because the date of Larry's supposed death was November 25th, "his favorable day . . . when everything good was shining on him." George, hardly interested, tells his sister that they must leave ("He simply told your father to kill pilots and covered himself in bed!") and dares her to deny Joe's guilt. Mrs. Keller tells Chris that he cannot marry Ann because "She's Larry's girl," but Chris replies, "And I'm his brother and he's dead and I'm marrying his girl."

"Never, never in this world," cries the mother, pushing her husband to exasperation with her delusion and he is finally driven to confront her about it. "Three and a half years," he says, "you been talking like a maniac," and then the playwright indicates a terrible moment as *Mother smashes him in the face*, for Kate Keller cannot consider the possibility of her firstborn's death. "He's coming back," she declares, "and everybody has to wait." She is almost in a trance. "Till he comes; forever and ever till he comes! . . . I'll never let him go!" When Chris says that *he's* let his brother go, she reaches the edge of her personal cliff.

"Then let your father go."

Here is the real reason she has refused to accept Larry's death, and confessing it brings release. She hadn't simply been refusing to accept the death of a son. "Your brother's alive, darling, because if he's dead, your father killed him. Do you understand me now? . . . God does not let a son be killed by his father."

She turns and walks into the house, leaving Joe Keller to whimper in self-defense, "He never flew P–40s . . . what, killed? How could I kill anybody?" And finally,

> You're a boy, what could I do! I'm in business, a man is in business; a hundred and twenty cracked, you're out of business; you got a process, the process don't work you're out of business; you don't know how to operate, your stuff is no good; they close you up, they tear up your contracts, what the hell's it to them. You lay forty years into a business and they knock you out in five minutes, what could I do, let them take forty years, let them take my life away? I never thought they'd install them. I swear to God.

The words are in the character's voice but even so, a howl.

Keller's defense is that he had counted on discovery of the damaged cylinder heads, but this never happened and then twenty-one American pilots died in the crashes. "They came with handcuffs into the shop . . . it was a chance I took for you."

Now it is Chris's turn, his recent army experience still vivid.

> For me! Where do you live, where have you come from? For me! I was dying every day and you were killing my boys and you did it for me? What the hell do you think I was thinking of, the Goddam business? Is that as far as your mind can see, the business? What is that, the world—the business? What the hell do you mean, you did it for me? Don't you have a country? Don't you

> live in the world? What the hell are you? You're not even an animal, no animal kills his own, what are you? What must I do to you? I ought to tear the tongue out of your mouth, what must I do? [With his fist he pounds down on his father's shoulder] What must I do, Jesus God, what must I do?

The third and final act is brief, a nine-page coda set at two o'clock in the morning, an hour of judgment. A stage direction indicates *Mother is discovered rocking ceaselessly in a chair*. A worried neighbor stops by and, hearing that Chris drove off after an argument with his father, guesses what it was about. It seems that everyone but Chris has suspected the truth all along, and he simply suppressed the suspicion because he hadn't the "talent for lying." He'll develop it, the neighbor expects.

Joe Keller, a stage direction indicates, *comes out from porch in dressing gown and slippers*, and after the neighbor leaves Mrs. Keller warns him that "this thing is not over yet . . . you better figure out your life." Without her to provide the backbone he is spineless, but she has "no strength to think any more." She suggests that he confess to his son and pretend to offer to go to prison. "He wouldn't ask you [and] maybe he would forgive you," but Keller refuses to feel guilty and blames the family for his actions. "You wanted money, so I made money. What must I be forgiven? . . . I spoiled the both of you. I should've put him out when he was ten like I was put out."

She argues that the excuse "done it for the family" won't satisfy Chris. His moral code is more important to him. Joe insists that "I'm his father and he's my son, and if there's something bigger than that, I'll put a bullet in my head!" which frightens her of course, but she is already rattled. Then a calm Ann comes out from the house to make the unexpected promise that she won't support a reopening of the case against Joe, but in return wants Mrs. Keller's admission that Larry is dead, setting Chris free to marry her. The mother remains obsessed and like a seeress predicts, "The night he gets into your bed his heart will dry up. . . . To his dying day he'll wait for his brother! . . . You're going in the morning." And so the play ascends to a level of final truths as Ann declares that she "knows" Larry is dead.

She asks Joe to leave and produces a letter ("I thought I'd show it to you only if there was no other way to settle Larry in your mind"). Mrs. Keller reads it with growing agony as Chris returns, having driven aimlessly through the night. Remorseful that "I suspected my father and did nothing about it," he has decided to leave home. Even now, he tells his mother, "I could jail him, if I were human any more. . . . You made me practical . . . and I spit on myself."

When Keller returns, Chris dreadfully warns his once beloved father, "I'm going to hurt you." Once again Keller states his belief in *the almighty dollar*, asking, "Who worked for nothin' in that war? . . . Did they ship a gun or a truck outa Detroit before they got their price? Is that clean? . . . What's clean? Half the Goddam country is gotta go if I go!" For Chris, though, this is exactly the point. "I never saw you as a man. I saw you as my father." This is the moment when Ann snatches the letter from Mrs. Keller and hands it to Chris. "Larry," she announces. "He wrote it to me the day he died."

Chris reads it aloud.

> Yesterday they flew in a load of papers from the States and I read about Dad and your father being convicted. I can't express myself. I can't tell you how I feel—I can't bear to live any more. . . . Every day three or four men never come back and he sits back there doing business . . . I can't face anybody . . . I'm going out on a mission in a few minutes. They'll probably report me missing. If they do, I want you to know that you mustn't wait for me. I tell you, Ann, if I had him here now I could kill him.

Keller, faced with his guilt, agrees to turn himself in. "Sure he was my son. But I think they were all my sons." As he goes into the house to dress, his wife pleads, "How long will he live in prison? The war is over! Didn't you hear?" But Chris is moving on to bigger issues. "Once and for all you can know there's a universe of people outside and you're responsible to it, and unless you know that, you threw away your son, because that's why he died."

A gunshot is heard from the house and as Chris weeps in grief, and in apology to his mother, she at last forgives him, her husband and herself. "Forget now. Live. Shhh . . ." and, Miller wrote, *As she reaches porch steps she begins sobbing as The Curtain Falls*.

This powerful play, Miller's first substantial, mature and fulfilled work, is virtually a guided tour of his past, present and future. In it are autobiographical aspects, elements of his early playwriting efforts, a new professionalism and sinew and signals of the mastery that lay ahead. In some ways and at some times *All My Sons* recalls the family life in *No Villain*. The browbeaten husband–dominating wife relationship of Joe and Kate Keller certainly has an Isadore–Gussie ring to it, and notwithstanding the Slattery inspiration and the Midwest setting, an occasional Jewish idiom can be found in the dialogue. Other elements of Isadore Miller are in Joe Keller (an echo name for *Miller*), for instance, his reference to going to work "when I was ten," and his slavish devotion to "the business." Isadore also can be heard in a Keller who refers to speaking in French as "talking dirty" and makes such remarks as "Everybody's gettin' so goddamn educated in this country, there'll be nobody to take away the garbage." Reminders of Gussie too are Mrs. Keller's dignity and strength, her intense involvement with her sons and her contempt for Joe. As to the Miller brothers so present in earlier plays, the brothers in this play are both present and absent—Larry, a brother even in death, and George Deever, in a real way taking his place.

The brothers Art and Kermit can be seen in various references to Larry's military history, even his baseball glove, and in an Arthurlike Chris holding moral values above family. Chris's final speech about Joe's responsibility to "people outside" is not so different from Arnie's climactic scene in *They Too Arise* ("You think that because you close your door in the front of the house then anything that happens outside doesn't have anything to do with you"). Also, like so many Miller protagonists, Chris is a vacillator, defending his father and damning him, ready to report him yet unable to.

Then again, at times Chris sounds more like Kermit than Arthur, as when he is described as someone who "makes people want to be better than it's possible to be." Arthur too may be seen in the moral outrage of George, a young man who shares his shirt collar size (15 1/2). Even so, if the play incorporates aspects of people in Miller's life, the combinations and variations make the characters ultimately his own.

Likewise the dramatic and moving story is Miller's, as he merely uses events described by Mary's mother as a starting point. By being specific about the manufacturing fault and using the vivid image of cracked engine cylinder heads, Miller intimately relates the malfunction to the pilots' deaths, and thanks to his experience with automobile parts, he knew what he was talking about. Miller was less knowledgeable about astrology. The play's original title *The Sign of the Archer* refers to Sagittarius, the astrological sign for late November into mid December, and Miller surely gave Larry a November 25 doomsday for just that reason; but in the world of horoscope the date of *birth* pertains. Larry's August birthday makes him a Leo or Virgo. Miller would have been better off dropping the whole astrological subject.

As to his Greco-Ibsen approach, Miller smoothly adapted a scheme of retroactive construction that effectively introduces facts of the past without making the dialogue uncomfortably expositional. The play's present action indeed hinges on past events. As to style, realism is supported by deceptively casual dialogue, born of what Miller's playwriting professor called *the ear for idiom*. This has always been Miller's gift, exemplified in *All My Sons* by such lines as "He'd been 27" and "the only one still talks about it," or the subtle elision in the line "There are certain men who rather see everybody hung before they'll take the blame."

Most important perhaps is the profound connection Miller discovers between dramatic structure and emotional weight. *Death of a Salesman*'s Biff and Willy Loman are anticipated when Chris cries to his father that ordinary forgiveness is not possible because "I never saw you as a man. I saw you as my father." This quality of meaningful heartbreak sits at the center of Arthur Miller's power as a playwright.

All My Sons also shares lesser qualities with Ibsen, melodramatic devices such as the letter and a final, offstage gunshot. The play reflects as well Ibsen's reputation for pamphleteering. Miller has argued fairly enough that *All My Sons* is not simply a condemnation of capitalism and wartime profiteering; yet he disingenuously denies that it is even about that, insisting instead that the play is strictly about a man's responsibility for his actions and the results of those actions.

All My Sons contains elements of Greek tragedy not only in its retroactive structure but also in a story that at times evokes Aeschylus's *Oresteia* and Sophocles' *Oedipus Rex*. Joe Keller can be viewed as a king whose hands are stained with a son's blood, and Kate Keller as a Queen who is suspended between shielding her husband and destroying him for love of a son. Keller's final entrance in a dressing gown certainly affords him a regal appearance and the play occasionally is staged to underline this, with Mrs. Keller in a formal robe as well and their home designed with touches of ancient Greece. Indeed the British director David Thacker believes that "the best way . . . is for the design element to be nonrealistic. Because . . . if it is trapped in a realistic setting, it confines the actual scope and scale of the play."

The Oedipal theme is carried further in Chris's behavior toward his parents and the terrifying mix of love, protection and vengeance in Mrs. Keller. Likewise Ann, George and their absent father might be viewed as the opposite of the Kellers, an ill-used and wrongfully deposed royal family of three; in their own way they are similar to Ophelia, Laertes and Polonius of *Hamlet,* another play with Greek overtones.

One added curiosity: The style of the script suggests that perhaps Miller never fully resolved the precise level of realism he sought. Mrs. Keller is regularly called Kate in the dialogue, but her name appears only as *Mother*. This may be left over from the original version of the play when there was no Keller name, just Larry, Chris, Mom and Pop.

The next step was to find a producer. Miller had acquired a new agent. "To have an agent," he would say, "is to have a kind of reassurance that you exist." Solid reassurance of a kind he had never known now came in the form of a tall, elegant and formidable woman named Katherine Brown, a playwright agent at MCA, a most impressive agency. As the giant of the industry, MCA bought out Leland Hayward and Company, which essentially meant acquiring its clients. Kay Brown was assigned to represent Arthur Miller and she would remain his agent for the next forty years.

For a start, she sent *All My Sons* to a couple of producers, one of whom promptly rejected it. When the other, the Theatre Guild, dallied over a decision, Miller urged Brown to try somebody else. He may well have been anxious. Eugene O'Neill's *The Iceman Cometh* had just opened on Broadway, only to close within a few months, a victim of mixed reviews by critics who overlooked a future American classic. Miller had seen the play and while scornful of the production and not particularly impressed with the grace of the writing, he appreciated the power and size of the play, acknowledging O'Neill's uniqueness and his "insistence on his vision." (Miller later described O'Neill as "The great wrestler, fighting God to a standstill.") The play's reception was doubly upsetting to Miller as a playwright. "There is no critic alive," he said, "who can tell the difference between a bad production and a bad script."

Eric Bentley, himself a critic, agreed.

> Whatever a man's estimate of the total intelligence of drama critics, high or low, he cannot fail to notice that—except for a Stark Young or Harold Clurman—they know far less about acting and directing than about literature. Which is another funny thing about this remarkable class of men. They know something of literature though they are anti-literary; they are pro-theatrical but know little about acting.

Yet playwrights cannot shake themselves free of critics, not even when thinking of them as lice. As a performing art, theater demands reaction. The reception accorded *The Iceman Cometh* angered Miller particularly. At the performance he saw, when it began there were "about thirty people in the audience" and four and a half hours later "there were a dozen people left." If this could happen to Eugene O'Neill, it could happen to Arthur Miller.

He asked Kay Brown to send *All My Sons* to Elia Kazan and Harold Clurman, a couple of old heroes from the late, beloved ("a society of saints") Group Theatre. The two had only recently formed a producing partnership, and they made an odd couple. Both were married directors who were attracted to the ladies and lived for the theater, yet they could not have been more different. Clurman was a man of the mind, Kazan a man of the stage; Clurman was a born teacher, Kazan a born magician.

Elia (pronounced eh-LEE-a) Kazan was born in Constantinople to the Kazanjioglou family, Anatolian Greeks who brought him to America in 1913 when he was four years old. His family, like Miller's, went down with the Wall Street crash, and his father, like Miller's, "put the yield of a life's labor into a stock [that] rumbled with all the others down the mountain of high finance." While it may be true that, as Kazan put it, "Arthur and I came out of the same experience, the Depression," Elia was six years older and so went through school worry free, graduating from Williams College then spending two years at Yale Drama School.

Several years later, in July 1934, "Gadget" (as everyone seemed to call him) Kazan joined the Communist Party, a political commitment that dictated his career choices. He studied with the Soviet director Vsevolod Meyerhold and taught at the New Theatre League, a Communist-front organization. He married a party member, Molly Thatcher, who was an associate director of *New Theatre*, a communist magazine, and a teacher of playwriting at the Theatre Union. One of their best friends was Clifford Odets, another party member, and when Odets became part of the ardently idealistic, left-wing Group Theatre, Kazan followed. There political convictions were inseparable from theatrical ideals, and Kazan immediately joined a nine-member Communist Party cell within the company.

At the Group Theatre "Gadg" started out as an office boy and soon became an assistant stage manager for a production of John Howard ("Jack") Lawson's *The Pure in Heart*. He finally got his chance to act, playing small parts in *Awake and Sing* and *Golden Boy* just as their author, Clifford Odets, was becoming the playwright of the hour. The breaking point between Kazan and the Communist Party came early in 1936, he recalled, when his cell was "ordered to take control of the Group Theatre." With that he resigned his party membership. Five years later the Group Theatre gave up the fight to survive and Kazan turned to Broadway.

Still a committed leftist, he was promptly successful as a director of such socially significant plays as Thornton Wilder's *The Skin of Our Teeth* and S. N. Behrman's *Jacobowsky and the Colonel*. The Theatre Guild's Teresa Helburn saw him in terms of such responsible material.

> Gadg works hard to get at the meaning of the play. [He] has an eye primarily for social implications. I sometimes think he finds social significance in a play whether it is there or not. This he carries over into his personal life. [He] looks rather like a young laborer, slightly unkempt, an appearance which he makes some effort to maintain.

As to Kazan's theatrical instincts, Helburn saw him as showmanly.

> He has a strong feeling for the basic idea of a play and for its architecture in building scenes. He always felt that there should be a big scene in the last act just before the curtain, that the success of a play depended on it.

His partnership with Clurman was uneasy, as might be expected of two dissimilar men in a competitive and ego-driven field. Their plan was to take turns directing the plays they produced and splitting the profits—of which there had been none thus far—but Kazan had begun directing movies and started with a success, *A Tree Grows in Brooklyn*. He was now preparing to make another, and so Clurman got to read *All My Sons* first. Without even consulting his partner Clurman offered to produce it. Miller accepted at once, much to the annoyance of Helburn's codirector at the Theatre Guild, Laurence Langner, who felt that the young playwright owed them something. As one of "Terry Helburn's proteges, discovered through the Guild's Bureau of New Plays as early as 1937 and encouraged by [its dramaturg] John Gassner," Miller might have shown some gratitude, thought Langner, by giving the guild "his first fully realized play. . . . We offered him a production . . . he chose another producer." Gratitude was never a particularly strong quality of Arthur Miller's, certainly not when it came to business.

Elia Kazan, not Clurman, ended up directing *All My Sons*. There need never have been any doubt of it. Clurman was a literary man, a theorist with a trusting, open nature, but Kazan was a born director, wily and manipulative. He knew how to get what he wanted out of people and out of life. He was the more aggressive figure, the more ambitious one and the better director—and Miller knew it.

A short man, Kazan had a high forehead, a long nose and immense charisma. He traded in charm and seems to have beguiled Miller from the outset, when he invited the playwright to watch him filming *Boomerang* on location in Connecticut. They became instant friends and he even put Arthur into the movie as an extra in a police lineup. Moreover, the casting of *All My Sons* began then and there as Miller found three actors in the movie, all alumni of the Group Theatre, to be perfect for his play: Ed Begley as Joe Keller, J. Arthur ("Johnny") Kennedy as Chris, and Karl Malden as George Deever.

Kazan began keeping a notebook, jotting down thoughts on a pocket-sized spiral pad. These notes vividly reveal a director's role as nothing less than creating life as he lifts the words from script to realization on stage. Kazan's notes demonstrate his invention of each character's psychology, so necessary to the actors. The playwright of course invents the character and provides the dialogue, but the director can fill in the blanks for the actor to imagine a real and complete person.

Elia Kazan's brilliance, social commitment, psychological acuity, commercial sensibility and personal magnetism must have lent him irresistible appeal for Miller. They also shared political commitments. Although Kazan had quit the Communist Party, leftist ideas were still on his mind, to judge by his preparatory notes for *All My Sons*. He makes frequent references to "the capitalist system" and "personal aggrandizement" and "the mad scramble for money . . . the jungle where one man exists only by the death of his neighbor."

Kazan's first note is dated November 18, 1946, on the eve of rehearsals, one month before *All My Sons* was to begin its tryout tour in New Haven. The Broadway premiere was scheduled for January 29, 1947. "Preparing the Miller play," Kazan noted. "First, what it should all mean. Second, each character's meaning. Third, what each character *does* in the inner sense. Fourth, how this is externalized."

Here the "inner sense" is the creation of the character's psychology, understandable from the actor's point of view. "Externalizing" is showing that psychology so that the audience can perceive it. Turning to the specific characters in *All My Sons*, Kazan dug beneath and between the lines of dialogue, seeking out what these people do not say. Although sensing a connection, he didn't read Joe Keller as simply Miller's father. Moreover, he wasn't a director who would tell an actor to imitate a real person. "Joe Keller," Kazan added to the man in Miller's play,

> is a character in conflict . . . attractive, jolly, lovable, playful, sexy . . . also ruthless, tough . . . so people say he is a very affectionate guy, but it is neurotic at base . . . it is to quell a guilt. After all, he has beaten the game. In Act One and Act Two you should feel he's hiding something . . . he only reveals his real self in Act Three. When the crisis of the cracked engine heads arose, he didn't really have a choice [but] he is a nice guy. All this conflict only exists because he is a nice guy. The neurosis only exists because he is a nice guy.

Kazan regularly referred to Kate Keller as "Mary," as though seeing the mother character—Freudian that he was—as Art's mother figure, his wife. Like other intense directors (notably Jed Harris), Kazan used psychology to insinuate his way into controlling relationships with playwrights. If a man's wife stood in the way, she would have to be shunted aside. "The real drive on Kate, or Mary," he wrote,

> is not from her femininity alone . . . but from the system. Kate is concerned with only one thing . . . keeping her children alive. She would not only lie to keep Larry and Chris safe. She would kill. Don't underestimate either her cunning, her strength or her ferocity. Kate and Joe are two tough hombres, no joke.

Surely because of this attitude Miller came to think of Kate Keller as having "a sinister side . . . critics see [my female characters] as far more passive than they are." He also felt that she was the play's central figure, and in a letter to Kazan he wrote,

> The way I see the Mother . . . a woman who mercurially rises to peaks, subsides, rises to a higher peak, subsides less, rises to a still higher peak . . . I believe it is a bad mistake to hold this woman back too consistently. The audience must feel she is capable of sudden and irrational, and wild surges of emotion of all kinds. And the slapping of Keller, and the revealing of his guilt is the highest of such surges.

Kazan seemed to think that the play was about Chris—or perhaps he was playing up to the author, taking this character to be the one with whom Miller identified. In any case, time and subsequent productions would prove Miller right in seeing Kate Keller at the play's center of gravity.

The last thing Kazan did (and would always do) before beginning rehearsal was to have his copy of the script rebound so that each page faced a blank sheet where he could mark ideas for the actors alongside their lines, invent stage business and suggest changes to the playwright. For instance, at the start of the process, Kazan noted in the script, "Keller has always been very frugal. Saves everything he finds around. Brings home pieces of metal he picks up on street, bits of lumber, boxes, etc." Later, as rehearsals brought actors into the picture, he wrote next to a scene between Joe and Kate, "This is the only time they look at each other during the scene."

As for Kazan's suggestions for changes in the dialogue, they tended to involve scene-ending lines, which he wanted to be active. He also disliked spelling out what the audience could already grasp, as in Mother's (Mrs. Keller's) praise for Ann, "No girl ever loved a boy like she did. They don't die so quick, do they, Annie? Tell them, darling." He would propose such a cut courteously, marking it in pencil, but Miller invariably acquiesced. He did in this instance.

With the start of rehearsals in early December 1946, Kazan's notes turned from working with the script to directing it on the stage. He began to deal with scenes and character relationships, deciding at the outset that the play's core relationship is between Chris Keller and his father. It was surely at Kazan's urging that Miller toned down the mother's powerful effect to allow for the conflict between Chris and Joe Keller. "In Act One," he wrote in his notebook, "Keller should dominate Chris. The power is in his hands. Chris in Act One never loses a certain filial awe of his parent. He breaks down in the following acts."

Kazan realized that the audience "thinks [Joe] is scared of Kate, and in a way he is . . . but his primary urge is to his own ego." Kate was played by Beth Merrill, an old-school thespian who could be upset by the deplorable sight of an improperly dressed actor. Kazan liked to come to rehearsal in blue jeans. He told Miller, "I thought that the years alone in that hotel had rubbed most of that Belasco crap off our lady but apparently not enough."

He came to the third act. It brought the play together, being

> the spine and the line a kind of dialectic process. The more Chris struggles and fights, the more he unearths, the more he has to fight, the more he thereby unearths, the more he has to fight, etc. in ascending spirals until the final terrible obstacle: namely that his father is guilty and that furthermore, he did it for Chris. This absolutely stops Chris. He is licked. He howls with the pain of his shame and frustration, his rage and his shame. Curtain.

Kazan had his big closing scene.

The final tune-up came the day before the world premiere in New Haven. Kazan wrote his notes to the company on Hotel Taft stationery then crossed out each one as he gave it to the individual actor. For Arthur Kennedy (Chris), "Don't flail about after Lois [Wheeler] breaks up your fight with George (Karl Malden) Stay disgusted." When Ed Begley (Keller) cries, "Jail?!!" Kazan notes for Kennedy, "Take more time before you respond." And on "You do, you do," Kazan scrawls, "More pain!"

He turned next to Miller. The author still was concerned, he wrote in a letter, about the link between the play's two story lines—Mother refusing to accept Larry's death and Joe Keller facing up to his guilt. Since a director deals with behavior it is not surprising that Kazan continued to insist on action above theme. "The spine of the play," he repeated, "is the spine of Chris . . . his effort to live with honor, to live like a man, in love and together with other people rather than against them."

The director concluded with a note to himself.

> It is important that the play start simply and winningly. The audience must 1. Recognize the people as themselves. 2. Like the people very much. But the play must not stay on that level. It must reach . . . the same size and stature as the theme. Just as Oedipus dealt with a basic huge moral issue, so this play. At the end it must be naked souls in the terrible darkness of this civilization.

After a second tryout engagement in Boston, the *All My Sons* company—cast, crew, sets, lighting equipment—moved to New York. On the eve of the premiere an apprehensive, hit-hungry Miller reminded Kazan of his original determination that every line should land, every scene must work.

> I think one thing, if nothing else, must be made clear to the actors now, because it can help even tomorrow's opening. Every moment of the play is of the highest importance. Meaning that every moment has to have an entertainment value. To sum it up—I think the lid is on too tight. . . . There is a sense of haste without movement, while what is needed is the excitement in the acting that you saw in the script when you read it. . . . There is too much goddamned 'interpretation' of lines, when they don't often know the literal meaning of the words involved.

Elia Kazan didn't need reminders about directing for entertainment value or excitement. When *All My Sons* opened at Broadway's Coronet Theatre on January 29, 1947, his staging was so intense that audiences seemed to fear for a son striking his father even before it happened. The actress Anne Jackson remembered, "That moment when Johnny Kennedy strikes his father, I thought I'd faint. It was like witnessing an accident. A screech of brakes and somebody is gone. That's what it was like, that kind of shock that Arthur was capable of and that Kazan knew how to build to."

Reviews were mixed, detractors generally accusing Miller of Ibsenism as if that were an automatic negative. Just as he had anticipated, the "Ibsenism" of which he was accused was not what he had studied and had in mind. Not untypically, Burns Mantle wrote in the *Daily News* that he'd been ready to leave the theater halfway through the play, but one review changed it all, that of Brooks Atkinson in the *New York Times*. "With the production of *All My Sons* last evening, the theater has acquired a genuine new talent. [It is] an honest, forceful drama, an original play of superior quality by a playwright who knows his craft."

This is perhaps the professional critic's role at its most important, recognizing nascent talent and encouraging it. Atkinson's influence affected other critics. The *New York Post*'s Richard Watts, Jr., for instance, introduced his qualified approval of the play with an all-important reminder of raves elsewhere. "I cannot," he wrote, "go as far in my enthusiasm for *All My Sons* as some of its admirers, who proclaim it a masterpiece and hail its author as already a first rate dramatist [but] I join in feeling that the drama is an interesting work by a promising man."

Calling attention to another, more enthusiastic review can have a multiplying effect. The morning after its premiere *All My Sons* was a hit and Arthur Miller felt that he was finally understood. "The Wonderful [his capital, his key word] was no longer something that would inevitably trap me into disastrously confusing works, for the audience gasped when they should have and I tasted that power."

In the decades after it was written *All My Sons* would be occasionally revived, but as Miller fell out of favor with the more intellectual critics such as Eric Bentley of *The New Republic* and his successor, Robert Brustein, the play was treated with disrespect and even contempt. Typically, Tom Driver, the regular critic for *Commonweal*, wrote in the *Tulane Drama Review*, "when all is said and done, the play seems to be only a play about an aircraft parts manufacturer in wartime. It has rapidly become dated."

Unimaginative revivals contributed to such an old-fashioned effect. Without creative direction, elements of Greek tragedy slipped away while the characteristics in *All My Sons* of the traditional well-made play came to the forefront. This is where the Greek–Ibsen structure ultimately leads, to straightforward dramas with beginnings, middles and ends. As the British director Michael Blakemore put it,

> The past determining the future is a very effective way of telling stories. Because the past *really does* work on the present. But it was so effective a way of telling stories that it was used by everybody. And so it [was] exhausted. It's not so much that it's associated with a particular sort of drama, but the device, the Ibsenite device of an expositional first act and then a developing second act, with a denouement in the third act—I think now seems tired.

Even so, half a century after the premiere of *All My Sons*, the "tired" play was not only being done but being done often, in New York, across America and abroad, and to ever growing acclaim.

The academic critics were always more respectful toward *All My Sons* than the professionals, acknowledging the influence of Ibsen as a good thing. Professor Christopher Bigsby wrote, "From the beginning, critics have recognized the traces of Ibsen's *Pillars of Society* in *All My Sons*." He suggests as well the influence of Ibsen's *The Wild Duck*, which

> also had taken as its subject two businessmen, one of whom had allowed the weaker partner to go to prison for a fraud which he had himself condoned and probably initiated. . . . In Miller's play, too, there is an intricate tracery of self-justification. . . . Chris's idealism conceals a compulsive need to justify his

own silence, the suppression of his own doubts. . . . To accuse his father is, ultimately, to affirm his own innocence.

Bigsby does not consider the Ibsen influence a negative element, but there is little admiration in the comment by the celebrated Harold Bloom that it has become a truism to call *All My Sons* "Ibsenite." The mischievously brilliant Bloom adds, "Joe Keller ought not to be the hero-villain of the play since pragmatically, he is a villain. But," the professor concedes, "Miller is enormously fond of Joe, and so are we." In minimizing the play's value, however, Bloom ignores its lasting appeal as well as its classic openness to reinterpretation. In sum, whether or not *All My Sons* is a great play, it can be presented in a great way. It certainly endures as do only a handful of American plays. It is repeatedly produced in other languages. The endurance and breadth of appeal can only mean that something about it continues to reach audiences.

In spring 1947 *All My Sons* was voted the season's best play by the New York Drama Critics Circle, triumphing over *The Iceman Cometh*. By May Miller was basking in the glow of recognition and relishing this rather delightful change in his financial condition. He promptly took himself down to an employment agency and got a $16 a week job in a Queens beer box factory, "putting dividers in wooden boxes . . . a moral act of solidarity with all those who had failed in life." It indicated the idealism of this thirty-one year old, the earnestness of his convictions and seriousness with which he took himself. Miller had not abandoned his identification with the working man, while at the same time, "I had the name now. They had to listen when I talked. And I didn't have to write another 'well made' play to keep from starving."

He lasted one week at the box factory.

6. Inspiration

I was lucky, I didn't get famous too quick. I don't envy people who are completely unknown on Monday and are celebrated around the world on Tuesday. That's a very difficult thing to bear.

—ARTHUR MILLER

THE SUCCESS OF *All My Sons* brought many rewards, but perhaps the most meaningful was simply the acceptance and approval of its author and his confirmation as a playwright. "It suddenly seemed," Miller said, "that the audience was a mass of blood relations and I sensed a warmth in the world that had not been there before."

There was also international recognition and the money that came with it. Productions of *All My Sons* were negotiated for Germany, France, Sweden, Austria, Switzerland, Hungary, Australia and New Zealand. Offers were pending from Czechoslovakia and Poland. Royalties from the Broadway production—10 percent of the gross receipts—were accumulating at the rate of $2,000 a week. He involved himself personally in negotiations for a movie sale and wrote Kazan, "Every day brings something new . . . [director] Robert Rossen came to New York . . . and he's hot to buy it at 100 G's down plus the percentage. We sent him back for more money." Rossen would ultimately write and direct the movie version of *All My Sons*, costarring Burt Lancaster and Edward G. Robinson.

The money part of Broadway success clearly was having a salutary effect on Miller's Depression-bred anxieties about shaky financial underpinnings. He wrote to his former college professor, "For the next four or five years, I can sit and do nothing but write . . . economic security, I can't say I'm quite used to it yet."

He would never get completely used to it. Miller would always take an active interest in the financial aspects of his plays and would always be careful with money, usually frugal and sometimes downright cheap. Nevertheless it had been a long time since he could enjoy *things*. As always, a car was high on his wish list and he got himself a new one to replace the Nash-Lafayette he'd bought for $250. Like the 1927 Ford, the Nash was destined to become a classic. The new car was a 1947 Studebaker convertible, created by the celebrated industrial designer Raymond Loewy. Miller's taste in cars was impeccable. The Studebaker would also become a collector's item.

He used some of the new wealth to finance a $28,000 converted stable house a short walk from the Brooklyn Heights Promenade. The house was at 31 Grace Court in their now familiar neighborhood where the Millers were comfortably ensconced in the artistic community. Their friends, Norman and Hedda Rosten, still lived nearby and Arthur's success made him a celebrity in the company of local aspiring writers such as Truman Capote, W. H. Auden and Norman Mailer. Within the year all would be making heady debuts, Capote with *Other Voices, Other Rooms*, Auden with "The Age of Anxiety" and Mailer with *The Naked and the Dead*. None of them became Miller's close friend but Mailer was already brash enough to boast, on first meeting Miller, "I could write a play like [*All My Sons*]." Norman Mailer eventually wrote one produced play, a 1967 dramatization of his novel *The Deer Park*—it played 128 performances Off-Broadway.

The house in Grace Court was big enough to provide an upper duplex for Art and Mary, and below, two income-producing apartments that were already rented. There was even a small top floor where the writer could write, and to do that, he bought himself a big Royal office typewriter. Miller also took advantage of an opportunity to buy a country place, a renovated farmhouse that belonged to Mary's new boss. She had left Reynal and Hitchcock to take a job as an editorial secretary for Sidney J. Jaffe, the editor and publisher of *Amerasia*. This seems to have been more than a job, for *Amerasia* was no ordinary magazine. According to Harvey Klehr and Ronald Radosh, authors of the rightist book *The Amerasia Case: A Prelude to McCarthyism*, the magazine had been at the center of "the first major spy case in the post World War II era." In January 1945, some months before the war ended, Jaffe had published an article about American and British intelligence operations in China at the start of the Chinese Communist Party revolution. The piece included the reprinting, virtually verbatim, of classified American intelligence documents.

The Office of Secret Service (OSS, predecessor of the CIA) promptly raided the *Amerasia* offices and discovered a cache of photographed top-secret documents. Jaffe and six of his employees were arrested (Mary Miller was not yet working there). They were charged with conducting espionage on behalf of the Chinese Communists. Had the case gone to trial, important issues of press freedom might have been raised, but for lack of evidence it was never prosecuted. Jaffe pleaded guilty to a lesser charge of unauthorized

possession of government documents and was fined $2,500. In a small New England town such as Roxbury, Connecticut, where Jaffe and his wife, Agnes, had a weekend retreat, such publicity could make life difficult. Locals were already calling him "the secretary of the Communist Party" (he ultimately amassed a 650-piece collection of Communist Party literature) and so the house was put up for sale. The Millers—a couple of Socialists becoming landlords—bought it in early 1947.

To Sidney Jaffe's credit, he refused to be intimidated by the government. While no editorial policy supported Mao Zedong outright, *Amerasia* simply and perhaps reasonably treated Chiang Kai-shek's resistance as hopeless and Mao's victory as inevitable. The magazine had an insignificant circulation and wasn't even Jaffe's primary business, but it was his primary concern and he published it as a matter of political conviction. Mary Miller's job there, it seems fair to infer, spoke for hers. Miller himself saw the Chinese Communist Party revolution as signifying "the long awaited rule of reason."

Mary remained at *Amerasia* as long as she could, but she was pregnant and on May 31, 1947, gave birth to a second child, a blond, brown-eyed nine-pound boy. He was named Robert Arthur, notwithstanding Jewish proscriptions against naming children after living relatives. "Mary and Bob doing fine," Arthur wrote Professor Rowe at the University of Michigan, "although I'm pooped out."

His fatigue was a result of directing a play for the first time in his life, or at least directing new actors going into *All My Sons*. Kazan was away in Los Angeles filming *Gentleman's Agreement*. In such a situation ordinarily the stage manager steps in to direct replacements, the same as with understudies; but also the stage manager's responsibility is to maintain a long-running play's level of performance, and Miller didn't think the job was being done. One actress was "every day starting up with that Stanislavsky crap" while another was "climbing the scenery" and, he immodestly wrote to Kazan, "If audiences still come after what's happened to it, it must be the words." Now he was rehearsing John Chalmers and John Forsythe as Chris and Joe Keller.

From time to time Kazan would offer directing advice ("The more differently you can direct each moment, even exaggerating the differences between the moments, the better off it will be"), but as Miller worked he grew into the job. He confidently predicted, "we'll do well with Chalmers, who is much more intelligent than Begley. I'm working on him now to make him act as ignorant as Joe Keller is. Begley didn't have that problem."

As for Miller's playwriting,

> I've got three stories or pieces of stories and can't make up my mind which to start. It is an agonizing process . . . but I've done it so often that it is possible now to control the necessary wanderings of the mind until that terrible moment when the paper is staring up at me with Act One, Scene One typed so ambitiously at the top.

He'd hired a maid to help Mary with both the baby and two-year-old Jane, and in June they all moved into the new house, incompletely furnished though it was. For the time being Mary and Arthur had their bed in the living room while the master bedroom was used for "Junior," as Miller sometimes called him (at other times it was "Mister Robert" after the current hit play), and the nurse. "There are so many women in the house," he wryly remarked, "I spend half my time raising the toilet seat."

Mary was already strong enough to begin decorating the place. For all her political commitment and eagerness to work, she was also a domestic creature and fixing up the house became her priority. One of its attractive features was a living room with a wood-burning fireplace and high ceilings. She had the room painted in two colors, cocoa for one pair of walls, yellow for the other. She hung a couple of Picasso lithographs and paintings by artist friends, for instance, a watercolor by Reginald Marsh and an oil painting of Robert Gwathmey's. She put in a pair of white lamps too, and Miller looked on, apparently content with domestic life. "Mary," he saw, "is now sitting and staring out the window, dreaming of thousands of yards of carpeting, linoleum, drapery materials." He certainly took to fatherhood, doting on little Jane while demonstrating a shamelessly conventional paternal pride in his infant son, regularly holding Robert in his arms and even feeding him. Miller found that between this comfortable family life, rehearsals, adjusting to success and getting the new house in order he had little time for writing, not even when there were lucrative screenwriting offers. He wrote to Kazan,

> You might be interested to know that Alfred Hitchcock asked Kay [Brown, the agent] if I could write *Rope*, his new picture. He saw the play and thought I would be the man to "give the picture passion." How do you like that? I suppose the much needed emotion is supposed to rise from the $2500 a week he's ready to pay. *Rope* yet!

At the time movies were considered a lesser form than theater and writing a screenplay beneath the dignity of a serious playwright. Whatever Miller's need for financial assurance, he would not do anything just for money and never considered accepting the offer. The screenplay for *Rope* was written by Arthur Laurents, while Miller, eager to begin a new play, told Kazan, "I simply have to get away or I'll never write another word again. I can't leave, though, till Mary is stronger and that will be a week or more."

As always, he signed the letter *Art*, but only after adding news of Norman Rosten, who had become Kazan's friend too. "It is always a solace," Miller said, "to regard him whenever I am feeling a little blue." Perhaps so, but work was the best cure for the blues and at last Miller thought he was on to something. "Finally," he told Kazan, "it has seemed like five years—I am able to sit down and direct the brain to the play." Called *Plenty Good Times*, it was going to be "a love story of working people in an industrial city." By then Kazan was completing *Gentleman's Agreement* and looking forward to a return east to stage Tennessee Williams's *A Streetcar Named Desire,* which the director considered "perfect except for a long bit in the last scene that was cut out."

Kazan appeared to be familiarizing himself with the perquisites of a Hollywood director, such as dictating his letters rather than typing them himself. A minor example perhaps, it still suggests a growing sense of male importance. As to *Gentleman's Agreement,* he wrote "Artie" that his contract with 20th-Century Fox included a guarantee "that I get through by Thanksgiving." He had better, because that was when the Williams play was supposed to start its tryout engagement. Busy but unhurried, the white-hot Elia Kazan concluded, "I'm looking forward to your play being ready by then."

It wouldn't be. By the time Kazan finished *Gentleman's Agreement* and was back in New York rehearsing *Streetcar,* Miller had set *Plenty Good Times* aside on a to-be-continued basis. As for the Tennessee Williams play, Kazan invited him to see it at the New Haven tryout. It is interesting to compare the two men's recollections of Miller's reaction to the play. As Kazan remembered it, "After the performance, he appeared to be full of wonder at the theater's expressive possibilities. He told me he was amazed at how simply and successfully the nonrealistic elements in the play blended with the realistic ones."

Miller's recollection of his reaction to Tennessee Williams's gorgeous and great play is in the lesser theatrical tradition of evasion. While praising "the radiant eloquence of the composition," he said nothing of the play's thematic material and plainly did not consider *Streetcar* substantial enough to qualify as important. "I don't care for theater that is absolutely personal and has no resonance beyond that," he said, calling such theater "exercises in personal psychology. A drama," he felt, "must represent a well defined expression of profound social needs." Drama must be "the creation of a higher consciousness and not merely a subjective attack upon the audience's nerves and feelings." Tennessee Williams, Miller thought,

> is primarily interested in passion, in ecstasy . . . the reality in the spirit rather than in the society . . . I am reasonably sure that [his] interest in the sociology of the South is only from the point of view of a man who doesn't like to see brutality, unfairness, a kind of victory of the Philistine.

That was selling Williams short. *Streetcar* certainly does trade in passion and ecstasy with rich language and emotional range, and it does decry brutish insensitivity, but it also sets the delicately refined, doomed Old South of Blanche DuBois on a collision course with the brawling, industrialized New South looming ahead, as personified by Stanley Kowalski. In its theme, humanity and poetic naturalism *A Streetcar Named Desire* invites comparison with Chekhov's masterpiece, *The Cherry Orchard.* Apparently Miller did not appreciate this. A more magnanimous Tennessee Williams freely praised *All My Sons,* telling Kazan he thought the play was "dynamite . . . the sort of eloquence this country needs very badly now. I will write

Miller my congratulations (though tinged with envy)." With his fragile ego and sensitive spirit Williams would always be the more giving of the two playwrights.

A Streetcar Named Desire had its New York premiere on December 3, 1947, and "took Broadway by storm," as Brooks Atkinson wrote in the *New York Times*. Although both Williams and Kazan already enjoyed success, they rose to an unprecedented level of cultural stardom. As for the play, more than being a smash hit, it opened a new era in American drama, sweeping aside a generation of playwrights with its imaginative construction, luxuriant language, sexual energy and deep feelings. The blend of Williams's writing, Kazan's theatrical realizations and the animal vibrancy of the actors—young Marlon Brando in particular—made the traditional dramas of the day seem like staged conversations. Rendered obsolete almost instantly were the talky and bloodless social plays of the writers who had been Broadway's ruling class for two decades—Robert Sherwood, Lillian Hellman, Sidney Kingsley, S. N. Behrman, Elmer Rice and others. Indeed Miller himself would narrowly escape inclusion in this group; in its more conservative elements *All My Sons* is of the same school. *A Streetcar Named Desire* would have a strong influence on Miller's next play, encouraging him to be imaginative and giving him, as he put it, "license to speak at full throat."

While Kazan, Williams and *Streetcar* were being celebrated in the early months of 1948, Miller dealt with the letdown of *All My Sons* closing on December 24, 1947. The play enjoyed a healthy run of 328 performances, but in the theater the end of an engagement is the end of a life, upsetting no matter how long-lived. A restless Miller took to roaming the streets of Brooklyn as he headed for the bridge to Manhattan (which he still called "the city"), passing through Brooklyn Heights's neighboring Italian community of Red Hook and its adjacent waterfront. Inevitably the dockworkers' roiling union situation attracted his interest. He had read a newspaper story about a longshoreman who disappeared after organizing a movement protesting the gangster-dominated leadership of the International Longshoreman's Association. "One evening during dinner," Miller recalled from the article, "the man was lured from his home by a phone call from an unknown caller and was never seen again. The movement he had led vanished from the scene."

Miller's sympathies were piqued. "The idea of a longshoreman standing up to the arrogance of such power," he said, "chilled me with awe." He also saw dramatic possibilities in the waterfront influence of the Mafia and decided to pursue this lead to its roots, which he thought might be found in Italy.

This first trip to Europe seems to have been particularly adventurous as Miller sought out the high and the low in educational tourism. Looking for antecedents of Italian gangsters in Sicily, he lunched with the exiled Charles "Lucky" Luciano. He patronized a bordello in Rome, toured the amphitheaters of ancient Greece, visited with Communists in Paris. He was aware of a postwar disenchantment with Josef Stalin developing among many leftists, but Miller's youthful sympathies were ingrained and not easily undermined. The Holocaust was recent and vivid and much more awful than anything then known of Stalin's own crimes against humanity. The Soviets had played an active part in putting an end to it. Miller felt that "Russian armies having . . . saved Europe from a thousand years of Nazism, it was not easy to credit tales of Stalinist terror."

He came home convinced that while the waterfront research could form the basis of an "Italian tragedy"—and he jotted down a note about that—it would probably work best as a screenplay. As Miller began to plot this out, however, another idea pushed it aside. Its seed had been planted during the tryout of *All My Sons,* in a fleeting moment that would barely qualify as an event. He had been standing under the marquee of the Colonial Theatre in Boston at the end of a performance when his uncle Manny appeared in the crowd spilling out of the auditorium. "Without so much as acknowledging my greeting," Miller recalled, Newman boasted about his son. "He said, 'Buddy is doing very well.' There was no 'hello, how are you?' He knew *All My Sons* was a hit. He was just competing with me."

Manny Newman's five-word non sequitur opened, in Arthur Miller's imagination, a psychological dossier of parental defensiveness, pain, envy, defeat, self-deception and even delusion. The man had been a salesman himself, a traveling man with a New England territory. A small fellow, he lived with his big and adoring wife, Annie, who was Gussie Miller's sister, in what Miller described as a "sad little house" across the street from his parents' home in Brooklyn. Manny's sons, Buddy and Abby (there were also two daughters), had been Arthur's occasional fishing companions, and as they all grew up—so it seemed to Miller—his uncle Manny came to see Artie and Kerm as "running neck and neck with his two sons in some race that never stopped." Miller supposed that in Manny Newman's mind it was a race that Abby and Buddy would always win. In sports, he remembered, "I lacked their promise," and in expectations, always the "insinuation of my entire life's failure before I was sixteen."

Buddy, the elder of the Newman boys, had been the athlete of the family, while Abby would "steal pointless volumes of candy from the local store." In their teens, Miller remembered, the brothers would "go on hiking expeditions like good Eagle Scouts . . . and find an old whore in a local tavern, use her up for the night and then cheat her with half pay."

In spring 1948 this modest little family, hardly apt figures for high drama, moved to the center of Miller's imagination. His sense of their tragic potential was inspired, and he expanded on that to conceive a play about "a salesman and it's his last day on earth." That is how he would describe the new play when weary of questions about its meaning. Of course it would be about much more, involving *two* death-bound salesmen. One, the central character, is a small fellow who is the archetypal little man. The larger salesman is the American economic and social system. The product it sells is the product the little salesman has bought: a materialistic value system promising that greed, guile and buying into the notion that business is its own justification—"business is business"—will be rewarded with the American dream, not merely the land of opportunity as advertised but opportunity fulfilled. That is the system's *line*, as in selling spiel—its *bill of goods*. In a greater sense, then, the play was to be about the death of that salesman, the discrediting of that bill of goods; the defeat of a system of specious values and empty promises offering reward without achievement, something for nothing.

Arthur Miller was not the first playwright to hit upon the symbolic potential of the American salesman. Only the previous year Eugene O'Neill had presented such a figure in *The Iceman Cometh*. His salesman, Theodore ("Hickey") Hickman, was a man determined to annul vain hope—the "pipe dreams" as he put it, that were the only consolation available to the hopeless and disillusioned drunks representing mankind in the meaningfully named Harry Hope's Saloon. Hickey is as deranged as Miller's salesman would be, although less of a fleshed-out character and more of a mythic figure. What Hickey is selling, his bill of goods, is the bitter truth, and he is peddling it to a saloon filled with lost souls whose lives are sustained by lies. Powerful and great though O'Neill's play is, its use of the salesman idea is less effective than Miller's would turn out to be, because in Hickey there is less of an individual and as a result, less of a heartbeat to the play. To contrast O'Neill's treatment of truth and hope with Miller's is interesting, especially as these plays are contemporaneous. In O'Neill's play the truth is destructive and hope a delusion. In Miller's play sanity depends on facing the truth and there is always hope, for the future is humankind's to make; indeed, making a better future is the obligation of being alive.

Thus Miller's new play would be a cautionary tale, or so it was intended. He never counted on its power being so overwhelming that the theme would become secondary.

With Manny Newman as the model for his salesman, Arthur Miller added qualities he'd observed in the suicidal Schoenzeit of his college story "In Memoriam" and included characteristics remembered from other salesmen he had seen in his father's business. Despite his claim, however, that the main character has no single model, and the absurd insistence that he barely knew his uncle ("a couple of hours with him in my entire life"), there is ample evidence that Manny Newman is the prototype for Willy Loman, as Miller named his man. Here is an almost identical echo name, Willy Loman–Manny Newman, and likewise the wife, Linda Loman–Annie Newman. Manny's sons too are without any doubt the prototypes for Loman's boys, whose names Biff and Happy are barely changed from their Newman family counterparts, Buddy and Abby.

Subsequent suggestions by commentators that the name Loman stands for *low man* are not implausible (for that matter it might be speculated that Willy is meant to suggest *wily*), although Miller scoffed at the idea. It is his stated opinion that if there is any source for the name Loman, it is *The Testament of Dr. Mabuse* (1933), a German movie directed by Fritz Lang in which a man urgently whispers into a telephone, "Hello? Loehmann? Loehmann!" Yet he offers no explanation as to why he would borrow that name. Perhaps he wished to prove that the author is a creator, that he invents his characters. If this was Miller's concern, he needn't have worried. Though Kazan has said, "Art had to have that living connection with a subject before he could make a drama of it," the characters in his play would be given a life, created with a humanity and believability perhaps unsurpassed in American drama.

Miller told Kazan that he was going to refresh his memories of the Newmans by researching the family. With this as background, he would reinvent them or as he put it, "find the facts first and then dream about them." He found Abby Newman living in Manhattan and arranged to "spend some nights with my cousin and get him started about his father." The surreptitious interviews proved fruitful, for the cousin was still boastful and it wasn't hard to get him talking. After being discharged from the army he seemed to have lived his life for sex. His brother Buddy had joined the navy and served with the Seabees. Their father "wanted a business for us," Abby said, "So we could all work together." Neither of the Newman brothers was working at anything of consequence or promise, and their father had died of "undisclosed causes"—or so Miller wrote in his autobiography. A decade later he would tell an interviewer that Manny Newman had killed himself, a perplexing inconsistency.

While Abby bragged about girlfriends, Art asked about the father. While Art asked about the father, Abby asked about the constrictions of monogamy. Miller replied that fidelity was not a requirement of marriage, which might have been a kind of boasting of his own. He seems to have still been a rather inhibited—or else moralistic—man, the Italian bordello perhaps marking the limit of his extramarital sexual ventures. Further exploration, however, seemed in the offing, given his straight-faced remark that success and inspiration filled him with "sexual desire, with love for my wife and, incredibly, for all women at the same time."

As the central character of Willy Loman evolved in his imagination, the style of the play followed. Manny Newman's non sequitur about his son struck Miller as typical of how the mind works. "The way we [all] think," he said, "is in non sequiturs. Connections we make are absurd." The notion led him to consider expressionist drama. Perhaps real people inspired the basic story, but the way it was told and its structure would be Miller's entirely. In an inspiration gilded with genius he began to conceive a dramatic scheme in which his play would cover twenty-five years of a man's life in twenty-four hours. Its salesman would live in two time frames at once, "the voice of the past . . . no longer distant but quite as loud as the voice of the present . . . working on two logics which often collide." This was a daring extension of the Greek-Ibsen principle of past events controlling present action. Ordinarily (as in *All My Sons*) the climaxes of such plays prove that what is happening now is a result of what happened then. In the new play no such proof would be necessary because the past would be actually visible in the present, and "The ultimate matter with which the play will close is announced at the outset."

His mind was churning, he was at the center of his creativity, that is unmistakable in a letter to Kazan describing the way he planned to do all this.

> I believe I am close to a method of knitting together his frames of mind, while at the same time connecting them to the very interesting little epochs of his past . . . I know a way of drawing in the past while keeping the central action in the present—a very tense central action; a way of having him soar out of a situation of the moment, and letting him follow what the situation suggested in his past.

Packing himself into his new Studebaker convertible, he drove the two-hour drive to the country house in Roxbury. The scenic drive into Connecticut took him past Danbury and into the foothills of the Berkshire Mountains. The colonial towns of Milford, Washington and Roxbury were destined to become expensive real estate—weekend addresses for successful writers, artists and theater people. At the time, however, they were simply small towns, even just post offices, surrounded by farmland. It was April, the start of spring, and Miller bought tools and lumber. He wanted to build a studio where he could write, a workshop in the woods beyond the house. Working "from sunrise to sunset" for six weeks, he nailed together "five windows and a door." Hardly even a shack, it was more like a shed and he furnished it just barely, with a table, a chair and some bookshelves, all of which he made as well. It was as if manual labor were an artistic calisthenic. (An interviewer at the time described him as a fellow who "gets a real joy out of building and fixing things.") When the little studio was finished, he moved into it, put a new ribbon in the typewriter and rubbed his mental hands in anticipation of starting to write."It's such a good feeling," he told Kazan. "I haven't written since January."

He had already bought a notebook for the new play. Like so many writers, he delayed an actual beginning. Its first entries describe his new little studio and the country sounds. "Roxbury. At night the insects softly thumping the screen like a blind man poking with his fingers in the dark. The evening sky, faded gray, like the sea pressing up against the windows, or an opaque gray screen (through which someone is looking at me?)."

He next put down a more specific description of the "Italian tragedy" that had occurred to him during his strolls along the Brooklyn waterfront. It grew out of a story he had heard in Red Hook about a man who turned in two illegal immigrants, violating the tribal proscriptions of the Italian community in Brooklyn. He noted that "the secret of the Greek drama is the vendetta, the family ties incomprehensible to Englishmen and Americans. . . . Much that has been interpreted in lofty terms [of] fate, religion, etc., is only blood and tribal survival within the family . . . Red Hook is full of Greek tragedies."

So was planted the seed of *A View from the Bridge,* which he would write eight years later. Then he began his notes for the central character in the new play. "In every scene," he wrote in his tight longhand, "remember his [small] size, ugliness." He wrote one scenario—a "line of action" he sometimes called it—after another, filling several speckled school composition books with notes. At first he used the latest thing, a ballpoint pen, but it skipped maddingly and he gave up on the invention to go back to a regular fountain pen.

The notes reveal a play in the birthing. The main character is first described in four short lines of poetry.

> *A man who doesn't build anything must be liked*
> *He must be cheerful on bad days*
> *Even calamities mustn't break through*
> *'Cause one thing, he has got to be liked.*

"Well liked" would become the character's catchphrase. Miller also plotted and replotted the scenario, began scenes only to scotch them and planned a third act, "a fantasmagoria," before deciding on a two-act format—novel at the time—with a short, final Requiem. He speculated that Loman could be resentful of his wife's "unbroken, patient forgiveness," not unlike Hickey in *The Iceman Cometh*. In Miller's play this resentment would have been based on Loman "knowing that there must be great hidden hatred for him in her heart." After brief consideration he rejected the notion. He even wrote complete speeches, for instance, Loman's "And don't worry about me. I'm not going crazy. That's one thing that's not in the book for me. I will never go crazy so if that's what's behind it, don't give it a thought." It was effective, but too on the nose for the character. He decided against using it.

The notebooks show that Miller could be a doodler, although not with drawings. Aptly for someone who lived in the mind he doodled with words. About, for instance, the Chinese Communist revolution, "China is going Communist. Now the West begins its final phase. We shall all have to learn Chinese." He doodled about his friend Rosten who, like his brother, Kermit, was "unable to believe in the existence of evil, and yet all his plays presuppose it." Most of all he doodled about women. Sex was surely on his mind. "Most women cannot bear the art of creation in a man. It is not supposed to be his business," and again, "Only a brilliant man can hold the interest of an intelligent woman. Anyone can do so with an intelligent man." And again, "A woman who talks a great deal is preoccupied with sex. So many draw their skirts down when they laugh." And similarly, "So many women contract narrowly when they laugh. All sorts of concealing gestures, tears, jerks, fixing of hair, as though their parts had faintly rattled."

He also made winceworthy jokes, "Hell hath no fury like a woman's corns."

When Miller finally turned to the typewriter and the play, "The first half," he would recall, "was very quickly written. Probably less than a week." The second act and the Requiem took much longer. The doodles in the notebooks might be considered resting places between long bouts with the play. "I know I started about January of 1948," he would say, "and I think I finished sometime in August." Then he gathered a few friends and read it to just them and Mary in the Roxbury living room. As he finished the Requiem, he looked up and in dismay, "saw nothing but glazed looks in their eyes." When he put down the script, "they said nothing." He took it to mean the worst. "The script," he recalled, "suddenly seemed . . . something I ought not admit to at all, let alone read or have produced on the stage."

Their silence only spoke for what was going to become a legendary, stunned reaction to the play. Relieved that his little audience approved, Miller sent the manuscript to Kazan, whose heady times had just become headier with an Academy Award for directing *Gentleman's Agreement*. Kazan took the new play along on a Connecticut weekend, "And the moment I read it," he would recall, "I thought it was perfect. I've had that experience only one other time. *Streetcar*."

He asked his wife, Molly, to read it, for she was a clever woman with a theatrical background. One evening they went out with the writer Garson Kanin and his wife, the actress Ruth Gordon, to see a Westport Country Playhouse production of a play that Elia had directed on Broadway, *The Skin of Our Teeth*, locally starring its author, Thornton Wilder. Afterward at dinner, the first thing Molly said was, "I've just read Arthur's new play."

Kanin looked up and asked, "Well?"

She turned to Elia and said, "You're gonna do it."

Death of a Salesman was conceived as an expressionist play. Miller had attempted the style before in *The Great Disobedience*, a relatively primitive college effort. *Death of a Salesman* was his first mature attempt to employ the technique, and he apparently began with a return to the principles of expressionistic theater that he had studied at Michigan. His influential playwriting professor, Kenneth Rowe, had stated in the textbook *Write That Play!*, "Expressionism is an attempt to lift the skullcap and look inside at the brain and see how it works." Miller all but took this definition verbatim for his original *Salesman* title, *The Inside of His Head*. He even said that one of his earliest visualizations of the play had been "an image of an enormous face the height of the proscenium arch which would appear and then open up and we would see the inside of a man's head. The play's eye was to revolve from within Willy's head, sweeping endlessly in all directions like a light on the sea." Within the head was, he said, "a mass of contradictions." The play thus was about the workings of a man's mind. Its structure mirrored the central character's "way of thinking at this moment of his life." Eventually this state of mind—a counterpoint of present and past—would be expressed in the subtitle *Certain Private Conversations in Two Acts and a Requiem*.

Less than a week after receiving the script, Kazan telephoned the playwright with his response. "That's about my family," he said. "It's a great play, Artie. I want to do it in the fall or winter."

Even before Arthur Miller wrote *Death of a Salesman* he told Elia Kazan that the play would begin with the salesman "telling his wife that he can't keep his mind on anything, that so many things keep crowding in on him from long ago." This is more or less how the play begins. Willy Loman enters wearily, carrying a valise heavy with samples and muttering to himself. He tells his wife, Linda, that he has cut short his sales trip because he was unable to concentrate on driving and the car kept veering off the road. In an upstairs bedroom, meanwhile, their thirtyish sons can be seen—Happy, who still lives there, and Biff, who is home for a visit. Like Abby Newman, Happy's main interest is "plenty of women" while Biff, like Buddy Newman, is a onetime athlete who has accomplished nothing in his adult life. Now he talks of buying a farm with an investment he plans to get from a former employer, a man named Bill Oliver.

In the living room Willy has slipped into a memory of returning from a more successful trip through his New England territory, a trip he'd made some seventeen years earlier. In the delusion his sons are polishing the car he used to own while he cries, "Wonderful!" to the empty room, and "don't leave the hubcaps, boys." Then his mind opens wide as Biff and Happy materialize—the same actors, dressed as youngsters.

Linda returns and enters into his fantasy, beaming, "The way they obey him!" but her appearance also pulls him back to reality as she frets about unpaid bills. Willy promises that he'll do better next week. "I'm very well liked in Hartford," he assures her, but contrarily adds, "You know, the trouble is, Linda, people don't seem to take to me."

"Well liked" is his litany. "Be liked," he advises his adoring sons, "and you'll never want." To Linda in the present, however, he confides the fear that he talks too much, jokes too much and is "foolish to look at." When his wife affectionately reassures him, he is guilt stricken about his infidelities on the road, and with that thought The Woman can be heard laughing in his memory. "I get so lonely," he tells Linda as his mind drifts through the past unmoored. He visualizes Biff's schoolmate Bernard, a superior student who lives in the house next door, and while the tearful Linda leaves her delusional husband in the kitchen, Bernard's father, Charley, in fact enters, curious about the loud conversation. He suggests a game of cards, and as they sit down, Willy confesses that he is virtually penniless. At the same time his hallucinations continue, now involving his brother Ben. Memory and reality overlap as Charley thinks Willy is talking to him when admitting to Ben that "I'm getting awfully tired." Getting a grip on himself, he tells the friend, "For a second there you reminded me of my brother Ben." In this way Miller calculates the precise caliber of Loman's dementia, that the man has enough self-control to wrench himself into present time when a memory threatens to overwhelm him. But when he continues talking to Ben, the visit deteriorates into acrimony and Charley leaves.

Willy then asks his brother, "What's the answer? How did you do it?" By setting out for Alaska, says Ben, to consider several properties. "When I was seventeen I walked into the jungle, and when I was twenty-one I walked out. And by God I was rich." Miller provides him with a magnificently preposterous explanation for how he managed to set out for Alaska and wind up in a jungle. "At that age I had a very faulty view of geography, William. I discovered after a few days that I was heading due south [from Nebraska], so instead of Alaska, I ended up in Africa."

This solemn nonsense extolling the magical opportunities of free enterprise only heightens Ben's surreal quality while mocking the get-rich-quick bill of goods that Miller found so despicable in the national sales talk, the delusion that success can be achieved without intelligence, talent or work. In the Loman family that delusion is reflected in Biff's refusal to study for exams and his expectation of a free ride on an athletic scholarship. As a boy, Miller himself had watched such a fantasy at work on the grand scale, when the soaring stock market sent his father and America chasing a zoom of effortless wealth headlong into the Wall Street crash.

As Biff and Happy deride their father's ranting, their mother defends him. "He's the dearest man to me and I won't have anyone making him feel unwanted and low and blue." When they insult him she responds with one of the American theater's most famous speeches.

> I don't say he's a great man. Willy Loman never made a lot of money. His name was never in the paper. He's not the finest character that ever lived. But he's a human being, and a terrible thing is happening to him. So attention must be paid. He's not to be allowed to fall into his grave like an old dog. Attention, attention must be finally paid to such a person.

She insists that her husband hasn't "lost his balance," just that "the man is exhausted," as well he might be, still on the road as a salesman at the age of sixty-three. Worse, after thirty-six years with the company his salary has been canceled and "like a beginner," he must depend on commission alone. Now he is suicidal, she tells them. She found a rubber tube that he'd fitted out to attach to a gas pipe in the basement. A concerned Biff promises that instead of buying a ranch he will use the money he raises to start a business for himself in partnership with Happy. It is an idea that Willy loves (much as Abby Newman had told Miller that his father "wanted a business for us") and as he and Linda prepare for bed, he asks her to sing him to sleep. With that the curtain falls on the first act.

The next day Loman sets off, promising that he will ask for a job in the home office as well as a cash advance to catch up on the debts. And don't forget, Linda reminds him, about meeting the boys for dinner, just the three of them. With his departure she implores Happy and Biff to "be sweet to him tonight. . . . Be loving to him. Because he's only a little boat looking for a harbor." Then the scene shifts to the office where Willy has gone to plead for his life with Howard Wagner, a boss who is more interested in showing off a recording of his children reciting state capitals. With the audience aware of Loman's humiliation, the borderline between emotional crisis and madness becomes fainter, all the more so when young Wagner disrespectfully asks Willy, "But where would I put you, kid?" Listen, he advises, "It's a business, and business is business." Willy angrily agrees. "Business is definitely business," a remark almost too close to the playwright's sense of irony, of which a character should not be aware. The actor should read this line as yesmanship rather than sarcasm. Willy then reacts to the rejection with a slammed fist and a reminder of Wagner's father. "There were promises made across this desk!" Wagner suggests that he pull himself together but left alone in the office Loman accidentally turns on the recording machine. His frightened cries bring Howard back and Loman surrenders. Alright, he says, he'll go to Boston as scheduled. No he won't, Wagner says, advising "a good long rest. . . . And when you feel better, come back, and we'll see if we can work something out." He cruelly adds, "Whenever you can this week, stop by and drop off the samples."

Alone again, Willy turns to Ben. "How did you do it? What is the answer? Nothing's working out." His brother suggests, "Get out of these cities, they're full of talk and time payments and courts of law."

Desperate for money, Loman goes to the office of the neighbor who has been supporting him. Charley's son, Bernard, now a successful attorney, happens to be visiting and asks after Biff. "Very big," boasts Willy, much as Miller's uncle, Manny Newman, had spoken of Buddy on the day the playwright ran into him outside of the Boston theater. In a verbal shorthand no doubt inspired by Uncle Manny's non sequitur greeting of Miller Willy says, "Bill Oliver . . . sporting-goods man. . . . Called him in from the West. Long distance, carte blanche, special deliveries." This facade of bravado crumbles as he implores Bernard for "the secret." If he could only be let in on it, "there'll be open sesame for all of us," as Willy says elsewhere. There simply has to be a secret of success, some reason why Bernard has achieved it and Biff has failed. Bernard replies that there is no secret. The reason is effort. Biff should have accepted the college athletic scholarship that had been offered. Willy refuses to say why this never happened. Instead he goes off to meet Biff and Happy at the restaurant, a stretch of playwriting that is extraordinary even in this thrillingly conceived work.

Happy is at the restaurant first, flirting with a woman who may or may not be a prostitute. By the time Biff arrives she has gone to find a friend for him. His interview with Bill Oliver, he tells Happy, was a disaster. After waiting six hours he saw the man for but a moment and wasn't even remembered. "I'm gonna tell Pop," Biff says. "He's got to understand that I'm not the man somebody lends that kind of money to."

When Loman arrives, Biff starts to tell the truth about his stupid life to the father who has lived by the lie. Loman stops him.

> I'm not interested in stories about the past or any crap of that kind because the woods are burning, boys, you understand? There's a big blaze going on all around. I was fired today. . . . I was fired, and I'm looking for a little good news to tell your mother, because the woman has waited and the woman has suffered. The gist of it is that I haven't got a story left in my head, Biff. So don't give me a lecture about facts and aspects. I am not interested. Now what've you got to say to me? . . . Did you see Oliver?

Thus with "facts and aspects" begins what can only be described as a scene written as a musical trio for actors. Willy *drives* (the playwright's direction) for good news about Biff's appointment, while Biff persists in telling the truth for once in his life. Happy lies as always. These character motifs play in counterpoint until Willy opens the resolving sequence on a bitter note, "You didn't see him, did you? . . . You insulted him, didn't you?" Demanding to be told exactly what happened but not wanting to hear, he is sucked into memory, reliving the day Biff's college hopes were dashed.

The sequence starts as young Bernard bemoans, "They won't graduate him" because he failed mathematics (which Miller himself did, but had the discipline to repeat the course). Linda insists, "They have to. He's gotta go to the university." Biff has already fled in search of his idolized father and the past now converges with the present, to integrate and then disintegrate. Willy hears Biff in present time, talking in the restaurant about the botched meeting with Oliver while at the same time he hears the Boston hotel operator of seventeen years ago calling up from the lobby to announce that Biff is there. In the restaurant Biff gets down to his father on bended knee, pleading that he come to his senses, finally (*desperately*) embellishing his report of the meeting with Oliver. It jerks Willy into present time, but when Biff fails to invent a story with a positive ending, Loman's mind reverts to the Boston hotel room and The Woman, and the teenaged son in the middle of the night looking for help from the father.

Simultaneously the women for Happy and Biff arrive. Willy, struggling with his senses as he is being introduced, is literally treated like a dog by Happy, who actually says, "Sit him down, Biff!" In Loman's mind he is also in Boston, refusing to open the door for young Biff. In the restaurant Happy is eager to get on with the dates and when his father wanders off with Biff in pursuit, he despicably tells the women, "that's not my father. He's just a guy."

Finally the Boston memory is played out to conclusion with Biff rapping at the door and Willy unable to stop The Woman's raucous laughter. Practically shoving her into the bathroom, he admits his son, who confesses that the mathematics teacher gave him a failing grade. "Would you talk to him? He'd like you Pop. You know the way you could talk." But The Woman is heard laughing in the bathroom, and when she emerges, the youth breaks down in tears and storms out, calling his father "liar" and "fake."

"Come back here!" Willy roars. "I gave you an order . . ." which he is now saying to the waiter in the restaurant.

"Your boys," the waiter tells him, "left with the chippies."

Willy can only mumble, "But we were supposed to have dinner together."

As he goes off in search of seeds to plant, the garden image is extended to Biff and Happy, who are guiltily coming home with flowers for their mother—that with righteous wrath she smashes to the ground. "Don't you care whether he lives or dies?" she cries. "Pick up this stuff," she tells Biff, "I'm not your maid any more. Pick it up, you bum, you!" She calls the two of them animals. "Not one, not another living soul would have had the cruelty to walk out on that man in a restaurant! . . . You louse. You . . ." she snarls at Biff. "Get out of this house!"

Willy can now be seen gardening by flashlight at the front of the stage while he tells Ben about a great idea, "'Cause she's suffered. . . . A man can't go out the way he came in, Ben, a man has got to add up to something . . . it's a guaranteed twenty-thousand-dollar proposition." Like all the scenes with Ben, this one is not out of memory but an utter fabrication as the brother warns, "They might not honor the [insurance] policy." When Biff appears, Ben fades away as the son confronts the father with the suicidal rubber tube. *Caged*, Miller notes, *wanting to escape*, Loman pleads, "I never saw that." But Biff is relentless as he dismisses such a suicide as a wasted one and warns, "There'll be no pity for you." He finally sees his family for what it is. "We never told the truth for ten minutes in this house! . . . I stole myself out of every good job since high school! . . . And I never got anywhere because you blew me so full of hot air . . . I had to be boss big shot in two weeks." He knows now that he doesn't belong in business or in an office. Here in the city, he says, "I'm a dime a dozen, and so are you!"

Loman summons up as much self-respect as he can muster. "I am not a dime a dozen! I am Willy Loman, and you are Biff Loman!" Reduced to tears, Biff pleads, "Will you take that phony dream and burn it before something happens?" As he flees the room, Willy turns to find Ben reminding him of the twenty-thousand-dollar proposition and telling him, "The jungle is dark but full of diamonds." Willy too has a diamond jungle, his own get-rich-quick scheme. He assures Linda that he'll be upstairs in a few minutes and, urged on by an impatient Ben ("The boat. We'll be late"), waves off his hallucinated voices like a swarm of bees, hushing them as he hurries off for the boat ride to fabulous wealth and total ruin, while Linda cries, "Willy, answer me!"

The stage is now empty, and at her cry of "No!" the sound of the car's engine is heard starting up with a roar, and as the car speeds off, *the music crashes down in a frenzy of sound, which becomes the soft pulsation of a single cello string*. The Loman family emerges from the house, dressed for a funeral, joined by Charley and Bernard. They move toward the audience to the front of the stage, where Linda lays flowers upon Willy's grave. This is the play's Requiem.

Nobody else has come to the cemetery. So much for being well-liked and, Linda asks, "where are all the people he knew?" It is so ironic, she says. "First time in thirty-five years we were just about free and clear. . . . He was even finished with the dentist." Happy insists "He had no right to do that," while Biff remembers "a lot of nice days [only] he had the wrong dreams." It is Charley, though, who voices the eulogy that would become classic.

> Willy was a salesman. . . . He don't put a bolt to a nut, he don't tell you the law or give you medicine. He's a man way out there in the blue, riding on a smile and a shoeshine. And when they start not smiling back—that's an earthquake. And then you get yourself a couple of spots on your hat, and you're finished. Nobody dast blame this man. A salesman is got to dream, boy. It comes with the territory.

Linda asks to be alone at the grave.

> Forgive me, dear. I can't cry. . . . Why did you do it? I search and search and I search, and I can't understand it, Willy. I made the last payment on the house today. Today, dear. And there'll be nobody home. We're free and clear. We're free. We're free . . . We're free . . .

A new play by Arthur Miller was news, and its being directed by Elia Kazan was even bigger news. This would surely be one of the major events of the 1948–1949 theater season. Word of it began to appear on the entertainment pages of the New York newspapers. The *Sunday New York Times* reported that although Kazan, Clurman and Walter Fried (who had joined them as a manager/partner) had presented *All My Sons*, they would not be producing *Death of a Salesman* because Clurman and Kazan had decided to concentrate on directing.

Fried was promptly invited to lunch by Kermit Bloomgarden, a producer with appropriate credentials. Like Kazan and Clurman he had roots in the Group Theatre, where he had been the business manager. Since opening his own production office, Bloomgarden had presented three consecutive hit plays, all of them serious and liberal minded, *Deep Are the Roots* by James Gow and Armand d'Usseau, *Another Part of the Forest* by Lillian Hellman, and the latest, *Command Decision* by William Wister Haines. At lunch Fried said he would be agreeable to coproducing *Death of a Salesman* with Bloomgarden, who telephoned Kazan. They were old friends. Bloomgarden had given Kazan his first job, as office boy at the Group Theatre. Now he asked if he might read *Death of a Salesman*.

"I read the play that night," Bloomgarden remembered, "and was so impressed and excited I could not fall asleep." At "exactly" nine o'clock in the morning, the middle of the night for most theater people, he telephoned Kazan, who "threw me a curve. He was delighted to hear how much I liked the play, but Cheryl Crawford had first refusal." Crawford was a closer friend of Kazan's, his cofounder (in 1947 with director Robert Lewis) of the already celebrated Actors Studio. Bloomgarden was sure "that was the end of that one. I could not imagine anyone turning this play down," but Cheryl Crawford did exactly that. Two days later Bloomgarden signed a contract to coproduce *Death of a Salesman* with Walter Fried. Immediately "Miller and Kazan went off to do some rewriting." Thus began the process of turning a written play into a stage work. In the course of that process a masterpiece would be created, perhaps the greatest of all American plays—but not before nearly being ruined.

Meanwhile the financial planning got under way. The production was budgeted at an even $100,000, which was expensive for the time. The money would be raised in the usual way, by selling shares, or *units*, in a general partnership. In this case there would be fifty units priced at $2,000 apiece and, given the celebrated director and prizewinning playwright, those units all but flew out the door. Many investors mailed in their checks without even seeing a script. When they did receive copies, their play-reading abilities were tested. That was when the financing became shaky. Miller's former agent, Leland Hayward, sight unseen had signed on for two units but after reading the play reduced his investment to $1,000, or a half unit. Another potential investor, Joshua Logan, the acclaimed director of musicals (*Annie Get Your Gun*) as well as plays, including the current hit *Mister Roberts*, told Kazan that he didn't understand what *Death of a Salesman* was all about. As Kazan told Bloomgarden, Logan was positive that "No audience would be able to follow the story, and no one would ever be sure whether Willy was imagining or really living through one or another scene in the play."

The intricate time scheme and the layered levels of reality were merely the crucial and most ingenious elements in the play. Yet, quite unbelievably, Kazan agreed with Logan. "Elia felt," Bloomgarden said, "that the flashbacks . . . slowed down the play's progress and detracted from the 'reality' scenes and he wanted Arthur to put them together in one section." Of course the play's expressionistic sequences are not flashbacks at all. They are projections of Loman's memory—the past in the present—and perhaps Bloomgarden's own difficulty in grasping this led him to support Kazan. To disagree with a director of such reputation would have been hard, anyway. Miller evidently respected Kazan's expertise too, because when Elia suggested that the play's time elements be simplified, he agreed to revise *Death of a Salesman* accordingly.

Collaboration is of course normal in the commercial theater. In the course of staging, naturally, the playwright must accept criticism and suggestions from his director. He must also listen to the producer, designers and actors. In the case of *Death of a Salesman* Arthur Miller was even accepting suggestions from his director's *wife*. Molly Kazan was very bright and Miller respected her intelligence. So did her husband, and she may well have contributed to Elia's conviction that the play's time elements were confusing. Miller said she urged him directly to "eliminate Uncle Ben and all the scenes in the past as unnecessary in the strictest sense."

All of this was based on reading the play, but as Bloomgarden himself put it, "Even people intimately involved with the theater often cannot tell from reading a script what will work and what will not." Thus is answered one of the most common questions asked of a failed play, How could anyone have ever thought that this would be any good? The answer is that nobody had been able to imagine what the script would play like. By the time they see it for themselves, the money is spent. The only choice then is to close the play or try to fix it—which often makes it worse.

Miller was already rewriting what was essentially a masterwork, in the process corrupting its dazzling concept. Meanwhile the money raising continued. When the new version of the play came in, Bloomgarden "was dumbstruck." His opinion was succinct.

"This piece of shit," he said, "I will not do."

Bloomgarden candidly conceded his role in this threat to *Death of a Salesman*. "On the surface," he recalled, Kazan's "ideas made sense." But even Kazan had unabashedly agreed that his suggestion did not exactly work out. The play was restored to its original form, and Miller later said,

> I've done rewriting in early stages of various plays, and on the whole I regret what I did. There were some improvements, but you have to trade with things you've given away. My plays are structured and once you begin unraveling that structure, the whole mechanism begins to shudder. If it's going to fail, let it fail the way I wrote it, rather than the way I rewrote it.

It is difficult to imagine what *Death of a Salesman* would be like without its elements of memory and alternate realities. The time phasing (or as Miller put it, "The past and the present . . . syncopated") and imaginative qualities in *Death of a Salesman* would prove not merely clear to audiences but crushingly effective, and soon enough. Yet now was the producer's turn for a lapse of judgment. Bloomgarden decided that "the title was a disaster," one that could "drive away a large part of our potential audience . . . we might lose six months of the run." His argument was that "the play was not in the end about salesmen," but this was a subterfuge. It wasn't the salesman in the title that he found worrisome. *Death* was the concern, too morbid to sell tickets, and his partner, Walter Fried, agreed. Miller was again amenable to reconsideration and Bloomgarden already had a new title in mind—*Free and Clear*, a phrase taken from the play's last scene. Miller agreed to consider it, but now it was Kazan who was the purist. He declared that if the title were changed he wouldn't direct the play. Nevertheless a survey was informally taken. "Of the people questioned," Miller recalled, when asked "if they would go to a play with my title . . . 98 per cent said absolutely not." Kazan didn't care what the survey demonstrated and he definitely was not amenable to reconsideration. He insisted that he was "absolutely against" any change and told Bloomgarden, "I'll bring all my influence on Artie."

"Do you mind," the producer asked, outside his office, "if we talk to him alone?"

Kazan suggested that he go right ahead, and whispered as Miller walked past, "Art, *no*." Then, as Kazan remembered, "He was in there about fifteen minutes and that was that."

It so happened that in the midst of all this, a play by Garson Kanin arrived on Broadway with the title *A Smile of the World*. "The reviews," Kanin recalled, "were uniformly rotten. I heard that Arthur got hold of all nine stinking reviews, brought them into Kermit's office and said, 'so much for happy, upbeat titles.'"

It was time to find the actors.

7. *Salesman*

IN A LETTER WRITTEN when *Death of a Salesman* was still in its germinating stage, and before even a single scene existed, Miller warned Kazan that "You are really going to have to hunt for an actor for this one . . . It will be a virtuoso piece for him at least." At that time he envisioned Willy Loman as "a very funny man sometimes, and a very frightening one at others." When he had finished the play, he provided more specific characteristics. Much like the playwright's uncle on whom he was modeled, Loman was "a very small man who wears little shoes and little vests."

In September 1948 Miller, Kazan and Bloomgarden began considering short and slender older actors who could handle the bravura role. The first to be offered the part was Ernest Truex, who turned it down. Walter Huston, the father of director John Huston, was briefly a favorite until it was learned that he was mortally ill. Bloomgarden then became enthusiastic about Fredric March, not only an excellent actor but a movie star with box office appeal. March's wife, Florence Eldridge, was a fine actor too, some thought an even better one, and the producer's idea was that she play Linda Loman. The public liked husband and wife teams playing husbands and wives; at least producers seemed to think so.

Fredric March was in London completing a movie called *Christopher Columbus*. Although Miller suspected that in reading the play the actor had been confused by its time shifts, March told Bloomgarden that he was excited about doing *Salesman*. However, he said, it was obviously a big and draining assignment and he was already weary from the film production. March asked whether the premiere might be delayed a year, but neither Miller nor Kazan had the patience for that and most likely the director already had Lee J. Cobb in mind for the role.

To anyone else, Leo Jacob Cobb (born Leo Jacoby) might have seemed an unlikely Willy Loman. At thirty-seven, he was twenty-six years younger than THE SALESMAN (Miller's capitals). He had never played a lead role in a major production. He was a quirky man with unpredictable moods, on stage and off. He was more interested in developing a movie career than working in the theater, and hadn't been on the stage since 1943. Not least, *Death of a Salesman* called for Willy Loman to be small and Lee Cobb was a big, hulking fellow; yet for all that, Kazan knew what he knew about the actor. They had worked together with the Group Theatre and had both played in *Golden Boy*. He had no trouble convincing Miller to hear the man out. The playwright, like his various vacillating protagonists, could be considered either reasonable or indecisive. Cobb was the one who had to be convinced.

He finally agreed to read for the part, but only on the condition that there be no one present except Kazan, Miller and Bloomgarden. The producer remembered the audition as being "wonderful," and when it was over, the stage-reluctant Cobb said, "This is my part. Nobody else can play this part. I know this man." He had the role. To accommodate his size, Miller merely changed one line so that instead of Loman seeing himself as a "shrimp" he said he was "fat" as well as "foolish to look at," and the actor's size would prove an asset. To watch a grown man fall apart is painful enough, but when he is physically imposing, it becomes pitiful. Cobb's rumbling, deep-chested baritone was only going to add to the effect.

No such search was necessary for an actress to play Linda Loman, because Kazan had already decided on Anne Revere. He had just directed her in *Gentleman's Agreement* where he thought she "was at the same time caustic and affectionate." These traits were also appropriate for Linda Loman; moreover, like Lee Cobb and Johnny Kennedy (who would play Biff), Anne Revere was a veteran of Kazan's old Group Theatre. There were so many of those people involved by now—actors who looked like real people, not models—that Miller thought *"Death of a Salesman* may well have been, unknowingly, the last gasp of the Group Theater." If so, that would have suited him just fine, the fulfillment of an old dream. "Oh God, I love those people," he would say, sounding more emotional about this organization than about his personal life. The Group's combination of commitments—artistic and political—seemed to get to him. "They weren't like anybody else," he said. "They were desperate about themselves."

As for Kazan's feelings about the Group Theatre,

> It died in 1941 but there were people who had been influenced by the Group or its leaders . . . and that thing, that element in the theater of a kind of spiritual realism still existed. It was alive within the actors, and the people I got in this play were part of my family. They were not stars. They were like people off the street, no one would recognize them. Humans. And they fitted Art's play perfectly.

When Anne Revere was lost to a movie assignment, another search became necessary, this time for someone to play Linda Loman. One of the first women considered was Mildred Dunnock. She was probably suggested by Bloomgarden, because she had played in his production of Lillian Hellman's *Another Part of the Forest*. A fine actress by anyone's standards, Dunnock wasn't even asked to audition, rejected by Kazan and Miller as being the wrong physical type (and besides, Kazan told Bloomgarden, her speech was "too good"). Miller saw Linda as "a woman who looked as though she had lived in a house dress all her life, even somewhat coarse and certainly less than brilliant." His first script described her as "taller, and much larger than Willy." Dunnock was a slender, refined, educated and well-spoken woman, in fact a former speech teacher. Theater people speak admiringly of *character actors* (those who play characters instead of themselves) but usually this is just paying lip service. Character actors are fine for grandparents and judges but typecasting has invariably been the rule for leading roles. How then could someone like Millie Dunnock play Willy's earthy wife, whom Miller still saw as his "big and broadchested . . . overweight" Aunt Annie?

Dunnock, unaware that she had already been considered, innocently inquired of Bloomgarden about "the older woman" she'd heard was a character in the new Arthur Miller play. By then some twenty actresses had been turned down for the part and she now learned that she had been the first of them. Undaunted and self-effacing, she asked if she might audition for the understudy, and this time the producer suggested that she "go get some padding."

Dunnock remembered,

> I think I added four inches to my waistline, but of course my neck and legs were the same. As soon as I walked out, someone called from the audience, "Take that stuff off!" I never was so humiliated. [Afterward] I went backstage, and there was Kazan. He said, "Are you married?" I said, "Yes." He said, "Have you any children?" I said, "Yes." "How many?" "One." He said, "Why don't you have any more?" I said, "I don't think that's any of your business."

Elia Kazan made it a habit of asking actors whether they had children. Personal questions disarmed them. Control seemed to be his first step in working with anyone, and he had already decided that Dunnock was his Linda. It was no longer important that the actress be a big woman. With burly Lee J. Cobb playing Willy, the wife couldn't very well be "much larger," and so with Arthur Kennedy (he had dropped the *J.*, although friends still called him Johnny) and Cameron Mitchell as Biff and Happy, the central roles were filled. The remainder of the company was completed without incident. Kazan promptly arranged to have dinner or drinks with each of them individually, which was more than just a social gesture. "By the time he got into rehearsal," Bloomgarden said, "he knew their weaknesses, their strengths and their neuroses."

The casting complete, Kazan turned to the problem of scenery.

Death of a Salesman has an extraordinary number of scenes, "almost sixty of them," Bloomgarden reckoned, anticipating a fearful production cost.

These scenes interweave such locations as the Loman kitchen, the two bedrooms, the garden, the driveway, the Boston hotel room and the company office. Making matters worse, the play is written to reflect Loman's mercurial mind shifts and so, as Kazan put it, "there was an immediate problem of how the hell to get this bit of scenery off and that bit on." Miller had suggested a basic, or unit, set around which the other settings might be attached, or merely suggested. One reason Jo Mielziner was hired to design the scenery was his experience as a lighting director, and much of the scenic work would be done with lights. As Kazan remembered, "Jo suggested that there be a vision of the man's life on stage all the time," so that if the script had Loman standing in the living room and imagining he was watching his boys polish the car in the driveway, the instant relocation could be accomplished through lighting, but the house would always be there to center the play. Designs thus were becoming part of *Death of a Salesman* in its transformation into theater.

Mielziner did make sketches of several painted backdrops, but only for such longer scenes as the restaurant, the Boston hotel and the boss's office. Even those "flats" were eliminated as the designer daringly proposed that there be no scenery at all, except for the Loman house with its living room and kitchen below, the bedrooms above. Props and lighting would accomplish the rest—for instance, when Willy goes from the house to the home office, the young boss would simply roll a table and recording machine on stage with him as he entered. At the same time the Loman house would be darkened. "The only piece of 'realism' that was left," Bloomgarden said, "was a funeral stone that rose at the end of the play on the forestage and even that would be eliminated. We all agreed that if the audience was accepting the way the play was staged, then the monument at the end would also be intrusive."

The director is a play's first critic. He explains it to the playwright from the staging point of view, dissecting the characters, outlining their interactions, pointing out the problems, suggesting the solutions. On September 13, 1948, Miller received the first of his director's notes. Kazan's focus was on tightening the script, then realizing the characters by conceiving psychologically dimensioned people for the actors to play. Once again he began by taking control of a personal interaction, in this case with the playwright. His first note to Miller was "You = Willy." Then he set down a series of fundamental statements.

> Basic: This play is about Willy Loman.
>
> Basic: This is a love story . . . the end of a tragic love story between Willy and Biff.
>
> Basic: He built his life on his son . . . But he taught the son wrong. The result: the son crashes and he with him.
>
> Basic: Without Biff loving Willy and Willy loving Biff, there is no conflict.
>
> Basic: The whole play is about love . . . love and competition.

> Basic: What the audience should feel at the end of this performance is only one thing: Pity, compassion and terror for Willy. Every dramatic value should serve this end. Your own feeling for your own father!

Kazan traced the play's dramatic line with bracing directness. "The viewer," he said, "is immediately made aware, first by the title, then by Willy's revealing that he found himself driving off the road, that we are gathered together to watch the course of a suicide." The director used the jargon of psychoanalysis to describe his first vision of the flesh and blood Loman to Miller. Willy, he said, was a man with "neuroses" and "anxiety," oppressed by an "unrelieved sense of worthlessness, insufficiency, which the salesman compensates for, hides, and comes up with his line of blarney." Kazan also suggested links to the classics, referring to *King Lear* as well as Greek tragedy, but he was on shaky ground there. His academic shortcomings are evident in his talk of "Inner Inevitability" and "Tragedy as in Greek Tragedy." He was also less than astute about the play's themes, citing as "The meaning of *Salesman* . . . the man didn't know who he was . . . the purpose of life is to get the better of your brother."

When dealing with the practicalities of performance, however, Elia Kazan came close to wizardry. Scene flow, physical action, these were his strengths, and character analysis his genius. One of a director's crucial functions is to provide the link between the playwright's words and the actor's realization, and The Salesman was already coming to life for Elia Kazan. Willy Loman, he decided,

> is one person to those he is sure of and someone entirely different to those he must please. He is arrogant to those who love him, but anxious, suppliant and charming to those who don't. Even his relationship to his children was one of perfect, unquestioning approval. On this basis, he loves them. When they left, he hated them. Biff and Happy, in the early scenes, *worship* the old man. They are merely extensions, tools for self worship, of his ego. When they grew up they found they had been raised with only one point, to win their father's praise. When this didn't work, they hated their father and he them.

Kazan, richly confident after *Gentleman's Agreement* in Hollywood and *A Streetcar Named Desire* on Broadway, was even more assertive with Miller than he'd been when they worked on *All My Sons*. Now he was specific about speeches that needed rewriting, shortening or even elimination. He suggested that Happy, the play's vaguest Loman, might achieve some individuality with a reference to being vain. "Willy and Hap," he said, have "the same pre-occupation with their weight . . . both have the same Biz [physical "business"] . . . feeling the flesh around their waists and under the chin." Miller responded by connecting vanity with Happy's insecurity, adding the line, "I lost weight, Pop. You notice?" He agreed to delete some of the repeats of "liked" and "well liked" and dropped several overly specific references involving Ben, one when he says he met "an old man in Alaska. A musician. He saw father die, William," and the other an exchange between Biff and Happy: "Has he come back from Africa?" "No, not since that visit when we were kids." This is the visit that recurs in Loman's hallucinations.

Kazan also convinced Miller to delete several fanciful remarks by Ben that would have only served to confuse, for instance, "So you're William. All my life I've been promising myself a trip to America to look you up." Miller also agreed to drop Willy's kiss ("Oh Linda, sweetheart!"), but he wasn't reflexively submissive. When Willy cries, "I am not a dime a dozen," Miller had Biff reply, "I'm gonna dump that dream!" Kazan crossed the line out. Miller restored it. Kazan crossed it out a second time and scrawled, "NO 'I'm gonna dump that dream.'" For him it was too on the nose. Miller finally conceded.

Virtually all of these suggestions were aimed at propelling the action, but one change seems to have weakened a scene, the painful one in the boss's office when Willy is forced to sit in humiliation, listening to a recording of a child's recitation. In Miller's first final draft, marked by Kazan, "the original script that Art gave me to read directly he'd finished it," the scene was played without interruption and included yet another appearance by Willy's brother Ben. In the revision young Wagner leaves the office, returning when Willy accidentally starts the recording machine. The intention seems to have been to prolong the vivid sequence, but instead its through line is broken. The scene is still cruelly effective, especially after the elimination of Ben's appearance, but it was even stronger when played straight through, and the accidental starting of the recorder would always seem like the contrivance it is.

One suggestion—and it wasn't Kazan's alone—the playwright absolutely would not accept. It was about the Requiem, "which everybody," Miller said,

> wanted me to cut out. They said the audience were never going to stay there because Willy Loman is dead; there's nothing more to say. Of course they did want to stay there [for] what is the point of a funeral? You want to think over the life of the departed and it's in there, really, that [the central point] is nailed down.

The Requiem would provide the play's ultimate crunch.

In the 1920s the New Amsterdam Theatre had been the most glamorous of the showplaces that lined both sides of Forty-second Street, between Seventh and Eighth Avenues. That glamour had since turned to several decades of sleaze and the glorious theater with its art deco interior had become a down-at-the-heels pornographic movie house by the time *Death of a Salesman* went into rehearsal.

An office building rose above the New Amsterdam with an entrance next door. A creaky elevator brought the company of actors from the drab little lobby to rehearsals in the indoor rooftop theater that had once sparkled with the *Midnight Frolic* revues of producer Florenz Ziegfeld. Like the theater below this one had also gone to seed, its plush seats torn, its carpeting filthy. Harsh rehearsal lights exposed the auditorium's grimy walls and peeling paint, but actors were at home in such places. Rehearsals were their real life while the shows were just performances.

Rehearsals for *Death of a Salesman* started on December 27, 1948, and began at the beginning, with Willy Loman's weary, muttering return home. Months earlier Miller had written to Kazan that Loman is "tired in the first second of the play." The early stage direction stated, *A pinpoint traveling spotlight hits a small area on stage left. The Salesman, Willy Loman by name, slowly walks into the light. He is dressed in a suit and a felt hat, carries a large valise.* To bring this to life Kazan created a full pantomime. Cobb enters with a weary mutter ("Oh, boy, oh, boy"), dropping the bag as if the load were unbearable. He opens the door to the house, picks up the bag again, enters the house, drops the bag again, takes off his hat and rubs his eyes with the heels of both hands.

It was already a sorry story, a man exhausted, when inspiration struck, as usual by accident. Loman's valise was to be a sample bag, the kind that Miller had seen dozens of salesmen carrying as they'd left his father's shop to make their rounds. Willy Loman, however, was a *traveling* salesman, which meant that he would be carrying a *second valise* packed with his clothes. Whoever thought of it, another bag was found and it makes a profound difference. One heavy valise pulls a person down to the side. With two of them a bigger-than-life image was created, a man bent to the earth like a plow horse. Was not a white-collar worker a worker too? Backbreaking labor, carried out by an older salesman wearing a hat and suit, spoke for the working man in every man. The hefty Lee Cobb seemed permanently stooped by a lifetime of making a living. The image of The Salesman loaded down with two valises would represent *Death of a Salesman* on its show cards (posters) and in advertisements, to be engraved on the consciousness of a generation of Americans forever.

As rehearsals got under way, Miller was worried. Cobb's part was enormous. Loman is onstage for virtually the entire play. From the outset the playwright feared that the actor's energy level was low. "He sat for days on the stage like a great lump . . . when it came time to speak lines, he whispered meaninglessly [looking] heavy eyed, morose, even persecuted," or else he was quarreling. The other actors, however, were neither bothered nor worried. Alan Hewitt, playing Loman's young boss, Howard Wagner, remembered that as the third week of rehearsals began, "Cobb did a lot of talking, not to say arguing over anything and everything, but he could not long have held back on 'acting' the play because, after the first two weeks of rehearsal, we staggered through complete run throughs every evening."

Kazan tried to set Miller's mind at ease. He said that Cobb understood Willy Loman in his gut. He dealt with the actor's low level of energy in a tactful way, couching his remarks in terms of the character. "The prototype of Willy," he said, "was not a mouse at all. He had strong, violent opinions . . . When he talked to himself on the street, he did so violently, and with sudden flares and flashes . . . he had high energy." Other notes were delivered to Cobb indirectly, for instance, in the opening scene when Willy speaks of having "such thoughts, I have such strange thoughts," Kazan made his comments not to Cobb but to Dunnock. "Every time he barks at you, in one way or another he immediately reassures himself of your affection and love. That is what holds you, Millie. You *know* he needs you. When Willy gets mothered, hugged and loved, he knows he's safe." Miller agreed, in fact he later wished he'd given Linda Loman even more strength so that the battle over Willy's life could have been more equal. Then again, he said in his usual equivocating way, "he wipes the floor with her from time to time . . . a woman who was thinking of herself more would simply not have been there one morning, or else she would have put up such a fight as to crush him."

This kind of back-and-forth thinking, which might confuse an actor, is only one reason why directors tend to discourage direct communication between a playwright and the company. To restrain an author, however, isn't always possible. "From time to time," Bloomgarden recalled, "Miller would ask Kazan to let him talk to the actors about the play. Kazan . . . would sit back silently in his chair while Miller would turn it on. After it was over, Kazan would take over as if Miller had never said a word."

The playwright insisted that "Willy wasn't crazy" and felt strongly that a production "shouldn't be about pathology." Rather, he told an interviewer, "I was trying . . . to set forth what happens when a man does not have a grip on the forces of life and has no sense of values which will lead him to that kind of a grip." The difference was more than semantic to him; it related Willy's drama of losing his senses to Miller's credo of controlling one's destiny. Kazan wasn't interested in such distinctions—these cannot be conveyed by an actor. "Willy," he said in his straightforward way, "is going nuts," and as for Biff, he left Arthur Kennedy almost completely alone. If Lee Cobb was the most complicated of the male actors in the company, Kennedy was the smartest, the most dependable and certainly the most mature. He could bring Biff to life on his own, just as he had done for Chris in *All My Sons*. Kazan was trusting with him, his suggestions concrete. "Biff and Willy," he said, "are each other's shame. . . . They see the worst of themselves much more closely in each other. . . . What Biff means when he says he can't look [Willy] in the face . . . is that he can't look himself in the face."

As for the rest of the cast, Kazan gave personal time to each. Alan Hewitt remembered,

> We were a very disparate group of people in that cast. We were not all from the Group Theatre, we were not all members of the Actors Studio, we had different sorts of backgrounds, but Gadg was able to talk to each actor in the lan-

guage that was right for him. He was chameleon-like in that capacity for sensing what is the best way to talk to that actor, and make the actor think that the actor himself, not Kazan, had done it.

Another aspect of Kazan's talent was his instinct for physical action. As the characters materialized during rehearsal, their physical behavior developed. At the climax of the restaurant sequence, after Biff's speech about being "a buck an hour" and not likely to bring any prizes home, Kazan told Kennedy to "turn and slowly start toward Willy—Willy speaks—Biff continues—silence—Willy prepares for an attack—Happy tries to intervene—Biff throws him out of the way; and at that moment he embraces Willy and bursts into tears." Then, Kazan decided,

> Biff starts toward Willy to beat some sense into his head. [His] rage bordering on tears comes from the fact that he can't wake the guy. He wants to shake him out of it, to beat him till he says, as Biff does, "I see, I see, I'm nothing, I'm nothing."

Kazan improvised that line. It was based on a partial misreading of the scene's intentions, which are not only about Willy recognizing Biff's inadequacies; the scene is also about Biff shaking his father free of hallucinations in the hope that he will recover his senses. In this lay the play's essential metaphor for confronting the delusion of unearned success created by a corrupt social system. Miller accepted Kazan's suggestion but adapted the line so that Biff addresses not only the truth about himself but also the desperate need for his father to face reality. With artful economy Miller rewrote the line, "Pop, I'm nothing! I'm nothing, Pop. Can't you understand that?"

The director himself rescued one of the play's most striking lines, which had slipped off the page during revisions. When Biff is telling his brother about the pathetic business interview, Kazan scribbled into the script, "So I took his pen." With this ridiculous theft the character tells the audience everything it needs to know about his senseless, self-destructive behavior and his inability to control it. On the blank page in the script opposite that line Kazan wrote, "Biff now must simply face the fact that he is a petty thief." For him to specify dialogue in a play was unusual, not only out of respect for the playwright but because Kazan had a less-is-more attitude. He was much more interested in action and behavior than in words. Indeed Kazan invented the stunning moment when Willy slaps his son in the Boston hotel room before falling to the floor. "Willy," Kazan said, "is now 'crazy,' down on all fours—like a crazy man—*King Lear*."

There can be a surfeit of such climaxes, and when they are contrived instead of organic to a play, they can seem false. *Death of a Salesman* was served by his staging invention, not dominated by it.

The director now tackled the play's toughest challenge, its memory scenes. If he didn't make these clear, the audience would be just as confused as were the play's early readers, Kazan included. How were the actors to play these unrealities, these delusions, these "stylization scenes," as he called them? All of his experience had been with traditional plays. He thrashed out the question with Miller, in the process getting an education in dramatic expressionism. Miller's own education in that style had of course come from Professor Rowe, who described expressionism as being not exactly fantasy but "an extension of realism inward to the areas of psychological experience and of abstract ideas." This is perhaps an elusive way of putting it. A clearer explanation is given by Professor George E. Wellworth of Pennsylvania State University. "One of the confusions about the term 'expressionism'" he wrote, "is the fact that it is used in literature, music, architecture and art as well as in the drama." Unlike impressionism, which "is an account of how the world of reality affects the describer," expressionism, Wellworth writes,

> is an imposition on the outside world of the describer's concept of it. . . . It is perhaps the most completely self-centered art form ever evolved. . . . Indeed, reality *per se* has no meaning for the expressionist . . . he takes the whole human race [and] shows it to us as it is seen through the eyes of one character.

The subjective reality that Wellworth describes is Willy Loman's alone. Elia Kazan, an apt student, promptly put this idea into concepts that actors could use. The characters, he said, are who they "really" are in the present-day scenes, but in the memory scenes they are seen as filtered through Loman's psyche. For example, Kazan said, Linda in Willy's memory scenes "is a figure fashioned out of Willy's guilt. Hard working, sweet, always true, admiring. 'I shouldn't cheat on a woman like that!' Dumb. Slaving. Loyal. Tender. Innocent. Patient. Always available for sympathy. But in [the 'real' scenes] she is terrifyingly tough. Why? She senses Willy is in danger. And she just can't have him hurt."

Miller seemed to think that Kazan had it more or less right. "Willy is all the voices . . . Happy and Biff are also presented as distorted in his imagination." As for Ben, the play never shows him in reality, only as seen through Willy Loman's psychological prism. Kazan again transposed that into terms his actor, Tom Chalmers, could grasp. Ben, he said, "is romanticized in Willy's memory and by Willy's necessity, into a godlike figure. And Willy is impressed."

At bottom, however, Kazan saw this brother as someone who should chill the audience.

> The point of the part is that Willy's ideal is wrong . . . that the model he holds up to his sons is a vicious and dangerous one. At the end of the play it should be felt that Willy's worship of this false ideal leads to his suicide. Ben represents *aggression*, Enterprise-ruthless! . . . He is a villain. Charming. Suave. But a villain.

As the one figure who is always imagined and never in present time, Ben would puzzle even the play's most ardent admirers. He was a hallucination, that was obvious enough, but had he *ever* existed? Working with Chalmers, Kazan offered clues to at least the appearance of the character, with "whips, spurs, big jewelry, hats and boots." He suggested that the actor think of the character as a "capitalist adventurer, like 'Barney' Baruch, but he never tells his secret." It is the secret about which Willy keeps asking, "What's the answer? How did you do it?" The Salesman needs to know "the open sesame" for instant success, but of course there is no magic formula for diamonds in and out of the jungle. This is the siren song of American capitalism, and Ben is capitalism incarnate. His existence still had to be explained, though. Audiences would accept him in the fullness of the play, but afterward many would wonder who exactly he was. Miller's own explanation remains the best.

> He's a real brother but Willy has invested him already with the whole mythos of that vast brutal success which is larger than life. Nobody can be that successful. Ben is an expressionist figure; every time he opens his mouth he is talking about diamonds, or wealth, or the land, or exploitation of some kind, and that's the way it would be for Willy. Willy wouldn't think of him excepting as the one who won, the victor.

In the third and last week of rehearsals the playwright watched yet another run through, and that time Cobb played without restraint. Miller was "elevated. I forgot I was in the theater. I was moved to tears by the wonder of his performance, the idea that a human being could do this. He peopled that block, that city. He created life. That was the most magical moment in my life in the theater." And so the play was almost ready to be seen in public.

On January 18, 1949, the *Death of a Salesman* company convened at New York's Pennsylvania Station and took a train to Philadelphia for the tryout engagement. Only a few more days of rehearsal remained before the single preview scheduled for Friday the twenty-first at the Locust Street Theatre. The world premiere would take place the following night.

The press agent for the show, Jim Proctor, had gone ahead with his assistant, Merle Debuskey. They were hardly the traditional advance men who concoct publicity schemes. Proctor had a history of working with serious-minded producers, while Debuskey was fresh from the Provincetown Players and the plays of Eugene O'Neill. Both were devoted to the causes of the Left, the same as Kazan, Miller, Bloomgarden, Cobb, Kennedy and Chalmers. This wasn't coincidental; it is comfortable to work with like-minded people.

Proctor and Debuskey were already arranging interviews and feature stories.[2] Their approach was that *Death of a Salesman* was unique. "At that time in American drama," Debuskey said, "a play had an antagonist and a protagonist and you knew they were individuals. In *Salesman*," he advised the local editors, "the antagonist is not an individual; the antagonist is society."

The two press agents were also charged with finding an audience for opening night. The preview was going to be invitational, which did not mean gala, it just meant free. "We'd been giving tickets away," Debuskey recalled, "just to get people to come." As for the rehearsals, he said, "We just worked on refining what we had. The somewhat odd circumstance that the second act played longer than the first seemed not to bother anyone."

Lee Cobb, however, was growing nervous and, Miller said, "Kazan caught the scent of [his] fears." If the playwright was tense too, he was not the type to admit it. The director—a devout believer in the power of music—suggested that both Cobb and Miller take a break and join him at an afternoon concert in the Academy of Music down the street. That same afternoon Mildred Dunnock was supposed to be meeting Kazan at the theater for a private rehearsal. "I'm a timid actress," she recalled. "Most actresses are insecure. . . . But you felt that you could do almost anything with Mr. Kazan . . . go whole hog with it . . . and not be humiliated." Dunnock continued, "I had a difficult scene, a monologue, and the end of it was the most quoted line in the play, 'Attention must be paid.' It was very difficult to find a way to play that lengthy monologue and give it the conflict that it needed."

She had been working on the speech, she said, "for a long time in Philadelphia," and finally Kazan took her aside and whispered, "I have a new attack for you, Millie." That was what the afternoon appointment was supposed to be about, but when Dunnock arrived at the theater she was told, "Mr. Kazan says he has been given tickets to the symphony. You're to come over, he's in the top balcony in the top box."

At the Academy of Music Kazan, Miller and Cobb were listening intently to the major work on the program, Beethoven's Seventh Symphony. It is a powerful piece of music, a series of increasingly propulsive movements. The fourth and last of them is relentless in its drive, some ten minutes of rising climaxes. Miller leaned forward in the upper box and whispered to Cobb, "Now *this* is the last ten minutes of the play." Cobb, he thought,

> had often yielded to the temptation of blowing all his forces well before his final climaxes. He was a terribly edgy horse, and sometimes, because he wanted every moment to count, nearly gave way to his emotions rather than the controlled arc of the play. Staring down at the orchestra, he nodded agreement, newly aware, I thought, of Beethoven's treatment of climaxes and his returning to them again and again until, in full possession of all his themes he smashed through the roof and into the heavens.

Dunnock, meanwhile, had arrived at the concert hall.

> I got in the back way and went way, way up. When I arrived, it was the last movement with every instrument playing *full blast*. We came downstairs after it was over, and Kazan said, "That's just what we're going to do tomorrow." It was very exciting.

The next day the director arrived at rehearsal with a conductor's baton. He told Dunnock, "I'm going to conduct you in this scene." He took a seat somewhere in the dark. She began her speech, "I don't say he's a great man." The director, sitting several rows back in the theater, shouted, "Louder!" Speaking up, she continued, "Willy Loman never made a lot of money."

"Louder! Louder!" cried Kazan.

"*His name was never in the paper*," she roared.

"I was screaming at the top of my voice," she recalled. "And I stopped and burst into tears and I said, 'I can't! I won't do it that way.'"

"That's *exactly* the way you'll do it," said Kazan.

"But tell me," Dunnock said, "where are all the nuances?"

"What?" Kazan asked.

"The neeeoo-ances," Dunnock replied in her best speech teacher's voice.

"Oh, Lord," said Kazan. "We'll come to those in a couple of weeks."

As the Philadelphia opening night neared, an excitement was building around the production. Theater people such as Lotte Lenya and Kurt Weill were coming down from New York, and Mary Miller too. She struck the press agent, Merle Debuskey, as "sweet and bright," but shy. "She never tried to become a significant part of the conversation . . . they seemed a very well suited, mated couple. The family was a very important function for her . . . She didn't come into the orbit we were in [but] the two of them were very much together and Art seemed consistently interested in his children." Only recently a newspaper interviewer had quoted Miller calling his son Bobby "a great man, though right now he's getting a tooth in the back of his mouth and he's unhappy about it." That was how Debuskey saw Miller, very family-oriented. "There was never any sense that he was looking for women," but Virginia Bloomgarden, the producer's wife, thought otherwise. She agreed about Mary's shyness and Art's sense of family, but thought she had a better understanding of the Millers' marital relationship. "Mary was very well read, very interesting to talk to. [But] I never saw her in a relationship with Arthur. I never had the feeling that they were close. I didn't think of her as being cold, the way I did Arthur . . . A big ego there, enormous. But there was such a remoteness. You could never get to know him."

The Friday night preview was the first public performance of *Death of a Salesman* and Cobb played it as though a man possessed. When he made his last exit he rushed off to prepare for the curtain calls, sponging off his perspiration as the soundman created the car crash. The actor was standing in the wings at stage left, watching the Requiem, but the curtain calls had been rehearsed for him to enter from stage right. He couldn't walk across the stage behind the set because it went all the way to the theater's back wall. So he had to go down a flight of stairs and walk under the stage in order to cross over to the other side. At the same time, Alan Hewitt had to do just the opposite. As Cobb remembered,

> I was, naturally, emotionally exhausted by this first public performance of the play . . . My ass was dragging. Hewitt and I pass each other underneath the stage. Neither of us stops but, just as he passes me, he mutters, "Been on yet?"
>
> We kept moving in opposite directions.
>
> Then it hit me. I had to stifle a roar of laughter. The son of a bitch brought me back to the world.

As they lined up for the play's first-ever curtain call, the thirteen actors peered through the stage lights, searching for their audience in the dark. The house was deathly quiet, no applause at all. Bewildered at first, they soon realized that, as Alan Hewitt put it, this was "an audience stunned into silence, with little strength left for applause." Then, as though relieved by a massive sigh, the crowd burst into vast and great cheers, waves of approval and gratitude that swept down the aisles and cascaded from the balcony. This play was surely going to be a hit—at least in Philadelphia.

One small matter remained. The critics would be coming to the official premiere the next night.

Once again, on January 22, 1949, the cast of *Death of a Salesman* took their bows before an eerily and utterly silent audience. This time, though, a sniffling sound began to emerge from the hush. It was a sound rarely heard in a theater—the sound of people weeping. Then they burst into applause.

"Because of the Saturday night opening," Hewitt remembered,

> the reviews did not appear until Monday. The company was told to relax on Sunday until a five o'clock call at the theater. Advance copies of some of the reviews were obtained and read. After the papers came out on Monday morning, the lines at the box office were so long that a second ticket window was opened.

All that remained was Broadway.

For weeks the New York theatergoing world had been hearing about the Philadelphia success of *Death of a Salesman*. That engagement had been a profitable one and with it the producers were pleased to find that the show came in for some $35,000 under its original $100,000 budget. Now a big advance sale was assuring financial success. A special rehearsal was called for Monday, February 7, 1949. Theaters come in different sizes and their acoustics vary accordingly. The Morosco Theatre on West 45th Street—now the Marriott Marquis Hotel—was shallower than the Locust Street Theatre in Philadelphia. With less projection necessary, actors tend to feel that vocal adjustments must be made and volumes brought down. Kazan minimized the effort and told his cast, "I love to hear actors without straining. You can be as loud as you please."

Only two previews were scheduled, on the evenings of February 8 and 9, before the New York premiere on Thursday the tenth. That night Miller went backstage to wish everyone a good show before taking his usual spot at the back of the theater. Restless while watching his play from behind the last row, he stepped into the theater lobby, where Bloomgarden was nervously puffing at a cigar. Miller told him to stop "smoking that cigar so loud" and went out through the front doors, walking down Forty-fifth Street toward Eighth Avenue before turning around and coming back to Broadway. When he finally returned to the theater, Bloomgarden was still in the lobby, now chewing on a dead cigar. Miller stayed with him until the end.

After the final curtain fell on that opening night performance the company came together on stage, glancing at one another in a bond of uncertainty. They had grown accustomed to sobbing audiences. Would Broadway opening nighters be too sophisticated for that, too blasé to be moved by their play? As the curtain whooshed upward, Alan Hewitt remembered, "There was a long, deathly silence. I held my breath for what seemed like an eternity and then the whole audience exploded. They cheered, hollered, clapped, hooted, screamed and would not stop. Even after the actors stopped taking curtain calls, they milled around and wouldn't leave."

One of those who wouldn't leave was Kazan's old friend Cheryl Crawford. She was blowing her nose, tears streaming down her cheeks, but it wasn't just for the tragedy of Willy Loman. In fact, she insisted to Kermit Bloomgarden, "That's not why I'm crying." She was miserable, she said, because she had turned down the chance to produce *Death of a Salesman*. "I had this play and let it get away."

Others in the audience had been so moved that they were still sitting, stunned, in their seats as liveried waiters from Louis Sherry's came down the aisles rolling tables laden with china, silver and champagne. Soon there was a crowd walking up the side stairs of the stage. Robert Dowling, the owner of the theater, had arranged an elegant party for a few dozen of his opening night friends. Neither the playwright, the director nor the actors were invited. Miller himself was refused a glass of champagne. He was annoyed and so was Bloomgarden, but there were more important matters at hand. Arthur and Mary, Elia and Molly Kazan, and Kermit and Virginia Bloomgarden walked the one block through Shubert Alley to Sardi's. In a private dining room upstairs they all sat down at a big table to distract one another until the notices came out. The only outsiders present were the actor Zero Mostel and his wife, Kate, and the Millers' friends, Frank and Nan Taylor.

Broadway's press agents, refusing to wait until the newspapers came out, had long since found typesetters who for a price would read the critics' reviews over the telephone. Miller leaned his head against the earpiece as Jim Proctor made the call to the all-important *New York Times*. The playwright would later insist that he could hear the "clacking of the typewriter" while Brooks Atkinson was writing the review, but that could not have been so. Atkinson had a benign understanding of show business urgencies, but he was not the kind of critic to allow anything so vulgar as having his review read over the telephone while he was writing it. The "clacking" that Miller heard was surely the sound of the typesetter's Linotype machine. All that mattered of course was the review.

> Arthur Miller has written a superb drama . . . rich and memorable. . . . It is so simple in style and so inevitable in theme that it scarcely seems like a thing that has been written and acted. For Mr. Miller has looked with compassion into the hearts of some ordinary Americans and quietly transferred their hopes and anguish to the theater.

"Simple in style" was not insulting but rather the highest praise. Miller's adaptation of expressionist techniques to suit a singular and ingenious scheme of time phasing, so challenging on paper, played out with a naturalness and clarity that signaled perfect execution.

Other reviews from daily critics were enthusiastic, too rushed for thorough analysis but ably communicating the nature of this theatrical experience. They certainly were *money* notices, from John Chapman in the *Daily News* ("one of those unforgettable times in which all is right and nothing is wrong") and Ward Morehouse in the *New York Sun* ("The most powerful and most exciting play that the season has revealed to date") to the *Herald-Tribune*'s tough-minded Howard Barnes ("a great play of our day has opened").

As dawn is followed by dusk, so are rave reviews followed by naysayers, usually among the critical intelligentsia. In this there is perhaps an element of power envy, these reviewers being commercially ineffectual by way of small circulations and publications printed too late to affect ticket sales. Yet their notices can also serve an important function as second thoughts, more seriously considered analyses that can fine-tune and sometimes correct the visceral reactions of frontline reviewers. After starting her criticism by referring to the play as *either* "Arthur Miller's or Elia Kazan's *Death of a Salesman*," Eleanor Clark, a *Partisan Review* punster, called the play "an ambitious piece of Confucianism . . . a hoax" drawn "straight from the party line literature of the Thirties." Mary McCarthy wrote that "Willy is a capitalized Human Being without being anyone, a suffering animal who commands a helpless pity."

This school of intellectual critics pursued the play long after it was established in the international dramatic repertory. In 1957 Tom Driver wrote in the *Tulane Drama Review* that the play "cannot make up its mind whether the trouble is in Willy or in society . . . at one moment [he is] the pathetic object of our pity and the next is being defended as a hero of tragic dimen-

Courtesy of Joan Copeland

ABOVE:
Isadore and Gussie Miller with Kermit

LEFT:
The young Arthur Miller

Arthur, Mary and three-year-old Jane, pictured in a 1947 magazine article

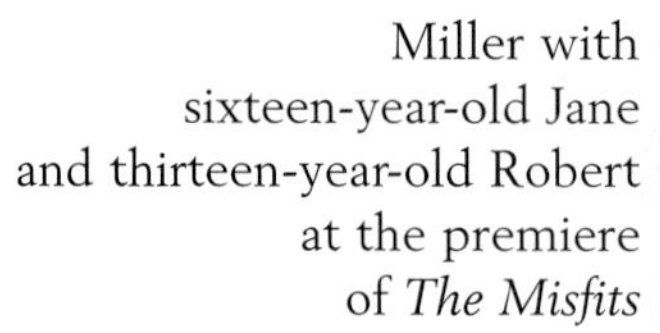

Miller with sixteen-year-old Jane and thirteen-year-old Robert at the premiere of *The Misfits*

PIC Magazine

Elia Kazan and Miller, early in 1949, during the tryout tour of *Death of a Salesman*

Photofest

The opening of the 1949 Waldorf Peace Conference, known officially as "The Cultural and Scientific Conference for World Peace": (left to right) A. A. Fadeyev, Secretary General of the Union of Soviet Writers, Norman Mailer, Dmitri Shostakovich, Miller and Dr. William Olaf Stapleton, the only British delegate granted a visa to attend the conference

Sam Schulman and Photofest

Miller announced his imminent marriage to Marilyn Monroe in the course of testifying at HUAC on June 21, 1956. The next day, the couple held a press conference on the sidewalk outside her Manhattan apartment, and it was there that this, their first photograph, was taken.

Corbis

Miller appealing the HUAC contempt citation with attorney Joseph L. Rauh, Jr.

Photofest

On their wedding day, June 30, 1956, with Isadore and Gussie Miller

Courtesy of Joan Copeland

Marilyn and Miller's sister, Joan Copeland

Photofest

On the set of
The Misfits

Photofest

With
Yves Montand

Photofest

Being met at London's Heathrow Airport by Laurence Olivier and Vivien Leigh before beginning work on *The Prince and the Showgirl*

Courtesy of Joan Copeland

Kermit and Frances Miller

Courtesy of Eli Wallach

Arthur and Inge

Corbis

Arthur and Inge

Photofest

Arthur Miller

sions." In 1963 Robert Brustein wrote in *The New Republic* "I have never been convinced that [*Salesman*] is a very important work, and I am certain that it is too familiar to need reviving." Not long after that Richard Gilman contributed an essay to the *New York Times* conceding only that "The play has minimal satisfactions . . . I think it is a melodrama." Still later, in 1984, James Wolcott wrote in *Vanity Fair*, "If *Salesman* is a classic, it's a square classic, full of homey wisdom and forlorn smoke curls of nostalgia . . . it makes its points with a rolling pin."

Noel Coward at least had the good taste to share his disapproval with only his diary.

> Went to *"Death of a Salesman."* I personally found it boring and embarrassing. . . . Lee Cobb overacted and roared and ranted. . . . The play is a glorification of mediocrity. The hero . . . is a cracking bore and a liar and a fool and a failure; the sons are idiotic. To me these ingredients do not add up to entertainment in the theater.

Regardless of such opinions, the value of *Death of a Salesman* is beyond dispute and as a masterwork has long since taken its place among the world's great plays. It is arguably the greatest of all American plays.

Mary and Arthur didn't leave the opening night celebration until the early morning hours and when they did leave, he left as someone else. Coming on the heels of the explosively successful *A Streetcar Named Desire*, Miller's *Death of a Salesman* completed a transformation of New York's parochial Broadway stage into a national phenomenon. Tennessee Williams and Arthur Miller were now the giants of a new American theater, linked by Kazan, towering above the cultural landscape.

As *Death of a Salesman* began its run, much was written about its sobbing audiences, who continued to amaze Kazan. "I'd never heard men sob in the theater. Night after night, I would stand there and you would hear these resonant, deep voices, expressing their pain." Miller seemed to take every opportunity to complain about this, insisting that he had not written a mere emotional entertainment. The play, he said, was supposed to make people think, not weep. Delivering a lecture at the New School of Social Research, he said that it was not a heartbreaking tragedy but a cautionary tale. "I was trying in *Salesman* to set forth what happens when a man . . . has no sense of values."

Yet the sobbing would not go away. The play's power is a function of its artistry and the author, despite his efforts to be a pure rationalist, finally admitted to the shattering effect his play was having and accepted the grateful adulation being given in return. The prominence that went with it, however, was not as welcome, nor was a new and nasty kind of publicity. Ed Sullivan, a gossip columnist for the *Daily News*, was sniping at Miller and the play as being Communist-influenced. "Sullivan," he wrote to Kazan, "will end up selling pencils on Broadway mumbling to himself if he keeps this up. [Still] at this stage, I'd just as soon my name didn't appear in the paper for any reason." Nor was Miller much impressed, he said, with the assorted prizes arriving in the form of medals, plaques and certificates—the Tony Award, the New York Drama Critics Circle Award, the Pulitzer Prize for Drama—and he wrote to Kazan (who was back in Hollywood preparing to film *Panic in the Streets*),

> Medals! Ribbons! Christ sake, I'll put them all on some day and look like a Russian ice skater. I don't know what the hell is wrong with me. I keep refusing to do things and go places, and still I haven't eaten at home but twice a week for a month.

Nevertheless he had already begun to change. "The person most affected by the success of *Death of a Salesman,*" Kazan wrote, "was the author . . . His eyes acquired a new flash and his carriage and movement a hint of something swashbuckling." Such was the new Miller self-image and then public image as the thirty-three-year-old playwright began evolving into a figure larger than life. As Garson Kanin observed, "At the time the play was in rehearsal, he was only a playwright named Art Miller.

"After it opened, he became *Arthur Miller.*"

Money had not been a problem for the Arthur Millers since the opening night of *All My Sons*. Although its New York engagement had ended, the play was still running in London and performed throughout Europe. Now more money began to come in as Broadway-sized checks resumed with *Death of a Salesman,* and it was estimated that he would earn $2 million from the play. Movie rights were also being negotiated and there was book money. The play was scheduled for publication by the Viking Press on May 18, 1949, and the first printing was already sold out. "With the Book of the Month [club]," Miller wrote to Kazan, "they tell me [sales] will go to half a million. Now Simon and Schuster want to make a pocket book edition, first printing, 250,000.

"I tell ya, kid, art pays."

He and Elia regularly called each other *kid,* although Kazan, having six years on Miller, sometimes referred to himself as *the old man*. The two considered themselves best friends and Miller dedicated the published version of the play to Kazan.

Success also brought entree into the greater outside world, with opportunities to meet people who until then had only been famous names. Miller received an invitation, for instance, to have dinner with Thomas Mann on May 9, 1949. "That ought to be interesting," he wrote to Kazan, "unless he talks only about himself, which Literary Figures are prone—or erect—to do."

Evidently he did not recognize such latent qualities in himself and at dinner, as it turned out, the eminent German novelist spoke admiringly and at length about *Death of a Salesman,* calling it "a lyric play" and adding, "You never tell them [the audience] what to think. It is simply an experience that they can't escape. If a European had written the play, there would have been a discussion of the theme by the characters."

Miller had consciously kept his characters within "their intellectual and emotional capacities . . . never [letting] them become aware of the play they are in." His point was to have their actions imply rather than specify the theme, an approach that he considered more artistic. He thanked Mann for "the greatest compliment" he had yet received, but suspected—whether or not with good reason—that the German novelist had been disingenuous, slyly expressing the "very European" attitude that "if the characters don't directly discuss the theme, it hasn't got one."

Deluged with requests for speeches and articles, Miller took every opportunity to defend what after all had been a rapturously received play. The first assignment he accepted was the most prestigious, coming as it did from the *New York Times*. Miller used his platform to respond to criticism from loftier critics who took offense at the comparisons he seemed to be making between *Death of a Salesman* and *King Lear*. The criticism was that however effective and affecting Miller's play might be, it was not high tragedy in the Aristotelian sense because its protagonist does not fall from a great height, nor does he come to any realization of his complicity in the event.

Artists tend to take praise as their due and criticism as a call to arms. Miller responded with a public exhibition of defensiveness and incipient arrogance, two not unrelated qualities. In an essay called "Tragedy and the Common Man" published in the *Sunday New York Times* on February 27, 1949, he asserted in effect that his play deserved to be ranked with the greatest of all tragedies. He invoked Oedipus and Orestes and reminded his readers that these were also figures of modern psychiatry, "which bases its analysis upon classic formulations." The Oedipus and Orestes complexes, he argued, were perhaps "enacted by royal beings, but . . . apply to everyone in similar emotional situations."

Miller's logic is simpler than his exposition. What he means is that since everyday people can suffer from Oedipus or Orestes complexes, they can be tragic heroes just like Oedipus and Orestes. There is charm, if not substance, in the naivete of this argument. Miller had little experience with dramatic theory and even less with expository writing. "Tragedy and the Common Man" was his first professional attempt at writing an essay, and his knowledge of classical drama was limited to what he'd learned in college. It was ingenuous to relate the Oedipus and Orestes complexes to their Greek eponyms in any senses other than the incestuous and matricidal.

Greek tragedy aside, *Death of a Salesman,* he argued, is a true tragedy because it evokes "a higher order of feeling" than a simple heartbreaking story with its pathos. One needed to distinguish between sad or "pathetic" plays and his own "higher order" of tragedy, he said. "The essential difference, and the precise difference, is that tragedy brings us not only the 'sadness, sympathy and identification' of pathos but also fear, and 'knowledge or enlightenment.'" He also related the tragic hero to a "struggle . . . to achieve his humanity. The possibility of victory must be there in tragedy."

If these arguments are not based on classical principles, they are at least the playwright's own. Because the essay isn't clear and sounds pompous, however, it may well have set the stage for the hostility ahead—a lifetime's worth from the upper critical community, which was already primed. It was not wise for a high-minded playwright to commit the offense of commercial success.

Oddly enough the most self-serving statement in Miller's essay is also the most affecting.

> There are among us today, as there always have been, those who act against the scheme of things that degrades them. And in the process of action, everything we have accepted out of fear or insensitivity or ignorance is shaken before us and examined, and from this total onslaught by an individual against the seemingly stable cosmos surrounding us—from this total examination of the "unchangeable" environment—comes the terror and the fear that is classically associated with tragedy.

Here is Miller's activist creed, even if it has only a tenuous connection with high tragedy. Obviously in Arthur Miller's mind the play's idea is not only that attention must be paid to such tragedies as Willy Loman's but that something must be done to correct the situation. The play never gets around to saying just what that something is, to its credit; it simply suggests that we must come to our senses if we are to prevail over social problems.

This first experience with a public forum would initiate a second career as an essayist. Besides writing about his plays, Miller would also write essays about the financial state of the theater, nostalgic essays about his childhood, essays about politics, international affairs, even crime, anything that stimulated his wide-ranging interests. The *Theater Essays of Arthur Miller* runs to more than 500 pages and these are only his theater essays.

On March 27, 1949, a month after the *Times* piece, Miller again took up the unnecessary defense of his enormously successful and for the greater part warmly received play. This time his pulpit was the Sunday theater page of the *New York Herald-Tribune*, but the longer he went on, the less convincing he became. "You are witnessing a tragedy," he wrote, "when the characters before you are wholly and intensely realized, to the degree that your belief in their reality is all but complete." Such pontificating would become habitual and did not serve him well. Miller was a playwright by profession, an essayist only by way of ego, and his breast-beating had little chance of convincing the likes of Professor Harold Bloom, who wrote,

> Miller has a fondness for comparing *Death of a Salesman* to *King Lear*, a contrast that itself is catastrophic for Miller's play. Ibsen, at his strongest, can sustain some limited comparison to aspects of Shakespeare, but Miller can not. Like Lear, Willy Loman needs and wants more familial love than anyone can receive, but there the likeness ends.

Nevertheless Bloom conceded that *Salesman*'s "strength . . . is beyond dispute. . . . Whether it has the aesthetic dignity of tragedy is not clear, but no other American play is worthier of the term, despite," the incorrigible professor was compelled to add, Miller's "palpable literary and dramatic limitations."

In academic circles *Death of a Salesman* has generally been considered with the seriousness it deserves—and it certainly has been considered. According to the teaching guide of the Modern Language Association (an organization of English professors), *Death of a Salesman* is the American play "most studied at the university level." Indeed more than 400 books, articles and theses have been written about the play. Many of them deal with the difference between classical tragedy and the everyday heartbreaking variety, but that is not the only subject of disputation. Columbia professor Eric Bentley considers *Death of a Salesman* essentially flawed on the grounds that the genres of tragedy and social drama cancel each other out. Like Bloom Bentley forthrightly concedes the play's emotional power, but he also ventures into dangerous speculation when he writes, "We are told that Mr. Kazan was virtually co-author of . . . *Death of a Salesman*, even to the extent of changing the character of the leading person; it is arguable that [the play] would have failed without his changes."

Elia Kazan's contributions to *Salesman* were considerable, especially in translating written word into staged performance, but as to his work with the script, coauthorship is an extreme and unsupportable suggestion. While Bentley's credentials are eminent, "changing the character of the leading person" is rash and inaccurate. Kazan's advice to Miller was certainly strong and specific, and even involved contributing an occasional line of dialogue, but *Death of a Salesman* was virtually complete by the time Kazan saw Miller's script. For that matter the director nearly undid the play with his recommendation to simplify and consolidate the memory sequences. A more accurate characterization of Kazan's role in this regard is that of editor.

Academics also discuss Miller's rural imagery and Biff as a symbol of rural ideals. Chester E. Eisinger, in "American Dreams, American Nightmares," has written of a Miller who "romanticizes the rural-agrarian dream." A more radical analysis was expressed by John V. Hagopian in 1962 in *Insight One*, where he argued that Miller didn't understand his own play because Biff Loman "achieves the most transforming insight" in the play and is therefore its true protagonist. Miller had in fact toyed with this approach himself. Shortly after the *Salesman* premiere he said, "I am sorry the self-realization of the older son, Biff, is not a weightier counterbalance to Willy's disaster in the audience's mind." Only a few years later he encouraged the director of a regional production to follow through on this notion.

> There are two plays running concurrently here. In one . . . Biff is the protagonist and Willy the antagonist, just as every son and father are in some degree. . . . Biff, being more conscious of what is wrong with his inherited attitudes toward society, is consciously trying to adopt a new idea of his place in it. In this sense . . . he is more protagonistic, being more positive. Willy, being more guilty, takes all fault upon himself, actually, and hence cannot project any objective idea of society at all; it is simply that he failed and must compensate for failure in various personal, private ways.

The play has stubbornly resisted such interpretation. No matter how it is directed, *Death of a Salesman* is the great and awful tragedy of Willy Loman. As to questions of whether it is a classical tragedy or why Willy is a tragic figure, these remain academic issues, as fruitless to pursue as why something is funny.

Are there autobiographical elements in *Death of a Salesman*? As a playwright's fame and reputation grow, audiences and critics are inclined to speculate about personal references. In the case of *Death of a Salesman*, Miller said, "People thought that Willy was my father, and Linda my mother," but he knew otherwise. While never admitting how thoroughly Willy Loman was based on Manny Newman, Miller would describe his uncle as "completely wrongheaded" and a pathetic "drummer," a common salesman, as opposed to his father, who had been a manufacturer, not a salesman, not competitive and not unhinged. "Nobody," Miller said, "could be further from my father than Willy Loman." (It is the neighbor, Charley, who is based on Miller's father.) He is less convincing in his denial that Bernard, "the boy next door who got all these great marks in school [is] me." As proof, he has said that he himself had received terrible grades in high school, but this is hardly the point. Bernard, the young neighbor who outlasts and surpasses the childhood competition with the Loman sons to become a Supreme Court lawyer, certainly bears a relationship to the Artie Miller who outstripped Buddy and Abby Newman and became a famous playwright. Kazan even told the actor playing Bernard, "That's Arthur." Likewise the relationships among the three boys are much as Miller described his youthful experiences with the Newman brothers.

Finally there is the question of the Loman family's ethnicity. The play offers no clues, and if Arthur Miller's background weren't known, it is doubtful that the characters' very occasional Jewish locutions ("attention must be paid," for example) would even be noticed. In his public statements Miller avoided the question of the Loman family's Jewishness until writing in his autobiography that they are "Jews light years away from . . . a Jewish identity." This is supposed to mean that they are Jewish even though they are not particularly conscious of it and show no signs of it. By this reasoning the Lomans are Jews, but only the playwright knows it. Perhaps he learned it belatedly. When *Death of a Salesman* was written, just a few years after the end of the Second World War, ethnic pride was an American irony. Racial and religious bias was a national pastime. Germany may have been defeated and Hitler dead, but the Holocaust was still fresh and many Jews preferred to remain unobtrusive, while others were eager to assimilate into the larger Christian world. Jewish performers Anglicized their names and Jewish plays were thought to have limited appeal, as Miller himself had learned with *The Grass Still Grows*. That play and its antecedents amply demonstrated that Miller could *write Jewish* if so he chose. He chose not to in *Death of a Salesman*.

Decades after its premiere, on the occasion of a revival with Dustin Hoffman, Miller told the director Michael Rudman, "The family is Jewish, the parents came over from Russia or somewhere . . . Willy had married this Jewish girl, Linda, but they never talked about being Jewish." All through his life, however, Miller would remain evasive on the matter. As late as 1999 he told an interviewer,

> Nobody ever denied that the Lomans were Jewish . . . but ethnic particularity seems to me such an artificial limitation. Why doesn't Beckett write his characters with Irish accents the way Sean O'Casey does? I think a lot of these ethnic identities are a way of hiding a vacuous center.

Does it matter whether the Lomans are Jews? Harold Bloom was positive that "Willy Loman . . . is not supposed to be Jewish," yet he suggests that intentionally or not, Jewishness is in Willy Loman's bones.

> Something crucial in him is Jewish and the play does belong to that undefined entity we can call Jewish literature. . . . His tragedy makes sense only in the Freudian world of repression, which happens also to be the world of normative Jewish memory. . . . That cosmos informed by Jewish memory is the secret strength or permanent coherence of *Death of a Salesman*.

One month after the play opened a distressed Mildred Dunnock called on Kermit Bloomgarden. The producer was in an expansive state. "The production was in great shape," he remembered with pride. "Business was fabulous, the critics were calling the play an American masterpiece." All of that notwithstanding, Dunnock, who had gone through so much to be cast in the play and had received such glowing personal notices, asked to be released from her contract.

"You know I am not a complainer," she said, "but I just can't take it anymore. Every night during the first act, when Lee [Cobb] and I go off together to sit behind the kitchen and wait for our cues, he whispers, 'What are you doing in the theater? You don't belong here. Why don't you go back to school teaching?'"

The producer persuaded her to stay, asking for patience. "After tonight's show," he promised, "I'll have it out with Lee," and he did. The actor promptly stopped misbehaving, at least with Dunnock. "Instead," Bloomgarden said, "he started going after every other member of the company." The only actor Cobb couldn't rattle was Arthur Kennedy. "Johnny Kennedy was an ardent Red Sox fan," Bloomgarden remembered, "and he would listen to their ball games in his dressing room. Cobb would spring at him out of corners and bellow, 'What's a baseball fan doing in a play like this?'"

Kennedy's reply would be a simple, "Fuck off, Lee."

The producer felt that

> The most unfortunate thing about Lee was that he could have emerged the biggest actor in this country. But he was impatient. He would not tour with the show, and all he could think about was getting out when his contract expired and heading for the Hollywood loot, which ironically and sadly, I don't think he ever managed to get. He gave one of the great performances of the century in *Salesman*, but he was a disturbed and unhappy man. His presence was always "heavy"—there is no other way to describe it.

Miller did not see it quite so gloomily. Not long after the premiere of *Death of a Salesman* he told an interviewer,

> I think of Lee Cobb, the greatest dramatic actor I ever saw, when he was creating the role of Willy Loman in *Death of a Salesman*. When I hear people scoffing at actors as mere exhibitionists, when I hear them ask why there must be a theater if it cannot support itself as any business must, when I myself grow sick and weary of the endless waste and the many travesties of this most abused of all arts, I think then of Lee Cobb making that role and I know that the theater can yet be one of the chief glories of mankind.

8. Movies

The Chinese people have triumphed over their enemies, changed the face of their country and founded the People's Republic of China. We the 475 million Chinese people have now stood up and the future of our nation is infinitely bright.

—MAO ZEDONG, SEPTEMBER 30, 1949

BY EARLY 1949 ARTHUR MILLER'S involvement with left-wing causes was beginning to resemble a public ideological commitment, and it was a bad time for this to happen. As so many studies of the period have shown, communism was becoming an American obsession and apprehension a national state of mind. In the tense atmosphere of an invisible "cold" war in a fearful atomic age an opportunistic American conservative bloc was waging a parallel war on its liberal opposite, and riding high by identifying liberalism in the general mind with leftism, leftism with communism, and communism with the Soviet Union. The American Communist Party's secretive tactics only exacerbated a spreading atmosphere of fear and suspicion, while the Chinese Communist Party's imminent victory over Nationalist China threatened to make the international situation even more dangerous. Within a year Chairman Mao Zedong would vow "to drive the American forces out of Korea," lending substance to warnings of a monolithic, international communist conspiracy.

In this testy political environment and for several previous years Miller had been actively engaged in the broad range of liberal causes, from civil rights and racial integration to the American Communist Party's right to exist. This range had a serious leftward tilt. Miller had "attended a few meetings of Communist writers in living rooms" sponsored by the Communist Party. He lent his name as a sponsor of a World Youth Festival in Prague as well as to such organizations as the Joint Anti-Fascist Committee and signed a Civil Rights Congress statement decrying legislation against Communists. He applied for a study course on Marxism. He signed a letter disseminated by the Civil Rights Congress' Veterans against Discrimination urging that the Committee on Un-American Activities be abolished. He protested the Smith Act, which would have made it illegal to teach or advocate the overthrow of the American government by force, and that came close to actually outlawing the Communist Party.

Some of these programs, organizations and petitions were frankly communist and some were simply liberal, while others were sponsored by *fronts*, which was a suddenly familiar term drawn from the dummy organizations, or "popular fronts," of the Comintern (Communist International), the Soviet Union's branch for exporting communism. It had ostensibly been dissolved in 1943 to allay wartime Allied suspicions of Communist ambition and subversion. The war over, the Comintern and the suspicions returned.

There is no way of determining whether Miller could separate the innocently liberal organization from the communist front but one may surmise that he was aware of at least the possibility of hidden sponsorships. He surely knew the risks that came with his public statements and activities, but he was willing to take those risks when the causes seemed just, if only to demonstrate that he had the right to hold opinions, sign petitions and go to meetings. To be a member of the Communist Party was not illegal, although it might as well have been.

Even for someone such as Arthur Miller, who'd had many contacts with Communists, it was probably difficult at times to tell whether an organization or a petition was or was not sponsored by the party. To some extent the times had forced it underground, but the underground was also home territory, given its traditional tactics of infiltration and subterfuge. Sometimes an individual's membership was even kept secret from other Communists outside a cell group, and in special cases party enrollment records were actually expunged to protect the member. Such special treatment accorded "members at large" was reserved for influential celebrities or, as Elia Kazan would later call them, "glamour intellectuals, elevated to the supreme status, membership without cards." Clifford Odets had such a status and so, Kazan suspected, did Lillian Hellman. He even implied through contrived understatement ("I didn't believe he'd been a Communist; he knew I had") that Arthur Miller may have been in this category as well. Whether or not Miller ever joined the party would never be certain, although there is some reason to suspect that he had. His friend Norman Rosten, who had enrolled when they were students at the University of Michigan, would only say, "Nothing was proved."

It hardly made a difference, for outside of political rhetoric, official "card carrying" membership seems to have been more significant to the Communists than to their hunters. The House Committee on Un-American Activities treated present and former party members alike, making the same demand that they admit membership and then renounce it. The Federal Bureau of Investigation was drawing few distinctions between party members, sympathizers, leftists and liberals. An FBI informer was already monitoring some of Miller's activities, such as the meetings with his weekly "discussion group," which involved some twenty writers. The group was looking, Miller said, "for ways to combat the rising hysteria in the country, the spreading fear of uttering any opinion that could be remotely interpreted as left, or even liberal, let alone pro-Soviet." Nor was he the only famous writer in the group. Other participants were Edgar Snow, the celebrated journalist and editor who had been the first westerner to interview Mao Zedong, and the novelist John Hersey, who "wasn't a communist," his then-wife Frances Ann remembered, "but then you didn't know who was a communist and who wasn't."

The FBI on at least one occasion also assigned agents to spy on Miller's house. After one dinner party the guests were followed home, their names and addresses reported to the bureau. He only learned about this surveillance decades later, through the United States Freedom of Information Act. Miller declined to release those FBI records. They are to become available to the public after his death.

The most public of Arthur Miller's leftist activities was a Cultural and Scientific Conference for World Peace scheduled for spring 1949 at New York's Waldorf-Astoria Hotel. Its sponsors included Albert Einstein and Eleanor Roosevelt. Among the participants were scientists, educators, composers and writers. Jim Proctor, the press agent for *Death of a Salesman,* was one of its organizers and he seems to have had little trouble convincing Miller to chair a panel on the fine arts.

The intention of the peace conference—innocent and perhaps naive—was the easing of growing tension between the world's two atomic powers. This was to be accomplished through civilized discourse by well-intentioned intellectuals. The conference was going to involve meetings and conversations among, as Miller put it, "the piano players, composers, playwrights and anthropologists [who] could appeal over the bureaucracies' heads for common sense." In a period when even the word *peace* had sinister (literally leftist) connotations, participation in such an affair all but guaranteed personal trouble. Miller has said that he was well aware of this but refused to be intimidated.

As the date of the two-day conference approached, the event was sensationalized in the press, and when the sessions finally began on March 25, 1949, the Waldorf-Astoria's entrance on Park Avenue became a setting for raucous demonstrations. While the police separated the competing persuasions (including a picket line of nuns), inside Miller was chairing a panel discussion by Dmitri Shostakovich, Aaron Copland, Clifford Odets and Olin Downes, the music critic for the *New York Times*. Lillian Hellman delivered a prepared speech to an audience that included Mark Van Doren and Norman Mailer as well as various liberals, progressives, left-wingers, Socialists,

Leninites, Trotskyites and assorted unaffiliated anti–anti-Communists. There were some 150 of these "delegates" at the Waldorf, including a cluster from the Soviet Union.

At the same time a counterconference for anticommunist intellectuals was organized by the social philosopher Sidney Hook. He had the cooperation of liberals who distrusted communism generally, for instance, the historian Arthur Schlesinger, Jr. and James Wechsler, the executive editor of the *New York Post*. Yet there was no escaping the red brush, not even by what one conservative journalist sarcastically called "other guardians of American liberalism, like Mary McCarthy and Dwight MacDonald [who] went to sessions of the conference in order to disrupt them," and disrupt them they did. One of the delegates, Madeleine Gilford, found herself barred from the hall just as Miller was starting his session. "There was a crowd of us locked out purposely on a stairway. Jack [Gilford, her husband] entertained them."

A week later *Life* Magazine published two full pages of postage stamp–size photographs identifying many who attended, a rogues' gallery of leftists. The magazine and its sister publication, *Time* Magazine, were known for an anticommunist bias, particularly since the rise of Red China. This editorial policy was presumably implemented at the behest of the *Time-Life* founder and chairman Henry Luce, who had been raised in Nationalist China by missionary parents.

As echoes of the Waldorf conference faded, Miller turned to another cause, that of his Brooklyn Heights neighbor, the Reverend William Howard Melish, whose Episcopal Holy Trinity Church was on Pierrepont Street. A few years earlier Melish had inherited the rectorship of this free church (no pew rent) from his father and proceeded to expand on its liberal traditions. A friend of Dr. W. E. Burghardt DuBois—who considered him "one of the few Christian clergymen for whom I have the highest respect"—Melish integrated the church's popular social functions and began to actively court Brooklyn Heights's growing black and immigrant population. DuBois, who also lived there, said, "It was not a large church but it was doing the best work among the young and foreign born of any institution in Brooklyn."

The Reverend Melish had strong ties with the Soviet Union. During the war he had been active in Russian War Relief. "He had become," Miller later wrote (as if he himself weren't), "a rather naive believer in the goodness of Soviet aims." Now the minister had antagonized his conservative superiors in the Episcopal Church by joining and becoming an officer of the National Council of American-Soviet Friendship, a high entry on the attorney general's list of subversive organizations. Under church pressure Melish was forced to quit that post, but he refused to resign from the organization itself, and for that he was charged with insubordination by the Bishop of Long Island, the Rt. Rev. James P. DeWolfe. Melish was then dismissed from his ministry.

He took the case to civil court, challenging the bishop's right to expel him for such a reason. Miller attended that trial, which he found prejudicial from the outset, when the judge barred evidence indicating that two-thirds of the Holy Trinity congregation had voted their support of Melish. "I tell you friend," he wrote to Kazan, who'd gone to Louisiana to film *Panic in the Streets*, "they will hang us all without so much as raising the voice. We have to be proving how anti-Communist we are every waking minute."

In New Orleans Kazan didn't appear concerned. Every morning he would show up at the movie location with a copy of *The Daily Worker* rolled up under his arm. Virginia Bloomgarden, visiting the site with Kermit, took the party newspaper to be no more than a prop, an affectation like wearing dungarees (as blue jeans then were called) to rehearsal to look like a proletarian. Miller had a more compelling sense of moral indignation and obviously needed to verbalize it. The Melish trial, he wrote Kazan, hit bottom when Bishop DeWolfe "lied outright, underhandedly, partly, almost, just about and then completely, as the occasion warranted," but notwithstanding DeWolfe, it was the judge who outraged him most,

> this Liberal jurist, this piss, has the effrontery to turn to old man Melish, who is 74 years of age and has never hesitated to place his "good name" in jeopardy, wherever justice was involved—this closely shaven hypocrite turns to the old man and says, "We have fought together many times for the good things, Dr. Melish, but now I must rule that your tenure as pastor of the parish is at an end."

Melish testified, "I believe it is not only the right but the duty of a Christian minister to consort with atheists, communists and anyone else who has or may have a humane concept for the running of this world." In the end, though, the judge ruled that on the basis of Canon law, Bishop DeWolfe had an absolute right of dismissal. A livid Miller wrote Kazan that the very bishop who in 1908 had formulated this particular item of Canon law had deposed that "he intended no such right as was being used in this case. Which will give you an idea how political men, for political reasons, induced by hysteria and hate, can twist even the 'sacred' things." And so, as W. E. B. DuBois would recall, Melish "lost his church, had his life work ruined, the church itself closed."

Soon afterward Arthur Miller spoke at a testimonial dinner honoring Reverend Melish given by the National Council of American-Soviet Friendship at the New York City Center. He began with the rather curious remark, "The concept of intellectual honesty does not apply when peace is at stake." Then he added, "I suggest to the FBI [and] I suggest to the powers diabolically leading our nation to fascism, that they should not be inquiring into what he is doing but why he is doing it." In Miller's autobiography he remembers that at the time of the Melish trial he "could only conclude that the country was intending to become a philosophical monolith where no real difference about anything important could be tolerated." He does not mention that several years later Melish chaired a dinner on behalf of this selfsame National Council of American-Soviet Friendship for the presentation of the 1953 Stalin Peace Prize to the Communist writer Howard Fast, with the participation of the previous year's recipient, Paul Robeson, another party member. Afterward Frank and Nan Taylor gave a cocktail party in their town house on West Fourth Street near Bleecker Street in Greenwich Village. As entertainment, Huddie Ledbetter, the celebrated folk singer known as Leadbelly, played the guitar and sang his signature songs, "The Rock Island Line," "Midnight Special" and "Good Night, Irene." The fabulous Robeson—a lawyer, professional football player, an operatic bass and acclaimed Shakespearean actor—loomed above the gathering with his booming voice and six feet five inches of robust height. "His wife," Nan Taylor remembered, "was a tall black woman, very handsome, wearing a turban" as well as, according to John Hersey's wife, Frances Ann, "more diamonds than anyone in the whole world."

Yet Miller held center stage. Success had given him new social confidence. The legend of *Death of a Salesman* and its sobbing audiences had carried his reputation across the country and it continued to grow. Nan Taylor recalled that even in a room with the magnificently gifted and bigger than life Robeson, it was Arthur Miller who "was the one with the social magnetism." His wife, Mary, never an extrovert, began to fade into his background, "meek," Nan Taylor observed, "beside him."

With such a reputation and the assurance it engendered Arthur Miller indulged his idealism, and whether or not he was a member of the party, that idealism was genuine. His willingness, eagerness and determination to express leftist opinions in so threatening a political atmosphere was certainly bold, even granting the privilege that his prestige allowed. Miller cared deeply, as is strikingly clear in his correspondences with Kazan, and if his expressions of conviction sometimes seem misguided or ingenuous, such are the handmaidens of earnestness. To scoff is certainly easier and safer than to endorse. Miller not only expressed his beliefs, he acted on them; it was the very reason that in liberal circles and even wider ones he was becoming an icon of moral probity.

Despite all the political activities, Miller did have time for work, and he was working on three projects at once. There was the endlessly gestating *Plenty Good Times*, his "contemporary play about a young man, set in New York," and a screenplay based on his waterfront research. There was also the last piece begun but the first to reach fruition, an adaptation of Ibsen's 1882 play *An Enemy of the People*. It may have looked like a way of bypassing the intimidating challenge of writing the play after *Death of a Salesman*, but in truth Miller was having domestic problems that were "making it impossible for me to go ahead with my own play until we move back into the city."

The problem was an infidelity that does not seem to have occurred. He confessed to merely temptation, telling Mary that he met a woman whom he very much desired. The marriage, he assured her, was essential to him and he had absolutely no intention of risking it. Mary flew into a rage that would not go away. She became generally suspicious and distrusting. Now they were spending the summer in the Connecticut house and he told Kazan it was "inadvisable, if you know what I mean, to leave the farm alone—there being more important things than starting a new play [namely] to stay close to home." Between the lines was couched a message—Kazan called it a "coded" message—about Miller's married life and the frustrations of monogamy. And so with three weeks remaining until school started for the children, Arthur, Mary, Jane and Robert remained in the country. Since research for a new play had to wait ("it's impossible for me to go ahead with my own play until we move back into the city") he used the time to finish the Ibsen adaptation "by working all day, every day" and completed it by Labor Day.

Ibsen had written *An Enemy of the People* just after *A Doll's House* and *Ghosts*. The play is typical of his middle period of social realism. Miller has said that his adaptation was suggested by another alumnus of the Group Theatre, director Bobby Lewis, who felt that Ibsen's theme was uncannily applicable to the current oppressive political climate. In that same letter to Kazan Miller more than agreed about the relevance. "My main interest in it," he confided to his brotherly friend, "is that through the guise of Ibsen—*ssssssh!*—I have managed to say things I wouldn't dare say alone."

Ibsen's own point, as George Bernard Shaw put it, was that

> Feeling the disadvantage of appearing in their true character as a conspiracy of interested rogues against an honest man [townspeople] pose as Society, as the People, as Democracy. . . . In attacking them [the protagonist] is thereby made an enemy of The People, a danger to Society, a traitor to Democracy.

If respecting the majority will is a basic principle of democracy, Shaw perceived *An Enemy of the People* as an admirable attack on that tenet, at least in regard to progress. The majority, Shaw wrote in *The Quintessence of Ibsenism*, tends to be conservative in that it resists change; it "is always wrong in its opinion of new developments [while] the pioneer is a tiny minority." Miller's adaptation took a more defensive position because in 1950 America's leftist minority was cast as the enemy of the American people. So he put Ibsen's central theme as "the question of whether the democratic guarantees protecting political minorities ought to be set aside in time of crisis." That, Miller wrote in the preface to his published adaptation, is also "the central theme of our social life today."

The play had another relevance for him. Miller found the problems of Reverend William Howard Melish to be "almost amazingly duplicated, down to a certain muddleheaded stubbornness in the main characters." *An Enemy of the People* also had personal resonances for Fredric March and his wife, Florence Eldridge. They were suing *Counterattack*, one of the self-appointed "watchdog" newsletters, for branding them as fellow travelers, or party sympathizers. Industry blacklists commonly fed off such unofficial sources and the couple had already lost work because of the accusation.

March told Miller that he and his wife were "interested in some response to the crucifying of left wingers." Also, the actor had already agreed to star in the movie version of *Death of a Salesman* and now, perhaps kicking himself for having missed the chance to create Willy Loman on the stage, he was eager for a second chance at an Arthur Miller play. Well rested after a long ocean voyage, he and Eldridge agreed to portray Dr. and Mrs. Stockmann in Miller's adaptation.

It hardly had commercial promise (and would do much better as the essential plot of *Jaws*) but a production of the play was personally important to Lars Nordenson, the young Scandinavian businessman who planned to finance it entirely himself. Nordenson, actually a Swede, even provided a dry, literal translation from the Norwegian original so that Miller would not be hampered by distortions in the available English versions. This gave the project added value, for in America, unlike England, translations of plays were too seldom written by the professional playwrights most appropriate to the task.

Arthur Miller's adaptation of *An Enemy of the People* is set, like Ibsen's play, in a Norwegian town where Dr. Thomas Stockmann is the medical officer of a newly built health spa that has set off a boom in local tourism. As the play begins, a chemical analysis that the doctor ordered has proven that the curative waters are contaminated by industrial pollution. The doctor's friends hail this discovery and he expects the town to do the same, closing the spa until it is made safe. Instead his brother, who happens to be the mayor, suggests that the scientific analysis may be unreliable. Moreover, he objects to Stockmann's proposed reconstruction of the entire water system. Aside from the expense and the delay, the mayor fears that "as soon as the rumor gets around that the water is dangerous, we won't have a visitor left." In short he intends to bury the laboratory report and demands that his brother disavow it. Refusing, Dr. Stockmann spells out Miller's second point—the contaminated waters as a metaphor for the capitalistic system—"We are getting fat by peddling filth and corruption to innocent people!"

In the next act the editor of the village's radical newspaper is planning to print Stockmann's exposé of the scandal, a story that will "put in a liberal administration once and for all." Yet when the mayor stops by and sees the article, he questions its facts, calling the story "the mad dream of a man who is trying to blow up our way of life!" The editor and his publisher are so intimidated that they join the forces of cover-up, and so Stockmann prepares to present the facts directly to the townspeople only to be undercut by his brother, who feeds the fears of lost tourism. The mayor's speech—thoroughly of Miller's invention—leaves little doubt that the American political climate is being addressed.

> God knows, in ordinary times I'd agree a hundred per cent with anybody's right to say anything. But these are not ordinary times . . . there are ruins of towns all over the world, and they were wrecked by people who, in the guise

> of reform, and pleading for justice, and so on, broke down all authority and left only revolution and chaos.

Dr. Stockmann then tries to read the laboratory report aloud only to be shouted down, and so he decries democracy as mob rule. "The majority is always wrong!" is the watchcry Ibsen gave him, a watchcry immediately reconsidered by the ever-equivocating, always reform-minded Miller. That is, Stockmann qualifies, "The majority is never right until it does right." So he is declared an enemy of the people.

As the third act begins, the doctor is being evicted from his home. He is offered various compromises, rejecting them all as offensive to his integrity, but at the end he won't flee. Instead he says he will start a school where "we'll turn out not taxpayers and newspaper subscribers but free and independent people, hungry for the truth."

The differences between adaptation and original are considerable, and some are improvements. Miller indeed succeeds in his intention to "transform [the] language into contemporary English." He also trimmed away considerable excess, consolidating Ibsen's five acts into three. He deleted many long and repetitious speeches, most notably Stockmann's racist remarks urging an aristocracy of the biologically brainier. In the play's preface Miller admits to eliminating this speech about "individuals bred to a superior apprehension of truths . . . and who have the natural right to lead," but he defends both the deletion and the original Ibsen by arguing that the play itself contradicts this statement. Besides, he adds in the preface, "Ibsen never really believed that idea," because some time after writing the play he spoke of an aristocracy of not birth or intellect but "an aristocracy of character, of will, of mind." This argument is not only specious but, some say, indicates a misinterpretation of the play. "Devastating" is what Professor Benjamin Nelson of Fairleigh Dickinson University calls Miller's "misreading of Ibsen, for he has done nothing less than interpret a polemic comedy as a glowering tragedy." Nelson concedes that Miller "closely" followed the plot, gave it "snappier" dialogue and made the action "more continuous and cohesive," but, the professor adds,

> Ibsen viewed his protagonist as both heroic rebel and fool. Missing this tantalizingly ambivalent attitude, Miller saw him essentially as the former, the individualist claiming his inviolable dignity in the face of adversity [and] allowed his unwaveringly solemn admiration to tip the play over into a loud and heavy-handed defense of everything for which his hero stands.

Despite such criticism, the Miller version has actually been included in some anthologies as a legitimate English translation. This is a disservice to not only Henrik Ibsen but also Arthur Miller, for besides being undistinguished and of dubious fidelity, the adaptation is only a blip on his artistic screen.

When the Ibsen-Miller *Enemy of the People* opened in New York on December 28, 1950, at the Broadhurst Theatre, it fared very well with the daily reviewers, who may have still been under the *Salesman* spell. The production was first class, with settings and lighting designed by the celebrated Aline Bernstein, whose turbulent, five-year extramarital affair with Thomas Wolfe had made tabloid headlines some twenty years earlier. In the *New York Times* Brooks Atkinson wrote, "You can hardly escape the power and excitement of a bold drama audaciously let loose in the theater by actors and stage people who are not afraid of their strength . . . Papa Ibsen was discharging thunderbolts in all directions. Mr. Miller has abetted him ably." The other notices were similarly enthusiastic, but Ibsen would always be a tough sell on Broadway and there was no convincing the public. The production closed after only thirty-six performances.

There are two ways of looking at this hybrid: As Henrik Ibsen's play, with the question, how faithful is the adaptation? or as Miller's play, with the question, how different is it from the original? The answer to the former is too faithful, the latter, too different. Stockmann's lectures violate Miller's stated principle of "never [letting characters] become aware of the play they are in." Instead these speeches are just what Thomas Mann had meant ("If a European had written the play, there would have been a discussion of the theme by the characters"). By combining the contributions of two great playwrights, *An Enemy of the People* only blurs their distinctions and subverts their separate artistries. It might be added that just the reverse was the opinion of director David Thacker who, through the 1980s and 1990s, staged almost all of Miller's plays in London. Having given this adaptation one of its rare revivals, Thacker considered it a

> fantastic marriage between Ibsen and Miller, two great playwrights shaking hands over the century. . . . This collaboration results in a play that couldn't have been written by either playwright individually. It starts very much like an Ibsen play and then progresses through the middle acts, where Arthur Miller rewrites most in the big public speech, and then it becomes more like a Miller. "The majority is never right until it does right." That is a fundamental Arthur Miller thought.

One of Arthur Miller's last thoughts on the subject of this play seemed to be about himself as well and his relationship to organized communism. Henrik Ibsen, he wrote in his preface to the adaptation, "was an individualist sometimes to the point of anarchism, and in such a man there is too explosive a need for self-expression to permit him to conform to any rigid ideology." This can be fairly taken as Miller's own attitude in February 1951 toward communist doctrine and its demands for unquestioning ideological conformity. By that time he would seem to have become disenchanted with organized communism and its party line.

With the play after *Salesman* out of the way Arthur Miller turned to getting his waterfront screenplay produced. He had been writing it on and off for two years. Random jottings in his notebooks reveal the drifts of his mind as he worked.

> I cannot quite believe that there ever was a playwright who did not really know it when he had written a good play or a bad one.
>
> A work of art is not finished, it is abandoned.
>
> Rule: the whole is written from point of view of the climax.
>
> If any of you have met an heroic person you know that there is no more gloomy and impossible human being.

And he was still writing poetry.

> *The wreckage of old buildings is not gay*
> *But their presence is unprofitable*
> *There we go from building to decay*
> *Trapped in memory's swaying stair.*

It was 1948 when he had been first struck by the suspicious disappearance of a Brooklyn longshoreman who had defied the corrupt, gangster-ridden International Longshoremen's Association. Back then, on November 26, Malcolm Johnson, an investigative reporter for the *New York Sun,* had started to write what would become a twenty-four-part, Pulitzer Prize–winning series of articles exposing "Crime on the Waterfront." Two days after the series began the union struck against its own president. He was Joseph Patrick Ryan, "the burly, barrel chested, 'lifetime' president of the ILA," Johnson wrote, who had negotiated a sweetheart contract with the shipowners.

Ryan had categorically denied graft and corruption in his union, insisting, as Johnson put it, that "there just wasn't any crime on the waterfront, no gangsterism or rackets in the ILA." In Ryan's own words he defied "anybody to prove there's any kickback in our organization. I don't care who says so and they have been saying it for years. . . . It's never been proved."

The rank and file won that strike against him, no little thanks to Johnson's articles that the following year were published in book form as *Crime on the Labor Front*. In one chapter Johnson described the waterfront "shape-up" as

> an archaic and degrading hoax—it leaves the hiring of dock workers entirely up to the union and opens up the gates wide for every type of racket and malpractice. At a designated hour, the longshoremen gather in a semi-circle at the entrance of the pier . . . As they stand there . . . their eyes are fastened on the hiring stevedore [representative of the unloading contractor]. At this crucial

> moment he possesses the power of economic life or death over them, and the men know it . . . they know that the hiring boss, a union man like themselves, can accept or reject them at will . . . under the terror of the shape-up, the longshoremen have learned from bitter experience to bow to the system.

Here was ritual drama in real life, a daily work event that was visual as well as meaningful—the kind of thing that must have stimulated Miller during his walking tours of the Red Hook waterfront adjacent to his Brooklyn Heights neighborhood. This is where he had begun the research, with the apparent murder of one courageous longshoreman, which in Miller's creative imagination provided an issue, a milieu, a story situation and a hero. He quickly learned that this longshoreman's immediate threat had been the head of the Brooklyn union local, a man named Anthony Anastasia, the brother of a major New York mobster. So he had a villain too.

Deciding that the material would best suit a movie, Miller began with a theme and a title. The theme, he wrote in his notebook, was

> the strange, mysterious and dangerous thing—the genuinely moral man. He is one with all the others, has received no more than they, but feels it more. Why? This is the story. It's as though a hand had been laid upon him, making him the rebel, pressing him toward a collision with everything that is established and accepted. And a point arrives when he realizes that it is no longer his choice to press on.

A genuinely moral man was the way Miller saw himself. He would repeatedly write in letters that "a hand had been laid" upon him, as if he had been chosen by destiny. His mother even spoke of him as "God's chosen."

His title for the screenplay was *The Hook,* referring to both the Red Hook section of Brooklyn and the longshoreman's ever-present baling hook, or *gaff,* the macho symbol of his occupation. Miller used this hook in his script's opening screen direction. It was sticking "out of the slanted breast pocket" of his longshoreman hero's "waist-length woolen jacket."

The first draft of *The Hook* was finished by May 1949, when Miller told an interviewer for the *New York Herald-Tribune,* "This is a subject which I didn't think could be properly covered in the stage medium. In the credits I am frankly going to call it 'a play written for the screen by Arthur Miller.'" He added that he, Kazan and Kermit Bloomgarden were "in the process of forming an independent company to produce it locally." Perhaps they sensed that its subject matter might prove too risky for a Hollywood studio. Bloomgarden even had his attorney draw up the papers for a partnership, but a year later Kazan felt differently. *Panic in the Streets* was finished and he was about to start the movie version of *A Streetcar Named Desire*. He needn't forego Hollywood's professionalism, distribution networks or money. Talent wasn't his only talent. Kazan was a master of arrangements and careerism. He had won every important stage and screen award. His work was hailed by critics and audiences, and it showed a respectable profit. His involvement with a play could guarantee a production and he had a six picture, nonexclusive contract with Twentieth Century-Fox studios. Some said it was the richest directing contract in Hollywood. Kazan could direct and produce virtually any play or movie he chose. He had been offered the new Tennessee Williams play *The Rose Tattoo* but turned it down to make *The Hook*—and he decided to make it for a major studio. Departing for Los Angeles and the filming of *Streetcar*, he left Arthur with the assignment of giving the screenplay one more rewrite.

The story's central character is the thirtyish longshoreman, Marty Ferrara, and in the opening scene he is joining a group of men who gather on a Brooklyn pier for the daily shape-up. With the screech of a whistle the hiring boss appears, and as the men gather around, he distributes brass checks to the chosen few who will work that day. When two of the checks go unclaimed, the boss tosses them into the air, to enjoy the scramble for them by the remaining "shape." A disgusted Marty Ferrara mutters, "Wonderful thing about the waterfront; a little mouse comes down here and he turns into a rat."

The work of unloading a ship proceeds, pushed to a frantic pace by Louis, the president of the union local, a man who—besides having gangster connections—is openly friendly with "the owner of the stevedoring company occupying this pier." Suddenly there is a jolting crash as a load of steel bars is dropped from a crane—a fatal accident, caused by the reckless work pace. Marty, frustrated by his inability to do anything about this, can only "puke into the river" while the men are ordered back to work. That evening he is still angry, *helplessly so*, according to a screen direction, and tells his wife, Therese, "They ain't gonna make no cattle outa me no more!"

Furious about the savage shape-up, the unsafe working conditions and the union local president's brazen selling of union memberships, Ferrara tries to quit the docks; but in a quiet scene set in a local playground he sits on a children's swing while telling Therese that although the situation on the waterfront is bad, "it's my trade, Terry, I like the ships." Yet he is also vaguely aware of having greater potential. "If I could [only] get some kinda job where I could show myself," he says, but instead he feels a failure. "My job on a ship, that's me, and look where I am." A typical Miller protagonist, he knows what is wrong but has difficulty acting on it and tells his wife, "I like it . . . and I hate it . . . I don't know what to do. [But] if I go back on them ships I start a revolution."

Marty tries working as a bookie for a racketeer relative but is guilt-ridden for taking money from needy workingmen. So he goes back to unloading ships until learning that some of the men are being cheated of legitimate overtime pay. That finally spurs him to action and he calls for a work stoppage. "I'm not askin' you to stand up for me," he tells the men. "Just stand up for yourselfs, that's all. Be human bein's for five more minutes," but they haven't the nerve and so he *goes down the gangplank, walks onto the pier. He walks down the length of the pier and out into the street through the tall wide doorway.*

Ferrara nearly gives up on reform until being convinced to make a speech at the next local meeting. "That's gonna make Louis very mad," he fears. "This afternoon I didn't even have no five guys stan' behind me." Besides, he "don't wanna be no leader." On the other hand, he says—Miller vacillating yet again—"I *wanna* be a leader so I can make a good life on these piers."

The union meeting, when it takes place, is not unlike the town meeting in *An Enemy of the People*. In this case it is Marty who is being called the enemy of the people—a "traitor"—by the local president, who reminds the men that "we got a contract with the shipowners and we gotta live up to that contract." Out of the crowd someone cries, "It's a fink contract! You ain't on our side. You're on the shipowners' side!" but strong-arms, or goons (Miller calls them *goofs*), materialize and the union men are intimidated. When the president of the local demands Marty's "book" (the union credentials that allow him to work), he leaps onto the speaker's platform and cries,

> These finks . . . they scared of us. . . . The kids used to say, "Go down the piers and you'll see the real big rats. The tough guys." I never seen no big rats on the waterfront. I only found little scared rats . . . [and] I seen rats kicked around on the ships . . . killed on the ships. So I says to myself, these ain't rats, these is little mouses. Only tonight, *We got big rats in the house tonight!* . . . If this fink can take from me my bread and butter, then I'm a slave in a chain! I was born in Italy [but] *this* is fascism!

He kisses his workbook and tosses it into the crowd. He is promptly suspended from the union, even turned away when he tries to work on the New Jersey waterfront. Now he is so poor that the electricity is turned off at home, the soles are coming off his shoes, he's picking up cigarette butts from the gutter, he is even stealing from drunks—yes, to buy jugs of cheap wine.

The ultimate humiliation that turns his life around is the repossession of his sofa and television set. With that Ferrara marches down to the local office and signs up to challenge Louis for the presidency. The turnout for the election is huge, and after Ferrara makes a courageous speech (*all heart,* Miller indicates, *with driving sense of rightness and hope*) the men vote. Louis takes no chances and counts the ballots personally, declaring himself the winner and locking the ballot box in a safe. A few hours later Marty and his work crew break into the union office, crack open the safe and count the votes themselves. By that time their sit-in has attracted a crowd of longshoremen. Then "Jack Uptown," the top union boss, arrives with his goon squad, only they aren't needed, for Louis really did win the election. The men were too fearful for their jobs to vote against the union–shipowner–stevedore company power structure. Marty himself is bought off with a soft, high-paying job as a "union delegate" and is seemingly pacified until the closing shape-up, when he grabs one of the brass work checks and shouts, "Don't dive for this! You ain't no cattle!"

It makes for an ambivalent ending, notwithstanding the final screen direction, *we pull back amid the shouting and confusion and flying arms of a first class riot, with shouts of joy and release coming from the [work] gang and the unmanageable soul of the brand new Delegate*. Ambivalence, however, was not what Elia Kazan looked for in finales. This was only one of his concerns about the much-revised—"half-ass" was his polite estimate—script.

In January 1951 Arthur and Elia boarded the 20th Century Limited at Grand Central Station and rode it to Chicago, where they changed trains for the Santa Fe Super Chief ("the rolling boudoir of Hollywood celebrities") on the way to Los Angeles. They were off to sell *The Hook*, along with a secondary purpose evidently in Kazan's mind. The manipulative director was ready to introduce his serious-minded young friend to the ways and byways of Hollywood, certain that Art Miller was "starved for sexual release."

Kazan had arranged a setting that could not have been more libidinous: a playboy club before Playboy Clubs, from a heated swimming pool and a collection of modern art to a nightly parade of beautiful young starlets streaming unaccompanied through the front door, implicitly available to the regular crowd of middle-aged movie men. The women were even instructed to arrive singly and in their own cars so as not to burden the gentlemen with such tiresome responsibilities as seeing them home.

The site of this midlife playpen was 2000 Coldwater Canyon Drive in Beverly Hills, the lavish home of Charles Feldman, a major Hollywood agent and the producer of Kazan's *Streetcar* movie. Elia had been Feldman's houseguest during the final weeks of editing the picture and had become familiar with his host's Sybaritic hospitalities. Molly and the children were 3,000 miles away and he was well in step with life in the movie colony. Only six months earlier he had been at the number-one table for the flashiest event of the 1950 Hollywood social year, a Meet the Oliviers party given at the Beverly Hills Hotel by Danny Kaye for 170 of the biggest names in the movie world. Kaye's wife, Sylvia Fine, had dictated that every couple be seated apart, designating herself as Laurence Olivier's dinner partner. Yet it was not Kaye but Kazan who was paired with Olivier's wife, Vivian Leigh, and he for one was not thrilled about the evening. The exquisite but exhausted Leigh had just left the London production of *Streetcar* to make the movie. Kazan would have preferred that she conserve her energy instead of dancing all night, but at least her exhaustion would be diverted to powerful screen effect. Leigh paid a terrible emotional price for her magnificent performance in the form of a nervous breakdown, but by then Kazan was on to another movie.

Marilyn Monroe was at that glamorous party too, although not as one of its stars. She was just another studio contract player, one in a crowd of such young women struggling for a break in the movies. She came as the date of her agent and lover, Johnny Hyde, the partner of Kazan's own agent, Abe Lastfogel. That was why Elia had met her before and now he noticed her again, there at the Olivier party, sitting, in his odd description, "at Johnny Hyde's side, like a frozen image." Monroe noticed him too and told a friend that she was interested in getting to know him. Elia Kazan was the hottest director in Hollywood. She was making little progress, moving from one minor role to another. He was about to cast his next picture, *Viva Zapata!*

There are many accounts of how Arthur Miller and Marilyn Monroe met, but the only actual witness to the event was Kazan. Monroe never described the encounter but both men put themselves at the center of it in their autobiographies, which were written some thirty years later. Miller gave his only interview for a Monroe biography in 1968 and that was as a favor for Frank Taylor, his old friend and Mary's former boss. Taylor had become an editor at McGraw-Hill and engaged Fred Lawrence Guiles to write *Norma Jean: The Life of Marilyn Monroe*. Even this account of that first meeting is something short of vivid since Miller, given editorial control by Taylor (not only of his own interviews but of the entire book), "couldn't remember the specific details." Presumably he had a better memory when he wrote his autobiography some twenty years later.

As for Kazan, he declined to be interviewed for the Guiles biography but a few years earlier had cooperated with one by Maurice Zolotow, probably because Zolotow's brother, Sam, was a powerful theater columnist for the *New York Times*. Kazan's recollection at that time was that he and Miller had been introduced to Monroe on the Twentieth Century-Fox lot by Cameron Mitchell, the actor who played Happy in *Death of a Salesman*. Kazan told quite a different story in his own life story published in 1988—not coincidentally a year after Miller's. There Cameron Mitchell isn't even mentioned.

While these competing versions cannot be reconciled, they nonetheless suggest the dubious credibility of autobiographies. More interesting is how jealously these two men of achievement guarded their experiences with the great American sex symbol of the twenieth century, reserving her for the stories of their own lives and putting themselves at the center of hers.

Despite the shortage of unbiased information regarding their first meeting, the overall facts of the introduction to Monroe have emerged, at least as many as might reasonably pertain here. On the trip west to sell *The Hook* both Kazan and Miller were invited to stay at Charles Feldman's home. The agent was out of town but the nightly partying continued—the stocked bar, lavish buffet tables, male regulars and the assembly line of single women. In this atmosphere Arthur Miller set up a worktable and typewriter near the swimming pool and continued to rewrite his script, for Kazan was still unhappy with it. Meanwhile there was the matter of selling the picture.

The first studio on Kazan's list was his home base, Twentieth Century-Fox. Lastfogel accompanied Kazan and Miller to an appointment with the studio chief, Darryl Zanuck. He had already read *The Hook* and peremptorily rejected it, Kazan recalled, simply because of its "subject matter." Lastfogel then left to try Warner Bros., a studio already excited about its imminent release of *A Streetcar Named Desire*. Kazan meanwhile remained behind with Miller, telling him that as long as they were at Twentieth Century-Fox, he wanted to look in on Harmon Jones, his former film editor, now directing a picture called *As Young As You Feel*. He seems, however, to have had an ulterior motive. Marilyn Monroe was playing a small part in that picture and Kazan knew that Lastfogel's partner—her boyfriend, Johnny Hyde—had recently died. It made her, in his word, fair "prey."

Despite having a powerful agent in her corner as well as her bed, Monroe's career had been floundering. She had been working frequently—six pictures in the past year alone—but only two were notable, *The Asphalt Jungle* and *All About Eve*, and not because of her performances (then again, little had been asked of her). The roles were small and Monroe had been cast strictly for her looks, which were special even in a city crowded with beautiful young women. She wasn't tall—just a shade over five feet five inches—but she certainly was good looking, her complexion creamy and her figure astonishing. It was a body she would always enjoy displaying, and with the bleaching of her natural brown hair to a honey blonde she made a strikingly lovely woman. At twenty-five, though, she was approaching the Hollywood age limit.

Kazan and Miller watched as, with obvious nervousness, Marilyn played her scene, finished it and fled the set. Kazan followed in pursuit and found her weeping in the corner of a dark and vacant soundstage. Although various Monroe biographers have attributed her upset that day to Johnny Hyde's death as well as to the shaky state of her career, it was more likely over her performance. She herself told a friend that Jones, the director, had "insulted" her, and she would always be prone to insecurity about her work, just as she was prone to it in her life.

The short, spectacular life of Marilyn Monroe has been well chronicled. She was born in Los Angeles in 1926 and never knew her father. She was named Norma Jean by her mother, Gladys Baker, whose parents and grandparents were either suicides, psychotics or both, and not much later Gladys herself would be institutionalized. "I was sorry she was sick," Monroe would later say, "but we never had any kind of relationship. I didn't see her very often. To me she was just the woman with the red hair."

Marilyn spent her childhood in a succession of foster homes before marrying at sixteen. When her husband enlisted in the navy, she went to work in a 1942 defense plant. She was already a young beauty and a photographer who was taking wartime publicity pictures at the plant suggested that she apply to a Hollywood school of what was then called modeling and charm. By 1946 she was divorced and a working model, even a magazine "cover girl." This led to the small contract she presently held with Twentieth Century-Fox, where a casting director had named her Marilyn Monroe (Monroe was her mother's maiden name).

Whatever the reason for her tears that 1951 afternoon on the dark soundstage, Elia Kazan knew how to comfort an actress. While soothing her hurt he walked her back to the *As Young as You Feel* set, where he introduced the soft-spoken young woman to Arthur Miller.

His physical attraction was instantaneous, he later claimed, but it was Kazan who began seeing Monroe and, soon enough, sleeping with her while Miller slept alone, elsewhere in the Feldman house, and stayed on for the continuing effort to sell *The Hook* after it was also rejected by Warner Bros. Meanwhile their host finally returned and promptly announced a party in Arthur's honor. The evening was to be so special that besides an orchestra for dancing, several grown-up women were to be invited, including Evelyn Keyes, the smart and beautiful actress who had just divorced the director John Huston. As for Marilyn Monroe, she was put on the guest list simply as "Marilyn—Kazan's date."

By the big night, Friday, January 26, 1951, Elia had other plans (a girlfriend of Howard Hughes to be exact, presumably under consideration for a role in *Viva Zapata!*) and he intended to work on that project before coming to the party late. As he headed for his rented convertible, he asked Arthur to stand in for him and provided Marilyn's telephone number.

Although she was planning to take a taxi to the party, Miller insisted on picking her up. It was not the way this party was supposed to work, but that was how he had been brought up. And so they made their entrance together, she in a dress so busty she looked to one catty observer like "the prow of a ship." For Miller the rest of the room seems to have disappeared. He focused his concentration so completely on her (and that "blatantly tight" dress, as he put it) that others in the living room could not but notice. Marilyn meanwhile seemed to bask in the guest of honor's attention, sitting beside him on the sofa with shoes off and legs folded up on the cushion while Arthur began to caress her foot. Nearby, Evelyn Keyes could see that he was "totally wrapped up" in her.

They were improbably different—the unschooled, unsophisticated California girl from a broken and dysfunctional home and the urban Jewish thinker, a master of theatrical success. What could his political concerns and psychological self-interest (Miller had recently started seeing an analyst) possibly have meant to her? And how could he grasp the flashy insularity of the movie scene and her life within it—to say nothing of their eleven-year age difference, a considerable one from a twenty-five year old's point of view? Yet Monroe probably had more experience than one needed, and Miller less. He was the innocent on the sofa, probably the only sexual innocent in the whole room, while in most other respects she was the innocent. For Miller was the educated, sophisticated and celebrated Pulitzer Prize–winning playwright, while Marilyn was only a Hollywood provincial and merely "Kazan's date."

In another sense, however, they were not so ill suited. Naivete was a quality they shared, with its elements of ingenuousness, trustfulness and earnestness. Still, she was sexuality incarnate while he was the virgin in the garden. In short, it was Eve herself whose toe Arthur Miller was beginning to caress.

By the time Kazan got there they were dancing. Sounding so much like a director considering a scene, he remembered watching them and thinking "how happy she was" with Miller, "tall and handsome in a Lincolnesque way." Monroe meant nothing more to Kazan than another body in bed and he was candid about that, even boastful. So he "did the right thing" and let Miller take her home, hinting smarmily, "I don't know what happened later that night, but Marilyn, without going into specifics, said that Art was shy." Obviously Kazan had asked.

None of this is mentioned in Miller's autobiography, where the Feldman party is dealt with only fleetingly. Monroe was among the crowd in Miller's version, but as he would have it they did not even speak. Rather it was Evelyn Keyes who, according to Miller, had been sitting on the sofa with Marilyn. Keyes in fact was witness to and the source of the descriptions of Miller and Monroe—and of course, the toe.

After that Miller, Kazan and Monroe became a friendly threesome—a psychological ménage à trois—and the New York playwright was proving to be something new in her life. He was serious and he seemed to take her seriously. He talked about writers and was interested in what she read. As they all three browsed through a Beverly Hills book shop, she told him that she was fond of poetry and he, the teacher, recommended Robert Frost, Walt Whitman, e. e. cummings. She bought a copy of *Death of a Salesman* and that was new to her, the world of Broadway and the theater. Of course he signed it, this tall, lanky, shy, bespectacled famous playwright.

She even tagged along when he and Elia went off to sell *The Hook* to Harry Cohn, the famously tyrannical head of production at Columbia Pictures. As a lark, Kazan passed off Monroe as his personal assistant, the director even providing his actress with props—eyeglasses and a stenographer's pad. This might have been funny had Cohn's reaction been different, but he was seriously concerned about *The Hook*'s characterization of organized labor as corrupt and gangster-ridden. Cohn insisted that Kazan and Miller meet with Hollywood's most important union man, Roy Brewer, who ran the International Alliance of Theatrical and Stage Employees as well as being chairman of the superpatriotic Motion Picture Alliance for the Preservation of American Ideals (with actor John Wayne as its president). In fact Cohn had already given Brewer a copy of the Miller script.

As Marilyn pretended to take notes, the discussion with Cohn turned to budgets, rehearsal dates and shooting schedules. It seemed to Kazan that the picture was going to be made, but Miller's mind was elsewhere. As he recalled, Marilyn Monroe was the only thing happening in Harry Cohn's office. She now was someone he "desperately wanted." That she was still sleeping with Kazan didn't seem to matter, for he wasn't going to do anything about it. He would never, he was sure, abandon Mary and the children.

There is no point in minimizing the power of sexual attraction or mocking it. Miller knew that it would be tough but necessary to flee if he were to escape with his married life intact. Yet he could not flee. He was in Los Angeles to sell *The Hook* and had a pending meeting with Roy Brewer, who was not only a movie union man but a veteran of the New York labor world and a friend of the longshoremen's union's Joe "It's never been proved" Ryan. In view of that, Brewer's reaction to *The Hook* was even more predictable than might have been predicted. Miller's script, he said, in Kazan's recollection, was downright unpatriotic, and no racketeers were involved with any labor unions. "The great problem in the unions is the Communist," Brewer informed Kazan and Miller, whereas the "racketeers are much less a menace to labor than the Communists." In short, he said, instead of gangsters and corrupt union leaders "the communists ought to be the villains." The union man and film critic suggested that the author of *Death of a Salesman* show "in the strongest possible way you can that Marty does not represent the so-called progressives." He even made specific suggestions for dialogue, proposing, for instance, that a reporter for *The Daily Worker* be introduced so that Marty can say, "We don't want any Commie sheets around here." Brewer was sure that this would be "a real way of showing he is not a Commie because a Commie would say he is not a Commie, he'd lie about that, but he'd never disavow an official Communist newspaper."

Kazan was not fazed. He was practiced at appeasing outsiders, whether they were producers, investors, even playwrights, before going his own way. Miller was not that coolheaded but he was practical, an idealist who wasn't wild eyed but rather was always looking for the other side of the argument. Even so they could get no reading on what to ultimately expect from Brewer, and therefore had little idea whether or not Cohn and Columbia intended in some fashion to make *The Hook*. As Kazan remembered, the meeting ended on this vague note.

Or did it? In Miller's autobiography *Timebends* he claims that he wasn't even there, that he had already left California. Rather, he wrote, it was Kazan alone who met with Cohn and Brewer, then telephoned him with an account of the meeting. In Kazan's version (with Miller present), written a year later, he claims to have a Miller letter to prove it (although it was not to be found in his archives at Wesleyan University in Connecticut).

Both Miller and Kazan nevertheless agree that the playwright all but raced for the Los Angeles airport; nor does it seem excessive to view his fleeing that place as a flight from his own freshly uncovered and terrifying (because compelling) sexuality. However radical Miller's politics, his morals were traditional. Yet this otherwise remote man now found himself taken by passion from the safeties of emotional constraint. As if to make escape even more difficult, Miller was escorted to the airport by not only Elia but Marilyn too, and thirty-five years later he still remembered the way she was dressed—"beige skirt, white satin blouse"—even the way she wore her hair, "parted on the right side."

Vivid in memory as well was what Kazan called the "specific detail" of his friend's sexual encounter with Monroe, a detail that Miller indelicately and unsubtly but unmistakably indicated in his autobiography, "her scent still on my hands." Yet his emotional state was more significant—a consuming sense of marital guilt ("my innocence was technical merely") and a belief "that I must flee or walk into a doom beyond all knowing."

This is certainly a dramatic way of putting it, but passion is passionate. Rather than being sexually liberated, as Kazan intended, Miller had been captured by sex and although he ran for his life, it affected his marriage immediately. He wrote from New York—in what Kazan called "a brotherly code"—about a worsening "situation at home," which seemed to elate Kazan.

> [H]e felt extra fine and had been thinking joyous thoughts. . . . He was a young man again, and in the grip of a first love, which was—happily—carrying him out of control. He didn't read like the constricted man I'd known. I remembered the lovely light of lechery in his eyes as he was dancing with Marilyn in Charlie Feldman's softly lit living room. I hadn't known he had it in him, that light in his eyes. I'd really done something for my friend, something he could not have done for himself.

This was a mischief maker's glee.

A now-smitten Arthur Miller shared his feelings with Kazan, asking him from New York to "look at" her once more, just for him. Elia more than obliged. He turned around and went right back to sleeping with Marilyn, undisturbed by and even boastful about the picture of Arthur that soon cropped up next to her bed.

9. *Betrayal*

ONCE HOME FROM CALIFORNIA Miller either (as Kazan had it) wrote a few modified scenes for *The Hook* to appease Harry Cohn, the studio chief, and Roy Brewer, the union man, or (as he had it) never for an instant considered making such revisions. Kazan claimed to have the rewrites that proved it, but if so, they are not to be found in his archives at Wesleyan University in Connecticut. They certainly are not incorporated in extant copies of the screenplay. There is no disagreement, however, about Miller's ultimate decision to withdraw it, only about his reason for making that decision. According to Miller it was a matter of principle, while Kazan considered it a decision made in fear, following several "frantic" phone calls to Molly.

Arthur Miller respected Molly Kazan much as he respected his own wife. Both women were strong, smart, opinionated and articulate. Their difference lay in morality. Mary Miller's righteousness was unwavering, her principles staunchly held, while Molly could and did change convictions like underwear, replacing her ardent communism, for instance, all but overnight with a rabid anticommunism. Likewise she could accept an unfaithful husband while Mary would not, but by the same moral token Molly Kazan could be a sympathetic confessor while Mary Miller's unyielding standards limited her capacity for forgiveness. "Art is acquiring all of your bad habits," she said to Elia, "and none of your good ones."

Molly told her husband that Arthur "sounded like a very nervous man" on the telephone, fearful that if he proceeded with *The Hook* he might be hauled up "for questioning" by the Committee on Un-American Activities. "They will ask me," Art reportedly said, "if I was a member of—" and then, Molly remembered, Miller stopped short. "There was a pause," she said meaningfully, "before he completed the sentence, '—of the Waldorf Peace Conference. I would have to say yes and that would finish me.'"

Kazan recorded this conversation with Molly in his autobiography *A Life*, a dastardly piece of smearing for it implied that Miller had started to say "a member of the Communist Party." Being a "member" of the Waldorf Peace Conference, as Elia Kazan well knew, would not have *finished* anyone. Obviously he suspected Miller of having been a party member, but rather than saying so forthrightly he took the furtive route of not so thinly veiled suggestion. "No one asked if his friend was a Communist in those days," Kazan wrote. "Art never offered to tell me." This is a gratuitous smear as well; in 1987, when Kazan wrote his book, there was no stigma in having been a Communist. This was informing long after the anticommunist mania had subsided, and for that matter the pause on the telephone could well have been misinterpreted. Miller might have been worrying—as he later would be—about explaining his mere attendance at meetings of Communist writers.

Still, worried he surely was, and Molly responded to those fears, Kazan said, by encouraging him to forget about any script revisions, in fact to forget about *The Hook* altogether. "Better not to expose yourself," she advised, and Kazan concluded his account with the bitchy aside, "Perhaps if she'd liked the script, she might have felt differently."

This is strictly Kazan's recollection. Miller never made any mention of such a conversation (although, as we shall see, he probably did make a HUAC-related telephone call to the Kazan house at that time). Miller did, however, withdraw *The Hook* from consideration by Columbia Pictures rather than comply with Cohn's demands to turn it into anticommunist propaganda. The studio chief fired off a telegram, IT'S INTERESTING HOW THE MINUTE WE TRY TO MAKE THE SCRIPT PRO-AMERICAN YOU PULL OUT. Cohn, not a man of subtleties, promptly announced to Kazan that "Miller is a Communist." Elia did not exactly fly to the defense of his best friend when he weakly protested that he "didn't think so." Cohn told him to forget it, *The Hook* was a dead issue. "We'll find something else to do together." That something else was going to be *On the Waterfront*.

At more or less the same time Miller received a telegram from Harry Cohn's secretary, a "Miss Baur," pressing him to get to work on the script and hurry back to Los Angeles with the revisions. This telegram of course was not from Cohn's secretary; it was from Marilyn Monroe, who occasionally wrote as "Miss Baur" to Kazan as well. Marilyn had already told Natasha Lytess, who was her acting coach and best friend, that she was in love.

"It was like running into a tree!" she'd said after the Feldman party. "You know—like a cool drink when you've got a fever. You see my toe? Well he sat and held it and we just looked into each other's eyes all night." They talked too, she said, Arthur about his next play and she about the roles she was being offered, which weren't characters but dumb blondes with great bodies. Arthur's first letter (he'd asked Elia for her address) was about this, and Monroe received it a few days after he left. "Bewitch them with this image they ask for, but I hope and almost pray you won't be hurt in this game, nor ever change." She wrote back, expressing her need to find someone she could respect. "Most people can admire their fathers," she said, "but I never had one. I need someone to admire."

Miller's reply—"If you want someone to admire, why not Abraham Lincoln? Carl Sandburg has written a magnificent biography of him"—suggests mixed motives, on one hand discouraging her from making him an object of admiration while on the other, by the very act of replying, maintaining the line of communication.

Perhaps this tutorial was also intended to capitalize on his Lincolnesque image. The popular press tends to focus on the person rather than the work and Miller was regularly described as looking like Abraham Lincoln with his high forehead, dark hair, chiseled features, pronounced cheekbones and lanky height. The comparison carried with it a suggestion that Miller also shared high principles with Lincoln. Whether or not he was using that image for flirtation purposes, Marilyn promptly went out and bought all six volumes of the then-celebrated Sandburg biography of Lincoln, along with copies of Arthur's novel *Focus* and his adaptation of Ibsen's *An Enemy of the People*. These were set alongside the copy of *Death of a Salesman* on her night table, near his photograph. Then his letters began to accumulate and they too were put on the crowded table beside the bed—the one in which Marilyn continued to sleep with his pal. Even in flagrante delicto (at least according to Kazan) she talked about how mad she was for Miller. Kazan claimed to have not been distracted by this, but no matter; the affair would end later that year, after—perhaps it was relevant—he had finished casting *Viva Zapata!*

As for Arthur, his letters to Monroe spoke of unhappiness in his marriage even as he was vowing to preserve it. He had already confessed his second bout of *impure thoughts* to his wife, this time telling Mary about the powerful sexual attraction that he had resisted in California. Not surprisingly it made her even angrier than the first incident; almost as angry as if he had consummated the attraction. He would later say, "I was as helpless to forgive myself as [Mary] was." Now she was disgusted with him, distrusting and disbelieving, which did not stop him from continuing to write to Marilyn and perhaps even encouraged it. He would manage to see her at least a half dozen times in the next few years, even while repeatedly saying that he was determined to save his life with Mary and the children. Monroe enlisted Kazan's support, writing to him that he must try to "cheer up" Arthur and "make him believe everything isn't hopeless," but Miller was giving every sign—almost—of trying to keep his resolve. Perhaps there was even the signal of a fresh start, or at least self-discipline, in his purchase of a new home for his family, a Federal-style town house that he described as "a mid–19th Century single family house at 155 Willow Street, one block from the river." Six-year-old Jane's room was next to Bobby's on the third floor, and their father's study was one flight below; he had a movie director's chair at the desk with his name on the back. This was the Millers' fifth home in eleven years, all within a seven-block radius in Brooklyn Heights.

Miller had already put *Plenty Good Times* aside to begin a new play about a young woman who is "the seeming truth bearer of sensuality," and who offers the protagonist a "revival of his life as she more and more comes to stand for the catlike authenticity of a force of nature." This character, Lorraine, is plainly (Miller said "rather distantly") modeled on Monroe, the character's name as usual echoing the real name. Making little progress with that play, he began blending it into yet another revision of *Plenty Good Times*, and now it was going to flourish, a major Arthur Miller play written at the peak of his powers. Miller wrote Kazan that it would involve "a lot of low grade conversations between a cop and the whole goddamned universe. And I will not be surprised that I have made myself out an idiot in it, that no woman will talk to me anymore, and that some will be ravished by it all."

He had already begun the additional research, having gone, he told Elia, "to see more of my friend the cop," meaning his boyhood pal, Sid Franks. As the *New York Times* later reported, the five-character play would deal with "a young married couple of the Depression generation," and that marriage was going to be a chilly and unfaithful one, riddled with recriminations.

Four years earlier, in 1947, the Committee on Un-American Activities had begun hearings on Communist Infiltration of the Motion-Picture Industry. The range of helpful-to-hostile witnesses had been broad and disparate, from the conservative novelist Ayn Rand to the German Communist playwright Bertolt Brecht, and from movie stars such as Gary Cooper and Robert Taylor, who were cooperative witnesses, to the "Hollywood Ten," screenwriters such as John Howard Lawson and Ring Lardner, Jr., who were "unfriendly" ones, united in the face of the committee's demands and refusing to answer any questions about their political convictions. Lawson's fate was particularly painful. Testifying on October 27, 1947, the respected academic, the playwright of *Success Story* and *Processional* (and the screenwriter of such lesser epics as *Algiers*) would not say whether he was or wasn't a member of the Communist Party, which he was. In this house of mirrored corridors an admission of ongoing party membership ensured professional punishment, while refusing to answer the question ensured criminal prosecution as well. After so declining, Lawson was cited for contempt of Congress. It would result in oblivion, for him in his lifetime and for his work afterward.

The essential question, which was asked of every witness, had developed an ominously comic ring. "It is a very simple question," said Committee Chairman John Parnell Thomas to Ring Lardner three days later. "Any real American would be proud to answer that question. Are you or have you ever been a member of the Communist Party?"

The congressman sarcastically added, "Any *real* American."

Lardner's reply was comic too, but intentionally so, in the manner of film noir heroines such as Barbara Stanwyck. "I could answer it," he said, "but if I did I would hate myself in the morning."

The substance and nature of these hearings were part of a billowing atmosphere of political persecution, an atmosphere that turned even darker in February 1950 when Senator Joseph R. McCarthy began his fiery moment in American history by accusing the entire U.S. State Department of being "full of Communists." By early 1951 Dashiell Hammett, writer of the Thin Man and Sam Spade mysteries, was being given a six-month sentence for refusing to name any contributors to a civil rights bail bond fund for which he was a trustee. Hammett was released after serving five months in prison, a man broken physically as well as professionally. In March of that year Julius and Ethel Rosenberg were convicted of conspiracy to commit espionage on behalf of the Soviet Union. They were facing possible death sentences even though in the history of the United States there had never been an execution for espionage in a time of peace.

So it was that in spring 1951 the Committee on Un-American Activities took the national aptitude for hysteria as an invitation to start a second round of publicity-rich Hollywood hearings. Its timing was so right, the grounds of fear so fertile, that leftists willingly emerged to confess past political sins that once had been acts of conviction, and to inform on others in the hope of saving themselves. In May the actor Jose Ferrer, an active supporter of left-wing causes, and the screenwriter Budd Schulberg, a former party member, appeared as cooperative witnesses, disassociating themselves from the values of their past to express their support of the criminalization of the Communist Party. Schulberg's justification for getting others into trouble was, "My guilt is what we did to the Czechs, not what I did to Ring Lardner." (Schulberg had named Lardner, confirming that he had been a member of the Communist Party.) Ringgold Wilmer Lardner, Jr., a superior screenwriter of such leftist propaganda as *Woman of the Year* and *Laura*, had been dismissed from Twentieth Century-Fox after refusing to answer the committee's questions. Like Lawson he was given a one-year prison sentence for contempt of Congress, while Schulberg's screenwriting career, insignificant until then, shot forward.

Elia Kazan, being the most important and successful ex-Communist in Hollywood, had every reason to anticipate a subpoena to testify before the committee. His movie career was soaring. *A Streetcar Named Desire* had received twelve Academy Award nominations, including Best Picture and Best Director (winning neither). His youthful membership in the party was no secret. He was bound to be called and confronted with a demand for the names of other members, a harrowing prospect. Compliance would mean betraying people—friends included—and putting their careers in jeopardy, while defying the committee could well ruin his movie career.

There was no such threat hanging over Kazan's theater work, for Broadway was unintimidated by HUAC. This was not a reflection of theatrical backbone but rather of theatrical unimportance. The committee was more interested in glamorous Hollywood, and as a result, Elia Kazan's stage career was still secure. Promoting *The Hook* had cost him Tennessee Williams's latest hit, *The Rose Tattoo* (he was still fuming about that, and still convinced that *The Hook*, which he had pursued instead, could have been made), but he had a new play to direct, George Tabori's *Flight Into Egypt*. Yet moviemaking was giving him immense satisfaction, not to mention a fancy income and a giddy life in the Hollywood power lane. So Kazan faced his dilemma while on location in Mexico, finishing *Viva Zapata!* How much longer could he delay a choice between informing and refusing to? How much longer would he be able to pursue moviemaking?

Ironically *The Hook*'s nemesis, Harry Cohn, and his Columbia Pictures released the movie of *Death of a Salesman* in 1951. Produced by Stanley Kramer from a screenplay by Stanley Roberts, the picture was directed by Laslo Benedek. Mildred Dunnock and Cameron Mitchell reprised their roles as Linda and Happy Loman, while Kevin McCarthy was brought in to play Biff. Fredric March was Willy.

One can only wonder what this movie would have been like had Kazan chosen to direct it instead of *A Streetcar Named Desire*. Certainly he knew which of the two plays had the greater cinematic potential (he thought Miller's the superior stage play, although he considered the Williams more beautifully written). In the end *Death of a Salesman*, which had so frequently been called cinematic, would prove too stagey on the screen. Inevitably Miller was unhappy with the picture.

> They made Willy crazier and crazier [and] they chopped off all the climaxes. . . . Sometimes it worked out. But it's very difficult to deal with this play, for the simple reason that already on the stage it has film making elements in it. The way the time changes, the locales, the way people appear and disappear. The dramatic tension of Willy's memories was destroyed by transferring him, literally, to the locales he had only imagined in the play. There is an inevitable horror in the spectacle of a man losing consciousness of his immediate surroundings to the point where he engages in conversations with unseen persons.

That horror was lost when Willy's imaginings materialized. Gone was the chilling sight of a man behaving as though he were (and convinced that he is) elsewhere when we can see for ourselves that he is not. As Miller pointed out, it is Willy's very realization that he is imagining things that scares the hell out of him. "His terror springs from his never-lost awareness of time and space." The movie instead placed him physically in his remembered places and there he was just crazy.

In addition to this conceptual problem, Columbia Pictures made matters worse by introducing the anticommunist mentality that had led to their scuttling of *The Hook*. In the case of *Salesman* Miller was told that the studio was adding a fifteen-minute introductory film, a series of interviews with business school professors analyzing Willy Loman and declaring him an exception to modern, happy salesmen. The playwright was shown this apologetic short in a Manhattan screening room and when the lights were brought up, the studio executives turned to him for reaction. He began agreeably enough, only to conclude, "But why the hell did you make the picture if you're so ashamed of it?"

This prologue evidently was never shown. Either way the picture was unsuccessful, commercially as well as artistically.

As the 1951 summer reached its midpoint, Miller wrote Kazan from Connecticut,

> Mary and the kids have been away all month at Vasarr—how the fuck do you spell that name? [He was an excellent speller but not world class—*aquit*, for instance]—where the kids get a kind of camp and the mothers find out things, or some shit of that kind. So I've been alone here, and buried in discarded sheets of paper. They'll be back August 2nd and a relief too, because I get lonesome sometimes, among other things.

The "among other things" is another one of his coded Marilyn messages, like the "thinking joyous thoughts" letter he had written to Kazan some months earlier. Why coded? To leave dangerous admissions unrecorded probably felt safer. Miller was a practiced hand at such writing between the lines. This is a fundamental of playwriting. Meanwhile he had been writing "reams" of the big new play.

> I am half finished—the first half. Actually I finished it a week ago, maybe ten days, but the third and last scene of Act One (it's in two) kept saying to me that it wasn't *all* there, you know? So I've been over and over it, and I've got it—by this date. I warn you—and myself—that I still don't know exactly, and somehow don't want to know exactly, where the end is, because I know the whole thing so well that I'd rather not figure it. All it is, so far, is true. And all I have is faith that if I tell the truth somehow they'll know it out there. But that may not be so, it isn't always.

He invited Kermit and Virginia Bloomgarden to Connecticut for a weekend. The motive was not only to have company; Miller always read his plays to friends, needing feedback on works in progress and even reassurances of his own playwriting ability. Once Kermit and Virginia became a captive audience he sat them down and picked up his play. He only read a six-page scene but was pleased with his producer's reaction, which, he wrote Kazan, was exactly what the reaction was supposed to be.

> He started to squirm! Oh shit, man, all of us are so the same and so unutterably naked, and still it's so discouraging to believe that people are no better than me . . . I may still stink it up . . . but one thing nice about it is the knowledge, absolute and unshakable now—that this is my trade.

Virginia Bloomgarden had an additional reaction.

> On the drive home we were talking about the scene and I said to Kermit, "I have the feeling that [it] had something to do with the problems that exist in Arthur and Mary's relationship." I knew Art and Mary were having marital problems, and that was what the play was dealing with. So I said to Kermit, "Something is wrong with Mary and Arthur. Boy, is he in trouble."

Was this "something" something he needed to express but was not the sort to talk about? Was writing plays his emotional outlet? Miller was already in psychoanalysis (as was Kazan and apparently almost everyone they knew), but he doesn't seem to have been changing much as a result of it. Whether or not there were psychological reasons for reading that particular scene to the Bloomgardens, the play covered a larger territory than marital wars of infidelity, guilt and recrimination. It reflected his lifelong fascination with the workings of the human mind. Just as *Death of a Salesman* originally occurred inside of Willy Loman's head, the new play's "plot," he told Kazan, "is what each one is thinking."

Much of the story revolves around the past life of Quentin (an echo name for Arthur's brother, Kermit) Strupp, a policeman who once lived in a handsome building overlooking the very park that is his beat. He is patrolling his past, as it were, and as a policeman he is emblematic of the protector, the safeguard.

In a scene involving his father Quentin's childhood is called into the present as the old man, once wealthy but now working as a messenger, tells him of delivering a package not only addressed to their former building but to the very apartment where they'd lived. "The piano is there," he tells Quentin, "and the harp, and the settee from Denmark . . . you sit in that room and you will expect Mother to walk in through the French doors."

He urges his son to go and see it and reestablish the connection with his past.

> A man must know where he comes from, a man must know what he is! . . . You don't know anything!—you are walking around and around and around and . . . Quentin, your mother had black hair, and she was shorter than I . . . You mean to tell me that that's right? Not to remember your mother?

A stage direction indicates that when the father leaves, Quentin seems "about to weep." There was weeping in almost every play that Arthur Miller had written thus far, which is interesting in view of the fact that in his own life he was so emotionally constricted. Indeed he regularly disavowed emotional fireworks in his plays, striving for the same balanced rationality in audience reaction that he believed underlay his own thinking. The point was to achieve clarity of thought rather than the blur of transport. Such emotionalism was perhaps easier for him to justify in this play, whose central character is based at least in part on his sensitive brother. Thus Quentin the policeman *moves almost in anger against his confusion, against his emotion and angrily raps his club on the bench back . . . he looks up toward the apartment's windows . . . fixes his tie . . . walks toward his adventure*. This adventure was going to be an adultery, and, he admits elsewhere in the play, "I do lie, I lie to my wife."

The autobiographical references are unmistakable, not just in the adulterous urge that Miller adds to Quentin's character, but in the childhood apartment near a park, its furnishings of cultural aspiration, even the old man's job of delivering packages. Isadore Miller, after losing everything, had taken a succession of such humiliating jobs. In the scene between father and son this is all enveloped in an atmosphere of reverie.

In another scene, after Quentin's father has died, he does visit the old family apartment, where he recognizes the current tenant as a woman he'd noticed in the park. This is Lorraine of the aborted Marilyn Monroe play, evolved into the "full bodied" Dorothy. She is playing the harp when Quentin rings her doorbell. She had noticed him as well, it turns out.

QUENTIN: I might've known . . . that you lived here . . . I called you before . . . about the harp.

DOROTHY: You're his . . . ??

QUENTIN: I'm Quentin Strupp. He was my father.

DOROTHY: He was your father. Well, gee whiz. (*Laughing*) I can't get over it. You patrol right across the street from your house.

QUENTIN: This hasn't been my house in a long, long time.

She tells him she'd suspected that he was not really a policeman but "an investigator of some kind" and talks about herself and of wasting too much time. "You obviously know what you're doing," she says. "Very few people know that . . . especially the men . . . You're very unusual. I mean for an intelligent man to feel at peace with himself is an unusual thing. Or don't you agree with that?"

The investigating—querying, questing—Quentin replies, "I don't get around much, I don't know." As to his being a policeman, he says, "It seems to me that most men don't have much choice as to what they're going to do with themselves."

Dorothy lets it slip that his father might have been ashamed of what Quentin does—"He said you were in the government." Yet Quentin defends his work and describes the many Depression-era college men who wound up on the force: "twenty two graduate lawyers in my police academy class and a whole raft of accountants." Like Arthur's friend Sid Franks, but also like Kermit, Quentin trades his potential for economic security so that he can take care of a father. "There was a time when I was feeding that man with a spoon, and five weeks earlier he had a wife and a family and three million dollars."

He takes her hands. "The whole problem of living," he says tellingly, or perhaps bitterly, "is to make as painless as possible the waste of your life. Unless you're willing to hurt other people. Otherwise you've got to sacrifice your life." This is in apposition to Quentin's brother Frank, who walked out on family responsibilities to become a successful lawyer—plainly a projection of Miller himself. The notion of choice between selfishness and otherness was becoming an ongoing concern of Miller's.

In a long and vivid speech Dorothy tells Quentin that she'd once been married because she had hoped it would make her feel like other women.

> They pretend they're completed when they get married. . . . I have an image. I'm saving it for a book. This is the image: People live under a lattice work; you ever see those overhead things in the country for vines to grow on? And in the daytime, the sun shines through and makes little squares of light on the ground. And each couple stands inside its own square, pretending that there's four hard walls around their lives, see, and nobody else existed outside. But at night, when there's no sun, those shadows vanish, and the squares vanish, and there's only a lot of separate men and women, a crowd mixed together in the undemarcated dark, with nothing to tell them who they belong to. I mean that in our hearts, down deep where we live, it's really always night. . . . You understand what I mean?

In these scenes Miller creates mood through understatement and implication as he establishes character within the sustained atmosphere of a dream. Another scene anticipates the terse dialogue and oblique tensions that would be found decades later in Harold Pinter's plays. The scene involves Quentin and Frank, classic Miller brothers, as they discuss buying the contents of the old apartment.

> FRANK: Did you want the harp?
> QUENTIN: I just wanted to look around.
> FRANK: Did you want the harp? Because it's yours if you want it, kid. I just assumed you had no interest in it.
> QUENTIN: Why'd you assume I had no interest in it?
> FRANK: All right, let's put it another way; I wanted it and I just didn't think of you.
> QUENTIN: In that case, take it.
> FRANK: It's just that I do have a house and it would go well in the living room; and my wife does play piano and she'd be interested in it.
> QUENTIN: I agree with you. So take it.
> FRANK: No, now that I see you want it, I want you to have it.
> QUENTIN: I don't want it, Frank.
> FRANK: What's the matter, Quent?

QUENTIN: Why do you always assume that you're taking something from somebody? (*They sit down to talk*) You know, Frank, some people don't want anything.

FRANK: I don't know where your animosity comes from, Quent. It's kind of shocking.

This perfectly written scene with its rhythmic and interactive dialogue establishes a delicate and ambiguous relationship, a connection that is warm, yet fraught with resentment. The passage is thoroughly playable and set within a free-form structure having neither time nor place nor common realism. Miller does not anticipate concrete scenery to be changed as he moves his locations from a park to the father's apartment to the brother's home. Once again his play is set in a state of mind.

Miller wrote many hundreds of such pages for this play. Its autobiographical antecedents are all but spelled out in his notebook jottings. Here Miller speculates about Quentin, incorporating elements of his own state of mind.

> In place of the old "morality," where adultery was religiously in the "wrong," there is presently its equivalent—the psychological "wrong"—a point must arrive when this is not so horrible. When in fact he can do without her, when he is free of the necessity to have her acceptance. When he does not need her, or "respectability" to feel "good."

And again,

> The important, decisive decision is whether he *wants* to throw away his neurosis, for it contains warmth and love for him, memory of his mother.—to him it means forgoing the claim and possibility of ecstasy.
>
> Question: can that be found with one woman, with his wife, anymore, *given the circumstances?*
>
> In other words, having found with another woman the heat of passion, is it possible to give that up and find the old happiness with a wife? Or any physical happiness?
>
> The adventure also reveals how terribly he—the trap he has "adopted." He never knew, until now, how much he had hated the life.

Those notebook ruminations are followed by a brief exchange between Quentin and his wife.

LILLIAN: I never knew you!

QUENTIN: That's right.

LILLIAN: The man I knew could never do this!

In Los Angeles Marilyn Monroe was emerging from the crowd of bit players jostling at the gateways to the film studios. She signed a new contract with Twentieth Century-Fox, and although her roles were still small, she was now playing alongside such stars as Ginger Rogers, Claudette Colbert and Cary Grant. By the end of 1951 she was being assigned her first big roles, costarring with Richard Widmark and Anne Bancroft in *Don't Bother to Knock*, to be followed by her first leading role, opposite Joseph Cotten in *Niagara*.

Just as the first of these pictures was being released, Marilyn was hit with a professional calamity, or so it seemed when a three-year-old nude photograph turned up in a calendar that was being promoted nationally. The photograph was called "Golden Dreams" and it showed a stunning Marilyn Monroe stretched full length and naked across a crimson velvet floor cloth. "I mean," she said, "there I am with my bare *tuchas* out."

What might have been catastrophic for another young starlet became a spectacular career opportunity for Monroe as she gave America its first glimpse of the guileless erotica that was going to make her the century's great sexual symbol. Rather than apologizing for the photograph or cringing from the subject, she approached it with the forthright cheer and fragile pluck that endeared her to the public, even as she oozed sensuality.

> I did have to pay the rent where I lived at the Hollywood Studio Club, and I was four weeks behind . . . That's no kidding. You can go there and check and find out. If you got a week behind, you got a notice in your box. I don't know why they let me stay over. I guess they thought I had possibilities. I did tell Tom Kelley [the photographer] I don't mind if your wife is there but none of your helpers please. And he said, okay, we can do it at night. Then when I got there and took everything off—they don't put any make up on, body make up, nothing—he put me out on this stretch red velvet. And it was drafty. He kept gasping, "Oh, my God," and I thought, well maybe it isn't too bad.

The calendar photograph proved to be one of her earliest star bursts, for it set her beyond the ordinary. Although Miller was not in contact with her during this period, he approved of "her laughing acknowledgment of the photo" and her freedom from "the illusions of a properly ordered life." That was not the way Joe DiMaggio saw it. The baseball star had come into Monroe's life with sudden seriousness and they were widely expected to marry. Whatever she still felt for Arthur Miller, he was a continent away and working on a marriage.

Monroe was plainly in the habit of using her beauty to promote her career—from the powerful agent Johnny Hyde to the celebrated director Kazan, the famous playwright Miller and now a great American sports hero. Many have observed that she sought out older men, father figures, and there is nothing particularly strange in that, but perhaps in these choices something was even more significant to Monroe, if only in an instinctual way. She seemed to have a sense of the mythic in the American culture, anticipating her future as an icon; and she was drawn to or sensed the suitability of an appropriately iconic mate. If Arthur Miller was on his way to becoming America's playwright of playwrights, a giant figure of high artistry and courageous social conscience, then Joe DiMaggio had comparable oversize as the country's elegant and dignified athlete of athletes. Both men matched Monroe's childlike sensuality with their unique and considerable male images, despite their opposite moral identities, Miller's code intellectual and liberal, DiMaggio's traditional and conservative.

The calendar picture made one man chuckle, the other seethe.

In New York Kazan was finally served with the subpoena he had been dreading, but he was not served the usual way. By his own description the delivery was almost friendly, accompanied with a suggestion that his cooperation with the Committee on Un-American Activities was anticipated, and with the assurance that his testimony would be given in "executive session." This meant that the interview would be conducted in secret and would not be made public. It was unusual but not exceptional, probably the work of his powerful ally, Spyros Skouras, the president of Twentieth Century-Fox Pictures, who had some influence with J. Edgar Hoover. It seems fair to presume that in helping Kazan, Skouras was not so much being paternal to a fellow Greek as merely pragmatic, a studio president protecting a property.

The secret session—its record suppressed for a half century—was held at two o'clock on the afternoon of January 14, 1952, in room 226 of the Old House Office Building. Five committee members were present, including Congressman Francis E. Walter, who had become chairman after his predecessor, the *real* American J. Parnell Thomas, was convicted of financial chicanery. Thomas served a one-year sentence in the same prison—the Federal Correctional Institution, Danbury, Connecticut—at the same time as Ring Lardner, Jr.

The questioning of Kazan was conducted almost deferentially by Raphael I. Nixon, the committee's director of research (Richard M. Nixon had been a member of the committee but was now in the Senate). Asked whether there was "anything in your experience . . . with the Group Theatre that would [confirm it] as a Communist group," Kazan called such a description "erroneous" and was not challenged on it. He said that his membership in the Communist Party—which he forthrightly admitted—was not related to his membership in this theater company. He did, he said, belong to a Communist cell "that was trying to influence the goings on in what they called the revolutionary theater," but added that he quit the party rather than follow orders to "further the democratization of the Group Theater."

At that point the big question was asked. "Were there other individuals to your knowledge who were members of this same cell of the Communist Party?"

Kazan replied, "I don't want to answer that question. I don't take any refuge in anything [i.e., Fifth or First Amendment protection] and I am not hiding behind any immunity of any kind. It is a matter of personal conscience." He wasn't challenged on that either, and when he was asked to name the person who had enlisted him in the party, he declined to answer that as well. Asked whether Clifford Odets were a party member, he also said, "I don't want to answer that question," and as for Harold Clurman, Kazan said, "The three members . . . who ran the Group Theater [Clurman, Strasberg and Crawford], were never members of the Communist Party. . . . They were extremely egotistical people, had an idea of what they wanted, and nobody shoved them around."

Nixon moved to a broader line of inquiry. "Have there been any individuals that have previously appeared before this committee . . . that were members of the Communist Party in this [Group Theater] cell?" Kazan responded,

> On coming down on the train this morning, I knew I would be asked this question, and I knew the risks I would run in connection with not answering it. I am not taking immunity. I just made up my mind not to answer, as a matter of personal conscience. . . . There were two names on the list you gave me, mentioned before this committee. There were two.

Nixon asked, "Would you care to identify those two?"

"No," Kazan said. "I wouldn't."

He added that he thought Communists generally "are a conspiracy" and that, whether in war industries or communications, "they should be exposed," but, he said, "for the life of me, I don't see how an actor saying someone else's lines can be subversive."

This too was accepted without comment, while the questioning took another tack, dealing with various organizations that he might have joined, petitions he might have signed. Kazan answered these questions straightforwardly until he was again presented with a name. "Do you know whether to your knowledge [*sic*] John Garfield was a member of the Communist Party?" Once again Kazan said, "I am not ducking you. I cannot remember. He was a kid from the Bronx. That is what I remember about him. I don't remember his having been very much interested in anything except girls and acting."

Finally he was asked a curious question: what it was he had meant by "personal conscience."

Kazan said, "I feel, if I did give these names, I would harm someone." Giving names to the committee was already being referred to as *naming names*, a catchphrase that connoted informing on other people and dooming them to subpoenas and ruined careers. A committee member commented that "several of the Hollywood witnesses we had here . . . were not penalized because they came here and made a clean breast." Kazan replied,

> Well, I may be wrong, but I feel if this were an open meeting instead of the one we are having now, the plans I am working on as a director of a picture would be off tomorrow. I may be wrong about it. But it's just that the pressure groups are so strong. And I understand about everyone's anxiety. God knows, I think you should investigate, and what you are doing is right. But I feel, myself, if this were known, if this were an open meeting, I would be out of a job.

With that the session was concluded and, as Kazan had been promised, no record of the proceedings was published. Spyros Skouras had apparently gained access to the committee chairman through J. Edgar Hoover, easing the treatment of his important director, and that might well have been the end of it. Kazan probably would have been out of the woods had it not been for—of all things—an informer. Someone leaked news of the secret session to the press and it was promptly reported that Kazan had refused to provide names to the committee. The repercussion was immediate, but not from HUAC. The Committee on Un-American Activities did not publish newsletters or disseminate lists of Communist Party members, fellow travelers, sympathizers or consistently liberal contributors. That work was done by patriotic volunteers, perhaps comparable to religious zealots who are stricter and more demanding than their church hierarchies. In much the same way unauthorized enforcers of the anticommunist crusade were harsher and more fanatic than official bodies. Whether or not HUAC acted on a witness's testimony, movie studio chieftains such as Skouras were intimidated by nongovernmental sources, for instance, watchdog newsletters (such as *Counterattack*) or blacklist keepers (*Red Channels*) and most particularly John Wayne's Motion Picture Alliance for the Preservation of American Ideals. Even though the committee thus had signed off on Elia Kazan's January 14 appearance without charging him with contempt of Congress, the director was *advised* by Skouras to request another session. He would provide those names, because if he didn't, the studio president said, he would be finished as a movie director.

There could be no better example of the essential role played by newspapers and the entertainment industry in the professional punishment of these witnesses. HUAC may have bred the blacklist, but the only punishment it could mete out was recommending a charge of contempt of Congress for refusing to answer questions. The committee could not cancel a job, blacklist a performer or refuse to hire a writer. The ultraconservative press and the cowardly executives of the movie and television industries had to take responsibility for that.

Eric Bentley, the respected critic, academic and author of *Thirty Years of Treason*, recalled,

> In the two months between the executive session and the open one, Kazan was under heavy pressure from his wife Molly, who had been a much more

> ardent Communist [and now] was much more of an anti-Communist. . . . When he was disinclined to name those names, Molly convinced him that it was his patriotic duty. It wasn't [for movie] money like the Communists said. I knew Molly and she was a very powerful woman and she had a great intellectual domination of him.

That both Kazan and Miller were married to strong women who dominated them even as they ran off to play games of princely entitlement is certainly curious. Kazan early on perceived maternalism in Mary's relationship to Arthur, yet he was unable to see a similar pattern in his own marriage to Molly, a woman eight years his senior. With her strong support of Skouras's demand that he cooperate with the committee Kazan agreed to the second session, which was not to be a secret one. Having that to look forward to, he began rehearsals of *Flight Into Egypt*. Its author, George Tabori, immediately noticed the director's anxiety. Kazan explained only that he was "under a lot of pressure right now" as he continued to work on a play that was about, of all things, betrayal. When its tryout began in New Haven, Kermit Bloomgarden was invited to a preview and was disappointed. Friend to friend, the producer told Elia, "Some very good actors [Zero Mostel among them] are giving some very questionable performances." The usually disciplined Kazan defended them, saying, "They're blacklisted," as if that were excuse enough. "Since when," asked Bloomgarden, "do we judge actors by whether or not they're blacklisted?" Kazan responded that such people deserved to be given some slack. "We owe them the jobs." Perhaps this was not hypocritical, but whether from reflexive liberalism or an advance payment on an anticipated debt of guilt, such an unprofessional, softhearted approach did not contribute to the quality of the production. *Flight Into Egypt* was badly received in New York, closing after the briefest of engagements.

Soon afterward, one afternoon early in April 1952, Bloomgarden was in his second-floor office at 1545 Broadway, near Forty-fifth Street, when something rattled against the window. On the street below Kazan was tossing coins to get the producer's attention, gesturing for him to come downstairs. They walked the one block to Dinty Moore's, a theater bar on Eighth Avenue, where Elia, making no mention of his earlier session with the committee, told Bloomgarden that he had been to Washington and met with J. Edgar Hoover and Spyros Skouras. He was under pressure to inform on others, "and if they call me," he said, "I'll give them some names. They know the names anyway." This was a common excuse offered by informers. As Bentley put it, "Usually the Committee knew the names already, though there was no way of knowing for sure." More to the point, careers were ruined and even suicides committed because of names the committee already knew anyway.

Bloomgarden coldly suggested that Elia do "what your conscience tells you."

"I've got to think of my kids," Kazan pleaded.

"Gadg," the producer said, "we both have kids. They're all friends and we teach them all the same thing. Not to tattle. Remember, this will pass but you'll always be an informer in the eyes of your kids." Kazan closed the conversation with the defense that he was at least going to telephone the names first, before naming them. He had already agreed with Clifford Odets, who was scheduled to testify in May, that they would name each other. He didn't say what he would do if anyone asked not to be named.

Bloomgarden was furious. Elia had been part of the Group Theatre with him, a core member of Broadway's liberal community. Not that long ago Kermit had seen him walking around with a copy of *The Daily Worker* and only a month earlier, Bloomgarden had told his wife, "Elia said that even though he wanted no part of the Communists, if [HUAC] wanted him to give names, he'd tell them where to get off." One had to wonder, if he proved to be a turncoat, could anyone be trusted?

When Bloomgarden got back to the office, he telephoned Miller and recounted the conversation he'd just had with Kazan. He asked Art to call Elia to try to change his mind about informing. This is probably the "nervous" telephone call that Molly reported to her husband, the one that Arthur didn't write about in his autobiography.

The terrorizing search for Communists—*McCarthyism*, as it was being called—was frequently characterized as a witch hunt, a reference to the historic events in 1692 Massachusetts when some 1,000 people were arrested in Salem for consorting with the Devil. Nineteen people were hanged during that hysteria and Miller was fascinated by yet another parallel between HUAC and Salem. Even though the anticommunist investigation was political, "the rituals of guilt and confession followed all the forms of a religious inquisition." With that "surreal transaction" in mind, he had been mulling over the idea of a play about those Salem witch trials as a parable. The strangeness of witch talk and demonology seemed to suit the current feverish political atmosphere, which he thought was "much more weird and mysterious" than was conveyed by the term *McCarthyism*. He was struck by "the fact that a political, objective, knowledgeable campaign from the far right was capable of creating not only a terror, but a new subjective reality, a veritable mystique which was gradually assuming even a holy resonance."

This analogy between McCarthyism and Salem's witch hunts was rejected by sophisticated conservatives such as Molly Kazan, who argued,

> Those witches did not exist. Communists do—here, and everywhere in the world. It's a false parallel. "Witch hunt!" The phrase would indicate that there are no Communists in the government, none in the big trade unions, none in the press, none in the arts, none sending money from Hollywood.

She was wrong. The analogy does hold, since Communists were just as innocent as women accused of witchcraft; they were guilty of nothing except holding unpopular beliefs. The only difference is that in Salem believing in witchcraft was more than unpopular—it was a sin, and even worse, a crime punishable by hanging, while in America believing in communism is a constitutionally protected right. The other parallels also hold. In Washington, as in Massachusetts, accusations of evildoing were leveled by self-styled moral paragons feeding on an intemperate political climate. Too, in twentieth-century America as in seventeenth-century Salem, once the heretic was accused no defense of innocence was available. Acquittal was possible only through confession and disavowal. This intrigued Miller, the notion of confessed sin—even sin falsely confessed—being the equivalent of virtue. In 1692 the only alternative was condemnation and death by hanging, while in twentieth-century America it was merely professional and financial ruin.

That contemporary political terror, said Miller, would underlie every word in *The Crucible,* as his play was going to be called, and so he temporarily set the big new play aside. The Salem project had an immediacy to it, through which he could say what had to be said. The case of Ethel and Julius Rosenberg seems to have brought his determination to an artistic boil. He would later tell Anne Jackson (when she was playing Ethel Rosenberg in the 1970 play *Inquest*) that he had been so enraged by the treatment of the Rosenbergs that he'd set out to write the witch hunt play "about them."

His first step toward writing it was reading *The Devil in Massachusetts,* a general history of the seventeenth-century witch trials by Marion Starkey. It strengthened Miller's belief in the subject's dramatic possibilities and he decided to drive up to Massachusetts early in April 1952 for a week of primary source research. He told Kazan about it of course; they were a team and surely Elia would direct any play he wrote, but just as Miller was about to leave Roxbury for Salem, Kazan, he said, telephoned from his country retreat that was also in Connecticut and nearby. There was "something" Elia wanted to talk about. In Miller's autobiography he writes that the possibility of Kazan turning informer first occurred to him during the drive to Elia's house. The circle of ruined careers had been drawing closer. Miller's friend and editor, Frank Taylor, having become a movie producer a few years earlier, had been called into the Twentieth Century-Fox executive offices and given the "chance" to resign. He was told that if he didn't resign that afternoon, his name would appear on one of the blacklists the following day. He had no choice and now it was Elia's turn. "I all but knew," Miller said of his drive to Kazan's house, "that my friend . . . whom I loved like a brother . . . would tell me he had decided to cooperate with the Committee." Of course he already did know because Kermit Bloomgarden had told him. Miller doesn't seem to remember that. He wrote that Kazan told him he

> had been subpoenaed and had refused to cooperate but had changed his mind and returned to testify fully in executive session, confirming some dozen names of people he had known in his months at the Party. . . . As [Elia] related to me, this great director was told that if he refused to name people whom he had known in the Party years earlier—actors, directors and writers—he would never be allowed to direct another picture in Hollywood.

Kazan would insist, however, that as they walked through the woods on his property that day, he told Art that he *was going to* cooperate with the committee and that this conversation took place *before* he provided the names. Other than this crucial distinction, both men agree that Arthur, while sympathetic, disapproved of Elia's decision. They also agree that Arthur was frightened and indeed Miller would recall thinking that "Had I been of his generation, he would have had to sacrifice me as well."

What did he mean by that? Kazan was only six years older. Was that enough for Miller to conjecture that had he been the same age, and had he been with the Group Theatre in the 1930s, he probably would have joined that party cell? Or is this an autobiographical writing between the lines, an oblique reference to his own membership in the party? He always sounded careful with his words when describing his Communist involvements.

To continue his recollection, he wrote that he had chilled to the possibility that "I could still be up for sacrifice if Kazan knew I had attended meetings of Party writers years ago." This too is a bewildering remark. Why would he have kept those meetings secret from Kazan? Moreover, if Elia had already named the names, why would that be a concern? Again, how could he "still be up for sacrifice?" Indeed why would Kazan have summoned him in the first place—just to describe what he had already done? Even Miller said that it was "almost as though he had not yet done what he had done."

Despite these described concerns, Miller wrote in *Timebends* that he was no longer worried when he left Kazan's home and started for Salem. One is led to speculate that perhaps this peace of mind was the result of a deal, a promise of protection in exchange for some promise of his own, but what could that promise possibly have been?

Research had been the basis of every Arthur Miller play thus far, but never so thoroughly as it would be for the Salem play. The actual words spoken during the witch trials are preserved in the official records of the seventeenth-century proceedings, stored in the town courthouse. As Miller studied this testimony, he later said, he began to see the shape of his play. "The fate of each character" would be, he said, "exactly that of his historical model." Ultimately he would be certain that "there is no one in the drama who did not play a similar—and in some cases exactly—the same role in history." Yet *The Crucible* would not be a documentary but a blend of research and dramatic invention, making for a stage work so different from *Death of a Salesman* (as that play was from *All My Sons*) that anyone unfamiliar with these plays would not instantly recognize that Miller wrote them all.

It is unusual too for a playwright to be so concerned with morality and willing to take the inevitable abuse engendered by righteousness. In Arthur Miller's view Salem, Massachusetts, was about sin. "Pure evil" was afoot in 1692, just as, it seemed to him, evil was afoot in the United States of 1952. In his introduction to the 1957 *Collected Plays* Miller wrote,

> I believe that . . . a dedication to evil, not mistaking it for good, but knowing it as evil, and loving it as evil, is possible in human beings who appear agreeable and normal. . . . The society of Salem was "morally" vocal. People then avowed principles, sought to live by them and die by them. Issues of faith, conduct, society, pervaded their private lives in a conscious way. They needed but to disapprove to act. I was drawn to this subject because the historical moment seemed to give me the poetic right to create people of higher self-awareness than the contemporary scene affords.

In short, the history would allow him a decisive protagonist.

Miller spent a week and a half in Salem, not just in the records room of the courthouse but also in the Witch House of the town Historical Society. Even drawings of the trials exist, but the transcripts of the testimony were the prize, verbatim accounts in the original Puritan dialect. Here is a playwright's treasure trove, a virtual textbook of period idiom. Miller also drew thematic material from the testimony. "What the research showed me," he later said, "and what I hoped the play would show the country and the world, was the continuity through [history] of human delusion and the only safeguard, fragile though it may be, against it—namely, the law and the courageous few whose sacrifice illuminates."

Although Miller was already familiar with these historic events, they had a deeper resonance when studied with the 1952 political climate in mind. "It was with the contemporary situation at my back" that he drew essential parallels between the eras, "particularly the mystery of the handing over of conscience which seemed to me the central and informing fact." Miller surely had another, less lofty intention for this play—namely, success on Broadway. With this in mind he determined to avoid the Pilgrim quality of school pageants and the stigma of the costume play, a rarely successful genre. As Max Gordon, a 1920s Broadway producer, said with showmanly simplicity, "I hope I croak before I put on another play where the guy writes with a feather."

Although the analogy with contemporary political witch hunts was Miller's original motivation, and while he had conceived a through line that would transcend transient relevance to provide a more timeless theme for the spine of his play, he still needed a human element and a dramatic story. He came to the start of that with the discovery in the court records of a girl named Abigail Williams, who had touched off the Salem hysteria with witchcraft accusations against one Elizabeth Proctor. The girl had previously been the house servant of the Proctors and through her Miller hit upon a sexual element for his play, one that not by chance related to his own marital situation. The real Abigail Williams had been eleven years old and John Proctor in his sixties. Miller decided to make her seventeen and Proctor thirtyish. In one of his first notebook entries he warned himself to "Remember: the point of the act—of the play—is to show him crippled by guilt." Thus had he found an opening into his own life and his "play's center, the breakdown of the Proctor marriage and Abigail Williams's determination to get Elizabeth murdered so that she could have John, whom I [decided] she had slept with while she was their house servant, before Elizabeth fired her."

It was the fact, Miller said, "that Abigail, their former servant, was their accuser, and her apparent desire to convict Elizabeth and save John, that made the play conceivable to me." Simply by making her older and Proctor younger, he had his "central image . . . a guilt ridden man, John Proctor, who having slept with his teen age servant girl, watches with horror as she becomes the leader of the witch hunting pack and points her accusing finger at the wife he has himself betrayed."

In the Proctors Miller would be able to interpolate the tense, mutually recriminating "young married couple of the Depression generation" the *New York Times* described from his play in progress. The element of judgment would then be pervasive. Abigail's desire for John would be her ulterior motive for leveling a witchcraft accusation against Elizabeth Proctor, while John's infidelity would provide him with a guilt in search of punishment, his wife already providing some of that punishment in the form of emotional and sexual withdrawal. Miller's remaining challenge was to blend the troubled marriage with the witch hunts, making for a play that would likewise blend the two themes, personal and social guilt. The link would be relative morality.

In terms of plot one question remained: If in Salem's man-made society witchcraft is strictly women's work, why would John Proctor be hanged? In the research Miller found that Proctor, like the Hollywood Ten, was convicted of being in contempt of court, "as one of the few who not only refused to admit consorting with evil spirits, but who persisted in calling the entire business a ruse and a fake." This not only provided John Proctor with a capital crime but also suited the play's connection to McCarthyism. Still, a motive more dramatic than political was needed for his "illuminated sacrifice," for this play was going to end with a suicide, just like Miller's previous professional plays. That motive was yet to be found.

Miller realized that the play would place him at personal risk by decrying the McCarthyism that threatened people exactly like him—but was not such bold assertion exactly what the Mary figures in his early plays demanded of their men? He does seem to have been addressing the play to her. Perhaps through this coded public confession of unfaithful impulses coupled with a forthright condemnation of McCarthyism he would be granted forgiveness; he would have made it up to his wife, "pleased" her, as John Proctor is trying to please Elizabeth at the beginning of the play.

In an introduction to the published script Miller's old friend Harold Clurman seems to go out of his way to point out these personal references, writing, "That there is an autobiographical base to this drama, is undeniable." Clurman may even have been rationalizing Miller's marital transgression in describing the play's protagonist, John Proctor. "Perhaps it is this forbidding quality in [his wife] which has betrayed him into a momentary adultery . . . a fall from grace in his eyes"—possibly a private double entendre, as Mary's middle name was Grace.

Not for the last time Miller was putting himself on trial for moral guilt. Perhaps this is why he dedicated his play *For Mary*, as though she were the keeper of his conscience and in thanks for a forgiveness she seems to have been on the verge of granting. But he was already leaving her. He just didn't want to know it. In the end writing this play and thereby giving vent to his frustrations would have a liberating effect on his psyche. More important for his work, he also had the idea—and the material—for the making of a great play. He could now go home and write it.

Elia Kazan wasn't even questioned during his second round with the Committee on Un-American Activities. As the official transcript indicates on that day, April 10, 1952, at 4:25 P.M. in room 330 of the Old House Office Building, Kazan appeared before a "Subcommittee of the Committee," meaning one congressman (committee chairman Francis E. Walter) and two staff aides, who accepted a written affidavit as his full representation. His was not as craven as the testimony of some of the other cooperative witnesses, who larded abject confessions and disavowals of past politics with present praise for the committee and declarations of patriotism. Kazan's written testimony began with the statement that he wished "to amend the testimony which I gave you on January 14," adding, "I have come to the conclusion that I did wrong to withhold these names before, because secrecy serves the Communists, and is exactly what they want." After some self-exculpatory remarks about peaceful Soviet-American relations at the time of his party membership and his sense that it seemed to be independent of the Soviet Union he came to the testimony that would haunt him for the rest of his life: the names of those people he had known—in an acting school, for instance, or in actors unions—whom he believed or thought to be Communists. Most crucially he gave the committee the names of his fellow Communists in the eight-member Group Theatre cell, or at least "the only Party members of the unit whom I recall."

The names were followed by a listing of his credits, his "entire career," as he put it, with a paragraph to justify each play and every movie that he had directed as being unimpeachably patriotic. The following day the testimony was published; then on April 12, 1952, the transcript of this nonconfrontational session appeared in newsprint. Along with it the *New York Times* ran an advertisement placed by Kazan but paid for, rumor had it, by Spyros Skouras. "In the past weeks," it began, "intolerable rumors about my political position have been circulating." The statement went on to describe, in some 700 words, Elia Kazan's conviction that "Communist activities confront the people of this country" and that it was essential to "protect ourselves from a dangerous and alien conspiracy." Kazan admitted his past membership in the Communist Party and proclaimed his decision to explain it to the House Committee on Un-American Activities. Now, he said, he was placing "these facts before the public and before my co-workers in motion pictures and in the theater." He concluded by insisting that "liberals must speak out," as he described his "passionate conviction that we must never let the Communists get away with the pretense that they stand for the very things which they kill in their own countries."

The advertisement backfired, only adding infamy to capitulation. Designed to justify what Kazan had done, it instead inflamed the community he had betrayed and probably did more to stain his reputation than the testimony itself. Unwelcome now in his natural constituency, he went over to the other side and evolved into a thoroughgoing anticommunist. His movie-making career had been saved, but at a terrible cost. Ironically he himself had been betrayed—not just by the committee leak but by the executive session whose secrecy was supposed to protect his dignity. Had that record been promptly released, the first session would have demonstrated that Kazan truly tried to protect people until pushed to the wall. This might not have excused his ultimate capitulation, but it would have modified the rage with which it was met. With his original testimony sealed, however, there was no way of showing that Kazan had first and rather courageously refused to name anyone.

And so he placed a curse, it is fair to say, on his reputation, his career, his sense of himself and his name. Ever after, rather than being celebrated for his phenomenal talent as a director, Elia Kazan would be vilified as a traitor to his kind. As Senator Joseph McCarthy had come to personify the mania of the anticommunist era, so Elia Kazan would become his dance partner, the era's quintessential informer. That made for another kind of guilt and he would punish himself for it. The penalty would be a lifetime of futile defenses of his actions. It would poison his talent. With but one telling exception he would never again create any movie to compare with the splendid works that had gone before. In the theater Broadway was about to exact its own revenge. As if by its will, but more likely because of his own psychology, Kazan would never again direct on the magnificent level that, during the previous decade, had set the standard for American theatrical greatness.

Miller remembered driving home from Salem, Massachusetts, after the week and a half of research and switching on his car radio as "the announcer read a bulletin about Elia Kazan's testimony before the House Un-American Activities Committee and mentioned the people he'd named." Kazan had indeed talked to him *before* testifying.

Arthur Miller would eventually develop compassion for Elia Kazan's experience with the committee, and a measure of understanding, if not forgiveness, for the options presented and the choice made. Kazan's had surely been a cruel position. Miller certainly disapproved of informing but he also knew that it was easier to demand action than to take it. "As usual," he later remembered, "I was carrying several contradictions at the same time." In the end they did not stop him from turning away, professionally and personally, from this closest of friends. It would be many years before he would ever have anything to do with Elia Kazan, and even then the relationship would never again be the same.

10. Crucible

MUSIC WAS ALWAYS an essential part of Arthur Miller's being. He called the first act of his witch hunt play *An Overture* presumably because he considered it an opening or introduction to the main action and because that action would have certain musical qualities in the form of cadenced and stylized language, even arias and set pieces for character groups.

The story begins with Reverend Parris praying over his mysteriously ill daughter, Betty, when a niece, Abigail Williams, enters. "Strikingly beautiful," she brings the suggestion from Betty's puzzled doctor that Parris "might look to unnatural things" as the cause of the illness. "The rumor of witchcraft," says Abigail, "is all about" and even now Parris's parlor downstairs has grown crowded with frightened villagers.

Abigail herself is partly to blame for the superstitious whispers. She and Betty were in the woods dancing (which was forbidden to Puritans) when Parris discovered them. At this point Abigail forthrightly regrets the panic she has caused. "I'll be whipped if I must be," she says, "but if they're speakin' of witchcraft, Betty's not bewitched . . . we never conjured spirits." But superstition has already ripened into alarm. A couple of the townspeople, Thomas and Ann Putnam, come into the sickroom talking about witches flying over their barn and fearing for their daughter, who has suddenly been struck dumb. They sense "the Devil's touch . . . forked and hoofed," and as a "precaution," Parris decides to call for Reverend Hale, a specialist in the demonic arts.

When the Putnams' servant girl arrives to report that their daughter has now started to walk "like a dead one" (sleepwalking), Abigail takes the maid aside and makes mischief. A no-nonsense leader who can easily intimidate her adolescent friends, Abigail convinces this girl and soon several others to confess that they all danced naked in the woods and even saw the dead rise out of their graves. Abigail in fact really did drink blood, "a charm," she privately admits, to kill her former employer, Elizabeth Proctor, who had dismissed her as a maidservant.

When Elizabeth's husband, the farmer John Proctor, appears, Abigail takes him aside to passionately sigh, "Gah! I'd almost forgot how strong you are!" She reassures him that all the noise about witchcraft is pure "posh!" and pleads for "a soft word" from him. Instead he tells her "that's done with." She reminds him how he "clutched" and "sweated like a stallion" until his wife threw her out when he confessed the adultery. "You loved me then," she insists, "and you do now!" He admits to longing for her but swears to never "reach for" her again. That brings down her confidence and she pleads for his return as lover and intellectual guru. Since Proctor is not written as an educated man, this particular detail seems to complete Arthur Miller's identification with him. Indeed Marilyn Monroe said, "At the beginning [ours] was a pupil-teacher relationship," and in *The Crucible* Abigail urgently says, "I look for a John Proctor that took me from my sleep and put knowledge in my heart! I never knew what pretense Salem was, I never knew the lying lessons I was taught by all these Christian women."

Suddenly Parris's daughter Betty sits bolt upright in bed and screams at the sound of a hymn being sung downstairs, as though she were unable to abide even the name of Jesus Christ. Her shriek brings on Giles Corey, a legendary figure from the Salem witch trials, and the benevolent Rebecca Nurse (not her occupation but a name Miller found in the court record). A calming influence, Rebecca dismisses the girls' alarming behavior as adolescent mischief, and Proctor agrees that the so-called witch incidents are but teenage pranks. Yet when Reverend Hale, the witchcraft authority, arrives, he accepts some of the phenomena as deserving of investigation and explains that he will consult his reference books where "all the invisible world [is] caught, defined and calculated. Here we see all your familiar spirits—your incubi and succubi; your witches that go by land, by air, and by sea; your wizards of the night and of the day."

Those Familiar Spirits would be the nineteenth title considered for the play, and the one announced following such suggestions as *Inside and Outside*, *If We Could Speak* and Kermit Bloomgarden's own offering, *Harlot's Cry* (as well as Mary Miller's joking *Death of a Salem*). Only on Christmas Eve 1952, four weeks before the Broadway premiere, was *The Crucible* finally chosen.

The Reverend Hale suggests that if Parris's daughter Betty "is truly in the Devil's grip we may have to rip and tear to get her free." When Abigail Williams blurts out that the Caribbean maid Tituba called for the Devil, he asks whether in the woods there had been "a sudden cold wind" or "a trembling below the ground." The girl insists that she herself "didn't see no Devil" until Tituba is brought in, whereupon Abigail cries, "She made me do it! She made Betty do it! She makes me drink blood." Abigail is exhilarated by the effect Tituba has on her and shouts, "I danced for the Devil . . . I saw Sarah Good with the Devil! I saw Bridget Bishop with the Devil!" Parris's ailing daughter sits up in her sickbed once again to join in this chorus, and on these "ecstatic cries" the curtain falls on an exciting first act, a real tale played out in an evocative, exotic milieu.

The second act is set a week later. John Proctor is at home with his wife. Although their conversation is adult and mutually respectful, he is behaving in a penitent way, plainly catering to her. Elizabeth recognizes John's efforts to please her, but this, Miller notes, is hard for her to express and "a sense of their separation rises." She tells him that witch trials have begun in Salem. "There be fourteen people in the jail now, and they'll be tried," and if they don't confess to witchcraft, "the court have power to hang them too." The only proof required is for Abigail and her girls to "scream and howl and fall down to the floor" at the sight of anyone who has been accused of consorting with the Devil. Elizabeth reminds her husband of what he'd said—that Abigail herself had told him that the witch stories were pure "posh." Such an admission would surely discredit the girl and Elizabeth, relentlessly moral like the heroines of Miller's early plays, insists that John "must tell them it is a fraud."

Proctor agrees, although fearful that it will be his word against Abigail's because "She told it to me in a room alone." This indication that he has seen the girl again, and privately, renews Elizabeth's distrust of him and John explodes.

> You will not judge me more, Elizabeth . . . I have forgot Abigail . . . You forget nothin' and forgive nothin.' Learn charity, woman. I have gone tiptoe in this house all seven month since she is gone. I have not moved from there to here without I think to please you, and still an everlasting funeral marches round your heart.

Their maid, Mary Warren, returns from Salem with a gift for Elizabeth, a rag doll or "poppet." Mary had made this doll while watching the trials. She says that there are now thirty-nine women in prison on charges of witchcraft and that one is going to be hanged merely for saying that she knew the Ten Commandments when she didn't; another, though, is being freed after "confessing" to a compact made with the Devil. Mary adds that Mrs. Proctor herself has been mentioned as a potential defendant. Scared now and jealous of as well as disgusted with her husband, Elizabeth begs him to "go to Abigail. . . . There is a promise made in any bed . . . [she] thinks to kill me, then to take my place . . . go and tell her she's a whore. . . . Whatever promise she may sense—break it, John, break it."

An earlier version of this scene was perhaps stronger.

> ELIZABETH: Will you go to Abigail now? Will you tell her . . . so she may know she has . . . no hope for you?
> JOHN: How are you sure it was Abigail accused you?
> ELIZABETH: Why not? Is she too too pure, too good, too—

JOHN: I would never call her good . . .
ELIZABETH: May I know what you do call her? So I may sleep again?

Suddenly (*as shot through the air*) Reverend Hale is at their door, come to observe "the Christian character of this home" because, he tells Proctor, there is "a softness in your record, sir"—a remark that perhaps too specifically nudges a political elbow in the audience's ribs. Then "as a test" as well as a dramatic contrivance, the Reverend asks Proctor to recite the Ten Commandments. He remembers only nine, predictably repressing the proscription against adultery.

As the unimpressed minister is leaving, a frightened Elizabeth, knowing that she is really the one under suspicion, urges her husband to prove to Hale that Abigail Williams's witch stories are false. Proctor tells Hale, "Mr. Parris discovered them sportin' in the woods. They were startled and took sick." However, when Elizabeth ("a woman," John says, "who nevert lied, and cannot") says frankly that despite biblical references to witches, she cannot believe in them, her arrest is all but assured.

More news arrives with old Giles Corey, who comes in crying, "They take my wife," and even Reverend Hale is upset when he's told that the devout Rebecca Nurse has been jailed too. "Believe me," he says, "if Rebecca Nurse be tainted, nothing's left to stop the whole green world from burning," and then a clerk appears to arrest Elizabeth. As Proctor angrily defends his wife, the clerk spies the poppet that the maid, Mary Warren, gave to her. It seems that Abigail has been "stabbed" with a needle and has accused Elizabeth of attempting to murder her through witchcraft. The clerk can see that beneath its ragged dress, this doll also has a needle stuck in it, and so, he says, the charge against Elizabeth Proctor will have to be defended. Hale points out that if she is innocent the court will clear her, but that only further enrages Proctor and his outcry is plainly directed at America's twentieth-century witch hunters.

> If she is innocent?!! Why do you never wonder if Parris be innocent, or Abigail. Is the accuser always holy now? Were they born this morning as clean as God's fingers? I'll tell you what's walking Salem—vengeance is walking Salem. We are what we always were in Salem, but now the little crazy children are jangling the keys of the kingdom, and common vengeance writes the law!

As Elizabeth is led away in awful chains, her maidservant Mary pleads to Proctor that even though Abigail saw her make the doll and store the needle in it, she dare not testify to that. "She'll kill me and charge lechery on you!" "Good," he grimly replies. "We will slide together into our pit; you will tell the court what you know [because] my wife will never die for me!" And with the terrified maid's repeated cries the curtain falls on this equally exciting and rich second act.

After the intermission (the play is written in four acts but played in two) an angrily protesting Giles Corey emerges from the offstage courtroom, followed by the Massachusetts Deputy Governor Danforth, who is running the witch show. He announces that already some four hundred women are in jail for witchcraft, seventy-two of them condemned to death. When Proctor and Corey claim to have evidence—and the servant Mary as a witness—proving the girls to be frauds, Danforth agrees that if true, the effect would be conclusive, for "the entire contention of the state in these trials is that the voice of Heaven is speaking through the children."

In written and oral testimony the Proctor maid swears that all the cries of Satanism, hers and the other girls', were "pretense." Danforth, more interested in continuing the trials than in their validity, tries to bribe Proctor with clemency for his wife. If Elizabeth is pregnant, as she claims (which comes as news to John), and if he drops his accusations, then "you shall have her living yet another year until she is delivered." Miller had written a note to himself while working on this section.

> Now we have a man conceiving himself a sinner, but superior to his society, his judges . . . Question: Am I trying to tempt him with 'confession?' Yes. I am trying to bring him to the act of will when he chooses to die rather than to lie. One force is the pressure of example. Nurse, Giles. The other must be Elizabeth letting him impregnate her.

Proctor won't withdraw his charges. He insists on proving the innocence of not only his wife but of all the women who have been falsely accused.

Acting as his own attorney, he is at a decided disadvantage, and Giles Corey, after testifying to the existence of corroborating witnesses, is ordered to "tell us their names." In one of the real Salem's closest parallels with the hearings in Washington, Corey refuses to inform on others and is charged with contempt of court. Danforth, however, must deal with the maid's testimony that she "never saw Satan and neither did the other girls." He summons Abigail, who brazenly lies to the court, but Miller sustains an uncertainty of outcome as Danforth once again asks whether "the spirits you have seen are . . . some deception." The young woman toughs it out, retorting that she has been "pointing out the Devil's people—and this is my reward? To be mistrusted, denied, questioned?" She even threatens Danforth. "Let you beware. Think you to be so mighty that the power of Hell may not turn *your* wits?" She then lapses into a holy fit (*Looking about in the air, clasping her arms around her as though cold*). Her cry, "It is a wind, a wind!" whips the other girls into a frenzy and they moan "Your honor, I freeze!" and scream "Lord, save me!" This is too much for Proctor and he grabs Abigail, crying, "How dare you call to Heaven! Whore! Whore!" Now realizing that he has no other recourse, he turns to the court and admits to the crime of lechery with Abigail. And where?

> In the proper place—where the beasts are bedded. . . . A man may think God sleeps, but God sees everything, I know it now. I beg you sire, I beg you—see her for what she is. . . . She thinks to dance with me on my wife's grave! And well she might, for I thought of her softly. God help me, I lusted, and there is a promise in such sweat. But it is a whore's vengeance, and you must see it. . . . You must see it now.

Danforth demands that Abigail respond to this accusation of harlotry, but she is arrogant in her power. Certain that the court dare not level a charge of contempt against her, she refuses to even dignify that with an answer. This builds to a climax as Danforth calls for Elizabeth Proctor to confirm that, as John testified, she dismissed Abigail for harlotry. Danforth instructs that—so as not to influence the witness—everyone will turn his back to her, while Proctor repeats that his wife has never lied, could not lie and would not.

When Elizabeth is brought in, she hesitates before answering Danforth's question, and tries to protect her husband through evasion, swearing that Abigail was dismissed because "she—dissatisfied me." Danforth corners her, demanding, "Look at me! To your own knowledge, has John Proctor ever committed the crime of lechery? Answer my question! Is your husband a lecher?"

"No, sir."

"Remove her."

"Elizabeth! I have confessed it!"

"Oh, God!"

Reverend Hale, the figure of religious moderation, cries out that Elizabeth's was "a natural lie," that he believes John Proctor, and that this "must stop now before another is condemned!" When he insists that Abigail has always struck him as false, she goes into another hallucinatory fit, and "with a weird, wild, chilling cry, screams up to the ceiling." The other girls join her, turning against Mary in their shrieking and wailing, and Danforth demands that the maid either confess to having seen the Devil or hang. Breaking under the pressure, she joins the other girls, telling Proctor, "I'll not hang with you," and swears that he has done the Devil's work. When Danforth demands to know whether Proctor is "combined with anti-Christ," his reply is, "I say—I say—God is dead!" and he adds,

> A fire, a fire is burning! I hear the boot of Lucifer, I see his filthy face! And it is my face, and yours, Danforth! For them that quail to bring men out of ignorance, as I have quailed, and as you quail now when you know in all your black hearts this be fraud—God damn our kind especially, and we will burn, we will burn together!

Miller had a weakness for fiery imagery. These judgmental flames recall similar ones in *Death of a Salesman,* when flames are related to Willy being "fired" from his job—"There's a big blaze going on all around . . . I was fired today"—and of course the rest of that speech, with Willy's fearful cries that "the woods are burning, boys, do you understand?" Even the early *The Man Who Had All the Luck* presents a hero accused of starting a fire "where nobody can see" as well as the symbol of a church in flames ("there never was a sign of God that was so clear"). The very title *The Crucible* was chosen by Miller because he "wanted something that would indicate literally the burning away of the impurities, which is what the play is doing."

With John Proctor's furious outburst he and Giles Corey are hauled off to jail while Reverend Hale denounces the proceedings and quits the court, ringing down the third act curtain on Proctor's heroic curse, "God damn our kind!" and a stretch of epic drama.

The fourth and final act begins in the prison. So many people have been arrested by now that "orphans [are] wandering from house to house, abandoned cattle bellow on the highroads, the stink of rotting crops hangs everywhere." Twelve women have already been hanged and Reverend Hale is urging the other prisoners to save themselves by confessing to witchcraft. He makes a final effort to save John Proctor, asking Elizabeth to meet privately with her husband, pleading,

> Life, woman, life is God's most precious gift; no principle, however glorious, may justify the taking of it. I beg you, woman, prevail upon your husband to confess. Let him give his lie. Quail not before God's judgment in this, for it may well be God damns a liar less than he that throws his life away for pride!

This raises a fascinating question of whether martyrdom—or by extension, any variation of self-sacrifice—is ever justifiable. Miller would pursue the issue again and again, but the question does not stump Elizabeth Proctor. She replies, "That be the Devil's argument," for she is more righteous even than the Puritans, a woman of immoderate morality.

Even Danforth urges her to save her husband. "Have the Devil dried up any tear of pity in you?" Chastened, she agrees to meet with John as Miller succeeds in maintaining a strong sense of bond in this strained marriage. Now man and wife alone together, Elizabeth tells John that already one hundred women have confessed to witchcraft but not, she points out, Rebecca Nurse. And not Giles Corey, who cried "more weight!" as he was being executed by means of "pressing," his chest crushed by stones. In short, some still hold to their principles even unto death. One of Miller's notebook entries suggests that at this "point when Elizabeth advises [John Proctor] not to lie, he does not know if it is . . . her desire to destroy him or her love for his unblemished soul." (Did Miller think that his own wife was in some way trying to destroy him?) Proctor declines, thank you very much, to take principle as far as martyrdom. "Nothing's spoiled," he tells Elizabeth, "by giving them this lie that were not rotten long before," and he asks her forgiveness for a false confession. Unyielding, she tells him that forgiveness "is not for me to give."

Miller then gives her leeway. His play was (or at least seems to have been) partly written as a supplication to his wife, Mary. He lends Elizabeth Proctor a measure of leniency, perhaps wishful thinking on his part, as she tells her husband, "Be sure of this. Whatever you will do, it is a good man does it. I have read my heart this three month, John. I have sins of my own to count. It needs a cold wife to prompt lechery." It is a speech for her that Miller originally wrote in quite lovely metered prose, "It needs a cold wife to prompt / Lechery. I counted myself so plain." And again, "Suspicion / kissed you when I did; I never / knew how I should say my love."

Only a week before the New York opening Miller chose to revise this as straightforward dialogue, so that Elizabeth merely concedes, "it were a cold house" and offers her blessing, "I never knew such goodness in the world!" (He told a friend—William Styron's wife, Rose—"Much of *Death of a Salesman* was originally written in verse. *The Crucible* was all written in verse.) This sudden softness, so out of character for Elizabeth—which is probably why Miller dropped the even softer verse—is also a device to prolong suspense. More than that, it reflects an Arthur Miller who cannot shake his inclination to equivocate, which is so desirable in logic and so diffusive in drama. From out of this conflict of principled resolve and survivalism, Proctor decides, "I will have my life."

The playwright now risks the headlong thrust of his narrative by pausing to have his characters speak of guilt and innocence, confession and absolution and comparative moralities. Proctor continues to treat Elizabeth as his moral superior, imploring her to judge the integrity of his confessing to a crime uncommitted. "Would *you* give them such a lie? You would not, if tongs of fire were singeing you, you would not!! It is evil.

"Good, then," the guilt-ridden, unfaithful husband cries in self-contempt. "It is evil and I will do it." He turns to the inquisitors and admits he has seen the Devil. Yes, he was bidden to do the Devil's work, and yes, he bound himself into the Devil's service.

Here Miller points the play directly at Elia Kazan. Asked to name names ("To your knowledge, was Rebecca Nurse ever—?"), Proctor refuses. This reflects a toughening of Miller's attitude toward Kazan's informing. His initial impulse had been generous. As always, he looked to both sides of an argument, and he'd felt some compassion for his friend's predicament. By the time he started writing the play his attitude had evidently hardened, for he begins to sound like the college playwright whose *Honors at Dawn* raged at informers ("Stand up, ya rat! . . . Ya' crept to 'em, didn't ya!"). Perhaps Mary had had something to do with it.

In *The Crucible* John Proctor, like Kazan after his first session with HUAC, is not punished for refusing to provide names. In both cases each is so respected in the community that the inquisition's purposes are better served by confession than conviction. In the play Proctor's confession is taken, put in writing and presented for his signature, which he refuses to provide. Miller here rises to the occasion by giving Proctor a heroic stance and the play a powerful conclusion as he stretches the man's final dignity across a stirring passage, plainly addressed to Elia Kazan. Proctor's decision to save his own life—unlike Kazan's decision to survive in Hollywood—is withdrawn when such a decision requires that he disgrace his name.

> I confess to God, and God has seen my name on this! It is enough! . . . God does not need my name nailed on the church . . . You will not use me! . . . I have three children—how may I teach them to walk like men in the world, and I sold my friends?

As Kermit Bloomgarden had said more than once on the subject of informing, "We teach our children the same thing. Not to tattle."

Asked once again why he will not sign his own confession, he makes a most magnificent speech, all but nailing Kazan's looming fate.

> Because it is my name! Because I cannot have another in my life! Because I lie and sign myself to lies! Because I am not worth the dust on the feet of them that hang! How may I live without my name? I have given you my soul; leave me my name!

Proctor tears up the confession, "weeping in fury," and as he is left doomed to the gallows, the play's last line is left for Elizabeth. It is telling, for it implicitly approves his suicide. "He have his goodness now. God forbid I take it from him!" Thus Proctor's self-punishment for his personal guilt of adultery.

Elia Kazan surely grasped the play's allusions to him, but he spoke only of its autobiographical references. "I had to guess," he said, "that Art was publicly apologizing to his wife for what he'd done." Clifford Odets also avoided the political implications of *The Crucible,* dismissing the work as "just a story about a bad marriage." The hostility that these former friends expressed was predictable to say the least, fresh as they were from helpful sessions with the Committee on Un-American Activities. (Odets had been a cooperative witness a few weeks after Kazan.) Even though they were on the prejudiced lookout for flaws in the play, however, the two men's knowledge of Miller's private life indeed was intimate and their take on personal aspects of *The Crucible* would seem incontrovertible. The play is not only dedicated to Mary Miller; in a meaningful way it is her play. John Proctor, with whom Miller so obviously identifies, has sacrificed himself not, as he cries, for the sake of his good name but rather to the gods of morality. Having betrayed Elizabeth he can never redeem his innocence. He can only commit an act of contrition—namely, the "illuminated sacrifice." Miller thus seems to have bought into the biblical premise that with knowledge of evil innocence is dead, leaving only guilt as the opposite of evil.

Early in the play Proctor had remonstrated to his wife, "I should have roared you down when first you told me your suspicions. But I wilted and, like a Christian, I confessed." Late in the play he accepts her accusations and concedes his guilt for betraying the marriage vows. It is a Catholic ritual—confession, penance and absolution. As Miller described it, "The whole process of self-condemnation now begins to join the process of social condemnation. And that was exactly what I was after, because without one you can't have the other." Another view of this is that of a child-man's marriage to a dominating, judging, punishing mother figure. This then is also perhaps a psychological ritual, a misbehaving child violating the maternal rules, to be punished and forgiven. With that is earned another play date—and inevitably another misdeed, another punishment, another forgiving. This was perceived early on by Elia Kazan, master director and instinctive psychologist, although he failed to notice the same pattern in his own marriage. Molly's politics and morality might have been the polar opposite of Mary's, but their psychologies were similar. Elia Kazan's penance to satisfy his wife seems to have been served in Washington, while for Arthur Miller the penance was his confession and ritual martyrdom in *The Crucible*.

If Arthur Miller indeed were guilt-stricken about his adulterous impulses, the confession in *The Crucible*—John Proctor's "self-condemnation"—certainly seems to have rid him of that guilt, and he had Mary to thank for it. She could hardly have realized that it left him free to grow up and leave her. This is an example of what Harold Bloom called "the influence of the work upon the life [rather] than the supposed influence of the life upon the work."

As for the real Elizabeth Proctor, she was not hanged; she was pardoned four years after John was hanged, and then she remarried.

When *The Crucible* was finished to Arthur Miller's satisfaction, he handed it over to Kermit Bloomgarden for production, both knowing that their first choice for its director was the last person they would ask. On July 28, 1952, the *New York Times*, playing the game of false naivete, offered no theory as to why Elia Kazan would not be directing *Those Familiar Spirits*, as Miller's play was still being called.

> Severed is the Damon and Pythias collaboration of Elia Kazan . . . and Arthur Miller. Despite his refusal to assign any reason, it is known that a disagreement—nothing to do with the play, though—exists between them that would make their future association incompatible.

It was as if the entertainment editors did not read their own newspaper's front page. They could hardly have been unaware of the significance of Elia Kazan's recent HUAC appearance. "Now," Bloomgarden recalled, "we had to find someone of Kazan's caliber to direct it."

While the producer registered *The Crucible* as "The Second Play" and prepared to raise its capitalization, his other important playwright, Lillian Hellman, began lobbying for the directing assignment on behalf of her current lover (aside, that is, from Dashiell Hammett, who lived with her)—the infamous Jed Harris. Once the theater's "wonder boy," virtually the inventor of Broadway, the "meteor" who had shot to fame and the cover of *Time* Magazine at the age of twenty-eight with four consecutive hits in the 1920s, Harris had crash-landed into oblivion. He was consumed by a director's psychology in extremis, driven to control, operate, dominate and then to destroy the very actors and playwrights who were essential to his success. This compulsion rendered useless his considerable talents as a producer and director. Ever since his landmark 1938 production of *Our Town* he'd had no luck on Broadway, with the singular exception of Ruth and Augustus Goetz's *The Heiress*. Since then Harris had been reduced to directing flops and concocting money-raising schemes, finally producing on *television*—and even that he could only feign. He had lost whatever confidence ever existed behind his arrogant front, and now virtually destitute behind a grand theatrical manner, he could only hope for an assignment as a director. When his friend, the press agent Jim Proctor, mentioned that Bloomgarden had a new Miller play and needed a director, Harris had his last chance for resurrection. So he had courted the producer's prize playwright, Lillian Hellman, a woman he privately described as "so ugly, I can fuck her but I can't dance with her."

Lillian Hellman wasn't so ugly when it came to theatrical success. She had enjoyed a string of prestigious hits, among them *The Little Foxes* and *The Children's Hour*. She was also the reigning heroine of the liberal community, for in May 1952, just a month after Kazan's Washington shame, she had defied the committee's demands for names with the grandly heroic statement, "I cannot and will not cut my conscience to fit this year's fashions." And she had gotten away with both the refusal and the grandiosity.

Theatrically and politically Lillian Hellman carried a lot of weight with Kermit Bloomgarden and he listened when she recommended Jed Harris to direct *The Crucible*, even though Harris, just fifty-two, was literally a has-been, not only dead in show business—and many thought he actually was dead; the rest just seemed to wish he were. "When word got out," Bloomgarden recalled, "that we were thinking of Harris, I began to receive calls. George Kaufman shouted into the phone, 'Are you out of your mind?'" (Among Kaufman's many legendary remarks was his hope that "When I die I want to be cremated and have my ashes thrown in Jed Harris's face.") Most people thought it was Harris who was out of his mind. "Wild and irrational," the producer Vinton Freedley said to Bloomgarden, "he'll destroy you."

Yet Jed Harris, while "dead broke," as he privately admitted, could still summon up the bravado to borrow his own former yacht—since repossessed—then collect Jim Proctor, who was also Arthur Miller's friend, and sail from Shelter Island across Long Island Sound to Westport, Connecticut, to have the playwright for dinner aboard the boat, which Harris of course passed off as his own. Arthur was certainly impressed, and not merely by the yacht and Harris's erudite conversation and elegant manner ("I had suspicions from the outset that he was just too classy for me"), which were not entirely phony, but almost. The man who said he was the Viennese-born Jed Harris had been born Jacob Horowitz in a shtetl in Eastern Europe. However, he indeed had gone to Yale, talking himself into the college and after three years leaving in disgust with its anti-Semitism.

But what impressed Miller most about the man was a memory of the 1936 Harris production of *A Doll's House,* which he still considered a once-in-a-lifetime experience. As for the Salem play, "Harris had done his research," Miller remembered, or so the director had made it seem. In fact Harris knew only what Proctor had told him on their ride across the Sound, but he was on his confidence game and Miller was "aware of a tremendous visceral force emanating from him. Because my play was so emotional, in story as well as in theme, I thought that this energy of his would help a production."

Therefore, and shortly afterward, Kermit Bloomgarden announced a fall 1952 opening of *Those Familiar Spirits* and mailed a letter to prospective investors offering, script unseen, shares in his production of Arthur Miller's first new play since *Death of a Salesman,* to be directed by Jed Harris, "America's most distinguished director."

Backers rushed to invest. Lillian Hellman signed on for $1,500. The actors Montgomery Clift and Karl Malden put in $1,000 apiece. The *New York Times* reported that

> the privileged few who have read one draft or another . . . are extremely enthusiastic about it. The excitement is not as wide as it was in the case of *Death of a Salesman* but only because before that play went into production, Mr. Miller was unrecognized as a playwright and more people had access to the script.

The play had been written in Connecticut during the 1952 summer in the twelve foot by eighteen foot freestanding studio that Miller had built for writing *Death of a Salesman*. Jed Harris would take much longer than that trying to get Miller to rewrite it. He was still up to his old trick of undermining a playwright's confidence through endless time spent together over repeated revisions. "He couldn't read a newspaper article," Miller said, "without telling you it needed a rewrite." This working relationship "horrified" Bloomgarden, who remembered a day he "came in on Arthur sitting typing a new scene as Jed pulled pages right out of the typewriter. This was my idea of how to produce hack work."

It was the Broadway style of creating on the fly, perhaps inevitable and even fun in lowbrow commercial theater but hardly appropriate to serious playwriting. Yet Miller was caught up in it because a part of him enjoyed the show business of Broadway and because Jed Harris was Broadway incarnate and Broadway did not distinguish between important plays and commercial plays. Some time would pass and be wasted before Arthur came to his senses, but meanwhile the premiere had to be postponed until early 1953.

As rewriting continued, Miller had to fight off Harris's demands for shared royalties and even a credit as coauthor, but this was one playwright not prone to intimidation and he finally lost patience with America's most distinguished director. "The only reason Arthur didn't fire Jed," Jim Proctor remembered, "was because they had worked so long on the script, past the point of no return."

As for the title, Miller was certain that his suggestion of *The Crucible* appealed to Harris "Simply because most people wouldn't know what a crucible was and he was a snob." Proctor had to issue a press release defining it as "a vessel, usually of earthenware, made to endure great heat, used for fusing metals, etc. The figurative meaning in which the word is used is 'any severe test or trial.'" This was just in case newspaper editors couldn't figure it out for themselves.

Casting the play was no problem except for the leading role of John Proctor. Miller had written it with his favorite actor Arthur Kennedy in mind, but Kennedy was already rehearsing another play and Harris didn't like him anyway, complaining, "He doesn't have class. He's just an Irishman from Worcester." Miller replied that class was not important since John Proctor "is just a peasant himself," but with "Johnny" Kennedy unavailable it didn't matter.

Harris was eager to have Richard Widmark in the part, but the actor's movie studio would not release him. Six weeks before rehearsals were to begin there still was no John Proctor. Many names were being considered, if not always with their knowledge, such as Richard Burton, Marlon Brando and Robert Ryan, but after Arthur Kennedy's play opened and failed Miller and Bloomgarden ganged up on a reluctant Harris and they signed him. The other roles were already cast, but as work on the production began, Beatrice Straight, playing Elizabeth Proctor, thought that while

> Jed's discussions and character insights were exciting and bold, company resentment was already building. He'd begun feeling out the cast. Who could he dominate? Walter Hampden [Danforth]. Who would he have to tolerate? E. G. Marshall [Reverend Hale]. Who could he abuse? Cloris Leachman [who fled Harris's punishment and was replaced as Abigail Williams by Madeleine Sherwood]. And who could Jed grapple with? Who was Jed's personal scapegoat for *The Crucible*?

Inevitably that was Kennedy, for Harris gleefully undermined his leading men (when he directed *The Green Bay Tree* he'd gone after Laurence Olivier). He got started on Kennedy the first day of rehearsal. "Go out and dye your hair black," he told the actor. "You'll come back two inches taller." There was no sense in this insidious taunting of an actor; it was psychological sadism. In his headlong drive toward self-destruction Harris spent considerable mental energy seeking out the vulnerabilities of his prey. Kennedy was a man of just average height. His hair was red and thin. In the interest of finding an actor's vulnerability vanity was always a good place to start.

Fortunately for Kennedy Harris's other problems soon distracted him. He could no longer mask his insecurities with cruelty. He may have cut a flamboyant figure (Bloomgarden described him as "looking like a 1920s bright young man, except that it was 1952") by showing up at rehearsal in a camel hair polo coat flung theatrically over his shoulders and a gray fedora pulled over one brow, but despite the desired effect, it was undone by the distinct quaver of his teetering confidence.

As Harris began staging the play, his work took on the eerie qualities of another era. The company was directed to address speeches to the audience rather than between characters. Directors commonly had the actors' positions chalked out on the stage floor, but this one instructed the cast never to move from those marks. He was creating a static tableau. More than once Harris referred to "Dutch Masters" as the look he wanted, referring to the illustration on a box of popular cigars, a formally arranged group of Pilgrims in seventeenth-century high hats and white collars, staring out from the cigar box lid.

This was certainly a change from Elia Kazan and even Proctor was appalled. The press agent who had been awed in the Jed Harris heyday now sensed "a quality of desperation" in the man.

> He was trying too hard. The values emerging were overly melodramatic, making it into a neat play with a beginning, a middle and an end instead of this rocklike, tumultuous, tremendously original thing that Miller had started out with. He was making a tremendous effort to have the whole business under control and acceptable as a commercial play.

Miller agreed that Harris was simply "terrified. I think he was afraid that he didn't know what to do with my play," and in such a mood and condition the *Crucible* company took the train to Wilmington, Delaware, on January 18, 1953, for the play's brief tryout engagement. Miller and Harris shared a private compartment, where the playwright spoke with a reporter from the *New York Times* while the director thumbed through a yachting magazine, looking up to make the occasional wry comment. He still had some of the old Harris charm. While the ever-serious Miller talked about morality and theocracy, inquisitions and hangings, Harris said, "In Andover they hanged a dog. The dog said, 'I'm not even human.' They said, 'That's what you say,' and they hanged the dog."

Miller insisted on being serious and went on about his play. "The idea," he told the journalist, "came to me a long time ago. I became fascinated with it because altogether these people of Massachusetts were quite ordinary people, and it is rare in history or in life that you get such a complete heroic tragedy occurring in reality." The remark seems to underscore the play as another example of *tragedy and the common man*. Miller must have had *Death of a Salesman* on his mind because he went on to say that *The Crucible* "has an aseptic form . . . it's less sensuous than *Salesman* . . . more pitiless, probably because . . . the witch hunt was fundamentally a business of prosecutors and lawyers, witnesses, testimony—" Harris interrupted. He could still flash some of his old, tough-minded theatrical sense, but in this case it came at the expense of the play, which is hardly helpful in terms of newspaper publicity. "It is a monster of a play," he told the reporter, and

> overwritten . . . Arthur has tried to cover too much ground, and there is enough in it for four plays. There are things here that are wild and mad. . . . I don't care about that. I know that there are flaws. But this play has a certain bigness. I think it has a certain power. And even that is not right for me to say. . . . What gives me a pain is this conception of Arthur as a big social thinker, a man sitting like a sort of Brooklyn Ibsen, sitting thinking about the ills of society.

However misguided and even harmful such remarks were, Harris did have a point. "*Art shmart* . . . if this play is any good," he told the man from the *New York Times*, as he had told many reporters over the years, "it can only be good for one reason. As a theatrical experience." Not for Miller. Finally alluding to his play's politics, he suggested, "there may be repercussions on this play. There may be those who will think it was deliberately written because of the present period through which we are living. But that doesn't matter [and] even if there are repercussions, I don't worry. I have had repercussions before."

That was real bravery. Jed Harris's attitude may have been appropriate to the kind of energetic, entertaining theater that he had pioneered, but it was an attitude that mocked higher aspirations. *Art shmart* indeed. *The Crucible* was saying something tremendously important in an artful way, and Miller's seriousness and political courage were more real than a diverting escapism.

The dress rehearsal in Wilmington was a disaster. Harris was all but delirious with fright and barred Bloomgarden from the theater. Kermit told Arthur, "Everything I heard about this man is true. Besides being a crazy son of a bitch, he is a moral and physical coward," but by then it was too late. On the Delaware opening night—the play's world premiere—Miller only intermittently watched from the back of the theater. His agent, Kay Brown, kept him company on his frequent nervous trips to the lobby bar, and there they sat as the final curtain fell. Then they came back to watch the curtain calls and judge the audience response, which was rapturous. There were cries for "Author! Author!" (a custom that, alas, has since disappeared) but as the playwright headed down the side aisle toward the stage, he saw his director saunter out from the wings to take the author's bow himself. Miller met Harris coming down from the stage, holding out a jacket lapel and sputtering, "They pulled me out like this. The actors." Kay Brown later said the man had to be mad. "What was he doing, taking Arthur's bow?"

Jed Harris probably didn't know what he was doing but at least the *New York Times* reported the opening night a success, even if it did not quite report the event accurately. "Shouts for the author were so insistent that Miller had to take a bow."

During the next few performances in Wilmington Beatrice Straight felt that Harris "had quit on the play." He was having his (and Ruth Gordon's) illegitimate twenty-two-year-old son give the cast their notes, which, it was roundly suspected, the son himself wrote, because Harris wasn't showing up at the performances. So it was a less than buoyant company that returned to New York for the play's January 22, 1953, Broadway premiere at the Martin Beck Theatre.

Many of Miller's friends were there that evening, including Kazan's replacement as best friend, the artist Alexander ("Sandy") Calder, a Roxbury neighbor. Even so the playwright was depressed. "The actors," he said, "were dried up from the tryout ordeal. They couldn't maintain a level of life."

That wasn't as the *New York Herald-Tribune* reported the opening night.

> Before the curtain rose, the audience sat in such expectant silence that one got the impression of being in a cathedral. Then, in the second act when the curtain was lowered for two minutes between scenes, these same spectators let loose a barrage of sustained applause rarely heard during the course of a dramatic offering. The bravos were resumed at the play's close and repeated cries of "author" finally brought Mr. Miller on from the wings.

This time, he took the bow himself.

Gloomy as usual, for once Miller had reason. The reviews were mixed, leaving theatergoers in the unaccustomed position of actually having to make up their own minds. "And of course," Miller said, "the play opened in the teeth of the McCarthy gale. As soon as the audience realized that's what it was about, they froze—and the critics likewise." This is less an accurate observation than a playwright's rationalization. A likelier explanation for the mixed critical reception was the memory of *Death of a Salesman* and its sobbing audiences, its emotional power. As Brooks Atkinson wrote in the *New York Times*, "After the experience of *Death of a Salesman*, we probably expect Mr. Miller to write a masterpiece every time. *The Crucible* is not of that stature and it lacks that universality."

Many critics considered *The Crucible* a chilly play, associating power with emotional heat. None of the major reviewers noted any relationship to the anticommunism then fevering America. Atkinson tried to be kind to his old favorite—not Miller but Jed Harris—writing, "No doubt the overwrought direction by Jed Harris is deliberate, for a specific dramatic reason." Yet the man from the *Times* did not speculate on what that reason might have been and ambiguously concluded, "Although the performance is brilliantly organized and paced, it becomes a little tiresome before the play is over." Other notices were likewise noncommittal, with a slant toward the downside. In the *New York Herald-Tribune*, Walter F. Kerr thought the play was message-driven and called it a "mechanical parable," although he did not explain the point of the parable. "Salem and the people who live, love, fear and die in it, are really only conveniences to Mr. Miller, props to his thesis. He does not make them interesting in and for themselves. . . . You stand and think; you don't really share very much."

Proctor's assistant press agent, Merle Debuskey, remembered,

> Wolcott Gibbs of *The New Yorker* was so drunk, he had to be carried into his seat. The next morning, Bloomgarden said to Proctor, "He can't possibly review the play. You have to talk to him." Proctor started the awkward conversation with Gibbs, only to be interrupted. "Jimmy, tell Kermit not to worry. It'll be a rave."

Such was the respect with which theater was treated on Broadway. Serious and artistic dramas were lumped together with musicals and comedies, all reviewed on the run—or the reel. Debuskey recalled that *The Crucible* had a mildly respectable engagement,

> but it certainly wasn't a great hit. In the Thirties and Forties, people were writing plays of, you should pardon the expression, social significance. These were accepted and eagerly looked to. A broad spectrum of people were going to the theater in those days. By the Fifties, that spectrum had begun to narrow and the lower classes were out of it altogether while the middle class had begun to become conservative like the president, Eisenhower. It didn't help that *The Crucible* was described as a political play, and with the pressures that were beginning to seep down from HUAC, it was even something to avoid.

Five months into a faltering run Miller was still flinching from the reviews that had accused his play of being cold and unemotional. Blaming the Harris production, he decided to restage the play himself. Although he had consciously intended "to go beyond [writing] a play to draw a tear," he now reinstated an emotional scene that had been cut during rehearsals. He also reduced the production's operating cost by removing the heavy realistic scenery that he never liked in the first place. This gave the play a more stylized look, as he had first wanted—"a physicalization of infinite space so that the play wouldn't be going on now or in 1692, but was instead going on forever." Always a visual person, Miller sometimes even sketched such suggestions for scenery. His preferred design for *The Crucible* had been symbolic, "two funnel-like openings that led the audience into a tunnel." The best he could do now was to have it played against a simple black drop cloth using basic props. A director's permission is usually required for such changes but Miller did not seek it and Harris did not complain.

Reviewing the revised production for the *Times*, Brooks Atkinson wrote,

> The changes have improved [it]. *The Crucible* has acquired a certain human warmth . . . a brief new scene between Abigail Williams and John Proctor . . . completely motivates their clash in the following scene . . . Mr. Miller has personally re-directed a good deal of the performance, giving it more variety and humanity than it had.

Good re-reviews, however, rarely undo the damage done by the originals, and the production closed on July 11, 1953, after only 197 performances, with Arthur Miller apparently failing to meet the challenge of following up on the tremendous success of *Death of a Salesman*. It was a challenge that Tennessee Williams had successfully met with *The Rose Tattoo* and the two playwrights were still being coupled as the princes of Broadway drama. Although a most unlikely couple, they understood and accepted that relationship, Williams always standing up for Miller and Miller sensing a kinship with Williams. "Tennessee felt that his redemption lay in writing," he said, "and I feel the same way. That's when you're most alive."

As for *The Crucible*, with the Broadway theater being essentially the only American theater, the play might have died the death of a flop. The European acclaim accorded *Death of a Salesman*, however, had made Arthur Miller not merely an American playwright but an international one. *The Crucible* would have an ongoing life in the continental repertory.

Reviewing its British premiere in the *Sunday Times of London*, Harold Hobson wrote,

> Mr. Miller does not allow his personal convictions to interfere with the dramatist's responsibility for presenting every one of his characters with understanding and sympathy. He shows that the witch hunting of bygone Salem generated hysteria, terror, cruelty, and injustice; that it degraded the nature of those taking part in it; that it brought ruin and death to the innocent. He protests against the brutality and stupidity with which evil was persecuted, but he does not claim either that the evil did not exist or that, existing, it was good.

This marked the beginning of a long-lasting love affair between the British and Arthur Miller, and the play would have a year's run in Paris too as *Les Sorcieres de Salem*. It was promptly staged in Munich, Berlin and Copenhagen, and productions were scheduled for Buenos Aires, Vienna, Cologne, Rome and Brussels. In addition there would soon be an American theater beyond Broadway with an audience seeking more serious-minded plays. Ultimately *The Crucible* would become a modern classic, a staple of the international theater, a subject of regular New York revivals and by far Arthur Miller's most frequently performed play.

In a preface to the first published edition Miller describes his play as revealing "the essential nature of one of the strangest and most awful chapters in human history"—a careful remark that might be taken as a reference to witch hunts instead of McCarthyism. In time—but for artistic reasons—he would try to distance his play from the political connection, preferring to emphasize its broader and more enduring theme of moral guilt. A half century later a slip of the tongue could betray his original impulse.

> A man like [Proctor] would literally shrivel up and die if he found himself dragging other people into this nest of vipers. . . . He has an idea of himself which is that of a leader of a sort, a moral example, perhaps, for others, so he's letting down a lot of people if he should accede to the committee.

Not the committee; there is no committee in *The Crucible*. Miller meant to say, "the inquisition." Yet the play's allusions to contemporary political events in the 1950s would never limit its universality.

One of several ways in which *The Crucible* is unique is that apart from the staged experience, a reading provides extratheatrical rewards. Still not satisfied that he had expressed himself fully, Miller wrote additional material for the first New York revival. That came in 1958, when the alternative Off-Broadway theater was in a formative phase.

The additions are not dramatic passages. These are essays recited by an actor cast as "The Reader" to "set the scenes and give the historical background of the play." About these narrative passages Professor Orm Overland of the University of Bergen, Norway, points out, "The narrator is hardly an innovation in the history of dramatic literature, especially when seen in relation to the chorus in Greek drama." Yet these narrations, he said, reveal a "reluctance to let a play speak for itself," suggesting that Miller implicitly felt that he had not been understood within the body of the play. In compensation the playwright thus took on "the roles of historian, novelist and literary critic, often all at once, speaking himself *ex-cathedra* rather than through his characters *ex scena*." Overland sees little difference between these and other essays by Miller on *The Crucible* except that "in the one instance, he is looking at his play from the outside, as one of its many critics, in the other he has added new material and has thus changed the text." It is a point well taken.

These narrations have invariably been deleted from subsequent productions of the play but the spoken essays are included in most published editions, making for an unusual combination of drama and expository prose. A reader may either skip them to continue with the action or pause to reflect, to learn more about a character and history, to enjoy the playwright-author's speculations about John Proctor or consider views on related matters, much as Shaw had done in his prefaces. It must be added that Miller, like Shaw, could be verbose, unconvincingly academic, convoluted and overbearing in such writings.

The first of these essays is an introductory Note on the Historical Accuracy of the Play. Here Miller explains that he has taken certain dramatic liberties, for example, making Abigail Williams older, John Proctor younger, and combining many real characters into a few, the hysterical girls, for instance, and the various judges. Then in the midst of the first act Miller provides a description of Proctor (fictitious of course and possibly self-referential) as "powerful of body, even tempered, not easily led . . . a sharp and biting way with hypocrites. [But] he is a sinner, a sinner not only against the moral fashion of the time, but against his own vision of decent conduct." A few pages later Miller writes at length about Francis Nurse, who barely appears in the play. This is factual. Nurse owned some 300 prime acres in Salem, a tract of property so envied that it became the subject of a squabble. Miller speculates that this property and Thomas Putnam's greed for it motivated the persecution of Francis and Rebecca Nurse, and that the people behind it were members of the extended Putnam family. He found in court records that it was the Putnams "who signed the first complaint against Rebecca [Nurse] and that Thomas Putnam's young daughter was the one who fell into a fit at the hearing and pointed to Rebecca." This then is his reason for making the Putnams the play's central alarmists.

The longest essay begins with an invented description of the Reverend Hale as "a tight-skinned, eager-eyed intellectual." Miller makes him out a witchcraft authority of humanist inclination ("his belief is not to his discredit"), and takes the occasion to discourse on the Devil and sin. "It is as impossible," he writes, "for most men to conceive of a morality without sin as of an earth without sky." The essay then becomes a discussion of political morality—capitalists embodying evil for Communists and reactionaries doing the same for leftists—before returning to theological Satanism as related to sin generally and sex particularly. "Our opposites are always robed in sexual sin," he writes, "and it is from this unconscious conviction that demonology gains both its attractive sensuality and its capacity to infuriate and frighten."

Miller then describes true events that occurred after the play is over, for instance, compensatory payments that the Massachusetts government made to victims, the church's rescinding of excommunications, Elizabeth Proctor's remarriage and in a gossipy footnote, "Legend has it that Abigail turned up later as a prostitute in Boston." On a somewhat more serious level he concludes, "To all extents and purposes, the power of theocracy in Massachusetts was broken." The British critic Malcolm Bradbury has suggested that these interpolated essays have "in effect, 'novelized'" the play. Maybe so, but they also provide an enlightening, provocative and complementary pleasure to seeing *The Crucible* performed. In many editions too the text of the play is followed by the second-act scene that Miller was unable to make up his mind about, first agreeing to its deletion then restoring it when he redirected the original production. In this scene John Proctor pays a late-night call on Abigail Williams. She thinks it is for love but instead he ridicules her hallucinations. She pleads conviction ("My spirit's changed entirely. I ought to be given Godly looks") and calls him the only good person in Salem, as Miller again uses fiery imagery, this time in her dialogue.

> [Y]ou taught me goodness . . . It was a fire you walked me through, and all my ignorance was burned away. It was a fire, John, we lay in fire . . . And then you burned my ignorance away . . . And God gave me strength to call them liars. . . . Oh, John, I will make you such a wife when the world is whole again.

But Proctor has come to threaten her. "If you do not free my wife tomorrow, I am set and bound to ruin you." He has proof, he tells her, that "you yourself bade Mary Warren stab that needle into [the doll]." Abigail rears back and cries, "No, this is your wife pleading, your sniveling, envious wife!" Besides, she incredulously asks, "You will confess to fornication?" Yes, he tells her. "You will never cry witchery again, or I will make you famous for the whore you are!" She embraces him, insisting, "You are at this moment singing secret hallelujahs that your wife will hang!" He calls her a "murderous bitch" and she responds that he is a hypocrite. "I pray," she says, "you will come again with sweeter news for me. I know you will—now that your duty's done . . . From yourself I will save you."

After Miller had restored this scene it was again dropped, this time from a 1965 production by the National Theatre of Great Britain at the suggestion of its artistic director Laurence Olivier, who insisted that it was superfluous. The scene is usually omitted from American productions, although it underscores contradictions in both characters and makes the worthy point that Proctor is himself in need of saving, and not in a religious sense but from his own guilt. (The speech for Abigail, "From yourself I will save you," was one of Miller's first lines for the play.) The scene's inclusion as an addendum to the published text allows directors the option of restoring it. Originally conceived to start the play, this scene was probably meant to introduce Proctor's own self-contradictions and hypocrisy, an adulterer who claims to be a moral man. This is one of Miller's precepts for the play, entered in his notebook at the outset.

> Abigail has absolute conviction that John's love for his wife is a formality and that she will get him after it is all over. Yes. This first scene should present him with one who really believes in his evil. And she is on the offensive against his, and all, hypocrisy.

Miller sketched another speech for Abigail in that early notebook, one that might have made a powerful and provocative impression in the play.

> If your wife had what I have under her dress, she'd be what I am . . . there never were a husband didn't linger at my bed to say good night. What's this "goodness?" They lie and call it goodness. That's why the world trembles at them. Because they're all liars, and I alone, I am the truth, for I am what they want, I am what the women hate with envy.

He decided not to use it, perhaps because this was Mary's play.

A particular quality of *The Crucible* is its dialogue, well described by the English director Richard Eyre as "a collage of language that is a marvelous blend of . . . biblical cadences, pastoral poetry, regional English dialect and muscular theatrical rhetoric." This invented language is a rich and stageworthy mix of past and present vernaculars that suggest but do not replicate the English spoken in Puritan rural seventeenth-century Massachusetts. This style enables Miller to evoke Salem in a twentieth-century sense, as in the following speech for Elizabeth Proctor.

> I cannot think the Devil may own a woman's soul, Mr. Hale, when she keeps an upright way, as I have. I am a good woman, I know it, and if you believe I may do only good work in the world, and yet be secretly bound to Satan, then I must tell you, sir, I do not believe it.

Or this common speech of a peasant.

> The girl, the Williams girl, Abigail Williams, sir. She sat to dinner in Reverend Parris's house tonight, and without word nor warnin' she falls to the floor. Like a struck beast, he says, and screamed a scream that a bull would weep to hear. And he goes to save her, and, stuck two inches in the flesh of her belly, he drew a needle out. And demandin' of her how she come to be so stabbed she [to John Proctor] testify it were your wife's familiar spirit pushed it in.

Inventing patterns of speech is an essential aspect of Miller's unique way of setting each play in a style suited to its purpose, much as a theater composer might suit the style of music to a libretto's subject. The Puritan idiom for *The Crucible* is a heightened version of the original, just as Miller's own family's idiom is heightened in *Death of a Salesman* ("So don't give me a lecture about facts and aspects," for instance, or "there'll be open sesame for all of us"). Miller is seldom given credit for his innovations in creating such appropriate as well as characteristic dialogue, perhaps because he exercised the ability so convincingly, perhaps because, as a result, his characters do not speak "beautifully."

Arthur Miller was not the first to see dramatic potential in the 1692 Salem witch trials. In 1868 Henry Wadsworth Longfellow wrote a verse play about these selfsame events, calling it *Giles Corey of the Salem Farms* and Miller was surely aware of it. Corey does appear in *The Crucible*, because "more weight" is simply too celebrated a watchcry in American folklore to be ignored, but his is a minor role in the Miller play, possibly just because he is central to Longfellow.

The two works share several other real-life characters—Magistrate John Hathorne, Tituba and Mary Walcot—and inevitably bear some similarities to each other. While Longfellow wrote his play in verse one hundred years earlier for a different America, his theme too is religious fever and social terror. The differences are greater. *Giles Corey of the Salem Farms* is written in metered verse and in Longfellow's own voice, even though he had ample research for Giles Corey, whose actual testimony was easily available. Miller, though, had no choice but to invent his hero's speeches. "The testimony of Proctor himself," the playwright found, "is one of the least elaborate in the records, and Elizabeth is not one of the major cases either." As to the relative playability of the works, Longfellow's is all but unstageable and in fact has no record of professional performance.

There are several parallel scenes. One is Giles Corey's refusal to inform on anyone. In Longfellow's speech (metric, although presented in a single paragraph) Corey says,

> If I deny, I am condemned already. In courts where ghosts appear as witnesses, And swear men's lives away. If I confess, Then I confess a lie, to buy a life Which is not life, but only death in life. I will not bear false witness against any, Not even against myself, whom I count least.

Miller's version is simpler, briefer and more affecting: "I will not give you no name. I mentioned my wife's name once and I'll burn in hell long enough for that. I stand mute."

With such speeches Arthur Miller could make courage come alive, and this is the most exciting difference between his and Longfellow's approach. An engine of righteousness propels *The Crucible* and its powerful declamation against the ignorance that begets, allows and sustains political evil.

On June 19, 1953, Ethel and Julius Rosenberg, she thirty-eight (about the same age as Miller) and he forty-one, were executed in the electric chair at Sing Sing Prison in Ossining, New York. They left two sons, Michael, seven (the same age as Miller's son), and Robert, three. In Paris John and Elizabeth Proctor were being played by Yves Montand and his wife, Simone Signoret, in *Les Sorcieres de Salem*—as adapted by Marcel Ayme (the couple later filmed it using a screenplay of Jean-Paul Sartre). When they had first read the play, Montand said, they immediately thought of the Rosenbergs. Once performances began, Signoret told interviewers that for emotional inspiration she used Ethel Rosenberg's letters written from prison. For the play's final scene between the Proctors she and Montand arranged for the staging to be modeled on a photograph that had become world famous. It showed Julius Rosenberg embracing Ethel just before the execution, his wrists in handcuffs.

11. The Little Red

WHILE MILLER HAD BEEN in Connecticut writing *The Crucible,* Marilyn Monroe was in California becoming a movie star. On her twenty-sixth birthday, June 1, 1952, she was announced for the costarring role in *Gentlemen Prefer Blondes,* a major Hollywood musical. Filming began six months later and when the picture was released in July 1953, the beautiful but insecure actress who "was brought up differently than the average American child," she said, "because the average child is brought up expecting to be happy," that actress turned into *Marilyn Monroe*.

To emphasize the movie's title her hair had been bleached from honey blond to platinum. It was the color of choice for Hollywood sex queens from Jean Harlow to, most recently and demurely, Betty Grable, the star Monroe was replacing at the Twentieth Century-Fox movie studio. Marilyn Monroe, however, appeared to be something new, a contemporary variation on the dumb blonde of burlesque sketches. Here was an endearing personality with a phenomenal body, offering the promise of a sexual liberation that awaited the country only a decade later.

To maximize that body's effect the studio engaged William Travilla as her exclusive costume designer. Billy Travilla was an unusual choice, for rather than being a movie designer he specialized in the outrageously provocative gowns that strippers wore at the starts of their acts and for not much longer. The studio's notion was for Travilla to take the same approach to Monroe's dresses, and so he used flashy fabrics and all but vulgar designs to create sheaths more suitable for burlesque shows than movie stories. He stretched his materials tight across Monroe's buttocks and cut her necklines to not merely reveal cleavage but plunge into an undercarriage that cupped and thrust her breasts upward and out. The architecture helped boost her into the bosomy territory that had recently been staked out by Jane Russell, her costar in *Gentlemen Prefer Blondes*. Russell pioneered the notion, such as it was, of breasts as movie star, but the Monroe bottom was just as pronounced as her top. It made for a heady package of sexual characteristics, a double act that she seemed to both love and despise; she was dependent on its ticket to acceptance yet resentful that it was all she was being taken for. She was also resentful of the disparity between her treatment and Russell's. There was little she could do about her contract with Twentieth Century-Fox, which paid her a fraction of what Russell received, but she was sure enough of her importance to answer smartly when advised that she wasn't getting the same pay because she wasn't a star.

"Yes," she nodded. "Well remember. *I'm* the blonde and it *is* 'Gentlemen Prefer Blondes.'"

She accepted the disparity because she had to, and appeared to revel in the look that Billy Travilla created for her, and didn't seem to need much encouragement to wear his costumes in her increasingly public private life. So as the romance with Joe DiMaggio made her a familiar figure in America's tabloid consciousness, the real Marilyn Monroe emerged, or seemed to, as being much like the girl on the movie screen.

The real Marilyn Monroe, however, was still living on a contract player's salary, sharing a $227 a month Los Angeles apartment on Holloway Drive with another young actress, Shelley Winters. Monroe was spending a great deal of time there too, because as filming began she'd had to suspend her New York weekends with DiMaggio. That left her idle during production breaks, and one rainy Sunday Winters was flopped across a bed, turning pages of pictures in a Hollywood players' directory and rating aloud the actors for sex appeal. "Wouldn't it be nice," Marilyn said, "to be like men and just get notches in your belt and sleep with the most attractive ones and not get emotionally involved?" Winters replied that a girl could already do that. The double standard, she said, was a thing of the past. A giggly Monroe found pencil and paper and suggested that they go through the directory, drawing up lists of the sexiest men. Winters had a better idea. "Why just actors? [Why not] any man in politics, music, science or literature who appeals to us?"

Marilyn's list began with actors as diverse as Charles Boyer and Charles Bickford (a character actor who had once been mauled by a lion). She named several movie directors, among them Jean Renoir, John Huston and Elia Kazan, not mentioning her actual affair with him. Her roster of ideal lovers—all of them older men—ended with Ernest Hemingway, Charles Laughton, Clifford Odets, Arthur Miller and Albert Einstein.

"Marilyn," Winters said, "there's no way you can sleep with Albert Einstein. He's the most famous scientist of the century. Besides, he's an old man."

"That has nothing to do with it," Monroe replied. "I hear he's very healthy."

The disappointing reception for *The Crucible* hardly damaged Miller's reputation. He had transcended common theater. The play's immediately relevant heroism—so rare on Broadway, so daring in that America—and its international success were also deepening the aura of moral and political courage that had begun to glow around him, adding yet another element to a developing dichotomy. He still spoke the language of artistic socialism ("it is not the masses we serve anymore, not the 'American people,' but . . . the more or less better-educated people, or the people aspiring to culture") at the same time relishing the blithely commercial traditions of old show business. He visited with the aging aristocrats of Broadway and plainly enjoyed theatrical veterans such as the producer John Golden. "In his office," Miller wrote for *Holiday* Magazine, "the walls are . . . dark and covered with hundreds of photographs. . . . There is an Oriental rug on the floor, an ornate desk at the distant end of the room [and behind it] leather bound plays he has produced. In a smaller, adjoining room is a barber chair."

The eighty-year-old producer told him,

> You fellows have a much harder time, much harder than the old days; nowadays every show has to seem new and original. But in the old days, you know, we had what you might call favorite scenes. There was the scene where the mother puts a candle on the window sill while she waits for her long-lost boy to come home. They loved that scene. We put that scene in one play after another. You can't do things like that anymore. The audience is too smart now. They're more educated, I suppose, and sophisticated. Of course it was all sentimental, I guess, but they were good shows.

A part of Miller missed those times. "The [John] Golden species of glamour," he lamented, "is gone with the masses." At the same time he was smitten with the current species of glamour, going to "Park Avenue apartments" like Josh Logan's, where there were star-studded parties "for a hundred people!" Miller was becoming theatrical himself as sex appeal was superimposed on his established image of a pipe-smoking, bespectacled, very serious dramatist, positively Lincolnesque. Even his wife bought into that image, showing little Jane Ellen Miller a shiny new penny and telling her, "Look, daddy on money." This Abraham Lincoln, however, was posing for newspaper photographers in a white tee shirt, suggesting Marlon Brando and the torn undershirt he had so recently worn to stardom in *A Streetcar Named Desire*. And Miller, while far from robust, was no longer skinny. He had gained thirty pounds since his string-bean youth and was now carrying 150 pounds on his six-foot three-inch frame. These looks, combined with his reputation for serious-mindedness, contributed to a new development in American culture, the author as matinee idol. Miller was becoming a celebrity and he didn't seem to mind it at all.

During the 1953 summer, as *The Crucible* was closing and *Gentlemen Prefer Blondes* opening, Elia Kazan was at home at 167 East 74th Street in Manhattan working on a Budd Schulberg screenplay, *The Golden Warriors*, soon to be retitled *Waterfront* and ultimately *On the Waterfront*. Its subject was corrupt labor unions and racketeering on the New Jersey docks, a notion brazenly similar to Miller's aborted screenplay *The Hook*. Elia had come up with the perfect way of first, responding to Art's charges in *The Crucible* ("as for Art Miller, the film spoke to him"), and second, striking back at the liberal community that turned against him with such a vengeance ("I was telling . . . my critics to go and fuck themselves"). Kazan was going to fulfill the longshoreman project whose cinematic possibilities still had him enthralled and make the waterfront movie that Miller wouldn't, couldn't and didn't write, at least not to everyone's satisfaction. In Budd Schulberg he had a ready screenwriter who, as a fellow informer, shared his need for self-defense. Together they were going to make not merely an anticommunist movie; they were going to construct a more powerful and subversive defense of informing than Hollywood's Harry Cohn and Roy Brewer could ever have imagined.

In the years that followed, Kazan, Schulberg and Miller were vague and inconsistent in their comments regarding similarities between *On the Waterfront* and *The Hook*. Miller in his autobiography makes no mention of Kazan's movie; instead he summarizes *The Hook* in such a way that the similarities all but leap from the page. The one time that he was directly questioned on the subject he was evasive in his own smart, sly way. *The Hook*, he said tersely, "was about longshoremen who were being victimized by this gangster union in combination with the ship owners." An expert at speaking between the lines, Miller is all but saying that this is also the basic plot of *On the Waterfront*. That movie, he continued, was made "later after [Kazan's] problem with the Un-American Activities Committee." Between these lines is the suggestion that Kazan had used the movie to defend his testifying. When pressed, Miller continued to be evasive but suggestive. "I have no way of knowing. Of course they are both waterfront pictures." His only specific was, "The one succeeded the other." In short, his came first.

Budd Schulberg claimed that he and Kazan had separately thought about waterfront movies even before Elia—at Molly's suggestion—came calling to suggest they make a picture together. "Coincidentally," said Schulberg, "both of us had been bitten by the waterfront bug. A project Kazan had begun with Arthur Miller had aborted."

Coincidentally too, said Schulberg, he had been approached by "a nephew of Harry Cohn" to dramatize for the screen the same series of newspaper articles, "Crime on the Waterfront" by Malcolm Johnson, that had provided Miller with some of the impetus to research *The Hook*. (Both Johnson and Miller had been awarded their Pulitzer Prizes in the same ceremony at the same time, spring 1949.)

Kazan admitted that *On the Waterfront* "did not start with Budd Schulberg, it started with Arthur Miller," but he insisted to an interviewer that the original idea was his, and that he'd told Art, "Let's do a story about the waterfront." This seems at best an end run around the truth, for he might well have suggested to Miller that the waterfront research, which of course had been Arthur's idea entirely, would be better suited to a screenplay rather than a stage play. In any event Kazan backed up Schulberg's claim of prior invention by saying that "Some years before, [Budd] had bought the rights to Malcolm Johnson's series, 'Crime on the Waterfront,' and written a screenplay based on the material." This would seem to validate the claim that Schulberg had been working on his own waterfront screenplay at the same time as Miller. The only problem is it isn't true. In a letter written by Johnson's agent, Annie Laurie Williams, to the publisher of Johnson's waterfront book the sale of the movie rights was acknowledged.

> We have sold the motion picture rights of Malcolm Johnson's book, "Crime on the Labor Front," which was published by the McGraw-Hill Publishing Company on October 20, 1950. As you know, when the motion picture rights of a book are sold, it is necessary to have the publisher sign a release.

The date of that letter, however, is not 1950 (the year of the Johnson book's publication) and it is not "some years before" the making of *On the Waterfront*. The date of the letter is February 17, 1953, only eight months before production began. Was that a last-minute precaution to avoid legal problems in regard to *The Hook*? A plagiarism case would seem weak, for there is no serious paraphrasing of Miller's screenplay in Schulberg's, and for that matter the plot of *The Hook* is hardly worth borrowing. What Kazan and Schulberg did use, however, was something more important—they used Miller's whole idea, the criminal corruption of labor unions on the New York waterfront and the struggle of one man, a reluctant and unlikely hero, to lead his timid coworkers against a system that was exploiting them.

Along the way a few story details were borrowed as well. The *Hook* protagonist, Marty Ferrara, is based on a real longshoreman who disappeared after trying to organize a movement protesting union corruption. Miller's ending suggests that Ferrara will probably suffer the same fate. The hero of *On the Waterfront*, Terry Malloy, is tricked into participating in a similar "accidental" death of a protestor, but he survives triumphantly by testifying against the men responsible.

Other similarities include Ferrara's wife, Therese, who, like so many Miller wives, is his conscience. She urges him to be decisive and do something about the terrible labor situation on the docks, but he fears that the longshoremen are too intimidated to back him up. ("They are the same guys let me walk off alone today.") In *Waterfront* Terry Malloy is likewise slow to act and Edie Doyle (the love interest) like Therese is trying to shame him into action. "Look out for number one," she says sarcastically. "Always number one. I think [Johnny Friendly] still owns you. No wonder everybody calls you a bum."

In *The Hook* Ferrara admits to his wife that he feels as if he failed to fulfill whatever potential he might have had. "Any job on a ship," he tells her, "that's me, and look where I am." This speech is reflected in Schulberg's justly famous "I could've been a contender" speech for Terry Malloy. ("I could've had class and been somebody. Real class. Instead of a bum, let's face it, which is what I am.") And as Ferrara is briefly bought off with a soft, high-paying job as a "union delegate," Malloy is offered "a slot for a boss loader . . . you don't have to lift a finger . . . It'll be three, four hundred a week." Still another similarity is a dance sequence. Miller himself especially enjoyed dancing and incorporated it into a scene for Therese and Marty, who tells her, "You don't understand racketeers, baby . . . forgive and forget, that's the notice!" Then he puts an arm around her and says, "Come on," as he begins dancing with her. In *Waterfront* Terry says to Edie, "You like that music? If I had my tuxedo I'd ask you to dance. Come on. Want to step?" She certainly does.

Other similarities include Miller's gangster bigwig Jack Uptown (Schulberg's is Mister Upstairs), but such details, if inherited from *The Hook,* are not important enough to add up to more than a bit of cribbing. They hardly detract from Schulberg's powerful screenplay, which is significantly inventive. Terry Malloy, the richly drawn protagonist, is a punchy ex-boxer, an inspired idea that provided the keynote for Marlon Brando's magnificent performance (Brando was himself an amateur boxer), and coming from Budd Schulberg it was not a surprising idea. He was a lifelong boxing aficionado and only a few years earlier had published *The Harder They Fall,* a popular novel about the fight game. The prizefight background adds a special quality to the character of Malloy as well as an extra element to the plot of *On the Waterfront.* Other richly drawn characters contributed by Schulberg are Terry's brother, Charley, the mob lawyer who sells him out, and Father Barry, the crusading Catholic waterfront priest, based on the real-life Father John Corridan. Interesting and original too are Schulberg's hints of religious allegory in carefully placed references to the Crucifixion and a Christlike hero with bloodied hands (from breaking a pane of glass). Schulberg used this to shape a parallel speech of Father Barry's into a defense of informing on others.

> Some people think the Crucifixion only took place on Calvary. They better wise up. Every time the mob puts a crusher on a good man—tries to stop him from doing his duty as a citizen—it's a crucifixion . . . And anyone who sits around and keeps silent about something he knows has happened—shares the guilt of it.

This relates to the central and most controversial of Schulberg's plot devices, the Waterfront Crime Commission. Here is a patent stand-in for the House Committee on Un-American Activities. The waterfront commission is investigating crime and corruption in the longshoremen's union. When it issues a subpoena to Malloy, his first impulse is to refuse to testify and to protect the union local's thuggish president, Johnny Friendly—that is, to respect the code against informing and not be a "stool pigeon." By the end of the movie the waterfront priest has convinced Malloy to do exactly that—testify against Friendly and the corrupt union. "One thing we got in this country is ways of fightin' back. Gettin' the facts to the public. Testifyin' for what you know is right against what you know is wrong. What's ratting to them is telling the truth for you." Now the priest says to Malloy, "You want to be brave? . . . Don't fight [Friendly] like a hoodlum down here in the jungle. . . . Fight him tomorrow in the courtroom—with the truth as you know it—truth is the gun . . . That is, if you've got the guts."

It costs Malloy what it cost Kazan as he is roundly rejected for being a squealer and a rat, reviled by policemen and even shunned by a young member of the *Golden Warriors*, the youth gang that he himself had started. There is dramatic danger in such theme-specific material. The message threatens to undo the drama, but Schulberg and Kazan were so artful in weaving it into the movie's fabric that there was no notable recognition of the HUAC subtext when *On the Waterfront* was released in 1954. Even Brando, who had needed convincing just to work with Kazan because of his informing, "didn't realize" until long afterward "that *On the Waterfront* was really a metaphorical argument by Gadg and Budd Schulberg; they made the film to justify finking on their friends."

Nevertheless the professional artistry and power of the movie cannot be denied. Kazan's hurt, anger and guilt proved to be formidable sources of energy as he put these negative forces to positive and creative use. As for Budd Schulberg, he may have been an inexperienced screenwriter but his screenplay suggests that he had learned a great deal while growing up in the movie business as the son of the head of production at Paramount Pictures. And of course he had the brilliant Elia Kazan as editor, director and collaborator. Kazan is the real connection between *On the Waterfront* and *The Hook*. In his conception of and approach to the picture is what Professor Christopher Bigsby calls the "pillaging" of Miller's screenplay and the directorial borrowings are unmistakable. In Miller's screenplay the opening sequence has Ferrara in a jacket carrying a baling hook. Kazan saves that for what theater people call the *eleven o'clock number*, the stunning finale of *Waterfront*, where the borrowed image is combined with Miller's notion of Ferrara as he "goes down the gangplank, walks onto the pier. He walks down the length of the pier and out into the street through the tall wide doorway." Also as in Miller's screenplay, in *Waterfront* a loading accident occurs in a ship's hold. Kazan uses as well a sadistic shape-up scene much as Miller described it, with the hiring boss tossing work checks into a crowd of longshoremen and letting them fight it out for the privilege of working that day. In both scripts the shape-up itself is much as described by Malcolm Johnson in his newspaper series and subsequent book, but the tossed work checks were Miller's idea.

Perhaps the most obvious example of exploiting *The Hook* is the celebrated glove scene in *On the Waterfront*. Set in a children's playground, it has Brando and Eva Marie Saint growing closer as he sits on a children's swing—

which lends him a childlike quality—famously improvising the putting on of one of her white gloves. Schulberg's dialogue has Terry admitting that despite the wrongdoing in the longshoremen's union and the investigation of it by the Waterfront Crime Commission, he intends to mind his own business and not get involved. When she demands, "Whose side are you with?" he replies, "I'm with Terry."

In Miller's screenplay Marty and Therese are also in the playground of a local park. He also sits down on one of the swings. He tells her that although the labor situation on the waterfront is hateful, he can't quit because "it's my trade, Terry. I like the ships."

Both scenes reveal the couple as close and the hero as boyish and indecisive, looking to a woman for strength and direction. Both scenes are tender this way, but Schulberg's screenplay mentions neither playground nor swing. Published in 1980 as *On the Waterfront—The Final Shooting Script,* it sets this intimate scene between Terry and Edie on "a dark waterfront street." It was Kazan, Schulberg recalled, who decided during production to instead play the scene in a park playground, with Malloy sitting on a children's swing.

Regarding the covert pro-HUAC theme, as Victor Navasky put it in *Naming Names,* "Whatever else it may be, *Waterfront* seems an allegory for 1950s anti-Communism, with the Waterfront Crime Commission an analog for HUAC." To be specific, Navasky wrote,

> it can be argued that his film, *On the Waterfront,* with its screenplay by Budd Schulberg (who also named names), makes the definitive case for the HUAC informer or at least is . . . a valiant attempt to complicate the public perception of the issue. . . . The movie is rife with talk of "rats," "stoolies," "cheesies," "canaries." Terry Malloy has to choose between the waterfront ethic, which holds ratting to be the greatest evil, and the Christian ethic, which suggests that one ought to speak truth to power . . . Terry . . . achieves heroic stature as he single-handedly takes on the mob at the risk of his life and in the process comes to true self-knowledge. "I been ratting on myself all these years . . . I'm glad what I done."

Yet Schulberg in an afterword to his published script (dedicated to Elia and Molly Kazan) makes no mention of the HUAC subtext, although twenty-seven years had passed since the movie was made and much had been written about its underlying theme. He even audaciously remarks that his screenplay was criticized by a trade newspaper as being "pretty communistic," and makes the rather startling suggestion that John Garfield "would have been good, maybe great" as Terry Malloy. Garfield, a major movie star throughout the 1940s, had been one of Hollywood's most prominent and tragic victims of McCarthyism. His career was undone by movie industry Red hunters and the blacklists even before he was handed a subpoena to testify in Washington. Garfield died awaiting that date, a thirty-nine-year-old ex–movie star reduced to playing small-time stage roles for minimum wages. The idea of John Garfield participating in Schulberg and Kazan's apologia for informing is one of lunatic irony. And all but unforgivably Schulberg adds that Garfield's "career and life were being destroyed by his pathetically 'Un-American' activities and he died of a heart attack before our project was underway."

Kazan, however, was perfectly frank about the movie's underlying message. "Hounded," he wrote, by liberal condemnation after the second committee appearance and "determined to reclaim my self esteem," *On the Waterfront*, he said,

> was my reply to the beating I'd taken. . . . When Brando, at the end, yells at Lee Cobb, the mob boss, "I'm glad what I done—you hear me?—glad what I done!" that was me saying, with identical heat, I was glad I'd testified as I had. I'd been snubbed by friends [surely referring to Miller and Kermit Bloomgarden among others] each and every day for many months in my old show business haunts, and I'd not forgotten nor would I forgive the men, old friends, some of them, who'd snubbed me . . . So when critics say that I put my story and my feelings onto the screen, to justify my informing, they are right.

Why didn't Miller complain about the usurpation and subverting of *The Hook*? Kazan claimed to have heard from Miller's lawyer that "If you go ahead with that waterfront picture, you'll never again get one of Arthur's plays to do again." This would not have been much of a threat as he wasn't likely to be asked. One theory might be that during their walk in the Connecticut woods on the day Kazan told Miller that he was going to give names to the committee, he assured his worried friend of protection. It created a debt and, whether explicitly or tacitly, it created a threat, making for an understanding, a deal: Kazan would not inform on Miller and in return Miller would not object to his making a movie about labor unions on the waterfront.

With the Elia-Art friendship broken so too was the American theater's powerful triumvirate of Miller, Williams and Kazan. The parts would never again be as great as the sum, but every subsequent production of *Death of a Salesman* and *A Streetcar Named Desire* would benefit from Elia Kazan's influence in transforming superlative drama into thrilling theater. The plays belong to Miller and Williams but Kazan's psychological insights and showmanship are inherent in the final working scripts.

Without Kazan Miller needed not only a new director but also a new correspondent. Writing letters seems to have been a lifelong way of expressing the many thoughts he felt compelled to verbalize. It had been four years since he had contacted Kenneth Rowe. He resumed the correspondence in December 1953, describing work on *Plenty Good Times*, his dormant "new play."

> I wrote *Crucible* to get my mind away from it. After New Year's I'll go up to the country and begin actual writing. I hope to have it done by Spring or maybe earlier . . . this one has been in active process since 1951, even a little before, and I ought to know what I'm writing about by now. This time I am saving a man. Things, you see, are getting brighter all the time.

A month later, while Marilyn Monroe was marrying Joe DiMaggio in San Francisco's City Hall, Miller was unexpectedly presented with a work break. He excitedly accepted an invitation from the American-Belgian Society for an all expenses trip to attend the March 9, 1954, premiere of *The Crucible* at the National Theatre of Belgium in Brussels. It proved to be a trip he couldn't take, canceled when his application for a passport was held up by the United States Department of State. He must have expected trouble because he had asked his friend, the actor Montgomery Clift, to accompany him when he applied at the passport office.

The reason for the rejection, the State Department vaguely informed his lawyer, was that Miller's presence abroad "would not be in the national interest." That was ominously vague, but the *New York Times* subsequently reported on March 21, "The State Department's spokesman said Mr. Miller's application, filed March 2 in New York, had been rejected under regulations denying passports to people believed to be supporting the Communist movement, whether or not they are members of the Communist Party;" Miller does not seem to have taken the incident very seriously. The Un-American Activities Committee's sessions with movie people were coming to a conclusion. The last scheduled witness was to be Lee J. Cobb, appearing in April, voluntarily and without subpoena. Cooperative, generously providing the committee with names, Cobb came directly to Washington after finishing work in *On the Waterfront*.

Not everyone was so eager to appease. On April 1 Tennessee Williams wrote an unsolicited and unpublicized (even Miller never knew of it) note to "The State Department, Washington, D.C."

> Dear Sirs: I feel obliged to tell you how shocked I am by the news that Arthur Miller, a fellow playwright, has been refused a passport to attend the opening of a play of his in Brussels. . . . I am in a position to tell you that Mr. Miller and his work occupy the very highest critical and popular position in the esteem of Western Europe, and this action can only serve to implement the Communist propaganda, which holds that our country is persecuting its finest artists and renouncing the principles of freedom on which our ancestors founded it . . . I have seen all his theatrical works. Not one of them contains anything but the most profound human sympathy and nobility of spirit that the American theater has shown in our time and perhaps in any time before.
>
> Yours respectfully,
> Tennessee Williams

There was no reply from the State Department, at least none to be found in the Williams Archives.

Meanwhile, the *New York Times* was reporting that Miller was "two thirds" finished with his new play.

> [H]e hopes to finish by August. . . . It is the one in which he is dealing with his own generation, the one that is now in its early forties, the one that went through the Great Depression [and] the intellectual ferment of the Thirties. . . . Set in the present, the play is supposed to be a love story. There will be many scenes but they will not be memory scenes.

The memory scenes—the ingenious counterpointing of time in *Death of a Salesman*—that Miller had been roundly urged to simplify were coming back to haunt him. In the desire for more of the same emotional effect, it was easy for observers to mistake that time element as the source of the *Salesman* power. Such pressures to replicate previous achievements are exerted too often and they directly threaten creativity.

Even as Miller was still blending his scrapped Lorraine, or Marilyn, play with *Plenty Good Times*, Kermit Bloomgarden took the first formal steps toward producing the big work. On May 11, 1956, he filed the necessary papers for "The Third Play Company" (the first two plays were his presentations of *Salesman* and *The Crucible*) with the Securities and Exchange Commission. He capitalized the production at $75,000 and told the *New York Times* that while the ever-evolving play was still "too long, unwieldy [and] had to be cut," that did not pose a problem. Arthur Kennedy, he added, was already cast in this "love story which takes place in New York City today and involves a young man and two women."

Elia Kazan, the *Times* mysteriously concluded, "will direct." Neither Kazan, Miller nor Bloomgarden ever recalled such a possibility. It didn't make much difference, for a month later Bloomgarden's press agent, Jim Proctor, told the *Times* that "the meticulous author has struck a snag and wants more time to polish the untitled script."

The meticulous author diverted his energies to helping Norman Rosten, whose new play *Mardi Gras* was having a shaky tryout engagement in Philadelphia. Miller's friend—of some twenty years now—had not enjoyed much success. His last performed work was "For My Daughters," a group of poems set to music by the American composer Ellie Siegmeister. It was not the stuff of which a living is made, but perhaps *Mardi Gras* was. The play had incidental music by Duke Ellington, and in Rosten's habitually arty manner was subtitled *A Summer Story with Music and Games*. Miller did what he could to fix his friend's play but the tryout engagement failed and *Mardi Gras* was never brought to New York. So Arthur came home just as Mary was getting seven-year-old Robert ready to join his sister Jane at the celebrated Little Red School House in Greenwich Village.

The Little Red, as it was affectionately called by progressives and derided by conservatives, was an expensive ($600 a year) private school in Greenwich Village. Neither little nor a schoolhouse, it was a full-sized redbrick building at 196 Bleecker Street with a reputation for superior education without the competitive pressures of traditional schools. Its emphasis was on creative abilities rather than mathematics, science or even spelling. Jill Rubin, a classmate of Bobby Miller and ultimately a clinical psychologist, remembered that "the idea was for education to be enjoyable . . . for the kids to feel good about themselves and have good relationships with the teachers." Reports were given instead of tests, and no grades other than general indications of accomplishment. Teachers were addressed by first names and students were allowed to wear casual clothes, even jeans, in an era when ties and dresses were the rule. The classes were small and there were only some thirty-five students in each grade. These were organized by age, as the Sevens or the Eights, for instance, rather than the second or third grade.

Progressive schools attract political progressives and more than a few of the students came from blacklisted homes. One of the Miller boy's classmates was Robbie Meeropol, the son of Ethel and Julius Rosenberg. Robbie and his older brother, Michael (who was in Jane Miller's class), had been adopted by Abel and Anne Meeropol after a protracted struggle with the New York State bureaucracy, which had been shuttling the children between various state institutions after their parents' execution. Abel Meeropol was a teacher at New York's DeWitt Clinton High School (later a college professor), but that was only his daytime job. Under the pseudonym Lewis Allen he wrote the music and lyrics for songs of social protest, most famously the Billie Holiday classic, "Strange Fruit." Such creative work and left-of-center convictions were typical of the parents at The Little Red, and the school must have seemed inevitable for the Rosenberg boys. "They were sheltered there," according to Madeleine Gilford, who had been blacklisted along with her actor husband, Jack, and whose daughter Lisa was also in Robbie Meeropol's class. "Nobody knew who they were, so they had a very normal childhood. The parents knew it but not the children."

She was wrong. Parents talk and children listen. The Meeropol boys' identities were common knowledge among the students. As Jill Rubin remembered, "It was a small school and everyone knew what everyone else was doing. We all knew that certain teachers had been blacklisted. The kids were very aware of the political atmosphere."

The Little Red School House was thus the obvious choice for Arthur and Mary Miller's children. "I can't imagine," Madeleine Gilford said, "where else they would have sent their kids," and soon enough the Millers were actively participating in school activities. Arthur even spoke at a graduation ceremony.

In the autumn of 1954 the brief marriage of Marilyn Monroe and Joe DiMaggio was all but over. A slapping incident apparently brought her to the limit and by the time *The Seven Year Itch* was made early the next year she was gone. The picture would establish her as one of the world's most famous, glamorous and alluring women, but success only seemed to add to her unhappiness. She was tired of being underpaid, cast in stereotyped roles, mocked as inane and ridiculed by the press. And she was tired of their taunting questions. When, for instance, she professed an ambition to act in *The Brothers Karamazov*, she was repeatedly forced to reply, "I don't want to play one of the brothers." She asserted her anger by quitting Twentieth Century-Fox and entering into a movie-producing partnership with Milton Greene, an ambitious and entrepreneurial photographer she had met while posing for a layout in *Look* Magazine. She was also determined to study serious acting. "First of all," she said, "I want to be an artist, an actress with integrity, and that includes all kinds of parts. If fame goes by, so long, I've had you, fame." She hoped to eventually act on the stage, and so she accepted Milton Greene's invitation to come east. Her motives were probably mixed—putting space between herself and Hollywood, studying at the celebrated Actors Studio, getting away from the scene of the DiMaggio divorce, and resuming the romance with Arthur Miller.

Milton and Amy Greene lived in a converted barn on an eleven-acre site in Weston, Connecticut, where Monroe began adjusting to the drastic changes in her life while looking for a way to contact Miller, a married man who worked at home. Elia Kazan might well have been the first person she asked. Whether or not she was aware of the chill in that relationship, she could depend on Kazan to know where Miller lived and who his friends were. Elia could well have been mischievous enough, manipulative enough, even vengeful enough to conspire in the reunion. As a starting point he would surely have suggested she get in touch with Arthur's friend and Brooklyn Heights neighbor Norman Rosten. If he couldn't arrange that—were Norman among the myriad Kazan haters, which he was—Monroe could go through Elia's regular still photographer, Stan Shaw, who was also friendly with Rosten and happened to be close to her as well. So it was that one wet Saturday afternoon in January 1955 Stan Shaw and Marilyn Monroe set out on a walking tour of Brooklyn Heights. The excuse was to take pictures. The foul weather was no problem since the real purpose was to find Miller. That was supposed to begin with Monroe meeting Rosten, which Shaw arranged by simply telephoning to ask whether he and a friend might come in from the rain. "I answered yes, come on," Rosten remembered, "you're both welcome."

As a bedraggled Marilyn Monroe appeared at the top of the stairs at 22 Remsen Street, wearing a camel hair coat and dark glasses, Rosten did not recognize her. She was not as tall as she seemed on screen. "No makeup," he remembered, "hair short and careless and wet." But as his wife, Hedda, put up a percolator of coffee, a friendship with the young—and as it turned out, famous—actress was begun.

All of this romantic intrigue in Brooklyn Heights, however, did not reunite Marilyn Monroe with Arthur Miller. That happened some five months later, and it happened in a more conventional way. Elia Kazan had eased her into the Actors Studio—he was after all one of its founders—by introducing her to Lee Strasberg, who had become its artistic director. Strasberg then invited her to attend the studio's twice-weekly sessions as an outside observer, which led to socializing with New York's theater set. It was inevitable that her path would cross Arthur's and so it did, perhaps not that accidentally either, at a party given by Lee and Paula Strasberg. Miller was alone and Monroe was standing and sipping an orange juice and vodka as he walked toward her. She told him about the Actors Studio, he talked about a new play and he did not ask for her telephone number. But he did call Paula Strasberg for it the next morning, and she gave it to him.

The Rosten connection that had not led to their reunion became important soon afterward, as an intense affair got under way. So it was that Mary Miller's friend Norman Rosten and his wife, her college roommate Hedda Rowinski, were now entertaining—even providing the occasional bedroom—for Arthur and his movie star girlfriend. Marilyn also brought him home, married or not, to meet the parents, as it were, introducing him to Amy and Milton Greene at a dinner in their Connecticut home. She now needed a place of her own and she found it in a three-room apartment on the twenty-seventh floor of the Waldorf Towers, the annex of the Waldorf-Astoria Hotel. Marilyn hung a large print above the bed—a portrait of Abraham Lincoln—and she started to write a poem.

So many lights in the darkness
Making skeletons of the buildings

Soon enough, Arthur was stopping by for afternoon socializing.

Several months earlier Miller had begun a new correspondence. It was with James Stern, some eleven years older, an Irish writer of fiction (*The Short Stories of James Stern*), nonfiction (*The Hidden Damage*, about his experiences in Berlin) and translations (most notably of Sigmund Freud). Stern had also worked at *Time* Magazine in the early 1950s, and it was in those days that he and his wife, Tania, met Art and Mary Miller. Then when the Sterns moved to London, Jim added Art to his long list of celebrated correspondents in the literary world, among them W. H. Auden, James Agee, Henry Miller, Djuna Barnes, Christopher Isherwood, Malcolm Lowry, Katherine Anne Porter, Samuel Beckett and Nadine Gordimer. Maintaining this load of correspondence must have been a full-time occupation, but as Stern's literary executor, John Byrne, understated it, he "was not reticent about his friendships with writers better known than himself. In a way it was a compensation for not writing other things."

The Miller-Stern correspondence was begun in early November 1954 when Arthur wrote about the American elections and a hopeful break in the power of Senator Joseph McCarthy, since "several of [his] closest supporters and imitators were beaten." He added that he'd just finished a "short novel" but had set it aside "because it is not whole yet." It never would be whole or published. He feared, "I am writing under a curse. I can't see why one writes excepting to say what has never been said, or at least to say what at all cost must be said . . . I fear I waste much [on material] that seems valueless to me."

He also wrote Stern about their mutual friend, his Connecticut neighbor Alexander Calder. "Sandy tended to drink too much wine and nod off at dinner parties, or else would insist that everyone get up and go dancing at some local night club." When that happened recently, Calder had "grabbed" a girl and started to dance, prompting the manager to object that it wasn't a nightclub. Calder "refused to sit down, paid the check and demanded that everyone leave to find somewhere else they *could* dance." Miller liked that and concluded, "There is something in him that is upholding the rights of man."

A month later on December 2, 1954, the United States Senate voted to censure Joe McCarthy, effectively concluding his terrifying stretch of power and perhaps beginning the end of the anticommunist mania. For Miller the times must have seemed good. By February he was acting positively chipper. Bicycles had always been signals of freedom, carrying him to escape in childhood and expressing liberated spirits ever after. He wrote Stern that he had bought himself a new one, an English racing bike with several gears, the kind that had lately become the rage. He was riding it, he said, "all over the city" and by more than coincidence Marilyn Monroe had just acquired an identical model. She told an interviewer who asked about her "handsome gearshift English bicycle" that she often rode it down Ocean Parkway in Brooklyn.

Marilyn Monroe bicycling along Ocean Parkway in Brooklyn? The incongruity could be explained simply enough. It was the neighborhood where Arty Miller had grown up.

He did not write Jim Stern about the intensifying affair or the ever more frequent and daring (or reckless) occasions that he went out in public with her. Oftentimes Norman Rosten played the beard. "I was a safe, nonrecognizable, nongossip companion," he remembered, although he didn't mind seeing his name in the papers. Walter Winchell reported that "Marilyn Monroe is cooing it in poetry with Norman Rosten," and Rosten was so tickled he boasted about the item. When it became clear what he was up to, another columnist called him the "cupid" of the Monroe-Miller romance. Despite the increasingly public nature of this secret romance, Miller wrote to James Stern, "The family is thriving. Mary is taking some kind of lessons in body movement or some damned thing. I always forget to ask her what it's about. But she does it in a class every week and is convinced she is growing younger." He seems to be trying to create an impression of marital stability. Such misleading may have been designed for self-deception too, as if he were seeking to satisfy both conscience and passion.

Insincere and hypocritical as such behavior appears, Arthur Miller may well have seen his life as newly and excitingly twinned—one valid life with one woman and a second equally valid life with another. In a lighter and perhaps infantile vein he may have felt, as men often do, that he could keep his two lives cheerfully zipping along on parallel tracks. Like a criminal who never considers the possibility of being caught he could leap lightly, even charmingly, between the two situations, dancing his way through a double life, mistress in place, family intact. The complicated love life with its illusion of male power and deserved rights even seems to have had a salutary effect on his work. He was hard at it, he wrote Stern, and meanwhile his friend Norman Rosten amused the idle Monroe. When she wasn't auditing classes as an observer at the Actors Studio, he would escort her (she would disguise herself, he recalled, with "dark glasses, crazy hat, no makeup, a loose coat") to museums and concert halls. Meanwhile, Miller told Stern that he was making progress on his ever gestating "large play." He also wrote to Stern of happening upon another, quite unexpected stage project.

> [A] director I know called up and asked if I had any one acts he might do for Sunday nights as a lark. I remembered sending you a memoir I had written—five or six pages of dialogue about the warehouse. So I have been writing. Title: *a Memory of Two Mondays*. And I have agreed to write another as a curtain raiser and we shall have a Broadway show all of a sudden. And if these two plays get published, you may find yourself dedicated to on the fly leaf.

Miller had written the "five or six pages of dialogue" several years earlier in 1952, and even read them at the 92nd St. Y. His present account to Stern was a shorthand version of what actually happened. An actor named Martin Ritt had been performing in a Clifford Odets play, *The Flowering Peach*, at the Belasco Theatre. Ritt aspired to directing and suggested to the play's producer, Robert Whitehead, that on dark nights he would like to stage several readings of new one-act plays, performed by the Odets cast for invited audiences. Whitehead was a tall, slender, handsome and charming man. As a patrician Christian from a leading Canadian family he was also an exotic creature in the generally middle-class and Jewish milieu of Broadway producers. His elegance seemed to entitle him to special credibility and by chance he deserved it. Bob Whitehead was going to become Arthur's regular producer and one of his closest friends, an exception to a general rule of keeping theater people out of his private life.

Whitehead thought that the scenery for *The Flowering Peach* could serve any play, since it looked "like a circus ring with an immense cyclorama behind it." After Whitehead agreed to the suggested Sunday night readings

Ritt asked several prominent playwrights for available scripts and Miller offered *A Memory of Two Mondays*. When his agent, Katherine Brown, heard about the project, however, she reread the piece and changed Arthur's mind. Whitehead agreed; *A Memory of Two Mondays* was "too good," they felt, for a one-performance reading. Instead Brown suggested that Miller write another one-act play to make for a complete evening. The playwright retrieved a manuscript he had begun and abandoned. So much of his work followed this sequence—started, dropped, revised, canceled and consigned to the scrap heap only to be redeemed and revised once again.

The play he now resuscitated was called *When the Submarines Came*, *submarine* being longshoreman shorthand for an illegal immigrant. It was the germinating Italian tragedy he'd described in a notebook some years earlier, while roaming through the Red Hook section in Brooklyn, before turning that waterfront research into *The Hook*. This was his chance to rescue that material, make it into a stage play and put it to good use as well. In early 1955 as he rewrote it, changing the title to *The Men from Under the Sea* (to indicate that his submarines were human), Miller effectively transformed the piece into a response to *On the Waterfront* and a rebuttal of Kazan's defense of informers. He for one had not missed the movie's subtext.

This "curtain raiser" was now eighty-two pages long, which made it twenty pages longer than *A Memory of Two Mondays*. It was also the more substantial work. As such there was no question that it would be performed last, and Whitehead joined Miller's regular producer, Kermit Bloomgarden, as a partner. Production of *The Third Play* was postponed yet again while a press release was duly sent out, announcing "Two short plays by Arthur Miller for a limited engagement early in May." The overall title was now *A View from the Bridge*, one play being set in Manhattan, the other in Brooklyn, the New York boroughs connected, actually, by three bridges. Then, the release continued, there would follow "a full length, contemporary play, to be directed by Mr. Miller for Kermit Bloomgarden." Whatever its title was going to be and even if it came fourth, *The Third Play* was very much alive.

As May came and went, *A View from the Bridge* was postponed until September. Martin Ritt was given the directing assignment, which was more of an opportunity than he hoped for when he first suggested a few Sundays of staged readings. The casting soon got under way and if Arthur Miller's fellow liberals wanted and expected his enmity toward Kazan to extend to all informers, such hopes were dashed when Lee J. Cobb was offered the leading role. The reason he didn't get to play it (Van Heflin did) had "nothing to do with politics," Miller insisted. "I do not believe in blacklisting," he said, and there is no reason to doubt him.

Heflin, recently of the movie *Shane*, considered acting before a live audience "the biggest gamble of my career," but he was so proud of this project that he committed himself to three years with the play, should it go that well ("limited engagement" was a common Broadway hedge against poor reviews). He also became its biggest individual investor, putting in $9,000 of his own money. Once again Bloomgarden had a quick and easy time financing an Arthur Miller play, and the partnership with Robert Whitehead made the job even easier. In addition to Heflin, other investors from the theatrical community included Lillian Hellman ($750) and Josh Logan ($500). Miller himself put in $2,250. Another investor was one Mary Miller of 155 Willow Street in Brooklyn. Mary put in $550 of her own money.

It was an investment that was not going to pay off for her. While she and the children were in Connecticut for the summer, Arthur and Marilyn were slipping off, escaping the steamy city for overnights at Lee and Paula Strasberg's beach house on Fire Island or visiting with Norman and Hedda Rosten at their summer rental in Port Jefferson, Long Island. Moreover, Marilyn told an interviewer that she'd "fallen in love with Brooklyn. I'm going to buy a little house in Brooklyn and live there. I'll go to the Coast only when I have to make a picture."

Meanwhile, casting *A View from the Bridge* was completed with Jack Warden, J. Carrol Naish, Eileen Heckart and Leo Penn, most of them performing in both plays. In August rehearsals got under way on the New Amsterdam Theater roof. Most days at the lunch break Whitehead and Miller would walk the few blocks to a Child's Restaurant at Broadway and Forty-sixth Street. Its windows looked out on a giant five-story Times Square billboard advertising *The Seven Year Itch*, which had become the top-grossing movie of the national summer. The billboard featured a renowned photograph of Monroe unsuccessfully keeping her skirt from flying up to her hips. At street level in Child's Restaurant the real Monroe regularly joined Whitehead and Miller for lunch. "She'd wear dark glasses and a babushka," Whitehead remembered. "She was seeing Lee Strasberg at the Actors Studio. I hadn't even known that she and Art were together. She would talk about the work she was trying to do at the Studio." The work meant private classes she was taking with Strasberg in his West Side apartment. He didn't usually give them but was making an exception in her case, he said, "before subjecting her to the terrific pressure of class work." Marilyn also attended those classes, the studio's regular sessions on Tuesdays and Fridays, from eleven o'clock until one, but she hadn't yet worked up the courage to play a scene. It would mean public criticism, a prospect, she said, almost as daunting as having to criticize the other actors herself.

Whitehead, as befitted a gentleman, was not of a suspicious nature and did not try to figure out why Monroe was joining Miller at lunch. He certainly did not speculate about scandal. In this respect he was refreshingly and delectably naive. "It still hadn't registered with me," he said,

> that something was going on between Arthur and Marilyn until he started talking to me about bicycles. "You've got to ride a bicycle," he kept saying. "It's good for you." Then one day I read in a column, we were toward the end of

> rehearsal, that Marilyn could be seen riding a bicycle in Central Park, early in the morning. And I thought, "I think Arthur got her on that bicycle."
>
> That's when I thought, they must be having some hocus pocus. But I didn't really know and Arthur didn't say anything.

One of her first new friends at the Actors Studio was Eli Wallach, and when she learned that he was starring in the play *Teahouse of the August Moon* (he had replaced David Wayne, who had been her costar in *How to Marry a Millionaire*), she went to see it. She insisted on watching the John Patrick play from backstage, standing in the wings of the Martin Beck Theatre because, she told Wallach, she wanted to see up close how stage actors perform a two-hour play. From up close Wallach well appreciated her appeal. "And I'll say this about Marilyn," he recalled. "She makes every male think that she is trapped in the castle tower and each one of them will rescue her. That was her ability to capture the male imagination." Intellectual types were equally susceptible to Monroe's sensuality. Delmore Schwartz, reviewing *The Seven Year Itch* in *The New Republic*, wrote,

> Nothing that Miss Monroe says in any role can be quite as meaningful as the ways in which she sways . . . her poise and carriage have a true innocence; have a spontaneity, an unself-consciousness which are the extreme antithesis to the calculated sex of the strip tease and other forms of the propagation of prurience. She can be understood only from one point of view, that of beauty.

After Wallach's performance he invited her to supper. They walked around the corner to Downey's on Eighth Avenue, another actors' bar in the theater district. It became a regular thing since Wallach's wife, Anne Jackson, was out in Los Angeles touring in a play called *Oh, Men! Oh, Women!* And not much later Arthur was joining Eli and Marilyn at the late suppers. "The best audience," said Miller one night, speaking like a playwright, "is youth." Wallach responded like an actor. "The best audience," he said, "is when it's raining outside." When their photograph was taken, all three, and hung on the wall in Downey's, they inevitably found their names in a gossip column. Jackson read it in California, and when she did, she telephoned Eli to ask, "Well? What is that all about?"

"Please, Annie," he laughed. "Think of Marilyn like my sister." Jackson turned with the telephone and repeated this to her costars, Gig Young and Larry Blyden, who were with her in the California hotel room. "They fell on the floor laughing," she told her husband, but he insisted, "I'm the beard for Arthur." Soon enough they were all friends and Monroe nicknamed Eli "Tea House."

When her former roommate Shelley Winters returned to New York and also began attending the Actors Studio sessions, she told Wallach about Marilyn's list of dream lovers and of the last name on it, Albert Einstein. The actor thought this was so amusing that he went out and bought a picture of

Einstein, signed it, "To my dear Marilyn. Love, Albert," and gave it to her. She put it in a silver frame and displayed the signed photograph on the lid of the white baby grand piano in her living room. When anyone asked whether Albert Einstein had really sent it, she would giggle, "Oh, that Eli Wallach!"

Anne Jackson was also a member of the Actors Studio—every serious actor in New York seemed to be—and when she returned to New York, the Miller-Monroe rumors were no longer just whispers. Even so, "I was so naive," Jackson remembered, "that I'd say, 'Oh, who says?' *Please*," and Miller's sister Joan Copeland was just as skeptical.

> Unless I see evidence of some hanky panky, I just don't believe it. I would hear snippets of rumors but I'd just pooh-pooh it because when you're in that position of celebrity, people are going to say and write all sorts of terrible things about you. So I was guarded against any kind of malicious rumor. I just didn't believe it and I didn't ask Mary or Arthur about it. But Marilyn would search me out at the Studio and we'd have lunch, talk about scenes. I guess she was trying to curry my favor, or maybe she just liked me.

Anne Jackson thought that a Monroe-Miller romance "seemed so unlikely," and the combination of Arthur Miller and Marilyn Monroe certainly did seem unlikely to people. Newspapers were already referring to the couple as "Sex and the Intellect." As Norman Rosten, a friend to both, described the pair, it was "The Brain versus The Body," and he understood why outsiders were wondering, "What? Why? How?" But he also sensed that the usual explanations did not apply with "people who are also symbols."

Rehearsals of the two short plays in *A View from the Bridge* were concluded by mid August 1955 and with the New York premiere scheduled for late September the production was readied for the tryout. The brief out-of-town engagement would include three days in New Haven and a two-week booking at Boston's Colonial Theater, starting September 12. Before those dates Bloomgarden and Whitehead decided to shore up the show's finances by testing it in summer stock. Vacationing audiences tended to be forgiving, and such an engagement would come as close as anything in the theater to guaranteed income. Thus in early August the company and the production of *A View from the Bridge* shipped out to the Falmouth Playhouse in Coonamesett, Massachusetts, on Cape Cod.

The scenery was trucked north, and while it was being set up at the Falmouth Playhouse, Whitehead recalled, "the show had the last part of rehearsal" there on the bare stage. It was scheduled to play from August 22 through Labor Day, two weekends sandwiched around three weekday evenings. Meanwhile, Whitehead said, "Art and Mary had a little cottage in Falmouth, not far from the theater." Just like any family man, the playwright had loaded up the car, settled the children—eleven-year-old Jane and eight-year-old Robert—in the back seat and taken the steering wheel beside his wife. Six hours later one of 1949's official "fathers of the year" arrived with the wife and kids for a summer's working vacation.

With the end of the Falmouth engagement—and the summer—Miller went on to New Haven and Boston with the production while Mary and the children came home to Brooklyn and began preparing for school. Gossip columnists were now regularly reporting the Miller-Monroe love affair. Walter Winchell identified Eli Wallach as Miller's "beard" in print. Earl Wilson asked Marilyn about rumors "that your attractions were driving this or that famous man to distraction . . . do you think it's all right for a single girl to encourage the attentions of married men?"

"Oh," she replied, "first of all, it just isn't so . . . I think everybody ought to do what they feel. Who am I to make any kind of rules?" And to another questioner she replied, "How can they say we're having a romance? Why he's a married man," just the sort of remark that suited her light-headed image. Naturally the rumors became the talk of Bobby Miller's class at The Little Red School House, but as to Mary Miller, the columnists reported nothing of her reactions.

She was not there when *A View from the Bridge* opened in New York on September 29, 1955, at the Coronet Theatre. Jane and Robert went with their grandparents. Marilyn Monroe went too. She sat alone, but during the intermission Gussie Miller—who had to be aware of the rumors but still, after all, had a daughter-in-law—walked over and boldly introduced herself as "Arthur Miller's mother." Monroe replied, "I admire Mr. Miller's plays. I'm a first nighter at all of them." That at least was how Isadore Miller described his wife's report of the conversation. The playwright himself was nowhere to be seen, which of course is the rule at opening nights, but it was a heady time for him. Perhaps there was also a marriage to be salvaged, but he was talking to his psychoanalyst, Dr. Rudolph Loewenstein, about that. He also had the excitement of a Broadway premiere, a certain amount of fame, an international reputation and a continuing, compelling, passionate hocus pocus with the most desirable woman in America.

12. A Bridge

AS ITS TITLE INDICATES, *A Memory of Two Mondays* is autobiographical. Yet even though factual, it is also fanciful, for this recollection of Miller's youth serves as a setting for poetry. He had since college days expressed and maintained an interest in dramatic verse. Even late drafts of both *Death of a Salesman* and *The Crucible* included stretches of poetry. This time he carried out the scheme. The combination of reportage and verse is certainly odd and the inspiration is possibly Irish. Most of the characters are from Ireland, and of course in the English-speaking theater Irish playwrights enjoy an unparalleled reputation for poetic language. Sean O'Casey is a playwright Miller admired particularly. "I recently read his last book," he wrote to James Stern. "No one has remarked on his continued warmth of feeling for the U.S. when, aside from Russia, he has very little good to say for any other country. A real Irish loony . . . aye, but you have to admire them."

The play is explicitly based on its author's youthful experiences as a stock clerk in the Chadick-Delameter automobile parts warehouse on the West Side of Manhattan. The theme is the spirit-stifling dreariness of such—indeed most—occupations and lives, and the importance of an adventurous spirit. Once again Miller deals with controlling one's life and making changes for the better, but escape to excitement and adventure always plays a part. In this case the self-described social playwright is writing about change on the personal level.

The time is 1933 at the depth of the Depression. The site is "the shipping room of a large auto-parts warehouse [in] an industrial section of New York." The bins of shock absorbers, generators and hubcaps are somewhere offstage, while the setting is dominated by a packing table and high, filthy windows that "seem to surround the stage." In keeping with the nostalgic mood of the piece is a program note of "warning" about the level of its realism. Although the place is gray and dusty, the playwright advises, "it is also romantic"—that is, "it is seen in this play with two separate visions." One of these visions is that of an unimaginative participant in life, reflected in drabness. The other vision is open to possibility and beauty, reflected in glorious light; and being a poetic way of seeing life, it is expressed in blank verse that can be read as dialogue. The vision and the poetry are why *A Memory of Two Mondays* is subtitled *A Poem*.

It is a summer's morning and already hot. The eighteen-year-old Bert (an echo name for Art) arrives carrying his lunch and a copy of *War and Peace* (although an audience could hardly notice that) as well as the *New York Times*. He has been reading about Germany's election of Adolf Hitler as chancellor, an event of which his supervisor knows nothing, suggesting the low level of awareness around the place. The conversation turns to Bert and his hopes of going to college ("that'll be another year . . . I've got to save it up first . . . I'm probably just dreaming anyway"). Meanwhile the other warehouse employees begin to arrive. After Bert exits one of them remarks about his college ambitions. "He must have a wealthy family. Still and all, he don't spend much. I suppose he's just got some strong idea in his mind . . . You can almost see it in him, y'know? He's holdin' on to sometin'."

As the work day starts, the big cast (of fourteen) takes the stage and some of the characters begin filling orders for "Maxwell differentials . . . Marmon valves and ignition stuff," while others hand out assignments to the truck drivers who deliver the parts throughout the city. The play's time is passed with small talk, most of it on the locker-room level, as are the crude flirtations with the secretary and telephone operator. There is nothing resembling a plot until some fifteen minutes into the play, and then it is merely the middle-aged Tommy arriving "in a dream," which is actually an alcoholic stupor. It is left to Kenneth, the only intelligent adult on the premises, to spell out the playwright's point and he does it in an "Irish" style.

> Ah, you can't blame the poor feller; sixteen years of his life in this place . . . There's a good deal of monotony connected with the life, isn't it? . . . Oh, there must be a terrible lot of Monday mornings in sixteen years. And no philosophical idea at all, y'know, to pass the time?

The small talk resumes with speeches seemingly assigned at random. There is merely a general, unconvincing illiteracy ("I brung over a couple a friend of mines") while the action, such as it is, arrives sporadically. One of the men, Gus, receives a telephoned message that his wife has died; the stupefied Tommy seems certain to lose his job. As his fogginess clears, he joins the others in finding excuses to exit, leaving Kenneth and Bert alone to give imagination's side of the story.

Kenneth starts this interlude with a reference to the begrimed windows that serve as the play's visual metaphor. "Bert? How would you feel about washing these windows—you and I—once and for all? Let a little of God's light in the place?" He then actually speaks in poetry.

> *Hey, look down there!*
> *See the old man sitting in a chair?*
> *And roses all over the fence!*
> *Oh, that's a lovely back yard!*

After more poetry from both of them, they start to scrub away the filth "and instantly all the windows around the stage burst into the yellow light of summer that floods into the room." This scene is written entirely in verse. "There's something so terrible here," Bert says of the warehouse, it makes him "so sad."

> *It's like the subway;*
> *Every day, I see the same people getting on*
> *And the same people getting off*
> *And all that happens is that they get older. God!*

As the lighting returns to normal, Bert urges Kenneth to escape to a more challenging life, but this man is only escaping into alcoholism and he versifies on the subject of defeated aestheticism. "And the streets full of strangers/ And not one of them's read a book through/ Or knows a song worth singing." He concludes the fourteen-line stanza with a few shouted lines from Walt Whitman's *The Ship of State* ("O Captain! My Captain! Our fearful trip is done!") but has forgotten the rest. "I hope you'll remember your poems again," Bert tells him earnestly.

Following this interlude and its magical stage transformation, the play returns to the realistic mode and in an effective time transition it is one year later, the title's second Monday. Defeated by his wife's death, Gus despairs about twenty-two wasted years in the warehouse. The sensitive Kenneth expects to take a civil service job, bitterly aware that "It seals the fate and locks the door." At least, he says, "a man needn't wonder what he'll do with his life anymore."

Symbolizing a moral corruption that hopelessness engenders, a whorehouse (possibly Miller's play on *warehouse*) has just opened for business directly opposite the freshly cleaned windows, replacing the "lovely back yard" that Bert had been able to see a year earlier, even through the grime. After general peeping and smirking the cast again clears the stage, this time leaving Bert alone in a pool of light to express once more his mournful sense of drudgery.

> *I don't understand how they come every morning,*
> *Every morning and every morning,*
> *And no end in sight.*
> *That's the thing—there's no end!*

He does realize, however, that a new chapter is beginning in his life and so he finishes the twenty-four-line soliloquy by promising himself that he will always remember these men, once again concluding with an exclamation.

And still I know that in a month or two
They'll forget my name and mix me up
With another boy who worked here once,
And went. Gee, it's a mystery!

When the news arrives that Gus has died, evidently of despair, the warehouse routine is barely disrupted and it is this glum cycle that Bert now departs. He takes his jacket from a wall hook for the last time and says his good-byes. Toasting the step toward life, Kenneth hails farewell—"The minstrel boy to the war has gone!"—concluding the play with the next lines in Thomas Moore's nineteenth-century Irish ballad, a poem that Bert has helped him to remember.

In the ranks of death you will find him
His father's sword he has girded on
And his wild harp slung behind him

Arthur Miller has called *A Memory of Two Mondays* the play closest to his heart, surely because it is so unabashed an ode to his youth. *A Memory of Two Mondays* is also his most immature and least consequential adult work. In its essential condescension toward a so-called average life it seems to share the mentality of its postadolescent hero. In this respect it sounds like the Arthur Miller of his unproduced *The Half-Bridge* of 1943. The dialogue is so monotonous and drab that only the author's word defies disbelief that he wrote it after *Death of a Salesman* and *The Crucible*. In a 1955 introduction to the published play (dedicated as promised to James Stern) he describes it as "a mortal romance" about "this fragmented world" and how "the goals, when won, are so disappointing. . . . It points the different roads people do take who are caught in warehouses, and in this play the warehouse is our world." This is an inflated description of a formless and weightless play vaguely related to Gogol's *Dead Souls* and O'Neill's *The Iceman Cometh* as a gathering of men in a gloomy and confining room—a representation of life as a depressing way station for teeming masses who have been beaten down, not by societal evils or bad luck so much as by their own defeatism. Kenneth's anticipation of a stifling civil service job is still another example of Miller's anger about the shelter-seeking effects of the Depression's economic insecurities. The use of graceless language and rhythms in verse serves little dramatic purpose, and the thoughts expressed are neither heightened nor emotional. They could as easily have been expressed in dialogue.

Dismissed by professional and academic critics alike, *A Memory of Two Mondays* is distinguished primarily by its original but unsuccessful blend of documentary realism and imagery, visual and verbal. Even so, it demonstrates Arthur Miller's unique approach of creating a style to suit each play.

A View from the Bridge, besides being the program's overall title, was the final name for the second play. It is the thematic opposite of *A Memory of Two Mondays*. That play celebrates a young man's freedom to escape the mundane and create his own future. *A View from the Bridge* portrays man as a prisoner of destiny in the manner of classical Greek tragedy. Corinthian columns stand alongside the essential setting, an apartment in a two-family Brooklyn house. A Greek pediment is suspended overhead and indeed the play begins with a Greek Chorus in the person of Mr. Alfieri, a lawyer who addresses the audience directly and in verse (which is the only apparent connection between this play and *A Memory of Two Mondays*).

His practice, he says, is largely on the nearby waterfront, and a couple of longshoremen are already onstage, tossing coins against a wall. As the playwright's surrogate, he speaks of "Sicily, from where these people came" and describes their Red Hook neighborhood as being linked to that past—to southern Europe, ancient Rome and Greece, its atmosphere so "timeless" that "when the tide is right . . . I see falcons . . . the hunting eagles of the olden time." He then turns from such musings to a current legal case involving one of the coin-tossing longshoremen. So the dramatic action begins as that man, the thirtyish Eddie Carbone, is chastening his niece Catherine, a seventeen year old whom he and his wife have raised from childhood. His remarks, partly in verse, are laced with innuendo as he reacts to the girl's sexy high-heeled shoes, but the verse is more organic to this play than to *A Memory of Two Mondays*. Here it is used for the more heartfelt speeches, those that would be sung if this were an opera. In fact the set pieces, the Italian characters and their story's elements of passion and violence expressed in verse "arias" are the reasons why the play is subtitled *An Opera*. So Carbone revealingly implores,

> *Take them off, will you please?*
> *You're beautiful enough without the shoes*

His wife, Beatrice, enters, expecting a couple of her cousins who have just arrived from Italy as stowaways. Eddie persists in his excessive interest in the young niece, calling her "Garbo," warning her about other men and telling her, "Don't walk so wavy like that." He also informs her and his wife (and the audience) about the corrupt longshoremen's union and its connection with the Italian-American gangster syndicate as he explains how illegal immigrants are smuggled into Brooklyn. A ship's captain, he says, "gets a piece, maybe one of the mates, a piece for the guy in Italy who fixed the papers for them. They're gonna have to work six months for that syndicate before they keep a dime for theirselfs; they know that, I hope."

Eddie also reminds his wife that "the Immigration Bureau's got stool pigeons all over the neighborhood" and tells both women that the stowaways will have to be passed off as relatives from out of town. "This," he warns, "is serious business. This is the United States Government." Then Beatrice tells Catherine about a local teenager who once informed on an illegal immigrant. His own family "pulled him down three flights . . . spit on him in the street," and he never dared return to the neighborhood. That is what happens to informers in Red Hook.

The cousins are the swarthy, stolid Marco, thirty-two, who has come to earn money for a wife and children in Italy, and the blond, unmarried, adventurous and exuberantly twentyish Rodolpho. They are welcomed by Carbone, who assures them of food and shelter. He promises the cousins that as long as they owe money to the syndicate, they will get work on the piers. The cousins in turn describe the impoverished but colorful life they left behind in Sicily. Now they are the versifiers as Rodolpho launches into a rhapsodic account of a motorcycle he hopes one day to buy ("A man who rides up on a great machine/ This man is responsible, this man exists"). It is an especially arioso speech and not by coincidence the young man proves to be musical.

Oh, I sing Neapolitan, jazz, bel canto
I sing "Paper Doll," you like "Paper Doll"?

He proceeds to sing that entire, warmhearted popular song of the day, and it is a delightful moment that "enthralls" Catherine but only spurs Eddie's jealousy, and he reflexively threatens, "You don't want to be picked up, do ya? Because we never had no singers here." As he darkens, the lawyer Alfieri portentously observes, "Who can ever know what will be discovered?/ Eddie Carbone never expected to have a destiny."

The dual role of lawyer and Chorus allows Alfieri to preside over a smooth time transition ("Now, as the weeks pass") during which a romance has developed between Catherine and Rodolpho. Jealousy is eating at Carbone, and his wife, Beatrice, vaguely senses the sexual nature of his attentions to the niece. "What you want, keep her in the house a little baby all her life?" She suggests that he keep out of it and "let her be somebody else's Madonna now," but when Catherine returns from an evening out with Rodolpho, Carbone takes her aside and tries to undermine the romance with scattershot accusations. Although he is only her uncle by marriage, his paternal attitude is underlined when he says, "if you wasn't an orphan wouldn't he ask your father permission before he run around with you?" Illegal immigrants marrying for citizenship papers, he adds, "is the oldest racket in the country."

And so, says Alfieri, Eddie came looking for a lawyer—"My first thought was that/ He had committed a crime/ But soon I saw it was only a passion/ That moved into his body, like a stranger." Is there any legal action, Eddie asks, that can be taken against this fellow who is romancing Catherine just "to get his papers" and who "ain't right . . . and when I think of that guy layin' his hands on her I could—I mean it's eatin' me out."

He's told that no legal action is available, with the unintended hint, "There's only one legal question here. The manner in which they entered the country." Alfieri then adds, "I want you to listen to me," which introduces an eleven-line aria about inappropriate love ("Sometimes it's a niece, sometimes even a daughter").

You know, sometimes God mixes up the people
We all love somebody, the wife, the kids—
Every man's got somebody that he loves, heh?
But sometimes—there's too much. You know?

And so he advises, "let her go . . . it's her life, wish her luck," which only leaves Eddie in turmoil, demanding, "Even if he's a punk?" (*Punk* had already been used by Miller in a college play, as a derogatory euphemism for a homosexual.) When Carbone significantly adds that "the son-if-a-bitch . . . is stealin' from me," Alfieri gets to the crux of the matter. "She wants to get married, Eddie. She can't marry you, can she?" Carbone's response is confused indignation and Miller notes that the man "feels the threat of sobs."

With Carbone's exit Alfieri returns to the role of Chorus, and stressing Greek parallels, speaks of fate and inevitability. "I knew where he was heading for/ I knew where it was going to end"—and, he adds while fading into darkness, "I was so powerless to stop it." At the same time the lights rise on the dinner table at the Carbone's. Catherine is enchanted by Rodolpho's adventures, but Eddie is hostile toward the young man and the cousins perceive it. "What," Marco asks, "does he do wrong?" The late nights out, says Eddie. Then "you come home early now," Marco tells Rodolpho, and Carbone adds, "He's gettin' careless . . . suppose you get hit by a car . . . where's your papers? . . . If he's here to work, then he should work [not] fool around."

This excellent scene grows still tenser as Catherine rebelliously puts on a record and asks Rodolpho to dance. He complies reluctantly, wary of Eddie, while Beatrice makes small talk to quell her husband's bubbling anger. It starts to boil over when Marco mentions that Rodolpho is a good cook. "It's wonderful," Carbone seethes. "He sings, he cooks, he could make dresses. . . . That's why the waterfront is no place for him," whereupon he abruptly offers to take both cousins to the prizefights. It is only an excuse for sparring with Rodolpho, which leads to a real blow. Rodolpho retaliates by asking Catherine to resume dancing while Marco, rising to Carbone's challenge, lifts a chair high in the air, holding it by one leg, ostensibly to demonstrate his strength. With it poised above Eddie's head "like a weapon," Miller notes, "he transforms what might appear like a glare of warning into a smile of triumph, and Eddie's grin vanishes as he absorbs the look." Such dramatics are very effective in performance.

The final step in the tragic ritual is taken when Catherine and Rodolpho are left alone in the apartment. The scene begins domestically, the girl ironing while the boy sits in a rocking chair, listening to jazz. When he tells her that he soon will have enough money for them to marry, she asks whether he would consider living in Italy. She is afraid of Eddie, she says, but she is also considering his accusation that Rodolpho is maneuvering for American citizenship. The young man responds in verse that it would be absurd to bring her "from a rich country/ To suffer in a poor country." This neatly manipulates the audience's uncertainty about his motives. She asks whether he would "still want to do it if it turned out we had to live in Italy?" He replies, "This is your question or his question?" and adds, "No, I will not marry you to live in Italy."

And tell him also, and tell yourself, please
That I am not a beggar,
And you are not a horse, a gift,
A favor for a poor immigrant.

Persuasive in its convictions ("You think I would carry on my back/ The rest of my life a woman I didn't love?"), it is a dignified and righteous speech.

Just to be an American. It's so wonderful?
You think we have no tall buildings in Italy?
Electric lights? No wide streets? No flags?
No automobiles? Only work we don't have

A tearful Catherine enters into the spoken duet, torn between the young man she loves and the father figure who "was good to me, Rodolpho/ You don't know him." And so she asks him to "just tell" Eddie that he would live in Italy. With male pride he insists on telling Carbone no more than that they plan to marry. "And you will not be frightened any more, eh?" With "longing in her eyes," she lustily suggests, "Now," assuring him, "There's nobody here." The scene makes for nicely romantic melodrama.

Melodrama not quite so wonderful but certainly operatic ensues as Eddie chooses just this time to come home drunk. Catherine emerges from the bedroom, her dress partly unbuttoned, Rodolpho behind her. Eddie orders him to leave and when she says she will follow, her uncle kisses her on the mouth. Then he grasps Rodolpho and kisses him as well, which was a startling stage action in 1955. When she reiterates that if Rodolpho must leave she will follow, Carbone threatens, "Don't make me do nuttin,' Catherine."

The scene ends with a blackout, and when the lights next arise, Alfieri speaks of a meeting with Eddie, "his eyes . . . like tunnels." This visit materializes as Eddie tells the lawyer that Rodolpho is refusing to leave; that even Beatrice is defending the young man even though the unresisted kiss surely demonstrated that he "ain't right." In fact the kiss seldom plays as if Eddie had meant it that way. Giving double meaning to physical action in theater is difficult. Carbone's kiss usually just makes him appear homosexually inclined.

Alfieri reiterates that nothing can be done about the romance and warns that if Carbone follows through on his impulse to inform on the two immigrants, "a river will drown you." The lawyer adds, now speaking for Miller in words surely directed at Elia Kazan (whose name is echoed in Eddie Carbone),

> *You won't have a friend in the world, Eddie!*
> *Even those who understand will turn against you*
> *Even the ones who feel the same will despise you!*

Then like Kazan Carbone names names, reporting the illegal immigrants to the government. Soon enough "two men in overcoats and felt hats" appear, stage mufti for detectives and G-men. Carbone is pleading with Catherine, "I never told you nothin' in my life that wasn't for your good. And look at the way you talk to me. Like I was an enemy!" "Immigration" is already knocking at the door, however, and Beatrice immediately grasps what her husband has done ("Oh, Jesus, Eddie"). Even as Carbone pleads innocence, Marco lunges toward him and spits in his face, crying, "That one! I accuse that one! . . . He killed my children!" Neighbors emerge to watch the arrest. "That one stole the food from my children!" Here is another strike at Kazan, evoking the loss of work suffered by the names named, and as Eddie–Elia keeps protesting ("I kept them like my own brothers!"), the neighbors turn away in disgust. Theirs, Miller has written, is "a solidarity that may be primitive but which finally administers a self-preserving blow against its violators."

With another blackout for transition it is the day of Catherine and Rodolpho's wedding, which Eddie forbids Beatrice from attending. "He's gonna come here and apologize to me or nobody from this house is goin' into that church today." Miller's dialogue now seems conclusively leveled at Kazan as Catherine turns on Eddie and cries, "Who the hell do you think you are? You got no more right to tell nobody nothin'! The rest of your life, nobody!" Turning to Beatrice, she demands, "What're you scared of? He's a rat! He belongs in a sewer! . . . He comes when nobody's lookin' and he poisons decent people!"

As Carbone raises a threatening hand at her, Rodolpho comes to the rescue, warning of Marco's approach. Eddie's response is direct.

Me get outa the house? Me get outa the house?
What did I do that I gotta get outa the house?

He insists instead that Catherine tell Rodolpho to leave. "I'll do somethin' if he don't get outa here!" She dashes for the door, but he catches her and again kisses her on the mouth like (according to the stage direction) "a lover, out of his madness," and cries, "It's me, ain't it?" Once more he calls Rodolpho, "you punk! . . . what are you going to do with a girl?" and rushes into the street as Marco is arriving. The neighbors are again watching as Eddie cries,

And now accusations in the bargain?
Makin' my name like a dirty rag?

But Marco snarls, "Animal! You go on your knees to me!" They fight, Carbone has a knife and of course he falls fatally upon it. Thus ends this tale of *betrayal, revenge and woe*. As in a Greek tragedy, the summation is left to the Chorus and as in a courtroom, it is left to the lawyer. Alfieri, being both, observes,

The waves of this bay
Are as the waves of Syracusa
And I see a face that suddenly seems carved,
The eyes look like tunnels
Looking back to some ancestral beach

Arthur Miller's earliest research for *A View from the Bridge* was being used for a second time. His 1948 wanderings along the Red Hook waterfront had led to the screenplay *The Hook,* with its focus on corrupt labor unions, racketeering and oppressive working conditions. The notebooks from this research paid off again as Miller expanded on the Italian Tragedy he first contemplated—a play based on an event that had passed into Red Hook lore, the tale of the longshoreman who had violated local unwritten law by informing on a couple of illegal immigrants. *A View from the Bridge* draws upon Miller's perception of ritualistic elements in that tale. The inviolable ethos of these immigrants—what he called "the built-in conscience of the community whose existence [Eddie] has menaced by betraying it"—suggested classical Greek tragedy to him. At the same time the Italian characters and emotional theatrics were suggestive of opera. Miller chose poetry to relate the two forms, linking the incantations of Greek drama with the emotional arias of Italian opera. This was the play's aspiration, its strength—and also its weakness.

The story is directly plotted with a clear, simple, elemental and forceful line of action—what Miller calls "the myth-like march of the tale." More mundane is the clichéd fall-on-a-knife ending with yet another Miller protagonist dying at the finale. Yet the scenes are balanced in terms of character interaction and move with satisfying directness, one to the next. The time transitions are smooth, except for a couple of abrupt blackouts, while the characters (but for Beatrice) are clearly delineated, with distinct personalities and speech patterns. This is most deftly accomplished in Alfieri, who is smoothly shuttled between Chorus and waterfront lawyer, acceptable in both roles without further explanation because his speaking style changes so markedly from one to the other. As the Chorus, he centers the play's aspects of Greek tragedy, while as the lawyer, he is a go-between. He weighs Eddie's notion of the law as a codified morality made by and for men to poise social need against personal interest, and balances it against Marco's notion of the law as a set of eternal principles laid down by the gods. For this Italian man such immutable and unappealable laws can be personally enforced, and rightfully so, in matters of honor and revenge.

Miller's use of the Greek chorus is not strictly correct. At times Alfieri serves as a conventional narrator, which isn't proper chorus work at all. In this instance, though, the combination does serve the play because narrators usually intrude on a play's make-believe. Here the chorus function justifies the narrator's presence, while establishing a tone of ritual.

Eddie is the most monolithic of the characters. He is primal in his instincts and his centrifugal force whips the work from one turn to the next. Marco is also drawn in a ritualized way, while Rodolpho and Catherine are less Greek and more realistic. They might be perceived as a Romeo and Juliet rescued from tragedy and rewritten to live ever after happily. The young man is made with a lyrical innocence and pride, while Catherine has her own youthful integrity as well as psychological conflicts. Miller notes that she is "moaning" when finally faced with a choice between Rodolpho and Eddie and at that point there is no mistaking her participation in the symbolically incestuous relationship with her uncle. That they aren't blood relatives doesn't matter because they have been treating each other as father and daughter.

Even in the fifth century B.C. Sophocles in *Oedipus the King* could spell out Oedipus's sexual relationship with his mother, while Euripides in *Electra* could only imply a daughter-father relationship with Agamemnon. Some twenty-five centuries later little had changed. Even though father-daughter incest was more common in society, the theater allowed only mother-son attractions to be depicted—probably because for all twenty-five centuries it was run by men. Miller's paraphrasing of such a relationship between Carbone and his niece successfully creates the incestuous impression, partly because, as he later realized, he was really thinking in terms of father-daughter incest when he wrote the play. "For years," he told Mel Gussow of the *New York Times*,

> I unthinkingly thought of Catherine as [Eddie's] daughter. In fact she isn't so there was no [designed] incestuous feeling but in my mind there was. And this

> incestuous line, of which I was not conscious when I was writing, emerged one day in a later production when I suddenly saw relationships in my own family that were reflected on the stage.

He decided that the uncle-niece relationship in *A View from the Bridge*—a play that, not incidentally, was written while Miller was in psychoanalysis—possibly reflected his relationship in his own life. As he wrote in *Timebends,*

> When I wrote this play I was moving through psychological country strange to me, ugly and forbidding. Yet something in me kept to the challenge to push on until a part of the truth of my nature unfolded itself in a scene, a word, a thought dropping onto my paper. I finally glimpsed something of myself in this play . . . I suddenly saw my father's adoration of my sister, and, through his emotion, my own.

Miller, seemingly disinclined to spell out the thought ("adoration" substituting for incestuous impulse), was implying that the "psychological country strange to me, ugly and forbidding," was his own "adoration" of his daughter, Jane. In a magazine article appearing the same year as the play's production, 1955, Miller dotingly described the eleven year old as "walking around the house in high heeled shoes with the lace tablecloth trailing from [her] shoulders." In the context of the era and its fascination with psychologizing—and considering Miller's own absorption by Freudianism and self-analysis—there may have seemed to him notable hints in his work of incestuous impulses in his relationship with this beloved daughter. These suggestions, which most objective observers would probably overlook, disregard or simply dismiss, plainly had significance for him. He would bring up the subject of his love for Jane yet again in a later play. The subject probably says more about Miller's relationship with himself than with his daughter.

In regard to the play's ritualism, Miller's lifelong commitment to free will would seem to have made him the wrong man for a story of predestination and inevitability, but he was plainly attracted to a Greek tragic scheme. As for the melodrama of opera, it is boldly introduced through poetry that, while emotive and musical, does not announce itself as verse with strictly measured cadences or rhymes. The rhythms and images are nonetheless subliminally effective in expressing emotional peaks.

Thus incorporating Greek tragedy and poetry, Arthur Miller had once again written a new kind of play, only this time perhaps with an ulterior motive. While *A View from the Bridge* on one level is about ancient rituals of natural law (in Miller's words, "ultimate law . . . the Grand Design") as opposed to human legal systems, on another level it is a direct response to Elia Kazan's usurping and corrupting of *The Hook* and a condemnation of his—and all—political informing. It is a rebuttal of *On the Waterfront*'s rationale justifying the naming of names; it is a declaration of contempt for Kazan's ignominious behavior in Washington and of disgust with his movie's congratulation of HUAC's cooperative witnesses. *On the Waterfront* characterized informing as heroic, transforming Miller's protestor Marty Ferrara into Budd Schulberg's Terry Malloy, the rat who is not a rat. In *A View from the Bridge* the rat is just a rat, reviled and expelled by his own. If Arthur Miller was evasive the one time he was asked about his reaction to Kazan's making *The Hook* into *On the Waterfront,* there is no evasion about it in *A View from the Bridge.* The play is his reaction, fashioned as the tragedy of Elia Kazan.

All of these factors result in a work that is perhaps overly ambitious in its attempt to relate Greek tragedy to Elia Kazan's history, but Arthur Miller could never limit his ambitions, nor could he separate his politics from his plays. He considered it obligatory for an artist to address the state of society and while he was at it, he addressed Kazan as well, expressing in a play the contempt that his equivocating disposition kept him from expressing personally. Even so, Miller's compassion lent Kazan's life the qualities of classical Greek tragedy. Kazan himself was a Greek, after all. Such compassion is also tucked into *A View from the Bridge,* making the story of Carbone–Kazan into the tale of a man whose moral lapse sets in motion an inevitable cycle of events leading to a doom that is as preordained and tragic as it is deserved. Thus in both senses of the term, the Greek as well as the colloquial, *A View from the Bridge* is a tragedy.

When the pair of one-act plays received its world premiere on August 29, 1955, at Cape Cod's Falmouth Playhouse, it hardly proved typical summer fare. The *New York Times* reported "a standing ovation" on the opening night, but after that, Miller said, "at least eight people walked out of every performance." Following a weekend layover in New Haven, the production began its major tryout on September 12 at the Colonial Theatre in Boston. The local censor insisted on minor deletions involving language but did not seem to notice the play's incestuous implications or homosexual allusions. Miller added a new scene to *A Memory of Two Mondays* and Marilyn Monroe came up for a one-day visit, but neither significantly helped the plays. They opened to mixed reviews, the comments on the longer piece ranging from "a superb drama . . . a stage work of power and stature" (Cyrus Durgin of the *Boston Globe*) and "a cause for deep gratitude and some wonder" (Elinor Hughes, the *Boston Herald*) to the inevitable comparison with *Death of a Salesman.* "Neither of the one acts," wrote Elliot Norton in the *Boston Post,* "is on the same level of achievement." Every play of Arthur Miller's would face comparison with and evaluation by that unattainable *Salesman* standard; it was the price of writing a masterpiece.

In New York a few weeks later Brooks Atkinson of the all-important *New York Times* dismissed *A Memory of Two Mondays* as a "pedestrian chronicle." He liked the story part of *A View from the Bridge* ("a grim, rasping drama") but preferred to take his realism in the conventional manner, uncomplicated by references to Greek tragedy. He read Miller's ambitiousness as pretentiousness. Atkinson, like other critics, made no mention of the play's poetry, which suggests that it succeeded subliminally (unless it didn't work at all). Alfieri's incantations as the Greek chorus, though, came in for heavy criticism, largely the mocking kind. Such instant and superficial reactions were a by-product of tight newspaper deadlines. At that time daily newspaper reviewers attended opening night performances, then had about an hour to get back to their offices, type their critiques and shoot them through pneumatic tubes to the Linotype machine operators. Under such circumstances it is perhaps remarkable that anything coherent could be written. In later years producers and critics would agree to make previews reviewable, thereby providing more time for the consideration and writing of opinions.

Among the elitist critics—those writing, as the mass-circulation reviewers sniped, for "the little magazines"—Eric Bentley's witty essay (in *Commentary*) is typical of the derision visited on Miller's artistic ambitions.

> When I received a printed copy of *A View from the Bridge* and found that a lot of the dialogue was in verse, you could have knocked me over with a feather. . . . I suspected Mr. Miller of many things, but never this . . . as for Greek tragedy, he would have been well-advised to let his story become Greek by its own poignancy and grandeur and not by choral tips to the audience.

Would the play have managed its Greek parallels without such choral tips or the visual ones of Corinthian columns and a pediment? Without them the parallels would probably have been apparent to only a small part of the audience. Need such references be recognized to enjoy the play? No, but to appreciate it yes, because they point to loftier intentions, add elements of ritual and timelessness that elevate the play above common realism, create a sense of inevitability—all of which endow an ordinary story with size. It might be Miller's way of making a smaller person iconic, solving the problem of tragedy and the common man.

In an afterthought written a decade later Eric Bentley graciously and publicly changed his mind, deciding that the play had been victimized by inadequate staging.

> [T]he directing was such as to underline the social drama and confuse the psychological issues . . . the injustice done to the script was reflected in nearly all the reviews of the production, including my own. *A View from the Bridge* was, I believe, the best American play of the 1955–1956 season.

Bentley viewed drama as art but in commercial terms this is most assuredly in the category of too little ten years too late. Miller's play had been written for Broadway, a marketplace for immediate consumption. The morning after opening night Walter F. Kerr of the *Herald-Tribune* admitted watching "with fascination; but we do not honestly like Eddie as much as we ought to." As for *A Memory of Two Mondays*, Kerr omnisciently suggested, "It might easily have been sacrificed in the interests of the larger work." In fact it would seldom be seen again.

The double bill ran only nineteen weeks, but the brevity of its engagement did not seem to embitter or discourage Miller about the theater.

> People keep coming into these five blocks because the theater is so simple, so old fashioned. And that is why, however often its obsequies are intoned, it somehow never really dies. Because underneath our shiny fronts of stone, our fascination with gadgets and our new toys that can blow the earth into a million stars, we are still outside the doorway through which the great answers wait. Not all the cameras in Christendom nor all the tricky lights will move us one step closer to a better understanding of ourselves, but only, as it always was, the truly written word, the profoundly felt gesture, the naked and direct contemplation of man which is the enduring glamour of the stage.

Nevertheless, the commercial nature of Broadway could not but be depressing. There, he said, a play "is judged almost exclusively by whether it works, or pays, or is popular." In Europe, however, where Miller had already earned a respect that had been accorded to perhaps only Eugene O'Neill among American playwrights, the critic and audience, he said, "are more interested in the philosophic, moral and principled values of the play." Certainly on Broadway his period of grace was over, and were it the only theater in which the work of Arthur Miller could be staged, that might have been the last ever heard of *A View from the Bridge*.

The play's anti-informer message was not lost on the Left. On November 8, one month after the New York premiere, the novelist Howard Fast wrote admiringly of *A View from the Bridge* in the Communist Party newspaper *The Daily Worker*. "To us on the left he has given beauty and tribute . . . I propose Arthur Miller as The American Dramatist of the Day." In those times a little praise from such a source could be a dangerous thing. The most attentive readers of the *Worker* seemed to be Communist hunters. Fred Woltman, a reporter whose specialty at the *New York World-Telegram* was Red-baiting, wrote to a friend, "Praise like that never just happens casually in the *Daily Worker*. And certainly never about anyone about whom the Party has any doubts."

Soon afterward Murray Kempton, a political columnist for the *New York Post*, expressed another complaint about Miller, this time from the Left. In an October column he related the new play to Miller's politics and in that respect unfavorably compared him with Sean O'Casey. Kempton considered the socialist Irish playwright's *Red Roses for Me* "immensely tolerant of the marvelous differences of humanity" as opposed to *A View from the Bridge* by "Arthur Miller . . . certainly our most respectable social playwright, and what are his concerns set next to O'Casey's vision?" Replying to his own rhetorical question, Kempton proceeded to cite

> a piece of theater gossip about [Miller's] new waterfront play. When he had finished it, the story goes, he sent it to Elia Kazan. Kazan is supposed to have sent it back with an enthusiastic assumption that he would be the director; and Miller is supposed to have answered that he sent it because he wanted Kazan to know what he thought of one who informs on former Communists.

Kempton sniffed at "a certain grandeur in this posture," calling it a "display of bad manners." Besides, he added, Kazan was beneath such contempt. "We are in a narrow little room when Arthur Miller cannot overlook Elia Kazan." Miller responded (as was printed in the *New York Post* ten days later) that unfortunately Murray Kempton had not bothered "to check his facts with me." Thus he was now forced to make an exception, he wrote, to "an old policy of refraining from answering newspaper criticism and attacks upon me." To be specific, he continued,

> I never offered Kazan *A View from the Bridge*, and if I had and he had accepted the job of directing it, I cannot conceive of a more boorish act than Kempton ascribes to me, namely, to then refuse him the project . . . I will offer Kazan a play of mine to direct when I have one which I believe would be best served by his kind of talent. I am sure he will accept or reject the job on the merits . . . What confounds me altogether is that [Kempton] finds it necessary to accept such an invention about one playwright in order to justify his appreciation of another.

Concluding, "It is no excuse to label [gossip as gossip] and then proceed as though it were fact," Miller added a foolish denial that his play was even about political informing. Arguing as though he had never heard of subtlety or writing between the lines, he used a common wriggle. "When I write a play about a political informer, he will be called a political informer." Kempton took issue with this in his own four-page private reply to Miller, written as though from one Communist to another. Kempton apologized for not verifying the gossip about offering the play to Kazan, and he confessed somewhat obsequiously to "an enormous admiration for your posture in times like these," even adding that he "would confess that admiration publicly." Kempton pointed out, "You have, after all, said what you thought of Kazan in a good many places; it would be hard for me not to have heard at least the echoes—and not just from my Communist friends—even on the fringes of your [theatrical] world." As to Miller's denial of any informer theme in *A View from the Bridge*, Kempton took that conspiratorially. "I know that living in the real world is an enormous problem," he said, careful with his words. He understood, he said, the practical need for a playwright to be oblique in expressing liberal attitudes such as condemning informers. "It is not so much the Communist who is forced to use Aesopian language in a society like ours as it is the artist who must get his work produced."

As for the possibility of Miller ever again working with Kazan, the columnist wrote in his letter, "I shall wait with patience for the first play of yours that [he] directs . . . my private assumption [is] that it will never be." Kempton then referred to the Howard Fast *Daily Worker* review that called Miller "The American Dramatist of the Day." He himself had telephoned Fast, "entirely off the record," to ask whether Miller had protested the piece. "He said you hadn't, and I take his word for it, although," he gibed, "I should hardly take his word for your having told mutual acquaintances that you liked it."

As a postscript Kempton included the response that was going to follow Miller's letter when it was printed in the *New York Post*. It began with an apology for the unverified gossip and then, regarding Miller's denial of any informer theme in *A View from the Bridge*, quoted Eric Bentley's (original) review of the play.

> One never knows what a Miller play is about, politics or sex . . . You may say of *Crucible*, it isn't about McCarthy; it's about love in the 17th Century. And you may say about *View* that it isn't about informing, it's about incest and homosexuality. Strange how this argument almost always constitutes a sort of alibi for the author.

Arthur Miller was bolder when speaking through his plays than when explaining them. In this respect he resembles so many of his early protagonists, courageous in theory, equivocating in action. It was nevertheless disingenuous of him to deny the obvious and insist that had he wanted to write a play about an informer he would have done so, directly and not undercover. He well understood the values of metaphor. Moreover, as he had said to Kazan regarding the message implicit in *An Enemy of the People*, "*ssssh!*—I have managed to say things I wouldn't dare say alone." Bentley and Kempton both perceived the perfectly apparent informer theme in *A View from the Bridge* and rightly scoffed at the author's denial that it existed. As they say, if it looks like a duck, walks like a duck, and quacks like a duck, it is a duck. Unfortunately it was not the best of times to be a duck.

October 1955 marked a critical turn in Arthur Miller's life. He had just opened a new production on Broadway and his prestige was such that hit or not it was a giddy experience, awash in spotlight and glamour. Disappointing reviews notwithstanding, he remained an established American playwright, albeit one no longer treated with critical kid gloves. At that time other, less ambitious plays were succeeding through emotional appeal. A second Kermit Bloomgarden production opened that same week, Frances Goodrich and Albert Hackett's *The Diary of Anne Frank*. A conventional work with immediate emotional appeal, the *New York Times*'s Brooks Atkinson called it a "lovely, tender drama" and its success intensified the already potent reputation of the Actors Studio because Lee Strasberg's daughter, Susan, was playing the title role. Her performance was rapturously received and, as Bloomgarden's wife, Virginia, remembered, "there were tremendous festivities surrounding the Studio, and lots of parties."

By then Marilyn Monroe was actively involved with the Actors Studio. She had even agreed to play her first scene in front of the full membership. She and Miller were venturing out in public ever more frequently, showing up together at theatrical parties. Virginia Bloomgarden remembered that "they seemed very happy" and so Miller's midlife crisis pulled within sight. This crisis had been coming for some time. It was heralded not only by his risky and passionate private life and not just in the qualified reception given his latest play but also in the intensifying abuse he was suffering for his left-wing positions, statements and activities. As if perceiving the life crisis ahead and accepting its inevitability, Miller in his public behavior all but invited it in.

The first jolt came in mid October when, for a fortieth birthday present, his wife threw him out of the house because of the Monroe affair. In the weeks leading up to this painful event Miller's son, Robert, remembered that "There was a lot of anger and tension around the house." Nine years old at the time, he had "tried to be a peacemaker," but Miller in *Timebends* wrote nothing about so touching an effort of a child to keep his parents together. Instead, the autobiography concludes, "The guilty parting with children and the wrenching up of roots seemed now the necessary price for what might truly be waiting just ahead, a creative life with undivided soul."

Nothing is said of the family tensions, the arguments, or breaking the news to the children, nothing even of guilt, a subject on which Miller was becoming a specialist. In his own account of his life others remain peripheral figures.

He moved into the Chelsea Hotel, the upper-bohemian artistic retreat at 222 West 23rd Street near Seventh Avenue, while Mary Miller insisted to reporters that Marilyn Monroe was not the reason for the separation. As a proud woman in a humiliating position, she remained aloof from her husband's open and well-publicized adultery, and this was one of her rare public statements on the matter. Then again it was one of the rare times that anyone asked for her opinion. Two of America's foremost celebrities were involved in a tabloid love affair, an affair all the juicier for being so unlikely as to seem ridiculous to many. In the bargain both of these lovers were married, Monroe to yet another national celebrity, as her divorce from DiMaggio was not yet final. In a matter of weeks it would be, but she was still identified with the baseball star and his popularity was immense. The iconic triangle had already gone beyond gossip to public debate and even ridicule. Why then would a reporter be interested in Mary Miller? After the Boston tryout of *A View from the Bridge* its coproducer Robert Whitehead "never saw her again. She just disappeared." As Virginia Bloomgarden put it, "Mary was just wiped out of existence."

During summer 1955, when *A View from the Bridge* had been in rehearsal and while Miller was still trying to keep his private lives on separate tracks, he had found the time and powers of concentration to take on yet another writing project. It was a screenplay commissioned by Combined Artists, Inc., an independent production company that wanted to make "an honest, unrelenting film dealing with the problems of 'juvenile gangs' in conflict with each other." Juvenile delinquency had become the social problem and catchphrase of the day. The movie, which Miller intended to be "*the* story of Juvenile Delinquency," was to be made on location in Gowanus, the tough Brooklyn neighborhood adjacent to Red Hook. The New York City Youth Board had already agreed to give him full access to its social workers and the city was going to partially subsidize the picture.

As always, Miller began a new project with research. While *A View from the Bridge* was rehearsed by day, he spent the summer nights "with various gangs . . . during periods of violence." He went to "secret mediation sessions, questioned every sort of person having any connection with or knowledge of the enormous and complex drama called Juvenile Delinquency." Then after the tryouts of *A View from the Bridge* on Cape Cod and in Boston and following its Broadway premiere he wrote a twenty-five-page movie treatment, as scenarios are called in the picture business. The working title was *Bridge to a Savage World* because its hero "is our bridge, our entryway into this subworld." Miller had a weakness for bridge imagery. It was his third such title.

The scenario's plot was only sketched out, its structure similar to that of *Situation Normal . . .*, Miller's wartime book about soldiers. His hero, "a faithful portrait of actual workers I have met," was called Jerry Bone, a peculiar name likely derived from a real social worker. He is an idealistic Youth Board worker who "is obviously on a quest," and such heroic intentions for the movie fit into the producer's hopes for "an uncompromising document of epic proportions." While Miller would always try to raise the mundane to lofty heights, he could also restore it to human size. As he concluded his treatment for the movie,

> These are children who have never known life excepting as a worthless thing. They have been told from birth that they are nothing, that their parents are nothing, that their hopes are nothing. The group in this picture will end, by

> and large, with a discovery of their innate worth . . . That is what this picture is about.

Gene Kelly immediately agreed to play Jerry Bone. Although he was Hollywood's reigning song and dance man, he was also a committed and outspoken liberal and was "thrilled at the prospect of working on anything Arthur Miller does whether it be a play or a movie." The project was challenged, however, on July 22, 1955, when the reactionary *New York World-Telegram* carried a front-page headline, "Youth Board Filmster Has a Pink Record." The story, written by Miller's nemesis at the newspaper, Fred Woltman, began, "Arthur Miller, who will write the script for a city sponsored full length movie on the Youth Board which the Board of Estimate approved yesterday, is a veteran backer of Communist causes." On the editorial page, where such opinions were supposed to belong, the Scripps-Howard newspaper urged the city to cancel the contract.

At more or less the same time the House Committee on Un-American Activities was preparing to hold four days of hearings in New York City, starting August 17. The committee was turning its attentions to Broadway and the star witness was going to be the actor Zero Mostel. Observers expected that Arthur Miller would be called as well. He wasn't, but a HUAC investigator suggested to the New York City Youth Board that the juvenile delinquency film project might be ill advised, as the search was on for proof that Miller had once been a Communist Party member. Evidently all the evidence was not yet in hand. In the meantime the board to its credit ignored such pressures. Following months of lobbying, however, by such right-wing groups as the American Legion and the Catholic War Veterans, a meeting of city commissioners was scheduled to deal with the matter. "Of the eight city commissioners or their deputies who were there," Walter Goodman wrote in *The New Republic*, "seven voted against Miller. 'I'm not calling him a Communist,' one of the majority said afterward. 'My objection is he refuses to repent.'"

It was a curious use of religious terminology. Shortly afterward the contract was canceled by the Youth Board, only because it "did not want to become involved in a controversy over Mr. Miller's loyalty." It emphasized, the *New York Times* reported, "that it was not passing judgment on the playwright's loyalty or his merits as an artist."

Miller provided an uncharacteristically terse comment for the *New York Herald-Tribune* of December 9, 1955—"Now let us see whether fanaticism can do what it never could do in the history of the world; let it perform a creative act, let it take its club in hand and write what it has just destroyed." He still refused to be circumspect about expressing his opinions. So many otherwise intelligent people were convinced that the right to hold liberal opinions was at the moment unequal to the danger in expressing them. Miller would not bend in that direction. Asked by two American anticommunist organizations as well as Moscow's Union of Soviet Writers to make a statement on the occasion of the seventy-fifth anniversary of Dostoevsky's death, he wrote, with delicate balance,

> I have always felt that the Soviet suppression of some of [Dostoevsky's] works and the outright banning of others was a particularly indefensible act of cultural barbarism . . . Were he alive today, I believe he would be in trouble in America for certain of his views . . . Here I am, a writer who has only recently been deprived of his right to create a screenplay in America; a writer who only a few years ago had his plays removed from the Soviet stages on the basis of his 'cosmopolitanism,' being asked to speak in celebration of an author who was exiled in his own time in Czarist Russia, whose works were forever being censored, and who until recently was suppressed by the Soviet Government. . . . The survival of Dostoevsky's work is a testament to the futility of censorship.

As for juvenile delinquency in the movies, it was going to prove a commercial subject. One of that year's most successful films was *The Blackboard Jungle*. Two years later the theme would sing out on Broadway and even be set to dance in *West Side Story*, a musical that would go on to become one of the most profitable movies of the era.

Anna Christie is the classic story of a whore with a heart of gold. Marilyn Monroe had been scheduled to perform a scene from the August Strindberg play before the full membership of the Actors Studio. This stage appearance, the first of her life, was postponed several times, which was either unprofessional and inconsiderate or fearful and evasive. Arthur helped her to learn the lines, cuing her and sounding by his own description "like a Southern cracker with a Scandinavian accent." They were working together in her new apartment on the eighth floor at Two Sutton Place South. The place was small but the view was stunning, looking out along the graceful Fifty-ninth Street Bridge over the East River and beyond.

She played the scene in February 1956, and although the Actors Studio's membership of some 250 professional actors included some of America's most celebrated players, Marilyn Monroe was now the main attraction and the studio's director, Lee Strasberg, was plainly catering to her. Before the performance even began he addressed the class of professional and in several instances renowned actors about "her courage" and her "willingness to make the effort, which is quite something, to appear in public for the first time." Strasberg would later recall an obviously nervous Marilyn Monroe proceeding to steal that *Anna Christie* scene from Maureen Stapleton, the experienced and respected actress who played it with her. "It was stolen," he remembered, "only by the sensitivity and tremulousness of her acting." Lee

Strasberg was heading for a profitable and prominent sideline as Marilyn Monroe's master teacher. He could foresee, he said, a long and rewarding career for her in the theater.

Arthur Miller wasn't at the Actors Studio the afternoon of her stage debut, perhaps because it would have made her nervous, perhaps because he considered Strasberg a self-promoter and a charlatan. The man's much publicized psychological interior "Method" approach to acting, he thought, "makes actors secret people, and makes acting secret, and it's the most communicative art known to man." As for Strasberg's talk of Monroe's acting "genius," Miller viewed it with more than a little skepticism. He himself saw her talent as "originality" and the rest as potential, but the evenings they had spent working on the scene did convince him that "she had a real tragic sense of what [Anna Christie] was like." He said he could see Marilyn's possibilities for stage greatness. He was not merely besotted with her; he was smitten. Norman Rosten saw that. "One thing is clear," he said. "Miller was in love, completely, seriously, with the ardor of a man released."

That 1956 February was a splendid time for her, in some ways her perfect month. Besides her stage debut at the Actors Studio, Twentieth Century-Fox pictures was about to make Marilyn the highest paid actress in the world. ("This was the studio," she laughed, "that said I was a bimbo.") She was also seeing her psychoanalyst, Dr. Margaret Hohenberg, on a daily basis. She needed that, she said, "to get through the days," as she needed barbiturates and vermouth to get through the nights.

part three

Middle Age and Crisis

The play is an attempt to order life.

13. The Committee

FOR SOMETHING PRIVATE the Marilyn Monroe–Arthur Miller romance could not have been more public. Reporters hounded the couple. Photographers camped overnight outside their apartment building. *Paris-Match* tried to rent an apartment on their floor. Publicity was to be expected as a result of fame, but this was extraordinary, and that was because it involved America's biggest movie star, a woman who symbolized sex, and one of its most celebrated playwrights, a man who symbolized intellect. "These two great planets in the sky," Miller's sister called them, and if not quite planetary, they surely were iconic.

"Sex symbol, I never understood sex symbols," said Marilyn.

> I thought they were those things you clash together. That's the trouble. A sex symbol becomes a thing. You hate to be a thing. I don't confine myself to that. But if I'm going to be a symbol of something, I'd rather have it be of sex than some other things they have symbols of.

She was dogged by the question of whether she was stupid and that lay at the core of the general bemusement—the sheer improbability of the coupling (whether he was a genuine intellectual was also questioned, but that was not nearly so humiliating). Miller himself was "aware . . . that our seeming so ill assorted"—what a British observer termed a *discordia concors*—"was part of what made us such news." *Ill assorted* they were to say the least, she a sweet, warm, uneducated and unstable provincial from the movie world, a product of a mentally troubled family and California foster homes, and he an emotionally constipated and complicated, politically minded, Jewish intellectual (or not) from New York City. He was surely in love with her, but he also realized that there was serious ego involved in having this beautiful movie star for his own. "Something in me," he confessed, "was proud of identification with Marilyn." In that his starlight was dimming behind hers. A playwright, no matter how esteemed, could not "hold stage" (as theater people say) with a movie star of movie stars. Miller was becoming only a featured player in this public drama. Even the liberal *New York Post*, ordinarily supportive of him, took as its headline for a weeklong series on the affair, "Inside Story of a Romance: Marilyn's Man."

In general the press treated the spectacle with titillation, astonishment, some disabuse and not a little ridicule. The *New York Daily News* quoted Miller on tragedy, "From Orestes to Hamlet, Medea to Macbeth, the underlying struggle is that of the individual trying to gain his 'rightful' place in society. . . . Tragedy, then, is the consequence of man's total compulsion to evaluate himself."

"Quite a change," the article smirked, "from television with DiMaggio."

In fact Miller hadn't said that, although he did say, "I have often wished that I had never written a word on the subject of tragedy." The newspaper had extracted the quote from his introduction to the published *Death of a Salesman*. Tabloid newspapers hadn't the time for niceties of relevance and once the scandalous element was removed—once he was separated from his wife and the existence of the affair was acknowledged—the scandal-chasing headlines turned into moralizing editorials. The couple was pressed for wedding plans since at that time respectable unmarried couples did not live together. Privately, Monroe would admit, "We had talked about [marriage] but it was all very vague." That was reasonable. Arthur already had a wife. He also had children to deal with. He had not yet met with divorce lawyers, his own or Mary's, and so Monroe was alternately evasive with reporters and defensive. Even while denying that she was taking a married man from his family she could regret, "I never want to be a home wrecker and I always am. I'm given that role in life." She could sympathize with Mary Miller ("I'm so sorry"), while insisting in familiar movie dialogue that the marriage "was on the rocks before I arrived on the scene." Miller, a man who trusted to reason but not necessarily to candor, regularly denied that they were having an affair at all. Perhaps he was protecting his children. Perhaps he was taking legal advice and protecting his flank. Perhaps he still considered himself a moral traditionalist, but he spoke as though he were involved in a pristine romance, on one occasion announcing to a reporter in all but Victorian parlance that he and Marilyn Monroe "have never been alone."

In fact he was usually in the Connecticut house, working on a lengthy introduction to a forthcoming collection of his plays that would be dedicated *To Marilyn*. He drove there in her car, one he had picked out himself, a dashing little black convertible coupe with white leather seats. He still had an unerring eye for future classics—this one was a 1956 Ford Thunderbird. Meanwhile she continued the twice-weekly classes at the Actors Studio on West Forty-fourth Street, private studies with Lee Strasberg in his Central Park West apartment, and daily sessions with her psychoanalyst. Her business partner, Milton Greene, tended to Marilyn Monroe Productions

(MMP), pursuing possible projects. Miller was already taking an interest in those, which did not sit well with Greene and forebode trouble.

The MMP materials chosen by Greene were superior to anything Monroe had yet done. Already set was *Bus Stop*, an adaptation of the William Inge play, to be filmed that spring in Los Angeles and on location in Arizona. Next Greene wanted to produce a film version of a Terence Rattigan play called *The Sleeping Prince: An Occasional Fairy Tale*. He had seen it in London and thought it a natural vehicle for her, a romantic comedy about a European prince and a chorus girl. Rattigan was England's most successful commercial playwright (*The Winslow Boy, The Browning Version, Separate Tables*) and this, his latest play, was already scheduled for Broadway in fall 1956. Even before that happened Greene hoped for Laurence Olivier—who would not do the play in New York—to repeat his stage performance in the movie version, with Marilyn replacing his wife, Vivien Leigh, as the chorus girl. So Greene sought out Rattigan for the film rights and the playwright came to New York to discuss the proposal.

Terence Rattigan was the personification of British theatrical elegance. As described by C. M. Franzero, an Italian journalist who accompanied him on the trip, he was

> the son of an ambassador and a handsome young man [with] the build of a grenadier, the body of an athlete, the head of Apollo and the manners of a diplomat . . . dressed with the greatest elegance with a gold cigarette holder by Faberge and a maharajah's Rolls Royce.

The forty-five-year-old Rattigan was instantly "Terry" to "Marilyn dearest" and, Franzero later wrote, when she was assured that Olivier—generally considered to be the greatest actor on the English-speaking stage—was to be her leading man, she "exclaimed, all of a tremble, 'Do you really mean to say that Sir Laurence Olivier is ready to act with *me*?'" Assured that he was, she agreed that Marilyn Monroe Productions buy the film rights. The reaction was somewhat less enthusiastic in "rarefied British theatrical circles" which, Franzero wrote, "have not yet recovered from the news that Sir Laurence Olivier has consented to play leading man to Marilyn Monroe."

Olivier, however, had not yet agreed and was in fact leery of the project, not only doubtful about Monroe's acting abilities but also wary of her reputation for tardiness and temperament. The wily Rattigan cabled the knighted actor, "Dearest Larry, Looks like deal completed. Monroe will now fight like mad thing to have you direct." Olivier went for the bait, his only movie directing offers having been the plays of Shakespeare. Rattigan then sold Greene on the idea of Olivier directing the picture and, but for a few details, the deal was made. The playwright turned to pacifying Olivier, who was demanding "complete collaboration" on the script, which Rattigan himself intended to write. The actor apparently wanted the freedom to improvise dialogue during production. "Dear Larry," Rattigan cabled, "Dialogue is not necessarily best when extemporaneous. Love and I mean love. Terry."

There was no disagreement about the incongruity of teaming Laurence Olivier with Marilyn Monroe but to Milton Greene's way of thinking the very incongruity was the stuff of fascination and box office attraction. In it too lay a variation on the classic beauty–beast theme, the sexuality of differences. A more general reaction to the pairing was that it was ludicrous—as ludicrous as the real-life pairing of Monroe and Miller which was clearly the subtext of this project. Monroe too seemed determined to prove that, as she put it more than once, she was "not a joke," on screen or off. In the meantime she prepared to leave for California and the making of *Bus Stop* while Rattigan wrote his screenplay and Miller arranged his legal separation.

As to his own work, besides the introduction to his plays Miller had begun expanding *A View from the Bridge* to full length. In the Broadway theater, he said, "A play is rarely given a second chance. [It] usually makes its mark right off or it vanishes into oblivion." Since he had developed a European audience, his plays had life after Broadway. There was already talk of a British production and that presented the possibility of perfect timing, *View* in London while Marilyn was there making *The Sleeping Prince*. In any event he was determined to go with her and when July 16 was settled as her starting date for work on the picture, he applied for a passport to travel to England. It was a dangerous action. The last time he made such an application to the State Department had been in 1954 for the Brussels production of *The Crucible*, and he never did get that passport. He surely knew the greater peril now; it was not the time for him to ask any favors of the United States government.

Other matters demanded attention, in particular his two children in Brooklyn. The pair of them, Jane and Robert, were being "buffeted around," according to his sister, Joan. "It was particularly difficult for Janie. At 12 years old, imagine your father leaving your mother for this goddess." He did take them to Connecticut for the occasional weekend but the atmosphere was tense. Children tend to get trapped in marital crossfire. An enraged Mary Miller threatened to inflict dire financial damage as the price for a legal separation. Her price grew even steeper when Arthur asked for a divorce. Early in February she finally agreed to terms, but they were harsh. Beyond child support payments, as alimony she was betting on his future and future rises in the cost of living. Rather than being paid a fixed sum she was to receive a substantial percentage of his income until she remarried (and she never would). Mary Miller would also get the Willow Street house in Brooklyn Heights while Arthur got the place in Connecticut as well as all the legal costs.

Then February 12, 1956, a few days after this settlement was reached, the powerful gossip columnist Walter Winchell broadcast a story on his regular

Sunday evening radio program that was planted, it was said, by J. Edgar Hoover himself. In a not very blind reference to "America's best known blonde moving picture star," Winchell announced that she "is now the darling of the left wing intelligentsia, several of whom are listed as Red fronters."

Norman Rosten would get another chance on Broadway. His dramatization of the Joyce Cary novel *Mr. Johnson* had been optioned for production by Bobby Lewis and Cheryl Crawford. Lewis was going to direct this story of a dignified native in racist British colonial Nigeria. Casting had already begun and the *New York Times* reported that Harry Belafonte was to play the title role. When Belafonte signed a movie contract instead, the search for a leading man resumed. Finally Earle Hyman, a respected classical actor, was given the part and the money-raising process began. Miller, supportive of an old friend, lent that process his name and Monroe did as well, for Hedda and Norman Rosten had become more than close friends—they were her listeners, supporters, consolers and confidants.

As Hyman remembered,

> We were invited to a big house in Brooklyn. There were about twenty people at a sit down dinner and I kept looking at this lady down the end of the table. She was so beautiful that I was blinded by her. Before the dinner, Norman Rosten had introduced me to Arthur, but it never occurred to me who this beauty was. Then, after dinner, we went into this enormous room and Bobby [Lewis] and I waited for these people, these potential backers to come in. Then after everyone was seated and we were ready to read, in walked this indescribable beauty. But there weren't any seats left except one chair just to my right. And she came over and asked, "Will it make you nervous if I sit here?" I said, like a fool, "What difference would it make?" Of course it certainly would make a difference, this stunning woman, and then it hit me with a bang! *Marilyn Monroe*. She was a star then, but on the screen she was different. In real life she was uniquely extraordinary.

As rehearsals for *Mister Johnson* moved to the stage of the Martin Beck Theatre where it was scheduled to open on March 29, Miller looked on, seated beside his friend a few rows back from the stage. Rosten needed the encouragement but even more he needed rewriting. As Amy Greene had noticed, "The Rostens didn't always know where the rent money was coming from," and Norman was desperate for this play to succeed. "Nothing," Hyman remembered, "was happening in the second act. That was where the work was needed and during one break, Norman told me that Arthur had given him several ideas for changes in the play, even for dialogue." Unfortunately the doctoring did not save the patient and the reviews were mixed on the downside. *Mister Johnson* deserved better but had to close after only forty-four performances.

At roughly the same time a play had opened that was destined to change the direction of the western theater. In so doing, *Waiting for Godot* would have a profound effect on Arthur Miller. The affair with Marilyn, his crisis with anticommunist America and the arrival of *Waiting for Godot* would create a divide in Miller's work. Everything written henceforth could be separated from everything written thus far in terms of his plays' ambition, theme, assurance, consistency of attack, public reception, critical attitude and certainly success.

Samuel Beckett's unique and poetic "tragi-comedy"—plainly a work of radical artistry—was being promoted as traditional Broadway fare, "the laugh hit of two continents." Already staged in Paris and London, its New York cast was headed by two of Broadway's most familiar and beloved actors, the stage comedian Tom Ewell, who had been Monroe's costar in *The Seven Year Itch*, and the bellowing clown Bert Lahr. Otherwise there was nothing remotely conventional about the play. *Waiting for Godot* is of a European sensibility and yet it is that rare creation, a universal, fully born original. The play evocatively blends a vaudevillian attitude with a bleak and desperate outlook, a mix that baffled New York's daily critics, who rejected the "terminal comedy," as it would later be called, as unfathomable. Like any masterwork, however, Beckett's play is beyond rejection. In a poll of playwrights, directors, actors and theater professionals taken at the centennial by the National Theatre of Great Britain, *Waiting for Godot* would be voted the most significant English language play of the twentieth century. *Death of a Salesman* placed second.

Second to *Waiting for Godot* among all English-language plays of the century was surely a satisfactory ranking to Arthur Miller in 1999 but it was hardly what he would have anticipated in 1956, when he viewed Beckett's play as ignoring the most basic elements of valid drama. *Waiting for Godot*'s portrayal of life's pointlessness and human ineffectuality, presented as man's endearing and brave dance at the outer limits of futility, was read by Miller as an offense against the concept of self-determination. Perhaps even worse, it wasn't anything like the plays he admired and more to the point *wrote*. In a moment of overkill Miller even indulged a spirit of theatrical McCarthyism, identifying the existentialism in Beckett's play with Nazi appeasement—"When they get too comfortable with the inevitable defeat of human hope, with man as a creature who is doomed to slip on a banana peel, I smell fascism around the corner." While Arthur Miller and the Broadway establishment might (and did) reject this seminal work, none of them could stop the theatrical revolution it began. A series of vivid and successful plays followed in *Godot*'s nonrepresentational style of *absurdism*, a term coined by the scholarly critic Martin Esslin in reference to "a sense of metaphysical anguish at the absurdity of the human condition." Esslin traced its roots to Albert Camus's *The Myth of Sisyphus*, where Camus explains,

> in a universe that is suddenly deprived of illusions and of light, man feels a stranger. His is an irremediable exile, because he is deprived of memories of a lost homeland as much as he lacks the hope of a promised land to come. This divorce between man and his life, the actor and his setting, truly constitutes the feeling of Absurdity.

With the absurdist plays a new and international generation of playwrights emerged to set the tone of New York theater: Europe's Jean Genet and Eugene Ionesco, England's Harold Pinter, and the American Edward Albee. Broadway's traditional dramas came to seem banal and hopelessly old fashioned. Soon the established playwrights were rejected, first by New York's burgeoning Off-Broadway movement, then by critics and finally by audiences. Some of Broadway's reigning dramatists tried to follow the new fashion—Williams, for instance (*The Gnadiges Fraulein*), Inge (*Where's Daddy?*) and Hellman (*My Mother, My Father, And Me*).Theirs was mistaken capitulation, an artistic self-denial leading unfortunately but inevitably to professional (and, in the cases of Williams and Inge, emotional) undoing.

Arthur Miller did not fall into this trap, but he had plenty to say about absurdism, all but blaming Samuel Beckett for his fall from Broadway grace, which happened, he would write, "when the Beckett thing hit." He allowed his anger with absurdism to push him toward a defense of its opposite, an absolute realism, as if relating that to being realistic in one's thinking; lucid, sane and positive, recognizing "the inexorable, common, pervasive conditions of existence in this time and this hour." Only through such realistic thinking, Miller avowed, can we recognize who we are and what we are and make our lives better—to fix what is broken, so to speak. As scientists "manipulate the material world," he said, so social scientists and artists must manipulate the social world. Thus he was offended by the existentialist philosophy that lay at the heart of so much absurdist theater. In those plays, he wrote, "the world would end with neither a bang nor a whimper but two people on a slag heap each trying unsuccessfully to make out what the other was implying." (A plain allusion to Beckett's *Happy Days*.) Miller came to insist that a play had to be comprehensible in terms of believable characters in believable situations, while sending a clear message of action to be taken. He continued this attack in a 1956 address given at Harvard University, where he asked, "Why has [realism] been assaulted from every side?" It is Ibsen's realism, he conclusively told the students, that mirrors the "family relationship in [a] play," while "unrealistic modes"—meaning absurdism—mirror the "social relationship." He insisted, "All great plays are about one issue, 'How may a man make of the outside world a home?'" The way to do it, he said, is through change; that is what mankind does to make life better.

For Arthur Miller change was necessary to get to paradise, "to find the safety, the surroundings of love, the ease of soul, the sense of identity and honor" that, he said at Harvard, for "all men" are related to the idea of family. It must have been the *idea* of family and *plays* about families to which he is referring and not the reality of his own family, for he would appear to have had a lifelong discomfort in playing the roles of son and husband and even father.

Miller's argument, at least in theory, was that a nonrealistic style is inappropriate to plays about families, that all great plays—plays about change—are family plays.

In later years, when *Waiting for Godot* had become an acknowledged masterwork, Miller would reconsider his opinion and "admire that play for the rebellion in it. It is an intimate statement. It has feeling and it has a brain. It enforces upon us a sense of the desolate—which is just what it is designed to do." Yet in 1956, when asked by the *Sunday New York Times* to write an overview of the Broadway season just past, he did not even mention the Beckett play. Instead he bemoaned the "trendless jumble" of boulevard entertainments and denigrated star vehicles such as *The Desk Set* for Shirley Booth or *Janus* for Margaret Sullivan, and while Miller conceded *My Fair Lady* to be "an exceptional musical," virtually all the serious dramas left him unimpressed. In an arbitrary slap at Lee Strasberg he dismissed *A Hatful of Rain* as "a sloppy improvisation from the Actors Studio." Of the dozens of plays produced on Broadway that season he found only three to be possessed of "a genuine creative vitality." These were Enid Bagnold's metaphysical mystery *The Chalk Garden,* Thornton Wilder's benign comedy *The Matchmaker* and Norman Rosten's *Mister Johnson*. For obviously different reasons he made no mention of Tennessee Williams's *Cat on a Hot Tin Roof* directed by Elia Kazan.

Concluding the *Sunday Times* overview, Miller cited as the year's "most enthralling dramatic experience" a play he had not seen at all but had only read. This was *Long Day's Journey into Night* and in his opinion so knowledgeably and articulately expressed, it was Eugene O'Neill's

> most moving work. It is as true as an oak board, a remorselessly just play, a drama from which all his other plays seem to have sprung. Excepting for a very few passages, when once again the dramatic strategy threatens to leave his people alone with their self-consciousness, or the author's, the work is written on an exactly-hewn plane of awareness which is only rarely violated—for his great previous fault, to my mind, was a mawkishness in voicing his themes. It is his most modern play, his most fluidly-written. It is as though here his symbol and his action came up out of him intertwined and at one with each other. His pity here, and his justice lift him as a writer to a genuinely philosophic height. Its only production took place recently in Sweden. I have not heard that there is a line of producers clamoring for it here, but it will surely be done and it must be for all our sakes. It will be good once again to watch a play which holds its prey with the teeth of a bulldog.

Long Day's Journey into Night was produced on Broadway the following year. It starred Miller's old friends from *An Enemy of the People,* Fredric

March and Florence Eldridge. The play won the 1957 Pulitzer Prize for Drama. O'Neill had already in 1936 won the Nobel Prize in Literature. Samuel Beckett was going to win it in 1969.

In 1956 many Americans in search of marital dissolution went to Nevada. A six-week stay was required to establish a fiction of residence, but the alternatives were a year's wait for a final decree elsewhere or a foreign divorce of uncertain legality. For many the six weeks in Nevada were an opportunity to either take a vacation on a dude ranch, gamble at the casinos or simply drink away the pain and guilt or regret of divorce. For Miller's month and a half of legal residence he took a cabin at the Pyramid Lake Guest Ranch some forty miles outside of Reno.

Pyramid Lake is eerie and beautiful, a flat, shallow, ice-blue island of water in the middle of the Nevada desert. Pyramid refers to a series of imposing primeval tufa rock formations rising out of the water near the eastern shore. Miller's cabin feasted upon that sight, but he had not come for the scenery. He brought along his typewriter, the ever-in-progress *Third Play*, the developing, full-length version of *A View from the Bridge* and the working introduction to *The Collected Plays of Arthur Miller*.

At the same time, just as the couple had planned, Marilyn left for California and the making of *Bus Stop*. She took Paula Strasberg with her and Hedda Rosten too—Paula as her drama coach and Hedda, educated to be a social worker, as her personal secretary, a euphemism for paid companion. Dr. Hohenberg, her psychoanalyst, promised to fly out at the first hint of emergency.

On settling into the Pyramid Lake cabin, one of two facing the lake, Miller returned to the big work that Kermit Bloomgarden had once registered with the Securities and Exchange Commission as *The Third Play*. It was the last play of Arthur Miller's first period, the last to be written in his original big hand and the revisions still showed that sweep. The structure was still open and free form, the setting beyond the confines of a given time or place. But there was a new, oblique approach to realism. In this version while Quentin remained the overly understanding self-sacrificing brother who became a policeman, the lawyer Larry has become the lawyer Frank. In one polished scene Frank comes to tell Quentin that their father has just died, using the moment to add that Quentin's lifetime sacrifice had been wasted. Their father had left a substantial sum of money that would have allowed Quentin to finish the engineering degree he had so dearly wanted.

QUENTIN: But I never knew he had anything.
FRANK: But surely you must have suspected . . .
QUENTIN: Why would I? He never said . . .
FRANK: Well what happened to the money from the sale of mother's antiques? Didn't you ever wonder about that?

QUENTIN: I . . . I guess I did, yes.

FRANK: Then why didn't you ever ask him point blank?

QUENTIN: Well we were living together in the same room; he saw how desperate I was to finish school; he knew I couldn't and support him too. What more did I have to ask him?

FRANK: (*leans forward, his arms hiked up on the chair arms as though ready to rise*) Yes, well . . . that's always the way he worked things. He had a talent for making other people feel dishonest. Although I'm hardly the one to be teaching you the facts of life.

LILLIAN: [Quentin's wife] Why do you say that?

After writing hundreds of pages of this version of the play, Miller put the work aside for a much different kind of writing, an essay that involved looking back on work already done. He had a deadline for the introduction to his collected plays. This fifty-seven-page overview would become the most celebrated of his theatrical commentaries, received in academic circles with a respect bordering on awe. In the *Tulane Drama Review* Professor Tom Driver called it "one of the major documents of American theater."

The introduction starts with "the assumption that the drama and its production must represent a well-defined expression of profound social needs." It proceeds to fundamental definitions, for instance, contrasting dramatic writing with literature and defining realism. His singular principle in reflecting reality, Miller wrote, is "to depict not only why a man does what he does, or why he nearly didn't do it, but why he cannot simply walk away and say to hell with it . . . the less capable a man is of walking away from the central conflict of the play, the closer he approaches a tragic existence." He criticizes "poetic" dramas, meaning plays about feelings (like the current hits *Dark at the Top of the Stairs* or *Tea and Sympathy* as well as Tennessee Williams's plays), and of course he dismisses the absurdists. He had become defensive about writing plays that have meaning. "Any attempt to 'prove' something in a play," he wrote, is considered "somehow unfair and certainly inartistic, if not gauche." Playwrights who teach, he says, are unwelcome, yet there cannot be "high seriousness" without teaching. The only issue is artistic and "the passion with which the teaching is made." The more skillfully the lesson is "embedded and articulated" the more possible it is for the play to seem not tutorial but "beautiful."

On May 12, 1956, Miller set the introduction aside to write a letter to his college professor, Kenneth Thorpe Rowe. He described the moonlike landscape surrounding the ghostly lake outside his cottage.

There is no living soul nor tree nor shrub above the height of the sagebrush. I am not counting my neighbors, Saul Bellow, the novelist, and his wife, because they are on my side against the lunar emptiness around us. I have done a great amount of work on a novel, which is really a finger exercise for a new play

> which, if I can pull it off, will blow up the whole theater and probably land me in jail.

Saul Bellow was working on a novel too, *Henderson, The Rain King*. He had stayed past the required six weeks to keep writing it. The wife with him was Alexandra Tsachacbasov, whom he'd married after his Nevada divorce. (This second marriage was destined to last but a year and the wife would become a central figure in Bellow's novel *Herzog*.) Saul Bellow had much in common with Arthur Miller, who didn't or chose not to remember the novelist's dismissive review of *Focus* in *The New Republic*. Both men were brainy, Jewish, sexually restless, roughly the same age and products of the Depression. Both too had worked with the Federal Writers Project of the WPA. By that time Bellow was a recognized and esteemed writer. Two years earlier he had established himself with *The Adventures of Augie March*, winning the first of three National Book Awards. He was already a fellow of the National Institute of Arts and Letters (Miller would be elected in 1958). These similarities, plus the oddity that Bellow was a trained archaeologist and a native Canadian who had become a quintessential Jewish American novelist, stimulated Miller to base a major character on him. So he began yet another revision of that unmanageable, unrelenting, immaturing *Third Play*. After five years he was still at it, as he wrote to Professor Rowe, "working at the form" of this behemoth, along with its "hierarchy of characters."

> [T]hree reams of paper stand beside me, all covered with dialogue not one page of which will I use, to say nothing of maybe six notebooks and God only knows how many reams thrown away. It will be an encyclopedic study of several couples against the context of this age, and the organization of the form is especially difficult because it needs to be flowing and precise at the same time. . . . I may have it written for the Fall, but perhaps not. Life has intervened several times to break me off from it, but now that life has a course again the play does too.

The latest was proving to be a wholesale revision. It included materials from Miller's research for the juvenile delinquency movie and it was jotted with philosophical speculations and disquisitions. The echo name he chose for Bellow was Weller and the working title became *Weller's Faces*. That this is not only unfinished material but work finally rejected by the author must be kept in mind. Its interest and significance therefore come purely from an evolutionary point of view, to study Miller's writing process and his development of materials into later versions.

In this incarnation Miller's earlier focus on the attorney brother, first Larry then Frank—the brother who is the more worldly and successful of the play's two—has been moved to Weller. Like Saul Bellow this man is an acclaimed novelist, teaching at a university (Bellow had taught at both Princeton and New York University). Miller's notes describe Weller at first as "a stooped man. He is surrounded with fear, and the sense of an undeniable challenge which he fears to face. In the course of Act One, the fear is made apparent, the challenge is suggested."

The policeman brother remained Quentin, the Kermit Miller–Sid Franks character who unnecessarily sacrificed his potential. "This is a fearful, talented man," Miller writes, but one who is too "desirous of pleasing everyone." In an apparent projection by the playwright the overly decent Quentin even admires Weller's self-centeredness, seeing it as a good quality while denigrating himself by saying, "Most people live to please others." Such idealization of egoism brought the socially responsible Miller close to justifying selfishness.

In his brief scenario for the new version Miller's identification with Weller is clear even in the abstruse remarks he jotted down in his notebook—"If one posited—Weller is guilty; he cannot see past it. His complaint: the coldness of his wife. . . . The theme is pity. Pity and science. Pity and utility." Such writing found its way into the dialogue as well, and this sort of analytical, circular dialogue and highfalutin oratory about the state of being, the country and the world was beginning to undermine Miller's dramatic strengths, although he could still create character and stage electricity with telling exchanges of dialogue and flourishes of nuance. And he still could exercise that strength, in the following scene, for instance, between Quentin and Weller. As in the play's earlier version, the setting is a park patrolled by Quentin. His brother, the novelist, is speaking.

> I think you're really the unusual one. I mean objectively—you've become a cop. I mean, with your scholastic record and your upbringing, it's not something anybody'd expect of you. For a man like you, being a cop is original. It's more radical than anything I ever did. To tell you the truth, I've thought of you very often.
>
> QUENTIN: Why?
>
> WELLER: Well, you're the only man I ever knew who took stock of a situation, decided what the intelligent solution was and carried it out.
>
> QUENTIN: Well you've done that all the time.
>
> WELLER: Oh God, no. I never know what I'm doing.

At this point Miller sketched out an exchange that was eerily personal, as though it were an invented conversation between himself as Weller and his brother, Kermit. The scene, set in the complacent America of the Eisenhower years, begins with Weller making yet another little speech to his brother.

> I feel we're in trouble. The whole country. The idea of it is going down. It's like we're living in the eye of a hurricane. You know the center of a hurricane?

It's supposed to be perfectly calm in there. But all around the wind is murderous. And nobody knows unless they happen to be standing on the edge of the center—just *where the wind begins*. Most of the people are in the dead center and the sun is shining on them. You ever feel that way?

QUENTIN: I never thought of it that way but that's just the way I see it. I always will.

WELLER: I think you did too, you know? I've thought about you a lot. I'll tell you the truth, I spent nearly a year working on a book in which you were the main character.

QUENTIN: Me?

WELLER: I got scared, I gave it up.

QUENTIN: What would you write about me?

WELLER: Well it wasn't really you, it was just my idea of you. But don't worry, I gave it up. I just couldn't understand you.

Miller tried that a second time.

> Well for one thing, I've known you since we were infants, practically. But it was mainly because I . . . well, I guess I have a great affection for you, for one thing . . . I don't know how to say it without possibly embarrassing you. (*He grins*)

Is this a reflection—even an admission—of emotional constriction? A few scenes later Miller wrote a speech that Weller addresses to his psychoanalyst, and it seems to come directly out of the playwright's own inhibitions.

> Do I dare to insist, to insist upon my own goodness? That this vision is valid? . . . Or maybe it is only hatred, hatred for myself, for my own cowardice—maybe I am only trying to shame others because I am not one of them and I feel guilty for not loving one of them.

For an evolving specialist in guilt, Miller, during his month and a half at the Pyramid Lake Guest Ranch, does not seem to have dwelled on the loss of his family or the betrayal and abandonment of his wife of sixteen years. He might have written abstractly about a "lifelong anguish of self-blame that sometimes verged on a pathological sense of responsibility" but there is nothing resembling anguish in his available correspondences. Even in *Timebends* describing these six weeks he says less about his feelings concerning the end of his marriage than he does about the Indian he talks to on a Nevada reservation, the Stetson hat of another divorce customer in his lawyer's office or that lawyer's comb-over hair styling. Almost as an aside, he mentions that "there would be no chance to explain to my children."

He certainly worked while he was there, writing scene upon scene for that *Third Play* and finishing the full-length version of *A View from the*

Bridge. He also managed to fly off for clandestine weekends with Marilyn in Los Angeles, where *Bus Stop* was in the final stages of production. That was in violation of Nevada divorce law but passion and love were plainly too powerful to resist and she had been telephoning ever more frequently, calling him "Papa," first in jest, then seriously and now regularly. It was in these conversations that they first talked about getting married, deciding to do it when they both got back to New York. She also needed sympathetic support, having been ill enough with bronchitis to warrant hospitalization. Her health was not helped by her drinking or by an ever-increasing dependency on sleeping pills, but she seemed safely with Milton and Amy Greene in their rented Beverly Hills house. As Amy Greene remembered,

> Arthur would come out on week-ends . . . they'd lock themselves up at the Chateau Marmont [Hotel]. He would arrive on Friday, she would go to the Marmont that night, come back to us Sunday night and she would be a mess on Monday. He was still married and she would be upset because she couldn't show this man off to everyone because he still had a wife and two children in Brooklyn.

Their secrecy was almost successful. Nobody knew about those weekends except the lovers, the Greenes and the Federal Bureau of Investigation.

The massive press coverage they attracted surely aggravated the political punishment that Miller had been absorbing. As has so often been observed, HUAC was significantly motivated by publicity, and Marilyn Monroe was publicity personified. When Miller returned from the last of these idylls to start his final week at Pyramid Lake, he was informed by his attorney in New York that his application for a passport had provided HUAC with an excuse to summon him to hearings. These were designed just for him and a few select others on "The Unauthorized Use of United States Passports." A subpoena would be served in his Nevada divorce lawyer's office and he was advised to be there to accept it. A ten-day postponement had already been granted so that he could finish the six-week residency. In his place the committee scheduled Paul Robeson, who testified on June 12, 1956.

To the big question (by now a litany) "Are you now, or have you ever been, a member of the Communist Party?" Robeson responded with a question of his own.

> What do you mean by the Communist Party? As far as I know, it is a legal party like the Republican Party and the Democratic Party. Do you mean which, belonging to a party of Communists or belonging to a party of people who have sacrificed for my people and for all Americans and workers that they can live in dignity? Do you mean that party?

Robeson proceeded to invoke the Fifth Amendment against self-incrimination to every question posed, excepting when he was asked whether he had ever suggested that black Americans would never go to war against the Soviet Union. The Metropolitan Opera star, the all-American athlete, the Phi Beta Kappa student and law school graduate, the sixty-eight-year-old son of a former slave replied in his resoundingly burnished and stentorian voice.

> Listen to me. I said it was unthinkable that my people would take arms in the name of an Eastland [the racist senator James O. Eastland of Mississippi] to go against anybody, and gentlemen, I still say that . . . the United States Government should go down to Mississippi and protect my people. That is what should happen.

Robeson went on to condemn the committee as "super patriots" and "un-Americans," while Arthur Miller was still in Reno being granted a divorce on the grounds of Mary Miller's "extreme mental cruelty." Several days later in between his divorce and his Washington testimony Miller was awarded an honorary degree from the University of Michigan. He was now single, an honorary Doctor of Humane Letters (LHD), and he had a June 21 appointment to appear before the House Committee on Un-American Activities, Chairman Francis E. Walter of Pennsylvania presiding.

Monroe was already home from California when Miller arrived at New York's Idlewild Airport, after a long and exhausting flight from Reno. Reporters were waiting for him as he came down the mobile stairs alongside the airplane and one of them sheepishly apologized. "We only bother you about this because people want to know." Miller, invariably polite even when irritated and all but pathologically reasonable, replied, "It is your job versus my privacy. That's a remorseless conflict." Only after another half hour of questioning was he able to extricate himself and telephone Monroe. When he finally did get back to the Sutton Place apartment, one of the first things they did was drive out to Brooklyn so that she might meet his parents. Gussie Miller—she had started calling herself Augusta—would later tell a reporter that she had no idea Marilyn Monroe was "the nice girl" Arthur was bringing home that day, but considering the massive press coverage of the romance this was rather unlikely. Gussie Miller was succumbing to the vanity of celebrity by association, responding perhaps too eagerly and sometimes inventively to reporters' questions.

With the parking of the Thunderbird out front on East Third Street she and Isadore, now in their seventies, came to the door of the plain little house. Children had already converged on the low-slung streamlined car and immediately recognized the movie star who climbed out of it. Marilyn signed autographs as Arthur led her arm in arm toward his parents, both of whom would later claim to have memorized every detail of the moment. Gussie recalled Monroe wearing a buttoned-to-the-neck black blouse and a gray skirt, with her platinum blond hair covered by a dark scarf, but she was not wearing her usual sunglasses. "This," Arthur said to his parents, "is the girl I want to marry." Marilyn kissed his father on the cheek, turned to Gussie and embraced her. As the four of them walked into the house, she asked whether she might call Gussie "mother," adding tearfully, "For the first time in my life, I have somebody I can call father and mother."

Then unprompted, or so Isadore recalled, she promised that the wedding was going to be performed by a rabbi. It meant that she planned to convert (she had been brought up a Christian Scientist) to Judaism and then, as Miller's mother told a reporter for the *New York Post*, "Marilyn opened her heart to me." In return, Gussie—now Augusta—said, she offered to teach the prospective daughter-in-law how to make chopped liver, chicken soup, borscht and gefilte fish.

That evening Arthur packed an overnight bag for his appointment with the Un-American Activities Committee. Marilyn was not to go with him. The attention she attracted would be too disconcerting. On the morning of Wednesday, June 20, 1956, he went to Pennsylvania Station and took the train to Washington with Lloyd Garrison of his New York attorney's office. Marilyn's parting words, he told Garrison, had been "worried" ones. "She hopes I don't get slaughtered."

He went directly from Washington's Union Station to the Georgetown home of Joseph L. Rauh, Jr., where he was to spend the night. The Washington attorney, a specialist in HUAC cases, was according to Anthony Lewis of the *New York Times* "the greatest of liberal lawyers" and he had a bemusing proposition in hand. Perhaps Marilyn Monroe would not be at the hearing, but her shadow was inescapable and it was the basis of the proposal. Apparently legitimate, its source a subcommittee member, it involved an offer by Chairman Walter to find a "painless solution" for the hearing in exchange for his being photographed with Monroe. Miller said that Rauh advised him to keep this to himself, as nobody would believe it, but recalling the event several decades later in his autobiography, the playwright described it as an offer to cancel the hearing entirely, which might indeed be beyond belief. He added that he laughed at the time but later wondered why he had never considered accepting the offer. There is no record of Monroe's reaction to it or whether he even mentioned it to her.

Shortly before ten o'clock on Thursday, June 21, Miller, Rauh and Garrison climbed the steps of the House of Representatives office building. The tall, lanky playwright was wearing a blue suit, a white button-down shirt and a dark, figured tie. He carried his pipe as he smiled at the knot of photographers backing up the steps in front of him. The Caucus Room just off a rotunda on the second floor was a big, high-ceilinged echoing place. Greek-style columns lined the walls and despite the midmorning hour, the

Venetian blinds were shut. All the frosted globes and chandeliers were turned on.

The committee's six congressmen entered, seating themselves in a row behind a long table on a raised platform. Each was provided with a microphone. Besides Chairman Walter they were congressmen Bernard W. Kearney of New York, Gordon H. Scherer of Ohio, Clyde Doyle and Donald Jackson, both of California and Edwin E. Willis of Louisiana. They peered down at the respondent, a physical relationship perhaps calculated to intimidate. At the small table below Miller and his attorneys had to look up at their inquisitors.

A plump, rosy-cheeked man was already pacing the area between the witness and the congressmen. This was the HUAC counsel and staff director, Richard Arens. The press looked on, seated behind Miller. Beyond them some 130 spectators filled the big room, with the overflow in the shallow balcony. There Eli Wallach leaned forward to watch the performance. He was in Washington on tour with *Teahouse of the August Moon*.

The announced purpose of the hearing may have been in regard to passports but, as Eric Bentley wrote in *Thirty Years of Treason*, the committee "also hoped to show that Miller had been an actual party member." The questioning began with Miller's identification—"I live at Roxbury, Connecticut. I am a playwright"—and went directly to his passport applications, the supposed subject of the inquiry. As he traced his international history for the committee, Arens asked the question that would link passports to the real subject of the hearing. "Did you, in your [Brussels] application, deny under oath that you had supported the Communist cause or contributed to it or were under its discipline or domination?" Apparently during the controversy over the juvenile delinquency movie Miller had referred to signing such an oath. Arens pointed out that there was no such oath on a passport application, and when Miller, after much evasion and obfuscation, finally replied that his reference had been an honest mistake, the committee counsel had a connection from passports to communism. Was it in fact true, Arens asked, that he had never contributed to the Communist cause?

"Maybe a dollar or two," Miller quipped, which only served to annoy the committee counsel. Arens then pressed for the names of subversive organizations that Miller had supported. "I am here to tell you the truth," the playwright said, trying to smooth things over, volunteering that he had not "warped" his juvenile delinquency script to support communist ideas. Arens turned to various leftist activities that Miller had sponsored and there were many to choose from as well as countless petitions signed. "These things," Miller said, "were coming across my desk. I did sign a lot of things in those days."

The committee's researchers had been thorough and, with all pretense of passport inquiry abandoned, he was asked about the Waldorf Peace Conference, about his support of Communist China and Spanish Civil War refugees. He was asked about anti-Fascist petitions, even a petition to abolish this very committee, but Miller was becoming more relaxed, less evasive, even bolder. "I would say," he conceded, "that in all probability I had supported criticism of the House Committee on Un-American Activities," adding that "people were being put into a state of great apprehension [of] just punishment and, in some cases, unjust punishment."

Arens asked about Miller's defenses of "twelve Communist traitors who were convicted in Union Square in New York City." He brought up Miller's twenty-three-year-old unproduced anti-HUAC sketch *You're Next*, and even read a scene from *Listen, My Children*, the one-act play that Miller had written with Norman Rosten in 1939. He pointed out that Rosten was a party member at the time. "I wouldn't know anything about that," Miller said, which was not very likely, nor did he know Howard Fast other than "I have met him." Arens reminded him of Fast's praise in *The Daily Worker*, which now came back to haunt him.

The counsel turned to the Smith Act and its proscription of "conspiring to overthrow the government of the United States by force and violence." Miller restated his opposition to it, "and I am still opposed to anyone being penalized for advocating anything." When asked by Congressman Scherer whether "a Communist who is a poet should have the right to advocate overthrow of the government by force," Miller replied, "if you are talking about a poem, I would say that a man should have the right to write a poem on just about anything. . . . I am opposed to the laying down of any limits upon the freedom of literature."

He vehemently and not quite truthfully denied criticizing Elia Kazan for being a cooperative witness. "I have never made a statement about Elia Kazan's testimony in my life. . . . The fact is, I 'broke' with him [but] I am not at all certain that Mr. Kazan would have directed my next play in any case." Certainly peculiar and interesting is that Miller would express sympathy for cooperative witnesses such as Kazan, Lee Cobb and Clifford Odets, while expressing none for courageous uncooperative ones such as Zero Mostel, Lillian Hellman or Paul Robeson. Questioned by Arens about his familiarity with another unreconstructed leftist, the playwright Armand d'Usseau, Miller impatiently asked, "Just what is the point?"

He knew what the point was. It was his point of greatest vulnerability, attendance in 1947 at meetings of Communist Party writers. Armand d'Usseau, the coauthor of the antiracist play *Deep Are the Roots* and of the movie about the Hitler youth *Tomorrow the World*, had chaired those meetings and Arens was nearing the crux of the matter as he probed the possibility of membership in the party. Miller admitted to having gone to "five or six [meetings] in someone's apartment. I don't know whose." Asked directly whether he had ever applied for membership, he said he'd "signed some form or other." Pressed to say whether it was an application for membership he replied, "I would not say that. I am here to tell you what I know."

Counsel Arens had a ready reply. "*Tell* us what you know."

He didn't know whether it was a membership application. It was "sixteen years ago," he said, "half a lifetime away. I don't recall." He was hardly off the hook. The committee counsel got to the dreaded question. "Who invited you there? Can you tell us who was there when you walked into the room?" Miller, answering very much as Elia Kazan had, all but begged not to be asked. Such confrontation with authority figures, even when they were inane politicians, seemed to bring out the child in these men, and they sometimes responded as if to disapproving and angry fathers. At the same time Miller spoke in the spirit and very nearly the words of *The Crucible*'s John Proctor.

> I want you to understand that I am not protecting the Communists . . . I am trying to, and I will, protect my sense of myself. I could not use the name of another person and bring trouble on him. These were writers, poets, as far as I could see, and the life of a writer, despite what it sometimes seems, is pretty tough—I wouldn't make it tougher for anybody. I ask you not to ask me that question.

In the balcony of the Caucus Room Eli Wallach reacted to the dramatic sequence as an actor would. "It was," he thought, "like one of those Restoration dramas. Or Shakespeare." Miller's interrogators would not let up. "These were Communist Party meetings," Arens asked, "were they not?" Miller tried to evade the issue. Arens repeated the question until Miller conceded that yes they were Communist meetings and the counsel then asked Chairman Walter "that the witness be ordered and directed to answer the question as to who it was that he saw at these meetings." Miller asked that the question be delayed, but finally Congressman Scherer said, "We do not accept the reasons you gave for refusing to answer the question, and it is the opinion of the Committee that if you do not answer the question, you are placing yourself in contempt."

At this point Arens became insistent in his demands for names, and that was when Arthur Miller parted company with Elia Kazan and stood his ground. "My conscience will not permit me to use the name of another person. My counsel advises me that there is no relevance between this question and the question of whether I should have a passport." Arens again asked that "the witness be ordered and directed to answer the question," adding a second part to it. Had a "Sue Warren" been at the meetings? The committee's only evidence of a Miller membership in the Communist Party was a card dated 1943 with which one "A. Miller," a "writer," of 18 Schermerhorn Street, Brooklyn—a former address of the playwright—had applied for membership in "the Stuyvesant Branch, 12th Assembly District, of the Communist Party." In the place on the card set aside for the name of the person proposing the new member was the signature of this Sue Warren.

Although she was a onetime acquaintance of Miller's, he would not tell the committee whether he knew her or any Sue Warren. This seemed to convince the congressmen that names would not be named that day, nor would any Communists be caught. Perhaps they had known it from the outset and even counted on it, defiance being more newsworthy than cooperation. The concluding question (by Congressman Kearney) was whether Arthur Miller considered himself "more or less of a dupe in joining these Communist organizations." Miller replied,

> I wouldn't say so because I was an adult, I wasn't a child. I was looking for the world that would be perfect. I think it necessary that I do that, if I were to develop myself as a writer. I am not ashamed of this. I accept my life. That is what I have done. I have learned a great deal.

It was over but it wasn't over. Congress would surely be asked to vote a charge of contempt against him. A prison sentence was a distinct possibility, but Miller had survived a hero; not, perhaps, a perfect hero out of fiction or a movie and not heroic in the way Paul Robeson had been, but rather a hero who wished to survive yet a hero still. He had done his share of evasion, backtracking, even pleading. He had denied that he'd ever heard of Ethel and Julius Rosenberg when he started to write *The Crucible*, which was absurd and untrue. (His rationale was that he began thinking about the play in 1938.) *The Crucible* was written a year after the Rosenbergs had been convicted of treason. In the end, though, he had been at the center of national attention with a spotlight on him as on no other, and he behaved bravely. He stood by his convictions and had not informed on anyone. He was risking imprisonment and it would win him a lifelong reputation for righteousness, courage and personal integrity. As Victor Navasky wrote in *Naming Names*, "Kazan emerged in the folklore of the left as the quintessential informer, and Miller was hailed as the risk-taking conscience of the times."

His impact as a moral hero can only be understood in the context of those times. A nation had been brought to its knees by the anticommunist juggernaut. Arthur Miller certainly was not alone in standing up to it. Others were even bolder and suffered for it, but he was in a position to seem alone in his valor and make headlines with it. A besieged community needs heroes. *Death of a Salesman* had already made a personage of him; with his principled and publicized stand before HUAC the evolving myth ascended to yet another level. His mother, already a woman of parental grandeur, ascended with her son. She told Arthur and his friend, the producer Robert Whitehead, as though the mother of Jesus Christ, "I was standing on the shore in Far Rockaway, and looking out to sea, and I was carrying you. And a star fell out of the heavens as I watched the ocean. And that was for you."

"Arthur," it seemed to Whitehead, "felt maybe his mother was right."

Such egoism—"his conceit was enormous," Whitehead admitted, and he was a friend—did not go unnoticed. As it was, some were less than awed by Miller's stand of conscience. The Red-baiting *New York Journal-American* printed a lead editorial calling his testimony "pretentious . . . and in some respects, pure literary humbug." The newspaper's notorious political columnist George Sokolsky wrote, "Julius and Ethel Rosenberg . . . may have been spies, traitors, evil people but at least they went to their deaths for what they believed to be true. They did not bargain with the State Dept for a passport to a honeymoon."

Despite such extremist views, the anticommunist fever was about to subside and Arthur Miller's valor contributed to it. In the process he achieved a kind of monumental status and it extended well beyond Navasky's "folklore of the left." With Marilyn Monroe in his picture, standing up to the anticommunists had become respectable, heroic, almost even patriotic and spangled by movie glamour. The spotlight had been focused on him and a massive public seemed to be smiling on what he had done. Marilyn Monroe had everything to do with that spotlight, but it was he who behaved as he had in its glare.

During the lunch recess Miller was besieged by reporters in the hall outside the Caucus Room. Their interest was not in HUAC, communism or his susceptibility to contempt charges but in his relationship with Marilyn and the answer he had given when Arens asked the objective of his proposed trip to England. "The objective is double," Miller had replied. "I have a production which is in the talking stage in England of *A View from the Bridge*, and I will be there to be with the woman who will then be my wife."

In New York Marilyn learned of the congressional wedding announcement by way of the radio and promptly telephoned the Rostens. "Have you heard?" she cried. "He told the whole world he was marrying Marilyn Monroe. Me! Can you believe it? You know he never really asked me!" This is not exactly true, and it was not even the first public mention of their intentions. A Hollywood gossip columnist had already reported her "telling friends here that she intends to marry Miller," and so when a reporter asked whether Arthur had ever formally proposed, Marilyn replied, "He never had to propose to me. It was simultaneous, a simultaneous feeling that overcame us both!"

The news was variously received. Miller's friend and producer Robert Whitehead

> thought it was kind of exciting that they were having an affair, but I was kind of surprised that he was going to marry her. He was the intellectual of the hour. Now he was going around hooked up to the biggest sex symbol in the world—this extraordinary child of nature. Arthur's own terribly innocent conceit couldn't resist it.

Elia Kazan's reaction (at least as he recalled it) had been similar but with a personal twist, as if he himself hadn't had the nerve to leave a dominating wife—and he expressed that timidity with barely concealed malice. While he contented himself with a string of lovers, keeping Molly at home with the children, Art Miller, he said, "couldn't be thinking of marrying her! Marilyn simply wasn't a wife. . . . He certainly wasn't going to upset his whole life, divorce Mary, leave his children; it was too absurd to even imagine."

In Washington reporters continued to press him. Suppose, one of them asked, Miller were denied a passport? "No matter," he said. "We will get married and when Marilyn goes to London she will go as Mrs. Arthur Miller." Six days later on June 27 the committee presented him with an ultimatum: Provide the names within ten days or face a citation for contempt of Congress.

With a wedding now imminent the media's pursuit of the couple—already relentless—became overwhelming. Upon Miller's return to New York City the morning after his testimony the couple was forced to give a press conference. Monroe's personal publicist, Arthur Jacobs, suggested that with the weather so warm, the apartment so small and the press entourage so big they answer questions on the Sutton Place sidewalk outside her building. Clearly Marilyn Monroe was a changed person. One journalist, Dorothy Manning, a reporter for a fan magazine, wrote,

> Gone was the shy, tense little girl voice, the slow groping for just the right word, the hesitation in answering a question . . . In its place was a poised woman . . . Gay, relaxed, less self-conscious, she came up in a few minutes with sprightlier conversation than most stars can manage in hours.

Not everyone was so charmed. One reporter, irritated after having been kept waiting for over an hour, asked, "Miss Monroe, do you plan to be on time for your wedding?" Marilyn peered at the woman for a moment then whispered, "Well, I guarantee that I'll be there." She got laughs with that and sympathy for her good nature. Then she asked for a few days of privacy while Arthur promised a full and lengthy press conference later in the week. Arthur Jacobs set it up for four o'clock on Friday afternoon, June 29, at the house in Connecticut. "In Roxbury, where Goldmine Road crosses Old Tophet," Miller helpfully told one of the reporters. "If they assign you the wedding watch, bring along a tennis racket. And your swim trunks. Frog Pond is just down the road." He expected a half dozen of them. Arthur Jacobs warned him that it would be "more like sixty."

On June 28 the local newspaper, the *New Milford Times* (Roxbury being too small to have its own paper), displayed classically dry New England humor with the headline, "Local Resident Will Marry Miss Monroe of Hollywood." The subheading added, "Roxbury Only Spot in World to Greet News Calmly."

> A Roxbury man will marry Marilyn Monroe within a few days and the news has created a furore [*sic*] in every part of the world except Roxbury, where townspeople took it in stride. . . . The presence of Miss Monroe in Roxbury has caused Norman Huirtbut, town clerk, much inconvenience. Hundreds of telephone calls from newspaper, radio and television newsmen inquiring about whether Mr. Miller and Miss Monroe have applied for a marriage license have kept him from his duties at his chicken farm. . . . The prospect of taking a back seat to the playwright's chores was faced by Miss Monroe again today. Cracks in the side of the pool were scheduled for repair, with Mr. Miller mixing the cement.

The Arthur Jacobs estimate that the Friday press conference would attract about sixty reporters proved to be on the conservative side. As one of those reporters, Maurice Zolotow of the *New York Times*, remembered,

> On all the roads leading to the intersection of Old Tophet Road and Goldmine Road, where the Miller place was located, scores of automobiles were parked. Hundreds and hundreds of men and women—I would guess as many as 400—were straggling about the property, waiting for Monroe to emerge [and] here we were, with the pencils and the folded copy paper . . . with the Speed Graphics and the Leicas . . . with the motion picture cameras on tripods . . . people from the magazines, the wire services, the newspapers of ten states, the weeklies and the monthlies, from England, France, Germany, Italy, waiting . . . trading morsels of gossip . . . rumors.

Catering to their impatience, Jacobs and his assistant publicist, John Springer, promised an imminent appearance of the celebrated couple while in fact they were down the road having lunch with the family at the nearby home of Arthur's cousin Morton. One of the reporters waiting at the Miller place—Mara Scherbatoff of *Paris Match*—managed to learn their whereabouts and with a photographer in tow had him drive her to the cousin's place, arriving just as they were emerging. Morton hustled Arthur and Marilyn into his green Oldsmobile and took off, racing down the narrow, winding road toward Old Tophet. In an eerie precursor to the Lady Diana accident of some forty years later Scherbatoff and her photographer took up the chase, their little white foreign car swerving out of control on the sharp curve approaching Miller's property. The car skidded, shot off the road and smashed into a tree, throwing Scherbatoff through the windshield while leaving the photographer unmarked.

Miller's cousin heard the crash, stopped the car, and they all three ran back to the site of the accident, finding the woman just barely alive. She was in so awful a condition that Arthur tried to hold Monroe off, but just leaning on the car door she was close enough to get blood on her yellow sweater. Hurrying on to the Miller house, Morton told a reporter, "Arthur's calling the hospital," and added, "My God."

The woman was dying but the press would not be denied and the conference proceeded on schedule. Monroe, however, was badly shaken, even describing the accident as ominous, and Miller decided to sidestep the carnival and get the wedding over with. That evening he and his cousin drove with her to the Westchester County Court House in White Plains, New York, where Judge Seymour Rabinowitz married the couple. Arthur borrowed his mother's wedding band for the occasion.

The following day marked the deadline for changing his mind about providing the committee with names. He obviously had no intention of doing so. Chairman Francis E. Walter, understanding the sentimental potency of this nationally publicized wedding, issued a statement posing the possibility that Miller could get both his passport and the contempt citation. It didn't make any sense except politically.

Sunday, July 1, they got married again, this time with two wedding bands of their own, hers inscribed *A. To M.*, his *M. To A.*, and both *June 1956. "Now is forever."* The ceremony as promised was a Jewish one, conducted at the Katonah, New York, house rented by Miller's agent, Kay Brown. Monroe's taste in clothes, along with her confidence, had become more refined. Amy Greene had been a successful model (a "Conover Girl") and she took a tutorial hand in teaching Marilyn about style. Speaking of herself in the third person, she remembered,

> Amy Greene had shopped for the shoes, the stockings. Amy Greene had gotten Norman Norell to dye the veil. Amy took off her own pearls and put them around Monroe's neck. She's wearing three layers of beige champagne chiffon. And it's tight but it isn't offensive. I had gotten the exact shading of the stockings from the head of Bendel's. She wore Amy's veil. Then a panic to get the right colored flowers. Beige flowers were not in great supply. Amy called Dorothy [Mrs. Richard] Rodgers who suggested orchids. "Not the purple kind. They should be beige orchids." She called Arthur Freed, the MGM producer, who was an orchid fanatic and had four greenhouses. An hour later, Dorothy called back: "It's done, you'll have it." And they arrived. And the Ferragamo shoes that were much later auctioned off for so much were *not* the shoes she wore at the wedding. She wore a pair of crummy sling backs she got from the studio.

Beige would seem to have been Monroe's color of choice. As for the groom, Miller was looking good himself, hardly robust but starting to fill out at 160 pounds and tanned from mixing cement out of doors. Instead of his usual baggy tweeds he was looking almost *Hollywood*, wearing a ("*chi-chi*" Amy Greene said) black suit as well as sunglasses, indoors and out, movie star style. The ceremony was held inside his agent's house for privacy's sake. Lee Strasberg assumed the traditional father's role, giving the bride away. Marilyn's dependence on him was obviously something with which Miller would have to learn to live. Rosten had been asked to be the best man but

"I got bumped at the last minute," he said, "by a late arriving relative," meaning Kermit. Hedda Rosten stayed on as the maid of honor.

The marriage was performed by Rabbi Robert E. Goldberg. Marilyn's "conversion" had consisted of a two-hour session with this very Reform rabbi. His condensed lecture on "the general theory of Judaism," Miller politely said, was perhaps not theological but "humanistic." Rabbi Goldberg also presented Monroe with what he called "The Five Books of Jewish Law," from which he asked her to "read for a short period every day." When she and Arthur returned from England, he said, he would provide further instruction. It was enough to convince her that she had become Jewish even though Miller wasn't sure just how Jewish that was. He told a writer that he was inclined to accept it as part of her intense desire at the time to please him, to become a vital part in his life. So she wore the traditional veil for the ceremony, lifting it to sip from a wine goblet. According to *Life* Magazine,

> The couple drank [the] wine, exchanged rings, and the bridegroom crushed [the ceremonial] goblet. Then, the 25 wedding guests—mostly Miller's friends and family—took off their coats and went outdoors. Over cold lobster, roast beef, turkey and champagne they settled down to boisterous banter.

The magazine, famous for its own pictures, credited these ones as "Exclusive photos by Milton H. Greene."

After the ceremony everyone went outside and into the brilliant sunshine. A bar and a long dinner table had been set up behind the house. Arthur and Marilyn mingled with their guests, who, besides his agent, included his parents, Kermit and his wife, Joan and her husband, Norman and Hedda Rosten, Lee and Paula Strasberg and Morton Miller. Arthur's children were there too. Having Marilyn Monroe as a stepmother made them the talk of The Little Red School House, but they spent most of the wedding day romping with her basset hound, Hugo.

In the milling and laughter Rosten nudged Marilyn away from Miller and whispered aloud and conspiratorially, "How come you're marrying that guy? He wears glasses and his teeth are crooked." "Oh," she beamed, "he's beautiful," and kissed Rosten. "Hey," Arthur cried, "cut that out," while Marilyn turned to her new husband and promised to "cook noodles like your mother." A tipsy Miller said, "Leave my mother out of it," and Rosten found his friend "wonderful to behold. He was happy and full of hope for the future . . . and Marilyn, too, blossomed with this new love."

Six days later on July 7, the day after the State Department issued him a temporary passport, Miller wrote to committee chairman Francis Walter,

> the meetings in question occurred nearly ten years ago. At that time the Communist Party, as far as I was aware, had not been declared a conspiracy but was legally recognized and accorded the privileges of a political party. . . . On the

> ground of their participating in legal actions, therefore, I cannot justify myself in naming these people.

The chairman's reaction, according to Miller, was "If that's his answer to the opportunity offered by the Committee to avoid contempt, then it seems to me he is inviting it." On July 10 the committee unanimously recommended that Congress cite Arthur Miller for contempt, which it did, by a vote of 379 to 9. Three days later the newlyweds were aboard an airplane halfway across the Atlantic Ocean.

Within the month the Roxbury place was put up for sale. The property included seven rooms with three baths, swimming pool, tennis court, terrace and two-car garage on a four-acre site. Miller himself had dug the cellar, poured the concrete foundation, installed the plumbing and put up the roofing in addition to building the shedlike studio where he wrote *Death of a Salesman*. He would sell it all for $27,500, holding on to the additional twenty-six acres that he owned, worth $9,000 at the time. He planned to find another place in Roxbury, perhaps even build it himself. "I began to dream," Miller said, "that with [Marilyn] I could do what seemed to me would be the most wonderful thing of all—have my work, and all that implied, and someone I just simply adored. I thought I could solve it all with this marriage."

14. *Movie Star*

ARRIVING AT NEW YORK'S Idlewild Airport for the flight to London, the newlyweds were engulfed by a mob of newsmen, fans and the aggressively curious. Miller described the experience as making him feel as though he were drowning, with no air to breathe, until the noises faded to a distant, muffled roar. The crush made Marilyn feel like "something in a zoo . . . everybody is always tugging at you. They'd all like sort of a chunk of you."

The pandemonium was no different at the other end of the trip. Sir Laurence and Lady Olivier were waiting to greet them at Heathrow Airport while the helmeted policemen, England's bobbies, restrained the throng of shouting fans jostling with a crowd of reporters, photographers and newsreel cameramen, all surging for a closer look at the sensational couple.

The momentum of publicity had been building in London since the earliest announcement of *The Sleeping Prince*—which had already been retitled to give Marilyn equal billing and was now called *The Prince and The Showgirl.* Souvenir shops were selling Marilyn Monroe scarves, sunglasses and the calendar with her nude photograph. One newspaper printed a special Marilyn Monroe section, and although such journalistic hysteria was no longer surprising to Miller, he would never appear to be comfortable with it. He couldn't, he said, even smile convincingly for the ubiquitous cameras, which he did try to do because he was being regularly described as looking "dour." If his cheek muscles were functioning when he tried to force a smile, he said, the photographs didn't show it, because they all made him appear grim. Perhaps that was an accurate representation of his state of mind, since Marilyn's drinking was becoming worrisome, all the more so in view of a developing dependency on barbiturates, currently Ambutal. She was staying up later, sleeping later, pulling herself together later and needing his company later, none of which made it easy for him to work. Several of Monroe's biographers describe the marriage as already disintegrating, but that seems like speculative hindsight. The couple's subsequent demonstrations of devotion and attachment as well as the sheer endurance of the marriage suggest a close bond at this early point and a desire for it to last. "I never thought in terms of being happy by myself," Marilyn said. "I thought marriage did that. . . . Happiness wasn't ever anything I ever took for granted." If both of them expressed moments of doubt, even at the start, that was not so unusual among the once divorced.

Living with a major movie star had already changed Miller's life in many ways. There was obviously a loss of privacy. "Being married to a girl like Marilyn," he said, not inventively but accurately, "is like living in a goldfish bowl." Every public appearance seemed to turn chaotic. He could hardly complain, though, about their private life; she had adapted hers to his, possibly because famous or unknown, she'd never really had much of one herself. And so they had been living in his world, their activities his choices, their friends his. And in theatrical circles at least he was still somebody.

As they climbed into the car that awaited them on the tarmac at Heathrow Airport, he experienced the first touch of changed *physical* circumstances. The automobile was a chauffeur-driven limousine followed on the drive from Heathrow to their temporary home by some thirty cars of reporters and photographers. From the relatively conventional, not very large apartment on Sutton Place and the modest farmhouse in Connecticut he moved into what Norman Rosten—who had tagged along with his wife, Hedda—called "one of the more modest stately homes of England." This stately home was Lord Charles Moore's "Parkside House," a ten-acre gated estate in the London suburb of Englefield Green in Eggham, Surrey. Its mansion, as Rosten recalled, had "a dozen rooms, a staff of six or seven, several acres of lush green lawn, inimitable English rose gardens and its back yard was enclosed by an iron fence and a gate that opened on Windsor Park, the private property of the Queen."

Likewise Terence Rattigan's welcoming party—Amy Greene called it "an honest to God ball"—reflected an old-guard British class system that was still very much in effect. The honest to God ball was a gala honoring the Millers. Rattigan had arranged it for Tuesday, July 24, 1956, at Sidale, his country estate in Swillington, not far from London. His master plan called for "one hundred guests, twenty chauffeurs, Cleary [his manservant] and four waiters, porter, chef, candelabra and six dozen gilt chairs." The guest list was divided among very important people, designated as "cups of tea," obligatory invitees, or "cosies," and, Rattigan added, "close chums to be invited for no other purpose but to give *me* entertainment and, I hope, Mr. and Mrs. Miller, but that is a secondary consideration."

The *cups of tea* were assorted titles as well as the American ambassador to the Court of St. James. The *cosies* were the cream of London stage society and its allied circles, including Dame Margot Fonteyn, Dame Edith Sitwell, Peggy Ashcroft, the Paul Scofields, the Alec Guinnesses, the Douglas

Fairbankses, John Gielgud, Margaret Leighton, Dame Edith Evans, Tyrone Power, choreographer Frederick Ashton, designer Hardy Amies and the writer Joyce Cary. To these Rattigan added the Hollywood gossip columnists Louella Parsons and Radie Harris. He did not bother listing the "close chums."

Marilyn, wearing a gold brocade gown from the wardrobe of *The Prince and the Showgirl,* was of course the center of attention but also the hit of the party when she danced the Charleston with Rattigan. Miller conceded that the reporters and crowds had no interest in him, and that the wisest course was to accept a background role, not that he had much of a choice. At the Rattigan affair, according to Amy Greene, he stood by sourly, bristling "like a porcupine . . . Whenever people came over to fawn over Marilyn he looked touchy, put down the crowd as aristocrats and snobs, and kept saying, 'Let's get out of here.'" Finally they did, and the following day, quoting a London rabbi, the *Daily Express* reported,

> Rabbi Goldberg gave Marilyn the Five Books of Jewish Law before she [left] New York. These books contain the basis of our faith. Mrs. Miller reads them for a short period every day. Rabbi Goldberg said she will receive further instructions from him when she gets back to New York. Then she will attend a synagogue ceremony, after which she will be recognized by all Jews as a believing and practicing Jewess.

With the party over work on the picture began.

Mornings at seven, Marilyn's car, chauffeur and bodyguard arrived for the forty-five-minute drive to Pinewood Studios. At the start Arthur came along, and for Marilyn the movie making was immediately unpleasant. When Olivier was dealing with "old friends," Rosten remembered—actors such as Dame Sybil Thorndike or Anton Walbrook—"he expressed his delight" but with Monroe his attitude became "patronizing" and "she was on guard . . . suspicious, sullen, defensive, with flashes of anger breaking out." Josh Logan, the director of *Bus Stop,* had written Olivier that "She's worth all the trouble," but the Englishman disagreed. Their relationship was fractious from the outset. Occasionally Marilyn would turn and walk away even as he was speaking to her, sometimes leaving the set entirely. She had always been sensitive to real or perceived disapproval of her acting and had been known to flee movie sets before. That after all was how she first met Arthur, but now her insecurities seemed to be thoroughly defenseless. She could, for instance, and did turn in flight simply because of Olivier's ineptly stated but harmless request, "All right, Marilyn, be sexy." On such occasions Miller would apologize for her, explaining that she was "distracted." Even so, she seemed to take him for less of an ally than the ever-present Paula Strasberg, who ran her through elementary acting exercises (such as shaking the wrists), dispensed vitamins and sedatives, rehearsed her every line and was driving Laurence Olivier out of his "squeaking mind."

In Amy Greene's inimitable description Paula Strasberg was "short, fat, dumpy, red haired . . . a bag lady before bag ladies were invented, muumuus she would wear." She would ultimately be squeezed or shoved off the movie set, but for the time being both Lee and Paula Strasberg were hovering about Monroe, he as a well-paid guru, she the acting coach. Miller considered the woman ridiculous and distrusted her husband, but he had "vowed" to himself that if Marilyn needed them, he would not oppose their presence. Another arrival was her psychoanalyst summoned from New York (and just as quickly replaced) to support the increasingly upset Monroe, who could read contempt in a simple British accent, starting with Olivier, who "came on," she said, "like someone slumming . . . Sir Olivier [*sic*] was enough Englishman for me."

Her edginess and unpredictable work habits were surely affected by ever-larger doses of barbiturates and a resulting prolonged morning grogginess. It was left for Miller to rouse her and get her off to work, which increasingly meant afternoon arrivals on the movie set and sometimes none at all. At such times Olivier had to hastily rearrange the day's shooting schedule, which led to friction with Milton Greene, who was producing the picture, and aggravation for Miller, who kept promising on the telephone to bring Marilyn to work while she asked him, "Why are you getting involved in this?"

"What was I supposed to do?" Miller later pleaded, "say, 'Here, have a glass of milk'?" Meanwhile, Rosten remembered, "behind the scenes, a struggle was taking place, with Greene and Miller and the Strasbergs competing for control over Marilyn's future career." Difficult or infantile or neurotic or not, she was a figure of immense financial significance. Kermit Bloomgarden wrote two letters to Miller suggesting that Monroe appear in *Maiden Voyage*, a Paul Osborne play he was producing. He insisted, "it was not her name that I [want] but her talent." Miller replied,

> when she gets onto a stage she will slaughter an audience and become one of the greatest stage stars we ever saw, but she is such a perfectionist that nothing seems like an accomplishment if she can do it. To the point—she is exhausted. It would be impossible for her to work this winter at all, not only for that reason but because we've got to settle down to a life, as soon as we get back.

He had begun playing the power behind the throne, not yet the mere prince consort—although it was she alone who would be presented to Queen Elizabeth—and it was just as well that she didn't do the play because *Maiden Voyage* failed even before reaching Broadway. Miller not only made that decision but would win the struggle to control Monroe's producing company, ousting Milton Greene and installing friends, including his sister Joan's husband, as the new board of directors of Marilyn Monroe Productions. With that, remembered Rosten, "Arthur was plunged into a world of daily crises, unspoken antagonisms, endless decisions [and] the necessity of providing Marilyn with almost constant support."

Miller insisted that he was only trying to boost what years later would be called the *self-esteem* of the woman. Deep down, he said, he admired Marilyn's naturalness, her rare spirit and her unique talent, even her potential for greatness as an actor, nor is there any reason to doubt it, although his admiration was perhaps maintained somewhat too deep down. Whatever the nature and extent of his support, however, it was profoundly undermined one weekend when Monroe came upon one of his spiral notebooks that he had left lying on a table in the drawing room. Whether it was open or if she thumbed through it and whether or not he had subconsciously meant for her to find it, she read a stunning entry. The Strasbergs were houseguests at the time and as Lee heard it from a shaken Marilyn, Arthur had noted "How he thought I was some kind of angel but now he guessed he was wrong . . . that his first wife had let him down, but I had done something worse. Olivier was beginning to think I was a troublesome bitch and he no longer had a decent answer for that one."

Miller accepted this as an accurate description of his entry but Marilyn told several friends of something else in the notebook, an even more painful remark—"The only one I will ever love is my daughter." When asked, he could not recall writing that. He believed the friends might have been confusing it with such a remark in a note mentioned in his later, patently autobiographical, play *After the Fall*. Its notebook admissions also include coldness and remoteness, and there is an understandable temptation to take such references for fact and that play for journalism because some of it is so obviously based on known circumstances and events. One is tempted, for instance, to read as Miller's own admission his central character's description of the notebook entry as a "letter from hell" from a man who "could not love." That would be a powerful and painful self-observation were it in fact a self-observation, but while the playwright surely identified with his protagonist in *After the Fall*, that is not necessarily the same thing as his own confession.

Arthur Miller may have been one of the original workaholics but his productivity had come to a standstill under the circumstances and conditions surrounding *The Prince and the Showgirl*. His lengthened version of *A View from the Bridge* was finished except for the inevitable adjustments that would be made during rehearsals. Since nothing was to be accomplished by going to Marilyn's movie set, he flew back to New York for a visit with his children. Upon his return the only writing he managed to do was a short story about a couple of men he had met in a Reno bar, cowboys who chased and caught wild mustang horses to sell for slaughter. He called this story "The Misfits, or Chicken Feed: The Last Frontier of the Quixotic Cowboy" (because, he said, "it is a short story about obsolete quests, a story with a touch of Don Quixote") and sent it off to *Esquire* Magazine, which bought it immediately and published it in May 1957. Then he idled away the time at Parkside House, sometimes at the typewriter, sometimes playing the piano in the drawing room, sometimes reading movie proposals that had been submitted for Marilyn's consideration, sometimes pasting up her scrapbook.

Finally work on *The Prince and the Showgirl* began to wind down. The London production of *A View from the Bridge* was imminent, but even as rehearsals were being scheduled under Peter Brook's direction, problems arose regarding a license required from The Lord Chamberlain, the office of the British censor. The issuance of this license (the origin of the term *legitimate theater*) was determined by whomever was designated as Lord Chamberlain. At the time it was the Earl of Scarborough.

In judging the moral propriety of *A View from the Bridge* the Earl—a man who came to work at St. James's Palace always dressed in a cutaway suit—managed to overlook the play's incestuous elements while objecting to its homosexual references. Among his specifics were not only Eddie Carbone kissing Rodolpho but the homosexual euphemism *punk*. At a meeting with the Earl, Robert Whitehead, gentlemanly and innocent producer that he was, insisted, "In America, 'punk' simply means 'no good bum.'" He was right and he was wrong. Miller knew what *punk* used to mean in America, and evidently still meant in England. He used it in a homosexual sense in some youthful plays as he now did in *A View from the Bridge*. The objections finally were not resolved but circumnavigated through a subterfuge that Whitehead had devised for Tennessee Williams's *Cat on a Hot Tin Roof*. The play was produced under the umbrella of a private theater club, outside the purview of the Lord Chamberlain. Theatergoers would automatically join the club by paying a small surcharge for their tickets.

The original purpose of Miller's revision was to expand the one-act play to full length, but with Peter Brook's patent encouragement of equal importance was the modification of it into a traditional, realistic drama. To that end the playwright removed the stylized elements, beginning with most of the poetry, although some of it was simply printed out as conventional dialogue. While the core of the one-act version remained with many speeches intact, the incantorial effect of spoken arias was eliminated as well as the other parallels with Greek tragedy. Scenes that were originally spare, simple and direct were stretched out with conversational doodling, or what Miller called "talk about this and that." Background details were added to lend dimension to the intentionally monolithic characters and coloration to the intentionally ritualistic events. One such background detail, involving sexual problems between Eddie and Beatrice, was perhaps more personal than Miller realized. When he wrote the first version of *A View from the Bridge*, he was married to Mary and struggling to resist his passion for Marilyn Monroe; while writing the second version he was being divorced and marrying her. He did retain his original view that "Everybody around of any intelligence would have told Eddie that it would be a disaster if he didn't give up his obsession [with his niece] but it's the nature of the obsession that it can't be given up." Now more than ever this seemed to apply to the playwright's obsession with Monroe, and he already knew the perils of it. In his *Introduction to the Collected Plays,* which he was finishing in London, he wrote,

> Both *The Crucible* and *A View from the Bridge* are about the awesomeness of a passion which, despite its contradicting the self-interest of the individual it inhabits, despite every kind of warning, despite even the destruction of the moral beliefs of the individual, proceeds to magnify its power over him until it destroys him.

Miller might well have been defending the desertion of his own wife by making Eddie Carbone's marital bed unfulfilled. He added a speech for Carbone to swear faithfulness, express sexual frustration and complain like John Proctor in *The Crucible* about conjugal coldness.

> I want my respect . . . What I feel like doin' in the bed and what I don't feel like doin' . . . You used to be different . . . The last year or two I come in the house I don't know what's gonna hit me. It's a shootin' gallery here and I'm the pigeon . . . A wife is supposed to believe the husband.

Whether related to Miller's life or not, such alterations added length to the play rather than depth. They amounted to perhaps not a bastardization but certainly a compromise of what had once been a play set in the modern day but rooted in classical Greek tragedy, with "the past," as Professor Rowe had taught the young Miller, "coming to life in the present and creating drama." Miller himself would later confess, "it had always seemed to me to be a one act play . . . the form was also influenced by my own curiosity as to whether we could in a contemporary theater deal with life in some way like the Greeks did."

Peter Brook began rehearsals by expressing relief about all such excised elements. "The British," he said rather glibly, "are terribly disturbed by any suggestion that the future is so closely determined by the present. If that were so, you see, we should have to blow our brains out." He assured Miller that a suggestion of tragic inevitability remained in the play but since "this is all happening in Brooklyn . . . they may allow it here." The most elementary alteration, the added intermission, was Miller's first concession. Greek tragedies were direct, concise and uninterrupted. He could live with that alteration along with the others, insisting that the ritualistic element was intact. "Everything," he said, was still serving "to advance the theme [with] no time for the character to reveal himself apart from thematic considerations."

He was kidding himself. His play's stylistic premise had been shelved and the work no longer presented monolithic characters behaving fatefully without psychological speculation. Length and realism had been achieved at the cost of mythic impulse. Eddie Carbone's tragedy (and by extension Elia Kazan's) was now human sized, the informer no longer a broken god but a man within the bounds of conventional tragedy enthralled by passion into a state of emotional anarchy. Carbone (and perhaps Kazan as well) was allowed a measure of sympathy, and a work written "in a mood of experiment" with ordinary people set upon a grid of ritualistic tragedy had been replaced by a play portraying realistic characters in a melodrama, where inevitability was superseded by conventional motivation.

The revision was reflected in production, the original scenic references to ancient Greece replaced by an elaborate traditional setting. As Miller described it,

> Two high wings closed to form the face of the house where Eddie lived, a brick tenement [that] when opened revealed a basement living room. Over and at the sides and across the back were stairways, fire escapes, passages, quite like a whole neighborhood constructed vertically.

Without allusions to "Syracusa" and with Alfieri more a narrator than Greek Chorus a ritual tragedy was turned into a family play, the statues brought to life, so to speak, surrounded by a real neighborhood with a crowd of extras for "neighbors." It oddly reflected a core tenet of the existentialism Miller so despised, the conviction that things are exactly what they seem and nothing more.

His willingness to make these modifications is regrettable but understandable. The play foundered on Broadway. He had not enjoyed a commercial success since *Death of a Salesman*. The international acceptance of *The Crucible* evidently did not make up for its disappointing reception in New York. Miller was still very much a son of old Broadway. For a play to be successful a play had to be *successful*. *A View from the Bridge* was now rearranged to be accessible in the manner of *All My Sons* and in London the strategy worked. Miller would alter the play yet another time at Brook's suggestion for the Paris production. This time the director suggested suiting the play to French audiences. Since they—or so he believed—appreciated suicides as curtain scenes, Eddie Carbone was rewritten to finally grasp his passion for Catherine and kill himself in shame.

On October 11, 1956, the full-length version of *A View from the Bridge* had its world premiere at the Comedy Theatre in London's West End under the auspices of the Watergate Club. The publicity surrounding Miller and Monroe pushed ticket sales to unexpected heights. In ten years of existence the little theater club had managed to enroll 20,000 subscribers, but in the first two weeks that tickets were on sale for the Miller play it signed up more than 12,000 new members. On the first night, Marilyn Monroe arrived in a scarlet evening gown with a neckline that plunged in a heart-stopping way. The United Press wire service reported,

> Never has London seen such an opening night . . . thirty policemen struggled to hold back the mob when the Arthur Millers, Sir Laurence Olivier and Vivien Leigh showed up. Marilyn smiled nervously, Miller looked glum and the crowd looked hysterical . . . Everyone stared at Marilyn's shimmering red satin dress, a large portion of which seemed to be missing.

London critics regularly did their homework and many compared the West End version of *A View from the Bridge* with the Broadway original. The best of them, Kenneth Tynan of the *Observer,* did so as well, but he was more interested in the play's subject matter. Tynan was not only a superb dramatic critic but also a political man, and his politics were leftward bound. He was weary of the genteel dramatists (Somerset Maugham, Noel Coward, Terence Rattigan) of the upper crust whose style and values long dominated London's professional stage. In May just five months earlier he had been galvanized by John Osborne's *Look Back in Anger* ("all scum and a mile wide. All the qualities one had despaired of ever seeing on the stage—the drift towards anarchy, the instinctive leftishness, the automatic rejection of 'official attitudes'"). Osborne's play deals with the young working class—bright and articulate characters disgusted with what was still considered the ruling class. If that anger delighted Tynan, it left the British theatrical establishment aghast. Such characters, language and manners were simply unimaginable in the theater. Laurence Olivier shared this disapproval but he had gamely come along for a second viewing when Miller chose *Look Back in Anger* as the play he most wished to see the day after arriving in London. Olivier even invited John Osborne to join them for after-dinner drinks while Monroe stayed home, recovering from the time change.

Leaving the theater, Miller told a startled Olivier how impressed with the play he was and by the time they joined Osborne at a nearby bar the great actor was convinced, even asking, "Mr. Osborne, would you consider writing a play for me?" The outcome would be *The Entertainer,* a relief from the actor's classical elegance and a performance that would broaden the range and use of his immense gifts. "As if in appreciation," the British critic Sheridan Morley said, "Olivier would [highlight] the National Theatre's new home with *The Crucible.*"

A View from the Bridge, like *Look Back in Anger,* was about gritty working-class people scrambling for dignity, and Tynan leapt to its praise as if Miller's play were confirming the new day begun by Osborne's. He wrote somewhat contradictively, the "masterly play falls just short of being a masterpiece," and he wasn't the only critic to applaud it. Thus the revised *Bridge* became the success that Arthur Miller needed, christening London as his artistic safe haven. Yet without seeming to grasp it (he insisted that with Carbone now seen "in his social context . . . the myth-like feeling of the story emerged of itself") he had done what he vowed never again to do after the near-emasculation of *Death of a Salesman.* He had betrayed his original design, and while the immediate purpose—commercial success—was served, Miller had forsaken his play's integrity. He would pay an enduring price for that. Once the two-act version of *A View from the Bridge* was declared the definitive text and included in his *Collected Plays* he would be saddled with a reputation for old-fashioned social realism. In England this was no bother, where tradition dominated, realism endured, theater was culturally embedded and change was incremental, as with the Osborne play—a matter of content first and style later. *Look Back in Anger* may have been about the working class, but it was just as photographic in depicting "kitchen sink" life as were the socialite plays and their drawing rooms. That is why, despite Tynan's exaggerated praise ("probably the most important British dramatist since Shaw") Osborne would end up a minor figure.

Miller immediately pronounced *A View from the Bridge* in both matter and manner "a rejection of that enervated 'acceptance' of illogic [i.e., Samuel Beckett's existentialist absurdism] which was the new wisdom of the age. Here, action had consequences again, betrayal was not greeted with a fashionably lobotomized smile." He was talking but New York wasn't listening. There dramatic realism was a dead issue. Terence Rattigan's *The Sleeping Prince,* due to open in a few weeks, would not even run a month, and Miller found himself first defending then representing a status quo that he had never belonged to or even endorsed in the first place. Thus his introduction to the *Collected Plays* would also serve as a conclusion to the four full-length plays in the volume—*All My Sons, Death of a Salesman, The Crucible* and *A View from the Bridge*. At the age of forty he was about to become an absentee playwright and an American theatrical anachronism, with his dramatic legacy—his most produced and best-respected work—generally considered behind him.

The very style of the introduction to the *Collected Plays* suggests a further reason for Miller's fall from grace in his own country. In 1950s America psychoanalysis exerted a fascination on not only the professional, artistic urban class but even on earnest innocents such as Marilyn Monroe ("seems like everyone I know is being analyzed"). To dig through and speculate about one's behavior and motives had become commonplace. Miller's essay introducing the *Collected Plays* to an unfortunate extent is symptomatic of that, an exercise in self-absorption, self-analysis and self-justification. Unlike Shaw, Miller could not easily separate his essays from his dramas. Miller's fascination with his own mind and the sound of his voice and his compulsion to rummage through his own psyche were leading him toward dramatics that got inside a protagonist's head like *Death of a Salesman* but stayed there, with no view from the outside. In the *Third Play* that he was writing and writing and writing too many central characters were starting to pontificate on his behalf instead of speaking in their own voices. The long introductory essay to *The Collected Plays of Arthur Miller* is stimulating and provocative and in many ways brilliant. It is hard to think of another American playwright who could have written such a treatise. Yet when its assertions and musings began to turn up in the mouths of characters, and pro-

Photofest

The original 1944 cast of *The Man Who Had All the Luck*, with (left to right) Karl Swenson, Eugenia Rawls and Dudley Sadler as David Beeves, Hester Falk and Amos Beeves

The original 1947 cast of *All My Sons*, with (left to right) Arthur Kennedy, Karl Malden, Beth Merrill, Ed Begley and Lois Wheeler as Chris Kennedy, George Deever, Kate and Joe Keller and Ann Deever

Photofest

Photofest

Photofest

LEFT:

Lee J. Cobb and Mildred Duinnock creating the roles of Willy and Linda Loman in *Death of a Salesman*

RIGHT:

Alan Hewitt played the young boss Howard Wagner to Cobb's Loman in the original production of *Death of a Salesman*

Photofest

LEFT: Thomas Mitchell with the two suitcases that became the signature image of *Death of a Salesman*

Photofest

LEFT: Dustin Hoffman was the first small actor to play Willy Loman as the "shrimp" Miller originally described.

BELOW: Brian Dennehey, Goodman Theatre, Chicago

John Haynes

Warren Mitchell, Royal National Theatre, London

George C. Scott

Theater Collection, New York Public Library

Photofest

Director Jed Harris playing psychological games with Miller, holding his wrist while discussing *The Crucible*. Producer Kermit Bloomgarden looks on with plain concern.

Simone Signoret and Yves Montand as Elizabeth and John Proctor in *Les Sorcieres de Salem*, the 1953 Paris production of *The Crucible*

The 1996 film version of *The Crucible* starred Miller's future son-in-law, Daniel Day-Lewis, as John Proctor and Winona Ryder as the sexy, dangerous, mischief-making Abigail Williams.

20th Century-Fox Pictures and Photofest

Photofest

A View from the Bridge was an unsuccessful one-act play in its original 1955 production. Its cast included (left to right) Jack Warden, Eileen Heckart, Van Heflin, Gloria Marlowe and Richard Davalos as Marco, Beatrice, Eddie, Catherine and Rodolpho.

Werner J. Kuhn and Photofest

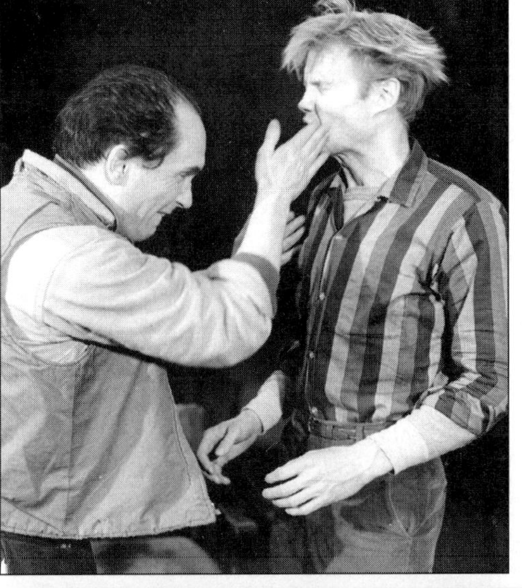

Robert Duvall and Jon Voight played Eddie and Rodolpho in the first American production of the full-length version of *A View from the Bridge* in 1965 off-Broadway.

Michael Gambon as Eddie and Elizabeth Bell as Beatrice in the Royal National Theatre Production of *A View from the Bridge*

Nobby Clark

A rare cheerful moment during the making of *The Misfits* as the cast and creators clowned around while posing for what would become a classic photograph. The tall, flanking gentlemen are producer Frank Taylor on the left and director John Huston on the right.

United Artists Pictures, Photofest

After the Fall with Barbara Loden and Jason Robards, Jr.

The Price with (left to right) Harold Gary, Pat Hingle, Kate Reid and Arthur Kennedy as Solomon, Victor Franz, Esther Franz and Walter Franz

Miller's sister, Joan Copeland, played Lee Baum, clearly modeled on their mother, in *The American Clock* when it premiered at the Spoleto Festival in Charleston, South Carolina, in 1980. John Randolph played opposite her as the Miller father figure, Moe Baum.

CBS Television, Photofest

Vanessa Redgrave as Fania Fenelon and Jane Alexander as Alma Rose in Miller's 1980 television play *Playing for Time*

Photofest

In the American premiere of *The Ride Down Mt. Morgan,* Patrick Stewart in fantasy heaven with both of his wives, Mary Silverstone as the younger Leah and Frances Conroy as Lyman Felt's first wife, Theo tagonists began to sound like polemicists, their theatrical force ebbed. As Miller once had expressed his emotions through his plays and in that sense escaped into them, he now rationalized feeling. In this focus on analysis and disquisition he seemed to be losing track of the emotive powers that had propelled him to the forefront of American theater. Curiously it was Marilyn who, talking about Miller, put it succinctly. "I suppose everyone needs a place to escape to. With some of us, though, maybe it's all up here," she said, pointing to her head. "I don't just mean the mind, I mean feeling."

Home again in October for Arthur's forty-first birthday, the couple began looking for another farmhouse in Connecticut while renting a temporary retreat in the oceanfront hamlet of Amagansett on the south fork of Long Island. The place belonged to a former stage manager named Jeffrey Potter and his wife, Penny, both friends of Miller friends. It was set on a one hundred-acre site that, like so much of the Hamptons, was once used for potato farming. To one side was a riding stable and on the other was the home of the artist Willem de Kooning. The farmhouse itself faced on winding, arboreal Town Lane, minutes from the painterly bay beaches at Louse Point and Barnes Landing, a few miles from the ocean dunes. Arthur and Marilyn would drive down to that Atlantic shore, rolling onto the beach at Napeague Lane in their new Jeep, at the time the only kind of car manageable in the sand. They would walk alongside the sea on this long stretch of beach with its sloping dune grass, a considerable change from the flat, wide duneless beaches she knew near Los Angeles. Here, as spring turned to early summer, Marilyn would watch Arthur flycasting in the surf (Robert Whitehead called him "a first rate carpenter, a second rate fisherman"). Wearing a red baseball cap and baggy gray swim trunks and less than muscular, he was not quite the male physical equal of even the now chubby Monroe, splashing in the surf in her one-piece white bathing suit.

Here in Amagansett he wrote a touching story for and about Marilyn and "her fierce tenderness toward all that lived." Called "Please Don't Kill Anything" (later published in *Esquire*), it is a short piece about a woman upset because a couple of flycasters, standing in the ocean surf, discard their inedible catch and leave the fish to die, floundering in the sand while still alive. The man who accompanies this woman is amused and charmed enough to help her throw the flapping fish back into the sea, while explaining the universal food chain and life's need for death. When their rescue effort is complete, she apologizes for having been so anxious, explaining that "they were alive, and if nobody's going to eat them. . . . " But rather than thinking her foolish the man is grateful, "a great happiness opening in him that she had laid his hand on the fish which were now swimming in the sea because he had lifted them." And "oh," she says, "how I love you."

The story would seem a fit parable about and testament to this marriage at its best and how Miller perceived it when happiest. To all the questions about what this unlikely and misfit couple had in common—what bound them to each other despite manifest differences, conflicts and displeasures, and what one got from the other—an answer can be found in "Please Don't Kill Anything" and its story of innocence and knowledge.

Then he turned to his legal problems. On February 18, 1957, following his letter to HUAC chairman Walter, Miller was indicted on two charges of contempt of Congress—refusing to acknowledge that Armand d'Usseau had been chairman of the Communist writers' meetings that he had attended in 1947 and refusing to name other individuals who were there. Early in May he wrote to James Stern that "the case of Miller vs. American civilization [begins] at the end of this week. I have to be in Washington to plead not guilty as the result of a crime which is not a crime and which it happens I have not committed anyhow."

This time Marilyn went with him, even though if she did, she remembered, "I was supposed to be finished." She had been threatened, she said, by a Twentieth Century-Fox executive. "Either Arthur named names and I got him to name names or 'You'll never be heard of again.' I said, 'I'm proud of my husband's position and I stand behind him all the way.'"

They went directly to the Georgetown home of Joseph Rauh, who was representing Miller once again. Perhaps the power of anticommunist America was beginning to ebb, but it had not yet failed. Even the American Civil Liberties Union, a supposed protector of liberal principles, declined to provide Miller with legal assistance. Ultimately the organization would tender an apology, giving him a $5,000 award for protecting the right to privacy during the period of anticommunist hysteria. In 1999 all the ACLU director could say was "God forbid, if something like [that] should happen again, we would be there for you." It was half a century too late but Miller didn't say so.

During the weeklong contempt trial in federal district court Rauh pressed the relevance issue. Whoever was present at the Communist writers' meetings, he argued, had nothing to do with Arthur Miller's passport application, the ostensible subject of his appearance before the House Committee. The government's argument was that the relevance lay in his credibility. The playwright himself did not testify. Nattily dressed now in a black silk suit he calmly doodled caricatures of the prosecutor as the legal scenario played itself out. He was feeling confident and wrote to Stern, "the lawyer and I were always laughing when we weren't under court duress not to." Their laughter notwithstanding, Judge Charles F. McLaughlin found Arthur Miller guilty of being in contempt of Congress. In the decision McLaughlin noted that

> however commendable may be regarded the motive of the defendant in refusing to disclose the identity or the official position of another with whom he was in association, lest said disclosure might bring trouble on him, that motive and that refusal have been removed from this court's consideration.

For a few weeks Miller had to live with the possibility that he might go to prison, perhaps not for the maximum term of a year given the Hollywood Ten, but prison nevertheless. On July 19 Judge McLaughlin handed down a one-year sentence that he reduced shortly after to a single suspended month with a $500 fine. It was only a slap on the wrist but it represented a conviction, which Rauh immediately appealed. One year later the decision would be reversed, although not the legal costs that according to Miller came to $40,000. "Nobody wants to be a hero," he commented, "but in every man there is something he cannot give up and still remain himself." That something, he said, was honor and repute, "his own name . . . If he gives that up, he becomes a different man, not himself." He was more than paraphrasing John Proctor in *The Crucible*; rather the play, its theme and its author seemed all of a piece. Perhaps it was true that nobody believed in Arthur Miller's moral heroism more than he did, but moral heroism it surely was.

Arthur and Marilyn were moving around a lot, which is never good for a writer. They had changed apartments in the city, turning the corner from Two Sutton Place to 444 East 57th Street. Marilyn had the decorator, John Moore, give the thirteenth-floor river view apartment a sophisticated look, lining its big living room with floor-to-ceiling book-filled shelves. She described the color scheme as "beiges and dark chocolate browns and whites." Providing a touch of Hollywood was a white baby grand piano opposite the wood-burning fireplace. She covered its lid with framed photographs, prominent among them the picture of Einstein that Eli Wallach had signed "To my dear Marilyn. Love, Albert." The most important element of the new apartment and main reason for moving, however, was an extra room so that Arthur could have a secluded place to work. Now he had a den, a desk, a chair and a door that he could not close behind him—Marilyn, he'd say, "fed off attention" while he needed quiet and privacy if he was ever to return to his work. She tried to leave him alone, going to museums with Norman Rosten or as often as not taxiing across town to visit with the Strasbergs, but that didn't make Miller any happier because he wanted both his privacy and her confidence. He told a specially trusted interviewer that he always wanted her to come to him so that they could sit down and have a "heart to heart talk." Some mornings they did just that, bicycling up Fifty-seventh Street, she in jeans and a kerchief, for a dawn breakfast at the corner coffee shop. But, Miller admitted, "communication was frequently short-circuited, leaving only the consolation of the bedroom."

Working conditions were no better in Amagansett. There the "farm," as Miller liked to call it, was quiet enough but now a rather gloomier Marilyn Monroe walked the water's edge, certainly on the afternoon their landlord invited them to lunch at one of the bay beaches. Wary of gawkers, Jeffrey Potter had chosen the waterfront deck at the nearby Devon Yacht Club just below the desertlike inland dunes where of all things the silent movie *The Sheik* had been filmed.

Marilyn removed her sunglasses as Arthur introduced her. "He was wearing sun glasses too," Potter said, "and he didn't used to." She startled him. He had not expected her to look "blowzy. She looked blown up in her bathing suit," Potter said, "almost as if by gas. It wasn't like fat. More like a rubber doll. Puffed up, the face, the whole body." He was also dismayed by her obvious distress. "She was very nice and very sweet," Potter insisted, "but there seemed a great sadness that was going on there [and] Arthur was so attentive, so concerned. He hung upon her every word. . . . He seemed so concerned for her that, if he could have, he would have physically *merged with her* and taken on her sadness." The only time that Potter remembered Marilyn "brightening" that afternoon was when she spied a sign with the motto of his dredging company, YOUR BOTTOM IS OUR BUSINESS. That gave her a giggle. Otherwise, he said, "She seemed *so sad.*"

In Amagansett they played records at home—Frank Sinatra for her, Bing Crosby for him—and visited with friends renting nearby: the Rostens, the Bloomgardens and Kermit's press agents, Jim Proctor on Shelter Island and Merle Debuskey in Montauk. "She was very relaxed in Amagansett," Debuskey remembered, "and anything but dumb. When the men were talking theater, she would curl up on the sofa and listen quietly, with interest."

Those days Monroe was wearing jeans all the time, along with sandals, a man's shirt and a floppy hat, and the two of them were unashamedly physical, constantly touching or leaning against one another. Debuskey was "amazed by the incredible amount of devotion she showed toward Arthur"—or *Arturo,* as she liked to call him among friends (*Papa* being reserved for their private life). With Debuskey's fiancée, Christine, she was girlish, leaning forward, for instance, to whisper advice about solving a wedding problem. They planned to get married in Baltimore, where Debuskey's family lived, and they wanted a Jewish ceremony but Christine was a gentile and they were having trouble finding a rabbi who would marry them. "Listen," Marilyn said,

> Don't worry. I tell you I can arrange for Chris to be converted and it isn't going to make her feel terrible. In fact it was one of the most rewarding experiences of my life, I'm so happy I did. I know a marvelous rabbi who has a congregation in Connecticut—a brilliant man. He marched in Selma, he's very anti HUAC. He's open minded and scholarly about Jewish history. He understands what makes sense in religion and what doesn't.

She arranged it too, "and," Debuskey remembered, "she was as happy as a little girl being mixed up in it."

Almost every day she bicycled north, up Abraham's Path to the Springs of Amagansett, where the Rostens had their summer rental. That left Arthur alone to write, but while he put in long hours at the typewriter, nothing of any use was rolling out of it. He was cursed, he said, by ideas that did not develop, scenes that were too talky and too many interior monologues. Although he used to save every scrap, every scene, every early draft that he wrote, he now found himself trashing bundles of manuscript, hundreds of pages at first, then thousands. He confided his frustration to Rosten during one of their meetings about the movie version of *A View from the Bridge*, which he was letting Norman write as a favor for an old friend.

That summer Marilyn was thrilled to learn that she was pregnant. She had been fearful that her many abortions had made it impossible for her to carry to term and she badly wanted a child. It was a regular subject when she was feeling down, which had become a familiar mood. One evening during a dinner party Rosten found her sobbing on his porch. When he asked what the matter was, she said she didn't know, adding, "Maybe it's the weather . . . Make believe I just was out here powdering my nose or something, okay? Arthur will only get upset."

He surely would have. He told one of her closest friends, a Hollywood press agent, that she had tried to jump out of a window in the Fifty-seventh Street apartment but he had pulled her back. "She was someone," the agent said, who "everyone knew was capable of suicide." Some months earlier she had asked for a series of gynecological examinations when she checked into Manhattan's Doctors Hospital—a place famous for handsome suites, East River views, four-star room service and second-rate medicine. The supposed reason for her being there was to possibly solve her pregnancy problems. This was the explanation given to newspaper reporters who learn about celebrity patients from paid informants at major hospitals. Arthur later conceded that the true reason for this hospitalization had been depression—"a wounded seagull could reduce her to weeping." The later news of pregnancy then lifted her spirits, but only temporarily, for in August a sudden and terrible abdominal pain was serious enough to knock her unconscious and warrant a two-and-a-half-hour ambulance ride into Manhattan. It was "a miscarriage," Rosten said, "an ectopic pregnancy. We visited her. She was resting easily, but her cheerfulness didn't fool anybody," and she wrote to him,

> I've got to make some decisions soon. Should I do my next picture or stay home and try to have a baby again? That's what I want most of all, the baby, I guess, but maybe God is trying to tell me something, I mean with all my pregnancy problems. I'd probably make a kooky mother. I'd love my child to death. I want it, yet I'm scared. Arthur says he wants it, but he's losing his enthusiasm. He thinks I should do the picture. After all, I'm a movie star, right?

Miller presented his devastated wife with a love offering, if perhaps as well one with a self-serving twist—the promise to turn his story about cowboys in Nevada—*The Misfits*—into a screenplay for her. He began it immediately. The screen story features a woman who had been peripheral in the original version. Even unseen her name had been Roslyn, an echo name for Marilyn, and Arthur researched her character by interviewing the original, taking notes on Monroe's "speech patterns . . . her attitudes toward life." He then began writing a scenario so elaborate that he would subtitle it *A Cinema Novel* (when published by Viking Press in 1972, the 132-page book would be called *A Story Conceived as a Film*). As a basis for her Roslyn character he said he was using Marilyn's depressions, nervousness, paranoia, insecurity and panic attacks. Then one evening he got up from the typewriter and once again came upon her unconscious. He had been keeping count of her Nembutal tablets and immediately realized that she had overdosed on the barbiturate (her throat diaphragm, he later learned, was "paralyzed"). After he telephoned the medical clinic in nearby East Hampton an emergency team came and revived her, which left her, he remembered, covering his hands with kisses.

Miller wrote to Stern, "The kids were here until a month ago when they left to be with Mary in Rockport, Mass. It took some adjusting but they, with Marilyn, are all together now, my three children."

Early in 1958 they found the Connecticut property they had been looking for, an old farm with a mailing address of 323 Tophet Road, not far from Miller's old place. Marilyn immediately wanted to raze the eighteenth-century white farmhouse—"kind of an old saltbox," she called it, "with a kitchen extension"—and replace it with a "dream house." She was anxious to have that house designed by the most famous architect in America, Frank Lloyd Wright. Soon enough the world-famous, ninety-year-old architect showed up. Upon being met at the railroad station by Miller's neighbor, Harold Birchell, who owned the adjacent farm, the rangy white-haired architect in the flowing cape and gaucho hat announced that even though it was already dark he wished to inspect the site. The bemused farmer drove the magisterial and theatrical architect to the Miller-Monroe property. Wright then proceeded to inspect the landscape by flashlight—which promptly entered Roxbury lore.

Shortly afterward and for a $100,000 fee the Millers received a portfolio with his architectural renderings of the proposed house. As described in *Architectural Digest*, it looked like

> a modernist *Xanadu*. It had a circular living room with a domed ceiling sixty feet in diameter supported by fieldstone columns, each five feet thick. A seventy foot swimming pool was cantilevered into the hillside, and Wright had also imagined a conference room, a chauffeured limousine in the driveway and a pennant flying from the roof . . . but there was only one bedroom.

The drawings left Miller less than enthusiastic and he told the magazine that he had declined to finance the great architect's proposal (not that he himself had the money to do so). As "a born carpenter and mechanic," he said, "I've always been able to visualize space. I failed algebra at Lincoln High School but I'm good at addition and I've been building things since I was seven." The pool alone, he figured, would have cost a quarter of a million (in 1958) dollars. Marilyn, he said, was going along with the alternative of "repairing and updating the existing house." So, he told *Architectural Digest,* dormer windows were being added and the roof was being raised over one wing to allow for an extra guest bedroom. As he wrote to his Irish pal, James Stern,

> We've been remodeling the old Ray Leavenworth house which is . . . within view of the [Alexander and Louisa] Calders. I have a fine little studio [twelve feet by fourteen] apart from the house with a fireplace and an electric heater and windows all around. And our basset hound Hugo lies faithfully at me feet.

When the renovations were complete, the Rostens were among the first to be invited. Arthur was dozing in the apartment bedroom when Norman arrived (Hedda staying home, nursing a cold). He was getting a ride to Connecticut in the Jaguar sedan that had replaced the Thunderbird, but Marilyn was taking her time, signing checks, answering the telephone, even having a fitting with a dress designer. Finally they all were out the door, she with a glass of champagne in her hand. After the usual end run through the building's basement, eluding the ever-waiting photographers, the three settled into the car. Once on the road Arthur said to Norman, "One thing about Marilyn. She can do anything she sets her mind on. She can become a great actress."

"You mean," she said, "I'm not there yet?"

"You will be dear," he replied. "Give it a couple of more weeks."

"He won't write a play for me," she said to Rosten. "He's afraid I'll forget my lines. And I could, too."

"You'd still be a hit," Miller said. "Just by being there, by letting them see you."

With that she leaned over and kissed him on the cheek and only once or twice complained that he wasn't paying attention when she was talking.

In Roxbury the only major concessions he'd allowed her whims had been the digging of an artificial pond and building a long, low stone wall in front of the property. As the masons began work on it, they accidentally cut into the roots of a two hundred-year-old elm tree. "When all of the leaves didn't come through that first spring," she told Rosten, "I knew the trees were hurt . . . punishing us for not appreciating them. But we loved them. Even in winter, without leaves . . . It was my fault. I wanted a stone wall to front the house."

During that weekend with Rosten there she tripped and fell down a flight of stairs. Her injuries were slight, "a bruised ankle," he remembered, "and a cut on her right palm from a broken whiskey glass."

With the completion of the interior decorating Marilyn convinced Arthur—"pressured" was the way he put it—to buy "as much of the adjoining property as I could, and I'm very grateful that I listened to her." Considering that he was all but bankrupt after his divorce settlement and had not been earning any significant money for several years, that he did the buying is doubtful. In his autobiography Miller does say that at the time "I had to sell some of my manuscripts to pay off our taxes." That is probably a mistaken recollection about a federal tax write-off for his subsequent 1961 donation of scripts, notebooks and papers to the Harry Ransom Library at the University of Texas. He would have a sudden burst of income that year, $225,000 for the *Misfits* screenplay. As to the additional property that was purchased in 1958, those 315 acres were worth some $100,000 at the time, bringing the total to 340 acres of ultimately prime Connecticut real estate. It was deeded in Marilyn's name, along with the house. She was not as business foolish or as profligate a spender as Arthur thought.

As a country retreat, it was his most elaborate yet, but as the most peaceful, he would remember the rented cottage in Amagansett. Instead of associating the cottage with Marilyn's anxieties or emergency hospitalizations he would remember, "Whenever there is any moment of mild despair in my life, what I would do is get in the car, drive down to Amagansett, drive past the Potter farm, come home and I'm a new man." As for his best working environment, the first Connecticut place had provided that. Now, as they began spending time at the new Roxbury house, he could isolate himself in a one-room work cabin (which he didn't build) but he couldn't get anything done. Miller had always been a disciplined writer. His lifetime work habit had been to write every day from dawn until ten or eleven o'clock in the morning, but with Marilyn's insomnia and her need for company he was often just getting to sleep at dawn.

Sometimes she was not asleep even then and would roll out her motor scooter to ride over to Birchall's farm and watch him milk the cows. After finally managing to doze off, she would leave Papa to his seclusion. Then waking late in the afternoon she would ride the scooter into the center of Roxbury, Hodge's General Store on Route 67. There Marilyn Monroe, known to the locals as Mrs. Miller, would listen to the local gossip while in New York newspaper items were beginning to suggest the possibility of her appearing in a new Arthur Miller play. On March 7, 1958, the *New York Times* reported that it could happen early the next season, the work being the still untitled *Third Play*. "The new drama was described by Mr. Miller as 'the tragedy and laughter of my generation'. . . . According to Mr. Miller, it will probably run for three and one half hours. This is the script Mr. Miller has been wrestling with since 1952."

Her role, the *New York Post* reported, "probably will be a secondary one," and Monroe was quoted as saying, "I am interested in good parts . . . but as far as writing a play for me, Arthur doesn't write for anybody." Six months later the *New York Times* had Miller uncertain "whether I'll get it on this season." He "confessed," the newspaper reported, that

> he now has 3,000 pages of manuscript from which he must winnow a playable version. . . . The play, whose subject Mr. Miller declined to discuss, will probably be in four acts; its setting is "various parts of the United States but basically New York. I hope it's about where we are and how we got here . . . It's written in a style I never wrote in before and it's spread out in time and space. It's not realistic and neither is it a so-called poetic play. What I'm trying to do is interpret a mystery" . . . Mr. Miller has a title, but he will not reveal it at the moment, having, as he said, had too many titles stolen from him.

The title he had in mind was *Music for the Deaf* and the play would not be produced that fall. He told the man from the *Times*, however, that he was "on the verge of finishing an original movie scenario." Called *The Misfits*, the picture was going to star Miss Monroe and possibly Jason Robards, Jr. Miller had already telephoned Frank Taylor, Mary Miller's onetime boss who had published and edited both of Miller's books and spent four years in Hollywood as a movie producer before being blacklisted. The telephone call was an invitation for the entire Taylor family, including the four sons, to come and visit with him and Marilyn in Roxbury. Frank reacted with skepticism, if not downright suspicion, since Arthur had never made any effort to sustain their friendship. The invitation was "not for lunch," Taylor told his wife, Nan, "and not for supper," and he reminded her that this was no friendship as he "hadn't heard from Arthur since his divorce from Mary."

Nan suggested that perhaps Arthur simply wanted them to meet Marilyn Monroe.

"Arthur never does anything *simply*," her husband replied, but he couldn't keep his family from being "very excited about the possibility of . . . meeting Marilyn Monroe." Unfortunately and despite Arthur's phony, he thought, greeting of him "with the warmth of a friend he saw often," there was no sign of her when they arrived. All six of the Taylors dutifully trooped after Miller as he showed them the pond that had just been dug ("more full of mud than water," Taylor noted) and the little cabin where he worked. He confided to Frank that the expense of buying and renovating the farm was driving him to distraction. Miller had become famously (at least in theatrical circles) parsimonious and in the bargain, "Not only was he in a money crunch" but, Taylor remembered, "Marilyn had plenty," which left him dependent on her and struggling to control the spending. As his reverse in so many ways, she, in apposition to his tightfistedness, had "a craziness about money," he told Taylor. To put in the pond, he said, "she took out all those trees," and it seemed to Frank Taylor that this "drove him absolutely up the wall," which didn't faze her at all. "She had said to him, 'Put in more. We can also build a guest house.'"

"You have to have a whole hill for that," Arthur said he told her.

"So?" Marilyn replied. "We'll put in the hill."

While the adults talked about renovation costs, the kids' frustration about the absent movie star only intensified. Miller and the Taylors sat down on the terrace while "Marilyn," Frank recalled, "wasn't even mentioned and the boys gave a superb performance of four brothers at play . . . [except] their games were in pantomime—not a sound . . . they didn't want to miss any announcements."

Abruptly, as he recalled, "a familiar prosaic sound came from the second story—a vacuum cleaner." That, Miller explained, was "Marilyn—she loves to vacuum, she's very domestic. She'll be down as soon as she finishes cleaning our bedroom." Then he revealed the true purpose of his invitation. "I would like to read you a screen play I just finished," and he began to read *The Misfits*, while the four boys fidgeted, hoping (their father was sure) that the vacuuming would soon end. Meanwhile Miller introduced the story, calling it "A quest for connection in the universe among three cowboys and a girl in Nevada." He did a good job of it too, Taylor thought, playing all the parts himself, "except when he read the woman's role, which was clearly based on Marilyn. It was," Frank was sure, "her spiritual biography. This is who she is and this is why life is so painful for her and always will be."

In the midst of the reading the vacuum cleaner was shut off. Famous footsteps were heard padding down the staircase. Momentarily Marilyn Monroe appeared, barefoot, wearing jeans and a white blouse, "no make-up," Taylor remembered, "her hair was disheveled and she was absolutely gorgeous. Within a minute, each of us had been seduced by a beautiful, shy, gentle Marilyn."

Turning to the boys she asked, "Well? Which of you wants to lie in the hammock with me?" From seven years old to seventeen they raced for the big white cotton mesh hammock while Monroe said to the Taylors, "It's the biggest one I could find at Hammacher Schlemmer," her favorite store, and she shouted to the boys, "There's plenty of room for all five of us!"

As Arthur prepared to resume reading, she turned back and suggested to Nan Taylor that later they make dinner for everyone, for there was neither cook nor maid. And when they did go to the kitchen, "She tied her hair back," Nan remembered,

> and put on an apron. She'd made a meat loaf and we put the potatoes in the oven to be baked. Marilyn used a big oven mitten to pull them out, but by the time they were done, Arthur was still reading. And he wouldn't stop until he finished, so we put more potatoes in to be baked.

After dinner and after Marilyn had washed the dishes, refusing assistance ("I'm used to it"), Frank told her that he was "very awed" by Arthur's script and asked what he planned to do with it. "Nothing," replied Miller. "Marilyn doesn't like it and neither does my agent. She doesn't want to send it to Hollywood." Frank thought that his friend, the film director John Huston, might be interested and later, when they were all sitting together over drinks, Arthur repeated that Marilyn "had not been too thrilled" with the screenplay. He did not mention that she once had put him on the line when she telephoned Norman Rosten to ask *his* opinion of it, having taken it on herself to mail him a script. She told Rosten that one speech in particular was "lousy . . . too goddamn long. I want this speech rewritten . . . this whole stupid speech. Are you there, Arthur? . . . What are you going to do about it?"

He had said, on the phone extension, that he would think about it. Now he was telling her that Frank liked the screenplay and even suggested sending it to John Huston. She said that she had enjoyed working with the director on *The Asphalt Jungle*. Taylor told Miller that perhaps Huston didn't have a reputation for being serious-minded or literary but in fact he was a voracious reader and had even staged the first American production of Jean-Paul Sartre's *No Exit*. Since Marilyn was about to start filming *Some Like It Hot* while Arthur was determined to finish that *Third Play*, they all agreed that he eventually send the script to Huston after one more polish and that they meanwhile get on with their various projects.

Miller intended to complete the play in Los Angeles while Marilyn was making the movie, but in August 1958 he wrote Stern from New York that after being "out there for ten days until two weeks ago [I] found it impossible . . . all she wants is to see work pouring out of me so I'm back here [but] I'll visit there every so often." As for the movie, he continued, she was "thoroughly dissatisfied with [it] but will be wonderful."

Marilyn was dissatisfied because in her view she once again was playing the "joke," yet like many actors she was addicted to giving the performance that had won approval in the past. Her work in *Some Like It Hot* would be perhaps the ultimate portrayal of "Marilyn Monroe" by Marilyn Monroe and generally considered the best acting of her career. As to Miller's claim of belief in and concern for her (he told Stern that he missed Marilyn "madly"), it was at some odds with the remembrance by the film's director, Billy Wilder. "There were days I could have strangled her, but there were wonderful days too, when we all knew she was brilliant." Yet, he said, "with Arthur it all seemed sour, and I remember saying at the time that in meeting Miller, at last I met someone who resented her more than I did." The Miller-Monroe relationship then was complex to say the least, and the complexities were by no means hers alone.

He had come home to a visit from Jane, now fourteen, and eleven-year-old Bobby and a long weekend with them in Connecticut before school resumed. He planned to drive them to the farm in the morning and had them sleep over in New York. With both of his children tucked into bed on that Friday night in September 1958 he sat down at the typewriter and composed a love letter to his "darling girl" (also called "Poo").

Jane, he said, who had canceled a party because there weren't enough boys, had already worn the white slacks Marilyn had bought her. Bobby had "enough dirt on him to start a farm." As to *Some Like It Hot*, he understood what Marilyn was "up against" while making the movie, but reminded her that he tries when he can to discourage her "belief in absolute disaster," assuring her that "you're my ideal girl, don't you know?" He told her about resuming his psychoanalysis and discovering "a ring of cause and effect" that might clarify his "troubles." He closed evoking "visions of unity" with her, saying he missed her so badly that "nothing seems properly marked out," and that the bed seems "a mile wide, empty as a field." Asking her to "love me" he confessed to sometimes finding "tears coming into my eyes for love of you." This long, typewritten single-spaced letter ended with all of his love, "Your Art."

Only a week earlier she had written to Norman Rosten, "Don't give up the ship while we're sinking. I have a feeling this ship is never going to leave port."

Meanwhile Miller set to work, as he wrote Jim Stern, on the never-ending play

> which began sometime in 1952. [It] has been through nearly four reams of paper and suddenly by dint, I suppose, of my old Jewish conviction that God will put his hand on my shoulder if only I'll stand still—I have hit the rock from which water is finally flowing. It is, as usual, out of my poor life but a hell of a funny tragedy, if I may say so. I am trying to set down the American disaster in the midst of the hilarity which accompanies it, *for in the laughter is the hope*.

While he worked yet again and again on this play, he held up finishing *The Misfits*. It would be in fact another year before the screenplay was finally sent to Huston. There was no rush, as the director lived in Ireland and had vowed never to make another picture in America. Miller turned instead to "My Wife Marilyn," an essay that *Life* Magazine had commissioned to accompany a Monroe layout photographed by Richard Avedon in which she interpreted a series of American sex symbols such as Lillian Russell, Theda Bara, Jean Harlow and finally herself. Miller wrote,

> In anything she does, she is "herself," whether playing with the dog, redoing the cleaning woman's hair, emerging from the ocean after a swim or bursting into the house full of news. Her beauty shines because her spirit is forever showing itself.

He wrote of "the spontaneous joy she takes in anything a child does [and] her quick sympathy and respect for old people . . . the child in her catches the fun and the promise, and the old person in her—the mortality." After that he packed up his typewriter and took it back to Los Angeles, where Marilyn was living in one of the cottages on the grounds of the Beverly Hills Hotel while continuing work on *Some Like It Hot*.

It became *The Prince and the Showgirl* all over again, as Miller would watch her decide each morning whether or not to show up for work, and if she did go, sit with her in a dressing room while she ran lines and practiced gestures with Paula Strasberg. Then she would go out on the set to play the role of Sugar Kane, sometimes gliding flawlessly through a scene, other times unable to get through a simple line like "It's me, Sugar." Miller was left to apologize and explain.

She wrote a Halloween note to Norman Rosten in New York. "It's too bad we can't be together. I might scare you," and added, "It's so spooky here! Arthur looks well though weaker—from holding me up."

Her mood swings could be ascribed at least sometimes to sedatives and tranquilizers. "Pills were so common," her local press agent said, "that Hollywood people played poker using pills for chips—yellows, reds." Miller's explanation for Marilyn's erratic behavior, as *Some Like It Hot* soared over budget while moving toward completion, was that she was pregnant again, which was true. Marilyn was already in her second month when photography was finally finished, and this time she meant to be careful—except for the sleeping pills. She would regularly rest in the hotel cottage and even had Arthur arrange for an ambulance to take them to the airport on the way back to New York. As for her performance in the brilliantly farcical film, while she was already considered a magical and magnetic screen personality, this was generally received as Marilyn Monroe's finest work to date. The baby was another matter. She miscarried in the third month of the pregnancy, toward the end of 1958.

To *The Third Play* Miller returned yet again. In spring 1959 after three years without contact he wrote Professor Rowe at the University of Michigan.

> I am at work on a kind of play which I think will sum up everything I know I am and which will combine everything into an image of what man is and might become. I have been years arriving at the stylistic problem which is to infuse intelligence with passion and visceral action with a kind of speech and construction that will throw not only heat but light into the audience's heart . . . if it does come off I hope very much that it may change the direction of our stage [and] say a good word for mankind, *finally*.

Kermit Bloomgarden was eager, to say the least, to present this big new play. Two years earlier he had been one of Broadway's most successful producers with four shows running concurrently, *The Diary of Anne Frank, The Most Happy Fella, Look Homeward, Angel* and *The Music Man*. Now he was at a standstill. He needed a major production and there hadn't been a new play from Arthur Miller in four years. Bloomgarden, as if to hurry it along, inquired whether Jason Robards, Jr. might want to star in such a work. Robards's agent wrote Miller about it and he replied,

> I do believe Jason Robards would be the right man for the lead in my play but it's impossible now to make the kind of commitment which only a completed work could justify. I am not certain that I will be satisfied with the work at any set time.

Back in New York Marilyn had resumed her classes at the Actors Studio while continuing to study privately with Lee Strasberg. She was also considering scripts for her next picture, leaning toward *Breakfast at Tiffany's*. That apparently was enough to push Arthur toward finishing *The Misfits* and sending it off to John Huston. On July 14, 1959, he wrote to the director at his home in St. Clarens Craughwell, County Galway. Sounding much less confident than when dealing with theater people, he began by saying that Frank Taylor had given him the address and that he had written an "original screenplay." He quickly summarized the story, set, he wrote, in the "Nevada back country," and about "two cowboys, a bush pilot, a girl and the last of the mustangs up in the mountains." He added that although Huston's agent had told him, "you wouldn't work in the U.S.," Frank Taylor suggested that "people change their plans." If that is not possible, he said, then perhaps Huston could think of a "foreign locale" that might pass for Nevada. He added that "Marilyn is available for the girl."

Huston, bemused by Arthur Miller's "unbelievable modesty," cabled back that yes, he was interested, but Miller then did something rather curious—on December 4, 1959, he wrote a letter to Elia Kazan. It may well have been their first communication in the seven years since Kazan had testified at HUAC. There is no evidence of any interim correspondence between the two. For certain the many public statements by Miller and others as well as his own autobiography are misleading in the assertion that he and Kazan did not resume communication until three years later.

In this letter to Elia he exulted about the possibility that his old friend, Montgomery Clift—who had just finished working with Kazan on *Wild River*—might join the cast of *The Misfits*. Making no mention of Huston possibly directing it, he added, "When [Monty] has read it, I wish you'd get it from him and if there's time, read it yourself." Perhaps he was floating the possibility of Kazan directing the movie. At the time Elia was at least as prestigious in Hollywood as John Huston, more powerful in terms of financing and a known quantity in Miller's artistic life. He also had no resistance to working in America. Nothing came of this, at least in terms of *The Misfits*, and there is no available record of Kazan's opinion of the screenplay, but with communication reestablished Miller and Kazan would sit down to a meal soon afterward.

Once Huston agreed to direct the picture events happened quickly. When Clark Gable, a far more bankable star than Jason Robards, Jr., agreed to play one of the lead roles, Seven Arts Productions, a division of United Artists, approved the financing. The studio even agreed to let Frank Taylor produce the picture, although he had only the slightest experience. More important evidently were the commitments of Clift and Eli Wallach to play the other leads as well as the signing of Thelma Ritter for a supporting role. Preproduction work on the picture was scheduled to begin in July 1959, and in anticipation of that Miller went to Nevada with Huston. They toured the actual locations in Reno and Pyramid Lake where Arthur had met the cowboys he had written about, and Gerlach, Nevada, where he'd seen a rodeo that was recreated in the script. Then all plans were postponed abruptly when Marilyn decided to first make a picture called *Let's Make Love* and satisfy an outstanding obligation to Twentieth Century-Fox. Perhaps she was hesitant about starting work on *The Misfits*. She had never been enthusiastic about the script.

In the meantime Miller's reputation began to erode among the higher brows in New York. In the midst of a 1962 review of the film *A View from the Bridge* in which the director Sidney Lumet's "lack of taste" was described as being "close to a lack of character," film and theater critic Stanley Kauffmann related the sparseness of Miller's output—"three plays, two short plays, one screenplay and some short stories and essays in fifteen years"—to the "shortcomings of the plays themselves." Dismissing *Death of a Salesman* as "one long autopsy," the critic suggested that "from the plays as well as from statements he has made, one can infer something about the difficulties he has in working." Kauffmann continued,

> In the deepest sense, Miller's crisis is religious . . . he could live to make dramas out of his life, dramas meaningful to his fellows and constructive of his society. Instead, he finds himself in a . . . desolate world in which to look for tragic art; and some of that desolation must necessarily be in himself.

Peculiarly psychological and personal, it was an ominous sign of an intensifying animosity toward Miller among the more serious critics. "This is not a premature obituary notice," Kauffmann generously allowed. "All men of good will can wish only well for a humane artist of good will . . . But Miller's artistic life—disconnected from a society that defies connection, searching for a temple it can serve—is a truer tragedy than any he has yet written."

Worse was to come from the critical fraternity.

15. *Misfits*

LET'S MAKE LOVE was supposed to costar Gregory Peck with Marilyn Monroe but after Miller read the Norman Krasna screenplay—which Monroe hadn't—she accepted his opinion that the movie belonged to Peck, for she had only four scenes in it. She pressured Arthur into revising the script and by the time he was through, having added plot motivation and what he called "humor of character" as well as material for her, Gregory Peck withdrew because of the diminished size of *his* role. That was as sensible a sequence of events as there would be during the making of this picture.

As to Peck's replacement, Yves Montand was appearing in concert on Broadway at the time. After seeing one of his performances Arthur and Marilyn invited the popular French cabaret singer back to their apartment with his wife, the actress Simone Signoret, as well as the Rostens. Montand, like Miller, was tall and dark haired, but his physique was muscular and athletic, more like Joe DiMaggio's. His nose was a considerable feature but its size only added somehow to his good looks. And despite his Italian background (his real name was Ivo Livi and Miller thought he was Jewish, which he wasn't), he was thoroughly French. He was also political, in at least that respect resembling Miller. In Montand's autobiography *You See, I Haven't Forgotten* he recalls being "born and raised in Communism."

Over late-night drinks they all talked about *Let's Make Love* and its need for a leading man. Montand's name came up as a candidate, a suggestion that Miller claimed to have made himself. The Frenchman did have acting credentials, specifically (also only) the film *Wages of Fear* and the Paris production of *The Crucible*. Arthur had liked that production and Montand's performance in it. He and Marilyn decided to recommend Yves for the part.

Let's Make Love is about an American billionaire in love with a minor actress, a variation it would seem on *The Prince and the Showgirl* except that this was a remake of a much older movie called *On the Avenue*. Any screenwriter confronted with a Frenchman being cast as the billionaire could have invented an explanation and worked around it; this particular French actor, however, barely spoke English. That too was considered no obstacle and after the picture's producer saw Montand's show in Los Angeles he agreed to the assignment, rationalizing that this after all was a musical and the tall, charming, good-looking chanteur could dance as well as sing. So it was that in February 1960 Arthur and Marilyn checked into the Beverly Hills Hotel for the start of rehearsals.

In hindsight Miller claimed to have known even then that the marriage was all but finished. They were barely speaking and Marilyn regularly sent him on "demeaning errands." If he objected, she would call him "Old Grouchy Grumps." He was reduced, he said, to being a guardian who "slept with her and counted her pills," the Nembutal count now standing at four a night, a very strong dose. Even so Miller "couldn't," he insisted, "turn off his feelings toward a person when something went wrong with the relationship." It was a singularly striking remark from someone who many observers felt had problems turning his feelings on. One is left to wonder whether such a remark was merely lip service paid to sensitivity reputation, and whether his attentiveness—in public, in letters, even in private—was the emotional equivalent of flexing the cheek muscles so as to appear to be smiling.

Soon enough he left behind her hostility, her "indignant and imperious protests" and Los Angeles, departing for Ireland, John Huston's home and work on *The Misfits*. He was greeted with a headline in the local newspaper, "Marilyn's Husband in Galway." In the meantime Montand rehearsed with Monroe and practiced his English while the director, the respected George Cukor, looked for further improvement of the script. Marilyn then once again asked for Arthur's help. Despite the animosity she showed toward him—possibly even as part of it, for she was already sleeping with Montand—she called him back to California after he had been in Ireland barely a week. Perhaps he did more work or perhaps he decided that he had done enough with a script he considered "not worth the paper it was typed on," but exactly when he did do the rewriting is uncertain. At this point an element of *Rashomon* enters the story. Miller conceded that although he "despised" the work, he had indeed done it because he was "trying to save her from a complete catastrophe." Yves Montand told another story. Miller, he said, "came running back to rewrite some scenes, pocketed a check and complained about prostituting his art." The way the Twentieth Century-Fox publicity office put it,

> Arthur Miller, the playwright responsible for *Death of a Salesman, A View from the Bridge* and other fine works, who is the lucky husband of *La Monroe*, read Krasna's script and suggested . . . that a deepening of the character of the role Marilyn was to play would enhance its value . . . whereupon Miller, without cash or credit, rewrote Marilyn's part.

Yet another version of this history is more troubling. On January 15, 1960, before Arthur and Marilyn had left New York, the Screen Writers

Guild called a strike. According to Sidney Skolsky, a producer who was also a gossip columnist, Miller made contributions to the screenplay in the midst of that strike, breaking the writers' ranks and becoming a scab, violating long-held convictions about the sanctity of organized labor. Hadn't he written in his first college play that were a true liberal to break a strike he would "be a lie . . . a lie through and through . . . like an animal"? Now, Skolsky said, "Arthur Miller, the big liberal, the man who always stood up for the underdog, ignored the Writers Guild strike and rewrote, silently. At night." Miller's version was that he used that time to tour Nevada locations for *The Misfits* with John Huston.

These recollections and allegations were all made after Monroe died and each might have had its own motivation. Montand's warm relationship with Miller, for instance, had been undone after he found himself simply unable to resist a Marilyn Monroe—his friend's wife after all—who was "beginning to throw herself at me." Skolsky, whether as a movie producer or a gossip columnist, stood on the Hollywood side of the East Coast–West Coast divide, a partisan in the era's competition between elitist theater and populist movies. Like many people, especially movie people, in search of an explanation for Marilyn Monroe's tragedy and someone to blame for it, Skolsky chose to blame Miller. The studio's press release spoke for itself and with shameless dishonesty, for Miller was paid $25,000 for his work on the screenplay. His autobiography makes no mention of this, nor does it even mention the screenwriters' strike. Possibly his rewriting was done before it began. The facts are unavailable, but the most reliable and certainly the most amusing recollection is Hal Kanter's, about what Miller actually wrote for *Let's Make Love*. Kanter, a professional comedy writer who was among this script's many contributors, remembered, "One day, I came in and George Cukor said, 'Here's a joke that Arthur Miller sent.'" In the sequence, Kanter recalled, "Montand and Monroe are walking and he turns to the doorman of a nightclub and says, 'Will you call me a taxi?' and the doorman says, 'Sure. You're a taxi.'"

"You got that from Arthur Miller?" Kanter remembered asking Cukor.

The director nodded.

"I don't think so, George," the writer said. "That's from Joe Miller, not Arthur Miller. That's the oldest joke in the world!" (Joe Miller was a 1920s vaudevillian best known for a collection of gags that he sold to small-time comedians, and this particular one had even been mocked as period banality in the 1952 musical *Singin' in the Rain*.)

Cukor said, "I never heard it before."

"Well you probably didn't hear it," Kanter said, "because you spend too much time with Somerset Maugham, but believe me, you *can't* have that joke, it's impossible to put that joke on the screen. Tell Mr. Miller to stick to *The Crucible* and stay away from the jokes."

Never expecting that this "humor of character" would actually be used, Kanter went to see the picture after it had opened. As he told it, he found himself watching "a scene where Montand and Marilyn are walking down the street toward a doorman." Kanter remembered turning to his wife and groaning, "Oh, my God, here it comes." The film continued with a close-up of the doorman. While Kanter squirmed, Montand asked the doorman to call him a taxi and the doorman replied, "Sure. You're a taxi," and, Kanter said, "That was the first laugh that came from that audience!"

There is no way of knowing exactly when Miller did the script doctoring or whether he had violated the writers' strike but whatever the truth of the matter, his work on this movie was part of a generally degrading period. As the strike ended and production of *Let's Make Love* got under way, the internationally celebrated playwright who had stood up to the House Committee on Un-American Activities now kept Marilyn Monroe company on the set, accompanied her to the first screenings and helped her to approve or reject publicity photographs. At the same time her behavior was becoming increasingly erratic, with lateness and absenteeism the least of it. One day while on camera, she lapsed into an acting exercise, flexing and shaking her wrists in the middle of a scene. In a notebook—the keeping of which she evidently picked up from Arthur—she wrote, "What am I afraid of? Do I think I can't act? I act, but I am afraid. I am afraid and I should not be and I must not be." Even such private thoughts became fodder for the press. An actor in the movie spied the journal in her dressing room, copied out her fearful notes and passed them along to a reporter who promptly printed them.

It may well have been such vulnerability, public betrayal and injury that would martyr Monroe, raising her beyond mere stardom to a kind of popular sainthood that would endure long after she died. As for Arthur Miller, it seems safe to say that no playwright ever suffered so public a private life. With the Montand-Monroe affair becoming a nationally advertised emasculation and playing field for tabloid newspapers Miller chose to leave the arena and head home to Connecticut. It was an act either of fear or fearlessness, situational suicide or survival, but certainly an abandonment of wife, marriage and pride, leaving Marilyn with and to Montand. Was he saving himself from this increasingly torturous, impossible, humiliating and destructive—for him as well as her—relationship? His flight surely was not calculated to save the marriage. Yet upon being settled in Connecticut he wrote a grateful letter to George Cukor dated April 30, 1960, appreciating "the way you have behaved toward Marilyn" and "the precious days and weeks of her life which your patience and skill and understanding have made humanly meaningful for her." In this handwritten letter—rare among his many, many typewritten correspondences—Miller wrote that he had never seen Marilyn so "happy" and "hopeful," and added, "You must know now some of the reasons why she is so precious to me. . . . I'm at work here . . . but I don't know how long I'll be able to bear the bachelorhood."

Marilyn was now openly with Montand, an affair that his wife seemed to accept as a Frenchman's prerogative. Norman Rosten, in Paris preparing for the filming of his screenplay of *A View from the Bridge* (it was being made in French), visited with Simone Signoret and brought up her husband's adultery. "Like any worldly woman," Rosten recalled, "the possibility of a brief affair did not unduly upset her." His nosiness inevitably alienated Miller, who would never be able to abide anyone inquisitive about—let alone interfering with—his private life. In later years strangers asking about Marilyn Monroe could send him into a frozen rage. Rosten's invasion of his privacy was only exacerbated by a subsequent exploitation of her in *Marilyn: An Untold Story* in which he wrote that "Miller's was the triumph of intelligence over feeling. It may well turn out that he was less the artist than she." Rosten even wrote a song about Monroe, "Who Killed Norma Jean?" with music by Pete Seeger, but the most serious offense would be his cooperation with Norman Mailer's 1973 "Novel Biography" *Marilyn,* which treated Miller viciously as

> a playwright with a workmanlike style, limited lyrical gifts, no capacity for intellectual shock and only one major play to his credit. . . . He begins to develop the instincts of a servant . . . a species of business manager, valet and in-residence hospital attendant. Her unvoiced resentment of him is . . . secretly sexual.

The twenty-two-year Miller-Rosten friendship would have as its epitaph a one-sentence mention of the longtime chum in Miller's autobiography. Even that is only in connection with Hedda, who is described as "an old college friend of mine . . . the wife of Norman, a poet and playwright who had also been at Michigan." With that "had also been at Michigan" Norman Rosten was quite literally excised from Arthur Miller's life story.

By the time Miller returned to California from Connecticut he had already made up his mind, he said, to leave the wife who had just been so precious to him, convinced that he could no longer help the marriage or her. Yet again he was of two minds about the matter, obviously so, as he certainly could have remained in Connecticut. He was sure that she'd never had a partner more supportive or protective, which is smug but probably true. He could also perceive that she had written him off forevermore as an untrustworthy husband who would not defend her every whim. With that for atmosphere *The Misfits* was still to be made.

At this time Elia Kazan was also in California, putting the final touches on *Wild River* and reading about the affair between Montand and Monroe. "When I heard about the infidelity," he recalled, "flagrantly conducted, I wondered, as did many others, whether Miller could take the punishment." Perhaps in sincere concern or perhaps pouncing, after years of estrangement, on his onetime friend at a vulnerable moment (had not Miller opened the door to reconciliation with his letter about *The Misfits*?) the director telephoned to suggest dinner. In the restaurant Arthur "didn't bring up what was going on. But," Kazan said, "I saw the pain on his face and some anger too." The acutely psychological director might well have had such perceptions. As Kermit Bloomgarden had observed during the production of *Death of a Salesman*, Elia Kazan made certain "he knew [actors'] weaknesses, their strengths and their neuroses." Perhaps he used similar tactical psychology to manipulate people offstage as well. He certainly was in the market for a major drama. His theater reputation had suffered since his infamy at HUAC and his subsequent work (*Tea and Sympathy, The Dark at the Top of the Stairs, The Sweet Bird of Youth*) had lost weight. A new Arthur Miller play directed by Kazan would have inherent gravity. A few months after the dinner, Kazan dropped Miller an affectionate note of empathy for his "troubles," conceding that there was no help he could offer but that "if there were I would." He also brought up an embryonic Lincoln Center project, even though it wasn't, he said, his reason for writing. "Both Bob [Whitehead] and I," he wrote, "would like to talk to you about" the Repertory Theatre. They wanted to christen it with a Miller premiere.

The Lincoln Center Repertory Theater was an ambitious project to create within just two years an American national theater modeled on England's great stage institutions. That meant a state-subsidized organization with a company of actors under contract for at least a season, performing a rotating program of plays. Robert Whitehead, who had coproduced *A View from the Bridge*, had been named as the executive producer of this fledgling theater and he had chosen Kazan to be his codirector and artistic counterpart. This was not as inflammatory a choice as might be imagined. While true that the liberal community would never forgive or forget the director's HUAC testimony, neither would Kazan himself. As Whitehead said, "Elia was always terribly anxious to know how you felt about his testifying . . . It never stopped haunting him." Yet theater people were a pragmatic and famously self-centered lot whose artistic and career needs usually transcended any political indignation (and perhaps that was not so different from most everyone else). Harold Clurman, for instance, who shared a thirty-year history with Kazan dating back to the Group Theatre—whose names Elia had named—was at first "outraged," Whitehead said, "that I got involved with Kazan. Then I said, 'I want you here too.'" That seemed to assuage his indignation. "Harold," Whitehead remembered, "decided that it was an important move for [Elia] to be involved" and so Clurman was brought on as a director and literary advisor. Miller never expressed any reservations about Kazan directing his play. "The only thing important to Arthur," Whitehead felt, "was the theater and his writing and the power to write." As for relinquishing the potential profits of a Broadway production, Miller seemed to sincerely believe that a subsidized institution offered a desirable alternative, although he wrote in the *New York Times*,

> I have never condescended toward "Broadway." Whatever there is of value in the American repertory of plays . . . was produced by commercial managers in the four or five blocks we call the American theater. [But] I have always felt a certain oppression at the thought of the tens of thousands of dollars riding on my words and scenes [and] I have felt it destructive to the imagination of all concerned that all esthetic innovation and risk should be instantly transformed into a financial risk.

That was almost sincere. Arthur Miller was never known to shrink from a profit, but the gestating institution offered compensatory attractions. Estimable Broadway people were involved, which added to the allure of a prestigious repertory company. Perhaps most of all he was eager to have Elia Kazan direct his forever-evolving *Third Play,* and this apparently was more powerful than any political grudge. Here Miller tried to have it two ways, getting the best director for his play while not quite forgiving him in public; indeed there is even a Kazan surrogate, a namer of names, in his play, the very play that Elia Kazan would be directing.

Although the two men had in fact been communicating for some time and even dined together, Miller in his autobiography suggests with some dishonesty that the decision wasn't easy.

> The issue became do I kick over what is maybe the only possibility for an art theater because of my differences with Kazan? . . . I would have to perpetuate a blacklist . . . I hadn't even seen him in all those years. . . . I still don't approve of what he did. I never have. But I understood his situation.

As to why he never offered the play to his regular producer, Kermit Bloomgarden, Kazan had to be the reason. Kermit would not ever forgive Elia, and Arthur Miller surely knew it.

Whitehead and Clurman agreed with Kazan that a new Arthur Miller play would be the perfect inaugural production for the Lincoln Center Repertory Theater. Whitehead was already envisioning an association "like Chekhov's with the Moscow Art Theater, or Molière's with the Comedie Francaise." Miller shared that vision. "My best hope," he said, "is that we can continue working together indefinitely. I would like to make it my own theater . . . in the sense that it would be available to me and I available to it." He was not available to it at the moment, however, being otherwise engaged. Directly from Marilyn's troubled and troubling experience filming *Let's Make Love,* he'd left with her for Nevada and making *The Misfits.* They had decided to be divorced but agreed to wait until the picture was finished before making a public announcement.

The temperature was exactly one hundred degrees on the July 1960 day that the Millers' plane landed at the Reno airport. They were met by Frank

Taylor (who was producing the movie), several local politicians, a publicity team from United Artists and a gaggle of reporters and photographers. The production was attracting international attention owing to its famous star, its celebrated author and their ancillary melodrama of adultery and betrayal.

The couple left the airport in separate cars, Marilyn with Taylor while Arthur rode in one of the production's rented limousines. Arriving at the Mapes Hotel in greater downtown Reno, he was asked for an autograph as "Marilyn Monroe's husband." Then he checked the two of them into the ninth-floor penthouse suite, completing the *Misfits* company, which immediately divided along battle lines. The solitary exception was Clark Gable, roundly known as the King of the Movies (and sometimes even called The King, but only behind his back), who had the stature to rise above any squabble and seems to have been everyone's favorite. Eli Wallach was a familiar face to Marilyn but also a friend of Miller's, and he sensed that she wasn't sure whose side he was on. Montgomery Clift was an even older friend of Miller's and remained that. "Arthur," he said, "represents to me such an ideal as an artist. I sort of face East every time I see him." But Clift's emotional availability made him a meet soul for Marilyn; his unprotected heart was evident in everything he did and he frankly admitted it. "The problem—the terrible problem of remaining vulnerable," he said, "is how to remain thin skinned and yet survive." It was a quality that heartened his work and a frailty he shared with Monroe, enough to reserve him in her trust.

In Arthur's camp certainly was the man's man, John Huston, although already distracted by the gambling tables, well on his way to losing piles of the chips that he stashed in the various pockets of his Italian-made, white hunter safari suits. Miller found his own style of dress, chino trousers and denim shirts, while Lee Strasberg showed up in a complete cowboy outfit, from hat to boots. His wife, Paula, wore a black ensemble of dress, stockings and shoes with a gold watch and chain around her neck. The whole business was swathed in a black caftan and capped by a black palmetto fan in one hand and black umbrella in the other, a wide-brimmed black straw hat on her head and a pair of black sunglasses. Thus "the spider," as she was roundly known. "My work," she would say theatrically, "is evident on the screen," and Miller so relished her absurdity that he wrote a spoof of her pretentiousness and name-dropping and gave it to Huston.

> It's like John [Kennedy] was telling Lee when he wanted him to come and direct the Inaugural and Lee couldn't do it so he tried to get me to go and at least get things placed professionally. . . . Rumors that I threatened to quit [*The Misfits*] are not Professional. It's simply that I had agreed to meet Adlai through a close friend whose name I can't mention and Josh [Logan] and Billy [Wilder] weren't set for the next picture I'm doing . . . I ought to get them to see Charley [Chaplin]'s new script, which I'm not at liberty to speak about although it's no secret it's in Oona's handwriting.

The send-up closed with Paula noting that "Bernie Gimbel ran into Gadgie at the party for Otto the same day Camus got killed."

As filming began, Arthur kept out of Marilyn's way, although not to the extent of staying back at the hotel. Instead of using his afternoons for rewriting he watched the making of this, his first produced screenplay. He sometimes tinkered with the script at the film location—*Life* Magazine published a photograph of him sitting on a canvas director's chair, downcast and rubbing his eyes beside an empty chair with Marilyn Monroe's name on it. Yet it was at the hotel that he meant to do the more serious revisions on what Frank Taylor still considered "the best goddamned screenplay that's ever been written." At night, as usual, he could hardly get anything accomplished. Marilyn would generally go to bed directly after their solitary dinners. He could only watch as she swallowed her pills and, if she became anxious, keep her company through the night, carefully avoiding, he said, anything that might irritate her. When he ventured into the bedroom, she would scream at him to get out. Oftentimes she wouldn't fall asleep until six o'clock in the morning, shortly before she was supposed to be ready for work. Nan Taylor finally arranged for a second room to serve as his study, but it was regularly darkened by electrical outages caused by a series of forest fires erupting in the nearby Sierra Nevada Mountains. At such times Miller would work by the light of a bare bulb that was connected to the hotel's emergency generator. Otherwise he would nap in that room until his power was restored.

Monroe's problems intensified. At times the makeup man had to come into their suite to do her face while she was still in bed. Her depressions were only exacerbated by the physical slowdowns caused by the barbiturates that were now being injected by, Miller remembered, a "scared young doctor." On the set she could exhaust Huston's patience by repeatedly reading a simple line, "Here we are," as "We're here." Even so, Paula Strasberg could tell Arthur's visiting sister, Joan Copeland, "You'll adore Marilyn in this. She just shot her 64th take and it was marvelous."

As for the united and companionable front that she and Arthur had meant to maintain, her shakiness and hostility were making that impossible. Miller and a British visitor were chatting in the hotel suite when Marilyn "slammed" through the door. "Thank goodness you've brought someone home," she said. "It's so dull." The Englishman thought Miller "looked as if he'd been struck." Another time, John Huston remembered, "I was about to drive away from the location—miles out in the desert—when I saw Arthur standing alone. Marilyn and her friends hadn't offered him a ride back; they'd just left him. If I hadn't happened to see him, he would have been stranded out there." The story was instant lore among the *Misfits* company, embroidered so that it became a slamming of her limousine door in his face. Yet she persisted in considering herself the victim. "To think, Arthur did this to me," she later confided to the Englishman. "He was supposed to be writing this for me, but he says it's his movie. I don't think he even wanted me in it." And, she added, "Arthur's been complaining to Huston about me, and that's why Huston treats me like an idiot."

During a break in the filming she flew off to Los Angeles for a widely reported visit with Montand, who was making a movie called *Sanctuary*. According to Eli Wallach, Miller acted as if he didn't know that she was even gone. When she returned, her emotional state was only worse for the respite and the national press was starting to scrutinize and psychoanalyze her every emotional tic. Miller even contributed to the process, something he would do increasingly and regrettably. *Time* Magazine summarized *The Misfits* as drawing on his short story about a couple of cowboys who refer to

> a vaguely mutual mistress named Roslyn. In the movie version, Roslyn has moved to the center and become, by the author's admission, a closely personal portrait of his wife. Like Marilyn, Roslyn is a fractured, manhandled woman always "searching for relationships." Helpless, yet flush with appetite.

Seven weeks into the ten-week production schedule she was all but falling apart. Her emotional state had become precarious, her barbiturate dependency dangerous. At times she was almost incoherent.

> My teacher, Lee Strasberg, has told me that acting isn't something you do. Instead of doing it, it occurs . . . You can have conscious preparation but you must have unconscious results. Lee always said two and two don't necessarily make four. Two apples and two pears make fruit salad. Two rabbits and two rabbits might make ninety rabbits.

On August 25, 1960, she left the movie location for California once again, this time accompanied by her husband. Frank Taylor told the company that she had suffered a "breakdown" and Miller brought her to Los Angeles's Westside Hospital where she was treated for barbiturate dependency and "exhaustion." She repeatedly tried to contact Montand, or so the Frenchman said, "by mail, by telegram, by telephone." She invited him, he said, to Manhattan; she threatened to come to Paris. Yet after a ten-day stay at the hospital she managed to return to Nevada and notwithstanding expectations to the contrary completed *The Misfits*. About the marriage Monroe publicly conceded, "I guess it's all over between us. We have to stay with each other because it would be bad for the film if we split up now." Even at that late juncture, Montgomery Clift said, "Arthur was doing some wish fulfillment. He identified with the character played by Gable. He wanted [Clark] to keep Marilyn because he wants her to himself," and she too seemed to sense his identification. "What [the characters] really should do," she said, "is break up."

Clift agreed. "Their marriage is over," he said, and Arthur "might as well face it."

Arthur Miller never wrote anything just for dramatic entertainment. Even after *The Misfits* had developed into an exploration of his wife's psyche its interior concern was ideological. The subject may have been Roslyn–Marilyn but the underlying theme remained as in his *Misfits* short story. It was a theme drawn from his 1955 essay "On Social Plays."

> Our society—and I am speaking of every industrialized society in the world—is so complex, each person being so specialized an integer, that the moment any individual is dramatically characterized and set forth as a hero, our common sense reduces him to the size of a complainer, a misfit.

Miller admitted, "I've always felt a misfit," and because he identifies with his heroes one may infer from his essay that he felt he was being perceived as a misfit in the nuisance sense—a political and intellectual malcontent—when he was actually a misfit in the nonconformist sense—an original. And a hero too. It would seem that Miller wanted his public image to be godlike and heroic but also feared that it might be the image of a maladjusted whiner.

If there is any hero in *The Misfits*, it is Gay Langland (Gable), an aging cowboy who won't take a regular job, "Because anything's better than wages." *Wages* is a recurring word in the screenplay meant to represent drudging jobs and conventionalism, and Langland isn't the only nonconformist in the story. He has a friend who won't work for wages either, Guido, a car mechanic (Wallach) nicknamed Pilot because he flies an airplane. The two of them spend their nights chasing women who are in Reno for divorces. When they meet Roslyn, a small-time singer in the midst of her six-week divorce residency, they are entranced. "You just walk in," Guido tells her, "a stranger out of nowhere, and for the first time it all lights up . . . because you have the gift of life . . . I hope it goes on forever." Gay does not go after her so directly. His approach is as a philosophical plain talker. "Dyin' is as natural as livin,'" he tells her. "A man who's too afraid to die is too afraid to live."

While they take turns failing to seduce her, they all go to the house that Guido had built for his wife and left unfinished when she died. There they dance and drink until the two men are struck by the idea of "mustangin'"—that is, chasing down the mustang horses who run wild in the desert, horses that were once bred to be children's pets but can now only be sold for dog food. After finding a third hand in a shaky rodeo contestant named Perce (Montgomery Clift) they all go off to hunt the horses—in Miller's words, "an auto mechanic whose wife died, a rodeo rider whose father had died and a cowboy whose marriage had died." Roslyn tags along on this hunt—a chase by airplane, truck and finally on foot whose ultimate purpose she hadn't anticipated. When she realizes that the horses are to be killed, she becomes hysterical. Protective of all animals and identifying with them as fellow innocents and victims, she runs into the desert calling the cowboys "dead men" and "murderers!" Ultimately they are won over by her compassion and free the horses they've captured.

The story is laden with symbols that are handicaps when noticeable. Its only sustained action is the chase for the horses, the one stretch in which the talk stops. Elsewhere the dialogue is dense and conspicuously meaningful. "I can't make a landing," says Guido the aviator, "I can't get up to God neither . . . How do you land?" Or Gay, "Nothing can live unless something dies . . . I hunt these horses to keep myself free." These self-presentations to Roslyn only cohere when seen as three Miller projections. Guido is the uncomplicated and spontaneous man he would like to be; Perce is the sensitive and caring man he would like to be; Gay is the manly and heroic fellow he wants to be most of all. And like most Miller protagonists Gay is an equivocator. Unlike the other two he refuses to succumb to Roslyn's plaintive pleas for the horses' lives and after they have been freed he seems to be speaking up for Old Grouchy Grumps when he tells her, "I been wonderin' who you think you've been talking to." Then with reckless physical courage he chases down one of the freed horses and ties it up—only to let it loose again. He just "don't want nobody makin' up my mind for me."

Two symbols are designed to provide the screenplay's theoretical underpinnings—the mustangs, whose meaning is clear enough, and the unfinished house, whose meaning is not clear enough. The character of Roslyn is drawn as an erotic waif who can evoke a man's fatherly impulses and inspire his moral standards, all the while setting his sexual blood to boiling. Gay, who is all over her, finally transcends his baser desires, ascending to an appreciation of her holy virtue. "I bless you girl," he tells her, and the screenplay concludes with Roslyn asking him, "How do you find your way back in the night?" His protective arm is around her. She snuggles up to him. They are driving in the dark and she is his. "Just head for that big star straight on," the older and wiser man tells her. "The highway's under it. It'll take us right home."

Despite such sentimentalities, a fair share of the dialogue plays well and the three male lead actors do well by it. Monroe, however, is in deep straits, palpably tentative in every scene except when the subject is animals. The timbre of her voice is a monotonous and infantile mewl, and even though the character she plays is based on herself—essentially the sensitive spirit of Miller's short story "Please Don't Kill Anything"—her acting is all but nonexistent. Her expression is almost always distracted, even vacant, while her interpretive efforts are transparent and sad, for she is plainly in scary condition, unable to make contact with her fellow players. The Marilyn Monroe who could be so disarming in comedies and so magnetic simply as a presence on a movie screen is not to be found in this picture.

That *The Misfits* is a serious-minded movie cannot be mistaken. As a production, it is much in the manner of such John Huston pictures as *The Asphalt Jungle, The Treasure of the Sierra Madre* or *The African Queen*, except for the director's fixation on Monroe's breasts and rear end, along with a fairly crude depiction of her embracing a tree. *The Misfits*, though, is ultimately a victim of its wordy screenplay. This was essentially Arthur Miller's act of devotion, a gift portrait of and to Marilyn Monroe—and a portrait of the painter as well—wrapped in the form of a plea for himself, that if she would only let him, he could be all men to her.

After the completion of photography and the move back to Los Angeles for postproduction work Marilyn asked Arthur to get out. He packed up and left their bungalow at the Beverly Hills Hotel, coming home to New York City and a *Daily News* headline—"Miller Walks Out On Marilyn"—that reflected her evolving image as a martyr. She went back to the Fifty-seventh Street apartment while he checked into the Chelsea Hotel and on November 11 the official release about their imminent divorce was issued to the press. *Life* Magazine reported,

> The most unlikely marriage since the Owl and the Pussycat has come apart. Pulitzer Prize winning playwright Arthur Miller, one of the country's foremost intellectuals, and Love Queen Marilyn Monroe, one of the country's foremost foremosts, were no longer as one.

This even attracted official attention from behind the Iron Curtain. The Soviet magazine *Nedelya* solemnly observed, "She found in Arthur Miller what she lacked. She exploited him without pity. He wrote scripts for her films and made her a real actress. Marilyn paid him back. She left him. . . . Another broken life on her climb to the stars."

By Christmas Miller had temporarily departed the Chelsea Hotel for the Hotel Adams at 2 East 86th Street. It was nearer the woman who would become his third wife. She was a photographer for the international picture agency Magnum, which held the rights to the *Misfits* still pictures. He met her during the Nevada moviemaking, no longer shy about women. Upon returning to New York he asked Nan Taylor for her telephone number. If there was any earlier flirtation, there is no evidence of it.

Her name was Ingeborg Morath—Inge—a dark, slender, tall, handsome, serious-minded thirty-seven-year-old European (Miller was then forty-five), the all but complete opposite of Marilyn Monroe. Born in Austria, she had grown up in Hitler's Germany where two of her brothers were in the *Wermacht*—the regular German army—as was her uncle, a general. That was not the fearsome Gestapo or the horrific SS, but even so, as Miller himself would point out in the later play, *Incident at Vichy*, the *Wermacht* was not exempted from enforcing the Racial Program. That did not necessarily make Inge Morath's family into Nazis but it did provide Elia Kazan with enough ammunition to taunt Miller for excusing them with the implication, in the forthcoming *After the Fall*, that all of humanity shared in the blame for the Holocaust and not just the Germans. Even Miller's producer and friend, Robert Whitehead, had to concede that such a notion, which "Inge [gave] him the motive to feel—that we're all guilty for the crimes of Germany—that was a bit of a stretch."

Inge Morath had gone to university in Berlin before fulfilling her wartime obligations by doing aircraft factory work and what she called menial "labor service." After the war and following a brief marriage she worked as a journalist, learned photography and moved in a sophisticated international circle that included the designer Cristobal Balenciaga, *The New Yorker*'s Janet Flanner, the actor Yul Brynner and the world-famous photographer Henri-Cartier Bresson. It was with Bresson that Morath, a fellow member of the Magnum photographers' cooperative, had come to Nevada to cover *The Misfits*. Most recently living in Paris, she had taken an apartment in New York.

The New York theater world had long been bemoaning Arthur Miller's absence from Broadway. It was five years since his last production. When asked whether the Monroe marriage were to blame for the prolonged silence, he said that an answer "would make news, I suppose, but I don't know whether it would make sense." He approved a supercilious description of his professional disappearance as resembling that of "most writers whose careers span a number of years and it was only coincidentally that much of [the] barren time came when he was with Marilyn." An interviewer from the *New York Herald-Tribune* wrote, "A new play from Mr. Miller would be a theatrical event of the first magnitude," but quoted the playwright as saying, "I can't make a play come out of a slot." On the day *The Misfits* had been pronounced as done at last somebody asked him for a pencil. Not only, he said, did he not have one but "I don't need one. I'm not going to write anything from now until doomsday." While the bitterness was understandable ("a terrible time, the lowest point of my life") his doomsday in a sense had just passed. He not only survived but was finally able to again write for himself. Indeed he was telling Frank Taylor that he was working on a new play "like a man possessed."

Most of that work was being done at the Roxbury farm, where he was staying "nine days out of ten." The farm was now his, thanks to Marilyn's generosity, and so was the Jaguar and even Hugo, the basset hound. Of her own memory that "we spent some happy years in that house," she would only ask for "a few odd pieces of iron porch furniture. . . . Sort of good luck, I mean hard luck pieces." She had hoped Arthur might be there when she came by to pick them up and "told him when I'd be there, but when I got there he wasn't." Her last words on the subject of the marriage were "I think he's a better writer than a husband. I'm sure writing comes first in his life."

There can be no argument that Marilyn Monroe's relationship with Arthur Miller had been the most important in her life. From start to finish it ranged over nearly a third of her thirty-four years. She would say that she'd wanted "some calmness, some steadiness in my life, and for a time I had that in my life with Arthur. That was a nice time. And then we lost it."

For him it was only an intermittent love affair and a brief second marriage, not nearly as enduring as the fifteen years and two children with Mary or the forthcoming forty years with Inge. Yet in a sense Arthur Miller's relationship with Marilyn Monroe was his most important relationship too, because ever afterward his life story would be inextricably bound up with hers. It would be impossible to conceive of Arthur Miller without relating him to Marilyn Monroe.

The rough first screening of *The Misfits* was held strictly for the benefit of Huston, Miller, Frank Taylor and some studio people. The reaction was disappointing. A publicity executive from United Artists privately told Taylor that John Huston, although usually a wonderful director, had reduced this "great script" to a movie about three men trying to get Marilyn Monroe into bed. He suggested that perhaps Huston, like most everyone else who had been involved with the picture, might have been smitten with the gallant and gentlemanly Clark Gable ("In life a true hero," Miller said, "I never knew anyone like him," and dedicated the published *Misfits* to him). Perhaps, the publicity man said, "Huston had excessively tilted the picture's focus toward him." The director accepted the overall criticism and went back to work in the editing room. When he was done, the publicity executive seemed to still be right—that the picture was tilted toward Gable and that it was about three men trying to get Marilyn Monroe into bed. And they were all Arthur Miller.

The picture was finally *finally* pronounced done on November 4, 1960, and the next day Gable had a heart attack. Two weeks later he suffered another and he was dead at fifty-nine. Some blamed his death on the picture's physical demands. One scene had Gable struggling with and being dragged by a horse in the extreme heat of the midsummer Nevada desert. Whatever the reason, the heart attacks had happened and United Artists rushed to release the film—a grisly and not unnoticed attempt to capitalize on the publicity and sentiment surrounding the star's death. A December 31 premiere was announced to meet the Academy Awards deadline but it was not met. There simply was too much work undone, the musical score, for instance. The first full screening was held on January 11. Its audience included studio executives, Taylor, Miller, Huston and all the leading actors except Monroe, who refused to attend. When the lights came up, Miller said, "I still don't understand it. We got through it. I made a present of this to her, and I left it without her."

At this screening Miller found the picture "quite miraculous . . . just like the original vision," and told a feature writer, "I was tremendously impressed . . . a wonderful motion picture." The general consensus was so enthusiastic that the studio increased its advertising budget and ordered 1,300 prints, a record number, for the upcoming national release. In the meantime Marilyn was on her way to Mexico to get the divorce. To avoid media attention her trip was scheduled to coincide with John F. Kennedy's presidential inauguration. She was back in a day and a half and the marriage was over. Marilyn Monroe's last words on the subject were

> When the monster showed, Arthur couldn't believe it. I disappointed him when that happened. But I felt he knew and loved all of me. I wasn't sweet all through. He should love the monster too. But maybe I'm too demanding. I put Arthur through a lot, I know. But he also put me through a lot.

The Misfits had its world premiere at the Capitol Theatre in New York City on February 5, 1961, and the reviews were not good, from the *New York Times* ("curiously uncongealed") to the short story's original source, *Esquire* ("the life slowly leaks out"). In *The New Yorker* under the headline "Misfire" Roger Angell managed to simultaneously find it "almost continuously absorbing" and yet "a dramatic failure of considerable dimensions." In general the criticism was on a yea or nay level, with little discussion of any point to the movie and little consideration of the screenplay in relation to its author's body of work.

His own response to the bad reviews was to change his mind about the picture. Miller now told the *New York Herald-Tribune* that he "wasn't satisfied with" what he had so recently thought "quite miraculous." The movie that had been "just like the original vision" suddenly "didn't conform to the vision I had when I started." Inconsistencies aside, he seemed to accept that his screenplay had been too much of a stage play and he was articulate on the differences between theater and film.

> The movie springs from the way we dream. The art of cutting follows the physiology of a dream. In the dream we accept because we see it. . . . The passivity of the dream is the essence of the dream. The dreamer is paralyzed. The same is true in a movie. . . . The play, on the other hand, is built on words. There's a basic conflict [in movies] between the word and the image. The greatest impact will come from the image. It's hitting us truly where we live. A man says on a stage, "I'm starving," but when you show a starving man in a movie, there is no question.

In "A Question of Standard," an insightful essay about *The Misfits* for *Film Quarterly*, John A. Barsness saw the movie as an exploration of "the gap between the myth and the reality of the West." It presented, he felt, the antithesis of Hollywood's West, with Gay Langland no ordinary cowboy hero.

> The central symbol of the whole absurd search is, of course, those pitiful wild horses which supposedly will keep them all from going to work for somebody else—that is, succumbing to a place inside of instead of outside of society. Not only are the wild horses mostly dead—as is, in the end, the dream of the Wild

> West itself—but going after them is now, as it has always been, exhausting, backbreaking, and cruel. Roslyn, the innocent harlot, poses the ultimate question of reality: is independence worth all that? In reality, the past and the present are far different from the myth; in reality, the cowboy on your right is your pal one minute and seduces your girl the next, and her morality itself is a thing not practiced but yearned after.

It was left to Robert W. Corrigan, the considerable theater academic and founding chairman of the Department of Drama at the California Institute of the Arts, to see the screenplay in the context of the Arthur Miller canon. He called it "the pivotal work in Miller's career as a playwright." Corrigan viewed the screenplay as the turning point between on one side *All My Sons, Death of a Salesman, The Crucible* and *A View from the Bridge* and on the other the playwright's "second period," which followed the marriage to Monroe. Corrigan saw *The Misfits* as a hinge that opened onto what lay ahead, which he analyzed as

> concerned with the dramatic possibilities of otherness. In *The Misfits*, the characters are less concerned with themselves than with finding ways to relate to each other. Gay and Roslyn move from two extremes of isolation until they meet and make a promise with full respect for the "otherness" of the other.

The way Miller put this, the picture has to do with "people trying to connect and afraid to connect." Likewise, Corrigan pointed out, Miller's post-*Misfits* plays deal with identity crises. When previously his "heroes struggled unsuccessfully to discover who they were," in the later plays "Miller is concerned with the effect his protagonists have had on others and their capacity to accept full responsibility for what they have or have not done." It will be interesting to keep this in mind while dealing with the later plays, but Corrigan continues with a speculation that seems more appropriate to a gossip column than to an academic critique. "Miller's marriage to Miss Monroe had a profound effect on his attitudes, his sense of the world, his view of himself and perhaps even on the nature of his dramatic form."

That was perhaps overstatement and Corrigan never clarifies what the "profound effect" was. It is true that the plays following Miller's long and painful dry spell would be markedly different from those that went before, but they would also be just as different from one another. There appears to be no reason to consider *The Misfits* as a causal or introductory factor; rather with each viewing it seems a split image, partly a quirky John Huston movie and partly an idea-laden Arthur Miller "play for the screen," the two parts never quite meshing. Yet *The Misfits* certainly was the eleven o'clock number in the strange spectacle that was Miller's Marilyn Monroe period, four and a half years of ironic laughter over this great playwright's lifelong effort to keep (his) life under control.

Miller's mother, an exception in an otherwise healthy family, was ailing. The seventy-eight-year-old Gussie had suffered myriad illnesses, including breast cancer and diabetes. Shortly after *The Misfits* was released her health began to fail, but she seemed to throw herself into remission when Isadore's heart momentarily stopped beating during a minor prostate procedure. As their daughter, Joan, told it,

> Dad went home and mother took care of him, but she was getting weaker, and more tired. Then the time came to take him back to the hospital to do the prostate operation. When she came back from the hospital, she told a neighbor, "Well I put Izzy in the hospital today. He's going to be all right, the doctor says, and now I can die." And she died that night.

That was March 7, 1961, and Marilyn Monroe went to Mrs. Miller's funeral in Brooklyn, along with Arthur and Inge. There is no record of any exchange among them, but a shaky Monroe held tight to Isadore Miller's hand in the chapel (she refused to go to the cemetery), and he was shaky too. They were both freshly discharged from hospitals. She had just been released from the Neurological Institute at Columbia Presbyterian Hospital following a short stay at the Payne-Whitney Psychiatric Clinic in New York Hospital, where she had thrown a chair through a plate glass window. She was "tired," she said, "of being Marilyn Monroe . . . it's become a burden, a what do you call it? An albatross."

In the little time she had left, Marilyn's devotion to Arthur's father would remain daughterly and she would even choose him to be her escort a year later, May 19, 1962, when she sang "Happy Birthday" to President Kennedy in Madison Square Garden. Afterward she took the old man to meet the president. "I just said," Monroe remembered, "'This is my former father in law, Isadore Miller.' He came here an immigrant and I thought this would be one of the biggest things in his life . . . I thought this would be something that he would be telling his grandchildren about."

During the 1961 summer Miller had written to James Stern,

> Things are once again simple and thank God productive. I am . . . in Roxbury, writing much . . . and living the life. I have 340 acres here, a two acre pond—fourteen feet deep—full of trout, a beautiful house. . . . I hope and believe I'll have a play again soon . . . for various reasons, I suppose, my stuff seems to bear little relation to what has gone before. I feel like a beginner and all that wonder.

Looking ahead to the debut of the Repertory Theater of Lincoln Center in 1963, Miller began reading scenes from the latest version of *The Third Play* to producer Robert Whitehead. Such readings often meant a work nearing consummation. It was now more than six years since the writing of *A View from the Bridge*. Whitehead knew that Arthur

> felt very rusty. But there was also a sense of exhilaration. The period with Marilyn had emasculated him a little bit . . . Arthur was terribly excited to find he could write again. . . . I think he worried about . . . the emphasis [still] being there in the same way. I think he felt a kind of health returning, an excitement that he was writing.

He had retained the nugget of an unhappy marriage from the early versions of this long-germinating play. From other stages of its development he took the policeman's name, Quentin, and gave it to the lawyer, who was now the central figure, "a guy," it seemed to Whitehead, "who was trying to sort out, through this evaluation of his life, whether he had any capacity for love." Miller also stripped most of the camouflage from the young woman who in earlier versions had been called Lorraine, then Dorothy. She is the Eve who introduces Quentin to passion and lures him from the innocent Eden of his first marriage into a realization of his sexuality and an explosive moral crisis. In the scenes Miller read to Whitehead she was a switchboard operator in Quentin's office, a girl who was crazy for popular songs. She soon evolved into an aspiring singer (like Roslyn in *The Misfits*), now clearly modeled on Monroe, who of course had been an aspiring actress when Miller first met her.

Miller married Inge Morath in Connecticut on February 17, 1962. The circumstances were somewhat calmer than his previous wedding. Some fourteen friends and relatives came to the champagne reception at a friend's home in nearby New Milford. When inevitably Marilyn was asked how she felt about his remarriage, she replied, "A little bit remains even when you break up. You can't let go completely . . . You feel he's wiping out the past with you by marrying again [but] that's silly. . . . Arthur and I could never live together again. It's over. Why shouldn't he get married again?" His conclusion about their marriage was harsher. "There was no way," he said. "She was beyond help. There was simply nothing but destruction that could [have] come, my own destruction as well as hers. A person's got to save himself."

Marilyn Monroe's destruction came six months later in the early morning of Sunday, August 5, 1962. She was found dead in the bedroom of her house at 12305 Fifth Helena Drive in Los Angeles, a victim ("probable suicide" according to the police report) of an overdose of Nembutal. In New York a memorial was organized by Lee and Paula Strasberg. Shelley Winters, in a novel approach to eulogy, chose the occasion to tote up her old roommate's sexual accomplishments. As she figured the number of dream lovers that Marilyn had succeeded in checking off on the lists they had compiled as starlets, Winters was certain of at least one success. "I don't know how many of her choices she achieved, but after her death when many of her possessions were sent to Lee Strasberg's apartment, there on Marilyn's white baby grand I saw a large framed photograph of Albert Einstein. On it was written, 'To my dear Marilyn, love, Albert.'"

Monroe's New York public relations representative, Arthur Jacobs, called Miller to personally deliver the news of her death. His terse response was, "It's your problem, not mine." Jacobs replied, "Arthur, you always were a shit," and hung up. Miller didn't attend the funeral at the Westwood Village Memorial Chapel in Los Angeles but his father did. Isadore Miller had tried, he said, to call Marilyn on the day before she died but couldn't reach her. The last time he had spoken with her, a week and a half earlier, "She sounded happy," he said, but when "she wanted help . . . nobody was near her."

Arthur didn't send flowers either. His only recorded reaction, in a letter written to a friend, was that "The earth shocks for a moment [but] her life-death will not enlighten many." The only emotional impact her death seemed to have was in terms of his work. He would deal with the subject in his play. This is always how he expressed himself and his feelings—in place of directly experiencing emotions he conceptualized them, and the years of psychoanalysis had done little to change that. Marilyn's was the second recent death to confront him with his remoteness. He admitted he had felt no pain at his mother's death. His play was going to be about exactly these observations. As one of his earliest notes for *After the Fall* describes it, the play is "Quentin's effort to mourn someone." Arthur Miller, unable to come up with grief himself, was setting out to deal with it by universalizing and dramatizing the issue; dealing with it if not by the heart then by way of the mind and his art. The notion was earnest, even courageous and surely daring, but it was destined to be misunderstood entirely.

This latest version of *The Third Play* was called *After the Fall*, a title with more than one meaning: It refers to mankind's fall from grace in Genesis and the loss of innocence; it also refers to Albert Camus's novel *The Fall*, which likewise deals with guilt and lost innocence. That book was once suggested to Miller as screenplay material. Although he would denigrate the Camus as being "apart from its philosophical conundrum [merely] about trouble with women," his play would be at least in part *after*—that is, a response to—*The Fall*. As Professor Derek Parker Royal wrote in "Camusian Existentialism in Arthur Miller's *After the Fall*,"

> The structural premises of *The Fall* and *After the Fall* are strikingly similar. Both are confessional monologues delivered to an absent audience: what is more, the fictional audiences are situated within the texts in ways that directly engage the actual audience, so that by the end of the novel or play, the reader or viewer becomes something of an accomplice to the action. [Moreover] like his Camusian counterpart . . . Quentin is a lawyer who has become obsessed with his fall from innocence. He laments the passing of the time when he felt that there was a clear sense of right and wrong. . . . This profound sense of moral discomfiture . . . is akin to Camus's notion of the absurd. The feeling of oneness with the world is lost the moment an individual becomes aware of his

or her moral position in that world and, as a result, experiences at first a sense of existential despair.

Miller would later concede this connection, going on to describe Camus's central character as a "moralist unable to forget that he had not tried to stop [a] girl from jumping to her death in the river." He added,

> I would put it differently. The question was not so much whether one had failed to be brave. The question in my play is what happens if you do go to the rescue. Does this absolve? Does this prevent the fall? Supposing he had run over to the bridge where he thought he heard someone fall and had become involved with her and found out that she had an inexorable lust for destruction. At what point and when would he see wisdom?

His projection speaks for itself. The *After* in Miller's title can also be taken as a reference to survival (originally in fact the play carried the subtitle *The Survivor*), the play being about the life that is resumed, continued or renewed not just after Marilyn's death but after any guilt-inflicting fall from righteousness. It was her death, though, that jolted the play into becoming what it was going to be. "All summer," Whitehead remembered, "Kazan and I had been up in Roxbury, working with Arthur . . . the first half was written." When Marilyn Monroe died in August, the producer suggested, "Why don't we all take off until Labor Day and forget about the whole thing for a month?"

On September 5, Miller wrote to Kazan, "Marilyn died the day after I had decided that Maggie [her echo name in *After the Fall*] must die in the play." In that letter nothing more was said about any reaction he might have had to the death. Instead, almost as if confused between reality and his play, even as if seeing the play *as* reality, he spoke of Marilyn's alter ego dying. "The fact that Maggie died so young, so full of possibilities, has no bearing on her possibilities. They are as it turns out, as real as her defeat of them, as real as her death. And that is precisely why she was tragic." Then turning personal and by mistake calling the character "Marilyn," he treated the real death in terms of his own life—how he personally is affected by it as without pause he connects it with Inge's pregnancy. "A great deal of this past month," he wrote, "was exploded by her dying and her ghost, as you can imagine. And at the same time we are preparing for a new baby which is any day now. The wonder of it all."

Curious of course is that seemingly without thought, pause or transition his subject slipped from the fictitious Maggie to Marilyn's death to the imminent birth of his child. Yet can we really believe that the very day before Monroe died Arthur Miller had decided—would have dared—to have her alter ego dead in his play? Astonishingly he seemed to believe that his Maggie was an entirely invented character inspired by Marilyn Monroe but only basically, and that he alone knew this; she now existed apart from

Marilyn Monroe and was never to be thought of as her. He himself did not think of her as Marilyn Monroe. Maggie, like Willy Loman and John Proctor and Eddie Carbone, existed on another plane and in another dimension from the person who was the prototype. It is chilling to contemplate how this play might have been received—and how Miller would have been crucified—had Maggie been dead at the start of the play while Marilyn was still alive.

Whitehead recalled,

> We got together in October and started work on the last half of the play. Then Arthur came up with some things that were really strange—things that weren't related to the play at all. He was writing images—about this dead girl, *her bones in the bottom of the sea,* I didn't know where he thought he was fitting it in. It was a different thing, all subjective. . . . It was as if Arthur almost had to write that. For his own system. For his own subconscious pressure and throb. Strange images. He never referred to them again.

As for Miller's absence from Monroe's funeral, he would still be defending it a quarter of a century later. "To join what I knew would be a circus of cameras and shouts and luridness was beyond my strength . . . to me it was meaningless to stand for photographs at a stone."

In the autumn of 1962 a notably "overjoyed" Arthur Miller telephoned Robert Whitehead to announce, "I have a son." He and Inge, he said, were going to name the boy Eugene. Possibly it was after O'Neill. "Arthur was in a high state of excitement," Whitehead recalled. The excitement was short-lived, and it all changed the following morning.

"He isn't right," Miller said on the telephone and the producer remembered that "Arthur was terribly shaken—he used the term 'mongoloid.'" The condition was Down Syndrome and Whitehead said, "I'm terribly sorry."

"I'm going to have to put the baby away," Arthur said, and so he and Inge did. The boy was named not Eugene but Daniel, and he was enrolled in the Southbury Training School a short drive from Roxbury, a "home for individuals with Mental Retardation" (later revised as "the developmentally disabled"). The institution, beautifully set on a 1,600-acre "campus," provided its "residents" with not only room and board but such programmed activities as farming, educational training and "sheltered workshops." It was where Daniel would live for the rest of his life.

"Arthur talked to me a few times," Whitehead said, "about a natural intelligence the child has. He said that when the doctors told him, he'd already suspected because the baby had lines in his hand [the so-called simian line] that revealed the condition." As for the reason, according to the National Down Syndrome Society, medical research has isolated "an error in cell division" as the all but certain cause. The incidence of births of children with

Down Syndrome tends to increase with the age of the mother. It is much more common for such babies to be born to women over thirty-five, and at Daniel's birth Inge Miller was thirty-eight years old. Moreover, evidence shows that inheritance might also play a role in creating the "extra genetic material" that demonstrably causes the syndrome. "The risk is higher," the society reports, "if one parent is a carrier of a transmuted cell." Arthur Miller did have a cousin who was born with Down Syndrome, "a helpless mongoloid," as he put it in his autobiography. He also had a close relative born with cerebral palsy and attendant mental retardation. His sister Joan feared that "something in the family genes" was the cause of Daniel's condition.

For the next forty years Inge would visit him almost every week at the Southbury Training School, but it seems that Arthur never did. That at least was Whitehead's understanding.

In *After the Fall* Inge's echo name is Holga, and Miller wrote a speech for her.

> I dreamed I had a child and even in the dream I saw it was my life, and it was an idiot, and I ran away. But it always crept on to my lap again, clutched at my clothes. Until I thought, if I could kiss it, whatever in it was my own, perhaps I could sleep. And I bent to its broken face, and it was horrible . . . but I kissed it. I think one must finally take one's life in one's arms.

Arthur Miller would never recognize or mention this son in any public fashion. His sister Joan said, "Daniel was a very difficult subject for Arthur." None of his official or professional chronologies includes the birth and Daniel does not exist in his father's autobiography.

part four

Endurance, Survival

I think art imputes value to human beings,
and if I did that it would be the most
pleasant thought I could depart with.

16. *The Fall*

> After the Fall *is a turning point . . . a signal step in the evolution of Arthur Miller as man and artist. The play's auto-criticism exposes him to us; it also liberates him so that he can go on free of false legend and heavy halo. Had he not written this play he might never have been able to write another.*
>
> —Harold Clurman

As After the Fall and the theater it was to inaugurate crawled toward completion, the building began to lag behind. Designed by Eero Saarinen and called the Vivian Beaumont Theatre, its site was still a mammoth hole in the ground at the corner of Amsterdam Avenue and Sixty-fifth Street. Yet there was an immense hopefulness about the place—high expectations for the institution ahead and an excitement about its inauguration with the first new Arthur Miller play in—it was now—almost eight years. Elia Kazan began a notebook before having seen a page of manuscript. The play was in constant flux with no second act, but the playwright and the director were eager to get started. And so Kazan dated his small, brown spiral notebook "April, 1963" immediately upon his return from Roxbury, where Arthur had read several scenes to him. Kazan had already concluded that the play was "about Morality and guilt. It's about Miller." Now he began his staging process with the first entry in the notebook.

> What is more heroic, more deeply *human* than the spectacle of man looking into himself . . . without deception . . . to judge himself?

Was Kazan writing about the play's protagonist or its author? His mind worked on a more concrete level than Miller's, attuned to people rather than ideas, which suits a director. The notebook entry suggests that while the director was trying to grasp the play's fiction in a broader context, he became drawn to the piece as being about Miller personally and, not incidentally, about himself as well. The scenes that were read to him apparently begged for autobiographical notice. So, Kazan entered in his notebook, "Arthur Miller has found his morality sterile [and] guilt-ridden. Everyone," the director said, "made him feel superior, a God, . . . and it turned out not to be so [because] *the person Art is most like is not* [a] *puritanical, always right eminence.* Now," Kazan noted, possibly projecting for his own sake as well, Arthur Miller "wants to join the rest of the human race, *the fallible!*"

In real life that fairly seemed the sum of it. Even icons need breathing room. In Marilyn Monroe's case she had come to resent playing *Marilyn Monroe*; in Arthur Miller's case he had wearied of believing he was *Arthur Miller,* America's moral paragon. He knew that it had become hypocritical but Kazan was too much of a cynic to understand that Arthur Miller was earnestly and profoundly committed to notions of virtue. His sense of moral inadequacy, if not hypocrisy, is what the play is about, but to direct *After the Fall* Kazan didn't need to understand that. To direct a play Elia had to treat it as being about a man named Quentin and not the erstwhile friend Arthur Miller. He had to see not Art but Quentin as the first-time wayward husband just discovering sex with not Marilyn but the open-bodied Maggie. Quentin the character is finding that this passion destroys his traditional family life—not with Mary but Louise. Kazan thus had to consider Quentin as emerging into a wiser maturity. But psychological acuity drew him otherwise.

As an unreconstructed Freudian, the director parsed the story for sexual elements.

> Maggie represents to Quentin [1] illicit passion (illicit yet!) Illicit = attractive? Illicit = not passion for my mother? Is that what it is unconsciously? At any rate, Art says that Quentin has to find out that it is *not* illicit. And [2] Maggie . . . represents to him *spontaneous truth*. She, Maggie, can do anything without *stain*.

Moreover, Kazan noted, "Maggie, stresses Miller, is a barbarian. She can barely read. What she does know she's learned from the whiplash of living, from everything else she's done (plenty!)." The director could take objectivity only so far. "I noticed," he wrote, "something about Art's voice when he was reading the part. He was always 'pleading.' And the particular significance of this was not only that Maggie thinks herself worthless, or that she can only 'get by' by taking the stance of worthlessness—but also that he, Art, enjoys being looked up to in that way."

That was a provocative reading of Monroe. Kazan's psychological sense was intact. If he found it difficult to separate the protagonist from the source, he didn't even try when it came to Maggie. "There are," he noted, "as there were with MM, sudden and real and unexpected hints of shyness," seeing as her basic attitude, "I am just someone men want to fuck. That is all I really have to offer [and] you are either in favor of my position [as] a waif or against it."

The director concluded in these notes from the March 31 conference, "This story is [Quentin's] attempt to join the human race without giving up the real values behind his posture." Although Kazan already seemed lost in a maze of theme analysis and psychological conjecture, the real test lay ahead: Whether he had lost any of his staging abilities, starting with the instinct for reading a play and visualizing it. Why and where had that and so many of his tremendous gifts been shunted aside while he directed superficially serious plays (*Tea and Sympathy*) and movies (*Splendor in the Grass*)? He hadn't found a stimulating playwright among the new lights. Tennessee Williams was already self-destructing, his latest plays (*Sweet Bird of Youth, Period of Adjustment, The Night of the Iguana, The Milk Train Doesn't Stop Here Anymore*) mocking the greatness of his major works. Kazan needed superior material to regain his stature. A reunion with Arthur Miller might have seemed like a chance for artistic rebirth, a salvaged name and a return to the glories of *Death of a Salesman*.

The former friends were now as wary of each other as any divorced couple. They even shared sexual history, and there was Marilyn Monroe in the play. Present too was another connection: Kazan's current mistress, an actress named Barbara Loden who, if the director had his way, would be playing Maggie. Finally Elia—a guilty man directing a play about guilt—was himself the basis for a character named Mickey, who was an informer, dishonorable and untrustworthy. Thus the fraternal, professional and political histories of Arthur Miller and Elia Kazan were woven into the fabric of this project, the background against which the production of *After the Fall* was set.

In those early months of 1963 when Arthur was just starting to work with Elia, he learned that Inge was pregnant once more. It was surely a worrisome development. Uncertainties about the cause of Down Syndrome made it difficult to predict the likelihood of another occurrence. Research conducted by the National Down Syndrome Society suggests that when one of the parents carries the extra genetic material—the transmuted cell present in virtually all cases of Trisomy 21, or *mosaic* Down Syndrome (the most common kind)—the risk of a second child being born with the condition narrows to about one in a hundred. At the time there was no way of determining whether Arthur or Inge carried that extra genetic material.

The couple was making Roxbury their home, but as *After the Fall* moved ever closer to production, Arthur needed a New York base. They took a permanent suite at the Chelsea Hotel to serve as both a workplace and pied-à-terre. There it was even easier for him to enjoy visits with his son, Robert, and his daughter, Jane, and he used this time to take a break from the big play and write a children's book for her. She seems to have been the child more upset by her parents' divorce, and perhaps Inge's pregnancy made Miller more keenly aware of it. Calling the story *Jane's Blanket,* he based it, he said, on his observations when she had been six or seven years old. Like so many children she'd had what he called a "night-night," a security blanket. In summation of his story, he said, "Jane wraps herself in the blanket, but somehow it gets smaller and smaller. It becomes the size of a handkerchief and then it disappears altogether. What happens is that as the girl gets bigger, the blanket gets smaller." In his story, "At night Jane's father came home. He picked her up and kissed her. Then he sat on the floor in front of her, and he played with her. . . . And she laughed, and her father kissed her."

At nineteen, Jane Ellen Miller was somewhat old for children's stories. Perhaps her father was making up for lost time, lost opportunities or just making up. He surely loved her a great deal and had no problem expressing it, but she would never be quite as expressive as Robert in forgiving the divorce. As for Inge's pregnancy, on August 7, 1963, she gave birth to a daughter they named Rebecca Augusta (after Miller's mother), a sound infant who would grow up to be healthy, brainy, beautiful and gifted, a talented actress and a prizewinning screenwriter and director.

Dramatists commonly protest any rummaging through their plays for connections with or references to their personal lives. Understandably they want to be taken at their word, expect to be and, like all artists, deserve to be. There is no need to speculate about any such connections or references to Arthur Miller's own life in *After the Fall.* There is hardly a scene, a speech or a situation in it that isn't rooted in fact, yet it is all fiction in the sense that he was doing what he had always done: dramatizing upon a bed of research. For him, that meant, as he had said to Kazan when preparing to write *Death of a Salesman,* "find the facts first and then dream about them." Kazan did not object but cautioned, "Just because something was 'true,' or had happened, doesn't mean it should necessarily be in the play. The important thing is to really decide what the play is about in concrete terms and from this standard and by this measure decide what belongs in the play and in what proportion."

This kind of cooperation existed throughout the writing of *After the Fall.* Was it also collaboration? From their individual recollections as well as correspondence it would seem that once again Kazan served as sounding board, advisor, editor, enthusiast ("May I just say again that I think you're writing better than you ever did") and catalyst rather than an actual partner in the writing. As for Miller, this time he was taking to the outer limit his method of factual research for fictive modeling. Here is his life story, perhaps more honest than in his autobiography, but set in an artistic mold and made into a separate drama. It is told as the mind works, from the inside out, the chronology rephased to play out as a kind of cubist composition of event and reflection, splintered in time, recomposed for theatrical cohesion then orchestrated. There is nothing quite like it in the western dramatic literature and it might have been recognized as such were there not the minor matter of a central character being recognizably the most famous movie star in the world whose marriage to the author—a marriage unmistakably portrayed in the play—had been the stuff of international headlines. Monroe's depiction was all the more problematic owing to her recent death, but the playwright didn't seem conscious of it. Indeed he insisted with winsome naivete that Maggie was not Marilyn. How touching his astonishment that she was taken for Monroe, yet how absurd his unawareness of the explosiveness with which the matter would play out.

After the Fall dramatizes a mental environment as did *Death of a Salesman*, but while that play reflects the distorted perceptions of a troubled mind, this one is set within a mind that is relentlessly sane, even excessively so in the sense that it is untouched by heart. The play is a dramatization of intelligent free association as it replicates what Miller called "the way the mind works," tracking the mental process through sudden, improbable and unpredictable excursions willy-nilly into the feelings and events of its past. In general the two plays *Fall* and *Salesman* are also alike in their concern with a man's chances of controlling his life or as Miller put it elsewhere, "How to make of this hostile world a home, that we may live with what we are doing."

In its simplest guise *After the Fall* describes one man's effort to be a human being. Quentin is afraid that he cannot love. That is where the play begins and ends, with the imperative to take care, not only about everyone but about someone. In short, otherness. The playwright was universalizing his own problem, the remoteness and chilliness of which he had always been accused. He was extrapolating from it to formulate a morality of emotional generosity.

The play's concept as a "mental geography" free in (but not of) form was selected and developed from the countless drafts and thousands of pages of *The Third Play*. As this particular incarnation starts out, the central figure confronts the audience, identifying himself as a lawyer who has abandoned "an important career." He has lost track of the point not only of practicing law ("I was merely in the service of my own success") but of life itself. He presents this to the Listener (which means of course audience), speaking as if to a friend or confessor or as Kazan presumed, a psychoanalyst, which could have made sense since the play had Quentin addressing the central issue of Miller's own psychoanalysis. Then again he might have been talking to God or what God represents, depending on how one takes his first words, "Hello! God, it's good to see you again!" For sure, on behalf of the playwright, he was feeling good about seeing a theater audience again.

Ultimately Miller believed that Quentin was in soliloquy, talking to himself about a decision to be made. Having been twice divorced, he is unsure whether he should or can make another commitment, this time to Holga, an archaeologist he had met in Germany. Yet this is more than a mere domestic crossroad he faces; he is at a juncture in his life where a choice must be made between withdrawing into himself permanently and no longer caring about anything or making a go at being part of the human race. So he has arrived at the confluence of all the strands, the real and psychological elements, in his past.

The dramatics begin as Quentin's mother appears. She is called Rose but only once, just as the father is once called Ike. Otherwise, as in earlier plays, they are addressed and listed in the cast of characters as Mother and Father. Having just died, she looms silently out of the dark and, he confesses, "I don't seem to know how to grieve for her." There are flash appearances of his second wife, Maggie (who calls out his name), and of the prospective third wife, Holga (asking about Mozart), as the stage pulses with memories. The first scene presents a meeting with Quentin's brother Dan—a character evoking Kermit Miller—who is fretful about giving the news of their mother's death to their father. Even as Quentin volunteers to be the messenger, he wonders whether he is doing so simply because he's "crueler" than his brother is.

His thoughts turn to a Jewish cemetery on the site of a Nazi concentration camp, a place he and Holga had visited, but even the death camp leaves him unmoved. "I swear," he says, "I don't know if I have lived in good faith." This is typical of Miller's fascination with word usage, which sometimes results in new meanings. Here he does not mean faith in the usual sense of believing something on trust. Rather he wonders whether he has ever been worthy of a more general sort of trust, for he shares none of Holga's grief over the slaughtered Jews.

As he stares at the Holocaust site, his mother returns to his thoughts, this time in his childhood as she dotingly shares with him her scorn of relatives. He asks himself, "What the hell has this got to do with a concentration camp?" but the mind has its own logic and his thoughts remain in his youth. There Mother scolds him for playing with matches and ridicules his father, a once "wonderful man," who is going bankrupt after the Wall Street crash. She, who was never interested in the family business, is now incredulous about its collapse ("Why didn't you say something?"), and Miller's stage direction reads *Father is gradually losing his stance, his grandeur* as she snarls, "Are you some kind of moron? . . . I ought to get a divorce!"

Overhearing that leaves the thirteen year old in tears and then he is his middle-aged self at the concentration camp staring up at the "slaughterhouse" watchtowers and asking Holga to swear her love. He is in awe of her benign view of humanity, which he cannot share, and she describes a recurring nightmare. This is the speech about kissing the broken face of her idiot child. She then disappears, leaving him alone with thoughts about being unable to say he loves her, followed by memories of his first marriage. That was so simple, he recalls—a wife, a family "and the world so wonderfully threatened by injustices I was born to correct!"

He flashes back to his first experience of sexual temptation (resisted) with the wife of his friend Lou, once his law professor, now a law partner, a good man who has been subpoenaed by the "Committee," one which hardly needs specifying. When Lou is treated like a child by his wife, Quentin's mind takes the cue and comes up with a memory of his mother berating his father as an "idiot." Then he is back with his first wife, Louise, who has decided to go into psychoanalysis. In a crisp cross-reference he asks why—"To take up your life, like an idiot child? Can anybody really do that? Kiss his life?" This is a marriage unraveling as Louise complains "You don't pay any attention to me." His egotistical, absurdly self-centered defense is, "Just last night I read you my whole brief." He adds, "Maybe I don't speak because the one time I did tell you my feelings you didn't get over it for six months," which is much as John Proctor complains to Elizabeth in *The Crucible*. Louise remembers that particular occasion scornfully—"You come back from a trip and tell me you'd met a woman you wanted to sleep with."

And why, he wonders, had he been so stupid as to confess that? To demonstrate some learned notion of a cleared conscience? It's the same old fantasy of innocence, he suggests to his audience. "The innocent are always better." The concentration camp watchtower again looms out of the dark, a recurring symbol of guilt. "Why," asks Quentin, "does something in me bow its head like an accomplice in this place?" Here the play is proposing—very debatably—that everyone's innocence was lost with the Holocaust and in that sense we are all guilty of it. Then his mind turns to Mickey, his law partner, who suggested, "Maybe you married too young. I did too. Although you don't fool around, do you?"

Mickey, who certainly does fool around, has been subpoenaed by the Committee. He confides that he is "going to name names" because "they" destroy anyone who doesn't. A shocked Quentin warns that "All this is going to pass" but Mickey, having been told it's either that or be dismissed from their law firm, has made up his mind. In earlier testimony he had refused to be a cooperative witness but now, he says, he has told the Committee he's changed his mind. Miller gives this character, bluntly based on Kazan, a full speech to justify his actions. He also has Mickey suggest to Lou that they name each other in a ploy to betray without betraying, much as Kazan had contrived with Clifford Odets. Unlike Odets, though, Lou insists that "You may not mention my name . . . You will ruin me" and adds, on the subject of betrayal, "If everyone broke faith there would be no civilization! . . . You are terrified! They have bought your soul!" When Kazan staged this speech, so accusatory of himself, he had Barbara Loden (playing the role of Maggie) at the same time crawl across the upper stage in a negligee. Miller at first overlooked this clumsy attempt to distract the audience but several weeks after the play opened Elia agreed to drop the diversionary tactic.

Mickey's cooperative appearance before the Committee ends the friendship as far as Quentin is concerned. His mind returns to his wife, who is proud that he is going to defend Lou in Washington until he confesses to a second bout of wishful infidelity, this time somewhat more than wishful. Louise's contemptuous reaction is that he'd gone out "to play doctor with the first girl he could lay his hands on" (seemingly an indelicate reference to Miller's first sexual experience with Monroe). In justification he blames his wife for turning away from him in bed. "Look Quentin," she says, "You want a woman to provide—an atmosphere . . . and you'll fly around in a constant bath of praise." Sorry, she says, "I am not a praise machine . . . and I'm not your mother! I am a separate person!"

This element of otherness, an awareness of other people and an involvement with them becomes an essential element in the play, one that Quentin (and by extension, Miller) finds hard to grasp. Quentin is intimate with other people only as society, and in that sense alone he can and does feel responsible for them. But his pathological detachment insulates him from other people as individuals. "When you've finally become a separate person," he cries, meaning an individual apart from society, "what the hell is there?" Maturity, his wife snaps—she means interaction with people. To her way of thinking a separate person can contact separate people; to her, caring about society and caring about other people are part of the same principle. Instead of total self-absorption she says, "You know another person exists."

Sexual passion being simpler to deal with—and succumb to—his mind again shifts gears, bringing him to the day when he met his second wife, Maggie, as he sat on a bench alongside Central Park. She approaches, looking for a Fifth Avenue bus stop and at the outset this beautiful young woman is both refreshingly unspoiled and scatterbrained ("I would like a dog . . . if I had a way to keep it, but I don't even have a refrigerator") while Louise bitterly reappears, "You think reading your brief is *talking* to me?"

The young woman knows him; she is the switchboard operator in his office. She is also on perpetual sexual exhibition. Even as they chat a stranger tries to pick her up. That, she says, happens to her "pretty often . . . they talk to me, so I have to answer." She is blithely devoid of guile or subtlety, believing everyone, distrusting nobody. Shaking off this distracting thought of her, Quentin turns to his wife, kissing her before being reminded that he's missed a parents meeting at their daughter's school. He's also missed a telephone call from his senior partner. It seems that the firm isn't happy about his defending Lou before the Committee. His wife says, "If you feel this strongly about Lou, you probably will have to resign," adding, "You have to decide what you feel about a certain human being. For once in your life. And then maybe you'll decide what you feel about other human beings. . . . [And] I don't care where you were tonight."

He tells her that while he was never unfaithful, he possibly acts as though he is because he wants to stop judging everyone else's morals. With that laborious rationalization he foolishly describes to this already distrustful wife his uncomplicated sense of Maggie ("she was just *there* like a tree or a cat"). His foolishness is the playwright's intention, but so is his earnestness. The endlessly rationalizing Quentin views candor as a moral act. Savoring another woman doesn't offend his conscience as much as not admitting it to his wife. Virtuous too he believes is his defense of Lou at a time when opposing the Committee was in some quarters "a kind of treason." He adds, pleading for the marriage, "I had a tremendous wish to come to you. And you to me . . . this city is full of people rushing to meet one another. This city is full of lovers."

Despite his protestation of wanting the marriage to prevail, Louise is snagged on the story of the girl in the park. Miller, as playwright and not merely the reporter of his own life, appreciates her anger and presents her fairly while he has Quentin, so dense about his wife's feelings and insensitive to everyone else's, blurt out, "Alright . . . it would have been easy to make love to her. [But] I didn't because I thought of you." Louise, less than moved by that, responds, "What do you want, my congratulations?" and promptly evicts him from the marital bed. A telephone call then comes with the news that Lou has killed himself. Quentin admits that he is relieved and that he was not the true friend as advertised. "I'd have stuck it to the end but I hated the danger in it for myself." Consumed with these assorted guilts, he returns to the site he sees as representing all human guilt, the Nazi extermination camp, which, he tells the Listener, "is not some crazy aberration of human nature to me. I can easily see the perfectly normal contractors and their cigars, the carpenters, plumbers . . . laying the pipes to run the blood out . . . grateful that someone else will die, not they."

His thoughts return to his wife and her anger, but also to a sound awaiting him, the strangulated rasp of Maggie's sickly, "difficult" breathing. He insists to Louise that he has only been honest with her, but from her point of view, he has been trying to be married and single at the same time, succeeding only in being deceptive. She doesn't believe him when he says that he has been struggling to maintain the marriage. As a matter of fact, she says, she's "waiting for the struggle to begin," and as she hands him an armful of bedding to sleep in the living room, he launches a strong, act-ending soliloquy about honesty and its drawbacks. "How do you live? A workable lie? . . . from a clear conscience or a dead one? Not to see one's own evil—there's power! . . . to kill conscience . . . And in the morning, a dagger in [my] little girl's heart" (referring to his daughter's discovery of the rift).

And so as Maggie calls out for him, the first act ends. It is also where the second act starts, a cry from Maggie coinciding with his meeting Holga on her arrival from Germany. He is still wondering whether to risk another relationship as his parents appear and he delivers a speech that describes the instant in which this play is occurring.

> You ever felt you once saw yourself absolutely true? I may have dreamed it but I swear, I feel that somewhere along the line—for one split second—I saw

my life; what I had done, what had been done to me, and even what I ought to do.

Then he runs into Maggie for the first time in years. She idolizes him, as had his mother, who reappears to celebrate his reputation as a great and famous moral hero, her glorious son. "I saw a star, and it got bright, and brighter, and brighter! And suddenly it fell, like some real man had died, and you were being pulled out of me to take his place, and be a light, a light in the world!"

This is very close to what Miller's mother had actually said to him, and now it is Quentin's youth again and Father wants him to help out at the shop. "You've got Dan" for that, Mother says, adding Quentin "wants a life!" As his brother loses out on college to stay and work and care for their father, Quentin remarks, "Yes, good men stay . . . although they die there," whereupon he is with Maggie, who has become a famous and famously sexy television star but also increasingly neurotic, fearing, in Marilyn Monroe's words (as she does several times in the play), that she is "a joke to most people." Recalling her desolate childhood, she gushes over him while his wife Louise is saying "The word is tart" and Quentin berates himself for even being attracted to Maggie, "Trying to take herself seriously! Why did I lie to her, play this cheap benefactor?" but he knows why—her heat and her reverence for him ("You're like a god!"). She saves clippings about his courageous liberalism and he patiently teaches her elementary concepts such as the meaning of "moral," which he simplifies for her as "To live the truth." She sighs, "That's you," to start a sequence that hopscotches in time as Quentin's memory springs from childhood to the present and from Louise to Maggie to Holga.

He is yanked back to a childhood betrayal when his parents tricked him into going for a walk with the maid while they took his brother ("because he's older") to Atlantic City for a weekend. That memory has also stayed with him, the psyche treating all hurts as equal. "God," he wonders, "why is betrayal the only truth that sticks? I adored that woman [Mother]. It's monstrous I can't mourn her!"

In such a time warp tense disappears. Quentin invokes the temptation of Maggie, the ingenuous whore ("I was with a lot of men but I never got anything for it. It was like charity"). He too is a naif in the innocence of his moral pretensions, for even as he struggles to resist her sexual magnetism, he invites it. "Don't be afraid to call me" he tells her, "if you need any help." His brother Dan says much the same thing to him, which is yet another reminder to Quentin of what a fraud he is, as when pretending to be sensitive by assuring Maggie that he could never laugh at anyone (like her). "I came to her like Dan—his goodness! No wonder I can't find myself!"

Midway through the second act, though, with the launching of the Quentin-Maggie relationship the play's time traveling is largely set aside. The scenes begin to cohere into a more sequential pattern, effectively but in a way that is inconsistent with the earlier dramatics. The story makes up for it as the affair with Maggie evolves. She swears her love. Experienced with married men, she buys odorless soap that won't arouse a wife's suspicions. Now he himself is summoned to testify before the Committee while she lies at his feet, kissing his trousers, begging to go to Washington with him, if only to be waiting naked in their hotel room, and he tells Holga, "It's all true, but it isn't the truth. I loved that girl."

Then he is marrying Maggie and in a powerful stretch of writing Miller paints a picture of Marilyn Monroe and her collapse that is so convincing, vivid and compelling that it poisoned his play's reception and stained his reputation in America for decades. Here is the portrait of a woman careening downhill from a peak of wedding day joy. "Good God!" Quentin cries on that day, "To come home every night—to you!" And she believes, "I have a king! But there's people who're going to laugh at you!" "Not any more, dear," he promises her. "They're going to see what I see." He helps to overcome her altar's edge doubts—her suspicions and insecurities—and then they are in a house that she is renovating, heedless of the cost; and they are dealing with her career, for he is in some ways becoming her manager. "Oh." She sighs. "I'm going to be a good wife, Quentin. I just get nervous sometimes that I'm . . . only bringing you my problems." Those problems are increasingly his, her demands for love that arrive as jealousy or as unfocused rage, her excessive drinking, the ordering of him to perform nasty tasks, such as firing musicians whom she suspects of sabotaging her singing. She is obsessed with a guru who is plainly a stand-in for Lee Strasberg; she is jealous of Quentin's love for his daughter; he is growing obsequious while she is becoming increasingly abusive. It is not unlike Mother's treatment of Father. "Should never have gotten married," Maggie snarls. "Every man I ever knew they hate their wives" and "Your mother tells me I'm getting fat . . . Slap her down." Finally, "What are you trying to make me think, I'm crazy? I'm not crazy! . . . I'm not going to work tomorrow . . . Look, you don't want me. What the hell are you doing here?"

Beyond the thickness of her drunken rage Quentin's mind registers *staying there*. He knows his history of abandoning people and, as if trying to convince himself that he has changed, tells Maggie "I'm here, and I stick it, that's what I am." She is now staggering under a mix of pills and liquor, while suggesting that he may be gay, dazedly asking him to leave— "Whyn't you beat it?" He carries her to a bed and lays her down, telling the audience, "If there is love, it must be limitless."

Time takes another turn and Mother is again calling Father an idiot, now in public, just as Maggie has started doing with Quentin, and then Lou is on a subway platform shouting Quentin's name as he leaps to his death. Abandonment comes in all these shades and shapes, whether as parents leaving a child behind on a holiday trip or as Quentin leaving his father and brother for college and freedom or Lou being left undefended. (Not included among these desertions is Quentin's abandonment of his first family.) And so the play returns to memories of Maggie in their cottage at the beach. "I was going to kill myself just now," she tells Quentin. Her only chance, he says, is "to start to look at what you're doing." Frightened that he will commit her to an institution, she begins to swallow pills but then begs him to stay. "We are separate people," he says, as if in defense of egoism and speaking of himself rather than of others. "I tried not to be, but finally one is—a separate person. I have to survive too." Thus the play's essential tension—the imperative to feel for another person, or *otherness*, as opposed to the *selfness* necessary for survival.

She lapses into a fantasy of her own childhood. "I want more cream puffs. And my birthday dress? If I'm good? Mama?" Drunk, reeling from the pills, she pleads with him to stay, even while fearing the worst—"Where you going to put me?" He is the only one, she says, who can be trusted with her pills. Right, he says,

> and then we fight, and then I give them up, and you take your death from me. Something in you has been setting me up for a murder. Do you see it? But now I'm going away; so you're not my victim anymore. It's just you and your hand.

She goes on,

> You know when I wanted to die? When I read what you wrote, kiddo, two months after we were married, kiddo . . . I was married to a king . . . and there's his desk . . . and there's his handwriting. "The only one I will ever love is my daughter."

He wrote that, he explains, because she'd called him "cold, remote." Hey, she snaps, "Don't mix me up with Louise," and he says, "That's just it. That I could have brought two women to the same accusation . . . that I could not love. And I wrote it down, like a letter from hell. . . . Maggie, we were both born of many errors [but] a human being has to forgive himself."

Resorting to sex, her first line of defense—and attack—she begs him to lie on top of her *just to keep her warm*. "It isn't my love you want anymore," he says. "It's my destruction." With that they struggle as she tries to swallow the rest of the pills—"Drop them, you bitch! You won't kill me!"—and, Miller wrote in a stage direction, *his hand, of its own volition, begins to squeeze her throat*. In Maggie's hysteria she screams, "You tried to kill me, mister . . . You're on the end of a long line."

Turning calmly to the audience, Quentin points out that "Barbiturates kill by suffocation . . . The diaphragm is paralyzed"—the rattling sound he had heard in her throat—and it made him glad, "like the footfalls of my coming peace . . . How is that possible? I loved that girl!" Maggie didn't die that time ("Her doctor tells me she had a few good months") but, he says to

Holga, he killed her just the same by turning his back, running out, saving himself.

"And no man lives," Quentin quietly says, as he stands in the cemetery at the former Nazi death camp, "who would not rather be the sole survivor of this place than all its finest victims! Who can be innocent again on this mountain of skulls?" He now knows that "we are all dangerous," but

> is the knowing all? To know . . . that we meet unblessed; not in some garden of wax fruit and painted trees, that lie of Eden, but after, after the Fall, after many, many deaths. Is the knowing all? And the wish to kill is never killed, but with some gift of courage one may look into its face when it appears, and with a stroke of love—as to an idiot in the house—forgive it; again and again . . . forever?

His last words, and the play's, are at a beginning. They are said about Holga. "She'll know what I mean," and then she tells him, "Hello," and he responds, "Hello."

In addition to *After The Fall* the inaugural season of the Lincoln Center Repertory Theater was to include Eugene O'Neill's seldom produced *Marco Millions* and a new play by S. N. Behrman, *But for Whom, Charlie*. The company was chosen with those three plays in mind. Some of the first actors to be signed, Geraldine Page and Maureen Stapleton, for instance, dropped out as the theater's construction dragged on. Those who stayed included Jason Robards, Jr., David Wayne, Hal Holbrook, Ralph Meeker and Faye Dunaway, who was not yet a movie star and was understudying Barbara Loden in the role of Maggie. The twelve weeks of rehearsals—far more than Broadway's usual—were scheduled to begin in October, anticipating an opening date in January 1964.

On the eve of rehearsals the producer Robert Whitehead got "the most bewildering" telephone call from the playwright. "Jesus," Miller said, "It just hit me. I'm awfully worried that this is going to seem like a play about Marilyn."

A "stunned" Whitehead said, "Of course they're going to think it's a play about Marilyn, Arthur. How could they not?"

"That's not the play I'm writing," he insisted. "What do we do about that?"

"It's a little late," said Whitehead. "We're going into rehearsal. You must be really crazy to be suddenly concerned about this." And the producer did think that this eleventh hour realization by the playwright was "almost obtuse . . . I thought, 'My God, doesn't the man know what he was writing?'" But a playwright, he concluded, does not always recognize the basis of what he is writing and "It's almost as if you have to believe it's someone else in order to write it." Perhaps, he thought, Miller was concentrating on the lesson drawn rather than the reality itself, as if he were saying, "I hope the truth of the play won't be destroyed by the facts behind it." But the actual and vivid identification of Maggie with Marilyn Monroe, while being the last thing to occur to the author, would be the first to occur to audiences and critics.

Rehearsals were held in one of Broadway's busier working halls, the two top loft floors at Central Plaza, so called because of the kosher restaurant on the street level. On the first day of work a long table was placed in front of the big windows overlooking lower Second Avenue. The newspaper people were asked to leave, although not before Miller told one of them, "All of my plays are autobiographical. This one less so." Then he sat down in the center of the table, flanked by Kazan and Whitehead. None in the facing company of twenty-five actors had yet read the play and the second act still hadn't been seen by either Kazan or Whitehead.

With the room settling to a hush Elia said, "Hello, my name is Elia Kazan, and some of you know this play is about an informer; and some of you know that I am an informer. Those of you who didn't know, know it now." That said, he continued,

> In this play, the real is the unreal. The psychoanalyst—the only "real" person who is in the "present"—is not there. He is the least real. On the other hand, the remembered figures are very real and affect the action. Not only are they in the action but they affect the course of Quentin. . . . There is no scenery. . . . The *rule* throughout is how the mind works, what the mind sees, remembers. The place is the inside of the mind. The life is the life which goes on within the mind. It is swift, immediate, very "sketchy"—the opposite of ponderous.

Ponderous was exactly the reaction Kazan feared about Quentin's philosophizing soliloquies. Miller meanwhile opened the 106-page leather-bound script and began to read ("a terrible reader," Jason Robards thought). When the playwright was finished, the Repertory Theater of Lincoln Center had begun to exist.

From the outset *After the Fall* was treated as autobiographical by everyone except the man who wrote it. "Arthur always talked about Quentin as if he were someone else," Whitehead said, "but the actors all thought of Maggie as Marilyn and they were calling the play *Miller's High Life*." Robards, who had the enormous role of Quentin, wavered between dislike for the playwright and concern that "there ought to be more give and take between actors and authors [but] I guess they think we're all shit . . . If Arthur were more like [his sister] Joan—now *there's* warmth." Nor was it a matter of Robards feeling awkward because he was playing a character based on Miller. "I chose to disregard that," he said. "I chose to keep that *over there*, somewhere." Aside from a disinterest in mimicry, he simply didn't connect with the man. "It's real difficult to get close to Arthur. He's always remote. Now it might have been the elements. There's Gadg. There's Barbara [Loden] playing the part of [Marilyn,] the girl that Gadg introduced him to" and, Robards continued, there was HUAC and Kazan's history as an informer.

> I certainly did think it was a little odd that [Miller] was working with Kazan. Especially since Gadg had been mixed up with Monroe. And in those first weeks of rehearsal, I thought that Gadg was shutting down. In fact, I almost quit the show. The atmosphere was so bad. I'd go off and get drunk. I said to Whitehead, "Get Miller out of the rehearsal." And they did. There was this thing underneath, he and Gadg, even though they'd said they had settled their differences.

Robards told his wife, Betty (Lauren Bacall), "It's a whole snake pit. I'm in a nest with *snakes*, here. I don't know *what's* going on at rehearsal." And then, he recalled, "*I* started misbehaving," by which he meant drinking. Kazan and Whitehead threatened to replace him with George C. Scott, another well-known stage alcoholic. Robards remembered telling them, "Why don't you get George C. Scott? That'll be great. He'll *never* show up." Scott was considered and rejected, and Montgomery Clift too, but Robards stayed.

Early in the rehearsal process Kazan received a "Late Bulletin" from Miller. It noted, about Quentin, "His innocence. Puzzling things out. Awkward. Childlike. All in all a bit of a schnook." Another late bulletin suggested that Louise "shivers with moral idealism." Then after seeing a November 10 run-through of his first act Miller told Kazan he found Quentin

> a little too un-guilty in relation to Louise's accusations. He [should] always believe that she is just a little bit right. He should generally be more defensive with her. He has a "free floating guilt" and especially through the first scene one should feel that one is watching a guilty man. In fact Quentin has long ago, and from the beginning made Louise the custodian of his conscience and just to look at her sometimes in her rectitude arouses his sense that he is guilty.

This was beginning to sound like Hickey in *The Iceman Cometh*, a role that was formidably identified with Jason Robards, and it wasn't the only reminder of Eugene O'Neill. The device of a character speaking his thoughts in soliloquy is an essential element of the playwright's *Strange Interlude*.

Miller was well aware that his play's soliloquies might be problematic. He asked Kazan for "more sense of man talking to himself." He accepted with qualification the director's approach that Quentin was talking to a psychiatrist but, Miller added,

> When he talks to [the] Analyst it is to himself. More internalness, interiority [*sic*]. Give him moments of silent thought. Make audience reach out for him. He now reaches for them too much . . . Quentin should summon up the memory figures more. As though they came out of his interior dialogues with self . . . there is too much *lecturing* of the listener.

Miller was sensing a problem with the play but was too close to do anything about it. Kazan could have helped him more there.

A play in rehearsal is a world unto itself, but just as this company finally began dealing with the second act, reality burst into the playhouse. On November 23 President Kennedy was assassinated in Dallas and when the news hit the rehearsal studio, work was shut down. All the Broadway theaters went dark. "Everybody collapsed," Robards remembered. "The next day, I was standing at the mirror knotting my tie when the phone rang and it was Gadg. 'We can't work today either,' he said."

A different sort of shock awaited Robards when rehearsals resumed.

> One day, just after a run-through, we were told that we were to go up to Arthur's at the Chelsea Hotel—to do cuts. It had been running four hours. Bob Whitehead and Elia were there. Barbara [Loden] and I sat on the floor and had a couple of glasses of wine. All of a sudden the hair dresser came in. He and Gadg took Barbara and went into Arthur and Inge's bedroom. I turned to the stage manager and asked, "What's happening, what's the cut?"
>
> He said, "Wait a minute."
>
> Arthur never said that she was Marilyn or that Quentin was him. Now Barbara came out with a blonde wig and she looked just like Marilyn. . . . She didn't say anything good or bad about it, but I was in shock . . . I went in early the next day so that she could talk to me about it. She said, "Well, that's the way it's got to be."

In hindsight Whitehead regretted the decision.

> We had endless discussions about it. We kept saying, she ought to have Monroe qualities, but not mimic. I think it had something to do with Barbara and Gadg. Arthur went along but we always kept talking, during rehearsal, about how it was a mistake to make her hair seem like Marilyn's. Barbara's natural features did the rest, but it was the hair that did it.

It was not only the hair. The way Kazan ran her performance, she whispered like Marilyn, she cooed like Marilyn, she moved like Marilyn, she was unmistakably portraying Marilyn Monroe. Miller would later insist incredibly, "It honestly never occurred to me that anyone was trying for a literal resemblance, or that the audience would see one, because I didn't see one." Nevertheless, Whitehead told Kazan, "It's going to be so related to Marilyn that I feel it's going to be a problem for us." Elia, always pragmatic and now eager for a success, replied, "It'll also be an asset in terms of public relations." Perhaps his perspective was beholden to theatrical effect or perhaps he wanted to make sure everyone did see Maggie as Marilyn Monroe. As "an asset," he was never more correct in terms of box office. He was also never more mistaken in terms of public relations.

Once the company was comfortable with lines, Kazan began putting *After the Fall* on its feet and setting it to movement. This is a particularly talky play and he wrote himself a note, "There must be a lot of simultaneous action, more than indicated in script. These people live continuously in his mind. They don't black out and come in. They only go from the background to the foreground and then back to a half light." He added,

> The law of entrances and exits, of overlaps, is the way the mind "works." That's all. Start scenes: as sound of bare feet on floor, sound of phone ringing, phone knocked off carriage, Frank Sinatra music, etc. Which are all the sounds he remembers. Also the sound of smashing glass ware! These elements are "separated" the way they are in the memory.

Kazan suggested to Barbara Loden that Maggie "stand with her legs apart. She unhooks her bra, releases by fits, stretches like an animal, rolls in the bed, crouches over Quentin." When Loden asked whether Maggie means "fuck me" when she tells Quentin she'd do anything for him, Kazan gave her a pantomime.

> The "fuck me, please" has become part of something more important. She has found her savior . . . What will happen when I direct this scene is that after Maggie says the last line in the scene ("Yes, you are like a God") I'll ask [you] to freeze into some attitude of adoration. Maggie will . . . offer him her whole life. I want her to kneel before him and slowly and gently take off his shoes . . . Then, as she unlaces the first shoe, Quentin will walk away and leave her there on the floor, unlacing his "shoes" and looking up at "him" adoringly throughout. He meantime comes forward and makes the speech to the audience.

Kazan's notes for Mariclare Costello, who was playing the first wife, suggested that Louise be "sitting, waiting, winding a clock. Combing her hair rather hopelessly. Since she judges perhaps she is more present than anyone else. She is dominated by the 'ought to.'" And, he added, "there is an outstanding element of revenge in Louise. For [her], Quentin is changing for the worse." The director might have been reminded of when Mary Miller had told him, "Art is acquiring all of your bad habits and none of your good ones."

In self-exposure Kazan jotted down a note for Ralph Meeker, playing Mickey, the character based on Kazan himself. Mickey, wrote Kazan in plain projection, first is

> a great and natural hedonist, full of energy and pleasure because he is not crippled with puritanism and the consequent guilt. Mickey is a "real guy" whom [Quentin] liked enormously . . . then dropped like a hot rock . . . and who aged, changed, after being dropped . . . expects Quentin to destroy him.

Yet for all these painstaking thoughts, Kazan seemed distracted during rehearsal and not at all the director he had once been. Virginia Kaye, who was playing Quentin's mother, could remember when he had been "a wonderful director for actors. And he was a playwright's director, but with *After the Fall,* he was there—but he was never *there*."

Actors who had suffered the blacklist, however, knew that he was there. At The Little Red School House, where *fink* and *rat* and *naming names* were everyday terms among the sadly knowledgeable student body, seventeen-year-old Bobby Miller heard about Kazan from his classmates. Now in tenth grade at the high school he was approached by Lisa Gilford, both of whose parents, Jack and Madeleine, were survivors of McCarthyism. "My parents want to know," she said, "how your father could work with Kazan."

The next day Bobby came back with an answer, "My father says that Elia Kazan has changed. He's sorry."

Madeleine Gilford would remember, "When Lisa brought that story home, Jack the quiet one, said to her, 'You tell Bobby Miller to tell his father that if Mr. Kazan takes a half page advertisement apologizing, like he did explaining why he finked, then we'll believe him.'"

Kazan, as rehearsals reached the midpoint, scrawled across a page in his notebook, "Molly Kazan had a stroke at about seven PM on December 13, 1963. She died in the emergency ward at Bellevue at 5:37 PM on December 14th." It was nine days after his wife's sixty-second birthday and she left him with four children. Elia, then fifty-four, would marry Barbara Loden a few years later.

When it became obvious that the Vivian Beaumont Theatre was not going to be finished in time for the play's scheduled premiere (it would not be completed for another year), an impatient Kazan and Whitehead convinced their board of directors to underwrite the building of a temporary theater. The chosen site was Washington Square Park in Greenwich Village. In just six weeks construction workers put together a prefabricated metal shell that contained a 1,100-seat replica of the interior dimensions of the company's future home. It was named the ANTA-Washington Square Theatre for the American National Theater and Academy and it was where the homeless Repertory Theater of Lincoln Center would play the inaugural season. This theater would be remembered ever after as being superior to the elaborate one that was finally built in Lincoln Center.

After the Fall was scheduled to begin its world premiere performance at 6:30 on January 23, 1964. When Arthur and Inge arrived at five o'clock,

Elia was already there. As the performance began, they stirred restlessly, shifting from the prop room to a dressing room to the cinder block corridor connecting the two. The backstage areas of the ANTA-Washington Square Theatre were even starker than most, reflecting the hasty construction and temporary nature of the place. The walls were bare, the carpeting thin and industrial. In back the place looked more like a locker room than a theater.

With the curtain up and the play progressing, the director, the playwright and the wife stared up at the small metal loudspeakers that were carrying the actors' voices. There was little conversation other than the occasional murmuring of "marvelous," or "wonderful," and a voiced concern about Jason Robards's hoarseness. Miller pushed his glasses up over his brow and rubbed an eye with the palm of his right hand, a familiar gesture in moments of stress. Both he and Kazan seemed overcome by a "simultaneous weariness, not despair," or so an observer remembered. Then it was over and Lady Bird Johnson, the country's First Lady of two months, escorted by Adlai Stevenson, led the audience in applause. Afterward she went backstage to congratulate the cast, "wowing" Robards. "What a great lady!" he remembered. "Sexy and funny and, oh, she was something!"

Arthur's father came backstage too ("a tall, lovely guy," Robards remembered, "with a tie and a fedora") but Arthur's brother, Kermit, was alienated by the play, evidently reminded of painful family history. His wife, Frances, seemed to side with Arthur. The morning after seeing *After the Fall* she sent him a note.

> Watching a great play I was supposed to experience a change of state. It never happened until last night. . . . You could not supply the courage I hope to find within myself as you did . . . Some day Kermit too will find the words to tell you how he feels. You touched very deep chords within him.

Miller also received congratulations from Martin Luther King, and, most grotesquely, considering the references to Auschwitz and the Holocaust, from Werner von Braun, the Nazi rocket scientist who had switched sides after his country lost the war. For some bewildering reason, Miller had sent him a copy of the play. As for the critical reaction, the press had been heralding the play and the subject matter for weeks. No drama in history, *Newsweek* dramatically reported,

> has been so eagerly awaited since the widow of Eugene O'Neill decided to countermand O'Neill's dying wish that *Long Day's Journey into Night* be withheld from the stage until a quarter century after he was gone. The promise was that *After the Fall* came out of the same autobiographical inferno as O'Neill's shattering record of the wreck of his own family.

Then the *Newsweek* axe fell.

> Instead of the mighty exorcism of guilt and storming of fate remembered from O'Neill, this audience got a documentary of one man's life with the man himself addressing the audience in a blurred rhetoric whose dominant note sounded like self-apology.

That was only the start of the critical assault. Instead of being recognized, like it or not, as a unique work of artistic ambition, *After the Fall* was perceived as two acts of confessional egoism, self-aggrandizement and the very heartlessness that it was desperate to expiate. In *The New Yorker* Kenneth Tynan most articulately led the attacks on the play's vanity, calling it "extravagantly personal . . . a tinted blow up of Mr. Miller himself." Tynan continued,

> He tells us the story of his life in a series of unchronological flashbacks linked by passages of self-flagellating narration. . . . His capacity for self-accusation is endless, and the operative syllable is self. You get the feeling that if only Mr. Miller's hero could expiate his multiple guilts, the future of Western civilization would be assured.

The New Republic's Robert Brustein raised the banner for Marilyn Monroe. Not content to merely abuse the play, he took its autobiographical aspects as license to criticize the playwright as well. *After the Fall,* he wrote, is

> A three and one half hour breach of taste, a confessional autobiography of embarrassing explicitness . . . an important reason for the tediousness of the evening is the author's superficial treatment of . . . "Maggie" Monroe. . . . It is astonishing that [he] could live with this unfortunate woman for over four years and yet be capable of no greater insights into her character . . . there is a misogynistic strain in the play which the author does not seem to recognize, nor does he recognize how much self-justification is hidden in his apparent remorse. . . . He has created a shameless piece of tabloid gossip, an act of exhibitionism which makes us all voyeurs.

For a final flourish he added the play is "first of all a wretched piece of dramatic writing."

Is a play's autobiographical aspect fair game for critics? Brustein's mentor, Eric Bentley, believed that the "critic shouldn't be concerned with whether it is autobiography but just with what kind of a play does it make." Tynan and Brustein were both formidable professional theater critics, but in this case they tended to discuss the ostensibly real prototypes rather than the characters in the play. Moreover, both critics seemed equally susceptible to the spotlight of reviewing a highly publicized play relevant to a movie star and a sensational real-life situation. Tynan was lured into critical pyrotechnics, while Brustein gave in to moral breast-beating; neither did his considerable reputation justice.

There would be some approval of *After the Fall*, particularly in England, where Miller's stock remained high. Of a later production Irving Wardle would write in London's *Sunday Independent* that Miller seemed to have declared

> an abdication from control of the past, that is, knowing what happened . . . knowing himself to be a prisoner of his own perceptions. . . . This is not the basis for the vigorous linear narrative proceeding to a conclusion where the writer strikes the patiently waiting nail on the head. It is, however, concerned with truth, and with creating dramatic patterns that fit the facts rather than the writer's convenience.

In academic circles Professor Dennis Welland of the University of Manchester was convinced that the play was "dramatic literature, deserving of closer critical attention than is possible in the theater. Its text can reveal to the student a carefully patterned structure and an integrity of approach." Such scholarly appreciation hardly mattered, though, in the commercial New York theater, where the devastating opinions of Tynan and Brustein were but the crest of a tidal wave of bruised sensitivities and offended principle, initiating the consignment of Arthur Miller to an American cultural purgatory. Of all the plays that Miller wrote, *After the Fall* is the most difficult and demands the most thorough and painstaking criticism, yet one's instant reaction inevitably centers on Marilyn Monroe. In the freshness of her tragedy the death cried out for a guilty party and the likeliest candidate was this dealer in guilt, a playwright who evidently had the ego to beat his breast at—but not actually at—her graveside. His play was seen as an aggrandizement of and an attack upon a beloved figure of vulnerability who was now dead and defenseless. Its vivid and cruel depiction of her made *After the Fall* seem sensationalistic and caused its author to be reviled by Marilyn Monroe's newest defenders among the literati, so many of whom had previously ridiculed her. In her life Marilyn Monroe may have been an object of derision, but in death she became loved beyond her most desperate wishes. Freshly sanctified as a goddess martyr, finally appreciated much as she deserved to be, her mistreatment at Miller's hands provided opportunity for defending her while punishing him with a vengeance. His image of moral integrity was destroyed as his portrait of Marilyn Monroe in *After the Fall* ushered in decades of hostility toward his work. Arthur Miller the playwright, the political figure, the celebrity—all of them were being buried under this storm of righteous rage.

"It is clear," Miller wrote to Kazan, "the Marilyn business has effectively overwhelmed the play for almost all the 'critics' and probably a good part of the audience as well." He was right. In addition to the critics' responses there would always be a sense of voyeurism in its audiences and an atmosphere of theatergoers having bought tickets for the privilege of righteous indignation. Feeling "charged with cruelty toward the memory of Marilyn

Monroe" by people who "cry in outrage that Maggie's suffering should be connected with Marilyn's," Miller felt obliged—just two weeks after the play opened—to defend himself in *Life* Magazine, the most popular if not the weightiest of journals. On its glossy illustrated pages he accused Monroe's defenders of hypocrisy. "It is in many cases precisely those who scoffed at her ambitions and in some cases those who were overtly vicious to her both personally and in print who now cry in outrage that Maggie's suffering should be connected with Marilyn's."

Even in this essay (which is not included in *The Theater Essays of Arthur Miller*) he refused to concede any connection between Maggie and Marilyn. "Despite appearances," he wrote in his perfected, between-the-lines way, "*After the Fall* is no more and no less autobiographical" than any of his previous plays. Of course all of them were autobiographical in one way or another but the facts had never been so publicly known. With like evasiveness he disingenuously added that his play's "other characters . . . are drawn, not reported." Miller insisted that the drama was only about "the inability of a man to live with the good and evil in his own nature" and that his protagonist, far from justifying his innocence, recognizes his "part in the evil he sees and abhors . . . taking on guilt even for what he did not do."

Such denials and defenses were evidently of little interest to *Life*'s editors, who laid out the essay with photographs of Miller with Monroe and pictures of Barbara Loden looking like Marilyn. Moreover, Miller's denial was further undercut by the headline "With Respect for Her Agony—But with Love," which any reader would easily take to mean Monroe, even though the words, drawn from the essay, refer to Maggie.

Some years later, in summer 1967, after six months of negotiation the film rights to *After the Fall* were sold to Paramount Pictures, with a Miller stipulation prohibiting any reference to Marilyn Monroe in publicity or advertising. This demand had undone an earlier sale to MGM. In the present case the purpose, according to a July 13, 1967, story in the *Hollywood Reporter*, was to establish "a safeguard against casting the leading role with a blonde look-alike of Marilyn—as was done in the stage play. Miller maintains final approval on the actress selected to play the part of Maggie, universally recognized as a projection of the late 20th Century Fox star."

The picture was never made.

If *After the Fall* is seen only as being about Marilyn Monroe and Arthur Miller, then it must be taken as his assumption of responsibility for her death. This is murder by abandonment, the result of his discovering immorality by giving in to temptation and passion with this vulnerable and unmalicious Eve. The play therefore is about his expulsion from the moral paradise of his first marriage, when he was innocent and virtuous and his life was dedicated to bettering the world. If the play is pure autobiography, it is about Miller moving on and surviving in two senses—living on after a spouse's death and enduring after a fall from grace.

But *After the Fall* is not just the story of Marilyn Monroe and Arthur Miller. It is also a play, a creation much the same as Strindberg's *The Dance of Death*, Williams's *The Glass Menagerie* and O'Neill's *Long Day's Journey into Night*, all of which are autobiographical. But we do not watch these plays with the authors' lives in mind because their lives are not part of our general experience. The same cannot be said of *After the Fall*. Miller's marriage to Marilyn Monroe became part of the national lore; their life had been international reading and Marilyn Monroe was becoming a twentieth-century myth, more vivid in death than in her lifetime. Movie exhibitors built festivals around her, biographers made an industry of her and intellectuals gave her cultural significance. Diana Trilling in her *Claremont Essays* wrote of "the myth of Marilyn Monroe" and the significant irony of her dying "alone, with no date, on a Saturday night," while remarking, "of Ernest Hemingway, for example, I feel much as I do of Marilyn Monroe."

Probably, no matter where or when produced, *After the Fall* will always evoke Monroe. When in 1990 it was produced at the Royal National Theatre in London, the director, Michael Blakemore, attacked the problem by casting Josette Simon, a black actress, as Maggie. His intention, nearly thirty years after Marilyn Monroe's death, was "to liberate the play from associations with [her] and to insure that its real meaning was not overlooked in a welter of celebrity speculation." While Maggie, he said, had "in fact been based on Monroe, as so many of Arthur's characters are based on his father or his mother. . . . I think the play, whatever it's derived from, has a life of it's own and that's the life you've got to try and realize."

Blakemore felt that "Kazan, a director I much admire, made a terrible mistake in encouraging Barbara Loden to do a Monroe." As to Blakemore's success in not doing a Monroe, it was the opinion of David Thacker, who directed almost every other Miller play in London, that this and all such attempts were doomed to failure. "Josette Simon," said Thacker, "is an absolutely beautiful, stunning, sexy black woman. She came on the stage and *within ten seconds* it was Marilyn Monroe. No matter how many times Arthur says that it isn't Monroe—there she is."

After the Fall is left as a paradox. If seen without Monroe in mind, it would stand as a flawed but powerful major work, but except for the rare place in the world that is beyond the reach of American popular culture, it cannot be seen without putting Marilyn Monroe in mind. As long as she is remembered it will seem invasive of her privacy and a work of confessional sensationalism, and even half a century after her death her image remains iconic. Yet even as the power of the play is strained by this undertow of celebrity recognition, the recognition and undertow themselves become part of it. The result is a unique equation of autobiographical and fictional drama, and a memory play that draws on the spectator's own attitude toward past events set in a unique dramatic form. Thus the sum and history of *After the Fall*, this considerable, unwieldy, ingenious, naked, unique and referential play, so singular and significant among the works of Arthur Miller, so essentially problematic.

As for Elia Kazan and the revitalization of his theatrical career, by the time the Vivian Beaumont Theatre was ready, he and Whitehead would be forced to resign as being *too Broadway* and lacking in classical credentials for the Repertory Theater of Lincoln Center—and Kazan would never again direct for the stage.

17. Price

IN FEBRUARY 1964 Arthur Miller took his wife Inge to Europe, combining a vacation with a visit to her family, and leaving behind, not incidentally, the fuss and fury surrounding *After the Fall*. In Germany he learned that Nazi war criminals were being tried in Frankfurt am Main. The accused had been officers of Heinrich Himmler's dreaded elite, the *SS*. Twenty-two of these paramilitary blackshirts were being charged with the murder of helpless Jews at the notorious Auschwitz–Birkenau concentration camp, and a "curious" Miller, having "never seen a real live Nazi," contacted the *New York Herald-Tribune* to propose covering the trial. He soon had his first reporting assignment since college days on the *Michigan Daily*, and the report appeared on Sunday, March 15, 1964. His Jewishness had been aroused.

> This trial will go on for about a year, during which time some 300 psychologically and physically scarred survivors will face the high tribunal in Frankfurt, living evidence of how one of the most educated, technically developed, and artistic nations in the world gave itself over to the absolute will of beings it is difficult to call human. And while that testimony fills the silent courtroom, and the world press prints its highlights, German industry will pour out its excellent automobiles, machine tools, electronic equipment, German theaters will excellently produce operas and plays, German publishers will put out beautifully designed books—all the visible signs and tokens of civilization will multiply and make even more abstract, more bewildering the answer to the riddle which the impassive faces of the accused must surely present to anyone who looks at them. How was it possible in a civilized country?

This time Miller didn't sound as if he and all of humanity shared the responsibility for the Holocaust. He must have decided, watching his first real live Nazis, that some crimes against humanity were more equal than others. Despite the recent battering he had taken for his moral exhibitionism, the Arthur Miller sense of decency evidently was intact, his righteousness undiminished. This could not have been easy, given the mockery and scorn that had been heaped on him.

Inevitably the indignant uproar over a thinly disguised Marilyn Monroe had resulted in a run on the *After the Fall* box office. Although Miller's status in the American intellectual and cultural community had suffered a body blow, good business consoled his producers. With a second season looming for the Repertory Theater of Lincoln Center, Whitehead and Kazan, unaware of their limited future, were eager for another new work from Arthur Miller. He wrote to Kazan from Paris on March 31, as always looking for material through research.

> I am going back tomorrow to Frankfurt, Germany. I may be wasting my time, but partly as a result of attending the Auschwitz trials there, and partly from my age-old fascination with Naziism as a human phenomenon, I have the feeling there is something there I can use. . . . I will stay a few days talking to prosecutors, lawyers, and others who have been up to their necks in some sinister stuff for years now.

He began the play soon after returning home in May, and finished it in three weeks. Written in one long (sixty-page) act, it wasn't the courtroom drama that might have been expected, possibly because the Nazi trials had already been the subject of a recent movie, *Judgment at Nuremberg*. Instead he found inspiration in a recollection by his former psychiatrist, Dr. Rudolph Loewenstein. A Holocaust survivor, Loewenstein had told him of a Jew who was rescued from the Nazis by a total stranger, a Christian who took his place in a police lineup. That self-sacrificing man, were he to be made a central character in a play, would have to be the Jew's opposite, someone with the least to fear from the Nazis. Miller got the prototype from Inge, who remembered a prince she had known in Austria, a Christian aristocrat who had refused to cooperate with the Nazis and paid for it.

These were people whom Miller could neither interview nor research. Now having a climactic event and two central characters, he was left with the challenge of inventing their personalities and the story that would lead up to that climax. Such invention had never been his strength but he wrote the play anyway and called it *Incident at Vichy*—a title not unlike *Judgment at Nuremberg*—describing it as a "companion piece" to *After the Fall*. The relationship between the two plays has to do with guilt, altruism, self-sacrifice and responsibility for one's fellow man. There certainly is no relationship in terms of dramatic approach, for unlike *After the Fall*, *Incident at Vichy* is a traditional drama. This might have been in part a matter of wariness. As Professor Orm Overland of the University at Bergen, Norway, wrote, "*Incident at Vichy*, written immediately after the critical disaster of *After the Fall* [is] clear and straightforward . . . no need for any Requiem or explanatory footnotes or narrator."

Whether or not it was a choice of caution, realism suited the new play's argumentative purposes. Having dealt with Jewishness only in the early novel *Focus* and never in a play (not since college, at least), Miller now planned to address the Holocaust itself. Only one notable drama had dealt with it in the twenty years since war's end—*The Diary of Anne Frank*. About that he felt, "There is something wrong when an audience can see a play about the Nazi treatment of a group of Jews hiding in an attic and come away feeling . . . gratification."

The scene is a Nazi detaining room in occupied France. Six men and a boy are awaiting interrogation. They have not been told why they are being held. Others are brought in, among them a bearded orthodox "Old Jew," a psychiatrist named Leduc and a prince, one Wilhelm Johann von Berg. Told only that their identification papers are to be examined, they suspect that for the Jews among them the outcome will be forced labor camps, but who is Jewish? All are mum.

One of them recalls that while working in the railroad yards, he had heard about "a quiet roundup of Jews," and of people being locked inside freight cars. The psychiatrist Leduc says that occupied or not this is French territory and he's "never heard of them applying the Racial Laws down here." Nevertheless a professor from "The Race Institute" is there to serve the Nazis as an expert Jew spotter. Leduc, speaking of those with forged identification papers, says that "Jews are not a race, you know. They can look like anybody." This leads to a brief exchange about circumcision as an identifying feature—a bad idea because even if seriously intended, a dialogue about circumcision is bound to invite a sense of smirk.

The discussion turns to the phenomenon of Naziism and the fact that "many cultivated people . . . did become Nazis," and that the Communists aren't much better, having been evasive about Hitler "until the Nazis turned against Russia; then, in one afternoon it all changed into a sacred battle against tyranny." Miller had apparently reconsidered his admiration for the Soviet Union and its armies that had "saved Europe from a thousand years of Nazism." Then the talk turns to racism in general. "The Russians condemn the middle class, the English have condemned the Indians . . . every nation has condemned somebody because of his race, including the Americans and that they do to Negroes." Such arguments imply that the Holocaust is just another example of racism.

In a growing dread that it isn't forced labor but death camps that await the Jews, the men start at each other. "It's people like you," one accuses another, "who brought this on us. People who give Jews a reputation for subversion." The psychiatrist Leduc suggests that some Jews suffer from a victim complex. A Nazi officer coming among them—a "good" Nazi—claims that "This is all as inconceivable to me as it is to you," but he refuses to help them escape. He fears for his own life and isn't persuaded by Leduc's offer to in exchange remember him as "a decent German." He responds, "You—goddamned Jews! Like dogs, Jew-dogs. Why do you deserve to live more than I do?"

The officer's underlying anti-Semitism thus revealed, he holds a gun to the psychiatrist's head, but he is only drunk. The conversation then settles into a dialogue between the aristocratic, unimpeachably gentile von Berg and the Jewish psychiatrist Leduc, who sermonizes,

> I am only angry that I should have been born before the day when man has accepted his own nature; that he is *not* reasonable, that he is full of murder, that his ideas are only the little tax he pays for the right to hate and kill with a clear conscience.

An offended von Berg, feeling unjustly included in this universal guilt when he is deeply committed in his hatred of the Nazis, retorts that there are still good people in the Christian world, "people who would find it easier to die than stain one finger with this murder . . . People for whom everything is *not* permitted . . . (Desperately) I ask for your friendship."

Leduc is unsparing. "I have never analyzed a gentile who did not have, somewhere hidden in his mind, a dislike of if not a hatred for the Jews." Whether or not such distrust of Christians speaks for Miller, it leads to a statement of the play's theme and the connection with *After the Fall.*

> Jew is only the name we give to that stranger, that agony we cannot feel . . . Each man has his Jew; it is the other. And the Jews have their Jews. And now . . . you have yours—the man whose death leaves you relieved that you are not him, despite your decency.

When von Berg once again insists that he is not anti-Semitic, Leduc reminds him that his cousin "helped to remove all the Jewish doctors from the medical school." That was something the prince had conveniently forgotten but, says Leduc, "It's not your guilt I want, it's your responsibility . . . you might have done something."

The aristocrat, shattered, is at that moment summoned for interrogation. When he emerges with the white card that is his pass to freedom, he slips it to Leduc, who asks, "What will happen to you?" That does not deter the psychiatrist from fleeing with the pass, leaving the chief Nazi and von Berg to stare at each other for the final curtain.

Intended as the highlight of the Lincoln Center company's second season, *Incident at Vichy* went into rehearsal under the direction of Harold Clurman. Miller immediately sat the company down and read them the play. Then he elaborated on the ideas behind it, an approach that the director considered less than inspiring. "Actors," Clurman had noticed, "are seldom stimulated by this sort of exegesis," but he couldn't excite them himself either. "Talking about what a play meant to our lives," producer Whitehead said, "and what it meant to the world, and exciting actors with that—it was Harold's strongest point." But with *Incident at Vichy* the dramatic pickings were too slim, as a one-sided debate is not the most exciting of events. The characters in this play are essentially sounding boards responding to Leduc's pronouncements, and he was not even Miller's intended hero. The prince was, and "What he discovers in this [police detention center] is his own complicity with the force he despises . . . his own secret joy and relief that, after all, he is not a Jew." That is hardly the stuff of heroics. Nor is it the stuff of a believable character but Miller would later concede that he "was not attempting to delineate psychological types. The characters were functions of the society, and I wasn't interested in whether they had any itches or not." It was a far cry from what he had recently said, "A play of ideas only, to my mind, is no play. My task is to deliver up the experience."

Incident at Vichy offers ideas without the dramatic experience. Its hero is not heroic. He is the rescued, not the rescuer, and at that a kind of coward, accepting another's sacrifice for his own sake. The tension, suspense and suppressed fright that ought to have provided the atmosphere for a dramatic situation and the characters with "itches" who are necessary to bring a play to life are instead subordinated to polemics, and even the ideas are unfulfilled. Despite Miller's zeal to grasp the meaning of something that doesn't make sense—a tantalizing notion—he never comes to grips with the monstrous genocide. Even the prince's martyrdom becomes questionable; it contradicts the playwright's contention that survival governs all human behavior. Ever open to reason, Miller would come to agree, saying, "The prince in *Incident in Vichy* shouldn't have behaved the way he did. He should have saved himself. But when the logic doesn't work with some people, they save the world." His logic doesn't quite work either, but one knows what he means.

Another problem is that Miller's play doesn't answer the question he first asked, "How was it possible in a civilized country?" and as dramatic carpentry, the play has clumsy fittings. Why is the psychiatrist's life worth more than the aristocrat's life? There are also patent contrivances, the revelation, for instance, that the prince's cousin is a Nazi, and such awkward choices as the Professor of Jewishness calling "Next" as though he were a barber.

Staging the play, Clurman was not strong enough to edit Miller, nor was he creative or theatrical enough to inject life into this tutorial script. The director's notion of a villainous Nazi officer was a man with a swastika and a limp, lacking only an artificial hand and a monocle to complete the war movie cliché. Clurman's own introduction to a Miller collection has little to say about *Incident at Vichy*.

Its premiere was on December 3, 1964, and in the *New York Post* even the benign Richard Watts, Jr. rejected the play as "self serving and self indulgent," while summing up the critical consensus, which was a non-consensus. Some, Watts reported (Taubman in the *New York Times*), saw *Vichy* as "a play of great distinction" while others (Kerr in the *New York Herald-Tribune*) felt that it shed "little new light." The elite press was less ambivalent. Going beyond their traditional and important role as the reaction, as if lying in wait for Miller's next and reserving special venom for one of their own kind, these tougher-minded critics seemed to relish the assault that could be visited upon the besieged American liberal icon. Their dissatisfaction with *Incident at Vichy* could well have been reasonable were not these reviews steeped in vengeance. The play proved an easy mark with its conjectures and lectures. Robert Brustein, a critic with considerable influence beyond his small readership, was the acknowledged leader of the anti-Miller brigade. He wrote in *The New Republic*, "Arthur Miller has a new entry in the Guilt Sweepstakes" and proceeded to demolish *Incident at Vichy* as though it were cancerous, citing its "noisy virtue . . . moral flatulence." Uncontent once again with merely criticizing a play, Brustein attacked the playwright—"It returns the theater . . . to the thirties, a period the author seems never to have left." Thus was Miller—indisputably a major twentieth-century playwright—dispensed with in print.

While now securely out of favor with the intelligentsia, Arthur Miller still had academic defenders. His play's most questionable element—the sacrifice of the aristocrat's life for the Jew's—was seen by Professor Robert Corrigan as "the mark of Cain."

> The murderer within us cannot stand the thought that someone else could and would give up his life for our sake. Such an act makes our guilt unbearable by destroying that balance of payments which we have created in an effort to justify our guilt. We cannot permit ourselves to be in someone else's debt. There must always be a price. . . . That is why there must also always be a Jew. The ending of *Incident at Vichy* reveals that otherness is an ambiguous reality.

Such approval mattered little to Miller. He had been bred in the commercial theater and couldn't relate to "the professors [who] were regarding the drama from a so-called academic viewpoint—with its relentless standards of tragedy and so forth." These professors, he said, "would cry 'Kitsch!' at anything capable of being admired by more people than could fit into a classroom." The public was even less interested in such esoterica, but neither was it concerned with the intemperate attacks of the critical elite. As a simple matter of entertainment, *Incident at Vichy* had little audience appeal. It played out its scheduled engagement in the repertory and was forgotten, notable among Miller's works only as being the playwright's first assertion (at least in a play) of any feelings about Jewishness. He dedicated the published script to Robert Whitehead but the experience left the producer with his own qualifications. "It's a marvelous idea," he said, "and it's a terrifying idea but I should have said, 'Arthur, you have to go back to the drawing board and do more on this.'" Whether more work could have improved *Incident at Vichy* is questionable. As it stands, it has never received a major revival.

Even as Miller tried to shake off his second consecutive set of nasty reviews, they were plainly beginning to eat at him. "I get to where it doesn't seem worth all the labor and the effort in view of the trendiness of criticism, which can kill you in the theater. . . . Most of my life," he said as he neared fifty, "I've been attacked. I rarely get a positive review. It's just that I persist and have managed to stay alive. And I don't now *have* to write anything." The impulse to desert the ingrates was understandable and his independence was true at least financially. *The Misfits* had provided him with a healthy bank account while regular productions of *Death of a Salesman* and *The Crucible* were earning dependable royalties. "I've made my living basically for many years now," he said, "on domestic and foreign amateur and semiprofessional productions . . . And I'm assured of productions in Paris, London, Italy, all over Germany."

With that as security Miller took temporary leave of the theater, escorted along the way by the departure of Whitehead and Kazan from the Lincoln Center company. They'd had no choice but to resign after learning of secret negotiations to replace them. Their replacements were chosen upon the recommendation of Robert Brustein.

Miller became a gentleman Connecticut farmer. Although a bred in the bone New Yorker, he had long since adapted to the rhythms of rural life. He cultivated a veritable tree nursery that included local seedlings and full-sized exotics as well as a wide range of plantings, from dogwood to imported katsura and locust. He was growing a small forest of evergreens, thanks to a 6,000-tree planting "when they were six inches," he said. They were already over twenty feet high and providing him with an annual business in Christmas trees. "And we have a garden that keeps our cold cellar full of fruits and vegetables all winter long." He grew banks of iris in front of the house, and built Inge a photography studio and darkroom in the barn, which he began painting a traditional New England red. He was fitting it out as a guesthouse and doing much of the work himself, installing the plumbing and building cedar closets.

With Hugo, the old basset hound, gone he and Inge got themselves a pair of German shepherds. He also bought two new cars. He still had his eye. These were a Volkswagen "Beetle" and a Mercedes-Benz 280 SEL, a pair of German cars soon to be classics.

He didn't stop all writing. The cabin was still his favorite workplace with its two plain chairs, simple day bed, desk, bookshelves, fireplace and no telephone. He kept a rifle leaning against a corner, occasionally aiming it through a window to take a shot at one of the gophers that were tunneling through the garden. Tacked to the walls were photographs of Inge and their daughter, Rebecca, and he even gave in to scientific progress, replacing the big old Royal office typewriter that had been with him since *All My Sons* with an even bigger IBM electric. "Once you begin a sentence," he said, "it completes it by itself. The motor in it hums faintly, saying, 'Well? Well?' until you oblige it and *write* something," but the something he was writing was not a stage play—it was a television play.

His children were growing up. At nineteen Robert was as lanky as Arthur had been and a sophomore at his father's alma mater, the University of Michigan. There the student radicals only looked different from those of Miller's era. "Bobby," he wrote to James Stern, "has the shaggiest mop of hair and the longest sideburns this side of the Beatles." His sister, twenty-two-year-old Jane, Miller said, "is beautiful, rather delicate in feature, a bit smaller than her mother. She's studying art at the New School and living illicitly with a sculptor." The next year Jane would marry that sculptor, "named Doyle, natch," her father said, meaning she *would*, wouldn't she, marry an Irish Catholic. Arthur Miller was less liberated from traditional Jewishness and more conflicted about his own Jewish identity than he seemed to realize (the only specifically Jewish characters in his plays so far were either Hasidic or Yiddish-inflected caricatures). As for Rebecca, his daughter with Inge, he told Stern that she "is now five years old, brilliant, beautiful and sophisticated, like her mother."

Inge had become a homemaker as well as a photographer, and she made the white farmhouse into a home with rural charm and urban sophistication. As Arthur's friend William Styron's wife, Rose, described it, with help from a neighbor, Olga Carlisle,

> The living room, glassed-in from the terrace, was eclectic, charming; white walls patterned with a [Saul] Steinberg sketch, a splashy painting by neighbor Alexander Calder, posters of early Miller plays, photographs by Mrs. Miller. It held colorful modern rugs and sofas, an antique rocker, an oversized black Eames chair, a glass coffee table supporting a bright [Calder] mobile, small peasant figurines—unique Mexican candlesticks and strange pottery animals atop a very old carved Spanish table—and plants, plants everywhere.

Inge was nearly the complete competent. She went into New York twice a week to teach photography at Cooper Union. At home she practiced yoga every day and swam laps in all but the coldest weather. Although she was herself a vegetarian, it did not limit her cooking and she was a versatile hostess, entertaining at dinner parties and serving inventive lunches for visitors from the city—Mexican tacos, for instance, with beer, pears and an assortment of cheeses for dessert. That was more interesting than Arthur's taste in food, which ran to coffee shop cheeseburgers and cheap cookies.

Clearly Litchfield County, Connecticut, was farmland no more. William Styron was but one of a number of celebrated writers in Miller's local circle of friends. Others were Philip Roth, John Steinbeck, Saul Bellow and Harrison Salisbury of the *New York Times*, and the circle extended beyond writers. Miller was also socializing with such Connecticut neighbors as the director Mike Nichols, the actor Richard Widmark and of course Alexander Calder, who had been his first Connecticut friend. Miller and Styron were particularly political—in fact Styron beat him out (by four votes) in an election for the Roxbury Library Board. Miller had much wider political interests but after his experience with the House Committee on Un-American Activities and throughout his marriage to Marilyn Monroe he had tempered his political involvements. He couldn't be constrained for long. When the conflict in Vietnam intensified, he began speaking at antiwar demonstrations. Upon returning from a "teach-in" at the University of Michigan in September 1965, he received an invitation to join a group of eminent American artists witnessing President Lyndon Johnson as he signed an Arts and Humanities Act. After the poet Robert Lowell declined the invitation because of the government's Vietnam policies, Miller followed suit and sent a public telegram to President Johnson.

> The . . . signing of the Arts and Humanities bill surely begins new and fruitful relationship between American artists and their government. But the occasion is so darkened by the Viet Nam tragedy that I could not join it with clear conscience . . . when the guns boom, the arts die.

Lowell's refusal had been formal and polite; Miller typically suggested a specific course of action. The playwright Paddy Chayevsky, who did attend the ceremony, was unable to find any connection between the war and refusing to attend an event devoted to subsidizing the arts. "The connection I saw," Miller said, "was that on that day some man in Viet Nam had probably had his family destroyed by some bomb we were dropping, and I would be standing up there congratulating the president on signing an arts bill." He wrote to James Stern,

> This war is a cancer . . . eating us alive. . . . You can't open a paper anymore without reading about some big executive or other turning out to be a Mafia member or a crook. The young people are almost entirely alienated and the smell of marijuana is all over. I spoke at Yale last week about the war but nobody upstairs is listening to anything but the generals' demands for still more troops. It's all a dream—nobody believes in the war and nobody can stop it!

In 1966 Miller joined an action by the Committee of Conscience against Apartheid in withdrawing accounts from Chase Manhattan and First National City Bank in protest of the banks' support of the economy of South Africa. The next year he participated in a "Poets for Peace" evening at Town Hall in New York City along with Lowell, Mark Van Doren, Stanley Kunitz and Richard Wilbur. Proceeds from the reading went to help civilians in Vietnam, and Miller's reading was from his essay "Why Kill a Nation No One Hates?"

In April 1967 he signed and contributed to the cost of a full-page advertisement that was to appear in the London *Times* protesting America's position in Vietnam. Miller's signature was joined by Mike Nichols, Marlon Brando, Joseph Heller, Allen Ginsburg, William L. Shirer and Benjamin

Spock. Philip Roth signed the protest and suggested that the organizers contact William Styron and Robert Brustein. Susan Sontag agreed to sign and supplied the addresses of Robert Lowell, Elizabeth Hardwick, Stella Adler and Jules Feiffer. Kenneth Tynan suggested Orson Welles. Those declining to participate included a couple of senators (Charles Percy and Ernest Gruening); Harrison Salisbury of the *New York Times*, who didn't think it appropriate for a newspaper editor to sign advertisements; and the historian Arthur Schlesinger, who wrote that he preferred to sign only those statements he personally wrote and moreover, he did not believe in criticizing the American government in foreign publications.

In 1968 Miller won election from Roxbury voters as their delegate to the Democratic Party convention in August. There he was excited by the event, the atmosphere, and by his contact with a middle American crowd he never saw on Broadway. "There was the American people," he said. "That's the audience I wish I had. They're not in my theater. And if they ever got into the theater, you would have something! You would have fever!" But the occasion was more appalling than exciting. This was the infamous Days of Rage convention in Chicago. Delegates were all but barricaded inside the amphitheater while hundreds of war protestors were being beaten or arrested by the police after gathering in Lincoln Park to hear speeches by the likes of Allen Ginsberg, Jean Genet, Black Panther Party Chairman Bobby Seale and Senator Eugene McCarthy.

He also accepted the presidency of PEN International, the writers' organization with some 8,000 members throughout the world, although none from countries that restricted artistic freedom—the Soviet bloc, for instance, Latin American dictatorships and apartheid Africa. The issue of free expression became a prime concern of Miller's 1965–1969 administration, and he helped to secure the release of Arrabal, the Spanish-French playwright, from a Franco prison. In that position with his passport problems long since resolved, he and Inge began to travel in earnest—to Hong Kong, Japan, Thailand and Cambodia and at long last to the Soviet Union. After that trip they collaborated on a book of photographs and essays called *In Russia*. At one time a visit there would have been a significant event in his life, but now the simple use of *Russia* in the book title indicated Miller's changed attitude toward the Soviet Union and international communism.

Some years earlier, after the London production of *A View from the Bridge*, Miller had pronounced its two-act version the final one. Given the play's unimpressive Broadway history, there was no commercial rush to present it anew. The New York stage was basically a theater of premieres. Even productions of Shakespeare were called *revivals*—then a dirty word on Broadway—and so the full-length *A View from the Bridge* was immediately made available to stock and community theaters. One of the first to present it was the Gateway, a small theater in Bellport, Long Island. The director was a young Belgian refugee named Ulu Grosbard and he cast Robert Duvall, "a kid just out of school," as the middle-aged Eddie Carbone. An actor–lighting man, Gene Hackman, played Marco. "We rehearsed a week," Grosbard said, "and played a week." Miller was satisfied with the production and in 1964 allowed the director to do the play in New York City, in a small Off-Broadway theater. Duvall repeated his performance but Hackman—who had been his roommate along with another aspiring actor, Dustin Hoffman—had by then gone to Hollywood. Grosbard gave the unemployed Hoffman a job as his assistant director, staging crowd scenes. A prettier young man was needed to play Rodolpho and the two finalists for that role were Christopher Walken, a Broadway chorus dancer with ambitions to become a serious actor, and Jon Voight, who had just played a brilliant Romeo at the San Diego Shakespeare Festival. Grosbard chose Voight and when rehearsals began, as Hoffman would remember with enduring awe, "My idol, Arthur Miller comes in. In acting class, the first scene I ever did was Biff in *Death of a Salesman*. Now he starts reading a play of his—to all of us." The dazzled twenty-seven year old could hardly have imagined that twenty years later he would himself be playing Willy Loman on Broadway.

The reviews for the revival of *A View from the Bridge* were generally favorable but Grosbard knew that "the tide was turning against Arthur. He had gone completely out of favor. There was Brustein and that whole line of attack. 'Let's get rid of naturalistic theater. Let's get with modern times.' They had turned on him and dismissed him."

Shrinking from that hostility, Miller started building a nine-foot-long cherry dining table—"an elliptical thing," he said. "Suddenly, I don't know why the hell I'm doing it. I escape through my hands, I guess." Yet he continued to write the television play along with a collection of short stories called *I Don't Need You Anymore*. "It's as though I'm saying to myself, 'I'm only doing this because I'm not writing a play at the moment.'"

After Grosbard made a success on Broadway directing *The Subject Was Roses* Miller asked him to read the television script, *It Is You, Victor,* about a director rehearsing a group of actors. It was, Grosbard found, "mostly scaffolding," by which he meant "aimless chitchat." Any vitality, he said, was limited to the scene that the actors were rehearsing, but that scene, he said with recollected astonishment, "was so resonant with meaning, it just *jumped out* from the script."

The scene had been salvaged from *The Third Play* and the reams of material that Miller had not used in *After the Fall*. It dealt with the family history and psychological legacy that a policeman and his brother inherited from their childhood, a legacy symbolized by furniture stored away in an attic when their father died. Just as *After the Fall* was only finished after Marilyn Monroe's death, so this scene was finally emerging only after Isadore Miller died—in 1966 at the age of eighty-one in a Long Island nursing home. On that day Miller saw no reason to cancel a speech he was to make at a New

York PEN Congress. Explaining his apparent lack of grief and evidently forgetting his concern about it in *After the Fall,* he said that he went ahead with the engagement because the "perfect spring" weather had made him feel "uplifted."

After reading Miller's television play the thirty-five-year-old Grosbard, with just one Broadway credit, suggested that the out of favor, fifty-two-year-old American playwright "Forget about the rest of the 90 page script" but "the scene in the middle is absolutely wonderful. There could be a one act play in it." Miller, knowing its history, decided otherwise. "That scene," he said, "is a full length play." He set out then with twenty pages of core drama and a scene for the final curtain, the playing of a laugh record. (Such records, peculiar to the 1920s, featured one or two men chortling for four minutes. Listeners were supposed to find the laughter contagious, which it occasionally was.) So Miller went back to writing plays. He resumed his regular work schedule, "seven days a week, from eight thirty until, some days, ten-thirty, sometimes eight hours or longer—even around the clock." He would

> work on the typewriter, plus three or four notebooks . . . I'll write a whole act sometimes and use only one scene, or a whole scene and use just one line. See, I'm discovering it, making up my own story. I think at the typewriter . . . I've got tremendous notebooks full of stuff I can't finish. There must be 100,000 words. But sometimes also there's another way of working; getting it all out in one burst . . . *Salesman* was that way . . . Boom! One burst and it was done. But *After the Fall* took me over a year and still many months.

He worked backward from that laugh record, deleting great swatches of idle conversation and adding a major second act event. And he took yet another approach to time. If *Death of a Salesman* occurs in the past and the present simultaneously, and if *After the Fall* takes place in a single instant of memory, then the new play was going to transpire in real time. Miller finished the revision in eight months and called it *The Price* because of the choices made in life and the prices paid for them. He gave the script to Robert Whitehead, who had resumed commercial producing, and the play was promptly announced for a February 1968 premiere on Broadway with Grosbard directing.

The setting is the attic of a small apartment house, significantly a condemned Manhattan walk-up. It is an attic "monstrously crowded" with "a whole houseful" of furniture. A harp is prominent, while a windup record player and a crystal radio date the rummage as from the 1920s. Here is a family history, the debris of the Wall Street crash of 1929, storage with ghostly "emanations," as Miller put it in his stage direction.

Moments after the curtain's rise a policeman enters—Victor, the same policeman who had been in the thousands of pages of *The Third Play*, followed on stage by his wife, Esther. Their last name is Franz and they seem a good couple, communicative and content. As Victor asks whether she wants to keep any of these things before the appraiser arrives, it becomes clear that they live on a tight budget and that the furniture belongs not only to him but also his brother, a wealthy and celebrated doctor whom Esther actively despises. "That son of a bitch," she says, cheated her husband of his life. Even now, with these men estranged since their father's death, Walter hasn't said whether he is even coming and Esther wonders why he should deserve half the proceeds anyway. She reminds her husband, "You made his whole life possible," by taking care of their father while Walter took care of himself and went to medical school. "There's such a thing as a moral debt," she says. "What law said that only he could study medicine? . . . And you were even the better student."

As Victor lingers over the relics from his past, an appraiser arrives, the rare, completely invented major character in an Arthur Miller play and the first funny one. Significantly called Solomon, he first appeared in a 1966 draft of *The Third Play* as the proprietor of "Solomon's Antiques." In *The Price* Gregory Solomon is a feisty ninety year old, breathless from climbing the four flights of stairs. He coughs and sputters, "Water I don't need, a little blood I could use." They are Arthur Miller's first Jewish locutions since his college plays as he brings to life this wily, Yiddish-inflected quipster with a touch of the sage.

The old man greets Esther—"How do you do, darling"—just as she is leaving to get Victor's suit from the cleaner, an acceptable contrivance to get her off stage. In leaving, she reminds Solomon to give her husband "a good price" and he tells her not to worry, "We'll take care everything one hundred per cent . . . I'm not sixty two years in the business by taking advantage. Go, enjoy the cleaner," and the famously dour playwright can be all but heard laughing behind the scene. With Esther's departure Solomon inspects the goods—the armoire, the chiffonier, the carved headboard, the harp. He doesn't suggest a price, but he does minimize the values. A cabinet is too wide to get through a modern door; a library table is beautiful but of little value when apartments don't have libraries anymore. There is also a long dining room table; the real one from Arthur Miller's childhood apartment would be on stage as part of this play's scenery.

"Are you going to make me an offer or not?" the exasperated Victor cries, "Because you talk about everything but money and I don't know what the hell you're up to. Every time you open your mouth the price seems to go down."

That is when Solomon pointedly says, "My boy, the price didn't change since I walked in." A beautiful line, it goes neatly to the play's subject, the price one pays for the roads taken. Miller is applying Ibsen's basic principle, the revealed past "no longer introductory but the center of the immediate conflict." He lends that history irony by setting it to a comic counterpoint, as Solomon takes a hard-boiled egg from his briefcase and asks, "There wouldn't be a little salt, I suppose?" Still inspecting the goods, he opens a drawer to find a lap robe for a car. "You had a chauffeur? . . . And from all this [your father] could go broke?" Victor nods at the "overstuffed armchair" around which, a stage direction indicates, "the area . . . appears to be lived-in." Gazing at this chair, "stilled by some emanation from the room," he says, "From a couple of million, and in less than five weeks." The line is virtually intact from *The Third Play* written decades earlier, when it was called *Plenty Good Times*.

Solomon went broke a few times too, says the old man, but he never gave up. "Well," Victor says, his father believed in "The system, the whole thing. . . . You tell your jokes, people fall in love with you, and you walk away with their furniture." Solomon offers a mere eleven hundred dollars for the lot, which stuns Victor, but, "The hell with it. Give it to me." As the appraiser hands over the money, the brother Walter appears in the doorway and the first act curtain falls. It is exactly where the second act begins, as the long-alienated brothers strain to bridge their separation while Solomon presses to settle the deal.

It seems that the only item of interest to Walter is the harp that their mother used to play.

> VICTOR: You want it?
> SOLOMON: Please, Victor. . . . The harp is the heart and soul of the deal.
> WALTER: I guess it doesn't matter.

This is the same style of off-center dialogue that Miller had perfected in earlier drafts dealing with the harp, which certainly is "the heart and soul of the deal" because it symbolizes the mother who ruled this family. As Miller's sister saw it, "My mother's dominating spirit hovers over the whole play." (Gussie Miller actually played the piano, but a harp is less bulky a prop.)

When Esther returns with Victor's suit, the brothers' reunion has already turned edgy with an element of one-upmanship. Walter makes it clear that he lives a life more luxurious and exciting than Victor's. He also questions Solomon's low appraisal and when Esther seconds that, Victor is only the more aggravated. He already resents his wife's obvious admiration and even awe of this brother whom she supposedly despises, and to make matters worse Walter too generously offers him the entire proceeds

Suddenly the old man feels faint and Walter takes him offstage for a checkup and a favor to the playwright. Alone with her husband, Esther asks, "Did you try to get him to go higher?"

> VICTOR: I don't know how to bargain and I'm not going to start now.

ESTHER: I wish you wouldn't be above everything. We're not twenty years old. We need this money. You hear me?
VICTOR: I've made a deal, and that's it. You know, you take a tone sometimes—like I'm some kind of an incompetent.

Making him feel worse, perhaps intentionally, Walter returns to suggest that instead of selling the furniture they donate it to charity and take a tax deduction—which his own income could justify—for an inflated price certified by this handy appraiser. Esther and Victor's share, he says, could come to as much as six thousand dollars. A "cornered" Victor asks for time and while Walter leaves the room to once again tend to Solomon, Esther asks, "can't you take [Walter] as he is? . . . You can't bear the thought that he's decent." It strikes her that Victor might be using his brother as an excuse for his own failure. "You can't go blaming everything on him or the system." And she delivers an ultimatum, "You throw this away, you've got to explain it to me . . . You take this money! Or I'm washed up."

After that the play's balance of sympathy is slyly shifted to Walter as the playwright puts to best use his alternative-weighing, rabbinical mind. (Miller would tell actors in various productions of *The Price* that Walter's and Victor's arguments should be evenly balanced. This is a trial that neither brother should "win.") When Walter returns, he is calm and reasonable as opposed to Victor's growing agitation. He offers his brother the whole tax savings, twelve thousand dollars, which he could present immediately and in cash. That was a tidy sum in 1968, enough to carry a modest family comfortably for a year. He speaks of healing the fraternal wounds. He also describes his own nervous breakdown that, he says, "simplified" his life. He is no longer driven to make pots of money.

> I never had friends . . . I do now . . . You start out wanting to be the best . . . you do need a certain fanaticism . . . until you've eliminated everything extraneous—including people. . . . And of course the time comes when you realize that you haven't merely been specializing in something—something has been specializing in you . . . And it finally makes you stupid. . . . One night I found myself in the middle of my living room, dead drunk, with a knife in my hand, getting ready to kill my wife . . . But there's one virtue in going nuts . . . You get to see the terror . . . the slow, daily fear you call ambition.

That is a striking notion, ambition as fear. "You wanted a *real* life," Walter explains to his brother, meaning a wife and family, "And that's an expensive thing. It costs." The terror that he is talking about began with the man who used to sit in the highlighted armchair at center stage and in a sense still does; their father is the reason for Walter's terror "of it ever happening to me—as it happened to him." So he has come to the core of Depression trauma, the morning after the nightmare when "the system broke down" and everything was lost in a trice. This is what has motivated Walter to over-achievement. If he is indeed a self-projection by the playwright (which seems indisputable), then Miller is seeing his own ambitiousness and success as driven by—and flight from—the memory of a flash flood of financial catastrophe. "We were both," says Walter, "running from the same thing. I ended in a swamp of success and bankbooks, you on civil service. The difference," he says, "is that you haven't hurt other people."

The same reference to hurting other people was in the earliest versions of *The Third Play*. It is a notion that bears some examination, for nothing in the text explains its relevance. If hurting other people is offered here as an unfortunate condition of achievement, it might well relate to the hurt that Miller inflicted—not just on his brother but also on his first wife and his children when he abandoned them on his way to fame and celebrity. And it could explain his recurring theme of human selfishness and survival—the latter defined not in the physical sense but survival as achievement, as getting what you want in life.

In *The Price* a seemingly conciliatory Walter offers his brother a position in the administrative wing of his hospital, but Victor cannot forget past grievances. "There used to be a man in that chair," he says, meaning their father. And he sacrificed his life for that man. Walter replies, "I told you that I was going to finish my schooling come hell or high water, and I advised you to do the same. In fact, I warned you not to allow him to strangle your life . . . He exploited you!"

As Victor sees it, he had no choice. "The icebox was empty and the man was sitting there with his mouth open." Choice is underlined as Solomon interrupts, quite willing to make the certified appraisal suggested by Walter. "I'm a dealer, he's a doctor and he's a policeman." This is no accidental remark. The men are prototypes. A dealer makes evaluations or judgments, a doctor tries to make things better, a policeman defends what is there. Solomon's estimate of Victor is a worrisome one, as in a biblical allusion he tells Esther, "You'll tear him to pieces . . . If they can't settle nothing they should stop right now." Yet again the play's scales shift balance. She reminds Walter that twenty-five years ago he'd refused to lend Victor the five hundred dollars that would have assured his college degree. "That," Walter concedes, "was despicable" but, he says, he had changed his mind and left a message about it with their father. The old man, selfish bastard that he was, never delivered it.

"Very convenient for you," says Victor, which tips the balance back toward him. The truth, he says, is that "You didn't give me the money because you didn't want to. If you want to help somebody, you do it." He is disgusted with Walter's effort to pay a moral debt and heal their wound "by offering me a job and twelve thousand dollars." Besides, he asks, "Why do you have to offer me anything? It sounds like I have to be saved." Is his brother trying to tell him, he asks, that his life has been wasted? Exactly so.

It is unspoken, but "There's a price people pay," Victor says, and it is paid by everyone.

> I've paid it. . . . Just like you paid . . . You've got no wife, you've lost your family. . . . This is where we are; now, right here, now. And as long as we're talking, I have to tell you that this is not what you say in front of a man's wife. [Frankly] we don't need to be saved. I've done a job that has to be done and I think I've done it straight.

In this family bloodletting, comparable in some ways to O'Neill's *Long Day's Journey into Night* (more so than *After the Fall*), Walter has saved the worst for last. While Victor was feeding his broken father with scraps scavenged from garbage cans, the old man had four thousand dollars, a fortune in Depression money, hidden away. He was certain that Victor would walk out on him sooner or later and had asked Walter to invest it, because "he couldn't understand . . . that you'd . . . stick with him like that. At such a cost to you."

A stunned Victor points out that Walter never told him about this, but in return Walter accuses him of having lived a fantasy, for he had to know that his father had money put away. There simply hadn't been enough to live on, especially after Victor moved out and got married. Why then did he keep sacrificing? "Jesus," Victor says, crawling through the rubble of revelations. "The man was a beaten dog, ashamed to walk in the street, how do you demand his last buck?"

But, Walter cries, "it was all an act! Beaten dog!" he scoffs. "He was a calculating liar! And in your heart you knew it!" But Victor in fact had confronted his father about a reserve of money. "He laughed. I didn't know what to make of it. . . . Like it was some kind of wild joke. . . . And I tried to figure out that laugh. How could he be holding out on me when he loved me?" Then in a speech almost too painful to bear he remembers the night the Depression terror began.

> The night he told us he was bankrupt, my mother . . . it was right on this couch. She was all dressed up—for some affair, I think. Her hair was piled up, and long earrings? And he had his tuxedo on . . . and made us all sit down; and he told us it was all gone. And she vomited. All over his arms. His hands.

After that Victor sacrificed his ambitions, he says, out of love and a drive to hold the family together. "But were we really brought up," Walter asks, "to believe in one another? We were brought up to succeed . . . Why else would he respect me so and not you? Was there any love here? When he needed [mother] she vomited. And when you needed him, he laughed."

He grimly concludes, "There was no love in this house."

Thus the final scene where Miller's habitual equivocating is finally exploited as powerful ambiguity. Victor, even acknowledging Walter's truths, cannot accept them because he won't be turned into "a walking mistake" and have his brother leave with "the old handshake [and] the respect, the career, the money . . . and you're one hell of a guy." Instead the brothers claw at each other as Walter cries, "You never had . . . a wish to see me destroyed? . . . with this mockery of sacrifice?" Victor is finally exhausted. "I don't need anything [and] I couldn't work for you. . . . I don't trust you." But Walter isn't spent yet, accusing his brother of trying "to prove with your failure what a treacherous son of a bitch I am!" As Esther begs him to leave off, he calls the two of them quitters and goes, although not before picking up their mother's gown and throwing it in his brother's face.

The appraiser reappears, settling the payment for the goods. Victor starts to change from his policeman uniform into the cleaned suit, but Esther tells him not to bother. In effect he is who he is, and with that they exit as Solomon puts on the Laugh Record, the laughter not unlike the father's in its defiance of reason. While it plays, one old man laughs at the cosmic joke along with the ghost of another old man as the curtain falls.

Miller would later say, "They'll never rid themselves of their father."

As *The Price* went into production, its misproduction began as well. Miller's favorite actor, Arthur Kennedy (Chris in *All My Sons*, Biff in *Death of a Salesman*, Proctor in *The Crucible*), was cast as Walter Franz, Jack Warden as his brother and Kate Reid as Victor's wife, Esther. Four days before the scheduled Philadelphia tryout Warden—who could not learn his lines—begged to be released and was. He was replaced with Pat Hingle, a dependable actor but possibly the most un-Jewish one in the entire professional theater. The other cast members were Irish. There are no suggestions in *The Price* that its characters are Irish, Jewish or of any ethnicity. Their family name, Franz, is nondescript like Loman, but Grosbard felt that this play "isn't like *Salesman*. This is definitely a Jewish play." He discussed that with Miller. "There was this whole business," Grosbard recalled, "about, if they're Jewish *is it less universal?*" He considered that "bullshit." The real reason seemed to be a fear of alienating Christian audiences, which hardly made sense when *Fiddler on the Roof* was beginning its fourth year on Broadway. But the decision was made, Grosbard's position was weakened and it seems fair to infer that the play's Jewishness was being consciously fudged by the author.

In Philadelphia David Burns (playing Gregory Solomon), the only Jewish actor in the cast, fell ill and left the show. Both Arthur Kennedy and Kate Reid complained about Grosbard's direction as being too detailed and Hingle refused to work with him entirely. One week before the scheduled Broadway opening night Miller himself had to take over the directing and the premiere was postponed for two weeks. "Arthur did not restage anything," Hingle recalled,

> but he did answer two questions I asked him. One, what is "the price?" He believes there is a price for everything you get in life. The "price" and "what you get" varies greatly in each individual. And each person has to honestly look into his own soul to know "the price" and "what you got." And second, what is Victor looking for? Victor knows the price he paid taking care of his father, but he doesn't know what he got for it.

Hingle added that *The Price* was "the only play I've done where I communicated directly with the playwright," but the difference was minimal. "Arthur wasn't much of a director," Whitehead said. "He doesn't go inside the actors' problems. He goes inside his own." Arthur Kennedy agreed, describing the author's direction as dialogue nit-picking, "telling us we're leaving out a 'the' or an 'and.'" That was the condition of *The Price* on the eve of its New York premiere, February 7, 1968, at the Morosco Theatre.

After the Fall may have brought accusations of autobiography down upon Miller's head, but *The Price* is the road map to his life. He denied that as earnestly as he had denied that the earlier play was about Marilyn Monroe. "In *The Price*," he said, "the characters were not based on Kermit and me. We were far different from these two, but the magnetic underlying situation was deep in my bones." The reasonableness of his denial is equal to the absurdity of it. The play is obviously rooted in personal history. The "magnetic underlying situation" possibly refers to an Arthur Miller who spent much of his adult life trying to prove himself better in the long run than his older brother, who had been the finer athlete, the superior student and the warmer hearted, more lovable fellow. Yet if *The Price* has autobiographical elements, it is also a work of invention and its historical roots are of no relevance to its dramatic qualities or lack of them. The play must stand or fall as fiction. Yet these selfsame elements are relevant because they suggest how Miller saw his life and what he saw in it. *The Price* could well be Arthur Miller's attempt to justify his life choices.

To make the play he combined characters and invented situations. In *The Price* Victor had dropped out of college and become a policeman. In real life, it might be remembered, Kermit dropped out of college to work with his father; it was Miller's boyhood friend, Sid Franks, who got his degree and then became a policeman. And it was Sid too who for a time lived with his ruined father in a Manhattan walk-up, Sid who was the friend Miller interviewed in 1952 when he was writing *Plenty Good Times*. Then again it was Kermit who, his sister said, "was the guy we thought would be the poet in the family." More to the point it was Kermit whose brother, the playwright of the matter, walked out on the family to save (and not share) his earnings, go to college and become so very famous and successful. And it was Arthur, whatever his selfishness, who became the parents' hero.

Had Isadore Miller "strangled" Kermit's life? Did Kermit's sacrifice make Arthur Miller's "whole life possible?" Did Kermit see it that way and was he as angry about it as Victor is in *The Price*? Miller's sister, Joan, said that Kermit's wife, Frances, certainly did feel "he should have done more," and like Esther in the play she was awed by Arthur Miller's success and celebrity. But "As far as Kermit having wasted his intellectual gifts," Joan said,

> that may be the way Arthur may have seen it, or he thought that's the way Kermit saw it, but I wouldn't say that there was wasted potential. [However,] as in *The Price*, one makes choices. Depending on how you look at it, either [Kermit] was forced to make the choice or he decided that it was the honorable thing to make that choice.

"How you look at it," as Miller's sister put it about her two brothers, is the floor plan of *The Price*. It is about ambiguities. As to accusations of Ibsenism, while *The Price* does revolve around "the past coming to life in the present and creating drama," it is not Ibsenesque in the sense of being well made, realistic and issue-oriented. "Critics dealing with complexity," Miller told the *New York Times*, "have to simplify in order to write about it, so you get a tag like 'Ibsenesque.'" Nevertheless in its misproduction the play settled Miller's reputation as a realistic playwright. As a result, in the following decades this sizable, singular and moving play would be mistakenly directed as a traditional drama, popular despite—even because—of that mistake, because audiences find traditional realism more digestible than stylized realism. Yet this is not a *well-made play*. It does not tell a story, nobody changes in it, wins or loses. It wants to be staged at a level once removed from reality. The exchanges between Walter and Victor are opaque and fraught with tensions and insinuations that are only gradually unspooled. There are mysteries too. Does Solomon, for instance, recall having once been an acrobat just for the sake of a laugh? ("I never heard of a Jewish acrobat," says Victor.) The old man mentions that his daughter had committed suicide. It is a reference of tantalizing sadness. What is its significance? (Eli Wallach, after playing Solomon in a revival of the play, suggested that Miller write a sequel about the old man and his daughter. The author wasn't interested in sequels.) Yet for all this *The Price* follows a clear line of interior logic, making sense on its own terms. As for the climactic issue of Depression trauma and the terror of sudden catastrophic loss, that was always in the play, powering the work throughout its two-decade evolution. In a 1950 version of *The Third Play* Miller wrote a speech for Victor, the policeman, then called Quentin.

> I guess I'm just afraid of being poor. I think sometimes I stayed with Pop too long. He was no fool . . . and that paper bag he turned into! It's a frightening thing. Except I see it all the time . . . The park is full of them.

The image of former businessmen sleeping in parks crops up in *The Price* too, but there the fear of becoming poor in a puff of smoke is better exploited. Finally, just as text, the central metaphor of the "price" as the cost of living centers the play and grounds it. Of *After the Fall* and *The Price* then—the two plays born of *The Third Play*—*The Price* has fewer pretensions but is more satisfying, even though the ambitiousness that drove the work for almost two decades was never quite fulfilled.

As for Miller's own take on *The Price* as well as perhaps his take on his brother and himself,

> Victor . . . is an idealist . . . in a sense the world depends on him . . . a terrific husband and father. He's carried that weight of his idealism through his life . . . his strict code of justice and injustice. [Then] there are creators, like his brother Walter . . . who are very cruel and destructive. But without them we are going to stand still. [The artist] takes risks lesser men wouldn't dare take . . . We need that guy, but Victor is much more careful about life. . . . He's got to hold back this creator or one day he'll probably blow up the world with his creating.

Despite the difficult birthing process, the production opened to reviews good enough for a 426-performance run, Miller's longest since *Death of a Salesman,* which played 742 performances. His nemesis, Robert Brustein at *The New Republic,* expressed amazement that the playwright was writing "social-psychological melodrama about family responsibility at a time when our cities are burning." This was the same critic who had defied anyone "to name a single work of art that ever changed anything." *The Price* and *After the Fall* may have been the eventual fruits of *The Third Play,* but separately or together they were not what that play had aspired to be. That—the major work "about where we are and how we got here," the play Miller thought might "change the direction of our stage [and] say a good word for mankind, *finally*"—was the cost and the price, so to speak, of Miller's eight years away from the stage. His boldness of intention and grandness of design had been lost along the way.

In the spring of 1968 Arthur Miller was subjected to the embarrassment of a public debate on his merits as a playwright, conducted on the pages of the *New York Times.* It began on April 14 with an essay by one of the more intellectual critics, Albert Bermel of *The New Leader,* who wrote, "Arthur Miller may have a new hit but [despite his] 'high seriousness' (mountainous solemnity is more like it) . . . he has not discernibly grown as a playwright since *Salesman.*" Bermel continued, with less vitriol but some critical insight,

> If Joe Keller and Willy Loman didn't even think of suicide; if Von Berg declined to give his clearance pass to Dr. LeDuc on the grounds that his own life was worth more to him than LeDuc's; if Eddie Carbone was too much of

> a coward to risk a brawl with Marco; if Victor Franz felt indignant about having paid the food and rent bills when his father had $4,000 socked away; if, in short, each play dealt with a man who remained fallible to the end, rather than turning into an exemplary figure, it would upset us because it would really be about us. We might then conclude what the playwright apparently wants us to conclude: that there is something fundamentally wrong with a society in which a man rats on his fellow men and doesn't pay a penalty . . . in which a salesman has been brought up to worship a creamy success he doesn't have the stuff to achieve.

The following Sunday under the headline, "The Merits of Mr. Miller," the *Times* printed a rebuttal by Harold Clurman. A writer and critic not nearly the equal of Bermel, Clurman faltered beneath the weight of his limitations but arrived at a stirring, if not analytic conclusion. "Miller's resolution," he wrote,

> to hold fast to a traditional morality is against the grain of our times, against much of our contemporary literature and drama which willy-nilly celebrate cynicism, negativism, collapse. . . . [That] defines Miller's signal contribution to the American theater of our day.

This did not refute anything, nor was it as specific as Bermel's analysis, but it did hit a mark.

An army of academics flew to Miller's defense and the *Times* printed a half page of their letters. Perhaps the most pertinent was from Professor Bernard F. Dick of Iona College in New Rochelle.

> Economical as it may sound, the dialogue [about Miller] represents one of the most vicious practices in contemporary criticism. The successful writer is forced to submit to a hazing session, and always under the pretext of "re-evaluation." The writer is stopped in mid-career on the supposition that such an analysis is healthy, therapeutic or even beneficial to his future growth.

This was not the first time that an important playwright had been punished in a public way by his lessers. Molière had been banned in Paris. Oscar Wilde of course had been imprisoned. Arthur Miller was merely humiliated. As to *The Price*, specifically, he wrote to his Irish friend James Stern that the "notices have ranged from ecstasy to sneers, which is my usual but the weight is on the good side and so is the public." Not that praise could renew his trust of reviewers. He granted the "reporter critics" token validity by conceding their "simple, primitive love of a good show. And if nothing else, you could tell whether that level of mind was genuinely interested or not." But such condescension was as far as he could go on behalf of a critic. In a letter to his college playwriting professor, Kenneth Rowe, he elaborated on the subject.

> The notices really would make a great subject for a doctorate. One would hardly know it was the same play they were reviewing. Kerr professes not to see the play's resolution, which several others quite easily summarize; similarly Watts. Others are absorbed by the action, still others find no action. I guess it will be my usual fate—it will take a few years and some European productions to establish the play . . . I suppose I've become paranoiac but I do think a certain school of critics truly hates me, and the more I succeed the more they can't bear it.

That did not discourage Miller and *The Price* would indeed become established, ultimately to be regularly produced as part of the standard repertoire. Miller, meanwhile, hoped to follow up on the box office success of *The Price*, dashing off a second note to Stern, "I'm about to get into another play . . . I feel fine and work a lot. Life now is the best it's been." He added,

> I am being importuned to come to London to join a protest meeting against the Soviet treatment of writers—end of March. As head of PEN I should go, but as I am sick of traveling . . . I've decided not to go . . . I'm tired of addressing protest meetings.

That was written in March 1968. A year later he finished his term as president of the writers' organization, but he didn't "get into" another play. He did write *Fame* for television, but there was little doubt now about his reputation's decline in America. *The Price* had to struggle through its yearlong Broadway engagement. His great years were apparently over. The Viking Press gave him a gold-tipped plaque of the cover page of *Death of a Salesman* to commemorate the millionth copy sold.

Like most radicals, Arthur Miller became more traditional as he grew older. His unmarried son Bobby announced that he was about to become a father and "this," Miller wrote to his friend Stern, "seems not unusually insane, which tells you what has become of my eroded standards. Jane was married this August but has no baby." For a specialist in the tragic he could laugh at himself. He was a man with an essentially sunny disposition, and he decided to exploit that.

"For 25 years now," the *New York Times* reported on August 2, 1972, "theatrical audiences have hired, so to speak, Arthur Miller to do their brooding for them—about the millstones of commerce that grind a man to dust, about political hysteria, incipient fascism, anti-Semitism, the tug and pull of family strife."

It was a witty introduction to an article about a new Miller *comedy*. It seems that America's playwright of conscience had so thoroughly enjoyed writing Gregory Solomon and had been so unexpectedly rewarded with audience laughter that he wanted more. "I've always loved to watch really good comedy," he said. "In fact, I like it better than the so-called serious drama when I go to the theater. The great moments of my life have come with good comedies." And so he wrote *The Creation of the World and Other Business*, a tongue-in-cheek adaptation of the Book of Genesis.

A comedy, perhaps, it marked a serious development in Miller's work, a departure from the higher ambition that had made his reputation. The long years of nonproductivity, when he had been involved with Marilyn Monroe, had caused more change, if not damage, than he seems to have realized. With the plays that immediately followed—particularly *After the Fall* and *The Price*—he had tried to pick up where he had left off. His approach was to exploit *The Third Play*, which had been written during the earlier period. *The Creation of the World* now was a turning of the page as he looked back on *After the Fall* and the scene of the crime to this time take a comic approach to mankind's loss of innocence. In addition to the first family the characters in his Genesis play include God ("He must never eat those apples") and Lucifer ("Then why have You tempted him?")—with the author providing the punch lines—"I wanted him to wake each morning, look at that tree and say, 'For God's sake, I won't eat those apples.'"

The idea of a mock Eden was not new. Mark Twain's "hieroglyphic" *Diaries of Adam and Eve* famously spoofed the biblical story. Unlike that acknowledged classic, however, Miller's version of Genesis was coy rather than whimsical, its humor heavy-handed and singularly unfunny. Inevitably perhaps he could not let a comedy be just a comedy. "What the play is probing," Miller said, "is whether there is in the human condition a force which makes man's concepts of high, low, good and bad, right and wrong, inevitable." His insistence on adding philosophizing to whimsy seemed to make an insufferable mix.

The Creation of the World played a shaky tryout engagement in Washington, D.C. The director, Harold Clurman, and one of the stars, Barbara Harris, were replaced. When it opened in New York on November 30, 1972, the critical response was devastating. Stanley Kauffmann, reviewing it as Brustein's successor at *The New Republic*, made sympathy synonymous with assault—"like going to the funeral of a man you wish you could have liked more. . . . The occasion seals your opinion because there is no hope of change."

The rest of Miller's reviewers had themselves a sitting target. *The Creation of the World and Other Business* closed after twenty performances, making it Miller's worst theater experience since 1944 and *The Man Who Had All the Luck*. "It is futile to criticize critics," he said. "It is quite enough to condemn them totally." It certainly was futile, and the play began a decade of failures and rejection, ten years that would finish off Arthur Miller as far as the American theater was concerned, and good riddance.

He spent the next two years sporadically working on an autobiography and writing a series of essays to accompany his wife's photographs for a travel book they called *In the Country*. He also wrote the libretto for a misbegotten musical version of *The Creation of the World and Other Business*, newly titled *Up from Paradise*. The score was composed by Stanley Silverman, and Miller even appeared (as a narrator) in the world premiere production at the Power Center for the Performing Arts at the University of Michigan. Ultimately given a modest New York production, the musical was reviewed in the *New York Times* as being "Not as far removed from *The Creation of the World* as one might have wished."

The published text of *The Creation of the World and Other Business* would be the only Arthur Miller play for which he did not write an introduction. Even so, he never disowned the play and his defense of it seems more than parental loyalty. "There are reverberations of all my plays in this one," he said. "It's wry, but with an underlying earnestness." It also served as an interval in his body of work, which folds out as if organized into distinct halves. *The Price* is an appropriately conclusive work following Miller's first and best-known group of plays. Written over two decades, it encompasses the themes, styles and dramatic rhythms of *All My Sons, Death of a Salesman, The Crucible, A View from the Bridge* and *After the* Fall. With *The Price* he left behind the aspirations to tragedy, the adventures in dramatic style and the themes that from the outset had dominated his work: guilt, fellow responsibility, controlling one's destiny and social morality. The plays that followed are, as Miller put it, "less subjective than the early ones."

On the wall above his desk in the Roxbury studio was pinned a calendar that was stopped at the month of April 1968. That was two months after *The Price* had opened.

18. Outcast

ENTERING HIS SIXTIES with his myth shattered and his work unwanted, Arthur Miller told a group of students that the ideal critic "should be small and invisible, deaf and dumb . . . I don't care whether he has a typewriter as long as nothing comes out of it. I never learned anything from critics. They are for the public and not artists."

Theater people have traditionally put on false fronts. They are "at liberty" when out of work, feign confidence when insecure and try to appear well off, *putting on the ritz,* when impoverished. It was most unusual then for Harold Clurman to openly acknowledge Arthur Miller's fall from favor, especially in a program note for a new work. As *The Archbishop's Ceiling,* Miller's first play in five years, was being readied for a pre-Broadway tryout and an April 23, 1977, world premiere at Kennedy Center in Washington, D.C., Clurman wrote,

> Conscience is not fashionable nowadays. Miller is therefore not fashionable now. We listen to him just the same, not simply because he writes with surprising humor, powerful theatrical impact and craft, with pith, compassion and eloquence, but because at bottom we feel that what he has said and continues to say in many different tones and forms, is basically true and contains the nourishment our dispirited souls so urgently need.

That was particularly kind of Clurman who, after all, had been replaced as the director of Miller's last play and was not directing this one (Arvin Brown was), but then he was a kind man. When Elia Kazan "bitchily," as Robert Whitehead put it, asked, "Would you work with Harold again?" Whitehead replied, "I'd work with him again forever," and hired Clurman soon after but he never worked with Kazan again.

The Archbishop's Ceiling was the only play besides *Incident at Vichy* to be set outside of the United States, excepting, one supposes, *The Creation of the World and Other Business*. The droll Mark Twain had located his Garden of Eden in Niagara Falls, which promoted itself as "The Honeymoon Capital of the World." The less droll Arthur Miller was less specific, merely describing "Paradise [as] the ultimate Garden."

The Archbishop's Ceiling is also indefinitely set. It takes place in "a capital in Europe" and draws on Miller's experiences as the president of PEN International. It was particularly suggested by an evening he spent with Czechoslovakian authors who suspected that their dinner table was wiretapped. At various times Miller would link the play to the McCarthy era or to Watergate and President Nixon's taped telephone conversations. Such ex post facto references were habitual for him; he once wrote that *The Price* was a reaction to not only "the seemingly permanent and morally agonizing Vietnam War" but also to "a surge of avant garde plays that in one or another degree fit the absurdist styles. I was moved to confront and confound both."

Such postscripts are best minimized if not ignored entirely.

At the time that *The Archbishop's Ceiling* was being written there was little mystery about artistic freedom in Soviet Russia and its satellites—there simply wasn't any. Aleksandr Solzhenitsyn had just been deported to the Gulag and under Leonid Brezhnev's harsh rule all political and artistic expression was restricted. The play provided Miller a chance to compare the reality of modern communism with the ideals of his youthful socialism. But eight years later much had changed within the Soviet system. Mikhail Gorbachev had introduced glasnost, and to Miller's mind it eased limits on artistic expression just as perestroika had led to a reconstruction of Soviet society. He was disabused of his optimism by the Eastern European writers he met. Glasnost did not make conditions ideal or even acceptable by western standards. "Greater" freedom was a relative term and artistic conditions, once harsh but definite, had become ambiguous, which was in some ways worse. In 1986 with a later British production of *The Archbishop's Ceiling* in the offing the uncertain atmosphere prompted Miller to revise the play. He had planned to anyway, feeling that "A lot of things were wrong with it." He restored some sections that had been cut, rewrote others, even dropped a major character. When he was finished, he had the final version of the play as well as the start of a serious turn toward an artistic haven in England. For the first time a work of his (this one) was going to be published there before it was published in America.

At this time Miller seems to have come under the influence of Harold Pinter, with whom he had traveled to Turkey in 1985 on behalf of PEN International. His presidential term having ended, he had become a vice president of the organization's American section. Pinter was his British counterpart and they were a pair of Jewish playwrights who could not have been more different. Miller, the New Yorker, then seventy years old, was a serious-minded man absorbed with politics and social problems, observant, objective and remote. Pinter, some fifteen years younger and much lighter in spirit, had grown up in London's East End and had been an actor before becoming the most important British playwright of his time. In temperament a man of the stage, he was often "on," being mischievous and mysterious, interested in theatrics and atmosphere. As he was about poetry, Miller was about journalism, as he was a social creature, Miller was a loner, as he played scenes, Miller made speeches. In short, they were much like their plays. With their friendship, Harold theatricalized Arthur while Arthur politicized Harold.

Pinter's fascination with the unspoken word and dynamics of human interaction had found an outlet in the psychological shadow lands of his plays, the famously Pinteresque. His off-center vision seems to have influenced Miller's reworking of *The Archbishop's Ceiling*. Miller had written his share of oblique dialogue before, but now, "I've become fascinated," he said, with "the question of reality and what it is, and whether there is any, and how one invites himself in." Here was a departure from the bedrock of reason on which he had always settled his certainties. The nervousness in these first steps toward an acceptance of the unsure is frankly conceded in a wry exchange midway through *The Archbishop's Ceiling*. "You don't like ambiguity," someone notices. "Oh sure," is the reply, "providing it's clear." With Miller's belated acceptance of some elements of the surreal the play became his tiptoe into the waters of absurdism. His approach was somewhat in the style of Franz Kafka, who appropriately was from Prague, where this play is presumably set, and who influenced Pinter as well.

Uncertainty suits *The Archbishop's Ceiling*. Its writer characters are never sure of the extent of glasnost. A Hilton hotel has been built in the middle of the city, but Soviet tanks hover on the outskirts. The play's ambiguities also reflect the inability of Americans to comprehend both the political situation and the Eastern European sensibility in general, not having even "the most primitive misunderstandings of what it means to live in this country." Most important, perhaps, the play is about writers forced to leave their countries and in this regard might be read as a parable about Arthur Miller's own situation at the time.

The play's action takes place in "the sitting room of the former residence of an archbishop . . . the ceiling symbolizes what happens below." Because of that the ceiling in a way is a character in the play. That is why Miller is so specific about its appearance, "first seen in high relief, the Four Winds, cheeks swelling, and cherubim, darkened unevenly by soot and age." He does not explain how a balcony audience is supposed to see this.

As the curtain rises, an important American writer called Adrian is searching the room for listening devices. He is visiting a woman named Maya and when she appears he says that he has come to research a new novel. He admits to having heard that she is not what she seems—an ex-playwright who has given up on being political to become a talk radio host. Rather it is rumored that she is an agent for her communist government, entrapping dissident writers with eavesdropping devices in this house.

Adrian insists, however, he does not believe that. She is nevertheless offended and asks him to leave, only to whisper in the foyer, "We can talk out here, 'it' is only in the apartment." She means a hidden microphone that may be in the sitting room ceiling.

Adrian does not leave but stays for a drink, and two of Maya's literary friends arrive. One is Sigmund (suggested by the playwright Vaclav Havel, later the president of Czechoslovakia), whose latest novel has just been confiscated by the state police. Maya considers the manuscript a masterwork, but she can only say this in the foyer. The other visiting writer, Marcus, may be a government agent—even though he denies it—since he has "privileges" and some kind of "power" with the state.

Marcus tells them that the government will not allow the publication of the novel and that Sigmund himself is in danger. Adrian is appalled by such artistic conditions that, he says, are like suffering "some kind of continuous crime." This strikes Maya as American naivete and she scoffs, "Where is not a continuous crime?" Adrian dares her to repeat her praise of Sigmund's book ("It will endure a thousand years!") within range of the listening device and this ends the first act.

After the intermission Marcus tells Sigmund that "they" are going to put him on trial for "slandering the state" in his novel. Maya pleads that Sigmund "Get out! He must leave the country!" Otherwise she and Adrian can only hope that the influential Marcus might help him avoid prison. "I am sorry," she says, "for Socialism. I am sorry for Marx and Engels and Lenin—I am sorry!" In this is a touch of *Darkness at Noon*, Arthur Koestler's classic 1940 novel of disillusionment with international communism. Miller, however, is after a more modern tone and like Beckett's tramps and their Godot his four writers await a mysterious woman named Alexandra, who supposedly will find a way for Sigmund to escape. "She's at some embassy dinner," says Marcus. "As soon as she can break away. Shouldn't be long."

They resort to tense small talk—about Marcus and his dentist, about Maya and her pets ("My bird died on Sunday . . . I finally found out . . . she was a male. And all these years I called him Lulu!"). Adrian asks about her radio program. "You ever get mail?"

> MAYA: Oh, very much. Mostly for recipes, sometimes I teach them to cook.
> SIGMUND: She is very comical. She is marvelous actress.
> ADRIAN: It's not a political show?
> MAYA: No! It's too early in the morning. I hate politics . . . boring, boring, always the same . . . You know something? You are both very handsome.

Concluding these elliptical remarks, she quotes W. H. Auden. "The world needs a wash and a week's rest," and then breaks the play's rhythm of terse speeches with a lyrical passage that describes the day she and Marcus met Sigmund.

> The snow was half a meter high on his hat—I thought he was a peasant selling potatoes, he bowed the snow all over my typewriter. And he takes out this lump of paper—it was rolled up like a bomb. A story full of colors, like a painting; this boy from the beet fields—a writer! It was a miracle—such prose from a field of beets. That morning—for half an hour—I believed in Socialism.

Bowed the snow is a noteworthy phrase. Adrian too now speaks a more expressive language and likewise at greater length, describing a novel he had been writing about living in "*unfreedom* . . . It's like a bad back—you simply learn to avoid making certain movements . . . like . . . whatever's in this ceiling; or if nothing is; we still have to live, and talk, and the rest of it." Sigmund, speaking in Middle European dialect, says that because of possible eavesdropping, "We must always making theatre." He does not mean mere wariness. As Miller said elsewhere—sounding positively postmodern—"We're all impersonators in a way, impersonating something including ourselves." In *The Archbishop's Ceiling* Sigmund says, "It is everywhere that people pretend."

The play's circles within circles begin to eddy as Marcus accuses Sigmund of playing up to this American. "Come on now, Adrian," he says, "Sigmund has been writing this story for you all evening! *New York Times* feature on Socialist decadence." Adrian then comes to a realization that it may not matter "anymore, what anyone feels . . . about anything. Whether we're not just some sort of . . . filament that only lights up when it's plugged into whatever power there is." Yet Adrian already has been revealed as a man whose convictions are simplistic, his perceptions sentimental. There is only one power, Marcus says, and that is society. He looks at the ceiling, once symbolic of the Catholic Church of which this house had been a part, now symbolic, because of the microphone, of the state. God has become, he says, "simply a form of art."

At this point a real-life miracle occurs. The mysterious Alexandra telephones with news that Sigmund's confiscated manuscript will be returned to him. Instead of accepting this as a good thing Sigmund takes it as a sly form of ridicule. Maya, in another religious allusion, thinks it is a demonstration that "they have the power to take it and the power to give it back." Sigmund replies that he's had enough of such games, such "theater," but he has become morose, for he is a writer who loves his country and knows its importance to his work. "I think I will not be able to write in some other country. . . . I must hear my language every day. I must absolutely understand who is speaking to me," and looking up at the ceiling he asks, "Who is commanding me?" Maya, although fearing what might "happen for what has been said here," declares, "we must begin to say what we believe." That—because she can't really mean it—is when Sigmund realizes that these two ostensible friends are there to "deliver" him and make sure that he leaves the country, not like Solzhenitsyn but voluntarily, to show that this is no totalitarian Soviet state but a glasnost government. The "game" Marcus says they have been playing is called "Power" and he suggests that when Adrian writes about what has happened,

> I hope you include the fact that they refused him a visa for many years and he was terribly indignant—the right to leave was sacred . . . now he has that right and it's an insult. You [to Sigmund] are a moral blackmailer. . . . But now you're free to go. . . . We have done what was possible; now you will do what is necessary.

Maya adds that should Sigmund go to America, he won't be able to write. Language is a writer's stock in trade; when there is limited comprehension and a tentative grasp of nuance, the writer flies blind. He will just be "another lousy refugee ordering his chicken soup in broken English . . . you will die of silence." This, Miller said, is "What happens . . . when people know that they are . . . at all times talking to Power, whether through a bug or a friend who is really an informer." Informing had been his bête noire since college days.

The sound of "a heavy brass knocker" is heard and "Sigmund lifts his eyes to the ceiling," saying for its benefit,"I will never leave." He asks Adrian to hold some letters for safekeeping. They are from brave writers: André Malraux, Heinrich Böll, Nadine Gordimer, "So many writers! Like snow . . . like forest . . . these enormous trees everywhere on the earth," and so the play ends.

The Washington premiere of the earlier version of *The Archbishop's Ceiling* had been met with a hailstorm of critical disapproval. One of the more forgiving reviewers was Gerald Weales in *Commonweal*. "I will settle for the playwright of earlier days. Come home, Arthur Miller." The producers (Whitehead, Roger L. Stevens and Konrad Matthaei), cutting their losses, closed the show rather than bring it to New York, a stunning humiliation for Miller.

At a party soon afterward a friend tried to console the author. "Stay with it, Artie," he said. "You'll make it yet." Miller replied, "Thanks, it's always nice to get a little encouragement."

His grimness was understandable but at the same time his British reputation was growing. Michael Billington, who had come to Washington to review *The Archbishop's Ceiling* for the *Guardian*, credited the playwright with "the European dramatist's belief in the need to ask daunting questions rather than provide comforting answers." Such questions were essential to this "comedy of disaster" whose crucial line is, "We don't even know . . . whether we're oppressed. We don't even know whether this whole thing is simply our paranoia."

Reviewing the London premiere eight years after the Washington debacle, Billington's praise was still greater—"a complex, gritty, intellectually teasing play." Among the academics Christopher Bigsby observed, "There is a metaphysical anxiety in the play which moves Miller closer to Beckett and Pinter than ever before." And after its publication American scholars came to the play's defense too. Professor William W. Demastes of Louisiana State University posed the question, "How, exactly, can authentic behavior be determined in a world that has become a stage for inauthentic performance?" Demastes also saw religious significance in the play—"the ceiling's soot covered relief [being] an invasion of Lucifer into God's former domain." Miller never ascribed such specific theology to *The Archbishop's Ceiling* but there are symbols in the play, certainly the ceiling with its connotation of a higher power. As to Sigmund's question—Who is commanding him?—Miller would only say, "It's like God. You never know whether he's there or not but you have to take account of him anyway." God was the name of whatever power ruled from above, if only ceiling high.

Academic attention and praise did not make much of an impression on him, but England was meaning more with every passing play. While *The Archbishop's Ceiling* was running in the Royal Shakespeare Company's Barbican Pit, the National Theatre presented *A View from the Bridge*. That production, directed by Alan Ayckbourn and starring Michael Gambon, was so highly praised that it was transferred to the West End for a six-month run. It gave Miller three plays on London stages in a single theater season. Even *Incident at Vichy* had been well received there, although he'd had to miss the first night because of a case of hepatitis that landed him in a Brighton hospital for a week. Treated under the National Health Service, the playwright informed a hospital spokesman that the same treatment would have cost him $5,000 in America. The information officer, apparently a theater man, told a reporter, "Nobody, I think, would like to lose Mr. Miller. He is needed to keep the human race up to the mark. We are happy to have restored his heart and mind, and of course his liver, to their accustomed brilliance."

His eminence in England was already considerable enough for an Arthur Miller Centre for American Studies to be formally instituted in 1987 at the University of East Anglia in Norwich, outside of London. On that occasion even *The Golden Years*, the Aztec epic that Miller wrote at twenty-five, was given a production by the BBC Radio Drama Department. But like Sigmund in *The Archbishop's Ceiling* he was still rooted in his homeland. "If you are weak enough to give it up," he said of becoming an expatriate, "I suppose you should give it up." Personally he was not ready to deal full time with the foreign language that was British English. "I must hear my language every day," Sigmund says in *The Archbishop's Ceiling*, and he could well have been speaking for the playwright. But also like Sigmund Arthur Miller was caught between Scylla and Charybdis, for his reviews at home were growing more savage with every premiere. Just as the Arthur Miller Centre was being dedicated in Norwich, two short plays, *Clara* and *I Can't Remember Anything*, were being presented in New York under the single title *Danger: Memory!* Like Eugene O'Neill, who had turned to one-act plays during his long period of disfavor, Miller seemed to find comfort in the less ambitious form. These were not works of consequence, but the British critics who came to see them praised the pair to an extent that suggested an evolving British-

American dynamic in regard to Arthur Miller. The English were in effect offering him comprehension and respect while in the *New York Times*, critic Frank Rich, after invoking the decades-old notoriety of *After the Fall* and Marilyn Monroe, wrote of the one acts, "The writing is studied and ponderous . . . essentially a [mystery] episode with middlebrow political ruminations substituted for suspense."

It appeared to Miller that "There seems to be a delight on the part of the critics to see that nothing survives. . . . I don't think we can remember one critic of Chekhov's, one critic of Strindberg's, one critic of Shakespeare's. Where are these guys?"

The relationship between Arthur Miller's daughter Rebecca and her half sister had grown comfortable enough for Jane to regularly ask the fourteen year old to take care of her baby. Playing nursemaid was something that Becky Miller plainly enjoyed, at least until the morning when the infant was found frighteningly still. It was a case of crib death, or what was then called SIDS—sudden infant death syndrome. *Syndrome* would soon be deleted when medical research discovered the specific cause of the tragedy (a lack of ascorbate, or liver metabolite), but it wasn't soon enough to save Jane Miller Doyle's baby.

"Rebecca somehow got it into her head," Miller told his friend Whitehead, "that she had a responsibility for it—and she adored that baby."

After that the producer and his wife, the actress Zoe Caldwell, would make it a point of asking Rebecca Miller to take care of their young sons, "To make Rebecca feel great about children again." She would grow up to have two of her own.

For a new year's feature in 1979 the *New York Times* had surveyed theater people for their choices of "The Perfect Plays," and published the results on January 14. Miller, dismissing the possibility of perfection ("smacks of engineering more than poetics"), placed *Oedipus the King* at the top of his list. "It is a play which, so to speak, supports itself, a thing of immense weight, yet so stressed within itself that it might be balanced on the tip of a blade of grass." He added, "it is a kind of play whose theme is its most important element. It is a play about political tyranny and at the same time an implacable confrontation with the processes of personal guilt, innocence and the human claim to justification."

He was managing to make *Oedipus* sound just like an Arthur Miller play. "After that," he said, otherwise strikingly objective and smart,

> it's all a matter of taste. Molnar's *The Guardsman* probably cannot be bettered in its kind, or Pirandello's *Henry IV* in its, but some kinds of perfection arouse

more affection than others and so Chekhov's *The Seagull* is my next choice. Of course, its characterizations are miraculously incisive, but just as fascinating is the mystery of its forward movement despite so little "happening." It accomplishes a sense of *being* almost without reference to events; it seems to banish everything in the theater except the spirit. Its greatness, I think, springs from an untroubled apportioning by the author of what his characters are conscious of and what belongs only to their fate.

As for Shakespeare, he wrote,

One can't leave out The Great Intimidator, but it is almost impossible to think of a "perfect" Shakespeare play. Indeed, we hardly ever see one that is not cut. . . . Probably the best piece of architecture, whose characters do not overflow their given outlines and whose events are always concise, thematically connected and dramatically apt, is *Julius Caesar,* a play I immensely admire but do not like. *King Lear* is far more profound, but to associate it with perfection is impossible.

More useful might be to ask for the most honorable plays—those that earn their conclusions and effects, which do not seek to create bogus mysteries but search out mystery to illuminate it with insight.

Arthur Miller's last play of the 1970s reached out in yet another new direction. *The American Clock* is a theatrical collage, an attempt, he said,

to rediscover my youth . . . In the Thirties, there was a different spirit in the country. We were all thrown together. It was truly a society. But in the Seventies, the basic feeling was, "Well, I'm all right, Jack." People, I thought, were becoming more and more separated from each other. There was no society left. It was all material goods and the brass ring.

The "different spirit"—the social warmth—he tried to evoke in the play proved to be laced with injury. *The American Clock* is a panoramic survey of America and Americans at the moment of the stock market crash and in the years that followed. He described it as a "mural" requiring an epic-style production to depict "the collapse of a society." Not really a play, it is more of a documentary-cum-fiction that is epic at least in production size, calling for a company of fifty actors telling a multiplicity of stories.

The focus of *The American Clock* is on the experiences of three groups during the 1930s. The first of these is a New York family whose fortune was lost overnight. Called Moe, Rose and Lee Baum, they are unabashedly based on Miller's own family (and given Jewish names at last). For the premiere production he even cast his sister, Joan, as the mother. The second group is the Wall Street sector, the bankers and stockbrokers and industrialists. The third group is the entire rest of America—factory workers, farmers, small-town people. Miller's resource for them was Studs Terkel's oral history of the Depression, *Hard Times*.

Like *The Archbishop's Ceiling*, this play too was revised for a subsequent British production. In 1985 Peter Wood staged it at the National Theatre, adding irony by introducing a touch of the music hall. This included to Miller's delight onstage musicians playing period songs such as "Million Dollar Baby," "My Baby Just Cares for Me" and "Once in a While." Hence the subtitle, *A Vaudeville*, and that is the final version.

The framework follows the pattern of most stage documentaries, for instance, one character adding to another's lines, while the chorus summarizes.

> ROSE: By the summer of 1929 . . .
> LEE: I think it's fair to say that nearly every American . . .
> MOE: Firmly believed that he was going to get . . .
> COMPANY: Richer and richer

There are also dramatic vignettes. A stockbroker named Robertson warns that the Wall Street bubble is about to burst, but nobody pays attention. A shoeshine boy is buying stock on margin and so is Moe Baum, across the stage in his "eleven room apartment." There his chauffeur ("I had the lap-robe dry cleaned") waits to take him and his wife, Rose, to a show while she is at the piano, accompanying the singing ("Rudy Vallee is turning green") of their son, Lee. At the same age of fourteen in 1929, young Miller also used to sing. Lee becomes the chronicle's narrator along with the stockbroker Robertson, both used as thread to connect the brief scenes. Robertson, for instance, strolls across the stage to a speakeasy where tuxedoed millionaires headed for bankruptcy drown their sorrows in liquor. As they talk of a banker who just jumped out of a Wall Street window, that man's sister comes through the door, bewildered because she has only forty cents in her purse and doesn't know "What has become of all the money?"

Another man in the speakeasy, the controlling stockholder of General Motors, already knows that the "gentleman . . . who has just put down the telephone is undoubtedly steeling himself to tell me that I have lost [that] control." He calmly advises the young woman to "shun paper . . . paper is the plague." Only then does she learn of her brother's suicide, while Moe Baum advises the audience that the man from General Motors wound up "managing a bowling alley in Toledo." Meanwhile in the Baum apartment young Lee is showing his mother a new bicycle.

> LEE: It's a Columbia Racer! I just bought it from Georgie Rosen for twelve dollars.
> ROSE: Where'd you get twelve dollars?
> LEE: I emptied my savings account.

Rose Baum is not buying anything. She asks the boy to take her diamond bracelet to a pawnshop. She is also "glad you bought that bike. . . . It's gorgeous!" This and virtually all of the material involving the Baums, from the Columbia Racer to the chauffeur, the lap robe, the pawnshop and their ultimate move to Brooklyn, come directly from Arthur Miller's life.

The play finally goes beyond New York (it calls for a map of the United States as a scenic backdrop) to deal with the Midwest and the auctioned sale of a repossessed farm. It soon returns, however, to the Baums and their son Lee, whose fine sense of moral outrage does not deter him from taking himself off to college. As narrator he also recounts a list of Depression tragedies, for instance, a once well-to-do man begging for food or a young man getting engaged in exchange for a rent-free apartment.

Miller called this play *The American Clock* because he meant to "give some sense of life as we lived it when the clock was ticking every day [and the] question was whether America . . . had a clock running on it." But the title only provided inspiration for such priceless critical witticisms as "This *Clock* is a bit off" (Barnes, the *New York Post*), "*The American Clock* is trying to tick away the past" (Watt, the *Daily News*) and "*The American Clock* has arrived on Broadway unwound" (Rich, the *New York Times*). A perhaps more informative review was Jack Kroll's in *Newsweek*, personal though it is. Aware of how overdrawn were Miller's autobiographical resources, Kroll suggested that the play "never finds its effective dramatic shape; it's part play, part chronicle, but mostly it's Miller's last evocation of the images and people that have haunted him more than any others in his life."

Not even the faithful academics could find much to analyze in this play, but when *The American Clock* was produced by the National Theatre in London, it was nominated for the Olivier Award as the best new play of the season. On Broadway, where it had opened on November 20, 1980, at the Biltmore Theatre, it closed after twelve performances. Still holding to his native country, Miller could and did look to the rest of America for stages hospitable to his work. Twenty major professional productions of his various plays were being mounted in 1985 and 1986. Nine more were already announced for the following year, but not only were these plays being done everywhere except New York, nearly all of them had been written thirty or more years earlier. Eugene O'Neill had been ill when he felt crushed by what his biographers Barbara and Arthur Gelb called an "accumulation of public-underevaluation." But Arthur Miller was in full possession of his mental and physical faculties when his work became unwanted. He had lost most of his hair and had filled out considerably since his lanky youth, but he was robust rather than heavy and altogether hale, a most alert, active and vital seventy year old. "I've always hated Broadway theater," he said. "They seemed to be absolutely brainless . . . It started to become a musical comedy theater." This did not sound convincing, particularly when he added, "All of which shouldn't have mattered, and wouldn't have mattered if I had some support around me."

England was becoming more attractive with every failing play. There *The American Clock* and *The Archbishop's Ceiling*—two plays, he said, "that at home had been branded null and void"—were received with respect, even prized. "In future," a British interviewer reported, "Miller declared, he would stage his plays beyond the shores of showbiz in some unnamed country where the words tragedy and doom were still part of the language."

"I'm becoming invisible in my own land," he bitterly remarked, adding,

> Perhaps interviewers would now stop asking what I had been doing through the Seventies and start looking into whether a significant number of worthwhile American plays had been chewed up and spat out by that lethal New York combination of a single all powerful newspaper and a visionless if not irresponsible theater management.

And, he said, "I can only tell you" what Chekhov said. "'If I had listened to the critics I'd have died drunk in the gutter.'"

In 1979 a young television producer named Linda Yellen had hesitantly approached Arthur Miller's agent to inquire about the possibility that he might write a television adaption of *The Musicians of Auschwitz*. Whatever Miller's theatrical problems, his reputation could still inspire awe among the young, certainly those in television.

The Auschwitz book, published in English as *Playing for Time*, was a memoir written by Fania Fenelon, a half-Jewish Parisian cabaret singer who had survived Auschwitz–Birkenau by entertaining the Nazis—playing in an orchestra made up of forty-seven Jewish women prisoners. Even before Miller surprised Yellen by agreeing to the project, she drew up a "wish" list of women to play Fenelon, actresses celebrated enough to sell television executives on the project. At the top of her list were Barbra Streisand, Jane Fonda and at Miller's suggestion Vanessa Redgrave, one of the finest actresses in the English-speaking theater. Fonda was committed to other projects while Streisand rejected the offer, but when Redgrave signed on, *Playing for Time* was bought by the CBS television network.

While Miller was writing the screenplay—which he finished in a month—and Redgrave was taking piano and singing lessons, a crisis arose over her public support of the Palestine Liberation Organization. There was an immediate protest from Rabbi Marvin Hier, the head of the Simon Wiesenthal Center of Holocaust Studies in Los Angeles ("Miss Redgrave's portrayal would desecrate the memory of the martyred millions"). Howard M. Squadron, the president of the American Jewish Congress, sent an open letter to CBS, stating, "The idea that Vanessa Redgrave, who publicly supported the terrorist cause and the PLO goal of destroying Israel, has been cast in the role of a concentration camp inmate is grotesque." Even within the film community the respected documentary producer David Wolper asked, "How low do you have to be to make controversy?"

Miller defended the actress in his trademarked, balanced-going-on-noncommittal way.

> Miss Redgrave was offered the role of Fania Fenelon as an actress suited to it. To fire her now for her political views would be blacklisting. Having been blacklisted myself in time past . . . I cannot participate in it now, but something more needs be said: No actress can possibly play Fania in this play without generating the profoundest sympathy for the Jewish people . . . if this attack is solely upon her past views and actions it ought to stop short . . . God help us, it may even be that the reconciling spirit has moved within her. I cannot know.

There was a farcical side to the controversy, a bomb scare at the movie's production office, when "an old Hasidic Jew," Yellen remembered, "threw this thing that was supposed to go off." The network was not amused since the controversy led to the film going without national advertisers, yet despite television's reputation for political cowardice, CBS backed Yellen, Miller and Redgrave. *Playing for Time* was filmed in November 1979 in Fort Indiantown Gap, Pennsylvania, where an abandoned army base had been used to detain German prisoners of war. The two-and-a-half-hour film was broadcast on Sunday evening, September 30, 1980, and it is a considerable accomplishment. Miller had learned much from the polemical conception of *Incident at Vichy* and the screenwriting mistakes of *The Hook* and *The Misfits*. Without resorting to either discussions or cheap emotional tricks his screenplay conveys the harrowing reality of the death camp and the irony of victims entertaining their killers with beautiful music. It was his most heartfelt Jewish expression and his most effective presentation of the survivor theme, effective because only implicit. In the process he mastered the differences between stage and screen writing, leaving plenty of visual space within terse bursts of muscular dialogue. In Miller's script is justification for the musicians ("We are artists. There is nothing to be ashamed of"), clear implication of theme ("For a beautiful woman to do such a thing—she's human like me, that's the problem") and irony in characterization. Doctor Josef Mengele, the "Angel of Death," is a music lover who has "rarely felt so totally moved." In the bargain Miller had the chance to indulge his love and knowledge of classical music.

Perhaps most notably in terms of his craft, he finally wrote with depth and variety for women. Certainly Linda Loman is a strong character as are, in their ways, Elizabeth Proctor and Esther Franz, but Miller's plays are essentially stories of men. The characters in *Playing for Time* are almost exclusively women and convincingly so.

Several years after the broadcast he decided to adapt the work for the stage. In theatrical form it is a singular and singularly unknown drama, a major, full-length Arthur Miller play that is not listed among his official stage works (his autobiography mentions neither the theatrical nor the television version). *Playing for Time* still had not received a major production—in America or England—in the seventeen years since it was given an obscure world premiere in the "Fringe" of the 1986 Edinburgh International Festival.

The stage work begins in the dark with the roar of a train fading as Fania Fenelon speaks from the floor of a boxcar. "We still weren't sure what was happening . . . where we were going, and why." The space is crowded with men, women and children who suspect that they are being taken to a labor camp. A needy young woman named Marianne tells Fania, "I still can't believe I'm sitting so close to you . . . I know all your songs by heart" and a man says, "Your music is for me the sound of Paris." As the train rumbles along in underscore, some of them nod off, some weaken, one dies. Suddenly there is a lurching stop, a burst of "blazing white light" and a couple of SS troopers funneling them off the train under the watchful eye of Mengele. A female guard has the women ("You Jew-shit!") give up their handbags, their coats, their earrings. As the group huddles fearfully—"What's that smell?" "When do we see our children?"—their clothes are stripped and the Jewish women among them have their hair shorn (the actresses wear wigs at the outset). Showers are heard in the dark and when the lights come up the stage is a barracks room with shelves for sleeping. Marianne, breaking down, cries to Fania, "Why are they doing this? What do they get from it?" then a guard bursts in to ask, "Does anyone know how to sing *Madame Butterfly*?"

As Marianne points to Fania the stage almost instantly becomes the brightly lighted work area for the "Orchestra Girls" with rows of music stands and a piano. The prisoner-conductor is Alma Rose, a Jewish musician who flaunts her Germanic discipline. As she looks on, Fania is ordered by Mandel, the women's commandant, to sing. Still in shock, she approaches the piano wearing "immense men's shoes . . . a fuzz of hair on her bald head," but after being accepted into the orchestra, she boldly tells the commandant that she cannot join unless her friend, Marianne, is taken as well. Mandel not only agrees to this but finds a better pair of shoes for Fania and even kneels to slip them on her feet.

The orchestra rehearsal begins. Originally a marching band, their conductor Alma has turned them toward "Bach and Brahms, giving concerts for the brass." It is a ragged sound they make but Alma is adamant that "This is not band music . . . Why can you not obey my instructions? Music is the holiest activity of mankind . . . you cannot simply repeat the same stupid mistakes." Fania is told the musical problem—no orchestrations exist for their weird combination of mandolin, guitar and accordion as well as violins and cellos. When she reveals that she studied orchestration, Alma is thrilled, but for nonmusical reasons. "Please try to hurry the work," she begs, "They're so very changeable toward us, you see?"

As 12,000 prisoners outside are being gassed daily, inside the full orchestra assembles with Alma on the podium, the Nazi officers forming the audience. They do not applaud for camp inmates; they only grant smiles of approval. The orchestra plays—it sounds like "caterwauling"—and then Fania is alone with Marianne, lecturing her. "After a year in this hell, I should think you could give up being a little child. When are you going to make peace with your situation, Marianne? You can't go on expecting something fantastic to happen. I mean, *this is where you are*."

She adds, on the subject of hoarding food, "I refuse to turn into an animal for a gram of margarine or a potato peel!" But the prisoners are already squabbling among themselves, building a hierarchy in which the Jews, certain to be gassed, are at the bottom. The women's nerves are soothed with Fania's girlish descriptions of Parisian styles in shoes (high heels), hair ("piled up curls") and stockings (none available, so the women paint their legs), and they cluster girlishly around the piano as she sings "The Man I Love."

Necessary outdoor scenes from the television play are effectively described in soliloquies, Fania peering through a window, for instance, to describe "hundreds of women with picks and shovels . . . go out and dig drainage ditches." When the orchestra is marching the prisoners off to work, Fania, though she needn't, insists on going outside to watch and a prisoner spits in her face for collaborating.

"What did you expect?" the conductor asks.

"I'm not used to being hated like that."

But as her orchestrating proceeds, she cannot concentrate, clapping her hands over her ears because of persistent gunshots and screams. Then she sees her friend Marianne taking food from a guard in exchange for sex. "What right do you have to judge anyone?" the girl asks. "You know what they think of us out there? We're no better than prostitutes to be entertaining these murderers. . . . Well, it doesn't matter . . . We won't live to get out of here anyway."

With a new group of arrivals the orchestra is given another assignment, "to play them into the gas." An officer tells Fenelon that her singing "is a consolation that feeds the spirit. It strengthens us for this difficult work of ours." Alma, the conductor, continues her strict, even physical discipline of the orchestra, all but breaking down as she tells Fania, "As it is, Doctor Mengele can just bear to listen to us. If we fall below a certain level, anything is possible," but Fania replies, "I will tell you the truth, madam. I really don't know how long I can bear this . . . Believe me, I recognize that your strength is probably what our lives depend on." Alma insists that whatever the circumstances, an artist has to be only an artist. As Fania walks out on that, Alma picks up her violin and plays an exquisite solo to end the first act.

While more of the prisoners have started whoring with the guards, the Nazi officers have decided that the women will play Beethoven's Fifth Symphony for the sick and mental patients in the camp hospital. "Doctor Mengele wants to observe the effects of music on the insane." But as they rehearse the Beethoven, it is learned that following the concert the patients will all be gassed. By this time Fania Fenelon has passed beyond despair. "My heart beats, so I'm alive . . . I could drive a nail through my hand, it would hardly matter." The Christian connotation is not stressed.

The Poles among these prisoners squabble with the Jews. The younger women realize that sheer terror has caused them to stop menstruating. They grow frail, steal, or succumb to romance with each other. "Why not?" Fania tells one. "After all you've seen and been through here, you're worried by a thing like that?" Suddenly the stage explodes with angry Nazis, searching for a favored prisoner and her lover, who have escaped. But at the same time there is word that the Allies have landed in France, and the women's commandant announces that "there will be no further . . . *selections* . . . from our camp." She has already taken a pet for herself, a prisoner's child.

When Alma is transferred out of the camp, it is decided that a Christian prisoner must replace her as the conductor, which terrifies Fania. As the woman proceeds to play a "foot-stomper" polka ("You'll send us to the gas! Mengele . . . won't stand for this racket") the escaping lovers are captured. The whole camp is called out to watch the hanging, after which Marianne has sex with the hangman. "You'd better be on the side of the executioners," she tells Fania, who is beginning to realize that "We may be innocent, but we have changed . . . we know a little something about the human race that we didn't know before." When she is asked, "How can you still call them human?" she responds, with perfect logic, "Then what are they?" So Miller has arrived at the center of it, the capacity of ordinary people to become beasts. At this point the "handsome" Mengele enters and solemnly informs them, "in memoriam," that their former conductor has been put to death. "If the Herr Doctor will permit me," Fania says, "The orchestra is resolved to perform at our absolute best, in memory of our beloved conductor." Mengele simply leaves.

Their haven apparently finished, they panic and wonder why Allied planes aren't bombing the camp. One says, "They don't want it to seem like it's a war to save the Jews." Then the women's commandant enters, "desolate" because the little boy she "adopted" has been put to death. For solace she asks the orchestra to play the duet from *Madame Butterfly* and Fania begins to sing with one of the others, while the commandant rocks, as if cradling a child. There are sirens, the roar of airplanes, the crashing of bombs. But the hospital concert is given as scheduled. "We played for the insane," Fenelon soliloquizes,

> who Mengele had been keeping for such an occasion . . . some began to dance . . . Some clung to each other like monkeys . . . as we played, they were one by one being carefully wheeled out to the gas chamber, some of them still waving their arms to the music.

And then German troopers—not the SS but the regular army—arrive to announce that the prisoners are to be evacuated. "The next thing I knew," Fenelon says, "a British officer was asking me to speak into a radio microphone . . . I began to sing! The *Marseillaise*!"

The former prisoners then reappear handsomely clothed in a restaurant. "I have two children," one proudly tells Fania. She tells a waiter to "Ask the chef if there is something absolutely extraordinary!" and the final curtain falls.

Miller wrote this powerful full-length dramatization of *Playing for Time* five years after the television broadcast. At the Edinburgh Festival the limited engagement received standing ovations and did not go unnoticed in the London press. Reviewing the play in the *Guardian*, Nicholas de Jongh called it "the true sensation of my Festival . . . There have only been two or three occasions in my theatre going life that I have been so wrenched, wracked and appalled." In the London *Times* John Hart wrote, "the impact of this, the UK premiere of Miller's play was far, far greater than that made by the film. It is a powerful drama." Film certainly has its advantages and for anyone who has seen the television version there are reminders of *Playing for Time*'s cinematic origins in the dramatization. But the living theater has the greater power of emotional transport because of the immediacy of the event and the physical presence of the actors.

While the stage version of *Playing for Time* must make accommodations for the exterior locations and scene changes of the television screenplay, Miller's devices of soliloquy are so artfully adapted to the style of the dramatization and so craftily executed that there is never any sense of compromise. As the author indicates in a production note, "There need be no set, as such. The few changes in locale should be made in full view of the audience." Perhaps because of the concurrent productions of *The Archbishop's Ceiling, The American Clock* and *A View from the Bridge*, however, this striking work was never brought to London. Arthur Miller's most emotional play since *Death of a Salesman* remains to be discovered.

Encouraged by the success of *Playing for Time*, which won an armful of television awards, Miller returned to the battlefield that theater had become for him. This time he chose a more protected environment for two one-act plays finished in 1982. They were produced by the nonprofit Long Wharf Theater in New Haven, Connecticut, whose subscription audiences guaranteed a six-week engagement, whatever the reviews.

One of these plays, *Elegy for a Lady*, is a two-character twenty-minute jewel. Once again Miller employed expressionism to dramatize the workings of the human mind. Based on his 1980 short story published in *Esquire*, the play, Miller explains, is not a dream but "a reverie" in which "The Man" deals with the likelihood that his lover is dying. He is "racing time to find out what they meant to each other."

The setting is a boutique where he is looking for a gift for the mistress. The only other character is the Proprietress, who is seen as this man perceives her—as a projection of his lover. As staged the boutique is surreal, some of its items "seeming to be suspended in space," and the playwright supplies a detailed description of the Proprietress's costume, "a white silk blouse and a light beige skirt and high heeled shoes." That was exactly as Arthur Miller described what Marilyn Monroe had been wearing on the day in 1951 at the Los Angeles airport when he fled his first passion for her.

The Man's first question of the Proprietress is whether she has anything "for a dying woman." As he talks about his thirty-year-old mistress, he admits, "I'm married—and a lot older, of course," but is the lover really dying? She isn't even in a hospital. "Not yet," he says, "although frankly, I'm not sure . . . they're evidently operating on her in about ten days . . . she's had this growth . . . she was told it was almost certainly benign." Anyhow every gift he considers "makes some kind of statement that is simply not . . . right." The Proprietress is terse but always amenable ("It sounds like you'd simply like to thank her") and positive ("I'm sure you're going to think of something"). The Man "can't get over it . . . walking in off the street like this and blabbing away," probably because the Proprietress reminds him of the lover. "Just about her age . . . Thirty . . . the last year to believe that your life can radically change anymore . . . so it's hard to think of something that won't suggest the end of all that." When the Proprietress finally speaks up, the exchange is tight with unfinished sentences. "The point does come . . ." or "Surprisingly, yes . . ." or "an effort to keep it uncommitted . . ." or "a kind of contradiction . . ." or "to care and simultaneously not-care . . . "

He is trying, he says, to "understand what she means to me. I've never felt this way about death. Even my mother's and father's." As to the lover's state of mind, she was not, he says, the panicky type. "Something like this must be like opening a shower curtain and a wild animal jumps out." That is dialogue worth noting. When the Proprietress unintentionally makes a gesture reminiscent of his lover—a slap of the thigh while laughing—the conversation turns more personal. "You're successful," he says, "but a baby would be better."

"Why? Do I look unhappy?"

"You look like you'd found yourself . . . for the fiftieth time."

She turns the conversation to him and almost convinces him that the mistress may not be dying at all, and as for his age, she says, "That's only an excuse to escape with." He admits that the arrangement with his mistress was mutually convenient and that his wife "is who I should be married to," because she is kind, he says, and "tremendously competent." Why then—why really—is he buying this gift for the lover? What is he trying to say with it? What is the meaning of an "appropriate" gift? The Man wonders whether "there is really nothing between us . . . but an . . . *uncommitment*." He wonders too whether the Proprietress is "condemning him." She says that she will "forgive everything, finally." And that, he replies, "is your glory." Now they are talking as if they are the lovers. "You can't," she tells him, "expect what you would have had if you'd committed yourself"—which would have been true pain "worn out with weeping . . . staggered with your new loneliness . . . clarified with grief, washed with it, cleansed by a whole sorrow. A lover has to earn that satisfaction." He does love, he insists, but his commitments and his age—"The whole thing is ludicrous . . . I can't bear the sight of my face in the mirror—I'm shaving my father every morning!"

Now the Proprietress can assure him that the lover will survive because the relationship was "perfect . . . it is all that it could ever have become. . . . She knows she'll live"—and Miller notes that the Proprietress "is filled with love and anguish." She comes to him with a kiss and "a last embrace" and says, "How gently! Oh, how gently!" And he finally finds the gift he had come for, a pocket watch on a chain, which she now gives to him. The watch of course represents time, and the play's elegy might well be not only for the lover but the Man, so wanting to love, so self-centered, so conscious of advancing age.

Touching, consistent, dreamlike, dealing once again with the inability to grieve or feel anything, *Elegy for a Lady* is an intimately perfect one-act play, but since there was now no commercial interest in Miller he coupled it with another—and lesser—work, *Some Kind of Love Story*, and sent them on their nonprofit way.

The twin bill, called *2 by A.M.* (later changed to *Two-Way Mirror*), had its premiere on October 26, 1982, in New Haven, but there was no hiding from the New York critics. In Miller's words the pair was "really blasted out of the water" ("Tiresome . . . maudlin . . . vulgar"—*New York Times*). These plays too would be rescued in London, its critics applauding the twin bill when it was produced at The Young Vic.

"A playwright expects to be misinterpreted to some important degree," Miller wrote in an introductory note for *Elegy for a Lady*. "But to confront total incomprehension on the part of the critics is a new experience." Unfortunately it was no longer a new experience for him.

The following spring the house in Roxbury was gutted by fire and the losses were incalculable. Destroyed were working scripts, scenarios, notebooks and most of Miller's archival materials. Inge lost irreplaceable negatives as well as art books, drawings and a closet full of Balenciaga originals that the designer had given her during their youthful days in Paris. With the remains of the farmhouse still smoldering the Millers decided to reject an architect's advice to tear down what remained and start fresh. Instead they rebuilt and restored. While that was happening, he accepted an invitation to direct a production of *Death of a Salesman* at the Beijing People's Art Theater. Even aside from his speaking no Chinese, it was a notion that made little sense. As Miller put it,

> China is more than 90 per cent peasant and most . . . have been taught socialist values which are the very antithesis of those Willy Loman strives for . . . but the Chinese insisted they didn't want just another naturalistic drama. What they wanted was something more poetic.

Taking Inge along for the adventure, he stayed for two months of rehearsal, working through an interpreter. He convinced the actors that they didn't need to make up as Westerners. He thought "It made them look like creatures from another planet." The Millers came home with accounts and photographs for a book, *Chinese Encounter*. By then—their architect's advice notwithstanding—they had their farmhouse back. "The impulse to fill this frame with life again," Arthur said, "was more powerful than I would have imagined."

Miller chose to ignore another piece of advice—his own. Speaking at the University of Pennsylvania, he had warned students about the dangers of space age technology. Too many of them, he said, "are up to their necks in computers and less involved in education." Just a year later his warning gave way to progress as he acquired his own computer. He kept the old Royal office typewriter handy, as though it were a security blanket, but a few years later he would be talking easily about floppy discs that were neither discs nor floppy. He was comfortable with the new writing machine, he said, but also amazed.

> Strange, isn't it? You do all that work and what do you end up with? A little piece of plastic. No one ever gets to see anymore where the author maybe had another idea, scratched things out, or made little corrections in his own hand. A manuscript is really one of the last man made things. Think about it, "manu" meaning hand, and "script" meaning written. And now it isn't there anymore.

That seems to have marked the end of his letter writing as well.

Arthur Miller's times might have become bad, but they were not hard. The most lucrative year of his life was 1984, when he himself coproduced a Broadway revival of *Death of a Salesman* that starred Dustin Hoffman. Finally Willy Loman was being played by a small man, as originally conceived. For the occasion Miller restored *shrimp* to the script but he could not restore what history had changed. Loman had come to be identified with a hulking actor and Hoffman would always seem to be wearing clothes several sizes too big. Robert Whitehead felt that more important than lacking physical size, Dustin Hoffman did not carry the Salesman's emotional weight, but he certainly had the box office magnetism, not that the play required it. *Death of a Salesman* would always do well on Broadway, whether with Lee J. Cobb, Thomas Mitchell, George C. Scott, Dustin Hoffman or Brian Dennehy. Yet as a movie star, Hoffman was a particularly strong attraction and as a coproducer (with Miller and Whitehead), he flexed that muscle. One of the oddest manifestations of it was his insistence that G. Gordon Liddy, the Watergate burglar, audition for the role of Ben Loman. Liddy, who had been released from prison some eight years earlier, was eager to play the role even though he had minimal acting experience. Miller did not complain. "It was," he insisted, "a very preliminary reading. We're just gathering people for the director to hear."

Perhaps so, but Liddy was even called back for a second audition (he didn't get the part). The production began what would be an extended, sold-out engagement at the Broadhurst Theater and Miller's partners in the venture, Whitehead and Hoffman, were starting to share in its immense profits. Shortly after the March 29 premiere, however, Whitehead had to leave for Australia to direct his wife, Zoe Caldwell, in a production of *Medea*. When he returned he was confronted with Hoffman's demand that the financial arrangement be changed. Whitehead said,

> Although Miller and Hoffman had the lion's share, Hoffman's lawyers got after me about giving up my connection, and Arthur went along with it. *The greed*. He was passive-aggressive. He wrote me a letter saying he regretted this terribly. He sort of indicated that it was Dustin who wanted to reduce the amount of money I was making. He didn't want to get involved in it, he said, but Dustin, who is a trashy character, couldn't have done it if Arthur hadn't gone along. The money was with Hoffman and Arthur went where the money is.

The money was considerable. Arthur Miller and Dustin Hoffman were each receiving 45 percent of the weekly profits, with Whitehead getting 10 percent. That came to $63,000 apiece weekly for the author and the star, leaving $14,000 for the producer. The engagement was twice extended, finally running some thirteen weeks. With Whitehead cut out Miller made nearly a million dollars and "Arthur liked money," Whitehead said. "He liked money more than a good left winger was supposed to."

The two old friends were alienated for three years, finally reaching a rapprochement, but "still," Whitehead said, "that made a big difference in my relationship with Arthur."

In November 1987 Miller published his autobiography *Timebends*, having once said, "The form of *Death of a Salesman* was an attempt to convey the bending of time." His experience and facility with time manipulation in drama did not apply to prose. The book is by turns fascinating and exasperating. Instead of presenting a linear account of the playwright's life it takes a dizzying route of free association, leaping back and forth through time, choosing select events to describe in extensive, untrustworthy detail, distorting others and omitting many entirely. Absent too is the good-natured Miller who in private company could be such a funny and quick man, easy to laugh.

Instead *Timebends* regularly presents his windier qualities with only an occasional glimpse of humanity, for instance, when he takes an opportunity to settle scores with "that great author," Norman Mailer, for the "grinning vengefulness" of the *Marilyn* book. Mailer, he wrote, was Marilyn Monroe "in drag." To his credit, Arthur Miller did not have Mailer's talent for vituperation.

Even so, for long stretches *Timebends* is beautifully written and absorbing, covering Arthur Miller's wide range of interests and describing many of the events in his adventurous life. His friend, Harold Pinter, provided the blurb, "tough, very moving . . . a book and a half."

Reviewing it in the *Sunday New York Times*, Roger Shattuck was respectful ("one of our most substantial authors") but qualified. "In spite of certain weaknesses, *Timebends*," he wrote, "is a work of genuine literary craftsmanship and social exploration." Calling the title "somewhat lame" in its reference to "the laminated free form construction," Shattuck points out that the book "does not advance to a steady narrative line." It "digs up," he said, "bucketfuls of past incidents ordered almost as much by association as by chronology." In all the review was inconclusive.

In *Vanity Fair* under the headline, "The Misfit," James Wolcott wrote,

> That Miller came to regard himself as a great thinker is one of life's terrible misunderstandings. . . . The honest Abe Lincoln of American letters, ministering from his marble throne to the ailing soul of the Republic. Since the success of *Death of a Salesman* he has been the traveling secretary of liberal humanism, a global delegate for peace and dialogue . . . If only he could give piety a rest.

Miller could hardly be blamed for seeking escape from a tidal wave of insult. "In England, Europe and Latin America," he said, "this book has been one of my best-reviewed works, while in my own country it was as often as not passed over when it was not aggressively dismissed by a few critics, even hated by two or three."

Of course in his primary market, the New York theater and establishment press, it had been open season on Arthur Miller for some time. It would seem that he had no choice now but to seek theatrical asylum in England, there to find receptive audiences, critical respect and appreciation for his body of work. He felt, in his words, "invisible in my own land."

19. Survivor

Take Hemingway. Given the real impact that man had on letters, it would have been hard to believe that nothing but a sneer would now greet the mention of his name.

—Arthur Miller

Rather than continue to seethe at home while creative energies were being sapped by anger, Miller made his British commitment, telling a writer for *The New Yorker* magazine that he no longer counted on his new plays being produced in America. His latest full-length work, *The Ride Down Mt. Morgan,* would receive its world premiere in London. That seems to have been a reluctant but rejuvenating decision; Miller was not about to quit the stage and slink away, remembered only for *Death of a Salesman* and *The Crucible*.

It is true that the writing of plays has historically been a young man's calling. Shakespeare was fifty-nine when he wrote his last play. Chekhov was forty-four when he finished *The Cherry Orchard* and died of tuberculosis. Molière's final work, *The Imaginary Invalid,* was written at fifty-one. At seventy-three Tennessee Williams had lasted somewhat longer, but only chronologically. His fall from favor was even steeper than Miller's had been, a twenty-year stretch of rejected plays that ended only when he was found dead in a hotel room on February 24, 1983. The author of *The Glass Menagerie* and *A Streetcar Named Desire* choked on a medicine bottle cap. That left only Miller and Kazan of the once awesome Broadway triumvirate, and the eighty-one-year-old Kazan was already suffering severe losses of memory and alertness.

Miller therefore was of an age that inevitably prompted mortal thoughts, especially as his personal friends had started dying off—John Steinbeck in

1968 and Alexander Calder in 1976. James Stern would die in 1993 and William Gaddis soon afterward. At seventy-five, however, Miller was a vigorous man. He was still writing as he approached the professional longevity of another robust dramatist, George Bernard Shaw, who had written into his nineties.

The Ride Down Mt. Morgan is the unlikeliest of Arthur Miller's plays and as such, best exemplifies his ingenuity of style. It is a deceptively benign, imaginative, comic and finally tragic play about a man with two identities, and unwilling—or unable—to choose between them. This work had been in progress, he said, for more than ten years, going through "about fifteen different versions" and that is understandable considering its refined balance of grimness and gaiety.

With his arrival in London for the start of rehearsals the change in atmosphere was immediate. The *New York Times* reported, "No other dramatist on either side of the Atlantic has the iconic stature Mr. Miller now enjoys in Britain."

"All his plays are big events here," Nicholas Hytner said, and another director, David Thacker, saw "Actors respond to Arthur Miller entering a rehearsal room as if Shakespeare had just walked in. The fact that *Death of a Salesman* was written forty or fifty years ago doesn't matter."

Miller's sister, Joan Copeland, was startled as

> Just walking down the street with Arthur was like walking down the street with the Queen Mum. People practically fell down on their knees. You don't know how they even knew who he was, and it wasn't just in Mayfair, or the theater district. Wherever you were, people would just come up to him, just enthused.

The *New York Times*'s London theater correspondent, Matt Wolf, reported,

> Almost play for play, one can contrast a failed New York production with its successful British counterpart. *The American Clock* closed quickly on Broadway in 1989, then ran a season at the National six years later, picking up an Olivier Award nomination for best play. *A View from the Bridge* flopped on Broadway despite praise for its star, Tony LoBianco, in the 1983 [revival], whereas Alan Ayckbourn's 1987 London production did so well at the National that it transferred for six months to the West End.

The playwright's American critics were not impressed with such appreciation abroad. Richard Gilman, an academic, briefly the *Newsweek* drama critic and a member of the Brustein anti-Miller bloc, told the *Times*'s Wolf that he looked upon the British enthusiasm for Arthur Miller's plays with "bemusement . . . [as] so much propping up the corpse." Why such personal enmity? Why were his plays so much more hospitably received in

London than New York? Revisions do not explain it; the New York critics would reject the revised version of *The American Clock* as peremptorily as they had the original. One explanation might lie in the nature of the dramatic experience. Emotional power and theatricality count for much on the American stage, while the dramatic tradition in England is more mental and linguistic. From Shakespeare to the Restoration playwrights and on to Shaw, Wilde, Coward, Orton, Stoppard and Pinter, the British drama has rested on language and ideas. That might explain why word- and theme-conscious American playwrights such as T. S. Eliot, S. N. Behrman and more recently David Mamet made the transition so successfully. Miller's gift for stageworthy, idiomatic, *characteristic* dialogue was consistently underrated in his own country.

Another possible explanation for the differences in attitude toward Arthur Miller's work might lie in the cultures themselves. American critics seem put off by his uncompromising morality, tending to be cynical about it, taking moralizers for preachers and preachers for hypocrites. "To enjoy those plays," director Thacker said, "you have to be capable of being moved by ethical dilemmas and of seeing the world in that kind of moral frame." Perhaps morals are not so suspect in England, and perhaps there too it is felt that standards hold whatever the weaknesses of the standard bearer. And perhaps British critics are not so competitive with playwrights and less eager to fell the mighty. A London review is less crucial to a play's success than one in New York, and so the British critic is not as tempted by power as his American counterpart might be. Certainly the London critics are not as apt to throw out the playwright with the play, as happens too often in New York. According to Thacker, the greatest factor in establishing Miller in England was the support of its institutional theaters—not only the Royal Shakespeare Company but the even greater championship of the playwright by "Peter Hall and Richard Eyre of The National Theatre, who were committed to doing his plays, as I was at the Young Vic. There would be at least one Arthur Miller play every year." Such institutions, Thacker felt, offered especially fulfilling performances of the plays.

> The way in which actors in Britain are used to cutting their teeth on Shakespeare, classical texts . . . if you bring that technique to Miller's plays it's quite helpful because they are plays that operate through language. However emotionally truthful and psychologically powerful your performances are, if you don't actually serve up the text, the text doesn't land, and these are plays where the ideas come thick and fast. You can't mumble your way through these things and hope that they are actually going to communicate themselves.

Audiences need technique as well. As Miller put it, "A play requires language, which takes an effort of listening and interpretation; consequently the effort becomes part of the enjoyment; but if you have an audience trained not to put out effort, it arouses impatience. Passivity always wins out because it's easier." He was definitely finding British audiences willing to invest the effort and they were definitely better trained than American audiences—after all, they liked his plays.

Some months before the start of rehearsals for *The Ride Down Mt. Morgan* Miller was invited by the British Broadcasting Company to interview Nelson Mandela shortly after his release following twenty-seven years of South African imprisonment. The playwright, having toured native townships outside of Cape Town, came to the meeting with deep forebodings about the country's looming desegregation and transfer of power. "All the wrong choices were made right down the line," he said, "and now the birds have come home to roost."

He spent two and a half hours talking with Mandela at his home in Soweto and concluded that the anti-apartheid leader was more pragmatic than some of his militant speeches suggested. "Had he been born into a peaceful society," Miller told the *New York Times*, "he would have been a judge. He's one of the most conservative people I've ever met." During the interview Mandela said, "All we want is jobs and houses and the rest of it. Whatever method will get us that is what we want." At the time the playwright was disheartened. The prospect of a bloodletting was a harrowing one. "It's like a dream paralysis," he said, "where you're reaching toward something and you simply can't extend your arm. I don't think it's hopeless. I think it's on the edge of a very narrow knife [and] could go either way."

It was not the first time he'd had an audience with a political leader. In 1985 he and James Baldwin had joined a group of fourteen western writers invited to Moscow. It was plainly a public relations event, the beginning of glasnost, the Soviet Union seeking to present an image of greater artistic freedom under Gorbachev. He told the group, as Miller remembered, "The past is not a guide anymore in the sense that we used to think of it. Marx never knew anything about the atom bomb, so we have to start from reality instead of from theories." The Soviet leader had asked Miller what he thought was the function of an artist. "To speak truth to power," the playwright replied, although he doubted, he said, that power would ever listen. "The reason it's power is because it *doesn't* listen." Then taking a private opportunity with Gorbachev he asked, "Are you a Stalinist or a Leninist?"

It was a question that only an old leftist would have asked.

"I'm no Stalinist," the party leader said, "I'm a Leninist, and I think we have to start a whole new approach to Marxism."

Miller read that as being "philosophically, spiritually at sea." He was so struck that he jotted down notes of the conversation and after coming home to Connecticut related the experience to a neighbor, Harrison Salisbury, a retired editor of the *New York Times.* Salisbury encouraged him to write an editorial essay on the meeting. Miller found,

> They couldn't believe it. I sent it to *The Washington Post*. They wouldn't print it either. That's when I learned that we have a party line. The party line was that the Russian government was Stalinist, incapable of any change, that the whole [Gorbachev] thing was some kind of gag. And that's how we ended up looking at a Soviet Union that was literally falling to pieces and refusing to believe it. Because the line was that they had the atom bomb, they had all these airplanes, they had the biggest army in the world, they *had* to be powerful. Here I'd just left a man who was saying, in effect, "We are lost. We don't know where the hell we're going." And I couldn't get a major paper to publish it.

Arthur Miller described *The Ride Down Mt. Morgan* in unusually simple terms as "a picaresque play about marriage." It starts out with the fiftyish Lyman Felt in a hospital bed, his foot in a cast after a car accident that happened while he was speeding down a nearby mountain in upstate New York. His wife and daughter have arrived, which is making him oddly angry. "They have to go back to New York right away!" he snaps. "It can't happen," he says to himself, "It mustn't happen!" whereupon he gets out of both the bed and the cast and leaves realism behind, setting the stage for his delirium and another Arthur Miller drama happening inside a man's mind. Momentarily the wife, Theodora, and Felt's grown daughter, Bessie, are seen in the waiting room as Theo murmurs, "Daddy loves life, he'll fight for it." Lyman is impressed and sighs. "God what a woman."

Another woman arrives, the thirtyish, fashionable, Jewish and sexy Leah, as Lyman looks on in horror. "No, she mustn't! It can't happen!" But it begins to, as Leah tells Lyman's daughter, "My husband, he cracked up the car on Mt. Morgan." When Bessie replies, "My father. It was a car, too," the playwright starts to spring the surprise that he has been leading the audience to anticipate. It is the most fun yet in a Miller play and his most inventive story too.

"If I could only get myself over to the window," pleads Lyman, "and out!" Meanwhile both Leah and the daughter, Bessie—still not sensing what the audience already does—are weeping. Theo smartly chastises both. "You still don't know how serious it is," she says, not yet realizing herself how serious, and Lyman has to admire Theo but he admires Leah as well. "What strong, definite characters. Luckily I'm not here and it isn't happening." The two women continue their little chat as Leah mentions that she has an insurance business there in Elmira. "Oh!" Bessie cries, "that's what Daddy does," and when Leah finally comprehends that Theo is Lyman's first wife, she can't understand why the hospital notified the woman. "So many years," she says, since "your divorce." That is when she learns that there was no divorce and that Theo is still his wife. The reason she was notified is that Lyman's car is registered at his city address (a minor slip—rural insurance is cheaper).

When a nurse appears asking for "Mrs. Felt," both women stand up, whereupon Theo faints, completing a playful, titillating and splendidly wry beginning.

In the space of a blackout the scene changes to the office of the Felts' lawyer, who is saying to Leah, "I assume he told you he'd gotten a divorce." Certainly, she replies, "We went to Reno together," and now she is in Reno with Lyman, who tells her that he "threw [the decree] away." But, she says to the lawyer, "It was all lies!" and he himself remembers Lyman having asked about prosecutions for bigamy (seldom, "it's a victimless crime"). As that earlier visit materializes, Miller gives Felt something odd to say—"A lot of people still think I turned in my partner to keep myself out of jail—which maybe I did, but I don't think so." Is this a reference to *All My Sons*? To informers like Kazan? To betrayers in general?

Felt turns to the subject of monogamy, infidelity and a wish to end all deception. "Maybe," he says to the lawyer, "it's simply that if you try to live according to your real desires, you have to end up looking like a shit." It sounds like straight-from-the-heart Miller.

Certain now that he has lost both women, Lyman groans. "Why did I drive into that storm?" whereupon Bessie and Theo are both at his bedside, preparing to abandon him. "I'm sorry," he tells his daughter, "I mean that my character's so bad. But I'm proud that you have enough strength to despise me." The tactic falls flat as Bessie snaps, "Who wouldn't?" and while Theo rattles on, Lyman pretends to doze off before climbing out of the bed, leaving his sleeping figure behind. It is a neat stage trick; then Leah comes into the room, which infuriates Theo until Lyman cries, "I want everybody to lie down!" whereupon both wives obediently join him in the bed. "Oh the double heat of two blessed wives," he cries. "This is heaven! . . . Let's delay [any decision] till we die!"

Abruptly he is alone with Leah, remembering how they met (at an insurance executives meeting) when he couldn't focus on her conversation because his "attention keeps wandering to a warm and furry place." When their affair began, he was so happy, he says, "your scent still on my hands!"—a verbatim quote from Miller's autobiography when he describes his first sexual experience with Marilyn Monroe. Then as Theo appears, demanding an explanation for the bigamy while threatening to strike Leah, Lyman brings down the first-act curtain with the mysterious remark, "My God!—again?"

The second act starts with Theodora and the lawyer. She is reluctant to leave without an emotional release, or, as they say, "closure." Leah comes in to say that according to the police, before Lyman raced down the mountain he pushed aside a barrier that was put up because of the icy road conditions. Theo wonders to her fellow wife, "Can it have been suicide?" and with that *Mt. Morgan* begins another fantastical sequence, the most playful of all. As described in a stage note, *Leah and Theodora are on elevated platforms like two stone deities . . . in kitchen aprons, wifely ribbons tying up their hair.* In

Lyman Felt's delirium they have both moved in with him and the scene is at once funny and chilling as they perform a skit of servitude. "I wouldn't mind at all," chirps Theo, "if you did some of the cooking," and Leah responds, "my gefilte fish is feather-light." Leah even asks, "Would you wash out my pants?" to which Theo is agreeable, "As long as he tells me my lies." So, Leah concludes, "You'll have your lies and I'll have mine." Then the wives embrace and take kneeling positions on either side of Lyman's bed, where each sucks one of his fingers—draining the life out of him until he "writhes in terror, gasping for breath."

Another fantasy comes fast upon it, this one of urinating into his father's hat. "Oh, what dreams," he cries, this time not so cheerfully. "God, how I'd like to be dead." Instead he awakens to memories of Leah's sensuousness and "slipping into her soft cathedral." The playwright had come a long way from the "vacant" juvenile deflowered by a prostitute and the abject confessor of lustful thoughts to his first wife. He was hardly recognizable as the inhibited fellow whom Elia Kazan had once considered "starved for sexual release." Having been duly released by Marilyn Monroe, the national symbol of desire, Arthur Miller had certainly exploited the freedom. He could now write knowingly of a man consumed by eroticism. His protagonist, Lyman Felt, realizes that it was his and Leah's treasury of sexual riches that made him marry her and, he tells the nurse, "those are all good reasons—unless you're married already." But it is his first wife who would probably take him back, at least so his lawyer thinks. Great, says Lyman, sounding like John Proctor, "I'd have to live on my knees the rest of my life." Anyhow, he says, he still wants both women.

Now Theo and Bessie return, the daughter utterly alienated, the wife ready to sign off on this "vulgar, unfeeling man." He glibly responds, "Well, I never had taste . . . taste to me is what's left of life after people can't screw anymore." She is not amused and Miller plays fairly with her. "When did you begin to fool me?" she asks. "I am trying to pinpoint when my life died." Miller plays fair with the daughter too as she tells Felt, "You have nothing to say anymore, you are a nonsense!" The airy style sustains this bitterness, as the major and minor keys of naturalism and fantasy make for a rather unique dramatic dissonance. It is certainly effective in underscoring this man's blithely egotistical reasoning, which is at once ridiculous, astonishing and logical. It was precisely because he had Leah, he tells Theo, "that you were happier in those last years than ever in our marriage." It was because, he says, he himself was never bored.

Unable to take much more of this, she calls him "simply a craving . . . you have never loved anyone!" Then how come, he asks, "I singlehandedly made two such women happier than they'd ever been in their lives?" As his first wife gapes with incredulity, he adds, "The only one who suffered these past nine years—was *me*!"

Theodora hoots her derision as, without any transition or blackout, Lyman gets out of bed to join wife and daughter—now wearing pith helmets—on the safari trip they'd taken some years earlier. They discuss bigamy while a monogamous species—a couple of lions—copulates and Theo explains why monogamy is a higher form. "It enhances liberty . . . when the family is weak the state has to move in; so the stronger the family, the fewer the police. And that is why monogamy is a higher form."

This simplicity delights Lyman ("I'm giving her an A-plus!"), but Theo advises their daughter, "Your father's sociology was on a par with his morals; nonexistent." Suddenly a lion roars and Lyman, after shoving his wife and daughter to safety, approaches the confrontation with a roar of his own, one king of the animals to another. It is an ode to machoism, egoism and infantilism.

> I am happy, yes! . . . That I'm married to Theodora and have Bessie . . . yes, and Leah, too! And that I've made a mountain of money . . . yes, and have no pending lawsuits! And that I don't sacrifice one day to things I don't believe in—and that includes monogamy, yes! We love our lives, you goddam lion! You and me both!

Felt's sense of his own lionlike quality is shared by characters in several of Miller's later plays—Walter Franz in *The Price*, Quentin in *After the Fall* and the protagonists in all the other versions of *The Third Play*. They are all in love with their own success in the male arena. In *The Ride Down Mt. Morgan* even a lion is intimidated by this amalgam of brains and testosterone. Lyman's wife and daughter are still gushing over his bravery as he exults, "The whole future is clear to me now!" The three of them will live an idyllic and literary life, he says, "and I'll spend every day with you—except maybe a week or two a month in the Elmira office!" And that is where he promptly is, with the pregnant Leah, as he promises to get a divorce and demands that she have their child. He even starts to ask Theo for his freedom, but can't go through with it and howls in frustration, "No guts. That's the whole story. No guts!"

Is that what Miller thinks of him? (Himself?) "Do you simply condemn the guy?" he asked. "These impulses exist in most people. Do you condone the thing? [You can't] because of the pain that it causes other people and the social chaos it could justify." Like so many of his protagonists, the playwright was weighing the options. Still fascinated by the mind, especially the reasoning process, he was again (as in *The Price*) leading an audience from one side of an argument to the other. Here he presents balanced reasoning as not debate but dilemma.

So Lyman Felt is on his back again, his leg in the cast, with Leah at the bedside demanding that he release any claims on their home and insurance office and provide an explanation to their nine-year-old son. He suggests honesty. "Only the truth is sacred," says this lion.

> LYMAN: To hold back nothing.

LEAH: You must be crazy—you held back everything! You really don't know right from wrong, do you!
LYMAN: Jesus Christ, you sound like Theo!
LEAH: Well maybe it's what happens to people who marry you.

That is when they learn that Theo has had a nervous breakdown and with her appearance—plainly naked under a coat—the play reaches for its peak, the comedy crashing through a series of unvarnished truths into the plane of tragedy. Theo concedes having schoolmarm faults, admits she subconsciously knew Lyman to be unfaithful and in her madness offers him the freedom to commute between herself and Leah, while Leah swears that she never trusted Lyman and didn't ever want to get married. He tells her he's "tired of this crap, Leah!—You got a little something out of this despicable treachery!" He swears that he loves them all. His daughter, who is the toughest among them, says, "You ought to be killed!" at which point all four burst into tears, a spectacle at once horrific and comedic—and that the play's London director, Michael Blakemore, considered unstageable.

In the end it is the daughter, Bessie, who tells Lyman what Arthur Miller seems to be conceding he had never learned, "That there are other people." It is the sense of, the need for, the lack of *otherness* that has haunted so many of his plays, a theme richer and possibly more meaningful than the morality and guilt on which he so frequently harped. So Lyman is deserted by them all and left with the nurse to beg for her company ("I love your warmth, Logan . . . you're a piece of the sun") while asking whether she hates him too. The play leaves him weeping and it is a tragic conclusion that might be devastating given the right production.

The Ride Down Mt. Morgan is in a sense Miller's *The Tempest*—a late play of summation and farewell, confronting the truths of his life in pitiful, wise, funny and grievous ways.

Lyman Felt is too odd a name to have been arbitrarily chosen. This is a man who does not seem to feel anything, a man whose self-serving lies are the essence of his being, as indeed his way of life is sustained by lies. "The point of the exercise," Miller said, "is to investigate some of the qualities and meanings of truthfulness and deception." Lyman is dishonest on the grand scale in a play about the capacity to care enough and trust enough to be truthful with another person. Like any criminal bigamist, he is living two dishonesties, one with each wife, but his duplicity involves more than the wives—his double life involves wholly separate identities. One self is the conventional insurance executive, the family man who never drives over sixty miles an hour and is married to a mature and intelligent woman his own age. The other self is a poetry-writing stallion who has a smart, young, sexy wife and (Miller being the car fancier) owns a Porsche, a Lotus and a Datsun "Z" besides having wrecked a Ferrari. In his life with Theo Lyman is afraid to fly; with Leah he pilots his own plane. Both identities exist in the one man, different selves within the self, each demanding satisfaction. The notion is expressed by Lyman in a speech.

> A man is a fourteen-room house—in the bedroom he's asleep with his intelligent wife, in the living room he's rolling around with some bare-ass girl, in the library he's paying his taxes, in the yard he's raising tomatoes, and in the cellar he's making a bomb to blow it all up.

Lyman Felt's bomb was the car that he drove down the mountain.

There is something else notable about his name, the suggestion of a possible connection between *The Ride Down Mt. Morgan* and the novel, *The Human Stain,* by Miller's good friend, Philip Roth. Written while the playwright was revising *Mt. Morgan* for its American premiere, *The Human Stain* is likewise about a man living a duplicitous life. Roth's protagonist has kept his identity secret from his wife and children for fifty years. In a mischievous Rothian twist, he is not a white Jew but a black gentile. As Miller's man is named Lyman Felt, Roth's is called Coleman Silk, "Coleman" possibly a play on "coal man" as "Lyman" is on "lie man." Silk is a 71-year-old classics professor who loses his position because of an accidental, politically incorrect classroom remark in which he innocently (or perhaps not so innocently) referred to a couple of missing students as "spooks," meaning ghosts, claiming to be unaware that the students are black and that "spook" was once a racist epithet. As Silk desperately pursues vindication, he finds a haven in an affair with a victimized, possibly illiterate woman half his age. In this brilliant, greatly praised and likewise picaresque novel, Roth explores the nature of honesty and deception in relation to the nondenominational version of original sin that he calls "the human stain."

That is familiar Miller territory, and as for the names Lyman Felt and Coleman Silk, their metric, sonic and connotive similarities cannot be easily dismissed. Moreover, the "R.M." to whom *The Human Stain* is dedicated is Ross Miller—Arthur's nephew, Kermit's son and one of Philip Roth's closest friends. In short, Miller and Roth might well have been having literary fun with these counter-references. If so, it would not have been Miller's first involvement in a Roth novel. Two years earlier, in *I Married a Communist,* Roth devoted three appreciative pages to summarizing the early Miller novel, *Focus*. That appreciation is particularly benevolent for, as Arthur Miller would doubtless be the first to admit, *Focus* is hardly in a class with Philip Roth's masterful fiction.

However, if the Lyman Felt/Coleman Silk stories are indeed a badminton between playwright and novelist, it would seem to be more than just a private amusement, as might be expected from such formidable artists. In *The Human Stain,* Roth takes advantage of the novel's form to speak of Coleman Silk's second life in a way that quite strikingly suits Lyman Felt's counterlife as well (and Roth's novel, *The Counterlife* deals with this same theme):

> Don't most people want to walk out of the fucking lives they've been handed? But they don't. And that's what makes them them, and this was what was making him him. . . . Didn't he get, from his decision, the adventure he was after, or was the decision itself the adventure? Was it the misleading that provided his pleasure, the carrying off of the stunt that he liked best . . . Was it the social obstruction he wished to sidestep . . . Did he ever get over the fact that he couldn't get over the fact that he was pulling it off?

This could well have been written about Lyman Felt's making a run at bigamy and two lives with two wives. And it bridges the essential difference between Roth's and Miller's philosophies. As Philip Roth considers it hopeless to make sense of one's life, Arthur Miller considers it essential.

Even for an Arthur Miller whose very signature was his refusal to have one, *The Ride Down Mt. Morgan* is his most uncharacteristic work. If it is at all related to any other of his plays, that would be *After the Fall*. In both the central issue is a man's moral worth. The difference lies in tone of voice. *After the Fall* is always serious and sometimes pontifical. *The Ride Down Mt. Morgan* takes a sardonic approach, bitterly laughing at what was so grimly decried in *After the Fall*, the death of morality. While *After the Fall* looks for power in Quentin's confessions as he in effect talks himself to life, *Mt. Morgan* taps the power of a loss of equilibrium, pulling the carpet out from under Lyman's dancing feet, to send him into emotional free fall. Those who cannot love are not loved, they are literally loveless. The hedonist is in love with himself and the man who tries to have everything without regard for others or for any moral code is an ethical anarchist. Suicide and madness are his only recourses and they are at the center of this play. As Lyman Felt's removal of the road barrier certainly does indicate, he was trying to kill himself.

The play leaves tantalizing mysteries in its wake. What is the meaning of "A lot of people still think I turned in my partner to keep myself out of jail?" Why does Felt cry, "My God—again?" at the end of the first act and why is he so enraged with his father as to treat anger as a joke, urinating into the man's hat? "Lyman Felt," in the end, the playwright said, "has everything except the main thing," but Miller does not say what the main thing is. He only conceded, "By the end of the play, we know what it isn't."

As the London premiere approached, the local critics were already familiar with dramatized midlife male sexual crises. Harold Pinter had dealt with the subject in *Betrayal* (1978), Peter Nichols in *Passion Play* (1981) and Tom Stoppard in *The Real Thing* (1982). In those plays the protagonists opt out of long-term marriages for younger lovers. The theme brought out the best in each of these considerable playwrights but not only was Miller's man the only one daring enough, or greedy enough, to choose both options; his play is as inventive as any. There is a high madness about *The Ride Down Mt. Morgan* and a horrific twinning of the cruel and the comic, as Miller finally and with artistic honesty faced up to his own egoism and emotional detachment.

The play received mixed notices following its opening night at Wyndham's Theater on October 11, 1991. The director, Michael Blakemore, concurred. "I don't think the production was right," he said, "and the first production of a play is very, very important. The whole future of the play can often depend on it." As well, perhaps the British were put off by this play's flaunting of the moral code with which Arthur Miller had always been identified, and by its implicit distinction between social values and personal ones. Even the playwright said, "I have an old quarrel with morality."

These might have been reasons why he had "wished to God that I could have opened this play in New York, but it's a minefield." In the end *The Ride Down Mt. Morgan* would not receive its American premiere (at the Williamstown Theater Festival in Massachusetts) for another five years. Robert Whitehead wouldn't even have produced it on Broadway three years later were it not for pressure exerted by his star, Patrick Stewart. By that time Miller had long since revised the work. "Having gotten the benefit of seeing [it] done once, I wanted to work on the script, to make it sharper and more pointed." Despite remarking to an interviewer that he "never rewrote anything after it was produced," he had in fact and with only two exceptions—*Incident at Vichy* and *The Price*—rewritten every play since *Death of a Salesman* (and of course *The Price* had been endlessly rewritten as *The Third Play* before the eventual production). Such postoperative industriousness, patience and discipline are all but unique among professional playwrights.

The new version opened on April 9, 2000, at the Ambassador Theater, but although some of the reviews were Miller's best in decades, a drama needed roaring approval to succeed on Broadway. *The Ride Down Mt. Morgan* ran for only 120 performances, or fifteen weeks.

There is no question that this work is hard to get right. Its tone of black whimsy is elusive and the challenge of clarifying what is reality, delusion, delirium or fantasy is even greater than that in *Death of a Salesman*. If the play is ever fulfilled in production, it should have a stunning effect. It may well be the best of Arthur Miller's later work.

Between the London production of *The Ride Down Mt. Morgan* and its New York revision Miller was interviewed on the stage of the 92nd St. Y, one of New York's cultural bastions. He attracted a full audience to its 1,000-seat auditorium. He was a cultural institution too, certified by such funereal awards as the Kennedy Honors in 1984 (with Gian-Carlo Menotti, Lena Horne, Danny Kaye and Isaac Stern) and soon to come, the National Medal of Arts. Such eminence could fill a thousand seats for a night and, relaxed and expansive, he responded in his usual articulate, New York–accented way to the questions of Professor Christopher Bigsby. The words, however, were not as amiable as the manner as he once again expressed his disapproval of the Broadway establishment, "the most ruthlessly commercialized theater in the world." The dramatic critics, he said, flattering his interviewer, were "more than likely to be ex–sports reporters or general journalists rather than scholars or specialists university-trained in criticism." He wasn't always so respectful of scholarship. On a different occasion he said that aside from *The Iceman Cometh* and *Long Day's Journey into Night*, "a lot of [O'Neill] is just plain academic stuff, and I have a feeling one reason his reputation grew was that it became available to academics. Academia harbors a lot of nonsense."

His prestige in England had not mollified his bitterness about New York. The man still had anger to spare. At the Y even theatergoers were subjected to his blame, having changed, he said, from a core audience "that loved theater [as] an absolute necessity for a civilized life" to "two or three very different levels of age, culture, education and intellectual sophistication." Professor Bigsby well understood the playwright's awareness of more appreciative audiences abroad. The youthful Broadway failure *The Man Who Had All the Luck* was at that very time, 1993, being enthusiastically received in a British production by the Bristol Old Vic. Its director, Paul Unwin, felt that "at a time when Europe was abandoning itself to tyranny and America abandoning Europe, Miller was testing the notion of individual responsibility. Do we affect events or are we simply their victims?"

That kind of discussion must have seemed more in tune with the playwright's thinking than the review appearing in the *New York Times* when *After the Fall* was produced in London that same year. The critic used the opportunity to take his turn at deriding the twenty-five-year-old cause célèbre, finding "it hard to take the self importance and pretensions of the soliloquizing protagonist Quentin, a Jewish lawyer who wraps himself in a half century's worth of guilt only to absolve himself of all blame by the final curtain."

There is no reference in *After the Fall* to Quentin being Jewish, although his family's names and their idiomatic speech certainly suggest it. Even so, that would hardly have been a reason for a critic to identify a character by his religion. Indeed what is meant by "a Jewish lawyer"? By this time, however, much of the hostility toward Miller was not reasonable, only habitual, and his exile seemed complete. Some time before his appearance at the 92nd St. Y, his five-minute playlet *The Last Yankee* had been performed in a seventy-five-seat theater near the Hudson River, up a flight of stairs beyond even Off-Broadway. When the scene was expanded to full one-act length and presented in more professional circumstances, the *New York Times* saw fit to merely assign its assistant drama critic to review the play, which he did not like.

The Last Yankee is the only Arthur Miller "problem" play, the problem being clinical depression (perhaps he was motivated by his friendship with the novelist William Styron, who had been writing about his own battles with the illness). The piece is direct in its connection of story to subject. The setting is a mental hospital, the characters two patients and their visiting husbands. In a nod to Miller's old theme of bad capitalism versus honest labor, the rich businessman husband is insensitive while the carpenter husband is receptive to the needs of the depressed, but that is a secondary point. Treating the illness is what this play is about and the conclusion drawn is dubious, platitudinous and possibly dangerous, suggesting a Christian Science for atheists—that medication only worsens the illness while psychiatry is not even worth discussing. In fact there seem to be no doctors at all in this hospital. As one of the patients says, "Being positive is the only way"—that is, with the support of caring friends the depressive, illness notwithstanding, can cure themselves through sheer willpower, just by taking it "one day at a time." For Arthur Miller, who had spent a fair amount of time in analysis, psychiatry's day was apparently done.

Several months after the play's resoundingly negative New York reception *The Last Yankee* was presented in the West End of London, where it ran for eight months.

During that same 92nd St. Y interview Miller mentioned a work in progress called *Gellburg*. It was inspired, he said, by a real person who had become mysteriously paralyzed, "a woman I knew when I was a teen-ager." He decided to relate such a condition to America's inertia at the start of Hitler's invasions. It was the playwright's second approach to the subject, the first having been his youthful epic *The Golden Years*. That, however, had dealt with German aggression; this time the subject was the Holocaust. *The Ride Down Mt. Morgan* had him face up to the selfness in his life, and the relationship between an inability to love and an intense need to be loved. The new play would confront his other enduring knot, his Jewish identity and his relationship to it. "To me," he said during that onstage interview, being a Jew was

> important only because I was born into a Jewish family and we had a certain amount of ritual, but nobody was all that bound up in it. I can't shred my identity and tell you which part of it derives from being Jewish. I guess I'm that mixed up thing, an American.

Yet even as he was saying that, the *Gellburg* play, which would eventually be titled *Broken Glass* (a reference to the 1938 *kristallnacht* in Berlin), was confronting what he seemed to have been evading all his life. He was writing a play about what Jewishness means and, specifically, about a man with conflicted, even tormented feelings about being a Jew.

Robert Whitehead insisted on doing the play in New York. Miller had not been represented by a new work on Broadway in fourteen years, an astonishing statistic. The prospect of once again offering himself up for critical target practice surely gave him pause. David Thacker urged him not to do it. The director knew that Miller himself "felt it would stand a better chance in London, but Mr. Whitehead was afraid of doing it that way because if it was a bad production or was poorly received, he would have a difficult time getting the money for it in New York." An American tryout engagement was scheduled then for March 1994 at the Long Wharf Theater in Connecticut, where the director, the leading actors and a great part of the audience were Jewish. In fact one leading actor was replaced because he wasn't acting *Jewish* enough (Miller felt he was playing a wealthy Jewish doctor "like Al Pacino"). When the play opened on Broadway, April 24 at the Booth Theater, unenthusiastic reviews led to a run of barely two months.

Once again England came to the rescue as the Royal National Theatre promptly scheduled *Broken Glass* for its Lyttleton Theatre under Thacker's direction. Miller began his revisions immediately. "The text of the New York production," the director would find, "bore very little relation to the final script."

In London the playwright and his wife took their regular room in the same hotel where he had stayed for every visit since 1974. On the eve of the production he told the London *Times,* "I've probably been influenced in selecting the theme by the recrudescence"—a pretty good word—"of anti-Semitism in this world." Just, he said, when you think, "'Well, that's over with, it's not going to happen anymore' . . . suddenly, there it is again."

Broken Glass takes place in Brooklyn and begins in a doctor's office, where a man named Gellburg—who doesn't like his name being mistaken for "Goldberg"—is waiting for news about his wife's sudden unexplained paralysis. He is prunelike, a "purse-mouthed" fellow, always dressed in black, running a bank's mortgage department—a busy and cruel place of foreclosures in those late-Depression times. He is reminiscent of Lawrence Newman, the inhibited anti-Semitic protagonist of Miller's novel *Focus,* except that Gellburg is an anti-Semitic Jew. He does not deny his Jewishness; he just doesn't like it.

The doctor, the exuberantly Jewish Harry Hyman (perhaps for *hymen,* perhaps for the anti-Semitic epithet *Hymie,* perhaps for both—or neither) has already examined Gellburg's wife and suspects her condition to be "a hysterical paralysis." Sounding like the author of *The Last Yankee,* he wants to keep her "out of that whole psychiatry rigmarole. . . . You get further faster, sometimes, with a little common sense and some plain human sympathy." The playwright clearly identifies with this doctor, a "scientific idealist," and indeed a minor pattern of reverence for science and doctors runs through many of his plays.

After some questioning Phillip Gellburg speculates that his wife's paralysis began "when they started putting all the pictures in the paper about these Nazi carryings on." That was when her legs suddenly "turned to butter." In particular Sylvia was horrified by a photograph of two old Jewish men being forced to clean a street with toothbrushes. They looked like her grandfather, she says, but neither Phillip nor Sylvia's sister Harriet can understand why she would become so upset over something that is happening so far away. Besides, Phillip says, these reports only give the American anti-Semites "fancy new ideas," and he adds, "It's no excuse for what's happening over there but German Jews can be pretty [snooty]. Not that they're pushy like the ones from Poland or Russia."

Asked by Dr. Hyman about himself, he boasts of working for Christian bankers and of being the only Jew who "ever set foot" on his chairman's yacht, "the only Jew ever worked for Brooklyn Guarantee in their whole history . . . It's a great firm." The doctor suggests he give Sylvia "a lot of loving," and adds with a touch of Yiddish that is certainly novel in an Arthur Miller play, "from here on out, *tuchas offen tisch,* okay?" (be forthright—literally, "put your rear end on the table"). At home Gellburg tries to put the doctor's suggestion of warmth and straightforwardness into effect, but Sylvia rejects the sudden display of ardor. If he wants sex now, she says, just go ahead and take it—"here I am, Phillip. . . . I'm here for my mother's sake, and [our son's] sake and everybody's sake except mine, but I'm here and here I am. And now finally you want to talk about it, now when I'm turning into an old woman?"

Giving up, he insists that she try to stand, which only causes her to fall to the floor. In the next scene the doctor is talking to her sister Harriet, curious about Sylvia's "fascination with the Nazis . . . the people in those photographs . . . They're alive to her." When he asks about Phillip, Harriet starts to say "the Jewish part of it," and the doctor completes her thought. "He doesn't like being Jewish." That's right, she says, and besides he is miserly, "tight as a drum" and impotent too. Even so, says Harriet, "it'll sound crazy . . . He adores her!" Making a house call (this was 1938), the doctor asks Sylvia to "Tense your hips . . . tense your thighs . . . come on, raise your knees . . . The depth of your flesh must be wonderful," but her legs won't budge. "Speak to me," he urges, "What is in your mind?" and she replies, "It's almost like there's something in me . . . something alive, like a child almost, except it's a very dark thing."

The physician's parting professional advice is odd, a suggestion that she imagine "I've made love to you. And now it's over and we are lying together. And you begin to tell me some secret things." The play returns to his office, where Gellburg is confessing assorted anxieties, including the conviction that his wife's paralysis "is against me . . . She knows what she's doing." For example, he says, last night he made love with her, only to be told in the morning that he had just "imagined doing it." The scene develops a chilling power as Phillip asks the doctor, "How could a man imagine such a thing? To invent such a thing?" When the doctor wonders whether he is sure that it really happened, Gellman shoots back, "How can you even ask me such a thing?" This effectively builds toward the act's end as Dr. Hyman inquires, "Has she said something about me?" To that odd self-interest Gellman responds,

> She is trying to destroy me! And you stand there! And what do you do! Are you a doctor or what! Why don't you give me a straight answer about anything? Everything is in-and-out and around-the-block!—Listen. I've made up my mind; I don't want you seeing her anymore.

As Gellburg "storms out," Dr. Hyman's wife, Margaret, who is also his nurse, suggests referring Sylvia to a psychiatrist because "Getting this hysterical about something on the other side of the world" simply is not sane.

> HYMAN: When she talks about it, it's not on the other side of the world, it's on the next block.
>
> MARGARET: And that's sane?
>
> HYMAN: I don't know what it is. I just get the feeling sometimes that she *knows* something . . . it's like she's connected to some . . . some wire that goes half around the world, some truth that other people are blind to.

He brings the first-act curtain down telling his wife, "it's real," meaning the events in Germany, and the second act begins with Gellburg's boss, the decidedly un-Jewish bank president, telling him that his recent real estate advice has only given a competitor named Kershowitz an advantage. Gellburg takes this as an accusation of Jewish conspiracy, an idea the president finds ridiculous. Then Dr. Hyman visits Sylvia while Phillip is away and she describes a recurring dream about a threatening crowd of Germans. One of them mounts her, "starts to cut off my breasts . . . I think it's Phillip . . . he was almost like one of the others." She weeps. "He doesn't like Jews."

When the doctor asks about Phillip's story that they'd had sex, she informs him, "We haven't had relations for almost twenty years," then addresses her obsession, the looming genocide in Germany. "How can those nice people go out and pick Jews off the street . . . and nobody stops them?" She cannot understand why anyone should think she is crazy for being upset about it. "What will become of us! . . . you mean if a Jew walks out of this house, do they arrest him? . . . What do they do with them? . . . Where is Roosevelt! Where is England!" Then climbing out of the bed as if to walk, she crumples to the floor as the play develops a palpable power, Gellburg arriving and demanding to know what the doctor is doing there. Hyman replies, "She is desperate to be loved" and leaves. As Sylvia is demanding to keep this physician, Phillip questions her tone of voice. "It's a Jewish woman's tone of voice!" she retorts. "They are smashing windows and beating children! . . . Don't sleep with me again. . . . You give me terrible dreams. . . . Maybe in a while. . . . You told him we had relations? You little liar! You want him to think I'm crazy?"

All he can reply is, "You will kill me," and he says this repeatedly. Thus the past is revealed in the Ibsen manner, so as to explain his impotence. It was her unhappiness about stopping work, which she loved, and her decision to have no more children that led to his feeling that she "didn't want me to be the man here [and] everything inside just dried up."

> GELLBURG: And maybe it was also that to me it was a miracle that you ever married me in the first place.

> SYLVIA: You mean your face? What have you got against your face? A Jew can have a Jewish face.

It is a direct suggestion of this Jew's self-hatred and Gellburg can only cry, "Do you want to kill me?" On the heels of this he is dismissed from his job and in shock suffers a heart attack. He undergoes an epiphany and tells the doctor, "When I collapsed . . . it was like an explosion went off in my head, like a tremendous white light. . . . I felt a happiness . . . Like I suddenly had something to tell her that would change everything."

He realizes that he was being used by the bank. "You got some lousy rotten job to do? Get Gellburg, send in the Yid. Close down a business. Throw somebody out of his house." And he asks the doctor,

> You're an educated man . . . I wish we could talk about the Jews. . . . Do you think about it much? . . . Why is it so hard to be a Jew . . . a full time job . . . How'd you come to marry a Shiksa? . . . It wasn't so you wouldn't seem Jewish?

Of Arthur Miller's three wives none was Jewish. The pattern had plainly occurred to him.

Dr. Hyman says that on the contrary, "I think *you* tried to disappear into the Goyim," and Gellburg begins to grasp that Jewishness is not a matter of religion; there can even be Jews without God's existence. He asks the doctor to tell Sylvia that he is going to change. "When the last Jew dies," he says, "the light of the world will go out. She has to understand that—those Germans are shooting at the sun!" Hyman takes it from there, telling Gellburg that Sylvia is afraid of him because "You hate yourself . . . you helped paralyze her with this 'Jew, Jew, Jew' coming out of your mouth and the same time she reads it in the paper." Digesting that, Gellburg now spells out his ambivalent feelings.

> [S]ome days I feel like sitting in the shul with the old men and pulling the *tallis* over my head and be a full-time Jew the rest of my life. With the side-locks and the black hat, and settle it once and for all. And other times . . . yes, I could almost kill them. They irritate me. I am ashamed of them and that I look like them. Why must we be different? Why is it?

The doctor responds rather platitudinously, "*Everybody* is persecuted . . . forgive yourself. And the Jews . . . and the Goyim." Phillip and Sylvia Gellburg, now alone, begin to heal. She realizes, "I can't find myself in my life . . . can't even walk." He admits, "I've been more afraid than I looked . . . of everything." He adds about Jews, "Why we're different I will never understand but to live so afraid, I don't want that anymore . . . I feel I did this to you! That's the knife in my heart . . . God almighty, Sylvia, forgive me!" and he "falls back" in his chair, "unconscious." His wife struggles up from her wheelchair to come to his aid, crying "Wait, wait!" and as she rises, taking a step toward him, the last curtain falls.

Although stocked with mysteries and ambiguities, the play is as essentially traditional in its realism and construction as *The Ride Down Mt. Morgan* is inventive and fantastical. Once again the playwright is suiting style to purpose. Still, *Broken Glass* does not entirely fulfill its intentions and there are questions left in its wake, starting with Miller's explanation for Sylvia's paralysis. The play, he has said, "is an investigation of a whole personal as well as political situation that brought this upon her. [Sylvia is] not a political person but she's living in that time when the menace of fascism was alive in the world and through various means she is affected by it." While this is confusing, elsewhere the playwright uses ambiguity to considerable effect—for instance, the uncertainty as to whether Sylvia and Phillip made love, or her remark, made more than once, that "It's almost like there's something in me . . . something alive." Pointedly ambiguous too are the doctor's sexual innuendos. It is even uncertain whether Gellburg has died at the end of the play. Miller said, "I've respected its ambiguities," but ambiguity is not always easy to stage. Thacker directed the play with Gellburg dying and he was pleased with its effect. "The image we're left with, simultaneously," he said, "is that the husband dies and the wife stands up. She can only stand when he dies. She can only stand *because* he dies." This interpretation pleased Miller. "The first night," Thacker remembered, "he was as happy as I've ever seen him. The play had gone very well. Inge turned to me and said, 'You've made it possible for him to write another play now.'"

There have been many Jewish playwrights, in Great Britain as well as in the United States, but with *Broken Glass* Arthur Miller became the only important one to write a play about what it means to be Jewish, apparently trying to deal with his own Jewishness. In an introduction to a 1995 reissue of his autobiographical *Timebends*, written immediately after the production of *Broken Glass*, he says,

> I may have forgotten the little Hebrew I knew as a child. I never go to synagogue, and even find it troublesome to accurately remember which high holiday is which and what they signify, but something in me suspects that there must continue to be Jews in the world or it will somehow end.

London's critics gave *Broken Glass* the Olivier Award as the best new play of the 1994–95 theater season. The author, speaking to an interviewer for the *London Independent*, compared its reception with that in New York. "Some plays fail because they are failures. This play, as a play, is precisely what I wanted it to be and it is beautifully performed . . . The conditions of . . . theater in New York are what have failed, not *Broken Glass*."

Director Thacker put the play in the same class with Miller's "four great plays at the beginning of his career plus *The Price* . . . plays that will be performed for all time."

On October 30, 1995, the PEN American Center sponsored a tribute to Arthur Miller at Town Hall in New York City. The occasion was his eightieth birthday, two weeks earlier. Selections from his plays were performed and tributes offered. Edward Albee remembered picketing with Miller on behalf of dissident Russian writers, the two playwrights carrying placards in front of the Soviet mission on East Sixty-seventh Street. "I think of Arthur," he said, "as a conscience," and there was no doubt of Miller's reemergence among his fellow writers as both a great artist and a figure of moral inspiration. "It's Arthur Miller time," said Albee, not the first to mock a current beer commercial, adding "and high time" in reference to the years of disfavor. Albee could well sympathize. He was himself in the midst of a long stretch of rejection.

After the speeches, performances of scenes and the lusty applause Arthur and Inge followed the PEN American Center officials and their invited guests across Times Square for a dinner at Sardi's, the theatrical haunt on West Forty-fourth Street. There, while Inge was engaged in conversation with Eli Wallach and Anne Jackson, Miller was approached by a young man in a sweater and sport coat. His name was Baird Jones and he was a reporter for the *Daily News*. His assignment was to gather material for the gossip pages.

The question, to be sure, was mischievous, if not downright baiting. Miller was agreeable to a quick interview and Jones kneeled beside the table, opening a notebook. "The way we were speaking," he recalled, "no one else could overhear any of the questions or answers." After jotting down the replies Jones wondered whether he might "ask one last question that was sort of personal." As Miller waited, Jones asked, "Do you ever dream about Marilyn Monroe?" He pressed on. "What kind of dreams are they?"

Miller (who later said that he doesn't answer questions about Monroe "unless some stupid jerk brings it up") suddenly brought his right-hand fist up to face level, "right by his jaw," Jones remembered. Rising from the chair, he said, "I'm going to knock your block off." In a "single moment," the reporter recalled, "his attitude escalated from quiet conversation to fighting speech. It was unmistakable—he was coming right after me. He was going to slug me."

One thing Jones knew, he said, "the interview was over." Moreover, "this man had just become an enraged bull," and getting up from his knees he began "back pedaling." Although he expected the playwright to promptly calm down,

> he started to go after me. The closer he came, the faster I back pedaled. Finally, about twenty feet from the table, he actually threw a punch, which hit me in

the shoulder. He was a big guy with huge arms, and this man had a heck of a lot of power behind that punch.

A witness said that "It looked like Arthur started to rush his punch," but it was a bizarre event, the famous playwright, six feet three inches tall and robust, but still eighty years old, physically attacking a five-foot nine-inch, modestly built thirty-one-year-old reporter. The blow knocked the younger man into the buffet table. "I slid along it," Jones said, "and he continued to plow after me. Then I looked down the table and saw a ham with, oh my God, a cleaver next to it." At that point Miller got a grip on himself, turned and went back to his table—where the confrontation had gone unnoticed. Yet it was not overlooked by a reporter for the *New York Post*. The raging playwright made the tabloid's headlines the following morning, a banner across its gossip page proclaiming, "MILLER GOES PUNCHY OVER MARILYN."

That Arthur Miller could lose control over a question about Marilyn Monroe, who had been dead for thirty years, surely betrayed myriad suppressed emotions. Obviously he had never resolved that relationship, nor understood his role in the public's ongoing obsession with her. Even at this date he could be commonly identified not as the author of *Death of a Salesman* but as the man who had married Marilyn Monroe. Her continuing myth only exacerbated the identification and it surely sat at the center of his angry reactions to questions about her.

Miller's American resurrection was just beginning as a movie version of *The Crucible* got under way in 1995 under the English director Nicholas Hytner. The playwright's son was coproducing the picture. Robert had been a production assistant for *Midnight Cowboy* and *The Producers*, among other movies. He had since been directing television commercials. *The Crucible,* he thought, was "the most cinematic of [my father's] plays. It's less introspective and more linear than most of the others." Unfortunately, he said, "I had no track record as a producer, and Arthur has not had good experiences with films. He had no reason to believe in me, but I kept pushing."

Given that nobody else was pushing, the younger (forty-eight-year-old) Miller convinced his father to give him an option on the play's movie rights and with a partner they sold Twentieth Century-Fox on the idea. When the studio agreed that Arthur Miller would write the screenplay, the project became a family affair. Even Robert's half sister, Rebecca, came along as the production's still photographer (she was between acting assignments, having played small parts in *Regarding Henry* and *Mrs. Parker and the Vicious Circle*). During the filming of *The Crucible* on location in Essex, Massachusetts, Rebecca Miller met her future husband, Daniel Day-Lewis, who costarred in the movie with Winona Ryder.

In the process of making the picture a kind of family therapy got under way. Father and son had not been in contact for many years. "Arthur," Robert said, "hadn't really had any experience of me as an adult. Our relationship was more or less the way it had been since I was 21. We needed something to glue it together. The film was the completion." As for that film, the older Miller ultimately said—much as he had about *The Misfits*—it was "the only time when what I imagined while writing actually showed up on the screen." Unlike *The Misfits*, however, *The Crucible* was well received and Miller got an Academy Award nomination for his screenplay (he lost to Billy Bob Thornton's *Sling Blade*).

His return from theatrical limbo continued the following year. New York's Signature Theater Company, which devoted itself to a single playwright each season, mounted a couple of secondary Arthur Miller works, *The Last Yankee* and *The American Clock*, along with a premiere, *Mr. Peters' Connections*. This is an eighty-minute piece that Michael Blakemore subsequently directed in London's Almeida Theatre. Blakemore compared it to "the late chamber works of Beethoven in terms of Arthur's achievements," a formidable comparison. Like the revered late Beethoven quartets, *Mr. Peters' Connections* gives an audience no easy way in. "Arthur himself told me," Blakemore said,

> he tried to write a play without any of the usual devices to keep people interested. He tried to write a play in which the narrative was simply the fluctuating moods and emotions of this old guy who has a nap in the afternoon. For most people, that doesn't constitute a play.

Mr. Peters' Connections thus is another interior work, here set in the dozing consciousness and fading life of an airline pilot named Harry Peters. He is imagining himself in a seedy nightclub where, as Miller put it, he vainly tries to "bring together the strands of experience." He wants to make some sense of his life, and so people and events from his past converge and depart, helped along by figures who never existed at all. In a number of details that are plainly autobiographical the play evokes a winsome grief as its author reflects on a life that has outlasted friends and values. The most obvious figure from his past is Marilyn Monroe. Anne Jackson, who had been friends with Monroe and was in the New York production of *Mr. Peters' Connections*, thought that "the Marilyn character was very different from Maggie in *After the Fall* . . . more of a forgiveness from him as a playwright."

Oddly the character drawing the most comment, because Miller made him out such a crude and violent man, is plainly based on Monroe's second husband, the baseball player Joe DiMaggio. As to these connections with real people, Miller only said, "It really came out of conversations with an actual pilot." The specific sources are not as important as the gentleness and float of this elegiac play.

Its London production opened during summer 2000, at the same time as the Royal National Theatre was presenting perhaps the finest and certainly the most acclaimed staging of *All My Sons* in that play's fifty-year history.

The British critics were kinder about *Mr. Peters' Connections* than their American colleagues, generally more perceptive and sometimes downright effusive, but reviews, good or bad, no longer mattered. Arthur Miller's reputation in England was settled. In some ways such respect, which was generally accorded abroad, was putting America to shame, but then the homeland correction was well under way. Just the previous year *A View from the Bridge* had again been revived on Broadway, but this time to enthusiastic reviews and two Tony Awards. Then *Death of a Salesman* was produced with Brian Dennehy as Willy Loman and was even more enthusiastically received, winning the Tony Award for his performance as well as for the production. While classified as a revival, *Salesman* was no more of a revival than would be a play by Chekhov.

The Price next was given a Broadway production along with *The Ride Down Mt. Morgan,* and both were nominated for Tony Awards, one as the best revival, the other as the best new play of the season. In 2001 *The Man Who Had All the Luck* had its first New York production since the original 1944 failure. Arthur Miller was now headlining the play advertisements, his name more prominent than the titles. He was being declared as a simple matter of fact America's Greatest Living Playwright. The long and miserable era of rejection was coming to an end.

An important and widely admired movie version of his early novel *Focus* was released, again coproduced by his son Robert, this time in partnership with New York City's mayor-to-be Michael Bloomberg. Later that season *The Crucible* was given a glamorous staging on Broadway, starring Liam Neeson and Laura Linney. While that production was playing to full houses, the eighty-five-year-old Miller was finishing—and misbegetting—a new full-length play called *Resurrection Blues*. It was his *Henry VIII* (Shakespeare's last and best forgotten—indeed generally forgotten—play), a heavy-handed political satire about the televised crucifixion of a modern-day Christ, set in a fictitious South American country. Clumsy in its satire, crudely making comic capital of the *erection* in *Resurrection,* the play left Robert Whitehead uncertain about producing it. The issue became moot when the producer died in 2001, and the play was ultimately presented by the Guthrie Theater in Minneapolis in summer 2002. It was not well received, although one of Miller's most loyal British champions, Michael Billington of the *Guardian,* came to America to review it as "his best play in years."

That year Inge had been complaining of severe backaches. She had been undergoing chemotherapy for lymphoma but, Miller said, "we thought we had it under control. . . . We thought she was licking it [and] then it exploded." On January 30, 2002, his wife of forty years was dead at seventy-eight, and within the week she was being memorialized in the barn where he had built a photography studio for her. Shortly afterward a major tribute was organized in a New York theater. "It was the first time ever," Joan Copeland remembered,

> that I had heard my brother read a prepared speech. It was almost as if he didn't trust himself to be impromptu. He was never at a loss for words, or thoughts. It was kind of the same speech he'd read at the first celebration of her life. He'd put all these thoughts together and it was a very tightly constructed memory of her. I suppose it's his way of preventing himself from showing emotion.

His wife's death left Miller alone for the first time in his adult life. He would occasionally visit his daughter Rebecca, who had a home in Ireland with her husband and children, but despite his on and off relationship with the United States, that was home—where his billing as America's Greatest Living Playwright had become a truism. That is how the playwright Terence McNally had introduced him at the PEN American Center celebration. After so much abuse, disrespect and lack of gratitude for patently important artistic accomplishment Miller's place in theater history, already secure elsewhere, was finally established in his own country. No critic can seriously challenge that, and the recognition is only bolstered by a renewed awareness of Miller's historic role in America's political past.

Rejection is the risk of high aspiration, but stature is its reward. Having endured contempt and even vindictiveness, Miller lived to see *All My Sons, Death of a Salesman, The Crucible, A View from the Bridge* and *The Price* become mainstays of the western stage. *The Ride Down Mt. Morgan* will likely join them, and perhaps also the stage version of *Playing for Time* that sooner or later will be produced. One day too the original one-act version of *A View from the Bridge* will be recognized for what it uniquely is.

Whether *Death of a Salesman* is the best play ever written by an American might be argued but cannot and need not be proved. Michael Rudman, who directed it twice (at the Royal National Theatre and for Dustin Hoffman on Broadway), even considered it "arguably the greatest play ever written." That such a suggestion could be made (Rudman made it not on literary grounds "but as a play, a crafted piece of dramatic art") is the highest of praise. If Miller had written just that play and no other, he would have made his mark. There have been playwrights—Strindberg, for instance, Beckett, Wycherley and Sheridan—who achieved classic reputation with just one or two acknowledged masterworks. Chekhov wrote only four major plays. Shaw, Ibsen and Molière each have bequeathed only a handful of classics. Shakespeare alone left a body of masterworks. That is the company Arthur Miller joined—remarkably during his lifetime. As the director David Thacker put it, "anyone who doesn't consider Arthur Miller a great playwright isn't to be taken seriously." For a man who has dwelled on the human imperative to survive, Arthur Miller not only survived, he triumphed.

List of Works

No Villain (1936) (play)

They Too Arise (1937) (play, based on *No Villain*)

Honors at Dawn (1937) (play)

The Grass Still Grows (1938) (play, based on *They Too Arise*)

The Great Disobedience (1938) (play)

Listen My Children (1939) (play, with Norman Rosten)

The Golden Years (1940) (play)

The Pussycat and the Plumber Who Was a Man (1941) (radio play)

William Ireland's Confession (1941) (radio play)

Joel Chandler Harris (1941) (radio play)

Captain Paul (1941) (radio play)

The Battle of the Ovens (1942) (radio play)

Thunder from the Mountains (1942) (radio play)

I Was Married in Bataan (1942) (radio play)

Toward a Farther Star (1942) (radio play)

The Eagle's Nest (1942) (radio play)

The Four Freedoms (1942) (radio play)

The Half-Bridge (1943) (play)

That They May Win (1943) (radio play)

Listen for the Sound Of Wings (1943) (radio play)

Bernadine (1944) (radio play)

I Love You (1944) (radio play)

Grandpa and the Statue (1944) (radio play)

The Philippines Never Surrendered (1944) (radio play)

The Guardsman (1944) (radio play, based on *The Guardsman* by Ferenc Molnár)

Pride and Prejudice (1944) (radio play, based on *Pride and Prejudice* by Jane Austen)

The Story of G.I. Joe (1944) (film)

The Man Who Had All the Luck (1944) (play)

Situation Normal (1944) (nonfiction)

Focus (1945) (novel)

Three Men on a Horse (1946) (radio play, based on *Three Men on a Horse* by George Abbott and John C. Holm)

All My Sons (1947) (play)

The Story of Gus (1947) (radio play)

The Hook (1947) (film)

Death of a Salesman (1949) (play)

An Enemy of the People (1950) (play, based on *An Enemy of the People* by Henrik Ibsen)

The Crucible (1953) (play)

A View from the Bridge (1955) (play)

A Memory of Two Mondays (1955) (play)

"The Misfits" (1957) (short story)

The Misfits (1961) (film, based on "The Misfits")

After the Fall (1964) (play)

Incident at Vichy (1964) (play)

I Don't Need You Anymore (1967) (short stories)

The Price (1968) (play)

In Russia (1969) (nonfiction, with Inge Morath)

Fame (1970) (television play)

The Reason Why (1970) (radio play)

The Creation of the World and Other Business (1972) (play)

In the Country (1977) (nonfiction, with Inge Morath)

The Archbishop's Ceiling (1977) (play)

Chinese Encounters (1979) (nonfiction, with Inge Morath)

The American Clock (1980) (play)

Playing for Time (1980) (television play)

Elegy for a Lady (1982) (play, aka *2 by A.M.* aka *Two-Way Mirror*)

Some Kind of Love Story (1982) (play, aka *2 by A.M.* aka *Two-Way Mirror*)

Salesman in Bejing (1984) (nonfiction)

Playing for Time (1985) (stage version)

I Think About You a Great Deal (1986) (play)

Timebends (1987) (autobiography)

I Can't Remember Anything (1987) (play, aka *Danger: Memory!*)

Clara (1987) (play, aka *Danger: Memory!*)

The Last Yankee (1991) (play)

The Ride Down Mt. Morgan (1991) (play)

Homely Girl (1992) (short stories)

Broken Glass (1994) (play)

Mr. Peter's Connections (1998) (play)

Resurrection Blues (2002) (play)

Chronology of Premiere Productions

The Man Who Had All the Luck. November 23, 1944, Forrest Theatre, New York City. Director: Joseph Fields. With Karl Swensen and Eugenia Rawls.

All My Sons. January 20, 1947, Coronet Theatre, New York City. Director: Elia Kazan. With Ed Begley, Beth Merrill and Arthur Kennedy.

Death of a Salesman. February 10, 1949, Morosco Theatre, New York City. Director: Elia Kazan. With Lee J. Cobb, Mildred Dunnock, Arthur Kennedy and Cameron Mitchell.

An Enemy of the People. December 28, 1950, Broadhurst Theatre, New York City. Director: Robert Lewis. With Fredric March, Florence Eldridge and Morris Carnovsky.

The Crucible. January 22, 1953, Martin Beck Theatre, New York City. Director: Jed Harris. With Arthur Kennedy, Beatrice Straight and E. G. Marshall.

A View from the Bridge. September 29, 1955, Coronet Theatre, New York City. Director: Martin Ritt. With Van Heflin, Eileen Heckart, J. Carrol Naish and Jack Warden.

After the Fall. January 22, 1964, ANTA Washington Square Theatre, New York City. Director: Elia Kazan. With Jason Robards, Jr., Barbara Loden, Salome Jens.

Incident at Vichy. December 3, 1964, ANTA Washington Square Theatre, New York City. Director: Harold Clurman. With David Wayne and Joseph Wiseman.

The Price. February 7, 1968, Morosco Theatre. Director: Ulu Grosbard. With Pat Hingle, Arthur Kennedy, Harold Gary, Kate Reid.

The Creation of the World and Other Business. November 30, 1972, Shubert Theatre. With Zoe Caldwell and Bob Dishy.

The Archbishop's Ceiling. April 30, 1977, Eisenhower Theatre, Washington, D.C. Director: Arvin Brown. With John Cullum and Bibi Andersson.

The American Clock. November 20, 1980, Biltmore Theatre, New York City. Director: Dan Sullivan. With Joan Copeland, John Randolph and William Atherton.

Elegy for a Lady/Some Kind of Love Story (Two-Way Mirror). October 26, 1982, Long Wharf Theatre, New Haven, CT. Director: Arthur Miller. With Christine Lahti and Charles Cioffi.

Clara/I Can't Remember Anything (Danger: Memory!). February 8, 1987, Vivian Beaumont Theater, New York City. Director: Gregory Mosher. With Mason Adams and Geraldine Fitzgerald.

The Ride Down Mt. Morgan. October 11, 1991, Wyndham's Theatre, London. Director: Michael Blakemore. With Tom Conti, Gemma Jones and Claire Higgins.

The Last Yankee. January 21, 1993, Manhattan Theater Club, New York City. Director: John Tillinger. With Frances Conroy, Tom Aldredge and Rose Gregorio.

Broken Glass. April 24, 1994, Booth Theatre, New York City. Director: John Tillinger. With Ron Rifkin, Frances Conroy, David Dukes and Amy Irving.

Mr. Peters' Connections. May 17, 1998. Signature Theatre Company, New York City. Director: Garry Hynes. With Peter Falk and Anne Jackson.

Resurrection Blues. August 9, 2002, Guthrie Theatre, Minneapolis. Director: David Esbjornson. With Laila Robbins, Jeff Weiss and John Bedford.

Notes

Chapter 1. Escape

p. 3 "But instead of working on a play": Miller's correspondence with Professor Kenneth Thorpe Rowe can be found in the Humanities Collections, Special Collections Library, University of Michigan. Most oof the information about Miller's youthful years, family history and description of their homes were provided by Miller's sister Joan.

p. 3 "try to understand the audience": The Theatre Guild play reader was John Gassner, a professor of drama at Columbia University who several decades later would write the two-volume college textbook *Drama: From Aeschylus to Arthur Miller*.

p. 5 "Arthur Asher Miller was born": Gittel Miller would be called "Gussie" and later took the name Augusta. See Zolotow, *Marilyn Monroe*.

p. 14 "The power that the father lost": Quote and details of Chadick-Delameter warehouse from Miller, *Timebends*.

p. 18 "He listed Stanford University": High school details from the records of Abraham Lincoln High School, Brooklyn, New York.

Chapter 2. Epiphany

p. 21 "While I the inferior student went off to college": Miller, *Timebends*.

p. 22 "One of their earliest conversations": Anne (Mrs. Charlie) Bleich.

p. 24 "The first time I saw Arthur": Mary Slattery Miller to interviewer Robert Sylvester for the *Saturday Evening Post*, 1949.

p.24 "Were dead history": Miller, *Timebends*.

p. 28 "contest for undergraduates" and "brooding young man": Helburn, *Wayward Quest*.

p. 29 "The general standard": Records of the Hopwood Awards Committee, Special Collections Library, University of Michigan.

p. 30 "This story is a more confidant work": "In Memoriam" was ultimately published in *The New Yorker* in 1995, on the occasion of Miller's eightieth birthday.

p. 30 "He saved what he wrote": The typed manuscript of the short story survived and can be found in the Miller Archives at the Harry Ransom Library of the University of Texas. Attached is Miller's note of thirty years later stating that it was "written when I was seventeen," apparently a mistake. For one thing, Miller was not able to type at the time. Moreover, he mentions that "I owned an old car." This indicates that "In Memoriam" was written *after* Miller had bought the 1927 Model T. This story was probably written in 1936 at age nineteen in memory of the salesman Miller had accompanied when he was seventeen and helping out in his father's business. This association most likely triggered the age he noted on the manuscript when donating his papers to the University of Texas.

p. 33 "administered the kind of criticism": *Michigan Daily*.

p. 33 "what is interesting or picturesque": Rowe, *Write That Play!*

p. 35 "The Ibsenite construction": Michael Blakemore, interview with author.

p. 36 "*By Corona*": *The Grass Still Grows*, manuscript.

p. 40 "You Miller?" and "He can't write without music": *The Gargoyle*, University of Michigan.

Chapter 3. Epic

p. 48 "the most truly experimental": Clurman, *Fervent Years*.

p. 49 "I feel a small, size 14 chain": Miller letter to Professor Rowe, 7 January 1939.

p. 51 "road company Jed Harris": Paul Streger, interview with author.

p. 51 "Moves fast, it is a comedy": Streger quoted in Miller letter to Professor Rowe, 10 November 1938.

p. 51 "between the teaching world": Eric Bentley, interview with author.

p. 54 "Now he shared his joyousness": Fortunately his old teacher had been saving young Miller's letters and would later donate them to the Special Collections Library at the University of Michigan. Flawlessly typed and single spaced, many of them five pages and longer, filled with serious ruminations as well as personal asides, these letters provide a unique insight into the thoughts and feelings of the youthful playwright. In fact he would be a prolific correspondent throughout his life with various and sometimes unexpected confidants. Many of those letters were also saved and donated to research facilities.

p. 59 "a powerful and accomplished drama:" Bigsby, *Cambridge Companion to Arthur Miller*.

Chapter 4. Debut

p. 63 "letter of frustration and despair": Written to Rowe, 1940.

p. 63 "scribbling a postcard": Miller wrote to Rowe on 14 May 1940. He married Mary Slattery on 5 August 1940. The Selective Service Act, America's first peacetime draft, took effect on 16 September 1940. Miller turned twenty-five on 17 October 1940.

p. 64 "opposed to marrying a Jew": Told to a British interviewer for the *London Independent* in 1994.

p. 65 "Arthur and Mary were already married": Joan (Miller) Copeland, interview with author.

p. 65 "We were married without a dime": Mary Miller to newspaper columnist Robert Sylvester.

p. 65 "This early parting": Miller, *Timebends*.

p. 66 "an uproar in the audience": Miller notebook.

p. 79 "[O]ne who, anticipatory of Larry Keller": Nelson, *Portrait of a Playwright*.

p. 80 "to fill two volumes": Gussow, *Conversations with Arthur Miller*;and Roudane, ed., *Conversations with Arthur Miller*.

Chapter 5. Hit

p. 87 "I can be disheartened": In response to an interview on *The South Bank Show*, London Weekend Television, 1980.

p. 89 "Arthur distances himself from intimacy": Frank Taylor, personal memorandum.

p. 90 "sale of the film rights": The picture was not made, but there was a 1962 television adaptation and ultimately an excellent full-length movie released in 2001.

p. 90 "Somehow a book": Miller, interview at the 92nd Street Y in New York City.

p. 92 "I had written thirteen plays": Miller apparently arrived at the number thirteen by including more than one version of some of the plays.

p. 92 "familiar events in a style": Gassner, *Reader's Encyclopedia of World Drama*.

p. 93 "In general, aside from the women": Miller, interview by Philip Gelb for the *Educational Theatre Journal*.

p. 98 "The third and final act": In the future, three-act plays would go out of style and *All My Sons* would be performed with only one intermission.

p. 101 "To have an agent": Essay in *Holiday* Magazine, January 1955.

p. 102 "Whatever a man's estimate": Eric Bentley, interview with author.

p. 102 "put the yield": Kazan, *A Life*.

p. 103 "Gadg works hard": Helburn, *Wayward Quest*.

p. 105. "each page faced a blank sheet": Kazan had learned this system at the Group Theatre, where Harold Clurman and Robert Lewis also had their scripts interfaced with blank pages.

p. 108 "The past determining the future": Michael Blakemore, interview with author.

p. 108 "From the beginning": Bigsby, *Critical Introduction*.

Chapter 6. Inspiration

p. 114 "decorating the place": Mary Miller to interviewer Robert Sylvester for the *Saturday Evening Post*, 1949.

p. 115 "After the performance": Kazan, *A Life*.

p. 115 "I don't care for theater": Miller, *Timebends*.

p. 119 "find the facts first": Miller in letter to Kazan, July 1947.

p. 119 "Seabees": American naval shorthand for Construction Battalion (CB).

p. 128 "I read the play that night": Kermit Bloomgarden, *American Theatre*, November 1988.

Chapter 7. Salesman

p. 134 "It died in 1941": Kazan, *A Life*.

p. 135 "I added four inches": Dunnock, Dramatists Guild Panel, Marymount College, New York City, 19 March 1981.

p. 137 "is one person": Elia Kazan notebook.

p. 138 "Delete several fanciful": Kazan annotated script, Kazan Archives at Wesleyan University, Middlebury, CT.

p. 138 "several decades of sleaze": In 1996 the interior of the New Amsterdam Theatre was fully restored, although not the rooftop theater.

p. 139 "Kazan tried to set Miller's mind": Kazan, Dramatists Guild Panel, Marymount College, New York City, 19 March 1981.

p. 140 "We were a very disparate group": Alan Hewitt, Dramatists Guild Panel, Marymount College, New York City, 19 March 1981.

p. 142 "One of the confusions": Gassner, *Reader's Encyclopedia of World Drama*.

p. 142 "The point of the part": Kazan notebook, Kazan Archives at Wesleyan University, Middlebury, CT.

p. 143 "'Barney' Baruch": Bernard N. Baruch, the financier.

p. 143 "He's a real brother": Miller, interview with Christopher Bigsby.

p. 143 "Proctor and Debuskey": Merle Debuskey, interview with author.

p. 144 "had often yielded": Miller's notes for a Penguin Music Classics recording of Beethoven's Seventh Symphony, conducted by Vladimir Ashkenazy and the Philharmonia Orchestra.

p. 144 "I got in the back way": Dunnock, Dramatists Guild Panel, Marymount College, New York City, 19 March 1981.

p. 147 "smoking that cigar": Bloomgarden memorandum.

p. 149 "I personally found it boring": Payn and Morley, eds., *Noel Coward Diaries*.

p. 150 "As Garson Kanin observed": Kanin, Dramatists Guild Panel, Marymount College, New York City, 19 March 1981.

p. 155 "The family is Jewish": Michael Rudman, interview with author.

p. 155 "A distressed Mildred Dunnock": Bloomgarden, *American Theatre*, November 1988.

Chapter 8. Movies

p. 158 "I didn't believe": Kazan, *A Life*.

p. 159 "wasn't a communist": Frances Ann Dougherty, interview with author.

p. 161 "lost his church, had his life work ruined, the church itself closed": Radical reform ran in the Melish family. During the student protest years in the Vietnam war era, Reverend Melish's son, Howard Jeffrey Melish, was a member of the extremist Weather Underground faction of the Students for a Democratic Society and was arrested in the Days of Rage demonstrations during the 1968 Democrat convention in Chicago. Miller attended this convention as a delegate from Connecticut. The Episcopal Holy Trinity Church was reopened in the 1970s as St. Ann and The Holy Trinity and continued its progressive tradition, sponsoring the first female ordained priest in Brooklyn.

p. 165 "Ibsen viewed his protagonist": Nelson, *Portrait of a Playwright*.

p. 166 "Fantastic marriage": David Thacker, interview with author.

Chapter 9. Betrayal

p. 179 "Sounded like a very nervous man": Kazan, *A Life*.

p. 181 "Bewitch them" and "If you want someone": Records of Natasha Lytess.

p. 182 "modeled on Monroe": As conceded by Miller in *Timebends*.

p. 182 "Hollywood Ten": The others were Alvah Bessie, Herbert Biberman, Lester Cole, Edward Dmytryk, Albert Maltz, Samuel Ornitz, Adrian Scott and Dalton Trumbo.

p. 184 "They made Willy crazier": Miller, in Bigsby, *Arthur Miller and Company*.

p. 185 "He invited Kermit and Virginia": Virginia Bloomgarden, interview with author.

p. 186 "the play covered a larger territory": Manuscript at Arthur Miller Archives in the Harry Ransom Library at the University of Texas.

p. 190 "my bare *tuchas* out": Unpublished section of Marilyn Monroe interview with Richard Meryman for *Life* Magazine, August 1962.

p. 193 "the session was concluded": The testimony was finally released in 2002.

p. 194 "In the two months between": Eric Bentley, interview with author.

p. 194 "immediately noticed the director's anxiety": George Tabori, interview with author.

p. 194 "Kazan was tossing coins": Kermit Bloomgarden, *American Theatre*, November 1988.

p. 195 "Bloomgarden had told his wife": Virginia Bloomgarden, interview with author.

p. 195 "the fact that a political": Miller, *Timebends*.

p. 195 "Those witches did exist": Kazan, *A Life*.

p. 196 "Marion Starkey": The preface to Miller's play credited his "primary and most used sources" as being "the trial record, on file in the Essex County Courthouse, Salem; and *Salem Witchcraft; with an Account of Salem Village, and A History of Opinions on Witchcraft and Kindred Subjects*, by Charles W. Upham, published in 1867." Oddly enough Miller did not credit *The Devil in Massachusetts* by Marion Starkey, which had been his first source.

p. 199 "previous professional plays": *The Man Who Had All the Luck* ends with its hero's suicide only a possibility.

p. 201 "Had that record been released": The testimony was finally released in 2002.

Chapter 10. Crucible

p. 205 "An earlier version of this scene": Miller notebook, Arthur Miller Archives in the Harry Ransom Library at the University of Texas.

p. 213 "so ugly I can": Proctor, interview with author.

p. 213 "cut my conscience": Hellman was not cited for contempt of Congress and her career continued unimpeded.

p. 213 "When word got out": Kermit Bloomgarden, *American Theatre*, November 1988.

p. 214 "He couldn't read a newspaper": Miller, interview with author.

p. 215 "Who could he dominate?": Beatrice Straight, interview with author.

p. 217 "On the Delaware opening night": Katharine Brown, interview with author.

p. 224 "A collage of language": Richard Eyre in a program note for the 2001 Broadway production of *The Crucible*.

p. 225 "Longfellow's approach": Tennessee Williams was also inspired by the Salem witch trials and wrote a short story, "The Yellow Birds," about them.

Chapter 11. The Little Red

p. 227 "engaged William Travilla": Spoto, *Marilyn Monroe*.
p. 228 "I hear he's very healthy": Winters, *Shelley*.
p. 229 "Kazan was at home": Notebook, Kazan Archives at Wesleyan University, Middlebury, CT.
p. 231 "We have sold": Legal department, McGraw-Hill Publishing.
p. 231 "In *The Hook*": Kermit Bloomgarden Archives, State Historical Society of Wisconsin.
p. 233 "to justify finking": Brando, *Songs My Mother Taught Me*.
p. 234 "it sets the intimate scene": *On the Waterfront—The Final Shooting Script*. Samuel French, 1980.
p. 234 "play the scene": Schulberg, interview with author.
p. 234 "would have been good": Introduction to *On the Waterfront—The Final Shooting Script*.
p. 235 "The plays belong to Miller and Williams": During the next few years Kazan continued to work with Williams but the heart seems to have gone out of him. None of their collaborations (*Camino Real, Cat on a Hot Tin Roof, The Sweet Bird of Youth*) approached the rich and poetic theater of *A Streetcar Named Desire*.
p. 236 "Dear Sirs": Tennessee Williams letter to U.S. State Department, Tennessee Williams Archives in the Harry Ransom Library at the University of Texas.
p. 237 "The Third Play Company": Kermit Bloomgarden Archives, State Historical Society of Wisconsin.
p. 238 "The idea was for education to be enjoyable": Jill Rubin, interview with author.
p. 239 "So long, I've had you fame": Unpublished section of Marilyn Monroe interview with Richard Meryman for *Life* Magazine, August 1962.
p. 240 "Hair short, careless and wet": Rosten, *Marilyn*.
p. 240 "Even providing the occasional bedroom": Amy Greene, interview with author.
p. 240 "Miller had begun a new correspondence": The Miller-Stern correspondence at the British Library in London.
p. 242 "Whitehead thought that the scenery": Whitehead, interview with author.
p. 244 "Other investors": Kermit Bloomgarden Archives, State Historical Society of Wisconsin.
p. 244 "She'd wear dark glasses": Whitehead, interview with author.
p. 245 "Bought a picture of Einstein, signed it": Eli Wallach, interview with author.
p. 246 "Unless I see evidence": Anne Jackson, interview with author.
p. 247 "Six hours later": Miller was one of several Fathers of the Year.
p. 247 "How Isadore Miller described": Wagenknecht, *Marilyn Monroe*.

Chapter 12. A Bridge

p. 253 "If this were an opera": In 1999 an opera version of *A View from the Bridge* was commissioned and produced by the Lyric Opera of Chicago; it was composed by William Bolcom to Arnold Weinstein's libretto. Earlier Renzo Rosselini, brother of the film director Roberto Rosselini, composed an opera version in Italy called *Un Siguardo del Ponte*.
p. 263 "Wrote to a friend": Eric Bentley, interview with author.

p. 266 "A lot of anger and tension": Stephen Farber, "Miller and Son," *Sunday New York Times Magazine*, 17 November 1996.

p. 267 "Never saw": Robert Whitehead, interview with author.

p. 267 "wiped out of existence": Virginia Bloomgarden, interview with author.

p. 267 "*Bridge to a Savage World*": Scenario at the Academy of Motion Picture Arts and Sciences, Los Angeles.

p. 270 "ardor of a man released": Rosten, *Marilyn*.

Chapter 13. The Committee

p. 273 "those things you clash together": Outtake from Marilyn Monroe interview with Richard Meryman for *Life* Magazine, August 1962.

p. 273 "Something in me": Miller, *Timebends*.

p. 275 "The son of an ambassador": Terence Rattigan Collection, the British Library in London.

p. 277 "We were invited": Earle Hyman, interview with author.

p. 277 "The Rostens didn't always": Amy Greene, interview with author.

p. 279 "when the Beckett thing hit": Interview with Dan Sullivan, *Los Angeles Times*, 15 November 1987.

p. 287 "Robeson went on": Robeson was subsequently found in contempt of Congress; an action was authorized but not taken, presumably lest he become a martyr.

p. 289 "The questioning began": The Testimony of Arthur Miller, accompanied by counsel, Joseph L. Rauh, Jr., 84th Cong., *Congressional Record*, Pt. 4, June 21, 1956 (Washington, DC: U.S. Government Printing Office, November 1956), 4660–90.

p. 293 "Have you heard?": Rosten, *Marilyn*.

p. 295 "On all the roads": Zolotow, *Marilyn Monroe*.

p. 297 "Rosten nudged Marilyn away from Miller": Rosten, *Marilyn*.

Chapter 14. Movie Star

p. 300 "I never thought in terms": Marilyn Monroe interview by Richard Meryman for *Life* Magazine, August 1962.

p. 300 "a dozen rooms": Rosten, *Marilyn*.

p. 300 "an honest to God ball": Amy Greene, interview with author.

p. 300 "His master plan": Terence Rattigan Collection, the British Library in London.

p. 301 "danced the Charleston": Monroe thank-you note to Rattigan, Terence Rattigan Collection, the British Library in London.

p. 301 "old friends . . . patronizing": Rosten, *Marilyn*.

p. 302 "short, fat, dumpy": Amy Greene, interview with author.

p. 302 "when she gets onto a stage": Miller letter to Kermit Bloomgarden, Kermit Bloomgarden Archives, State Historical Society of Wisconsin.

p. 303 "his own confession": While Miller contributed many notebooks to his archives at the Harry Ransom Library at the University of Texas in Austin, this London notebook is not among them.

p. 304 "Lord Chamberlain The office of the British censor": The term *Lord Chamberlain* derived from a sixteenth-century acting company called The Lord Chamberlain's Men, of which William Shakespeare was a member.

p. 304 "In America, 'punk' simply means": Robert Whitehead, interview with author.

p. 305 "seemed to me to be a one act play": Miller in 1985 conversation with Professor Matthew C. Roudane, in the *Michigan Quarterly Review*.

p. 307 "As if in appreciation": Sheridan Morley, interview with author.

p. 309 "Willem de Kooning": Willem de Kooning would paint a portrait of Marilyn Monroe. It is hanging in the Museum of Modern Art.

p. 310 "I'm proud of my husband's position": Marilyn Monroe, interview with Richard Meryman for *Life* Magazine, August 1962.

p. 312 "More like a rubber doll": Jeffrey Potter, interview with author.

p. 312 "She was very relaxed in Amagansett": Merle Debuskey, interview with author.

p. 313 "For an old friend": Directed by Sidney Lumet and starring Raf Vallone and Maureen Stapleton, the film version of *A View from the Bridge* was produced in 1962.

p. 313 "Hollywood press agent": Patricia Newcomb.

p. 314 "by flashlight": Howard Birchell, interview with author.

p. 315 "She tripped and fell": Rosten, *Marilyn*.

p. 316 "federal tax write-off": Such write-offs were permissible at the time.

p. 317 "Arthur never does anything *simply*": Frank Taylor, personal memorandum.

p. 318 "I'm used to it": Nan Taylor Abell, interview with author.

p. 322 "Sounding much less confident": The Academy of Motion Picture Arts and Sciences, Los Angeles.

p. 323 "In the deepest sense": *Show* Magazine, January 1962.

Chapter 15. Misfits

p. 326 "Demeaning errands . . . couldn't turn off his feelings": Guiles, *Norma Jean*, as verified by Miller.

p. 327 "A lie through and through": *No Villain*.

p. 327 "silently, at night": Skolsky, *Don't Get Me Wrong*.

p. 327 "Miller's version": Guiles, *Norma Jean*. Arthur Miller had editorial control over the book.

p. 327 "call me a taxi": Interview with Hal Kanter, Academy of Motion Picture Arts and Sciences, Los Angeles.

p. 328 "the way you have behaved": George Cukor files, Academy of Motion Picture Arts and Sciences, Los Angeles.

p. 330 "I just want to say I'm sorry": Kazan Archives at Wesleyan University, Middlebury, CT.

p. 332 "It's like John was telling Lee": John Huston Collection, Academy of Motion Picture Arts and Sciences, Los Angeles.

p. 333 "British visitor": A. J. Weatherby, Jr., of the *Manchester Guardian*.

p. 333 "I was about to drive away": Huston, *Open Book*.

p. 334 "My teacher, Lee Strasberg": Goode, *Making of the Misfits*.

p. 334 "Their marriage is over": Goode, *Making of the Misfits*.

p. 338 "thanks to Marilyn's generosity": The property had originally been deeded to Monroe.

p. 338 "And then we lost it": Weatherby, Jr., *Conversations with Marilyn*.

p. 340 "When the monster showed": Weatherby, Jr., *Conversations with Marilyn*.

p. 342 "Dad went home": Joan Copeland, interview with author.

p. 342 "Things are once again simple": James Stern Archives, the British Library, London.

p. 344 "It's your problem": Arthur Jacobs' assistant, John Springer, interview with author.

p. 344 "She sounded happy": Wagenknecht, *Marilyn Monroe*..

p. 344 "Arthur didn't send flowers": Arthur Jacobs' assistant, John Springer, interview with author.

p. 346 "He isn't right": Robert Whitehead, interview with author.

p. 347 "Daniel was a very difficult subject": Joan Copeland, interview with author.

Chapter 16. The Fall

p. 351 "Brown spiral notebook": Kazan Archives at Wesleyan University, Middlebury, CT.

p. 354 "*Jane's Blanket*." Viking Press, 1972.

p. 354 "May I just say": Letter to Miller, Kazan Archives at Wesleyan University, Middlebury, CT.

p. 363 "It just hit me": Robert Whitehead, interview with author.

p. 364 "Hello, my name is Elia Kazan": Cast member, Paul Mann.

p. 364 "a terrible reader": Jason Robards, interview with author.

p. 365 "Late Bulletin": Letter from Miller to Kazan, Kazan Archives at Wesleyan University, Middlebury, CT.

p. 367 "Kazan suggested to Barbara Loden": Kazan Archives at Wesleyan University, Middlebury, CT.

p. 368 "If Mr. Kazan takes a half page advertisement": Madeleine Gilford, interview with author.

p. 369 "Arthur's father came backstage": Jason Robards, Jr., interview with author.

p. 372 "picture was never made": Ultimately there was a television movie of *After the Fall* with Christopher Plummer and Faye Dunaway.

p. 373 "in fact been based on Monroe": Michael Blakemore, interview with author.

Chapter 17. Price

p. 375 "*SS*": An acronym for *Schutzstaffel*, or "protection squad."

p. 376 "*Judgment at Nuremberg*": Released in 1961 and written by Abby Mann, who later collaborated with Miller on a screenplay for *After the Fall*.

p. 377 "realism": Miller wished to qualify the realism of *Incident at Vichy*. "It deals with a group of people who are faced with the need to respond to total destruction, and when that is the situation, you are not in what can normally be called a realistic situation."

p. 381 "fruits and vegetables": Miller, interview with Josh Greenfeld, *New York Times Magazine*, 13 February 1972.

p. 383 "Mike Nichols, Marlon Brando": The British Library, London.

p. 385 "Christopher Walken, . . . Jon Voight": Ulu Grosbard, interview with author.

p. 385 "My idol, Arthur Miller": Dustin Hoffman, *The Making of "Death of a Salesman."*

p. 385 "playing Willy Loman": Hoffman also played Loman's young boss, Howard, in a 1965 audio recording that reunited Lee J. Cobb and Mildred Dunnock of the original *Death of a Salesman* cast.

p. 386 "work on the typewriter": Josh Greenfeld, *New York Times Magazine*, 13 February 1972.

p. 393 "nit-picking": Laurie Kennedy, interview with author.

p. 398 "the biblical story":Barbara Harris, who was playing Eve in Miller's version, had even taken the same role in *The Apple Tree*, a musical adaptation of Twain's story.

Chapter 18. Outcast

p. 401 "a group of students": In 1973 Miller was an Adjunct Professor for part of a semester at the University of Michigan.

p. 402 "Watergate": In his introduction to *The Archbishop's Ceiling* Miller terms the 1970s "the era of the listening device . . . the White House was bugged . . . Watergate and the publication of the Pentagon Papers demonstrated that the Soviets had little to teach American presidents about domestic espionage."

p. 402 "glasnost": In his introduction to *The Archbishop's Ceiling* Miller describes *glasnost* as "at bottom a Soviet attempt, born of economic crisis, to break up the perfection of its own social controls in order to open the channels of expression through which the creativity, the initiatives, and the improvisations of individual people may begin to flow and enrich the country."

p. 403 "mischievous and mysterious": Harold Pinter, in the company of the author.

p. 406 "a metaphysical anxiety": Bigsby, *A Critical Introduction*.

p. 407 "BBC Radio Drama Department": 6 November 1987.

p. 408 "crib death": Robert Whitehead, interview with author.

p. 408 "make it a point": Zoe Caldwell, interview with author.

p. 409 "rediscover my youth": Miller in *TV Guide*, 21 August 1993.

p. 411 "I've always hated Broadway": Miller, interview with Christopher Bigsby.

p. 412 "Barbra Streisand, Jane Fonda": Recalled by Linda Yellen, interview with author.

p. 417 "published in *Esquire*": "An Elegy for a Lady" was the full title when the story was originally published.

p. 419 "on their nonprofit way": *Some Kind of Love Story* was later filmed as *Everybody Wins*, with a screenplay by Miller. An inconsequential movie, it starred Debra Winger and Nick Nolte.

p. 422 "Shattuck": *New York Times*, 8 November 1987.

p. 422 "Wolcott": *Vanity Fair*, November 1987.

Chapter 19. Survivor

p. 423 "medicine bottle cap": Leverich, *Tom*.

p. 425 "Thacker felt": David Thacker, interview with author.

p. 426 "Some months before": December 1990.

p. 432 "Philip Roth": *The Human Stain* (Houghton Mifflin, 2000).

p. 432 "R.M.": Miller's sister Joan, interview with author.

p. 432 "Two years earlier": Philip Roth, *I Married a Communist* (Houghton Mifflin, 1998).

p. 433 "The director": Michael Blakemore, interview with author.

p. 435 "the review appearing": Frank Rich, *New York Times*, 30 August 1990.

p. 435 "Jewish lawyer": More pertinent and informative perhaps might have been the unique setting for this production. As Blakemore described it,

Our set was based on *The Golden Section*. The Golden Section is a relationship that the Greeks found. It is based on a ratio of roughly one to 7.38. You can enscribe a rectangle with that ratio, and having enscribed it, you can then make another rectangle at the end of it, which has the same proportions—except that the long side of the second rectangle is the short side of the first. And you can keep doing that, and doing it and doing it and doing it . . . and finally you will find that those diminishing rectangles will create a spiral. And that spiral is found throughout nature—this relationship can be found in the human hand. If the human hand is relaxed, the fingers—their position—begin the spiral of The Golden Section. . . . It's a relationship that exists throughout nature, [even] when a wave breaks.

When our designer told me about it, I was astonished. And it worked wonderfully for the play, because what we had was this huge spiral. It was possible for people to appear through different crevices of the spiral—on different levels. And they would just be there. And they'd play a scene, and then they'd go. And when the man jumps to his death in front of the subway train, we simply had two lights getting bigger and the roar of the train as it approached and he sort of jumped. It was very effective, being based on The Golden Section. (Hogarth described this curve as "the line of beauty" and put it onto the painter's palette in his self-portrait.)

p. 436 "felt it would stand": David Thacker, interview with author.

p. 436 "One leading actor": Ron Silver.

p. 442 "Jones kneeled beside the table": Baird Jones, interview with author.

p. 443 "Most cinematic": Stephen Farber, *New York Times Magazine*, 17 November 1996.

p. 443 "experience of me as an adult": Robert Miller as quoted in the *Sunday New York Times Magazine*, 17 November 1996.

p. 445 "Whitehead uncertain": Robert Whitehead, interview with author.

p. 445 "The first time": Joan Copeland, interview with author.

p. 446 "Anyone who doesn't": David Thacker, interview with author.

Bibliography

Bentley, Eric. *Thirty Years of Treason*. Viking Press, 1971.
———. *What Is Theatre?* Atheneum, 1968.
Bigsby, Christopher. *Arthur Miller and Company*. Methuen Drama, 1990.
———. *The Cambridge Companion to Arthur Miller*. Cambridge University Press, 1997.
———. *A Critical Introduction to Twentieth Century American Drama*. Vol. 2. Cambridge University Press, 1984.
———. *File on Miller*. Methuen, 1968.
Brando, Marlon. *Songs My Mother Taught Me*. Random House, 1996.
Clurman, Harold. *The Fervent Years: The Group Theatre and the Thirties*. Harcourt Brace Jovanovich, 1975.
Corrigan, Robert W. *Arthur Miller: A Collection of Critical Essays*. Prentice-Hall, 1969.
Eisinger, Chester E. "American Dreams, American Nightmares." Southern Illinois University, 1970.
Gassner, John. *The Reader's Encyclopedia of World Drama*. Ty Cromwell, 1969.
Goode, James. *The Making of the Misfits*. Bobbs-Merrill, 1963.
Guiles, Fred Lawrence. *Norma Jean: The Life of Marilyn Monroe*. McGraw-Hill, 1969.
Gussow, Mel. *Conversations with Arthur Miller*. Nick Hern Books, 2002.
Hamon, Herve, and Patrick Rotman. *Yves Montand*. Alfred A. Knopf, 1992.
———. *You See, I Haven't Forgotten*. Alfred A. Knopf, 1992.
Hayman, Ronald. *Arthur Miller*. Heinemann, 1970.
Helburn, Teresa. *A Wayward Quest*. Little, Brown, 1960.
Hellman, Lillian. *Scoundrel Time*. Little, Brown, 1976.
Huftel, Sheila. *Arthur Miller: The Burning Glass*. Citadel Press, 1965.
Huston, John. *An Open Book*. Knopf, 1984.
Kanfer, Stefan. *A Journal of the Plague Years*. H. Wolff, 1973.
Kazan, Elia. *A Life*. Alfred A. Knopf, 1988.
Leaming, Barbara. *Marilyn Monroe*. Crown, 1998.
Leverich, Lyle. *Tom: The Unknown Tennessee Williams*. Random House, 1998.
Mailer, Norman. *Marilyn*. Grosset and Dunlap, 1972.
Margolick, David. *Strange Fruit: The Biography of a Song*. Ecco Press, 2001.

Martin, Robert A. *Arthur Miller: New Perspectives*. Prentice-Hall, 1982.
Martin, Robert A., and Steven R. Centola. *The Theatre Essays of Arthur Miller*. DaCapo, 1986.
Miller, Arthur. *The Collected Plays*. Vol. 1. Viking Press, 1957.
———. *The Collected Plays*. Vol. 2. Viking Press, 1981.
———. *Echoes Down the Corridor*. Viking Penguin, 2000.
———. *Focus*. Reynal and Hitchcock, 1945.
———. *I Don't Need You Anymore. Collected Stories*. Viking Press, 1967.
———. *Jane's Blanket*. Viking Press, 1972.
———. *The Misfits*. Viking Press, 1957.
———. *On Politics and the Art of Acting*. Viking Penguin, 2001.
———. *Salesman in Beijing*. Viking Press, 1983.
———. *Situation Normal . . .* Reynal and Hitchcock, 1944.
———. *Timebends*. Grove Press, 1987.
Miller, Arthur, and Inge Morath. *Chinese Encounter*. Farrar, Straus and Giroux, 1979.
———. *In Russia*. Viking Press, 1969.
———. *In the Country*. Viking Press, 1977.
Moss, Leonard. *Arthur Miller*. Twayne, 1980.
Navasky, Victor. *Naming Names*. Viking Press, 1980.
Nelson, Benjamin. *Arthur Miller: Portrait of a Playwright*. David McKay, 1970.
Payn, Graham, and Sheridan Morley, eds. *The Noel Coward Diaries*. Little, Brown, 1982.
Rosten, Norman. *Marilyn: An Untold Story*. New American Library, 1967.
Rosten, Norman, and Stan Shaw. *Marilyn Among Friends*. Crescent Books, 1992.
Roudané, Matthew C., ed. *Conversations with Arthur Miller*. University Press of Mississippi, 1987.
Rowe, Kenneth Thorpe. *Write That Play!* Funk and Wagnalls, 1939.
Schulberg, Budd. *On the Waterfront*. Samuel French, 1980.
Skolsky, Sidney. *Don't Get Me Wrong—I Love Hollywood*. Putnam's, 1975.
Spoto, Donald. *Marilyn Monroe: The Biography*. HarperCollins, 1993.
Tynan, Kenneth. *Curtains*. Atheneum, 1961.
Wagenknecht, Edward. *Marilyn Monroe: A Composite View*. Chillen Book, 1969.
Weatherby, A. J., Jr., *Conversations with Marilyn*. Mason Charter, 1976.
Winters, Shelley. *Shelley: Also Known as Shirley*. William Morrow, 1989.
Zolotow, Maurice. *Marilyn Monroe: The Uncensored Biography*. Harcourt Brace, 1960.

Acknowledgments

So many contributed to the resourcefulness of this book and they are very appreciated. Arthur Miller was particularly helpful in describing the writing, rehearsing and production of *The Crucible*. Then—and foremost—were the helpful and forthcoming people who passed away before the publication of this book and are sorely missed: Harold Clurman, Jason Robards, Jr., Jack Gilford, Robert Whitehead, Paul Streger, Peter Cookson, Frances Ann Dougherty, Beatrice Straight, James Proctor, John Springer, Del Hughes, Josh Logan and Katherine Brown. I am grateful for the time, memories and uncanny details provided by Nan Taylor Abell, Bonnie Beacher, Eric Bentley, Michael Blakemore, Anne Bleich, Harold Bloom, John Byrne, Zoe Caldwell, Virginia Kaye Chilewicz, Joan Copeland, Merle Debuskey, Bob Dishy, Madeleine Gilford, Amy Greene-Andrews, Ulu Grosbard, Clive Hirschhorn, Earle Hyman, Anne Jackson, Herb Jaffey, Baird Jones, Hal Kantor, Frances Kazan, Laurie Kennedy, Harvey Klehr, Floria Lasky, Ruth Leon, Blanche Marvin, Sheridan Morley, Victor Navasky, Jeffrey Potter, Michael Riedel, Derek Parker Royal, Jill Rubin, Michael Rudman, Theodore Sayers, Gerald Schoenfeld, Budd Schulberg, George Tabori, Curtice Taylor, David Thacker, Eli Wallach, Tony Walton and Linda Yellen.

University libraries and archives were particularly fertile sources and I received generous access and assistance from Kathryn L. Beam, Curator of the Humanities Collections, Special Collections Library at the University of Michigan; William Davis of the National Archives and Records Administration, Washington, D.C.; Christopher Fletcher, Curator of Literary Manuscripts at the British Library, London; Jeanine Basinger, Curator, and Leith Johnson, Co-Curator, and Joan Miller, Archivist at the Elia Kazan Archives of the Wesleyan University Cinema Archives; Barbara Hall and Harold Prouty at the Academy of Motion Picture Arts and Sciences Center for Motion Picture Study in Los Angeles; the Arthur Miller Archives of the Harry Ransom Library at the University of Texas in Austin; and, inevitably and eternally, the Theatre Collection at the Library of the Performing Arts in Lincoln Center, New York City, with particular appreciation for the advice and help of Rod Bladel.

Finally, one must acknowledge the immense benefits provided by the World Wide Web and its search engines, particularly Google, in making available an unprecedented range of resources.

On the more personal level, my editor, John Radziewicz, has been simply the best, providing support, encouragement, newfound friendship and even occasional praise. If my writing is pleasing to any extent, it is to the credit of Michael Wilde, the most thorough and theaterwise copy editor in my publishing experience. As for my agent, Elaine Markson, there simply is no other to compare.

Index

abortion, 46
absurdism, 278–279
ACLU. *See* American Civil Liberties Union
Actors Studio, 240, 242, 244–246, 266, 269–270, 322
The Adding Machine (Rice), 28
Adler, Stella, 384
The Adventures of Augie March (Bellow), 283
Aeschylus, 33, 101
The African Queen, 336
After the Fall (Miller), xi, 303, 337
  autobiographical elements in, 189, 352–353, 354–355, 364–365, 370–373
  character in, 188
  critics and, 369–372
  Death of a Salesman vs., 355
  dream in, 188
  film rights to, 372
  Incident at Vichy vs., 376, 378
  Kazan and, 351–353, 355, 357, 364, 365–368
  as "mental geography," 355
  Monroe and, 345–346, 352, 355, 360–361, 366–367, 370–373
  mood in, 188
  otherness in, 358
  paradox of, 373–374
  plot of, 185–189, 355–363
  production of, 365–369
  The Ride Down Mt. Morgan vs., 433
  title of, 344–345
  See also A View from the Bridge
Agamemnon, 259
Agee, James, 240
"The Age of Anxiety" (Auden), 112
Ah, Wilderness (O'Neill), 28
Albee, Edward, 279, 442
Alfieri, 254–255, 257, 259, 306
Algiers (Lawson), 182
All About Eve, 173
Allen, Lewis, 238
Allen, Woody, 65
All My Sons (Miller), x, 306
  autobiographical elements in, 99–100
  critics and, 107–109
  Death of a Salesman vs., 100
  Greek tragedy and, 101, 108
  Ibsen's influence on, 93, 100, 108–109
  The Iceman Cometh vs., 109
  Kazan and, 104–107, 111
  Miller's creative process and, 71
  movie version of, 111
  No Villain vs., 99
  origins of, 70–72
  plot of, 93–99
  production of, 101–107
  retroactive construction in, 100
  success of, 111
  They Too Arise vs., 100
Amerasia, 112
The Amerasia Case: A Prelude to McCarthyism (Radosh), 112
America, 64
  anti-communism in, xi
  anti-Semitism in, 31, 51
  appeasement of Nazi Germany and, 58–59

communism in, 157–158
economic system in, 31
juvenile delinquency in, xi
Nazi sympathizers in, 53
organized labor in, 23
Second World War and, 72
Wall Street crash of 1929 in, 11–15
American Civil Liberties Union (ACLU), 310
The American Clock (Miller), 409–411
revision of, 425
"American Dreams, American Nightmares" (Eisinger), 153
Amies, Hardy, 301
Anastasia, Anthony, 168
Angell, Robert, 340
Anna Christie, 269
Annie Get Your Gun, 129
Annie Hall (Allen), 65
Another Part of the Forest (Hellman), 128, 135
anti-Semitism
in America, 31
Focus and, 88–89
in Germany, 155
The Grass Still Grows and, 51
Miller's first experience with, 19–20
The Archbishop's Ceiling (Miller)
critics and, 406–408
Pinter and, 402–403
plot of, 403–406
setting of, 402
Architectural Digest, 314, 315
Arens, Richard, 289–291, 293
Aristotle, 33
Arrabal, 384
Arthur, Robert, 113
Arthur Miller (Moss), 90
Arthur Miller Centre for the Advancement of American Studies, 59, 407
Ashcroft, Peggy, 300
Ashton, Frederick, 301
The Asphalt Jungle, 173, 319, 336
As Young As You Feel, 173
Atkinson, Brooks
All My Sons and, 107
The Crucible and, 218, 220
Death of a Salesman and, 148
The Diary of Anne Frank and, 266
An Enemy of the People and, 166
A Memory of Two Mondays and, 262
Nazimova and, 35
A Streetcar Named Desire and, 116
Atlantic Monthly Press, 70
Atomic Age, xi
Auden, W.H., 112, 240, 404
Auschwitz, 369, 375, 412
Australia, 111
Austria, 111
Avedon, Richard, 320
Avery and Julie Hopwood Awards in Creative Writing
The Great Disobedience and, 43, 48
No Villain and, 22, 24, 29
Awake and Sing (Odets), 39, 103
Ayckbourn, Alan, 407
Ayme, Marcel, 225
Aztec Indians, 3

Bacall, Lauren, 365
Bagnold, Enid, 280
Baker, George Pierce, 33, 48
Baker, Gladys, 173
Baldwin, James, 427
Balenciaga, Cristobal, 338
Balsam, Lee and Esther (uncle and aunt), 12
Bancroft, Anne, 190
Bangkok Star, 66, 67
Bank of the United States, 18
Bara, Theda, 320
Barnes, Djuna, 240
Barnes, Howard, 81, 148, 411
Barnett, Grandpa, 6, 9, 13, 65
Barnett, Rose (grandmother), 12
Barry, Father, 232
Barry, Philip, 33
Barsness, John A., 340
Baruch, Bernard, 143
Battle of Angels (Williams), 51, 69
Beckett, Samuel, 240, 278, 279, 281, 406, 446
Begley, Ed, 104, 106, 113
Behrman, S.N., 28, 33, 103, 116, 363, 425
Belafonte, Harry, 277
Bellow, Saul, 89–90, 283–284, 382
Benedeck, Laslo, 184
Benet, Stephen Vincent, 68
Bentley, Eric, 102
After the Fall and, 370
All My Sons and, 108
Death of a Salesman and, 153
The Grass Still Grows and, 51
HUAC and, 289
Kazan as informer and, 193–194
A View from the Bridge and, 262, 265
Bermel, Albert, 395–396
Bernstein, Aline, 166
Betrayal (Pinter), 433
Beyoum, 29
Bickford, Charles, 228
Bigsby, Christopher, 59, 108–109, 233, 406, 434
Billington, Michael, 406, 445
The Blackboard Jungle, 269
Black Panther Party, 384
Blakemore, Michael, 35, 108, 373, 433–434, 443–444
Bleich, Charlie, 22, 39
Blitzstein, Marc, 48
Bloom, Harold, xii, 25, 109, 152–153, 212

Bloomberg, Michael, 445
Bloomgarden, Kermit, 161, 185, 266
The Crucible and, 204, 212–216
Death of a Salesman and, 128–131, 133–136, 143, 147, 155–156
The Hook and, 168
HUAC and, 196
Kazan as informer and, 194–195, 211
Monroe and, 302, 312
Plenty Good Times and, 237
A View from the Bridge and, 244, 246, 281, 321, 330–331
Bloomgarden, Virginia, 145, 161, 185, 266, 267, 312
Blyden, Larry, 245
Böll, Heinrich, 406
Bone, Jerry, 267–268
Boomerang, 104
Boston Globe, 261
Boston Herald, 261
Boston Post, 261
Boyer, Charles, 228
Bradbury, Malcolm, 222
Brando, Marlon, 116, 215, 229, 232, 233–234, 383–384
Braun, Werner von, 369
Breakfast at Tiffany's, 322
Brecht, Bertolt, 35, 182
Bresson, Henri-Cartier, 338
Brewer, Roy, 175, 176, 179, 230
Brezhnev, Leonid, 402
Brichell, Harold, 314
Bridge to a Savage World (Miller)
juvenile delinquency and, 267
plot of, 267–268
Bristol Old Vic, 82
Broadhurst Theatre, 166
Broadway
Harris and, 51
HUAC and, 183, 268
language of, 91
Theatre Guild and, 28
Broadway (Harris), 51
Broken Glass (Miller)
Jewishness in, 436–437
realism of, 440–441
Brook, Peter, 304, 305
The Brothers Karamazov (Dostoevsky), 239
Brown, Arvin, 401
Brown, Katherine, 101, 102, 217, 243, 296
The Browning Version (Rattigan), 275
Brustein, Robert, 108, 149, 371, 374, 384, 395
Brynner, Yul, 338
Buechner, Georg, 35
Bureau of New Plays, 28, 31, 103
Burns, David, 392
Burton, Richard, 215
Bus Stop, 275, 276, 281, 301
But for Whom, Charlie (Behrman), 363
Byrne, John, 241

Calder, Alexander "Sandy," 218, 241, 382, 424
Caldwell, Zoe, 408, 421
Camus, Albert, 278–279, 344–345
"Camusian Existenialism in Arthur Miller's *After the Fall*" (Royal), 344
Capote, Truman, 112
Carlisle, Olga, 382
Carnovsky, Morris, 60, 69
Cary, Joyce, 277, 301
Catholicism
The Golden Years and, 56–57
The Great Disobedience and, 48
Miller's hostility toward, 64–65
Cat on a Hot Time Roof (Williams), 280, 304
CBS, 52
Chalmers, John, 113
Chalmers, Tom, 142, 143
Chamberlain, Neville, 59
Chapman, John, 148
Chayevsky, Paddy, 383
Chekhov, Anton, ix, 92, 115, 331, 408, 423, 446
The Cherry Orchard (Chekhov), 115, 423
Chiang Kai-shek, 113
The Children's Hour, 213
The Children of the Sun (Miller). *See The Golden Years*
Chinese Communist Party, 112–113, 121, 157
Chinese Encounter (Miller), 420
Christopher Columbus, 133
City College of New York (CCNY), 20, 61
Clara, 407
Claremont Essays (Trilling), 373
Clark, Eleanor, 148
Clift, Montgomery, 214, 236
After the Fall and, 365
The Misfits and, 322–323, 332, 334, 335
Clurman, Harold, 48, 51, 60, 61, 128
After the Fall and, 351
All My Sons and, 102
Communist Party and, 192
The Creation of the World and, 398
The Crucible and, 200
The Half-Bridge and, 69
Incident at Vichy and, 378–379
Kazan and, 103
Lincoln Center project and, 330
Miller's fall from favor and, 401
poster plays and, 39
The Price and, 396
Cobb, Lee J.
Death of a Salesman and, 133–135, 139–140, 143–147, 155–156, 420
HUAC and, 236, 290
A View from the Bridge and, 243

Cohn, Harry, 175, 179, 180, 184, 230
Colbert, Claudette, 190
cold war, xi, 157
The Collected Plays of Arthur Miller, xi–xii, 198, 281, 305, 308–309
Colonial Theatre, 117, 261
Columbia Pictures, 175, 180, 184
Columbia Workshop, 52
Combined Artists, Inc., 267
Comedie Francaise, 331
Comedy Theatre, 306
Command Decision (Haines), 128
Commentary, 262
Commonweal, 108, 406
communism
  in America, 157–158
  anti-, xi
  development of world, xi
  Federal Theatre and Writers Project and, 54
  organized labor and, 23
  Soviet Union and, 157–158, 183
Communist Party
  beliefs of, 31
  Chinese, 112–113, 121, 157
  Group Theatre and, 102–103, 191
  HUAC and, 158
  Kazan and, 102–103, 104, 158
  Miller and, 26, 179–180
  University of Michigan and, 40–41
Cooper, Gary, 182
Copeland, Joan. *See* Miller, Joan Maxine
Copland, Aaron, 159
Corey, Giles, 204, 206, 207, 209, 225
Cornell University, 19
Corridan, John, 232
Corrigan, Robert, x, 341, 380
Costello, Mariclare, 367
Cotten, Joseph, 48, 190
Coughlin, Father, 64, 74, 88
Counterattack, 163, 193
The Counterlife (Roth), 432
Coward, Noel, 92, 149, 307
Cowden, R.W., 29, 70
The Cradle Will Rock (Blitzstein), 48
Crandall, Frederic O., 36
Crawford, Cheryl, 48, 129, 147, 192, 277
The Creation of the World and Other Business (Miller), 398–399
Crime and Punishment (Dostoevsky), 19
Crime on the Labor Front (Johnson), 167–168
Cross-Section: A Collection of New American Writing, 75
The Crucible (Miller), x, xi, 58, 305, 306, 307, 311
  critics and, 218–220
  Death of a Salesman vs., 198, 218, 220, 224, 216–217
  dialogue in, 224
  fiery imagery in, 209, 223
  international success of, 220, 228–229
  McCarthyism and, 196, 199–200, 221
  movie version of, 443
  plot of, 198–199, 203–208
  poetry and, 249
  production of, 212–220
  research for, 196, 197–199
  self-condemnation in, 212
  title of, 204, 215
Cukor, George, 326, 327, 328
Cultural and Scientific Conference for World Peace, 159–160, 179–180, 289
cummings, e.e., 175
Czechoslovakia, 58, 111

d'Usseau, Armand, 128, 290
Daily Express, 301
Daily News, 107, 148, 149, 337, 411
The Daily Worker, 161, 176, 263, 265, 290
The Dance of Death (Strindberg), 373
Danforth, Governor, 207–208
Danger: Memory!, 407
The Dark at the Top of the Stairs, 330
Darkness at Noon (Koestler), 404
Day-Lewis, Daniel, 443
Dean, Alexander, 29
Death of a Salesman (Miller), x, 32, 181, 261, 306, 307, 397
  After the Fall vs., 355
  All My Sons vs., 100
  autobiographical elements in, 153–154
  characters in, 118–119
  critics and, 146, 147–149
  The Crucible vs., 198, 216–217, 218, 220, 224
  dialogue in, 224
  expressionism and, 122
  fiery imagery in, 208
  importance of, ix–x
  Kazan and, 119, 122–123, 128–131, 133–145
  King Lear and, 137, 141, 151, 153
  The Man Who Had All the Luck vs., 78–79
  memory in, 129, 141–142, 237
  Miller's critical defense of, 151–153
  movie version of, 184–185
  origins of, 117–122
  plot of, 123–128
  poetry and, 249
  power of, 118, 149–150, 237
  production of, 128–131, 133–156
  reality in, 129
  research for, 119
  revival of, 420–421, 444
  structure of, 122

style of, 122
success of, 150–151, 162
themes of, 118, 137
time in, 129–130, 237
as tragedy, 151–152
Debuskey, Merle, 143–144, 145, 219, 312
Deep Are the Roots (Gow and d'Usseau), 128, 290
The Deer Park (Mailer), 112
de Jongh, Nicholas, 417
de Kooning, Willem, 309
Demastes, William W., 407
Democratic convention (1968), xi
Dennehy, Brian, 420, 444
Depression. *See* Great Depression
The Devil in Massachusetts (Starkey), 196
DeWolfe, James P., 160–161
Diaries of Adam and Eve (Twain), 398
The Diary of Anne Frank, 266, 321, 377
Dick, Bernard F., 396
Dickens, Charles, 10
Dickstein, Samuel, 53
Dies, Martin, 53–54
Dies Committee, 53, 60
See also House Committee on Un-American Activities
DiMaggio, Joe, 190, 191, 228, 236, 239, 266–267, 325
Doll, Jim, 27
A Doll's House (Ibsen), 34–35, 163, 214
Don't Bother to Knock, 190
Dostoevsky, Fyodor, 19, 269
Dowling, Robert, 147
Downes, Olin, 159
Down Syndrome, 346–347, 353
Doyle, Clyde, 289
Driver, Tom, 108, 148, 282
DuBois, Blanche, 115
DuBois, W.E.B., 160
Dunaway, Faye, 363
Dunnock, Mildred, 134–135, 140, 144–145, 155–156, 184
The Dupont Cavalcade of America, 73
Durgin, Cyrus, 261
Duvall, Robert, 385

East Anglia, University of, 59
Einstein, Albert, 159, 228, 245–246, 311, 344
Eisinger, Chester E., 153
Eldridge, Florence, 133, 163–164, 281
Electra (Euripides), 259
Elegy for a Lady (Miller), 417–419
Eliot, T.S., 48, 425
Elizabeth, Queen, 302
Ellington, Duke, 237
An Enemy of the People (Ibsen), 92, 170, 181
critics and, 165–166
Miller's adaptation of, 162–167
plot of, 164–165
setting of, 164
theme in, 163
Engels, Friedrich, 404
England
appeasement of Nazi Germany and, 58–59
Miller's acceptance in, 82, 220, 407–408, 411–412, 435
The Entertainer (Osborne), 307
Esquire Magazine, 304, 309, 340, 417
Esslin, Martin, 278–279
Euripides, 33, 259
Evans, Edith, 301
Ewell, Tom, 278
Eyre, Richard, 224, 425

Fairbanks, Douglas, 300–301
The Fall (Camus), 344
Falmouth Playhouse, 246, 261
Fame, 397
Fast, Howard, 162, 263, 265, 290
Faulkner, William, 25
Federal Theatre and Writers Project, 4, 36, 48, 49
Communism and, 54
drawbacks of, 55
HUAC and, 54, 55–56
Miller's acceptance to, 52–53
regulations of, 52
Feiffer, Jules, 384
Feldman, Charles, 171, 172, 174, 175
Fenelon, Fania, 412, 414, 416–417
Ferrer, Jose, 183
Fiddler on the Roof, 392
Fields, Joseph, 81
Film Quarterly, 340
Fine, Sylvia, 171
First Stop to Heaven (Rosten), 68, 69
Flanagan, Hallie, 48
Flanner, Janet, 338
Flight into Egypt (Tabori), 183, 194
The Flowering Peach (Odets), 242–243
Focus (Miller), 181
anti-Semitism in, 88–89
criticism of, 89–90
dialogue in, 89
Jewishness in, 377
movie version of, 445
plot of, 88–89
publication of, 89–90
style of, 89
theme in, 90
Fog, 9
Fonda, Jane, 412
Fontanne, Lynn, 28
Fonteyn, Margot, 300
Forsythe, John, 113
France, 111
Franco, Francisco, 64
Franks, Sidney, 9, 52, 64, 187, 284, 393
Franzero, C.M., 275
Freedley, Vinton, 213
Freud, Sigmund, 240
Fried, Walter, 128, 129
The Front Page (Harris), 51
Frost, Robert, 175

Gable, Clark
  death of, 339
  The Misfits and, 322, 332, 334
Gaddis, William, 424
"Gadget." *See* Kazan, Elia
Gambon, Michael, 407
Garfield, John, 192, 234–235
The Gargoyle, 40
Garrison, Lloyd, 288
Gassner, John, 51, 60, 103
Gelb, Barbara and Arthur, 411
Gellburg (Miller), 436
General Motors, 23, 36, 37, 410
Genesis, 398
Genet, Jean, 279, 384
Gentleman's Agreement (Hobson), 90, 113–115, 122, 134
Gentlemen Prefer Blondes (Fields), 81, 227, 229
Germany. *See* Nazi Germany
Getting Gertie's Garter (Hopwood), 22
Ghosts (Ibsen), 35, 92, 163
Gielgud, John, 301
Giles Corey of the Salem Farms (Longfellow), 225
Gilford, Jack, 160, 368
Gilford, Lisa, 368
Gilford, Madeleine, 160, 238, 368
Gilman, Richard, 149, 424
Ginsberg, Allen, 384
The Glass Menagerie (Williams), 87, 373
The Gnadiges Fraulein (Williams), 279
Goetz, Ruth and Augustus, 213
Gogol, Nikolai, 252
Goldberg, Robert E., 297
Golden, John, 229
Golden Boy (Odets), 103
The Golden Warriors (Shulberg). *See On the Waterfront*
The Golden Years (Miller), 436
  appeasement of Nazi Germany and, 58
  beginning of, 55
  Catholicism and, 56–57
  as epic play, 55
  flaws in, 58
  language in, 58
  plot of, 56–58
  rejection of, 61
  research for, 55, 63
  response to, 59–60
  setting of, 56
  style of, 5
  tragedy of, 3–4, 58, 66
Goodman, Walter, 268
Goodrich, Frances, 266
Gordimer, Nadine, 240, 406
Gordon, Max, 198
Gordon, Ruth, 34–35, 122, 218
Gow, James, 128
Grable, Betty, 227
Grant, Cary, 190
The Grass Still Grows (Miller)
  autobiographical elements in, 50
  comedy in, 3, 50, 51
  Jewish milieu of, 51
  praise of, 52
  rejection and, 51
  response to, 50–51
  as revision, 49–50
Gravesend, 12
Great Depression, xi
  American economy and, 22–23
  effects of, 15–20
  Federal Theatre and Writers Project and, 48
  Miller and, 15–20
  No Villain and, 25
The Great Disobedience (Miller)
  action and cautiousness in, 67
  arty staging of, 55
  autobiographical elements in, 46
  Catholicism and, 48
  as dramatic fiction based on research, 47
  "ex- or impressionism" of, 66
  flaws of, 47
  Honors at Dawn vs., 47
  Hopwood Awards and, 43
  idea for, 43–44
  No Villain vs., 47
  plot of, 45–46
  prison as metaphor in, 44
  reality in, 47
  rejection of, 48
  setting of, 44
  style of, 122
  They Too Arise vs., 47
Greek tragedy
  All My Sons and, 101, 108
  The Children of the Sun and, 3–4
  Death of a Salesman and, 151–152
  playwriting and, 93
  A View from the Bridge and, 120, 253, 258–261, 304–306
The Green Bay Tree, 215
Greene, Amy, 239–240, 277, 296, 300–302
Greene, Milton, 239, 240, 274–276, 286, 297, 302
Grosbard, Ulu, 385, 386, 392
Gross, Sid, 32
Group Theatre, 48, 60, 102
  Communist Party and, 102–103, 191
  The Grass Still Grows and, 51
  Kazan and, 134
  Lawson and, 92
Gruening, Ernest, 384
Guardian, 406, 417
Guiles, Fred Lawrence, 172
Guinness, Alec, 300
Gussow, Mel, 259–260
Guthrie, Woody, 82
Gwathmey, Robert, 114

Hackett, Albert, 266
Hackman, Gene, 385
Hagopian, John V., 153
Haines, William Wister, 128
The Half-Bridge (Miller)
action and cautiousness in, 67
homosexuality in, 67, 68
plot of, 66–68
production of, 69
research for, 65–66
response to, 69
as wartime melodrama, 66, 68
Hall, Peter, 425
Hamlet (Shakespeare), 101
Hammett, Dashiell, 183, 212
Happy Days (Beckett), 279
Harcourt Brace, 49
The Harder They Fall (Shulberg), 232
Hard Times (Terkel), 410
Hardwick, Elizabeth, 384
Harlem, 8
Harlow, Jean, 227, 320
Harper and Brothers, 65
Harris, Herbert H., 75
Harris, Jed, 105
Broadway and, 51
The Crucible and, xi, 212–218, 219
A Doll's House and, 34–35
tempo and, 51
Harris, Radie, 301
Hart, John, 417
Harvard, 33
Hathorne, John, 225
Heckart, Eileen, 244
Hedda Gabler (Ibsen), 50, 92
Heflin, Van, 243–244
The Heiress (Goetz), 213
Helburn, Teresa, 28, 29, 36, 60, 103
Heller, Joseph, 384
Hellman, Lillian, 128, 135
Broadway and, 116, 279
Communist Party and, 158
The Crucible and, 212–214
HUAC and, 290
A View from the Bridge and, 244
Waldorf Peace Conference and, 159
Hemingway, Ernest, 68, 228, 373
Henderson, the Rain King (Bellow), 283
Henry VIII (Shakespeare), 24–25
Herald-Tribune, 81, 148
Here Is Your War (Pyle), 73
Hersey, Frances Ann, 159, 162
Hersey, John, 159, 162
Herzog (Bellow), 283
Hewitt, Alan, 139, 140–141, 146, 147
Hickman, Theodore "Hickey," 118, 121
The Hidden Damage (Stern), 240
Hier, Marvin, 412
Hillel Players, 36
Himmler, Heinrich, 375
Hingle, Pat, 392–393
Hitler, Adolf, 22, 53, 58–59, 155, 250, 290, 337, 377
Hobson, Harold, 220
Hobson, Laura Z., 90
Hoffman, Dustin, 155, 385, 420–421, 446
Hohenberg, Margaret, 270
Holbrook, Hal, 363
Holiday Magazine, 229
Hollywood Reporter, 372
Hollywood Ten, 182
Holocaust, 117, 155, 337, 369, 375, 377
homosexuality, 257, 304
Honors at Dawn (Miller)
characters in, 38–39
The Great Disobedience vs., 47
Hopwood Awards and, 36
Marxism and, 39
organized labor and, 38
plot of, 36–37
The Hook (Miller)
Kazan and, 168–169, 171
On the Waterfront vs., 230–235
origins of, 167–169
pitching to Hollywood of, 172–176, 179–180
plot of, 169–171
Hook, Sidney, 160
Hoover, J. Edgar, 191, 193, 194, 277
Hopper, Edward, 82
Hopwood, Avery, 22
Horne, Lena, 434
Horowitz, Jacob, 214
House Appropriations Committee, 55
House Committee on Un-American Activities (HUAC)
blacklisting and, 194, 196
Broadway and, 183, 268
Communist Infiltration of the Motion-Picture Industry and, 182
Federal Theatre and Writers Project and, 54, 55–56
Hollywood hearings of, 183–184, 236
Kazan and, 183–184, 191–197, 200–202
McCarthy and, 182–183
Miller and, x, 179–180, 288–293, 297–298, 310–311
opposition to, 158
purpose of, 53–54
WPA and, 54
Houseman, John, 48
Howard, Sidney, 28
How to Marry a Millionaire, 245
HUAC. *See* House Committee on Un-American Activities
Hughes, Elinor, 261
Hughes, Howard, 174
The Human Stain (Roth), 432
Hungary, 111
Huston, John, 133, 174, 228
The Misfits and, 319, 320, 322–323, 326–327, 332–334, 336, 339

Huston, Walter, 133
Hyde, Johnny, 172, 173, 190
Hyman, Earle, 277
Hytner, Nicholas, 424

Ibsen, Henrik, ix, 50, 162, 181, 446
  All My Sons and, 93, 100, 108–109
  An Enemy of the People and, 166
  influence on Miller of, 34–35
  realism of, 92–93, 163
  writing and, 34–35
I Can't Remember Anything, 407
The Iceman Cometh (O'Neill), 121, 252
  All My Sons vs., 109
  American salesman in, 118
  criticism of, 101–102
Ideology and Utopia (Mannheim), 44
I Don't Need You Anymore (Miller), 385
The Imaginary Invalid (Molière), 423
I Married a Communist (Roth), 432
Incident at Vichy (Miller), 337
  After the Fall vs., 376, 378
  critics and, 379–381
  Holocaust and, 377
  plot of, 377–378
  realism of, 375–376
  research for, 375–376
Inge, William, 275, 279
"In Memoriam" (Miller), 30
Inquest, 196
In Russia (Miller), 384
The Inside of His Head (Miller). *See Death of a Salesman*
Insight One (Hagopian), 153
In the Country (Miller), 398
Ionesco, Eugene, 279
Ireland, 52, 249, 326
Isaacs, Edith J.R., 29
Isherwood, Christopher, 240
It Can't Happen Here (Lewis), 48
It Is You, Victor (Miller), 385

Jackson, Anne, 107, 196, 245, 246, 442
Jackson, Donald, 289
Jackson (Michigan) State Penitentiary, 43
The Jackson Prison Play (Miller). *See The Great Disobedience*
Jacobowsky and the Colonel (Behrman), 103
Jacobs, Arthur, 294–295, 344
Jaffe, Agnes, 113
Jaffe, Sidney J., 112–113
Jane's Blanket (Miller), 354
Jaws, 164
Jesus Christ, 204
  The Golden Years and, 58
Jewishness, 6–7, 51
  See also anti-Semitism
Joe the Motorman, 51–52
Johnson, Lady Bird, 369
Johnson, Lyndon B., 383
Johnson, Malcolm, 167, 231, 233
Jones, Baird, 442
Jones, Harmon, 173
Judgment at Nuremberg, 376
juvenile delinquency, xi, 267–269

Kafka, Franz, 88
Kanin, Garson, 122, 131, 150
Kanter, Hal, 327–328
Kauffmann, Stanley, 323, 398
Kaye, Danny, 171, 434
Kaye, Virginia, 368
  See Bloomgarden, Virginia
Kazan, Elia, 104, 114, 337, 374
  After the Fall and, 351–355, 357, 364–368
  All My Sons and, 102, 104–107, 111
  background of, 102–103
  Cat on a Hot Time Roof and, 280
  Communist Party and, 102–103, 104, 158
  The Crucible and, 210–212
  Death of a Salesman and, 119, 122–123, 128–131, 133–145
  end of stage career of, 374
  Gentleman's Agreement and, 113, 114–115, 122
  Group Theatre and, 102, 134
  The Hook and, 168–169, 171, 179
  HUAC and, 183–184, 191–197, 200–202
  as informer, 183–184, 191–197, 200–202, 290–292
  marriage of, 102, 194, 212
  Miller's correspondence with, 120, 161–163, 182, 185, 322
  in Miller's plays, 210–212, 257, 261, 264–265, 306
  Monroe and, 172, 174, 175, 181, 190, 228, 294, 345
  moviemaking and, 183–184
  On the Waterfront and, 229–235
  A Streetcar Named Desire and, 115
  theatrical instincts of, 103
  A View from the Bridge and, 329–330
Kazan, Molly, 171, 179
  death of, 368
  Death of a Salesman and, 129
  Kazan as informer and, 194–195
  marriage of, 212
Kearney, Bernard W., 289, 292

Kelly, Gene, 268
Kempton, Murray, 263–265
Kennedy, J. Arthur "Johnny"
All My Sons and, 104, 106, 107
The Crucible and, 215
Death of a Salesman and, 134, 135, 143, 156
The Price and, 392
Kennedy, John F., 340, 342, 366
Kerr, Walter F., 219, 263, 379
Keyes, Evelyn, 174, 175
King, Martin Luther, Jr., 369
King Lear (Shakespeare), 137, 141, 151, 153
Kingsley, Sidney, 116
Klehr, Harvey, 112
Koestler, Arthur, 404
Kowalksi, Stanley, 115
Kramer, Stanley, 184
Krasna, Norman, 325
Kreymborg, Alfred, 29
Kroll, Jack, 411
Ku Klux Klan, 54
Kunitz, Stanley, 383

Lahr, Bert, 278
Lakewood, Ohio, 93
Lancaster, Burt, 48, 111
Lang, Fritz, 118–119
Langner, Laurence, 28, 51, 103
Lanier, Thomas. *See* Williams, Tennessee
Lardner, Ring, Jr., 183, 191, 182
Lastfogel, Abe, 172, 173
The Last Yankee (Miller), 435–436
Laughton, Charles, 228
Laura (Lardner), 183
Laurents, Arthur, 114
Lawson, John Howard, 54, 92, 103, 182
Ledbetter, Huddie, 162
Lehmann-Haupt, Christopher, 422
Leigh, Vivien, 171, 275, 307
Leighton, Margaret, 301
Leland Hayward and Company, 50–51, 101, 129
Lenya, Lotte, 145
Let's Make Love, 323, 325–328
Levine, George, 17, 73
Lewis, Anthony, 288
Lewis, Robert, 129, 163, 277
Lewis, Sinclair, 48
Liddy, G. Gordon, 421
A Life (Kazan), 179
Life Magazine, 160, 297, 320, 337, 372
Lincoln, Abraham, 181, 229, 240
Lincoln Center for the Performing Arts, 19
Lincoln Center Repertory Theatre, 330–331, 342, 363, 364
Linney, Laura, 445
Listen, My Children (Miller and Rosten), 60–61, 290
The Little Foxes, 213
Livi, Ivo. *See* Montand, Yves
Locust Street Theatre, 147
Loden, Barbara, 353, 357, 363, 367, 368, 373
Loewenstein, Rudolph, 247, 376
Loewy, Raymond, 112
Logan, Joshua, 129, 229, 244, 301
Loman, Biff, 79, 118, 124–128, 134, 135, 138, 140–142
Loman, Happy, 79, 118, 124–128, 135, 137–138, 140–142
Loman, Linda, 32, 118, 123–128, 133, 134, 142
Loman, Willy, 79, 118, 119, 123–128, 133–134, 136, 139–142
London *Times*, 383, 417, 437
Long Day's Journey into Night (O'Neill), 280–281, 373, 391
Longfellow, Henry Wadsworth, 225
Long Wharf Theater, 417, 436
Look Back in Anger (Osborne), 307–308
Look Homeward, Angel, 321
Look Magazine, 239
Lowell, Robert, 383, 384
Lowry, Malcolm, 240
Luce, Henry, 160
Luciano, Charles "Lucky," 116
Lumet, Sidney, 48, 323
Lunt, Alfred, 28
Lytess, Natasha, 180
Lyttleton Theatre, 437

Macbeth (Welles), 48
MacDonald, Dwight, 160
MacLeish, Archibald, 52
Magnum, 337, 338
Maiden Voyage (Osborne), 302
Mailer, Norman, 112, 159, 329, 422
Malden, Karl, 104, 106, 214
Malloy, Charley, 232
Malloy, Terry, 232–234
Maloney, Russell, 75
Malraux, André, 406
Mamet, David, 425
Mandela, Nelson, 427
Mann, Thomas, 150
Mannheim, Karl, 44–47, 57, 67, 75
Mantle, Burns, 107
The Man Who Had All the Luck (Miller), 94
criticism of, 81–82
Death of a Salesman vs., 78–79
dramatization of, 73, 75
fiery imagery in, 209
flaws of, 82
origins of, 69–70
plot of, 75–80
production of, 81
revival of, 445
setting of, 76
theme in, 76, 80
Mao Zedong, 113, 159

March, Fredric, 133, 163–164, 184, 280–281
Marco, 254–255, 257, 259
Marco Millions (O'Neill), 363
Marcus, 404–406
Mardi Gras (Rosten), 237
Marianne, 414–415
Marilyn: An Untold Story (Rosten), 329
Marilyn (Mailer), 329
Marilyn Monroe Productions, 274–275, 302
Marina, 56
Marsh, Reginald, 114
Marshall, E.G., 48
Martin Beck Theatre, 218, 245, 277
Marx, Karl, 404
Marxism, 39, 43, 427
The Master Builder, 82
Matthaei, Konrad, 406
Matthews, Caroline, 46–47
Matthews, Victor, 46–47
Maugham, Somerset, 307, 327
MCA, 101
McCarthy, Eugene, 384
McCarthy, Joseph, xi, 182–183, 201, 241
McCarthy, Kevin, 184
McCarthy, Mary, 148
McCarthyism, 234
  The Crucible and, 196, 199–200, 221
  Salem witch trials and, 195–196
McGraw-Hill, 172
McLaughlin, Charles F., 310
McNally, Terence, 445
Medea, 421
Meeker, Ralph, 363, 367
Meeropol, Robbie, 238
Meeropol, Abel and Anne, 238
Melish, William Howard, 160–162, 163
A Memory of Two Mondays (Miller), 243
  autobiographical elements in, 249
  critics and, 253, 261–262, 263
  dialogue in, 252
  plot of, 250–252
  poetry and, 250–252
  realism of, 253
  setting of, 249–250
  A View from the Bridge vs., 253
The Men from Under the Sea (Miller), 243
Mengele, Josef, 413, 414–416
Menotti, Gian-Carlo, 434
Mercury Theatre, 55
Meredith, Burgess, 74
Merrill, Beth, 106
"Metamorphosis" (Kafka), 88
Mexico, 63
Meyerhold, Vsevolod, 102
MGM, 372
Michigan Daily, 23, 31, 37, 375
Mickey, 353, 357–358, 367–368
Midnight Frolic revues, 139
Mielziner, Jo, 136
The Milk Train Doesn't Stop Here Anymore (Williams), 353
Millay, Edna St. Vincent, 28
Miller, Arthur
  British acceptance of, 220, 407–408, 411–412, 435
  children's story of, 303–304, 354
  Communist Party and, 26, 166, 179–180
  critics and, x
  Depression and, 15–20
  domestic problems of, 162–163, 177
  early life of, 5–20
  education of, 9, 18–19
  as essayist, 151–153, 320, 335, 340–341, 383
  financial concerns of, 4, 22, 23, 51, 111–113
  health of, 407
  HUAC and, 179–180, 268, 288–293, 297–298, 310–311
  importance of, ix–x
  Inge and, 337–338, 342, 343, 381–382
  Kazan as informer and, 201–202
  left-wing ideology of, 32, 382–384
  Monroe and, x, xi, 171–177, 180–182, 239–240, 241–242, 244–246, 270, 273–278, 287–288, 293–298, 299–305, 325–330, 338–340, 442–443
  notebooks of, 70, 91, 167, 189, 258
  personality of, ix, xi, xii
  physical appearance of, 13
  poetry and, 54–55, 70, 167, 249
  politics of, 24, 35, 43, 157–162
  postgraduate life of, 48–61
  pseudonyms of, 29, 36, 43
  radio scripts of, 4, 51–52, 68, 73
  rejection and, 3–5, 48, 83, 87, 446
  as reporter, 23–24
  reputation of, 228–229, 308, 323, 397
  short stories of, 4, 30, 309, 385
  student plays of, 24–40, 43–48
  style of, 43
  success of, 112, 265–266
  television scripts of, 385–386
  theater and, 90–91
  themes of, xi–xii, 43
  at University of Michigan, 19–20, 21–41, 43–48
  work and life of, xii

Miller, Daniel (son), 346–347
Miller, Frances, 72, 369
Miller, Gittel "Gussie" (mother)
background of, 8
death of, 342
Depression and, 16–17
education of, 8
illness of, 342
Jewishness of, 7
Miller's early life and, 5–6
in Miller's plays, 99
Monroe and, 247, 287–288
temperament of, 6
as "typical" Jewish mother, 11
Wall Street crash of 1929 and, 12–15
Miller, Grandpa, 6, 8
Miller, Henry, 240
Miller, Isadore (father)
background of, 8
business failure of, 30–31
death of, 385–386
illness of, 342
immigration of, 8
Jewishness of, 7, 8
Miller's early life and, 5–6, 11
in Miller's plays, 99, 187
Miller's relationship with, 14–15
Miltex Coat and Suit Company and, 10
Monroe and, 247, 288, 344
sensitivity of, 11
Wall Street crash of 1929 and, 11–15
Miller, Jane Ellen (daughter), 163, 229
birth of, 74
death of baby of, 408
family life of, 181, 247, 319–320, 382
Little Red School House and, 237–238
marriage of, 397
Miller's adoration of, 260
story written for, 353–354
Miller, Joan Maxine (sister), 6, 35, 50, 72–73, 246, 276, 342
Daniel and, 347
Depression and, 16–17
early life of, 9–11
Inge's death and, 445
Miller's marriages and, 65
Monroe and, 333
Miller, Joe, 327
Miller, Kermit (brother), 5, 6, 50
After the Fall and, 369
discharge from army of, 91
early life of, 9–10
education of, 14, 21
Miller's financial concerns and, 51–53
in Miller's plays, 76, 99–100, 284, 356, 393–394
Miltex Coat and Suit Company and, 15–16, 18
in Second World War, 72–73, 82–83
as student, 9
Miller, Mary. *See* Slattery, Mary Grace
Miller, Mary (wife), 29, 41, 49
Amerasia and, 112–113
Catholicism of, 64
character of, 65
The Crucible and, 200, 210, 211
Death of a Salesman and, 122
divorce and, 276, 305
domestic problems of, 162–163, 177
Jean and, 48
The Man Who Had All the Luck and, 69
married life of, 63–65, 112, 113–114, 145
Miller's marriage to, 68
in Miller's plays, 105
Monroe and Miller and, 241–242
pregnancy of, 74, 75
righteousness of, 179
socialist political convictions of, 24
A View from the Bridge and, 244
Miller, Rebecca Augusta (daughter), 354, 382, 408, 443, 445
Miller, Robert (son)
as adult, 397
family life of, 163, 181, 247, 319–320, 353–354
Kazan as informer and, 368
Little Red School House and, 237–238
Monroe and Miller and, 266, 276
physical appearance of, 382
Miller, Samuel (grandfather), 8
Miltex Coat and Suit Company, 5, 10, 19
Depression and, 15–16, 18
failure of, 11, 30
Wall Street crash of 1929 and, 13
The Misfits (Miller)
critics and, 334, 339–341
flaws of, 336–337
Miller's critical defense of, 340–341
Monroe and, 313–314
plot of, 335–336
production of, 322–323, 326–327, 332–335
theme in, 335
The Misfits: A Story Conceived as a Film (Miller), 314
"The Misfits, or Chicken Feed: The Last Frontier of the Quixotic Cowboy" (Miller), 303–304
Mister Roberts, 129
Mitchell, Cameron, 135, 172, 184
Mitchell, Thomas, 420

Mitchum, Robert, 74
Modern Language Association, 153
Molière, 331, 396, 423, 446
Monroe, Marilyn
  Actors Studio and, 240, 242, 244–246, 266, 269–270, 322
  After the Fall and, 352, 370–373
  background of, 173
  calendar picture of, 190–191
  career of, 173, 190–191, 227, 302
  The Crucible and, 204
  death of, 343–344, 345
  depression of, 313, 333
  DiMaggio and, 190, 191, 228, 236, 239, 266–267
  intelligence of, 273
  Kazan and, 172, 174, 175, 181, 190, 228
  Let's Make Love and, 323, 325–328
  marriages of, 236, 239
  Miller and, x, xi, 171–177, 180–182, 239–240, 241–242, 244–246, 270, 273–278, 287–288, 293–323, 325–330, 338–340, 442–443
  in Miller's plays, 182, 187, 313–314, 335, 343, 345–346, 352, 355, 360–361, 366–367
  The Misfits and, 323, 333–335
  Montand and, 328–330, 334
  myth of, xi
  pregnancies of, 313
  The Prince and the Showgirl and, 299, 301, 303, 304
  as sex symbol, 190–191, 227–228, 273, 320
  Some Like It Hot and, 319–321
  stage acting and, 269–270
  substance abuse of, 286, 299, 302, 314, 315, 321, 326, 333, 334, 343
  temperament of, 302, 321, 328, 333, 342
Montand, Yves
  The Crucible and, 225–226
  Let's Make Love and, 325–328
  Monroe and, 328–330, 334
The Montezuma Play (Miller). *See The Children of the Sun*
A Moon for the Misbegotten (O'Neill), 28
Moore, John, 311
Moore, Lord Charles, 300
Moore, Thomas, 252
Morath, Ingeborg, Miller's marriage to, 337–338, 342, 343, 346–347, 352–354, 381–382, 420, 445
Morehouse, Ward, 83, 148
Morley, Sheridan, 307
Morosco Theatre, 146–147
Moscow Art Theater, 28, 331
Moss, Leondard, 90
Mostel, Kate, 147
Mostel, Zero, 147, 194, 268, 290
The Most Happy Fella, 321
Mourning Becomes Electra (O'Neill), 28
Mr. Johnson (Cary), 277–278
Mr. Peters' Connections (Miller), 443–444
Muni, Paul, 69
Murder in the Cathedral (Eliot), 48
Murphy, Brenda, 81–82
Music for the Deaf. *See The Misfits*
The Musicians of Auschwitz, 412
The Music Man, 321
My Mother, My Father, and Me (Hellman), 279
My Sister Eileen (Fields), 81
The Myth of Sisyphus (Camus), 278
"My Wife Marilyn" (Miller), 320

Naish, J. Carrol, 244
The Naked and the Dead (Mailer), 112
Naming Names (Navasky), 234, 292
Nathan, George Jean, 81
National Down Syndrome Society, 346–347, 353
National Theatre of Great Britain, 223, 307, 410, 411
Navasky, Victor, 234, 292, 293
Nazi Bund, 53
Nazi Germany
  All My Sons in, 111
  anti-Semitism in, 51, 155
  appeasement of, 58
  Hitler and, 337–338
Nazimova, 35
NBC, 73
Nedelya, 337
Neeson, Liam, 445
Negro People's Theatre, 48
Nelson, Benjamin, 79, 165
New Amsterdam Theatre, 138–139
New Deal, 54
The New Leader, 395
Newman, Abby (cousin), 12–13, 117, 118, 119, 154
Newman, Buddy (cousin), 13, 118, 119, 154
Newman, Manny and Annie (uncle and aunt), 12, 117, 118, 119, 154
The New Masses, 40
New Milford Times, 294
The New Republic
  After the Fall and, 370
  All My Sons and, 108
  The Creation of the World and, 398
  Death of a Salesman and, 149
  Focus and, 89

Incident at Vichy and, 380
Miller and Communist Party and, 268
The Price and, 395
The Seven Year Itch and, 245
Newsweek, 369–370, 411, 424
New Theatre, 102
New Theatre League, 102
New York Daily News, 274
New York Drama Critics Circle, 109
The New Yorker magazine, 53, 338, 340, 370, 423
New York Herald-Tribune, 268
The Crucible and, 218, 219
Death of a Salesman and, 152
The Hook and, 168
Incident at Vichy and, 379
Miller's playwriting and, 338
Miller's reporting and, 375
The Misfits and, 340
A View from the Bridge and, 263
New York Journal-American, 54, 81, 293
New York Post, 160
All My Sons and, 107
The American Clock and, 411
Focus and, 89
Incident at Vichy and, 379
The Misfits and, 316–317
Monroe and Miller and, 274, 288
A View from the Bridge and, 263–265
New York Sun, 83, 148, 167
New York Times, 35, 72, 75, 81, 82, 159, 172, 288
All My Sons and, 91, 107
The American Clock and, 411
The Creation of the World and, 399
The Crucible and, 199, 214, 216–218, 220
Death of a Salesman and, 148, 149, 151
The Diary of Anne Frank and, 266
An Enemy of the People and, 166
Focus and, 89
HUAC and, 268
Incident at Vichy and, 379
Kazan's ad in, 201
Lincoln Center project and, 330–331
Miller's British acceptance and, 424
Miller's career and, 397
Miller's meeting with Mandela and, 427
Miller's one acts and, 408
The Misfits and, 316, 317, 340
Monroe and Miller and, 295
Mr. Johnson and, 277
Plenty Good Times and, 182
The Price and, 394, 395, 396
A Streetcar Named Desire and, 116
Two-Way Mirror and, 419
A View from the Bridge and, 237, 259, 261
New York University, 14
New York World-Telegram, 263, 268
New Zealand, 111
Niagara, 190
Nichols, Lewis, 81
Nichols, Mike, 382, 383
Nichols, Peter, 433
The Night of the Iguana (Williams), 353
Nixon, Raphael I., 192, 191
Nixon, Richard M., 191, 402
Nize Baby!, 32
No Exit (Sartre), 319
Nordenson, Lars, 164
Norma Jean: The Life of Marylin Monroe (Guiles), 172
North, Sterling, 89
Norton, Elliot, 261
Not About Nightingales (Williams), 44
No Villain (Miller)
All My Sons vs., 99
family life in, 99
The Great Disobedience vs., 47
Hopwood Awards and, 29–30
as Miller's first play, 25–28
organized labor and, 26
plot synopsis of, 26–27
revision of, 31–33
setting of, 25
theme of, 29
See also They Too Arise
Nurse, Rebecca, 204, 206, 210, 222

O'Casey, Sean, 249, 264
O'Neill, Eugene, 33, 35–36, 51, 143
The Iceman Cometh of, 101–102, 118, 252
illness of, 411
Long Day's Journey into Night of, 280, 373, 391
Marco Millions of, 363
Theatre Guild and, 28
Observer, 307
Odets, Clifford, 61, 242, 290
Communist Party and, 158, 192
The Crucible and, 211
Group Theatre and, 60, 92, 102–103
HUAC and, 357
Monroe and, 228
"poster plays" of, 39
Waldorf Peace Conference and, 159
Oedipus Rex (Sophocles), 35, 101, 259, 408
Office of Secret Service (OSS), 112
Olivet College, 29
Olivier, Laurence, 171–172, 215, 223, 275–276, 307
Monroe and, 299–323, 301–302, 303

A View from the Bridge and, 307
"On Social Plays" (Miller), 335
On the Avenue, 325
On the Waterfront, 180
The Hook vs., 230–235
Kazan and, 229–235
origins of, 229–231
subject of, 229–230
Oresteia (Aeschylus), 101
Orestes, 151, 274
organized labor, xi, 23, 24, 26, 38
Orpheus Descending (Williams), 69
Osborne, John, 307–308
Osborne, Paul, 302
OSS. *See* Office of Secret Service
Other Voices, Other Rooms (Capote), 112
Our Town, 213
Overland, Orm, 221, 376

Pacino, Al, 437
Page, Geraldine, 363
Panic in the Streets, 150
Paramount Pictures, 372
Paris Match, 273, 295
Parsons, Louella, 301
Partisan Review, 40, 148
Passion Play (Nichols), 433
Patrick, John, 245
Pearl Harbor, 72
Peck, Gregory, 325
PEN International, 402
Penn, Leo, 244
Pens and Pencils, 61
People's Art Theater, 28
Percy, Charles, 384
Period of Adjustment (Williams), 353
Pillars of Society (Ibsen), 108
Pinewood Studios, 301
Pinter, Harold, 279, 402–403, 406, 422, 433
Playing for Time (Miller), 412–417
controversy over, 412–413
critics and, 417
plot of, 414–417
success of, 417
playwriting
audience and, 91
critics and, 101–102
dialogue and, 25
directing and, 33
drama and, 34
fiction and, 87
Greek tragedy and, 93
movies and, 114
production and, 69
research and, 43
social problems and, 43
writing vs., 25
"Please Don't Kill Anything" (Miller), 309–310, 336
Plenty Good Times (Miller)
development of, 114–115, 162, 181, 235–236
production of, 237
revision of, 182
Poetry Magazine, 40
Poland, 58, 111
Poore, Charles, 89
Porter, Katherine Anne, 240
poster plays, 39
Potter, Jeffrey, 309, 311–312
Potter, Penny, 309
Power, Tyrone, 301
The Price (Miller)
autobiographical elements in, 393–394
critics and, 395–397
plot of, 386–392
production of, 392–393, 394
revival of, 444–445
setting of, 386
theme in, 80
The Third Play and, 395
The Prince and the Showgirl, 299, 301, 303, 304
Processional (Lawson), 54, 92, 182
Proctor, Jim, 143–144, 148, 159, 213, 215, 216, 219, 237, 312
The Proud Pilgrimage (Rosten), 40
Provincetown Players, 143
Provincetown Playhouse, 28
The Pure in Heart (Lawson), 103
Pyle, Ernie, 73

"A Question of Standard" (Miller), 340
The Quintessence of Ibsenism (Shaw), 163

Rabinowitz, Seymour, 296
racism, xi, 31
Radosh, Ronald, 112
Rand, Ayn, 182
Rashomon, 326
Rattigan, Terrence, 275–276, 300–301, 307, 308
Rauh, Joseph L., Jr., 288, 310–311
Ray, Nicholas, 48
The Real Thing (Stoppard), 433
Red Channels, 193
Redgrave, Vanessa, 412–413
Red Hook, 120, 168
Red Roses for Me (O'Casey), 264
Reid, Kate, 392
Renoir, Jean, 228
Resurrection Blues (Miller), 445
Return Again, Traveler (Rosten), 68
Reuther, Walter, 23
Revere, Anne, 134
Reynal and Hitchcock, 89, 112
Rice, Elmer, 28, 48, 116
Rich, Frank, 408, 411
The Ride Down Mt. Morgan (Miller), 423–424
After the Fall vs., 433
critics and, 433–434
plot of, 427–433
Riders to the Sea (Synge), 34
Ritt, Martin, 242
Ritter, Thelma, 323
Robards, James, Jr., 317, 321–322, 363–366
Roberts, Stanley, 184
Robertson, 410
Robeson, Paul, 286–287, 290, 292

Robinson, Edward G., 28, 111
Rogers, Ginger, 190
Roosevelt, Eleanor, 159
Roosevelt, Franklin D., 18, 54, 72
Rope (Laurents), 114
Rosenberg, Julius and Ethel, 183, 196, 225–226, 238, 292, 293
The Rose Tattoo (William), 169, 183, 220
Rossen, Robert, 111
Rosten, Hedda, 112, 244, 277
  marriage of, 49
  Monroe and, 240, 300, 312, 315, 329
Rosten, Norman, 40, 50, 244, 290
  Broadway debut of, 68, 69
  career of, 237
  The Children of the Sun and, 56
  Communist Party and, 158
  Federal Theatre and Writers Project and, 56
  Kazan and, 114
  Miller's correspondence with, 321
  Miller's success and, 112
  The Misfits and, 319
  Monroe and Miller and, 239–242, 246, 270, 296–297, 300, 302–303, 312–313, 315, 320, 321, 329
  Mr. Johnson and, 277
  Olivier and, 301
  poetry of, 68
  postgraduate life of, 48–50, 60–61
  Second World War and, 68
  A View from the Bridge and, 329
Roth, Philip, 382, 384, 432
Rowe, Kenneth Thorpe
  Communist Party and, 40–41
  expressionism and, 122
  Greek tragedy and, 305
  Greek tragedy and playwriting and, 93
  Ibsen and, 34–35
  marriage of, 49
  Miller's correspondence with, 3–5, 51, 52, 54–56, 60, 61, 63, 66, 68, 69, 113, 235–236, 282–283, 396
  Miller's education and, 142
  narrative construction and, 48
  playwriting guidelines of, 44
  seminar of, 33–34, 43
  Theatre Guild and, 28–29
  University of Michigan and, 33
Rowinski, Hedda. *See* Rosten, Hedda
Royal, Derek Parker, 344–345
The Royal Hunt of the Sun (Shaffer), 59
Royal National Theatre, 373, 437
Royal Shakespeare Company, 407
Rubin, Jill, 238
Rudman, Michael, 155, 446
The Rudy Vallee Show, 51
Russell, Jane, 227–228
Russell, Lillian, 320
Ryan, Joseph Patrick, 167
Ryan, Robert, 215

S. Miller and Sons, 8
Saarinen, Eero, 351
Saint, Eva Marie, 233–234
Salisbury, Harrison, 382, 384, 427
Sanctuary, 334
Sandburg, Carl, 181
Saroyan, William, 28, 68
Sartre, Jean-Paul, 319
Scherbatoff, Mara, 295
Scherer, Gordon H., 289, 290, 291
Schlesinger, Arthur, Jr., 160, 384
Schwartz, Delmore, 245
Scofield, Paul, 300
Scott, George C., 365, 420
Screen Writers Guild, 326–327
Seale, Bobby, 384
Second World War, xi, 63, 68, 72, 82–83
Seeger, Pete, 329
Separate Tables (Rattigan), 275
Seven Arts Productions, 322
The Seven Year Itch, 239, 244, 245, 278
sexuality, 17–18, 121, 171, 358
Shaffer, Peter, 59
Shakespeare, William, 408
  forgery of papers of, 52
  Henry VIII and, 24–25
  invention and, 33
  revivals of, 384
Shane, 243
Shattuck, Roger, 422
Shaw, George Bernard, 80, 163, 222
  as issue-oriented playwright, 92–93
  longevity of, 424
  Miller's analysis of, 92–93
  Theatre Guild and, 28
Shaw, Stan, 239
The Sheik, 312
Sherwood, Robert, 116
The Ship of State (Whitman), 251
Shirer, William L., 384
The Short Stories of James Stern (Stern), 240
Shostakovich, Dmitri, 159
Shubert Theatre, 9
Shulberg, Budd, 183
  On the Waterfront and, 229–235
Shumlin, Herman, 74
Siegmeister, Ellie, 237
The Sign of the Archer (Miller). *See All My Sons*
Signoret, Simone, 225, 325
Silverman, Stanley, 399
Simon, Josette, 373
Singin' in the Rain, 327

Situation Normal (Miller), 74–75
Sitwell, Edith, 300
The Skin of Our Teeth (Wilder), 103, 122
Skolsky, Sidney, 327
Skouras, Spyros, 191, 193, 194, 201
Slattery, Julia, 64, 70
Slattery, Mary Grace. *See* Miller, Mary
The Sleeping Prince: An Occasional Fairy Tale, 275, 308
A Smile of the World (Kanin), 131
Smith, Gerald L.K., 74
Snow, Edgar, 159
socialism, xi, 31, 44
society
  art and, 43
  individual and, 43
  knowledge and, 44
Sokolsky, George, 293
Solzhenitsyn, Aleksandr, 402, 405
Some Kind of Love Story (Miller), 419
Some Like It Hot, 319–321
Some Shall Not Sleep (Miller). *See Focus*
Sontag, Susan, 384
Sophocles, 33, 35, 101, 259
South America, 65–66
Soviet Union
  admiration for, 31, 43
  artistic freedom in, 402
  communism and, 157–158, 183
  realism of, 43
  socialism and, 31
Spanish conquistadors, 3
Splendor in the Grass, 353
Spock, Benjamin, 384
Springer, John, 295
Squadron, Howard M., 412
Stalin, Josef, 116–117
Stanford University, 18–19
Stanislavsky, Konstantin, 28, 113
Stanwyck, Barbara, 182
Stapleton, Maureen, 269, 363
Starkey, Marion, 196
Steinbeck, John, 82, 382, 423–424
Stern, Isaac, 434
Stern, James, 249, 252
  death of, 424
  Miller's correspondence with, 240–242, 310, 314, 315, 319, 320, 342, 383, 396–397
Stern, Tania, 240
Stevens, Roger L., 406
Stevens, Wallace, 25
Stevenson, Adlai, 369
Stewart, Patrick, 434
Stockmann, Thomas, 164–166
Stoppard, Tom, 433
The Story of G.I. Joe, 73–74
Straight, Beatrice, 215, 218
Strasberg, Lee, 48, 192, 240, 244, 269, 274, 296, 302, 360
  The Grass Still Grows and, 52
  The Misfits and, 332
  Monroe's death and, 343
  Monroe and, 303, 322
Strasberg, Paula, 240, 244, 301, 321, 332–333, 343
Strasberg, Susan, 266
A Streetcar Named Desire (Williams), 114–116, 149, 168, 183, 229
Streger, Paul, 50–51, 60, 74
Streisand, Barbra, 412
Strindberg, August, 373, 408, 446
Styron, Rose, 382
Styron, William, 382–383, 384, 435
The Subject Was Roses, 385
Success Story (Lawson), 92, 182
Sullivan, Ed, 149–150
Sunday Independent, 371
Sunday New York Times, 128, 151, 280, 422
Sunday Times of London, 220
Sweden, 111
The Sweet Bird of Youth (Williams), 330, 353
Switzerland, 111
Synge, John Millington, 34

Tabori, George, 183, 194
Taylor, Frank, 74–75, 147, 162, 196, 338
  Focus and, 89, 172
  The Misfits and, 317–319, 322, 331–332, 339
  Monroe and, 334
Taylor, Laurette, 35
Taylor, Nan, 74–75, 147, 162
  Inge and Miller and, 337
  The Misfits and, 317–319
  Monroe and, 333
Taylor, Robert, 182
Tea and Sympathy, 330, 353
Teahouse of the August Moon, 245
Terkel, Studs, 410
The Testament of Dr. Mabuse, 118–119
Thacker, David, ix, 101, 166, 373, 424, 425, 446
  Broken Glass and, 436
Thatcher, Molly
  Death of a Salesman and, 122
  marriage of, 102
That They May Win, 73
Theater Essays of Arthur Miller, 152
Theatre Arts Monthly, 29
The Theatre Essays of Arthur Miller, 372
Theatre Guild, 48, 60
  Battle of Angels and, 69
  Broadway and, 28
  Bureau of New Plays of, 28, 31, 36, 103
  The Grass Still Grows and, 51
  Miller's plays and, 3
  Williams and, 51
They Knew What They Wanted (Howard), 28
They Too Arise (Miller), 36. *See also The Grass Still Grows*

All My Sons vs., 100
characters in, 31–32
The Great Disobedience vs., 47
humor in, 32
plot synopsis of, 31
production of, 36
social responsibility and, 32
subplot in, 32
See also No Villain
The Third Play. *See A View from the Bridge*; *After the Fall*; *The Price*
Thirty Years of Treason (Bentley), 193, 289
Thomas, John Parnell, 53–54, 55, 182, 191
Thorndike, Sybil, 301
Those Familiar Spirits. *See The Crucible*
A Three Act Prison Tragedy (Miller). *See The Great Disobedience*
Timebends (Miller), ix
critics and, 422
Franks and Miller and, 52
The Hook and, 176
Kazan as informer and, 197
Miller's divorce and, 285
Miller's education and, 33
Monroe and Miller and, 266
problems in, x
publication of, 421–422
A View from the Bridge and, 260
Time Magazine, 160, 213, 240, 334
The Time of Your Life (Saroyan), 28
Tobacco Road, 9
Tomorrow the World, 290
"Tragedy and the Common Man" (Miller), 151
Travilla, William, 227, 228
The Treasure of the Sierra Madre, 336
A Tree Grows in Brooklyn, 103
Trilling, Diana, 373
Truex, Ernest, 133
Tsachacbasov, Alexandra, 283
Tulane Drama Review, 108, 148, 282
Twain, Mark, 398
Twentieth Century-Fox, 115, 169, 172–173, 183, 190, 227, 228, 270, 323, 326
Two-Way Mirror (Miller), 419
Tynan, Kenneth, 307, 308, 370, 371, 384

United Artists, 322, 332, 339
United Auto Workers, 23
United Press, 306
University of Michigan
campus of, 21–22
Communist Party and, 40–41
Miller at, 19–20, 21–41, 43–48
student radicalism at, 24
University of Missouri, 36
Unwin, Paul, 82
Up from Paradise (Miller), 399
Up in Mabel's Room (Hopwood), 22
utopia, 44

Van Doren, Mark, 159, 383
Vanity Fair, 149, 422
Vietnam War, xi, 383–384
A View from the Bridge (Miller), x, 321–322
completion of, 342–343
critics and, 261–265, 307–308, 323
expansion of, 276, 281–286
failure of, 306
as family play, 306
Greek tragedy and, 120, 253, 258–261, 304–306
homosexuality in, 257, 304
incest in, 304
Kazan and, 329–330
A Memory of Two Mondays vs., 253
moral propriety of, 304
movie version of, 329
origins of, 120–121
plot of, 253–259
production of, 243–247, 304–306, 330–331
research for, 116–117, 258
revival of, 384–385, 444
setting of, 306
See also After the Fall
Viking Press, 397
Viva Zapata!, 172, 174, 181, 184
Vivian Beaumont Theatre, 351, 368, 374
Voight, Jon, 385

Wages of Fear, 325
Wagner, Howard, 125, 138, 139
Waiting for Godot (Beckett), 278–280
Waiting for Lefty (Odets), 39
Walbrook, Anton, 301
Waldorf Peace Conference. *See* Cultural and Scientific Conference for World Peace
Walken, Christopher, 385
Wallach, Eli
HUAC and, 289, 291
Miller tribute and, 442
The Misfits and, 332
Monroe and, 245–247, 311
Monroe and Miller and, 334
The Price and, 394
Wall Street crash of 1929, xi, 11–15
Walter, Erich, 27–28
Walter, Francis E., 191, 200, 287, 296, 297, 310
War and Peace (Tolstoy), 250
Warden, Jack, 244
Wardle, Irving, 371
Warner Bros., 173
Warren, Sue, 291–292

Watergate, 402
Watts, Richard, Jr., 107–108, 379
Wayne, David, 245, 363
Wayne, John, 175, 193
Weales, Gerald, 406
Weber, Bruce, 82
Wechsler, James, 160
Wedekind, Frank, 35
Weill, Kurt, 145
Welland, Dennis, 371
Welles, Orson, 48, 55, 384
Wellworth, George E., 142
Wermacht, 337
West Side Story, 269
Wharton and Gabel, 69
When the Submarines Come (Miller). *See The Men from Under the Sea*
Where's Daddy? (Inge), 279
Whitehead, Robert, 242–243, 267, 292–294, 309
  After the Fall and, 345, 363–364
  Broken Glass and, 436
  end of stage career of, 374
  Incident at Vichy and, 378–379, 380
  Inge and Miller and, 337–338
  Kazan and, 401
  Lincoln Center project and, 330
  Monroe's death and, 345
  The Price and, 386, 392
  A View from the Bridge and, 244–247, 304, 342–343
Whitman, Walt, 175, 251
"Why Kill a Nation No One Hates?" (Miller), 383
Widmark, Richard, 190, 215–216, 382
Wilbur, Richard, 383
The Wild Duck (Ibsen), 108
Wilde, Oscar, 396
Wilder, Billy, 319
Wilder, Thornton, 103, 122
Wild River, 322, 329
William Ireland's Confession, 52
Williams, Annie Laurie, 231
Williams, Tennessee, 36, 69, 149, 169, 279, 353, 373
  Battle of Angels of, 51, 69
  Broadway success of, 87
  career of, 423
  Cat on a Hot Time Roof of, 280, 304
  HUAC and, 236
  Miller and, 220
  naturalism of, 44
  Not About Nightingales of, 44
  penitentiary play of, 44
  The Rose Tattoo of, 169, 183, 220
  A Streetcar Named Desire of, 114–116
  Theatre Guild and, 51
Willis, Edwin E., 289
Wilson, Earl, 247
Winchell, Walter, 241, 247, 276–277
The Winslow Boy (Rattigan), 275
Winters, Shelley, 228, 245, 343
Wolcott, James, 149, 422
Wolf, Matt, 424
Wolfe, Thomas, 166
Wolper, David, 413
Woltman, Fred, 263
Woman of the Year (Lardner), 183
wonder, xi–xii
Wood, Peer, 410
Woodrum, Clifton, 55–56
Workers Alliance, 60
Works Progress Administration (WPA), 4
  Federal Theatre and Writers Project of, 36, 48
  HUAC and, 54
World Youth Festival, 157–158
WPA. *See* Works Progress Administration
Wright, Frank Lloyd, 314
Write That Play! (Rowe), 122
writing
  playwriting vs., 25
  rewriting and, 31

Yale University, 29, 33
Yellen, Linda, 412, 413
You're Next (Miller and Rosten), 60, 290
Young, Gig, 245
You See, I Haven't Forgotten (Montand), 325

Zanuck, Darryl, 172
Ziegfeld, Florenz, 139
Zolotow, Maurice, 172, 295
Zolotow, Sam, 172

DISCARDED